Street by Street

NORTH ESSEX

PLUS BISHOP'S STORTFORD, FELIXSTOWE, HAVERHILL, IPSWICH, SUDBURY

Enlarged Areas Chelmsford, Clacton-on-Sea, Colchester, Harwich

Ist edition May 2001

© Automobile Association Developments Limited 2001

This product includes map data licensed from Ordnance Survey® with the permission of the Controller of Her Majesty's Stationery Office. © Crown copyright 2000. All rights reserved. Licence No: 399221.

Published by AA Publishing (a trading name of Automobile Association Developments Limited, whose registered office is Norfolk House, Priestley Road, Basingstoke, Hampshire, RG24 9NY. Registered number 1878835).

Mapping produced by the Cartographic Department of The Automobile Association.

A CIP Catalogue record for this book is available from the British Library.

Printed by G. Canale & C. s.p.a., Torino, Italy

The contents of this atlas are believed to be correct at the time of the latest revision. However, the publishers cannot be held responsible for loss occasioned to any person acting or refraining from action as a result of any material in this atlas, nor for any errors, omissions or changes in such material. The publishers would welcome information to correct any errors or omissions and to keep this atlas up to date. Please write to Publishing, The Automobile Association, Fanum House, Basing View, Basingstoke, Hampshire, RG21 4EA.

Ref: MX027

Key to map pages	ii-iii
Key to map symbols	iv-1
Enlarged scale pages	2-15
Street by Street	16-273
Index – towns & villages	274-275
Index – streets	275-294
Index – featured places	294-297

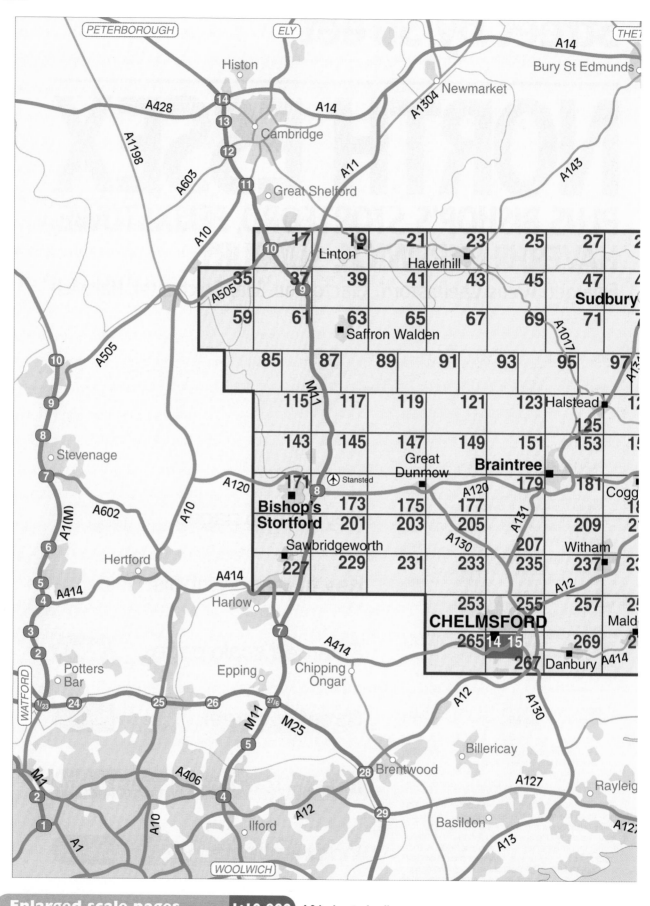

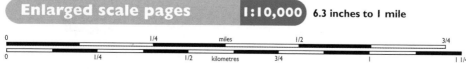

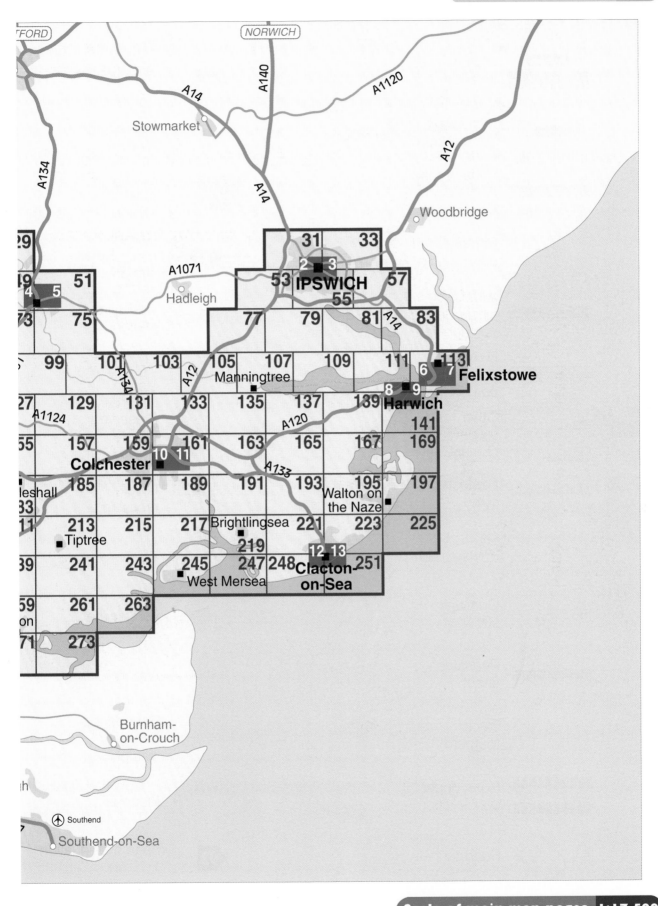

TFORD)

NORWICH)

A14

Stowmarket

A140

A1120

A12

Woodbridge

A134

29

19

51

A1071

31

33

4

5

53

2

3

57

Hadleigh

IPSWICH

55

73

75

77

79

81

A14

83

99

101

A134

103

A12

105

107

109

111

113

Manningtree

6

7

Felixstowe

127

129

131

133

135

137

139

8

9

Harwich

A1124

141

55

157

159

161

163

165

167

169

Colchester

10

11

A133

185

187

189

191

193

195

197

leshall

Walton on
the Naze

33

11

213

215

217

Brightlingsea

221

223

225

Tiptree

219

39

241

243

245

247

248

12

13

251

West Mersea

Clacton-
on-Sea

59

261

263

on

71

273

Burnham-
on-Crouch

h

Southend

Southend-on-Sea

3.6 inches to 1 mile   **Scale of main map pages   1:17,500**

0   1/2   miles   1

0   1/2   1   kilometres   1 1/2

2

Junction 9	Motorway & junction
Services	Motorway service area
	Primary road single/dual carriageway
Services	Primary road service area
	A road single/dual carriageway
	B road single/dual carriageway
	Other road single/dual carriageway
	Restricted road
	Private road
← ←	One way street
	Pedestrian street
	Track/ footpath
	Road under construction
⌐⌐⌐⌐⌐⌐	Road tunnel
P	Parking

P+	Park & Ride
	Bus/coach station
	Railway & main railway station
	Railway & minor railway station
	Underground station
	Light railway & station
┼┼┼┼┼┼┼┼┼┼┼	Preserved private railway
LC	Level crossing
•—•—•—•—•—•	Tramway
------------	Ferry route
··············	Airport runway
—·—·—·—·—	Boundaries- borough/ district
ᐯᐯᐯᐯᐯᐯᐯᐯ	Mounds
◀93	Page continuation 1:17,500
7	Page continuation to enlarged scale 1:10,000

	River/canal lake, pier	♿	Toilet with disabled facilities
	Aqueduct lock, weir	⛽	Petrol station
465 ▲ Winter Hill	Peak (with height in metres)	PH	Public house
	Beach	PO	Post Office
	Coniferous woodland	📖	Public library
	Broadleaved woodland	i	Tourist Information Centre
	Mixed woodland	⚔	Castle
	Park	🏛	Historic house/ building
	Cemetery	Wakehurst Place NT	National Trust property
	Built-up area	Ⓜ	Museum/ art gallery
	Featured building	†	Church/chapel
⊓⊔⊓⊔⊓⊔⊓⊔	City wall	⛹	Country park
A&E	Accident & Emergency hospital	🎭	Theatre/ performing arts
🚻	Toilet	🎥	Cinema

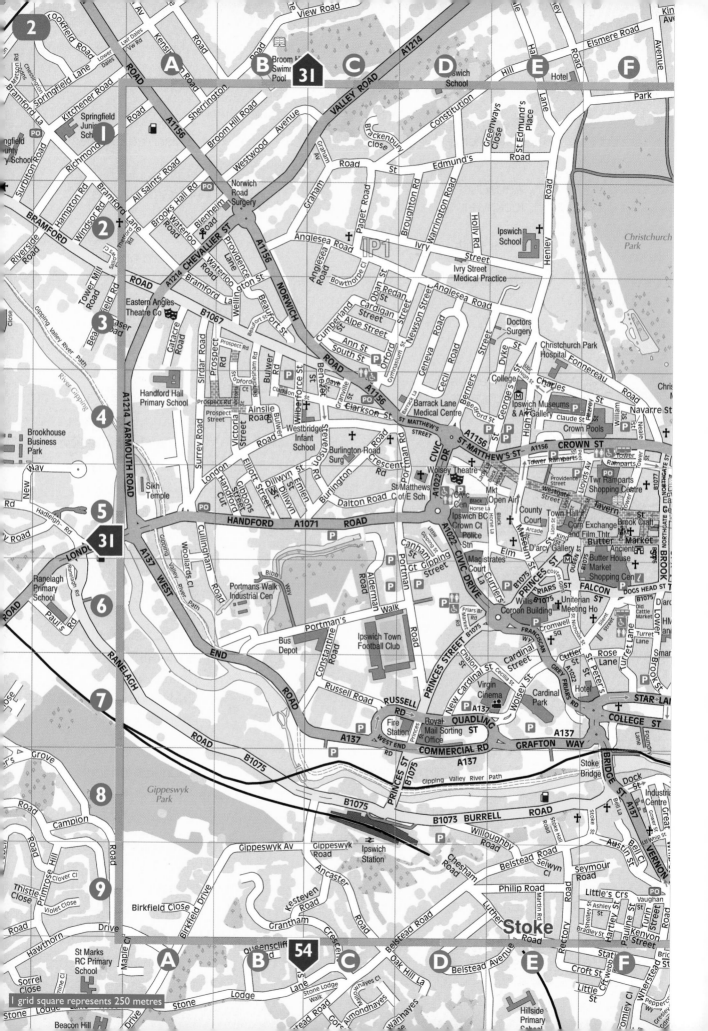

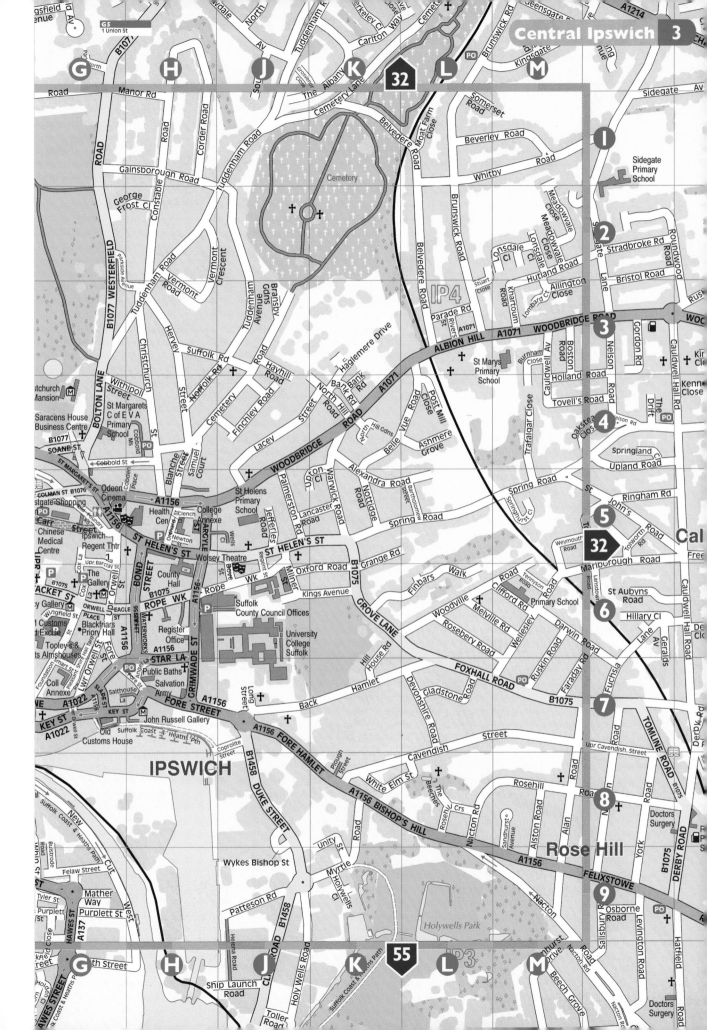

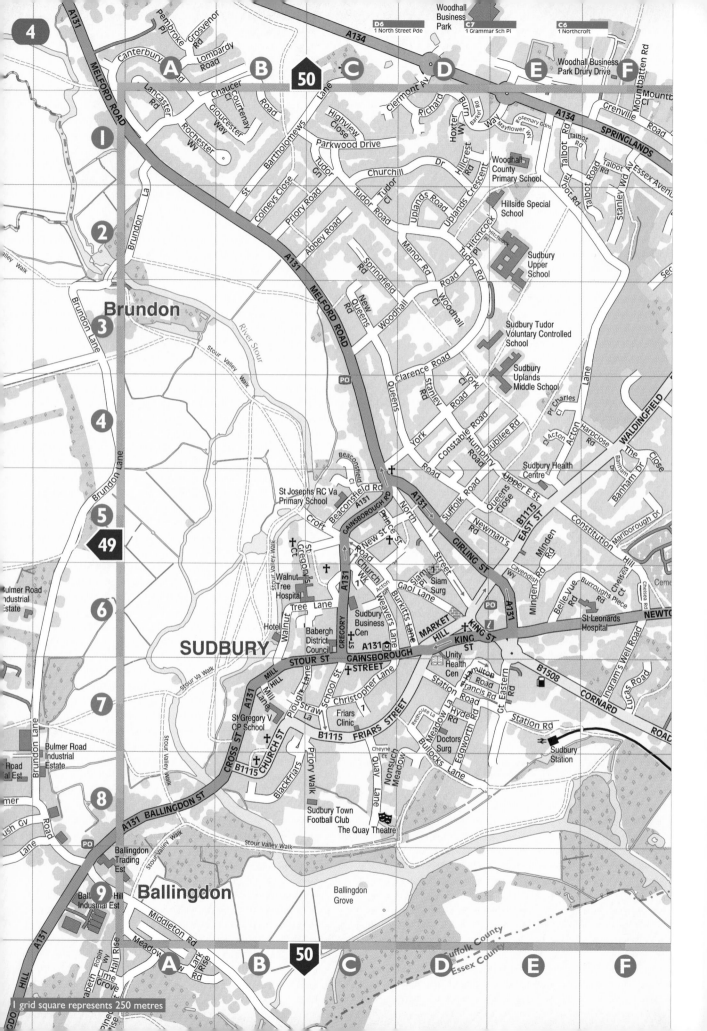

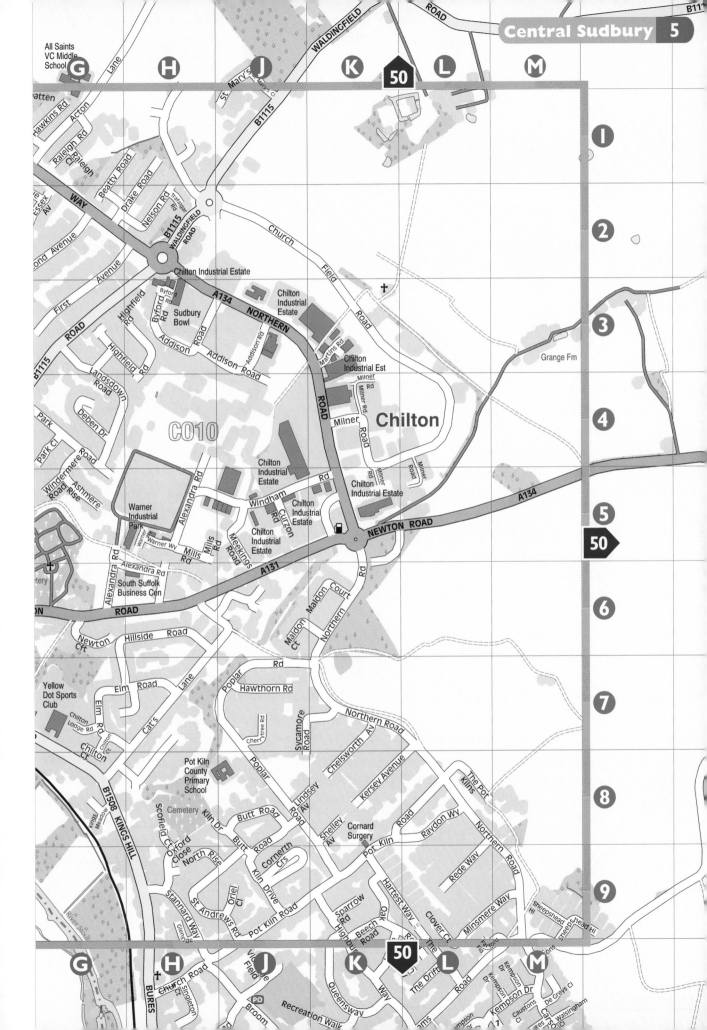

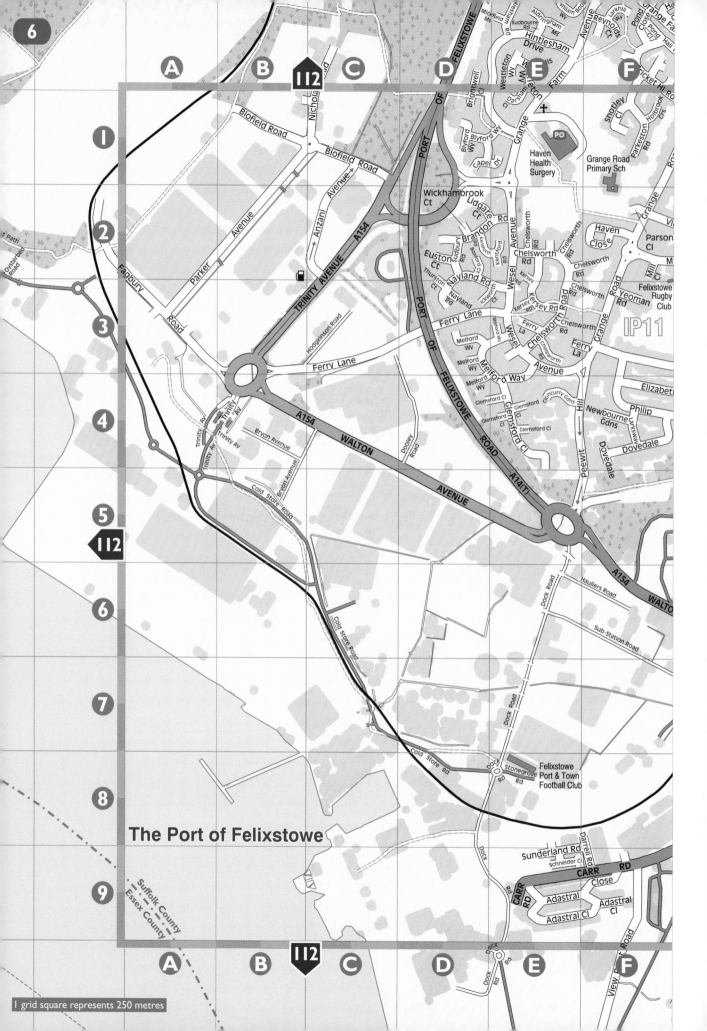

The Port of Felixstowe

1 grid square represents 250 metres

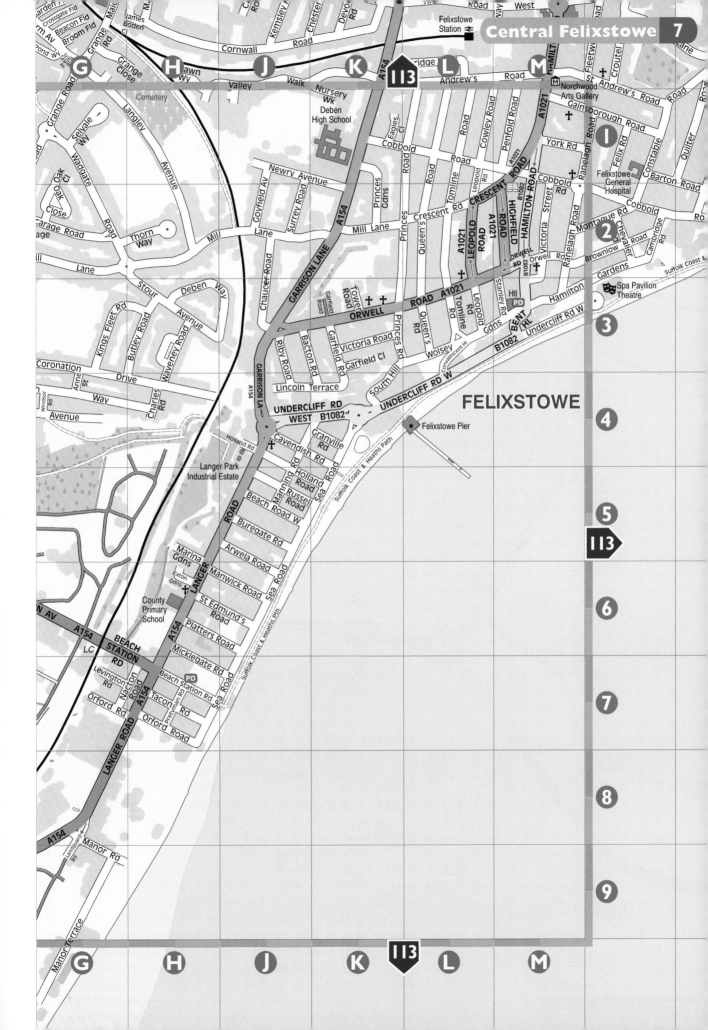

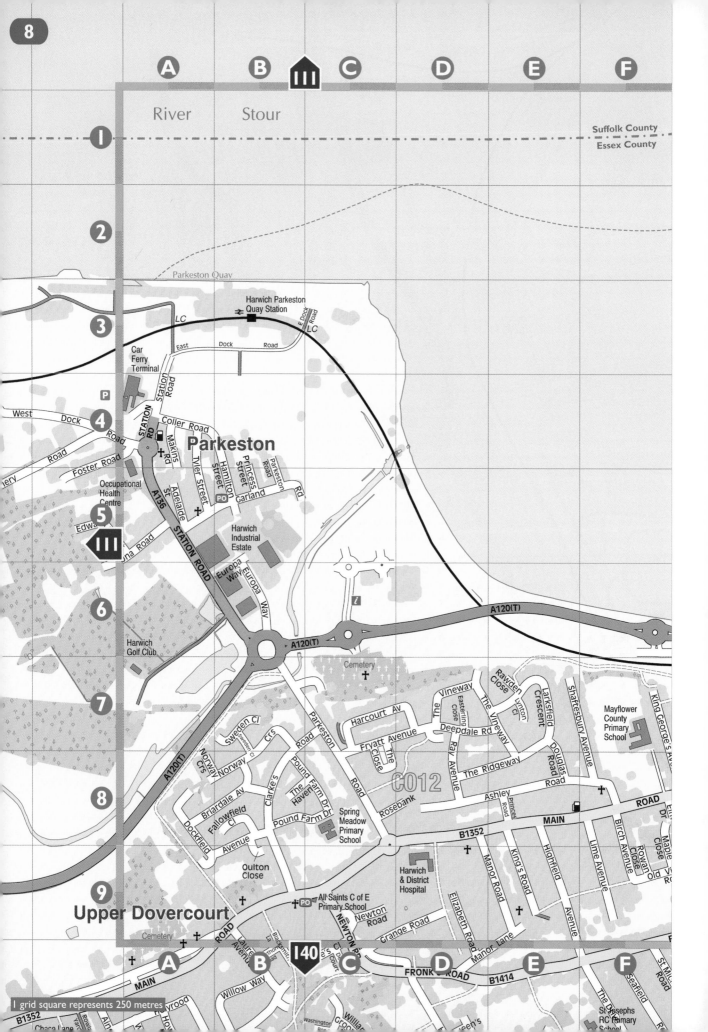

A **B** **C** **D** **E** **F**

1

River Stour

Suffolk County
Essex County

2

Parkeston Quay

3

Harwich Parkeston
Quay Station

LC

East Dock Road LC

East Dock Road

Car
Ferry
Terminal

4

West Dock Road

P

Coller Road

Parkeston

Station Road

STATION RD

Makins Rd

Tyler Street

Hamilton Street

Princess Street

Parkeston Road

Foster Road

Occupational
Health
Centre

PO

Garland

Adelaide

A136

5

Edwa

Harwich
Industrial
Estate

Una Road

STATION ROAD

Europa Way

Europa Way

6

Harwich
Golf Club

A120(T)

A120(T)

7

Cemetery

Sweden Cl

Sweden Cl Crs

Norway Crs

Parkeston Road

Harcourt Av

Fryatt Avenue

The Close

Deepdale Rd

Eastering Close

The Vineway

The Vineway

Ray Avenue

Rawden Close

Larksfield Crescent

Lynton Crs

The Ridgeway

Shaftesbury Avenue

Douglas Road

Mayflower
County Primary
School

King George's Av

8

A120(T)

Briardale Av

Fallowfield Cl

Dockfield Avenue

Clarke's

The Haven

Pound Farm Dr

Pound Farm Dr

Spring
Meadow
Primary
School

Rosebank

C012

Ashley

Princes Road

B1352

MAIN

Highfield

Manor Road

King's Road

Lime Avenue

Birch Avenue

Rowan Close

ROAD

Maple Close

Old Vi

9

Upper Dovercourt

Oulton
Close

Cemetery

All Saints C of E
Primary School

PO

Newton Road

Harwich
& District
Hospital

Grange Road

Elizabeth Road

Manor Lane

Seafield

A **B** 140 **C** **D** **E** **F**

MAIN ROAD

Willow Way

Laurie Avenue

Blacksmith

NEWTON RD

FRONK ROAD

B1414

St Mic Road

B1352

Chase Lane

William

St Josephs
RC Primary
School

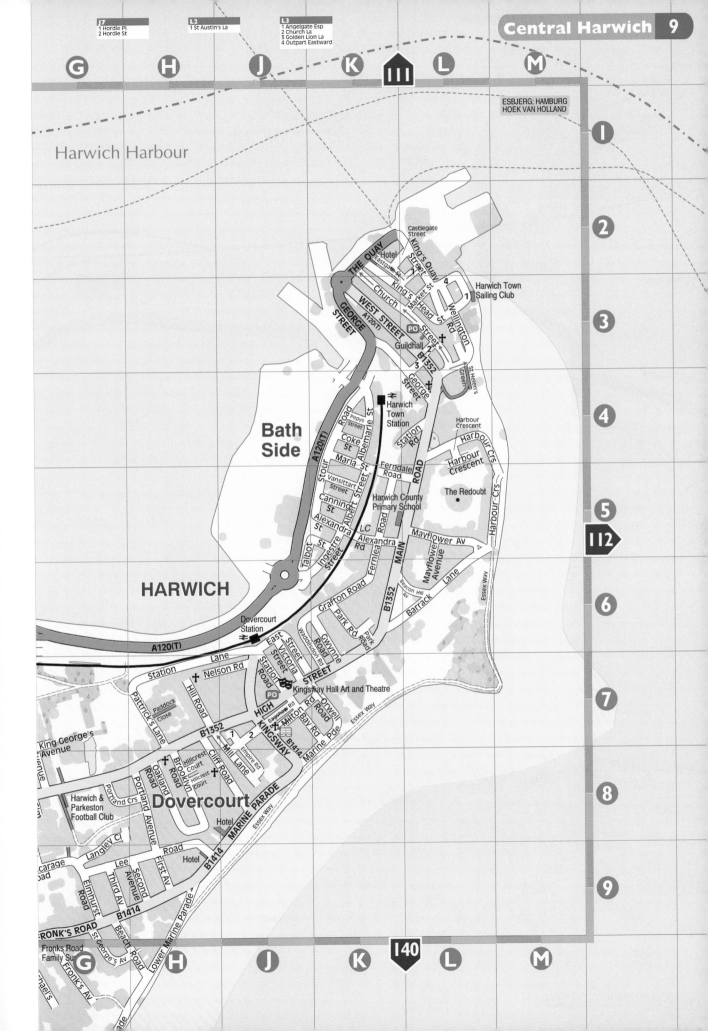

L1
1 Hordle Pl
2 Hordle St

L2
1 St Austin's La

L3
1 Angelgate Esp
2 Church La
3 Golden Lion La
4 Outpart Eastward

G H J K L M

ESBJERG; HAMBURG
HOEK VAN HOLLAND

1

Harwich Harbour

2

Castlegate
Street

King's Quay
Street

THE QUAY
Hotel

Eastgate St

Church

WEST STREET
A120(T)

GEORGE
STREET

King's Head St
Market St
Wellington Rd

Harwich Town
Sailing Club

3

PO

Guildhall

George Street

St Helen's Green

4

Harbour Crescent

Harbour
Crescent

Harbour Crs

Harwich
Town
Station

Station Rd
ROAD

Bath
Side

A120(T)

Pepys
Street

Coke
St

Maria St

Albemarle St

Ferndale
Road

Harwich County
Primary School

The Redoubt

5

Stour

Vansittart
Street

Canning
St

Alexandra
St

Talbot
St

Ingestre
Street

Albert Street

Alexandra
Rd

LC

Fernlea
Road

MAIN

B1352

Beacon Hill
Av

Mayflower Av

Mayflower
Avenue

Barrack
Lane

Essex Way

Harbour Crs

HARWICH

6

Dovercourt
Station

A120(T)

Grafton Road

Park Rd

Gwynne
Road

Park
Road

Waddeston Rd

East
Street

Victoria
Street

STREET

7

Station
Lane

Nelson Rd

Hill Road

Station
Road

HIGH

PO

MILTON Rd

Bagshaw Rd

Kingsway Hall Art and Theatre

Orwell Rd
Bay Rd
Marine Pde

Essex Way

Paddock
Close

Pattrick's Lane

B1352

KINGSWAY

7 2

Mill Lane

Empire Rd

B1414

8

King George's
Avenue

Oakland Road

Brooklyn Road

Hillcrest
Court

Cliff Road

Hillcrest
Court

Portland Avenue

Portland Crs

Harwich &
Parkeston
Football Club

Hotel

MARINE PARADE

Essex Way

9

Langley Cl

Lee Road

Road

First Av

Second Avenue

Third Av

Hotel

B1414

icarage
Rd

Elmhurst
Road

B1414

FRONK'S ROAD

Fronks Road
Family Su

Beach Road

St George's Av

Lower Marine Parade

Fronks Av

St
ichael's

Dovercourt

I
2
3
4
5
6
7
8
9

112

140

G H J K L M

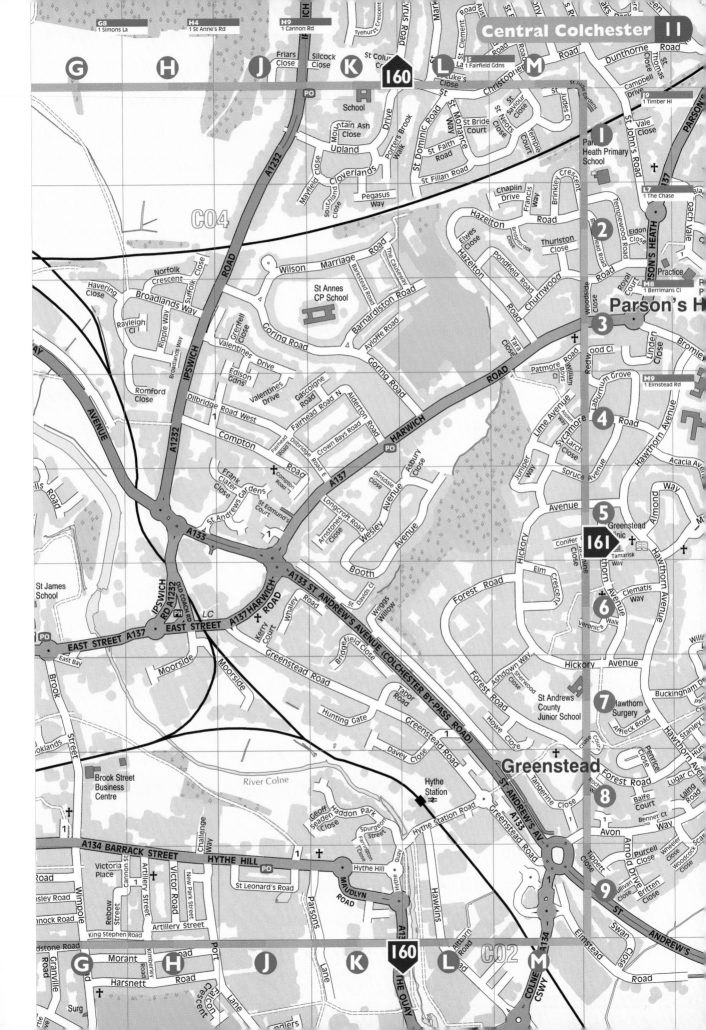

G **H** **J** **K** **L** **M**

Friars Close
Silcock Close

St Column
Cr

St Luke's St

St La
1 Fairfield Gdns

160

PO

School

Tyehurst Crescent

St Clement

Austin

Campbell Drive

J9
1 Timber Hi

Dunthorne Road

Thomas

Mountain Ash Close

Upland

Porter's Brook Walk

Drive

St Dominic Road

St Way

St Monance

St Bride Court

St Neots Close

Temple Court

St Jude's Gardens

St Jude's Ci

St John's Road

Vale Close

Park Heath Primary School

PARSONS

1

Cloverlands

Mayfield Close

Southland Close

Pegasus Way

St Faith Road

St Fillan Road

Chaplin Drive

Francis Way

Brinkley Crescent

St Saviour Close

Bridgebrook Close

Mead Road

Templewood Road

Eldon Close

L7
1 The Chase

The Chase

A1232 ROAD

C04

Hazelton Road

Elwes Close

Hazelton Road

Pondfield Road

Churnwood Road

Woodside Close

Royal Close

M8
1 Berrimans Ci

Practice

Parson's H

2

Wilson Marriage Road

Barkstead Road

The Causeway

St Annes CP School

Barnardiston Road

Ayloffe Road

Goring Road

HARWICH ROAD

Patmore Road

William Boys

Redwood Cl

Laburnum Grove

Linden Close

Bromle

3

Norfolk Crescent

Suffolk Close

Broadlands Way

Havering Close

Rayleigh Cl

Ripple Way

Broadlands Way

Grenfell Close

Valentines Drive

Edison Gdns

Goring Road

Tara Close

Lime Avenue

Aspen Way

Sycamore

Larch Close

Road

Hawthorn Avenue

Acacia Avenue

4

IPSWICH ROAD A1232

Romford Close

Dilbridge Road West

Valentines Drive

Gascoigne Road

Fairhead Road N

Alderton Road

Crown Bays Road

Dinsdale Close

Asbury Close

Juniper Way

Spruce Avenue

Avenue

Almond Way

AVENUE

A1232

Compton

Fairhead Road S

Dilbridge Road E

HARWICH

A137

PO

Avenue

Wesley

Longcroft Road

Hickory

Elm Crescent

Jasmine Way

Conifer Close

Tamarisk

5

161

Greenstead Clinic

Frank Clater Close

St Andrews Gardens

Compton Road

St Edmund's Court

Arnstone's Close

Avenue

Booth

St Davids Cl

Weggs Willow

Forest Road

6

Clematis Way

Veronica Walk

A133

IPSWICH RD A1232

OLD COACH RD

PH

LC

EAST STREET

A137 HARWICH ROAD

Kerry Court

Whaley Road

Bridgefield Close

ST ANDREW'S AVENUE (COLCHESTER BY-PASS ROAD)

Forest Road

St Andrews County Junior School

Ashdown Way

Sherwood Close

Hickory Avenue

Buckingham R

7

Hawthorn Surgery

Affleck Road

St James School

EAST STREET A137

East Bay

Moorside

Moorside

Greenstead Road

Hunting Gate

Tabor Road

Greenstead Road

Howe Close

Forest Road

Penrice Close

Lugar Road

Laing Road

8

Brook Street

PO

River Colne

Davey Close

Hythe Station

Tangerine Close

ST ANDREW'S AV

Greenstead Road

Greenstead

Forest Road

Balfe Court

Bennet Ct

Brooklands Street

Brook Street Business Centre

Challenge Way

Geoff Seaden Close

Haddon Park

Spurgeon Street

Farrington Close

Hythe Station Road

Quay

Hawkins

Greenstead Road

A133

Avon Way

Purcell Close

Wheeler Close

Woodcock Scan

9

A134 BARRACK STREET

HYTHE HILL

PO

Victoria Place

Cannon St

Artillery Street

Victor Road

New Park Street

St Leonard's Road

Hythe Hill

Maudlyn Road

Parsons Lane

Altbarn Road

Elmstead Road

C02

Tippett Close

Sullivan Close

Arnold Drive

Britten Close

ST ANDREW'S

Rebow Street

Artillery Street

King Stephen Road

Kimberley Road

Port Lane

COLNE CSWY

A134

Swan Close

Road

G **H** **J** **K** **L** **M**

Morant Road

Harsnett Road

160

THE QUAY

Granville Road

Surg

CLACTON-ON-SEA

Clacton Pier

Clacton Station

Clacton Leisure Centre

Clacton County High School

Clacton Rugby Club

Windsor School Clacton

Holland Park Primary School

Clacton Covered Market

Town Hall

Bull Hill Industrial Est

Windmill Park

The Great — Surgery

CO15

OLD ROAD

VALLEY ROAD B1027

HOLLAND ROAD

B1032

A133 ANGLEFIELD

CARNARVON ROAD

HIGH STREET

HOLLAND ROAD

MARINE PARADE EAST

Marine Parade East

222

250

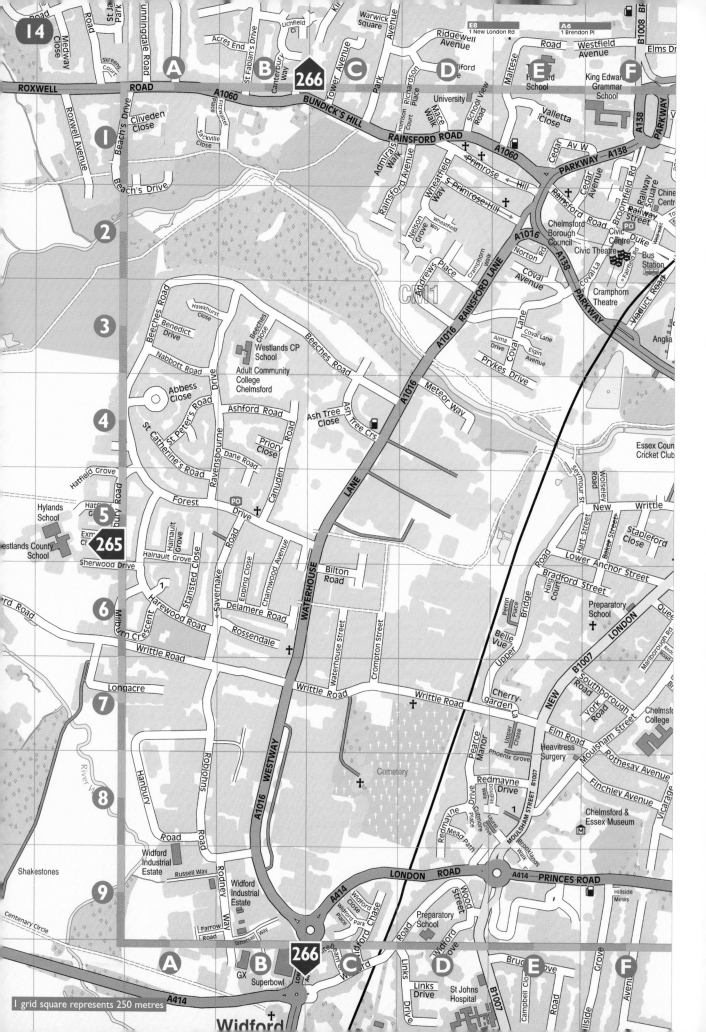

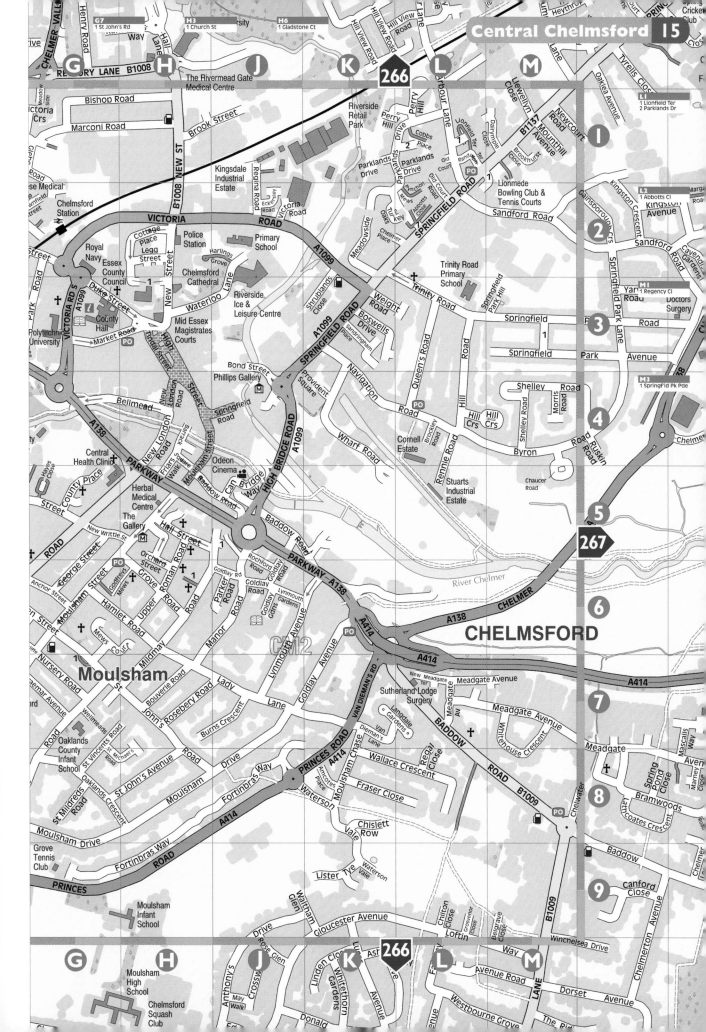

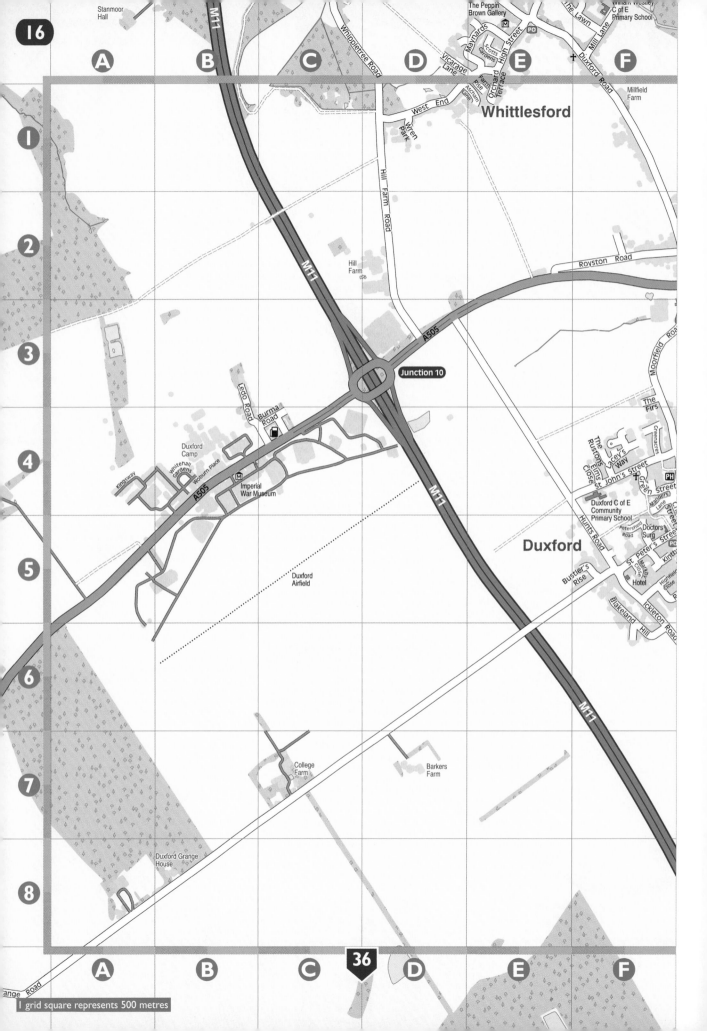

A   B   C   D   E   F

I
2
3
4
5
6
7
8

A   B   C   36   D   E   F

Stanmoor
Hall

M11

Whippletree Road

The Peppin
Brown Gallery

Maynards
Scotts
Gardens
Orchard Farm
Terrace
Ascham Lane
Vicarage
Lane
High Street
PO
The Lawn
Mill Lane
Duxford Road
William Wesley
C of E
Primary School

West End

Wren
Park

Whittlesford

Millfield
Farm

Hill Farm Road

Hill
Farm

Royston Road

A505

Junction 10

Moorfield Road

The
Firs

Ledo Road

Burma
Road

Duxford
Camp

Whitenall
Gardens

Kingsway

Woburn Place

A505

M

Imperial
War Museum

M11

Greenacres

Lacey's
Way

The
Rustons
Elms
Close

St John's Street

St John's Street

Green Street

PH

Duxford C of E
Community
Primary School

Doctors
Surg

Petersfield
Road

Manners
Lane

Street
Close

Street

Duxford

Hunts Road

St Peter's Street

PO

Kintb

Bustler's
Rise

Hotel

Highfield
Close

Blakeland
Hill

ckleton Road

Duxford
Airfield

College
Farm

Barkers
Farm

Duxford Grange
House

ange Road

M3
1 Clover Ct
2 Dolphin Cl
3 Rhugarve Gdns

G   H   J   K   L   M

Little Chilfords

CAMBRIDGE ROAD A1307

Little Linton

The Woodlands

Back Road

Cherry Close
The Grove
Crabtree Croft

Maple Close
Granta Leys
Symonds Lane
Flaxfields
Palmers Close
Meadow Lane
Joiner's Road
Joiner's Court
Market Lane
Horn Lane

Linton Village College

Station Road

CAMBRIDGE ROAD

HIGH STREET
High St
B1052

Chalklands
Hillway
Coles Lane
Church Lane

BALSHAM ROAD

Linton C of E (aided) Infant School

Linton Health Centre
PO

Cemetery

Tower View
River Way
River Close

Balindon Lane
Wheat Cfr
Fairfield
The Hamlets
Barley Way
Parsonage Lane
Mill Lane
Green La
Elmson's Close
Granta Vale
Beech Way

Linton Heights Junior School

Rob Battice Crescent
Brinkman Way
Millers Close
Wheatsheaf Way
Crossways
Finchan's Close
Bartlow

Horseheath Road
Bartlow
Baker Lane
Harefield
Lonsdale
Mac La
Rise

Lin
Lin

Icknield Way Path

I
2
3
4
20
5
6
7
8

CAMBRIDGE ROAD
A1307

THE GRIP
Long Lane

HADSTOCK ROAD

Linton Zoological Gardens

B1052 LINTON ROAD

Icknield Way Path

Icknield Way Path

Cambridgeshire County
Essex County

Bartlow Road

Cambridgesh
Essex Co

Icknield Way Path

Orch
Pightle End
Back
Billy's Ly
Moules Lane
Siguin's La

WALDEN ROAD
Church Path

Hadstock

Pen Farm

B1052

Hadstock Common

Icknield Way Path

G   H   J   39   K   L   M

B1052

A   B   C   D   E   F

A3
1 Pembroke La

I

Horseheath
Lodge

B1052
ROAD

A1307

2

Linton

BAM
Balington
Lane
Wheatsheaf Way
Brinkman
Road
Bawdtree
Crescent
Hollybush
Way

Linton Heights
Junior School

2

Horseheath Road

Wave

3

Lonsdale
Martins
Lane
Baker's Lane
Harefield
Rise
Kenwood
Gdns

Simpson's
Close

Willow
Finchers
Close

The Ridgeway

A1307   A1307

4

19

Barham
Hall

Cambridgeshire County
Essex County

5

River Bourn

Icknield Way Path

Dean   Road

6

Bartlow

Camps   Road

Bartlow Road

PO

†

Harcamlow Way

Westoe
Farm

7

Hills Farm

Harcamlow Way

8

A   B   C   D   E   F

River Bo

1 grid square represents 500 metres

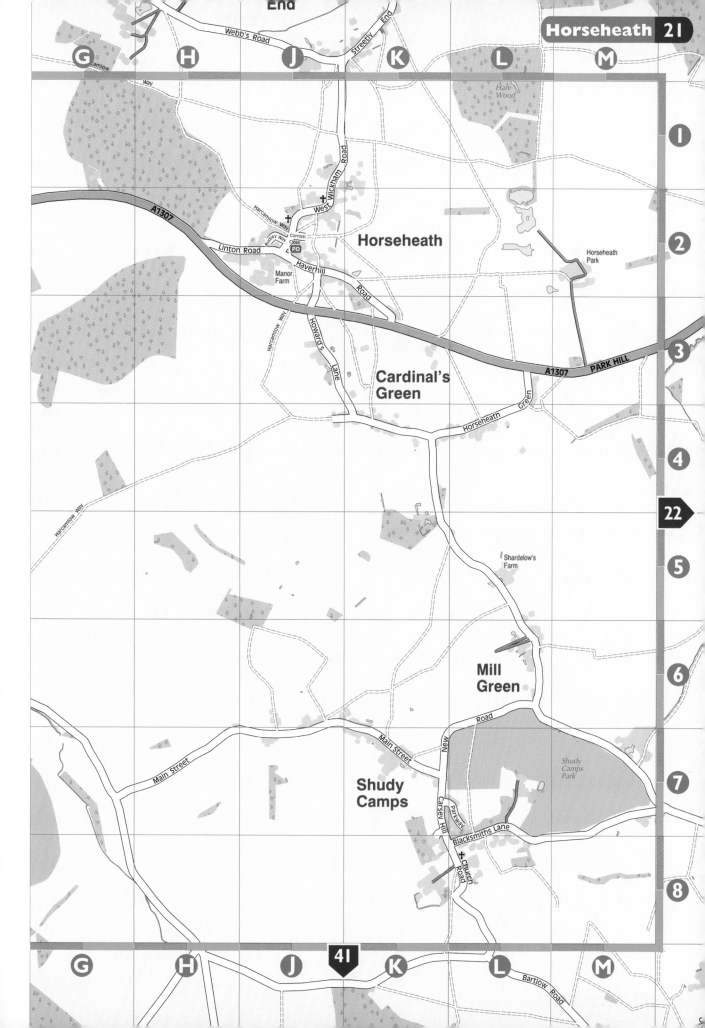

End

Webb's Road

Streetly End

G H J K L M

I

2

West Wickham Road

Hare Wood

Harcamlow Way

Audley Way

Cornish Close

PO

Horseheath

Linton Road

Haverhill

Manor Farm

Horseheath Park

A1307

3

Harcamlow Way

Howard's Lane

Road

Cardinal's Green

A1307 PARK HILL

Green

Horseheath

4

Harcamlow Way

22

Shardelow's Farm

5

6

Mill Green

Road

Main Street

New

Shudy Camps Park

7

Main Street

Shudy Camps

Carsey Hill

Parkval

Blacksmiths Lane

Church Road

8

G H J K L M

41

Bartlow Road

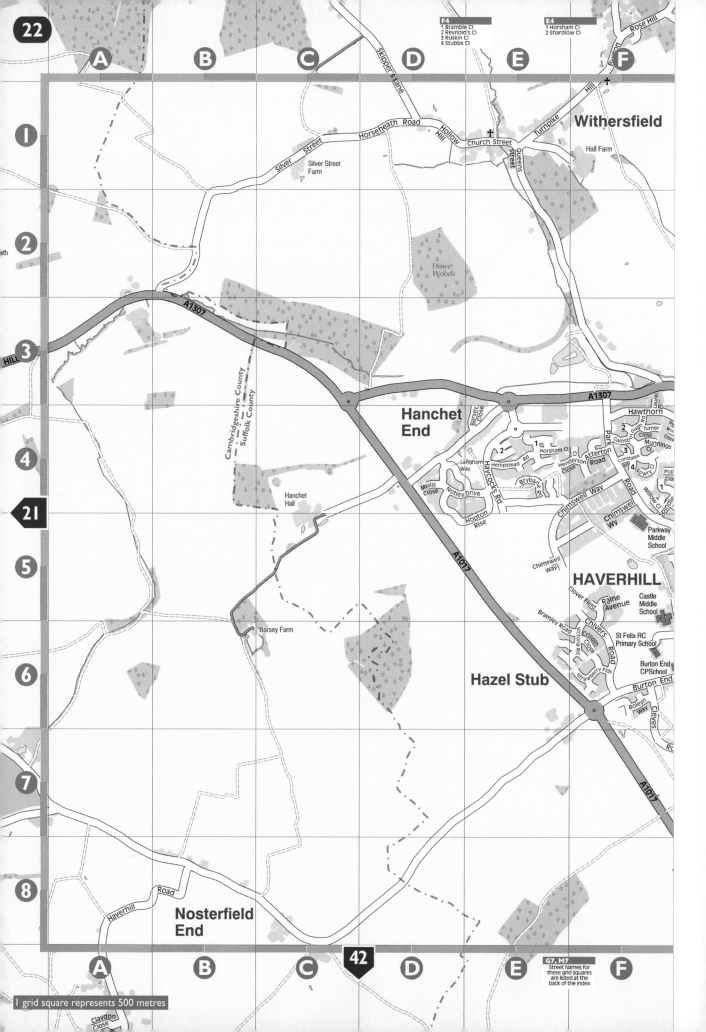

A B C D E F

F4
1 Bramble Cl
2 Reynold's Cl
3 Ruskin Cl
4 Stubbs Cl

E4
1 Horsham Cl
2 Shardlow Cl

I

Withersfield

Silver Street
Horseheath Road
Hollow Hill
Church Street
Queens Street
Turnpike Hill
Hall Farm

Silver Street Farm

2

Howe Wood

3

HILL

A1307

A1307

Cambridgeshire County
Suffolk County

Hanchet End

Hawthorn

4

Barsey Close
Park Road
Gainsborough Close
Turner Close
Munnings Cl
Horsham Cl
Atterton Road
Constable Cl
Henderson Cl
Lowry
Hempstead Rd
Langham Way
Bryhan Rd
Mellis Close
Notley Drive
Willow Cl
Sandle
Pop Clos
Haycocks Road
Hopton Rise
Chimswell Way
Chimswell Wy

21

Hanchet Hall

5

Chimswell Way

HAVERHILL

Parkway Middle School

Clover Field
Raine Avenue
Castle Middle School

Barsey Farm

Bramley Road
Chivers Road
Crispin Close
Victoria Rd
St Felix RC Primary School

6

Hazel Stub

A1017

Strawberry Flds
Burton End CP School
Burton End
Boleyn Way
Cleves

7

A1017

8

Haverhill Road

Nosterfield End

42

A B C D E F

G7, M7
Street Names for
these grid squares
are listed at the
back of the index

Claydon Close

1 grid square represents 500 metres

24

43

Little Wratting

CB9

G4
1 Cambridge Wy
2 Hawthorn Rd
3 Meadowsweet Cl

G5
1 Castle Wk

G6
1 The Causeway
2 Greenwood Cl
3 Horseshoe La
4 Yerril Gdn

H4
1 Cardinal Wy
2 Carlton Cl
3 Chaplains Cl
4 Chapple Dr
5 Markhams Cl
6 Moneypiece Cl

H5
1 Edmund Cl
2 Stephen Cl

M6
1 Fisher Cl
2 Hadrian Cl
3 Marcus Cl
4 Shannon Cl

L6
1 Stockley Cl

L7
1 Hudson Cl
2 Jupiter Cl

L5
1 Kingfisher Cl

K6
1 Elmhurst Cl
2 Pentlow H'ke Cl

K7
1 Ashlea Cl

J6
1 Helions Park Gv
2 Waveney Ter

H6
1 Clayhive Dr
2 Priory Av

J5
1 Dove House Rd
2 Murton Slade

Essex County

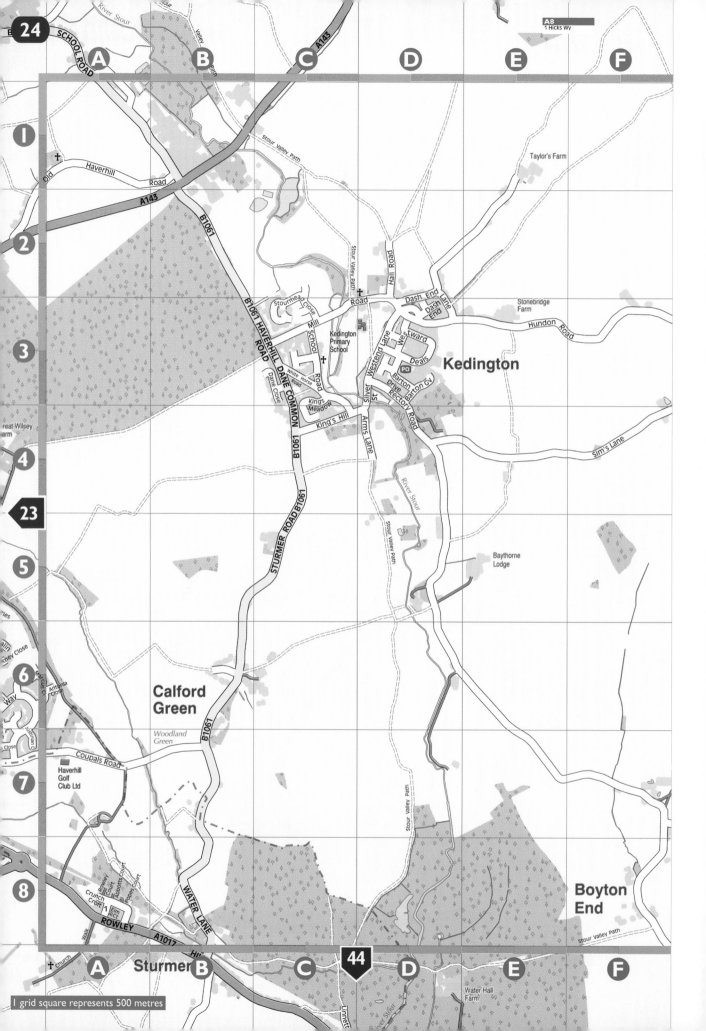

G · H · J · K · L · M

Mount Pleasant

Clare Road

Buntry Lane

Clock Hall

Green Lane

Brockley Green

PH

Parsonage Farm

Maple Hill

Ch tr

Lords Wood

Crooks Hall

Bank Way

Lane

Leys F

26

Canham's Farm

California Farm

Stonard's Farm

Cain's Hill

Farmer's Farm

A109

A1092

Moor Hall

G · H · J · K · L · M

Blacksmith

A1092

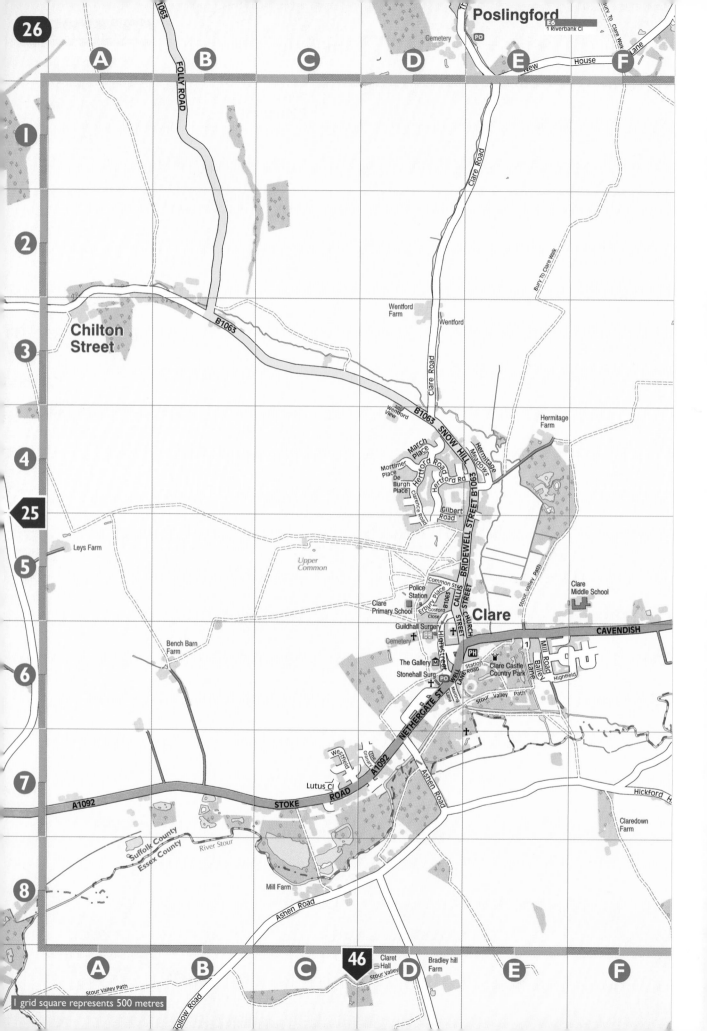

Poslingford

E6
1 Riverbank Cl

A   B   C   D   E   F

1

2

3   Chilton
     Street

FOLLY ROAD

1063

B1063

B1063

Wentford
Farm

Wentford

Clare Road

Clare Road

Bury To Clare Walk

4   SNOW HILL

     Hermitage
     Farm

     March
     Place
     Mortimer
     Place
     De
     Burgh
     Place
     Hertford Road
     Hertford Rd
     Clarence Road
     Gilbert
     Road
     Hermitage Meadows
     BRIDEWELL STREET B1063

25

5   Leys Farm

     Upper
     Common

     Common St
     Police
     Station
     Clare
     Primary School
     Erpury Place
     Gosford
     Close
     CALLIS STREET
     CHURCH STREET
     Clare
     Clare
     Middle School
     Stour Valley Path

6   Bench Barn
     Farm

     Guildhall Surgery
     Cemetery
     The Gallery
     Stonehall Surg
     High Street
     Well Lane
     Maltings Lane
     PH
     PO
     Station Road
     1
     Clare Castle
     Country Park
     Mill Road
     Bailey
     Highfield
     CAVENDISH

7   A1092

     NETHERGATE ST
     Westfield
     Lutus Cl
     Grove
     Green
     A1092
     STOKE ROAD
     Ashen Road
     Hickford H
     Claredown
     Farm

8   Suffolk County
     Essex County
     River Stour

     Mill Farm

     Ashen Road

     A   B   C   46 D   E   F
     Claret
     Hall
     stour valley
     Bradley hill
     Farm

     Stour Valley Path

     Bacon Row Road

L3
1 Manor Cl
2 Peacocks Cl

M3
1 Church Cl

G H J K L M

Ducks
Hall

Colt's
Hall

Blacklands
Hall

Water Lane

Peacocks

Peacocks Cl

Nether
Hall

Nether Rd

Road

Cavend

Stour Valley Path

Houghton
Hall

Stour Valley Path

Stour Valley Walk

Cavendish
Primary
School

PH PO

A1092 HIGH ST LOWER
ST

Sue Ryder
Foundation

Pentlow

Grey's
Close

POOLE STREET A1092

River Stour

Pentlow

STOUR STREET

Cavendish
Hall

A1092

Mill
Lane

ROAD A1092

River Stour

Bower Hall

Larks in the Wood

Paine's
Manor

Shearing
Place

Pannell's
Ash

I
2
3
4
28
5
6
7
8

G H J **47** K L M

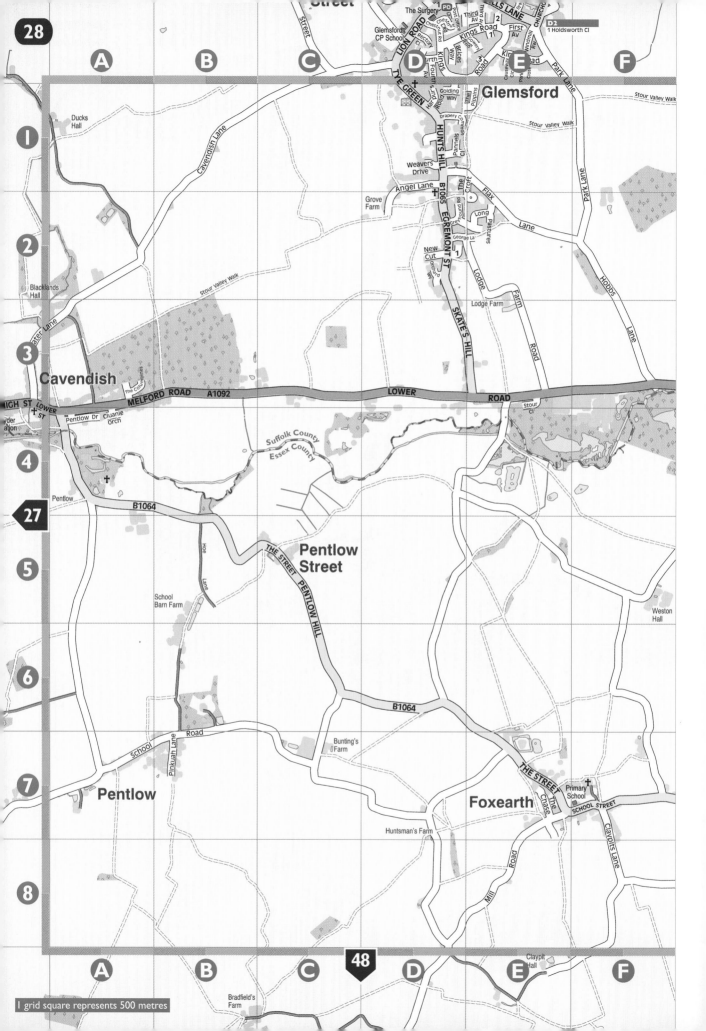

A   B   C   D   E   F

Street

The Surgery
PO Post Office
Wells Lane
CHURCH
D2
1 Holdsworth Cl

Glemsford
CP School
LION ROAD
Chestnut Rd
Rectory
Kings Road
Third Av
First Av

Ducks
Hall

Kings
Way

Glemsford

Stour Valley Walk

Cavendish Lane

Stour Valley Walk

TYE GREEN

Golding
Way

HUNTS HILL

Pannells Cl

Stour Valley Walk

Weavers
Drive

Angel Lane

Grove
Farm

B1065

The
Croft

Flax

Long
Pastures

Lane

Blacklands
Hall

Stour Valley Walk

EGREMONT ST

George La

Park Lane

Hobbs

New
Cut

Orchard
Wy

1

Lodge
Farm

Lane

3

Cavendish

Water Lane

The Columbines

MELFORD ROAD   A1092

LOWER   ROAD

SKATE'S HILL

Lodge Farm

Farm Road

Stour Cl

HIGH ST

LOWER
ST

Ryder
station

Pentlow Dr
Cluanie
orch

4

Pentlow

†

27

B1064

Suffolk County
Essex County

Pentlow
Street

Hoe Lane

THE STREET   PENTLOW HILL

5

Weston
Hall

School
Barn Farm

6

School   Road

Pinkuan Lane

Bunting's
Farm

B1064

THE STREET

The Chase

7

Pentlow

Foxearth

Primary
School

SCHOOL STREET

†

Claypits Lane

Huntsman's Farm

MILL   Road

8

Claypit
Hall

A   B   C   **48**   D   E   F

Bradfield's
Farm

1 grid square represents 500 metres

G H J K L M

LS
1 Steeds Meadow

B1066

Lumpit
Wood

River Glem

Cranmore
Green Farm

Stour Valley Walk

Kentwell
Hall

Stour Valley Walk

High Street
Farm

1

Parsonage
Farm

Cranmoregreen Lane

St Edmund Way

HIGH STREET

A1092

2

Harefield

3

Burton's
Farm

A1092

WINDMILL HILL   WESTGATE STREET

Church Wk

A1092

B1064

Cranbrook Lane

School Lane

Melford
Hall (NT)

4

River Stour

Chad Brook

B1064

Smaley La
Spicers La

Hotel

Lakforthi

Sam Palmerswent

Jason Dr

5

Liston
Garden

Chantry
Cock And
Bell La

PH
PO

Gallery
Woollards
Gdns

The Long Melford
Practice

1

Cordell Road

Cordell
Place

Shaw Road

Chadburn
Road

Middle
Way

Raile Walk

Hill
Cl

The
Limes

Olivers
Cl

Olivers
Cl

6

Meeting
Fld

View Rd

St. Catherine's Rd

HALL ST

Laurel
Dr

Long Melford
Primary Sch

Swan
Lane

Swanfield

Swanfield

Rivish
La

Roman
Way

LONG
MELFORD

Liston

Liston Lane

Stour Valley Walk

Stour Valley Walk

LITTLE ST MARY'S

SOUTHGATE ST

Southgate
Gdns

Cordwoa Dr

Clopton Dr

7

B1064

STATION RD

RODBRIDGE HL

The
Drays

The
Stephen
Clips

Martyns Rise

Westcrops

8

G H J K L M

Brook Hall

Ropers
Lane

Rodbridge House
Lane

Mills

BORLEY
ROAD

B1064

A134

**Rodbridge
Corner**

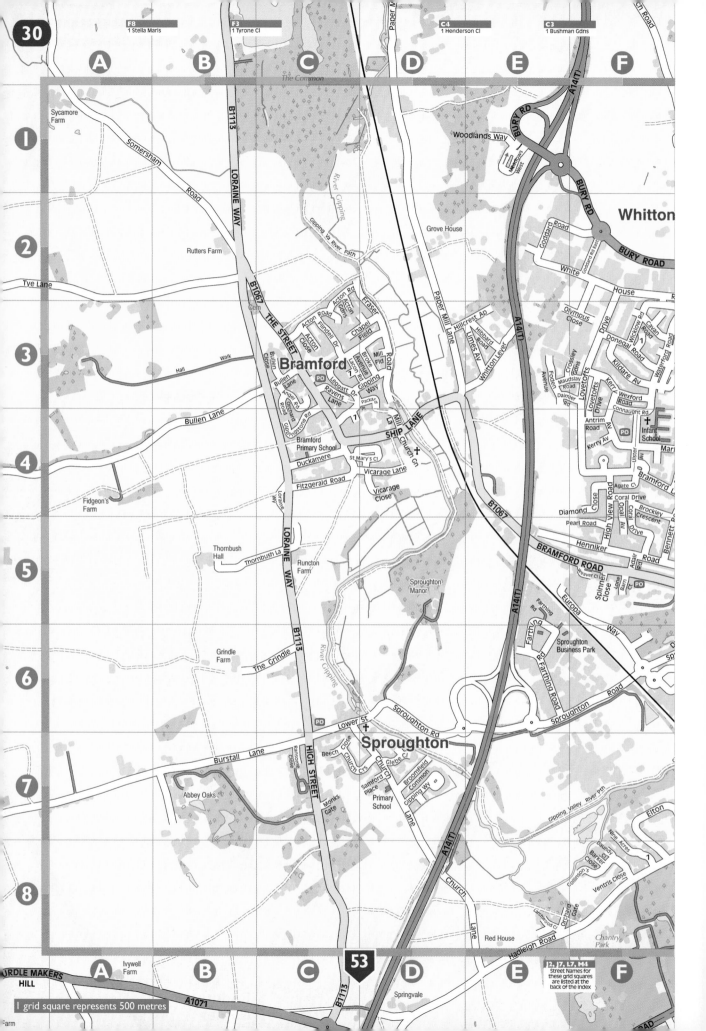

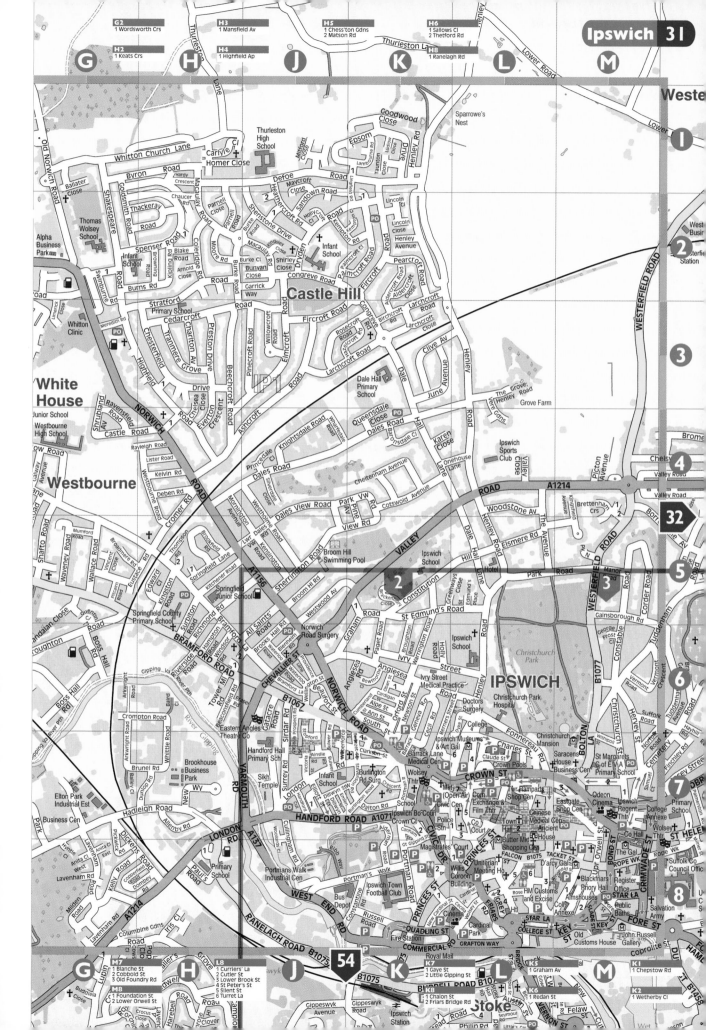

G2
1 Wordsworth Crs

H3
1 Mansfield Av

H5
1 Chess'ton Gdns
2 Matson Rd

H6
1 Sallows Cl
2 Thetford Rd

H2
1 Keats Crs

H4
1 Highfield Ap

H8
1 Ranelagh Rd

Weste

Lower

West
Busi

sterfield
Station

WESTERFIELD ROAD

Chelsy

Valley Road

Valley Road

Brome

A1214

Brettenham
Crs

Bore

Picton Avenue

Kingsfield Avenue

The Avenue

WESTERFIELD ROAD

Gainsborough Rd

George
Frost
Constable

Manor
Road

Constable
Road

Corder Road

Tuddenham

Vermont
Crescent

Vermont
Road

B1077

Christchurch
Park

Hayhill

Tuddenham
Avenue

Suffolk
Road

IPSWICH

Christchurch
Mansion

Christchurch Park
Hospital

Doctors
Surgery

College

Fonnereau Rd

Saracens
House
Business Cen

St Margarets
C of E
Primary School

Bolton La

Finchley Road

Withipol

Cemetery

Norwich
Road

Henley
Road

Hervey
St

Christchurch
Park

G
H
J
K
L
M
I

Goodwood
Close

Sparrowe's
Nest

Thurleston La

Thurleston
High
School

Epsom
Close

Henley Rd

Mitford
Close

Ludlow

Meadow

Taunton
Close

Lambourne Rd

Whitton Church Lane

Carlyle Cl
Homer Close

Byron Road

Defoe Road

Maycroft
Close

Sandown Road

Lincoln
Cl

Lincoln
Close

Henley
Avenue

Ballater
Close

Hardy
Crescent

Heathercroft Rd

Holly Cl

Kempton

Kempton Rd

PO

Thackeray Road

Chaucer
Rd

Macaulay
Road

Parnell
Close

Parnell
Road

Shenstone Drive

Dryden

Burke Rd

Palmcroft Cl

Palmcroft Road

Fircroft

Pearcroft Road

Shakespeare

Thomas
Wolsey
School

Alpha
Business
Park

Coldsmith Road

Spenser Road

Coleridge Road

Blake
Road

Browning
Road

Kipling Rd

Moore Rd

Burke
Road

Arnold
Close

Burke Cl

Bunyan
Close

Shirley
Close

Macaulay
Road

Infant
School

Congreve Road

Aldercroft Road

Aldercroft
Close

Birchcroft Rd

Larchcroft
Road

Larchcroft
Close

Limerick
Close

Whitton
Clinic

PO

Infant
School

Burns Rd

Stratford
Primary School

Cedarcroft

Tramere
Grove

Charlton Av

Chelsea
Crescent

Everton Rd

Pinecroft Road

Willowcroft
Road

Elmcroft

Fircroft Road

Castle Hill

Congreve Road

Rosecroft
Road

Rosecroft
Road

Larchcroft Road

Clive Av

Henley

June
Avenue

The Grove,
Henley Road

Grove Farm

Vere Gdns

White
House

Junior School

Westbourne
High School

NORWICH

Shrubland
Av

Ravensfield
Road

Castle Road

Rayleigh Road

Beechcroft Road

Drive

IP1

Dale Hall
Primary
School

Queensdale
Close

Dales Road

PO

Dale Hall

Dale

Karen
Close

Baronsdale Cl

Onehouse
Lane

Ipswich
Sports
Club

Valley
Close

Westbourne

low Road

Kelvin Rd

Deben Rd

Cromer Rd

Lister Road

Mornington
Avenue

Princedale

Dales Road

Knightsdale Road

Silverdale
Close

Wharfedale

Dales Road

Dales View Road

Park Vw

Cheltenham Avenue

Cotswold Avenue

Valley

ROAD

Woodstone Av

Henley Road

Dale Hall
Road

Elsmere
Road

Hotel

Railway

Shafto Road

Wavaney Road

Wallace Road

Mumford
Road

Broadmere Rd

Vincent
Close

Eustace Rd

Edward
Cl

Kingston
Road

Springfield Lane

Brookfield
Road

Thompson
Rd

Kitchener Road

Springfield
Junior School

PO

Sherrington Road

Broom HI Rd

Westwood Av

Pine
Av

View Rd

Lwr
Vw

Dales
Rd

Kensington

Broom Hill
Swimming Pool

Ipswich
School

Constitution

Greenways
Close

St Edmund's Road

Edmund's
Place

Ipswich
School

Park Road

2

Brackenbury

Mahdalan Close

Quentin
Road

Boss
Rd

Pitcairn
Rd

Subiton
Road

Richmond
Road

Hampton
Road

Bramford
Lane

Windsor
Rd

Fraser
Rd

All Saints Rd

Brooks Hall Rd

Blenheim

Bramford

Norwich
Road Surgery

Providence

Paget Road

Graham Road

Broughton
Road

Brunswick Road

Warrington Road

Ivry St

Ivry
Street

Holly
Street

Doctors
Surgery

Ipswich
School

3

Boss
Hall

Crompton Road

Arkwright
Road

Whittle Road

Baird
Road

BRAMFORD ROAD

Tower Mill Rd

Beaconsfield Rd

River Gipping

River Path

A1156

YARMOUTH
RD

CHEVALLIER ST

Catacre Rd

Sirdar Rd

B1067

Orford

Orford St

Waterloo

Bramford

Anglesea
Road

NORWICH
ROAD

Cardigan

Cumberland St

St Ann St

Newson St

Cecil St

Berners Street

Anglesea
Road

Geneva St

Alpe St

Berners
Street

College
St

Ivry Street
Medical Practice

Ipswich Museums
& Art Gal

Charles St

Claude St

Elton Park
Industrial Est

Business Cen

Dunlop Rd

Bailey Rd

Brookhouse
Business
Park

New Wy

Brunel Rd

Eastern Angles
Theatre Co

Handford Hall
Primary Sch

Sikh
Temple

Surrey Rd

London
Road

Prospect St

Victoria St

Ainslie Rd

Dillwyn St W

Dillwyn St E

Clarkson St

Burlington
Rd Surg

Barrack Lane

Barrack
Road

Medical Cen

Wolsey
Thtr

Misty's
(Open Air)

Civic Cen

Com
Exchange &
Film Thtr

Crown Pools

Ipswich Museums
& Art Gal

CROWN ST

Chinese
Medical Cen

Eastgate
Shop Cen

Qdeon
Cinema

Ipswich
Regent
Thtr

College
Annexe

Wolsey
Thtr

Primary
School

ST HELE

Hadleigh Road

Dickens Road

Kelly Road

Pickwick

Anita Cl
West

Copperfield Road

Dombey
Road

Paul's
Road

A137

LONDON
RD

St
Paul's
Primary
School

Cullingham Road

Portmans Walk
Industrial Cen

Portman's

Portman Road

Ipswich Town
Football Club

Bus
Depot

Cardinal
Park

WEST END RD

Russell
Road

Fire Station

Constantine Road

Gt Gipping St

HANDFORD ROAD A1071

Crown Ct

Dalton Rd

Ipswich Bo'Court

Crown Ct

Police
Stn

Civic
Dr

Co
Court

Town
Hall

Magistrates'
Court

Princes St

Willis
Coroon
Buildings

PRINCES ST

Unitarian
Meeting Ho

Ancient
House

Butter Mkt
Shopping Cen

FALCON

B1075

Cinema

Cardinal

Rose HM Customs
and Excise

Blackfriars
Priory Hall

Colly
Annexe

D'Arcy Gal

TACKET ST

Almshouses

Public
Baths

Salvation
Army

ROPE WK

STAR LA

The Gal

Co Hall

Co-op

ROPE WK

Register
Office

Suffolk Co
Council Offices

Mildenhall
Road

Lavenham
Road

Crocus Close

Grove

Columbine Gdns

Iris
Road

A1214

RANELAGH ROAD B1075

54

B1075

COMMERCIAL RD

QUADLING ST

GRAFTON WAY

Royal Mail

John Russell
Gallery

Old
Customs House

Coprolite St

HAM

G
H
J
K
L
M

M7
1 Blanche St
2 Cobbold St
3 Old Foundry Rd

L8
1 Curriers' La
2 Cutler St
3 Lower Brook St
4 St Peter's St
5 Silent St
6 Turret La

K7
1 Gaye St
2 Little Gipping St

L7
1 Graham Av

K1
1 Chepstow Rd

M8
1 Foundation St
2 Lower Orwell St

K6
1 Chalon St
2 Friars Bridge Rd

L6
1 Redan St

K2
1 Wetherby Cl

Buddleia
Close

Gippeswyk
Avenue

Gippeswyk
Road

BURRELL ROAD B10

Austin St

New

Felaw

VERNON ST

Stoke

Ipswich
Station

Seymour

Philip Rd

Wet

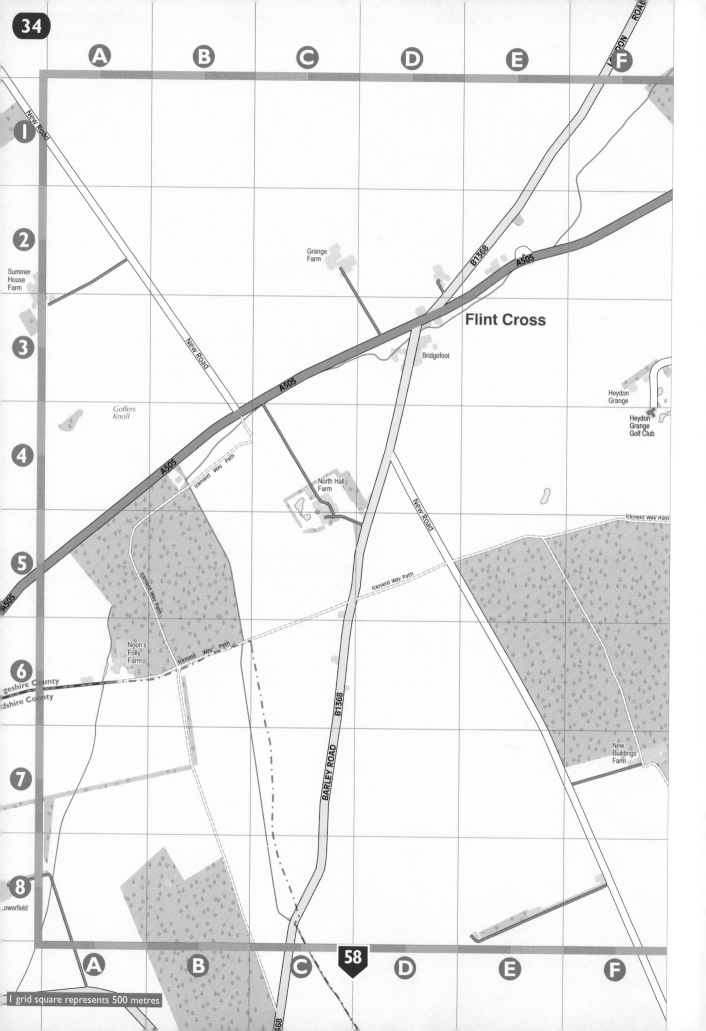

A B C D E F

1

New Road

2

Summer House Farm

Grange Farm

B1368   A505

3

Flint Cross

Bridgefoot

New Road

Heydon Grange

Goffers Knoll

Heydon Grange Golf Club

A505

4

A505

Icknield Way Path

North Hall Farm

New Road

Icknield Way Path

5

A505

Icknield Way Path

Icknield Way Path

6

Noon's Folly Farm

Icknield Way Path

...geshire County
...dshire County

BARLEY ROAD   B1368

7

New Buildings Farm

8

...owerfield

A B C D E F

1 grid square represents 500 metres

G H J K L M

A505

Grange Road

I

2

3

Dottrell
House

A505

Fowlmere Road

Chrishall
Grange

4

36

5

6

Icknield Way Path

7

Cambridgeshire County

Essex County

Hertford La

Cra ey
End

8

Heydon

Fowlmere
High Road

Close

Heydon Lane

Abram's Lane

Mill Causeway

Crawley End

Crawley End

Icknield Way Path

Pinkeneys

Engleric

59

Harcamlow Way

G H J K L M

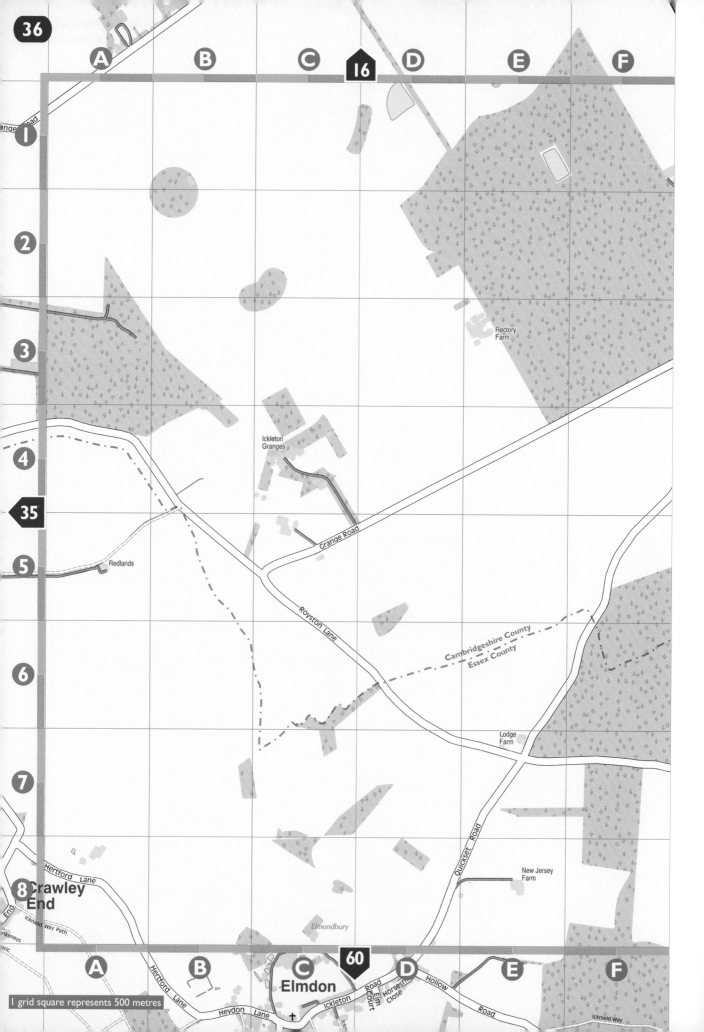

A   B   C   D   E   F

16

I

2

3

4

35

5

6

7

8 Crawley
End

A   B   C   D   E   F

60

Elmdon

Rectory
Farm

Ickleton
Granges

Grange Road

Redlands

Royston Lane

Cambridgeshire County
Essex County

Lodge
Farm

New Jersey
Farm

Quickset Road

Hertford Lane

Icknield Way Path

kenteneys

Elmondbury

Hertford Lane

Heydon Lane

Ickleton

Ickleton
Road
Elm
Court

Horsestih
Close

Hollow
Road

Icknield Way

I grid square represents 500 metres

J2
1 Icknield Cl

M2
1 Wakefield

Cemetery

Brookhampton St

G

H

J

17

K

L

M

I

Butcher's Hill

Mill Lane

PO

Church Street

River Cam or Granta

M11

Abbey Farm

Abbey Street

Southfield

Birds Close

Back Lane

Priory Close

Ickleton

The Stackyard

Coploe Road

Frogge Street

M11

B1383 NEWMARKET ROAD

Carmen St

Hyll Close

Wil

Lane

ROA

B1184

2

The Elms

Meadow Rd

Jackson's Rd

Four Acres

The Willows

Spencer Rd

Rookery

Rose L

Eastgate

High Stre

Carmen St

Pilgrims Cl

PO

Church Street

Primary School

The Surg

3

Great Chest

Frogge St

Ickleton Road

School St

School Street

South Street

Manor Lane

Rose L

LC

School Street Surgery

Granta Close

LONDON ROAD

Ickleton Wy Path

Great Chesterford Station

Ash Gn

4

38

B138

Junction 9

Icknield Way Path

M11

5

Valance Farm

6

Strethall Field

7

The Poplars

8

G

H

J

61

K

Strethall Road

L

M

Strethall

Howe Wood

Strethall Road

Strethall Road

Catmere

38

A   B   C   **18**   D   E   F

Cow Lane

Farm

A3
1 Bartholomew Cl

I   B184

Burtonwood
Farm

Icknield Way Path

2   WALDEN ROAD

Stanley Road

Jackson's

The Four Acres

Spencer

The Willows

Cow Lane

Icknield Way Path

Rookery

Rose

The Surg

High   Street

Primary
School

Rose Lane

3   **Great
Chesterford**

Rectory
Farm

Chesterford Park

4

River Cam or Granta

37   B1383

Emanuel
Wood

5   Bordeaux
Farms

High   Street

WALDEN ROAD

**Little
Chesterford**

6   B1383   B184

Springwell

7   B1383   SPRINGWELL ROAD

Rowley Hill
Farm

8   Westley
Farm

Westley
Lane

A   B   C   **62**   D   E   F

B1052

rethall Road   CAMFIELD ROAD   Roman Way   3

1 grid square represents 500 metres   2   1   Walden Road

Northend

G   H   J   **19**   K   L   M

Hadstock Common

Icknield Way Path

B1052

Monk's Hall

Bowsers Lane

Bowsers

Park Farm

Bowsers Lane

B1052

Ravenstock Green Farm

Petts Lane

Mitchells

Little Walden

B1052

Sadlers Farm

Harcamlow Way

LITTLE WALDEN ROAD

THE SLADE

Butlers Farm

Butlers Lane

Harcamlow Way

Walden Road

Ashdon Road

Hales Wood

Byrds Farm

Redgate

G   H   J   **63**   K   L   M

I   2   3   4   **40**   5   6   7   8

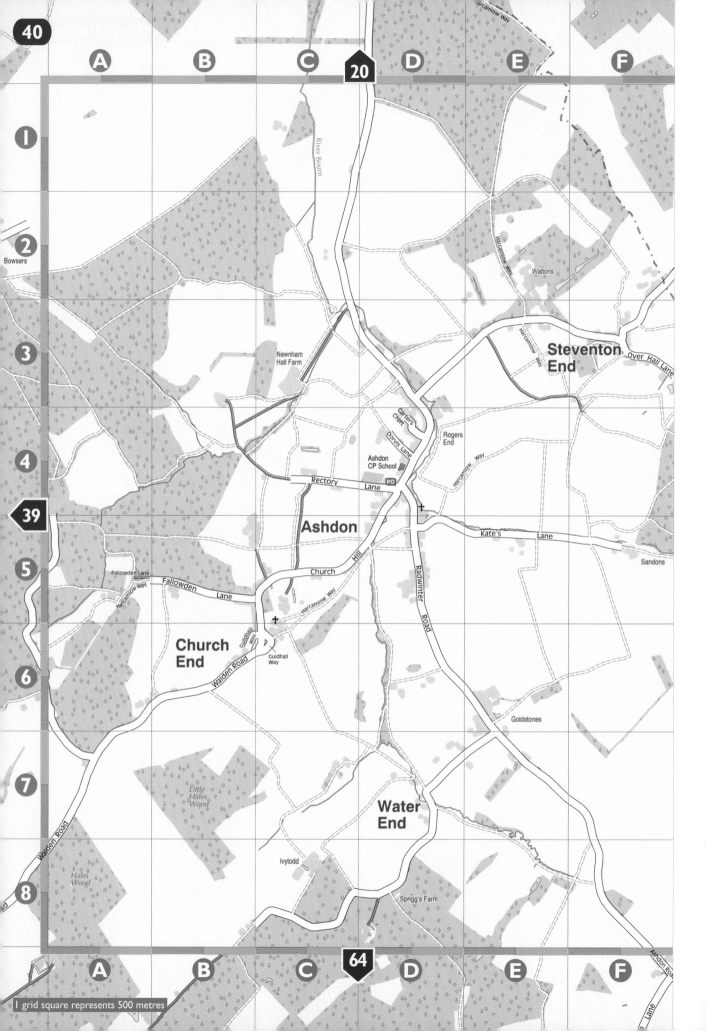

40

A B C 20 D E F

I

2
Bowsers

3

4

39

5

6

7

8

A B 64 C D E F

Newnham
Hall Farm

River Bourn

Harcamlow Way

Waltons

Steventon
End

Over Hall Lane

Carters
Croft

Dorvis Lane

Ashdon
CP School

PO

Rogers
End

Rectory Lane

Harcamlow Way

Ashdon

Kate's Lane

Sandons

Church Hill

Fallowden Lane

Fallowden Lane

Harcamlow Way

Harcamlow Way

Radwinter Road

Church
End

Guidhall Way

Guidhall
Way

Walden Road

Goldstones

Little Hales
Wood

Water
End

Walden Road

Ivytodd

Sprigg's Farm

Hales
Wood

Ashdon Road

Lane

1 grid square represents 500 metres

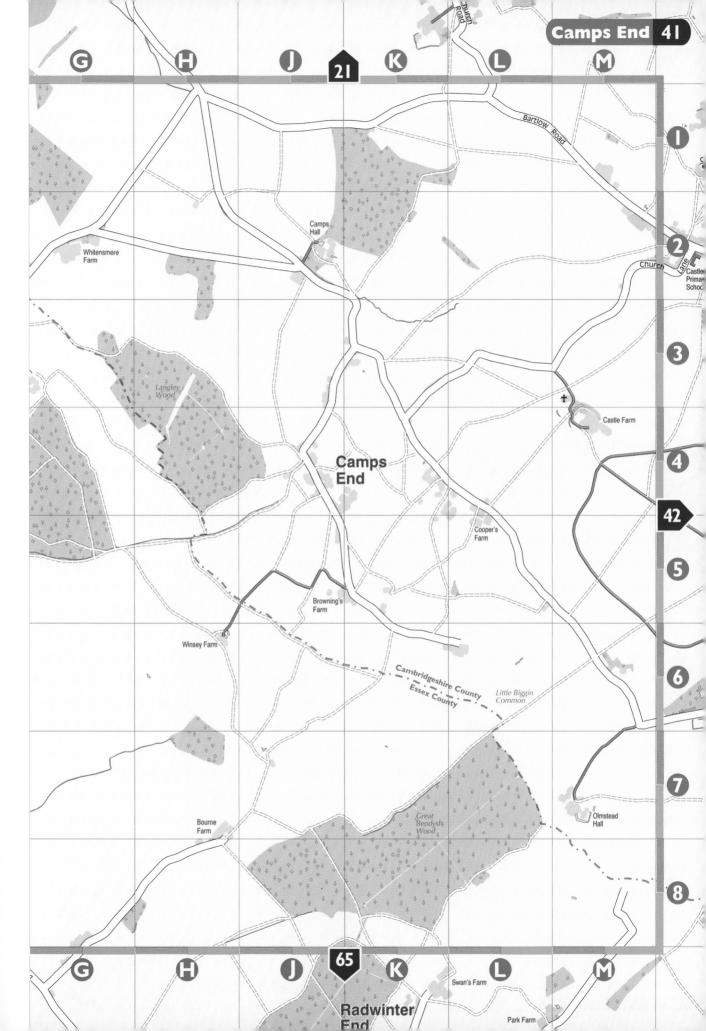

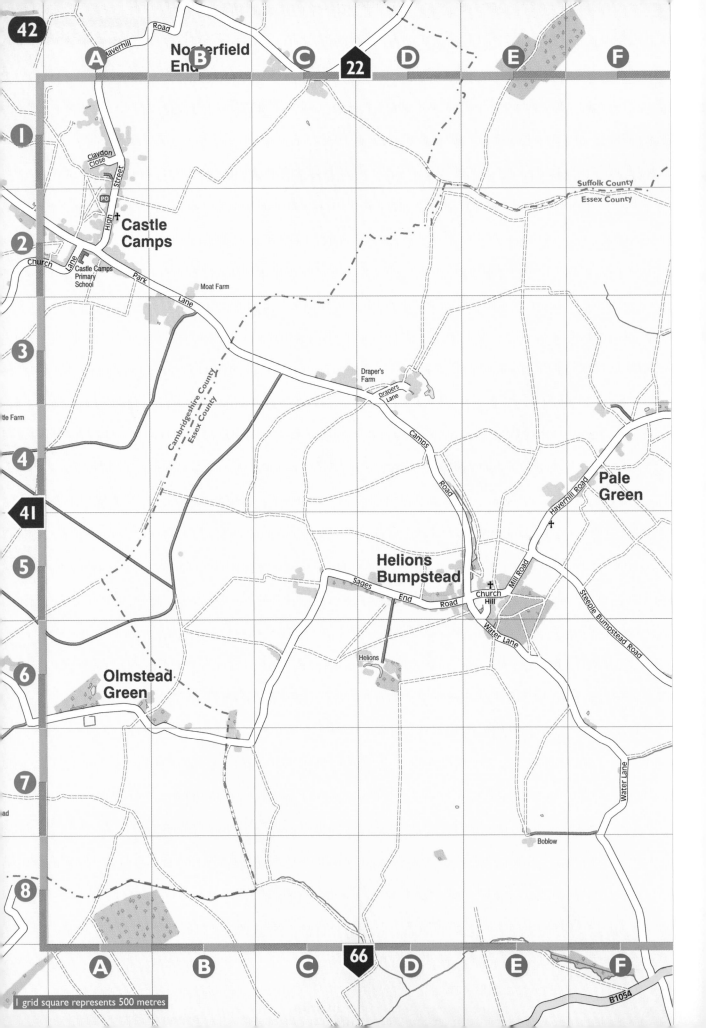

A Haverhill Road B Nosterfield End C 22 D E F

I

Claydon Close

High Street

PO

+ Castle Camps

Church Lane

Castle Camps Primary School

Park Lane

Moat Farm

2

3

Castle Farm

Cambridgeshire County
Essex County

Draper's Farm

Drapers Lane

Camps Road

Pale Green

Haverhill Road

+

4

41

5

Helions Bumpstead

Sages End Road

Church Hill

Mill Road

Water Lane

Steeple Bumpstead Road

Olmstead Green

Helions

6

7

Water Lane

Boblow

8

A B C 66 D E F

B1054

I grid square represents 500 metres

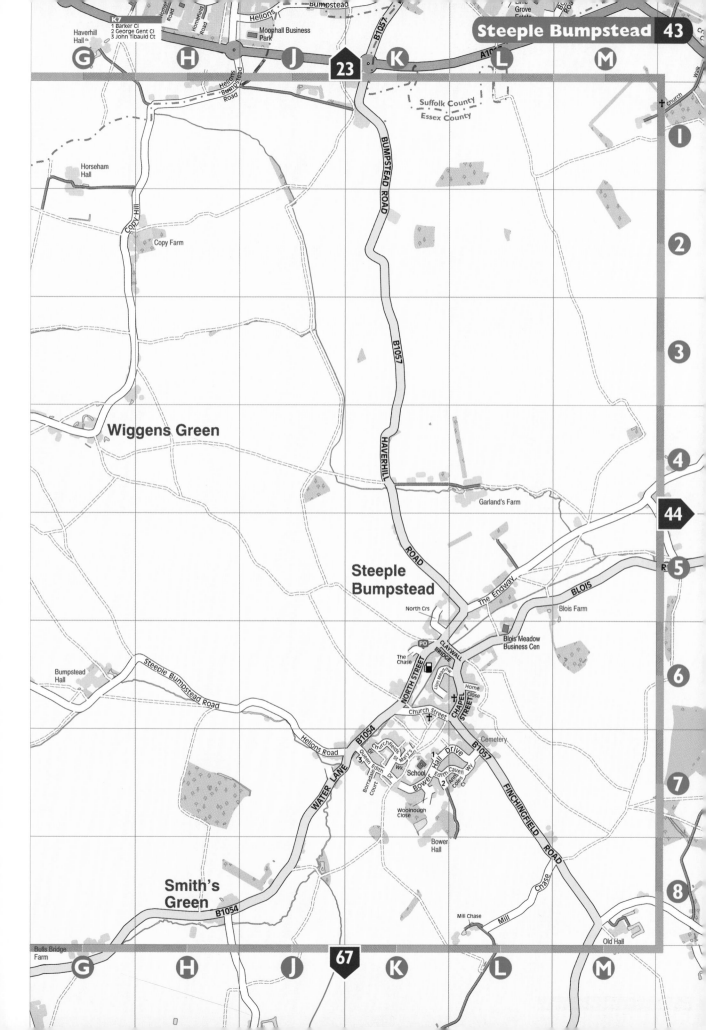

G H J **23** K L M

1 Barker Cl
2 George Gent Cl
3 John Tibauld Ct

K7

Haverhill
Hall

Homefield
Road

Hellions
Bumpstead
Road

Moophall Business
Park

Suffolk County
Essex County

A1017

† church

1

Horseham
Hall

Copy Hill

Copy Farm

BUMPSTEAD ROAD

B1057

2

3

Wiggens Green

HAVERHILL

Garland's Farm

44

4

**Steeple
Bumpstead**

ROAD

North Crs

The Endway

BLOIS

Blois Farm

R

5

Blois Meadow
Business Cen

Bumpstead
Hall

Steeple Bumpstead Road

PO

The Chase

CLAYWALL
BRIDGE

NORTH STREET

Lion Meadow

Home
Close

CHAPEL
STREET

6

Hellions Road

B1054

Church Street

Cemetery

B1057

Churchfields

Queen Edith Dr

Borradale
Court

St Mary's
Wk

School

Bower Hall Drive

Cavell Wy

Anne
Coles
Cl

Edith

FINCHINGFIELD

7

WATER LANE

Woolnough
Close

Bower
Hall

**Smith's
Green**

B1054

Mill Chase

Mill
Chase

ROAD

Old Hall

8

Bulls Bridge
Farm

G H J **67** K L M

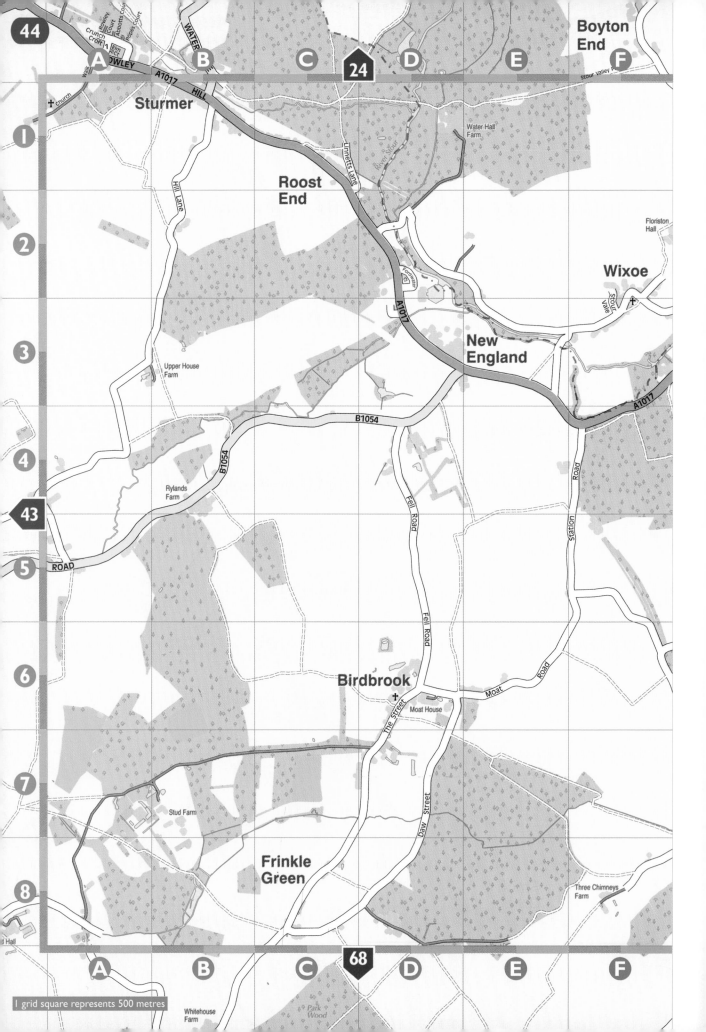

Boyton
End

A **B** **C** 24 **D** **E** **F**

stour Valley P

✝ church

Sturmer

Crunch
Croft
Pope's Court

WATER

WL

OWLEY

A1017

HILL

1

2

3

43

4

5

6

7

8

Roost
End

Hill Lane

Linnetts Lane

River Stour

Water Hall
Farm

Floriston
Hall

Fordwater

A1017

New
England

Wixoe

✝

Stour Vale

A1017

Upper House
Farm

B1054

B1054

Rylands
Farm

ROAD

Fell Road

B1054

Station Road

Fell Road

Birdbrook

✝

Moat House

The Street

Moat

Road

Stud Farm

Daw Street

Frinkle
Green

Three Chimneys
Farm

Hall

A **B** **C** 68 **D** **E** **F**

I grid square represents 500 metres

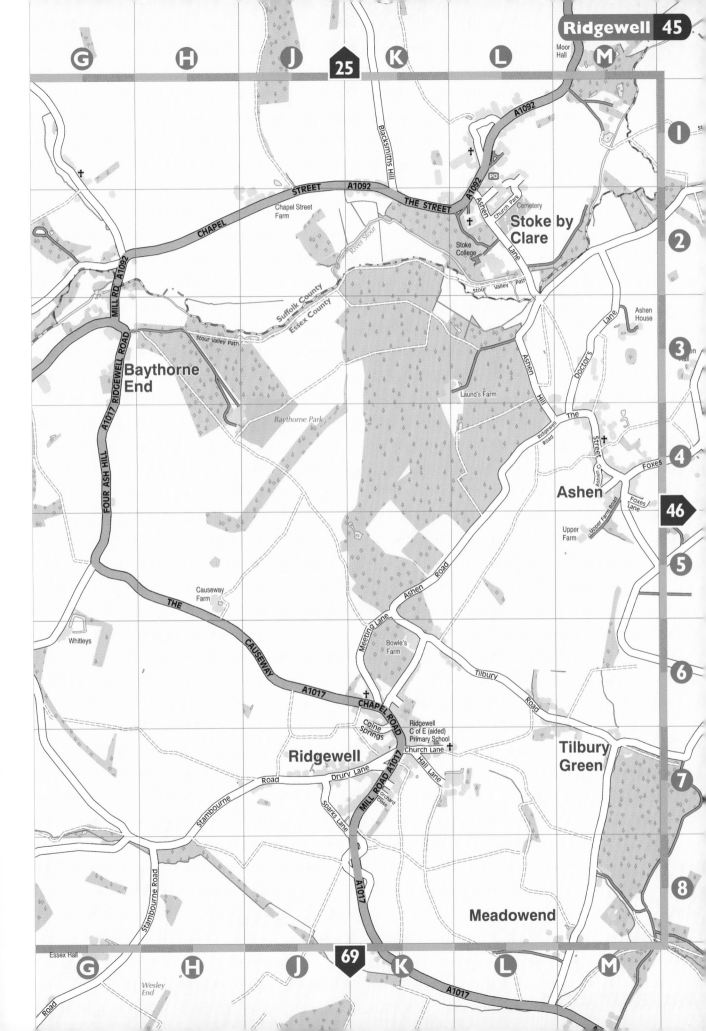

G H J **25** K L M

Moor Hall

I

A1092

2

Chapel Street Farm

CHAPEL STREET A1092

THE STREET

A1092

PO

Church Park Cemetery

Ashen Lane

Stoke College

River Stour

Stoke by Clare

Blacksmiths Hill

Suffolk County

Essex County

Stour Valley Path

Stour Valley Path

Ashen House

3

Ashen Hill

Doctor's Lane

The Street

Baythorne End

MILL RD A1092

A1017 RIDGEWELL ROAD

FOUR ASH HILL

Baythorne Park

Laund's Farm

Ridgewell Road

Ashen Close

The Street

4

Foxes

Foxes Lane

Ashen

46

Upper Farm

Upper Farm Road

5

Causeway Farm

Whitleys

THE CAUSEWAY

A1017

Ashen Road

Meeting Lane

Bowle's Farm

Tilbury Road

6

Coine Springs

CHAPEL ROAD

Ridgewell C of E (aided) Primary School

Church Lane

Tilbury Green

7

Ridgewell

Road

Drury Lane

Stambourne

MILL ROAD A1017

Hall Lane

Sparks Lane

Orchard Close

Stambourne Road

A1017

8

Meadowend

Essex Hall

G H J **69** K L M

Wesley End

Road

A1017

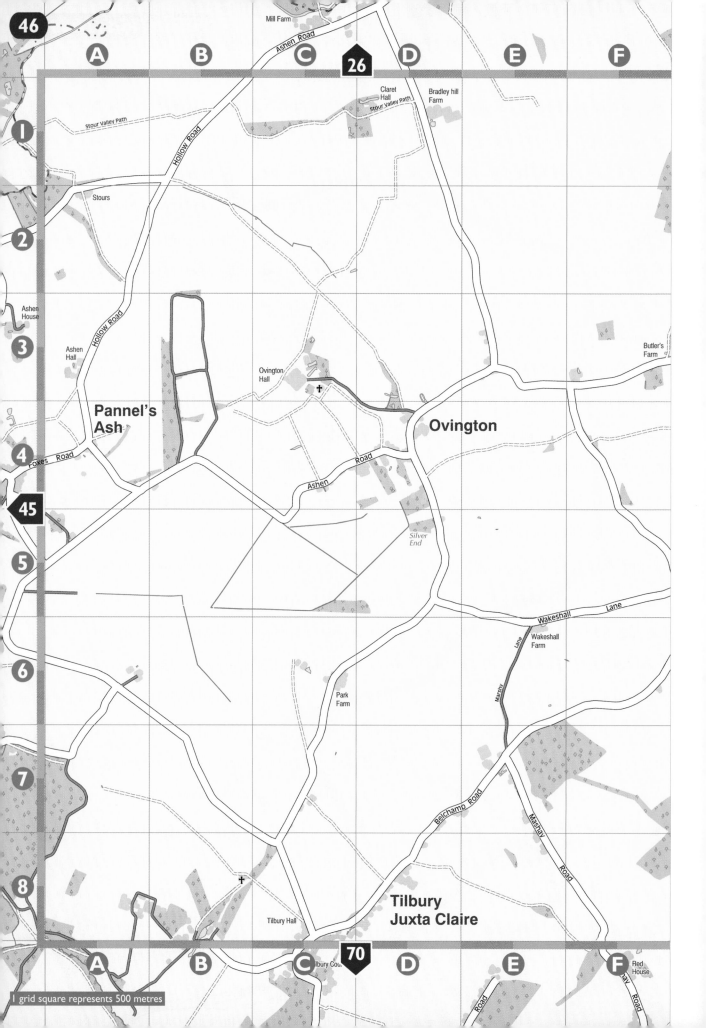

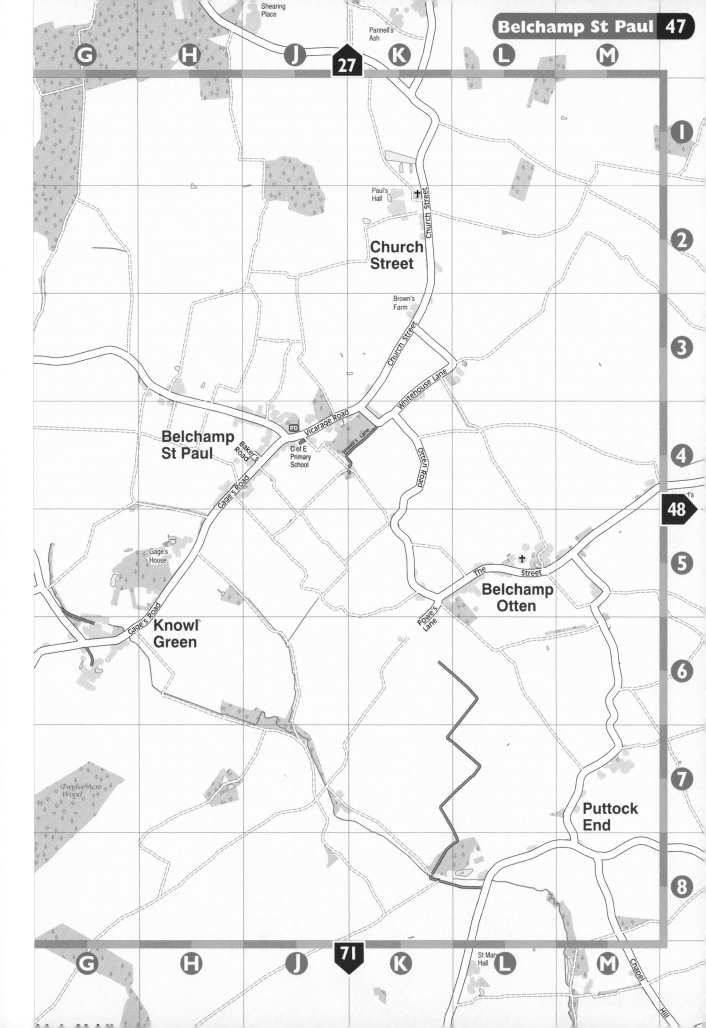

G H J **27** K L M

1
2
3
4
48
5
6
7
8

Shearing Place

Pannell's Ash

Paul's Hall

Church Street

Church Street

Brown's Farm

Whitehouse Lane

PO Vicarage Road

Sewell's Lane

Otten Road

Belchamp St Paul

Baker's Road

Gage's Road

C of E Primary School

Gage's House

Gage's Road

Knowl Green

Twelve Acre Wood

Fowe's Lane

The Street

Belchamp Otten

Puttock End

G H J **71** K St Mary Hall L M Chapel Hill

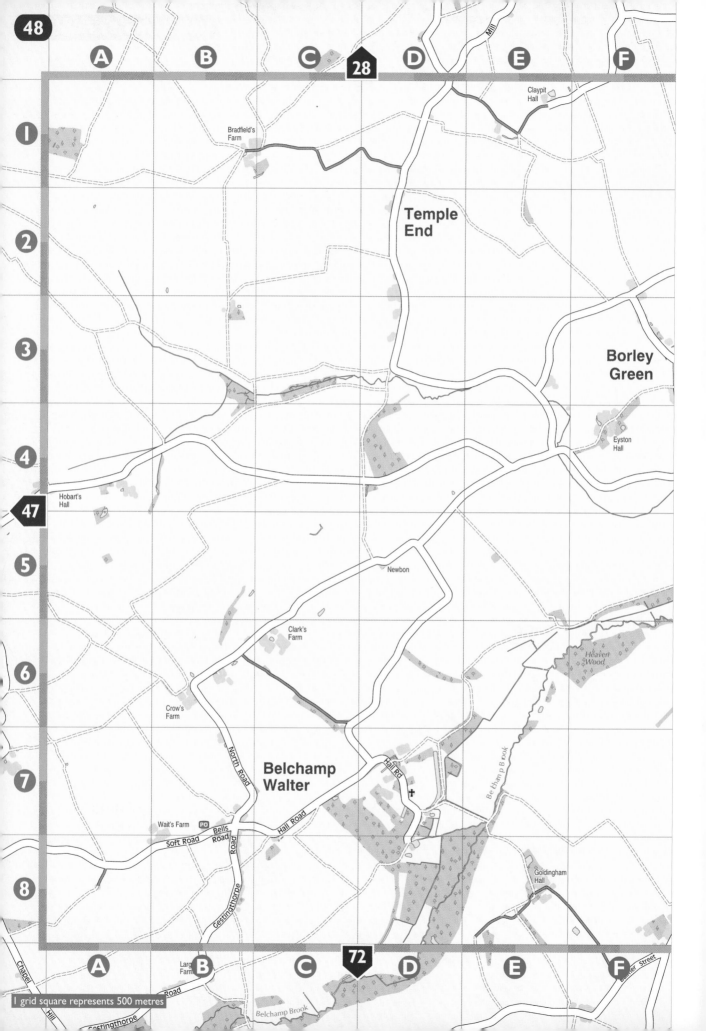

G   H   J   **29**   K   L   M

M3
1 Courtenay Cl

M8
1 Lark Ri

B1064

The Wash
Draws

RODBRIDGE HL

Ropers
Lane

Rodbridge House

Mills Lane

I 1

Brook Hall

BORLEY
ROAD

**Rodbridge
Corner**

B1064 SUDBURY ROAD

A134

Lower Road

Stour Valley Walk

CO10

A134

2

+**Borley**

Hall Road

Borley
Hall

River Stour

Pembroke Pl

Grosvenor Rd

Lombardy Rd

Canterbury Road

Lancaster Rd

Chaucer Road

Rochester Way

St Bartholomews Lane

Highview Close

Parkwood

3 +

4

Colneys Close

Priory Road

Abbey Rd

Tudor

Stour Valley Walk

The Valley
Walk

MELFORD

Brundon La

A131 ROAD

River Stour

Stour Va Walk

4

Queens Road

Brundon

50

The Rookery

Essex County

Suffolk County

Brundon La

St Josephs RC
Primary School

Croft Rd

Beaconsfield

A131

A1

5

Smeetham
Hall

Smeetham Lane

Finch Hill

Bulmer Road
Industrial Est

Brundon Lane

SUDBURY

Walnut Tree
Hosp

Hotel

Walnut Tree La

Babergh
District
Council

A131

A131

Sudbur
Centre

New

6 +

Kitchen Hill

Bulmer Road
Industrial Estate

Bulmer Road
Industrial Est

Bulmer

Bush
Grove

BALLINGDON STREET

PO

Ballingdon
Trading Estate

STOUR

CROSS ST

Plough

CHURCH ST

FRIARS STRE

School

Christopher

Blackfriars

Priory
Walk

Friars Clinic

Sudbury Town
Football Club

Stour Va Wk

Sudbury Road

Sandy Lane

Ballingdon Hill
Industrial Estate

Ballingdon

Ballingdon
Grove

7

+

Street

The
St Andrew's Rise

Vicars
Orch

PO

Bulmer

Church Road

Sandy Lane

A131 BALLINGDON HILL

Elizabeth
Way

Robin Wy

Pinecroft

Lime Gv

Hall Rd

Meadow View
Road

Middleton

stour valley Path

Suffo

Ess

8

+

G   H   J   **73**   K   L   M

Auberies

Armsey
Farm

I grid square represents 500 metres

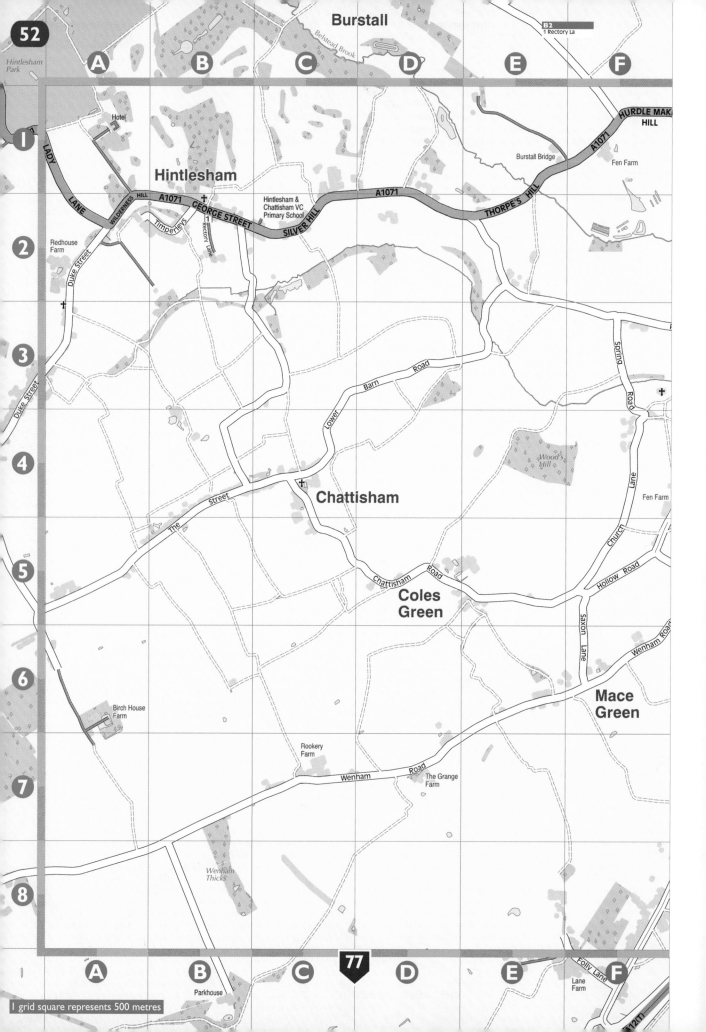

Burstall

B2
1 Rectory La

A   B   C   D   E   F

Hintlesham
Park

Hotel

HURDLE MAK
HILL
A1071

1

LADY LANE

WILDERNESS HILL
A1071
GEORGE STREET

Hintlesham

Timperleys

Rectory Lane

SILVER HILL

Hintlesham & Chattisham VC Primary School

A1071

THORPE'S HILL

Burstall Bridge

Fen Farm

2

Redhouse Farm

Duke Street

3

Duke Street

Barn Road

Lower

Spring Road

4

Street

Wood's Hill

Chattisham

Fen Farm

Church

5

The Street

Chattisham Road

Coles Green

Hollow Road

Saxon Lane

Wenham Road

6

Birch House Farm

Mace Green

7

Rookery Farm

Wenham Road

The Grange Farm

8

Wenham Thicks

Folly Lane

Lane Farm

A   B   C   D   E   F

Parkhouse

77

B12(t)

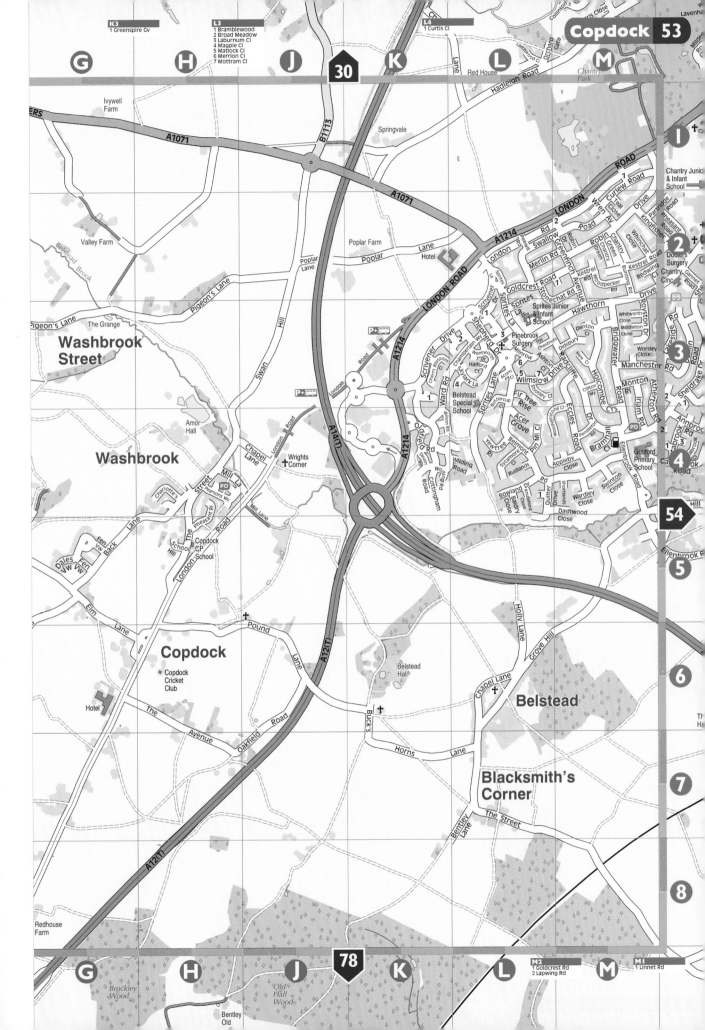

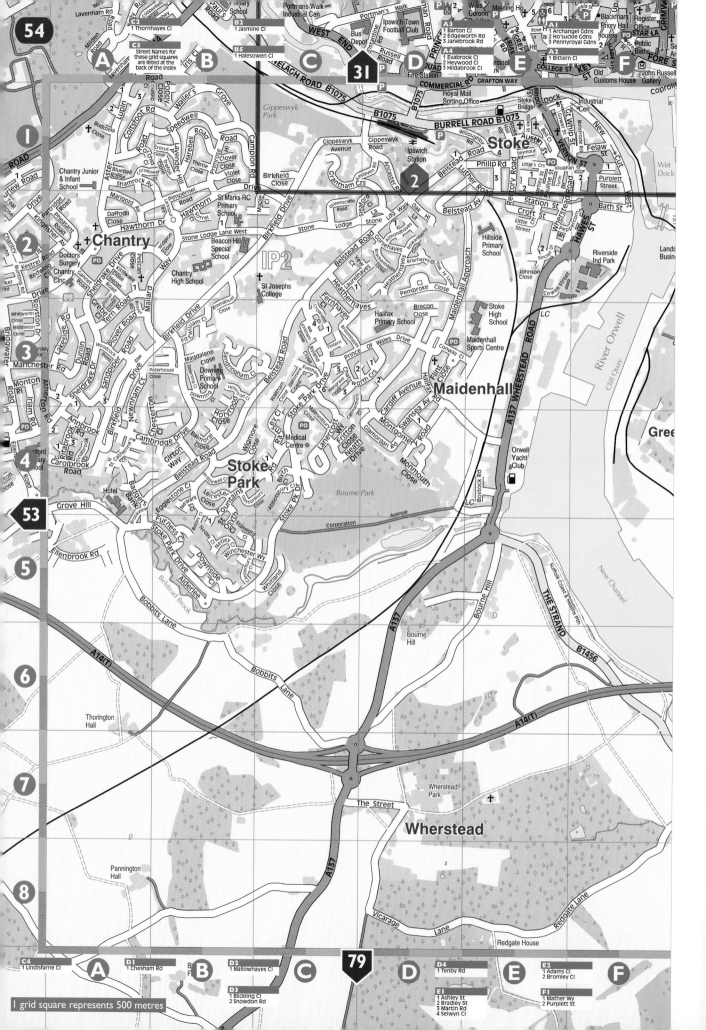

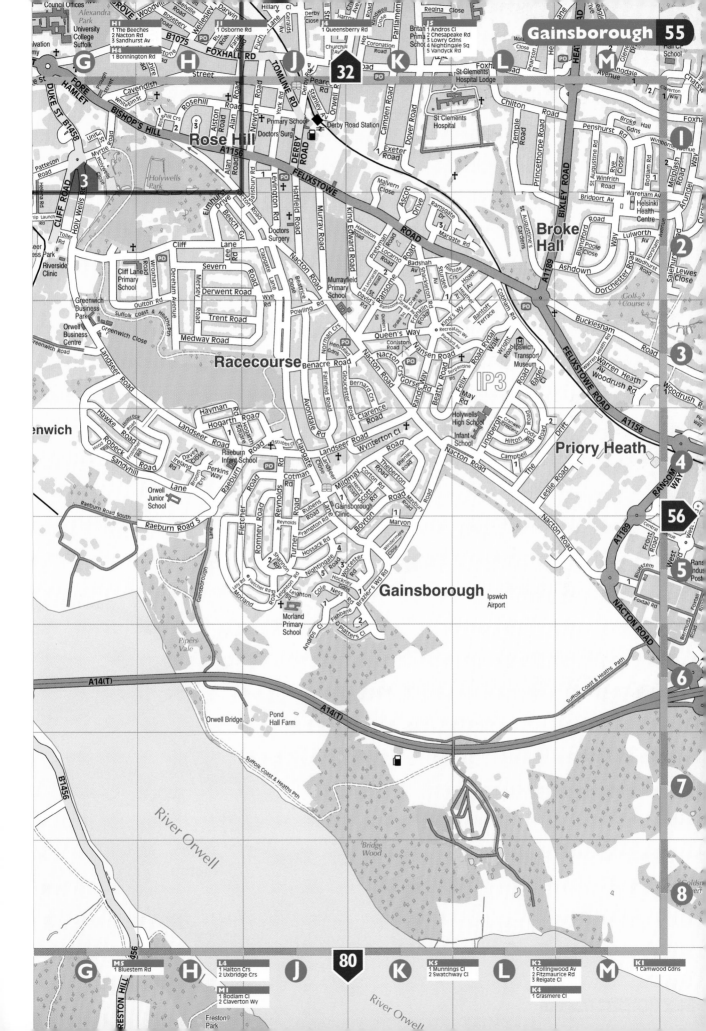

B4
1 Greenbury Cl

34

A B C D E F

1

2

3

B1039

B1368

CAMBRIDGE ROAD

ROYSTON RD

Bakers Lane

PICKNAGE ROAD B1039

The Surgery

HIGH STREET

B1368

Hanaper Dr

Barley

PO

Barley Vp School

Church End

Shaftenhoe

CHISHILL ROAD

B1039 BARLEY ROAD

Chishill Windmill

Cambridgeshire County

Hertfordshire County

4

LONDON ROAD

The

Mr

PH

Smith's End Lane

Pudding Lane

School

Churchfield

End

Road

Bogmoor Road

Little Chishill Road

Smith's End

Shaftenhoe End

5

CAMBRIDGE ROAD

Bogmoor Road

Abbotsbury House

6

Newsells

sells

7

B1368

Barkway Hill

Bogmoor Road

BARKWAY HILL

GE ROAD

Cross Leys

8

Cokenach

Walk Wood

A B C D E F

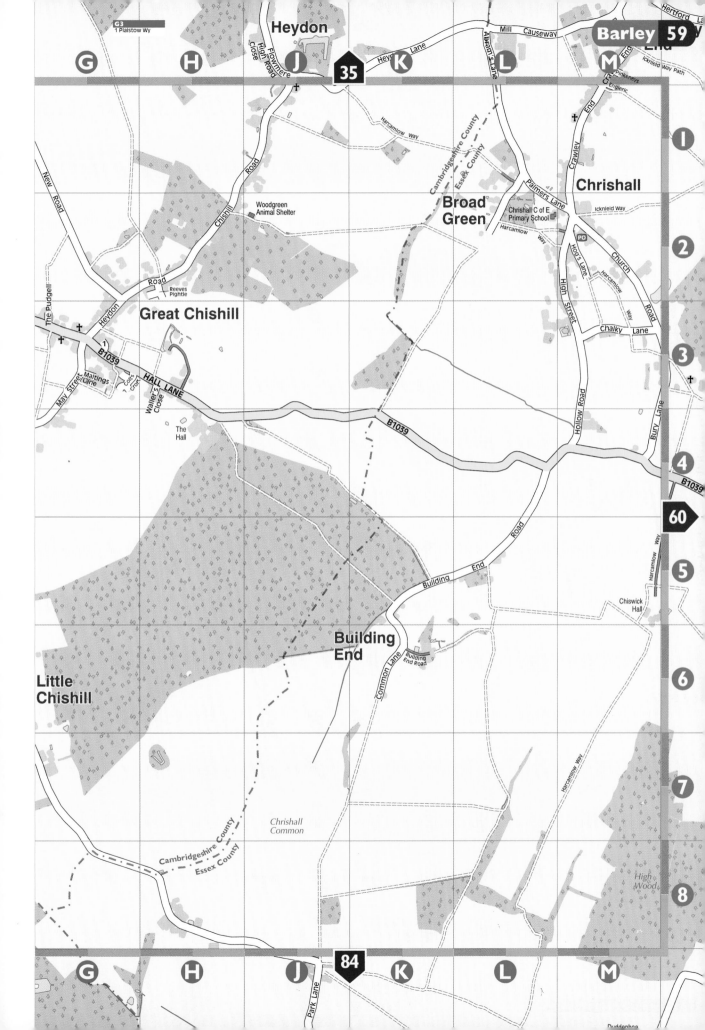

G3
1 Plaistow Wy

Heydon

G   H   J   35   K   L   M

Mill Causeway

Hertford Le

Icknield Way Path

I

Pinkeneys Ct

Ct Engleric

Flowmere High Road

High Close

Heydon Lane

Abram's Lane

Crawley End

Harcamlow Way

Cambridgeshire County

Essex County

Broad Green

Palmers Lane

Chrishall

Chrishall C of E Primary School

Icknield Way

Woodgreen Animal Shelter

Chishill Road

Reeves Pightle

Road

Great Chishill

Heydon

Hog's Lane

High Street

Harcamlow Way

PO

Harcamlow Way

Chalky Lane

2

Church Road

Bury Lane

3

The Pudgell

May Street

Maltings Lane

Lane Croft

Waller's Close

HALL LANE

B1039

B1039

Hollow Road

4

B1039

60

The Hall

Harcamlow Way

5

Chiswick Hall

Building End Road

Road

Building End

Building End

6

Little Chishill

Common Lane

Building End Road

7

Chrishall Common

Cambridgeshire County

Essex County

High Wood

8

G   H   J   84   K   L   M

Park Lane

Duddenhoe

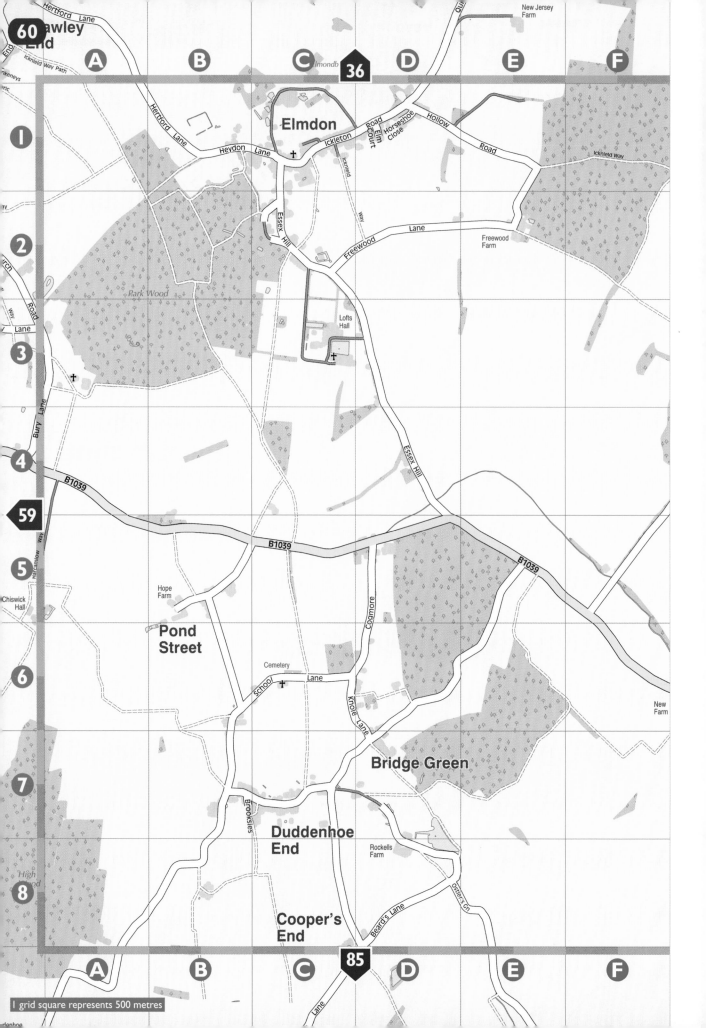

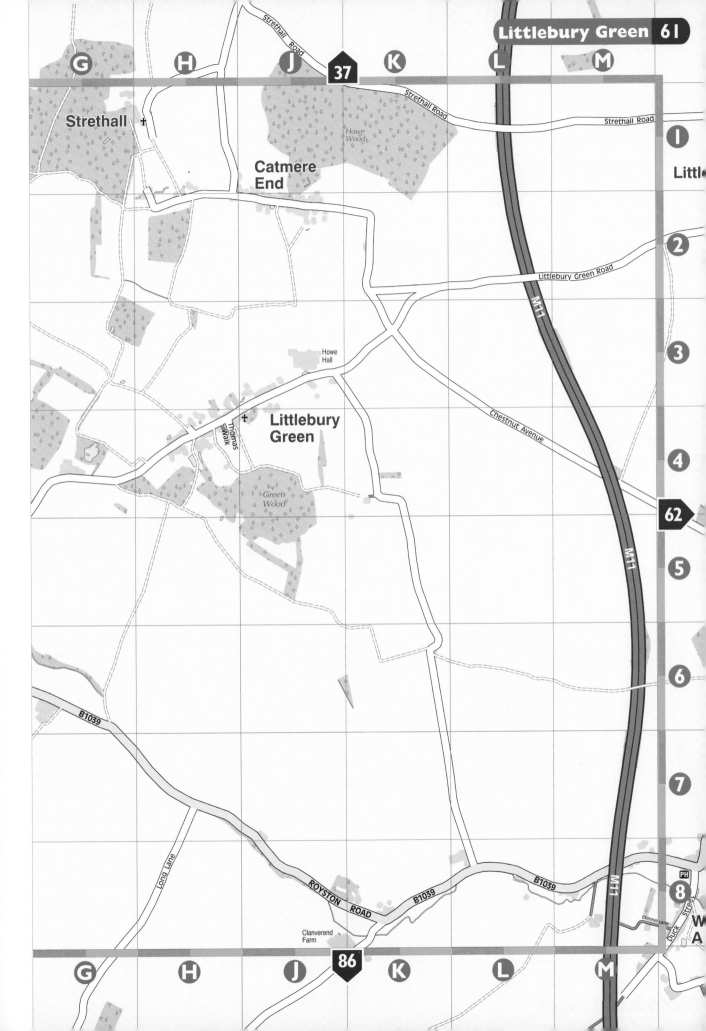

G H J **37** K L M

Strethall Road

Strethall

Catmere End

Howe Wood

Strethall Road

Strethall Road

I

Littl

Littlebury Green Road

2

M11

3

Howe Hall

Chestnut Avenue

Littlebury Green

Thomas Walk

4

Green Wood

62

5

B1039

6

7

Long Lane

ROYSTON ROAD

B1039

B1039

M11

PH

8

Chinnel Lane

Duck Street

W A

Clanverend Farm

A
B
38
C
D
E
F

Grethall Road

Roman Way

CAMBRIDGE ROAD

Northend

Littlebury

Walden Road

Church Walk

PH

HIGH ST

Mill Lane

Peggy's Walk

River Cam or Granta

WINDMILL HILL

The Vineyard

Spring Wood

B1383 LONDON ROAD

Golf Course

B184

Saffron Walden Town Football Club

St Marys Primary School

Castle Street

Little Walden Road

Catons Lane

B1052

Saffron Walden Golf Club

New Pond Lane

BRIDGE ST

Castle Street Surgery

The Museum

Kenneth Mark Practice

August 12th Art Gallery

Church street

Park Lane

Abbey Lane

HILL STREET

PO

HIGH STREET

Oasthouse Court

Gibson Close

Gibson Gardens

Station street

AUDLEY END ROAD

Harcamlow Way

Audley End

Audley End Road

Spring Hill

Audley End Road

Doctors Surgery

Beck Road

Saxon Way

LONDON ROAD

Copperfields

AUDLEY ROAD

Station Rd

West Close

Boytons Acre

Denden Close

Mount

61

M11

Chestnut Avenue

M5

St Marks College

Abbey Farm

Wenden Road

Saffron Walden County High School

Adams Court

B1052

Springhill Road

Summer Hill Road

Mandeville Road

Rowntree

Birdbush Avenue

Friends Way

Pleasant Valley

B1383 LONDON ROAD

Beeches Close

NEWPORT ROAD

Gallows Hill

Blacklands Close

Secdop Close

PO

Laws Close

Hunters Way

St Close

Orchard Close

Landscape View

Walden Road

Fulfen Way

Compits Way

Wards Croft

Seven Devils Lane

B1039 STATION ROAD

Nats Lane

Church Street

PH

Bearwalden Business Park

Audley End Station

MUTLOW HILL

Sparrows End

Harcamlow Way

Duck Street

M11

Chinnel Lane

Wendens Ambo

SPARROWSEND HILL

B1052

87

1 grid square represents 500 metres

G2
1 Aspin Ms
2 Buckenhoe Rd
3 Byrd's Farm La
4 Chalklands
5 Cornwallis Pl
6 Doddenhill Cl
7 Fair Leas

G4
1 Longhedges
2 Newcroft
3 Victoria Gdns

G5
1 Corn Mill Ct
2 Northfield Rd
3 Pennystone Rd

G6
1 Ansgar Rd
2 Church Fld
3 Mannings Cl
4 Ozier Ct
5 Reddings Cl
6 Well-green Cl

M4
1 Dragon's Gn

J3
1 Ferguson Cl

H5
1 Burnsall Cl
2 Stanleys Farm Rd

H3
1 Bradley Ms
2 Dawson Cl
3 Hamilton Ms
4 Nightingale Ms
5 Whiteshot Wy

G7
1 Plantation Cl
2 Ross Cl

H6
1 Peal Rd

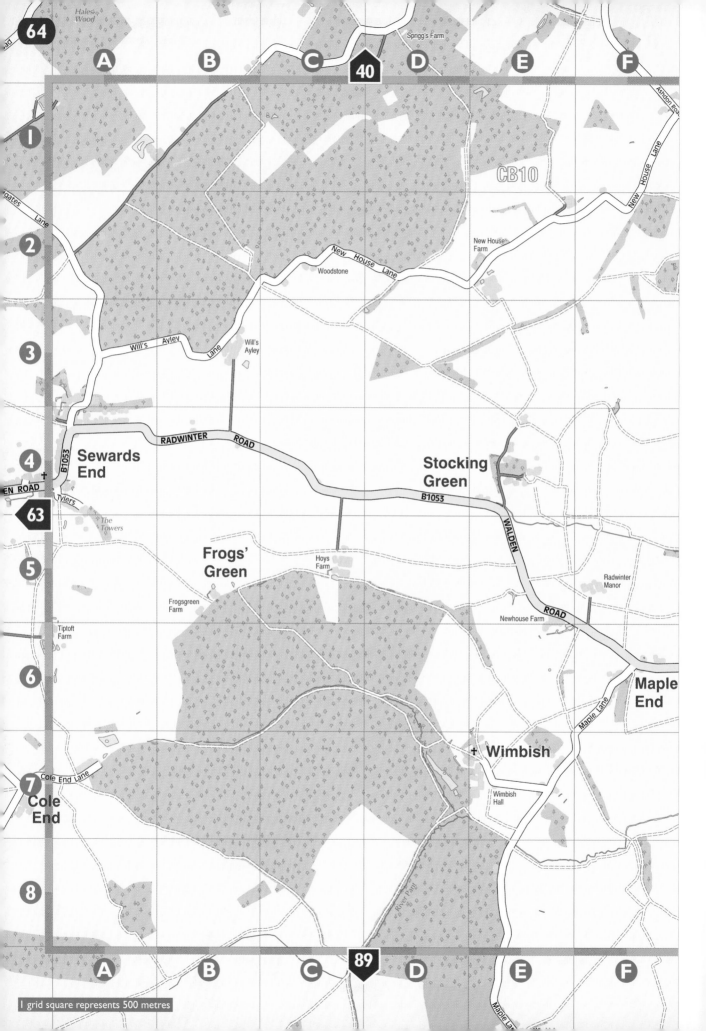

A　　B　　C　　D　　E　　F

40

I

Hales Wood

Ashdon Road

New House Lane

CB10

2

gates Lane

New House Lane

Woodstone

New House Farm

3

Will's Ayley Lane

Will's Ayley

RADWINTER ROAD

4

Sewards End

B1053

Stocking Green

63

EN ROAD

Tylers

The Towers

B1053

WALDEN

5

Frogs' Green

Frogsgreen Farm

Hoys Farm

Radwinter Manor

Newhouse Farm

ROAD

Tiptoft Farm

6

Maple End

Maple Lane

+ Wimbish

7

Cole End Lane

Cole End

Wimbish Hall

8

River Pant

Sprigg's Farm

A　　B　　C　　D　　E　　F

89

Maple La

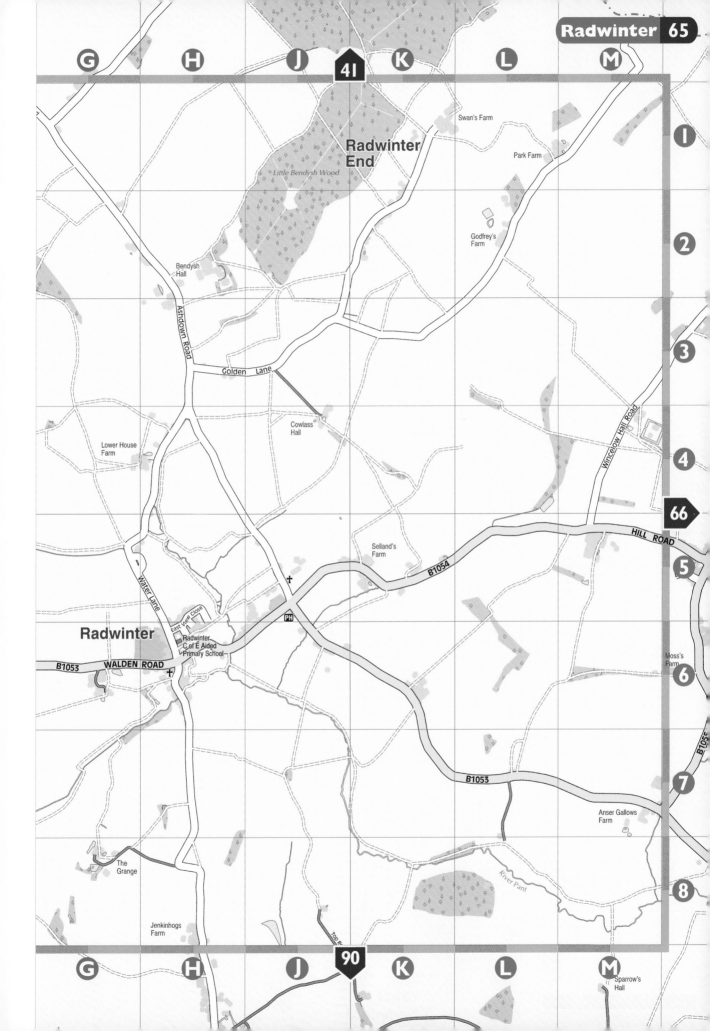

G H J 41 K L M

I

2

3

4

66

5

6

7

8

Swan's Farm

Park Farm

Radwinter End

Little Bendysh Wood

Godfrey's Farm

Bendysh Hall

Ashdown Road

Golden Lane

Cowlass Hall

Wincelow Hall Road

HILL ROAD

Lower House Farm

Selland's Farm

B1054

Moss's Farm

Water Lane

East View Close

Radwinter

Radwinter C of E Aided Primary School

PH

B1053 WALDEN ROAD

B1053

B1055

Anser Gallows Farm

The Grange

River Pant

Jenkinhogs Farm

Top Rd

G H J 90 K L M

Sparrow's Hall

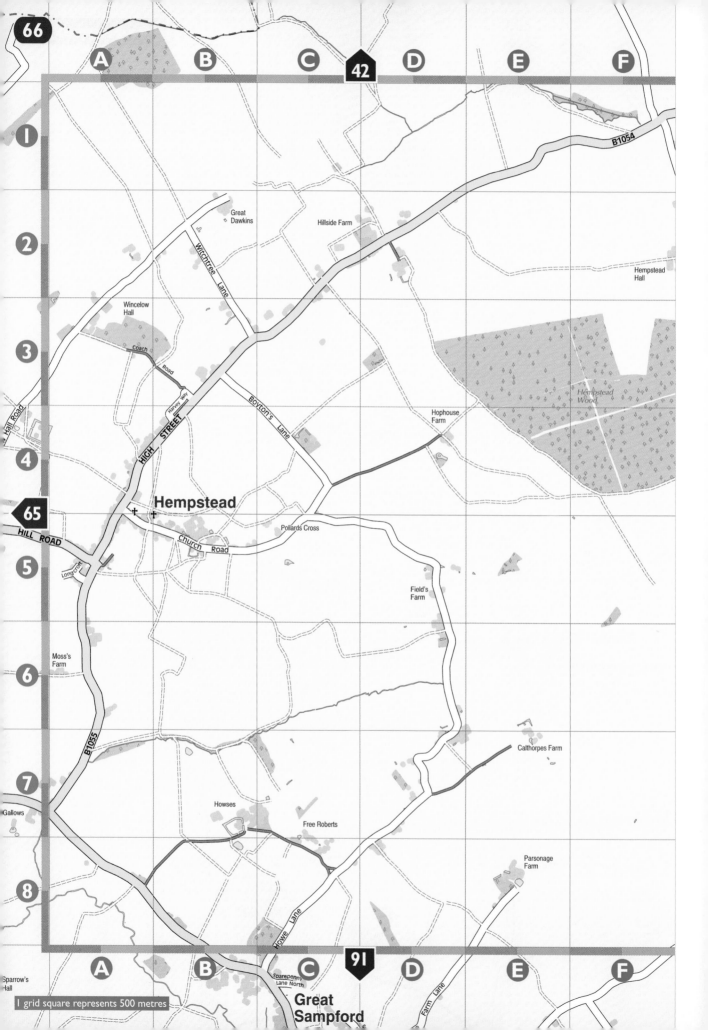

66

A   B   C   42   D   E   F

I

B1054

2

Great
Dawkins   Hillside Farm

Hempstead
Hall

Wincelow
Hall

3

Coach
Road

Hempstead
Wood

Witchtree Lane

Boyton's Lane

Hophouse
Farm

Hall Road

4

Harvey Wy

HIGH STREET

65

Hempstead

HILL ROAD

Pollards Cross

Church   Road

Longcroft

5

Field's
Farm

Moss's
Farm

6

B1055

Calthorpes Farm

7

Gallows

Howses

Free Roberts

Parsonage
Farm

8

Sparrow's
Hall

A   B   91   C   D   E   F

Sparepenny
Lane North

Howe Lane

Farm Lane

Great
Sampford

I grid square represents 500 metres

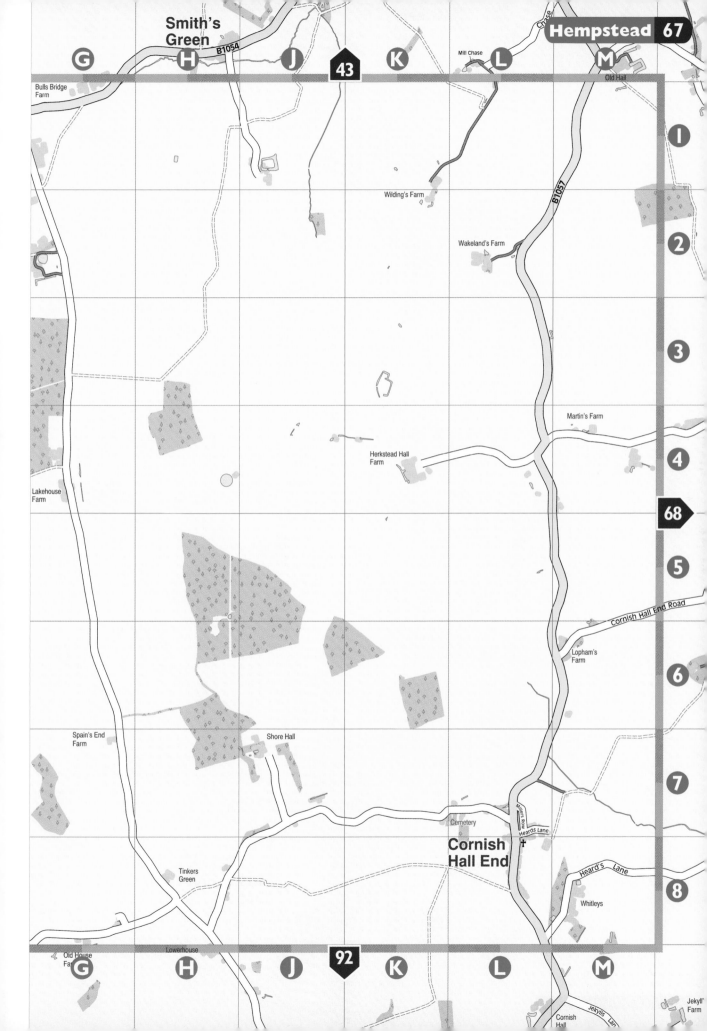

Smith's Green

G H J K L M

B1054

43

Bulls Bridge Farm

Mill Chase

Old Hall

Chase

1

Wilding's Farm

B1057

2

Wakeland's Farm

3

Martin's Farm

Lakehouse Farm

Herkstead Hall Farm

Cornish Hall End Road

4

68

5

Lopham's Farm

6

Spain's End Farm

Shore Hall

7

Cemetery

Villiers Row

Heards Lane

Cornish Hall End

Heard's Lane

8

Tinkers Green

Whitleys

Old House Far

Lowerhouse

Jekylls Lan

Cornish Hall

Jekyll' Farm

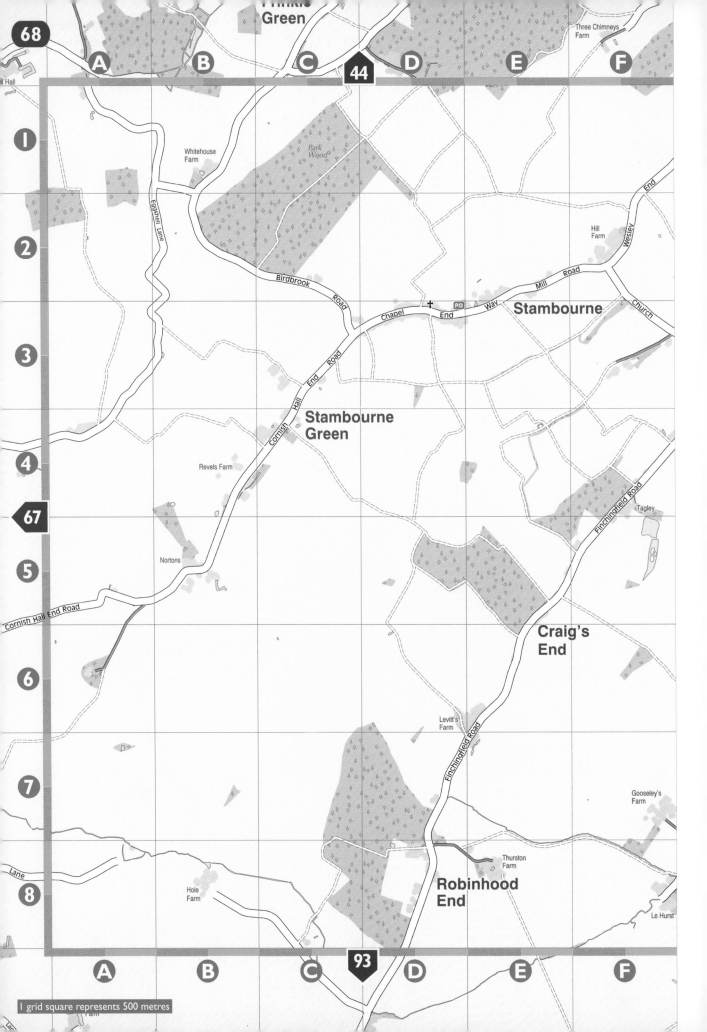

68

44

A **B** **C** **D** **E** **F**

1

Hall

Whitehouse
Farm

*Park
Wood*

Three Chimneys
Farm

2

Eggshell Lane

Birdbrook Road

Hill
Farm

Wesley End

3

Chapel End Way

Stambourne

PO

Mill Road

Church

Cornish Hall End Road

Stambourne
Green

4

Revels Farm

67

Finchingfield Road

Tagley

5

Nortons

**Craig's
End**

Cornish Hall End Road

6

Levitt's
Farm

Finchingfield Road

7

Lane

Gooseley's
Farm

Thurston
Farm

8

Hole
Farm

**Robinhood
End**

Le Hurst

A **B** **C** **D** **E** **F**

93

1 grid square represents 500 metres

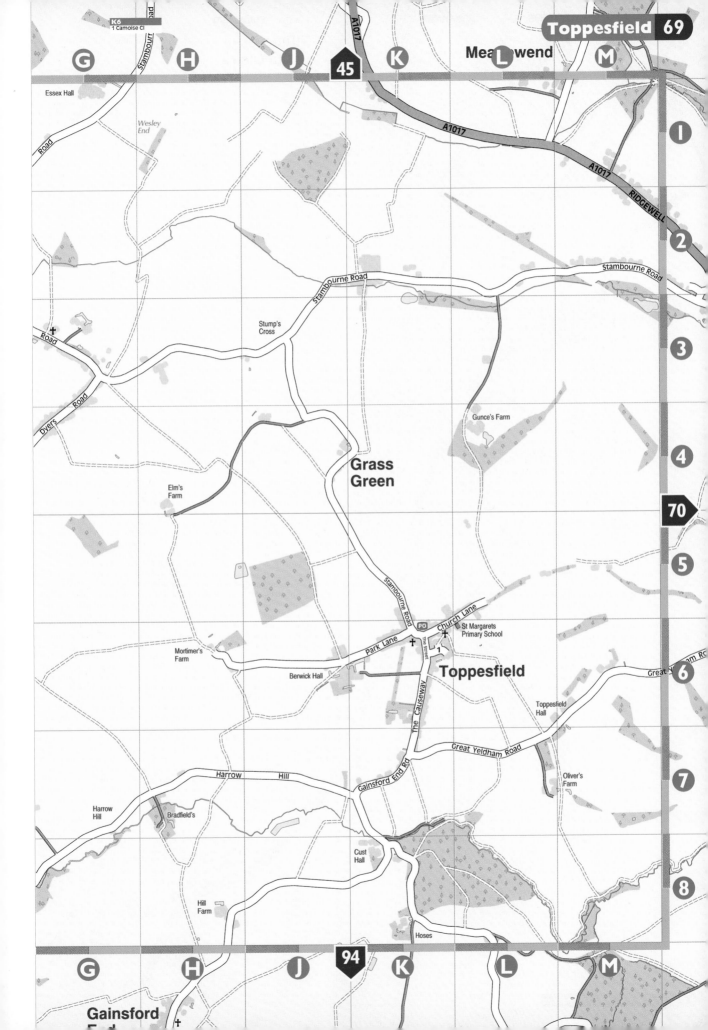

K6
1 Camoise Cl

G   H   J   **45**   K   Mea L wend   M

I

Essex Hall

Wesley
End

A1017

A1017

Stambourne Road

RIDGEWELL

2

Road

Stambourne Road

Stambourne Road

Stump's
Cross

3

Road

Dyers Road

Gunce's Farm

**Grass
Green**

4

70

Elm's
Farm

5

Stambourne Road

PO   Church Lane   St Margarets
Primary School

Mortimer's
Farm

Park Lane   The Street   1

Toppesfield

6

Berwick Hall

Great Yeldham Rd

The Causeway

Toppesfield
Hall

Great Yeldham Road

Oliver's
Farm

7

Harrow   Hill

Gainsford End Rd

Harrow
Hill

Bradfield's

Cust
Hall

8

Hill
Farm

Hoses

G   H   J   **94**   K   L   M

**Gainsford
E**

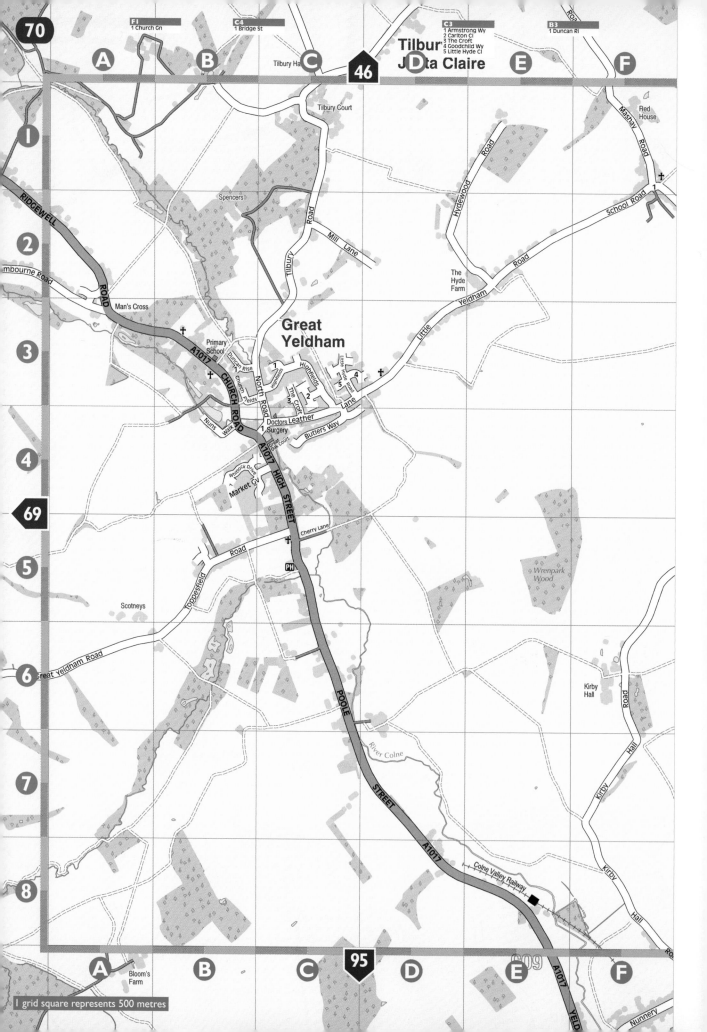

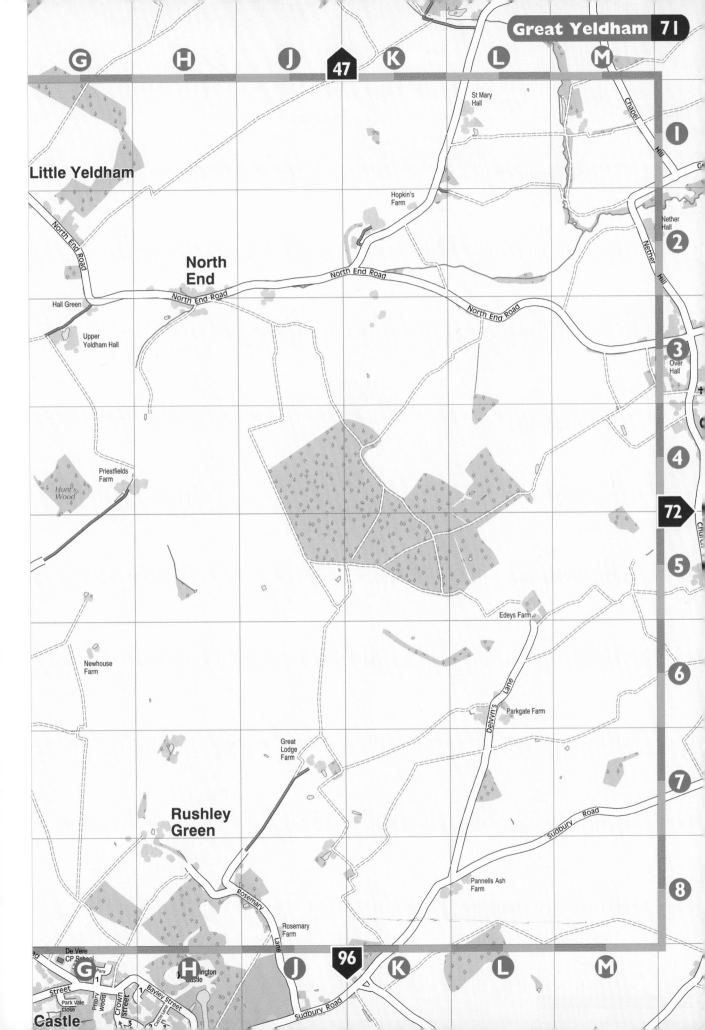

G H J K L M

47

St Mary
Hall

Little Yeldham

1

Chapel Hill

Nether Hall

2

Hopkin's
Farm

North
End

North End Road

North End Road

North End Road

North End Road

Hall Green

Over Hall

3

Upper
Yeldham Hall

Nether Hill

4

Priestfields
Farm

72

Hunt's
Wood

5

Church

Newhouse
Farm

Edeys Farm

6

Delvyn's Lane

Parkgate Farm

Great
Lodge
Farm

7

**Rushley
Green**

Sudbury Road

8

Pannells Ash
Farm

Rosemary Lane

Rosemary
Farm

De Vere
CP School

G H J K L M

96

Park Vale
Close

ington
Castle

Priory
Wood

Park

Street

Crown
Street

Bavley Street

Castle Lane

Castle

Sudbury Road

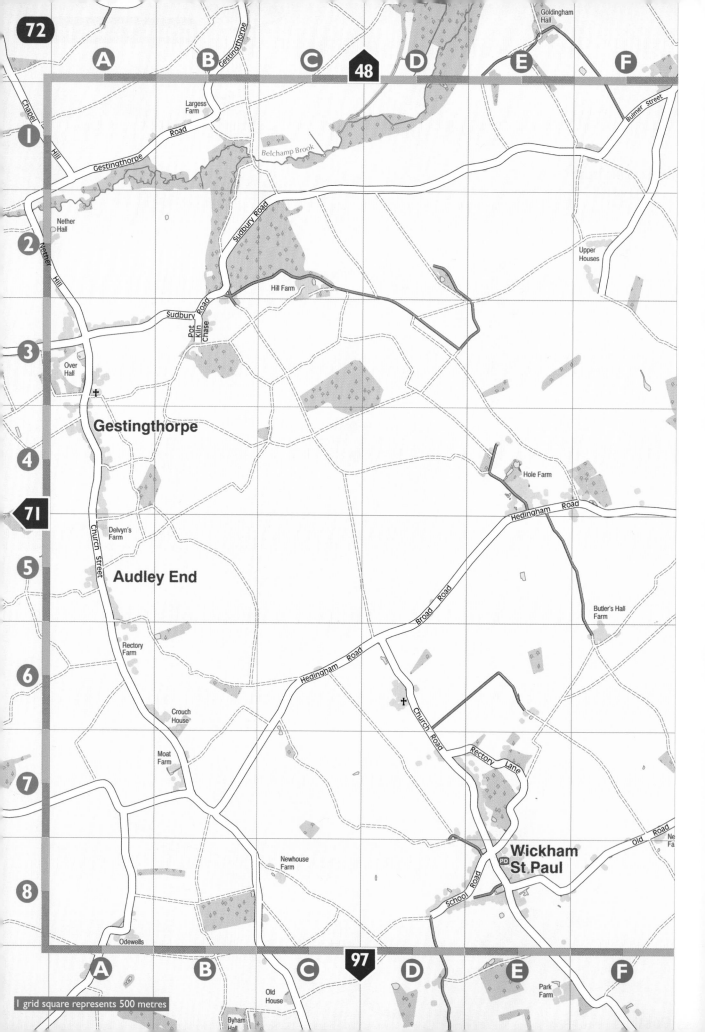

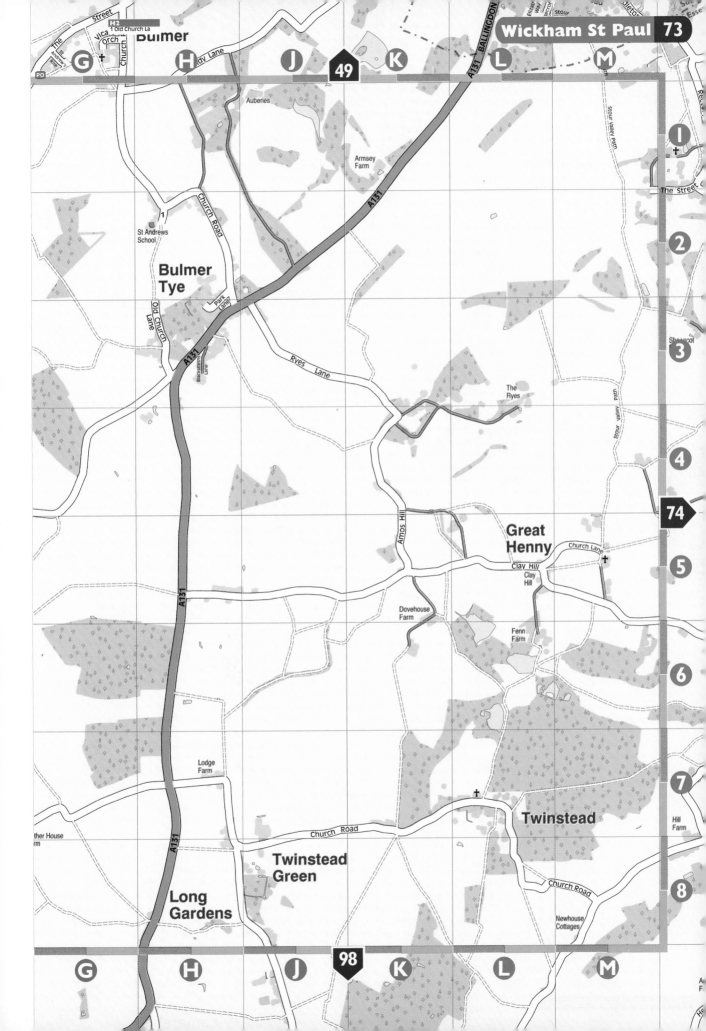

Street

H2 Old Church La

Bulmer

Vica
orch

Church

The
St
Andrew's
Rise

PO

G ✝

Hady Lane

H

J

49

K

A131 BALLINGDON

L

M

Auberies

Armsey
Farm

Stour valley path

Stour

I
✝

The Street

2

Church Road

1

St Andrews
School

**Bulmer
Tye**

Park Lane

Old Church Lane

A131

Blacksmiths Lane

Ryes Lane

The Ryes

Sheepcot

3

Stour valley path

4

74

Amos Hill

**Great
Henny**

Church Lane

✝

Clay Hill

Clay
Hill

5

Dovehouse
Farm

Fenn
Farm

6

Lodge
Farm

✝

Twinstead

7

Hill
Farm

ther House
rm

Church Road

**Twinstead
Green**

**Long
Gardens**

A131

Church Road

Newhouse
Cottages

8

G

H

J

98

K

L

M

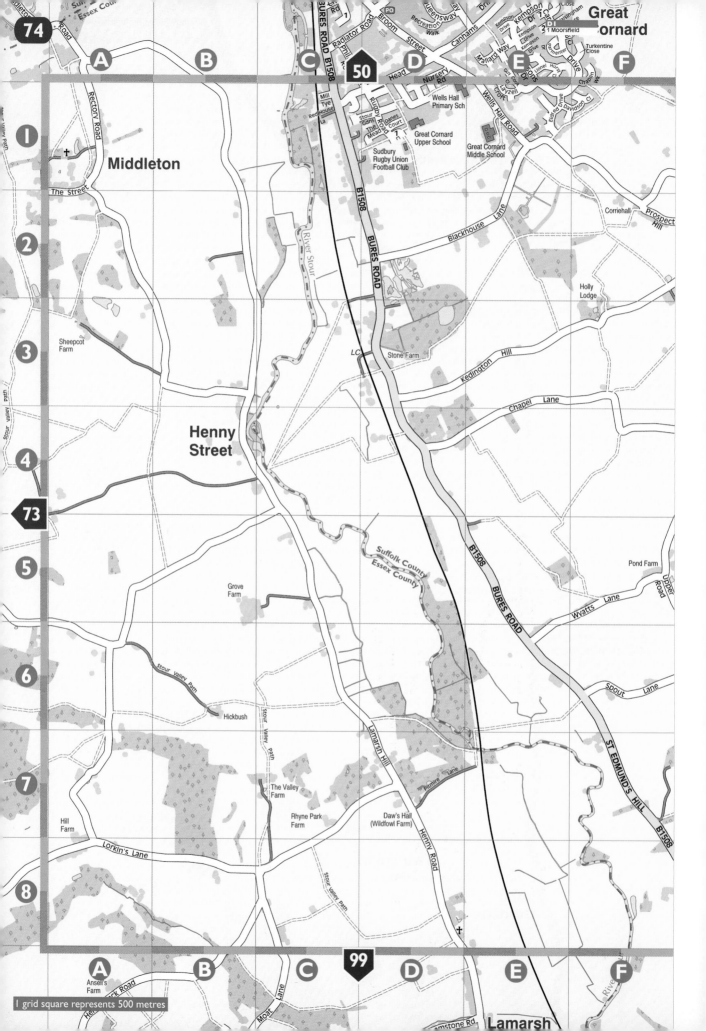

Leys

Rotten Ro

G   H   J   **51**   K   L   M   I

Joes Rd

Rotten Row

Sackers Green

Rectory Road

Kingswood
House

FURTHER STREET

Great
Greys

Goulding's
Farm

Dyers Lane

2

East
Farm

†

Little Cornard

Lord's
Wood

3

Assing

4

Costens
Hall

Mumford's
Wood

Severals Farm

Assington
Thicks

5

Ro
Gr

Upper Road

6

**Workhouse
Green**

Sawyer's

Stantons
Farm

se Gr

Moor's Farr   7

**Dorking
Tye**

8

B1508

G   H   J   **100**   K   L   M   Tiger
Hill

Corn
Hall

High Pale
Farm

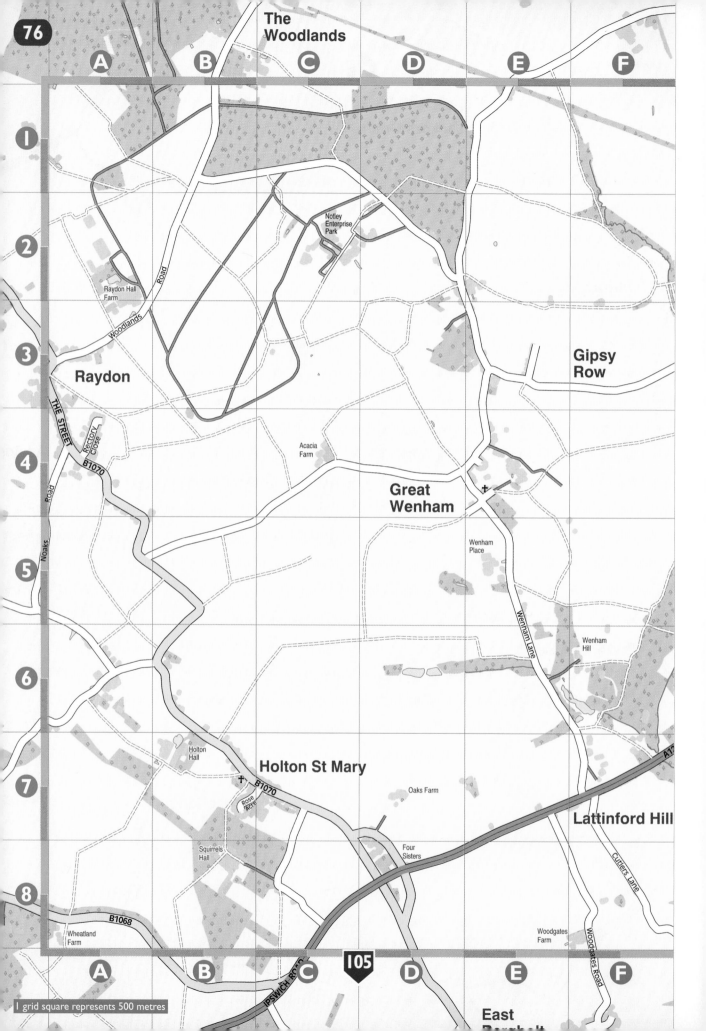

The Woodlands

A   B   C   D   E   F

1

2

Raydon Hall
Farm

Woodlands Road

3   Raydon

Gipsy Row

THE STREET

Rectory Close

4   B1070

Acacia Farm

Great Wenham

Noaks Road

5   Wenham Place

Notley Enterprise Park

Wenham Lane

Wenham Hill

6

Holton Hall

7   Holton St Mary

B1070

Rose Acre

Oaks Farm

Lattinford Hill

Cutlers Lane

Squirrels Hall

Four Sisters

8   B1068

Wheatland Farm

Woodgates Farm

Woodgates Road

A   B   C   D   E   F

IPSWICH ROAD

105

East Berholt

1 grid square represents 500 metres

A   B   C   53   D   E   F

Redhouse Farm

1   Brockley Wood

Old Hall Wood

Bentley Old Hall

2   Old Hall Lane   Bentley Manor   Hubbard's Hall Farm

3   Pond Hall   Bentley Park

4   Church Road   A137   White Horse Hill   School Road   Tattingstone White

77

5   Potash Lane   Grove Farm   Falstaff Manor

Potash

6   Church Road   Bentley Primary School   Tattingstone   The Box Gallery   The Close   Church Road   Glebe Cl   Green La   Tattingstone C of E V CP School   Lemons Hill

Bentley   Case Lane   West Mill Garden   East Mill Grn   Highfields   Back Lane   Pond Hall Farm

7   Station Road   PO   Grove Road   Church Road   Silver   Station Road   Church Road   Tattingstone Place

The Heath

8   A137   Tattingstone Wonder

Stutton Lane

A   Dodn Priory Farm   B   Coppey Farm   C   Folly Farm   107   D   Vale Lane   E   White House Farm   F

1 grid square represents 500 metres

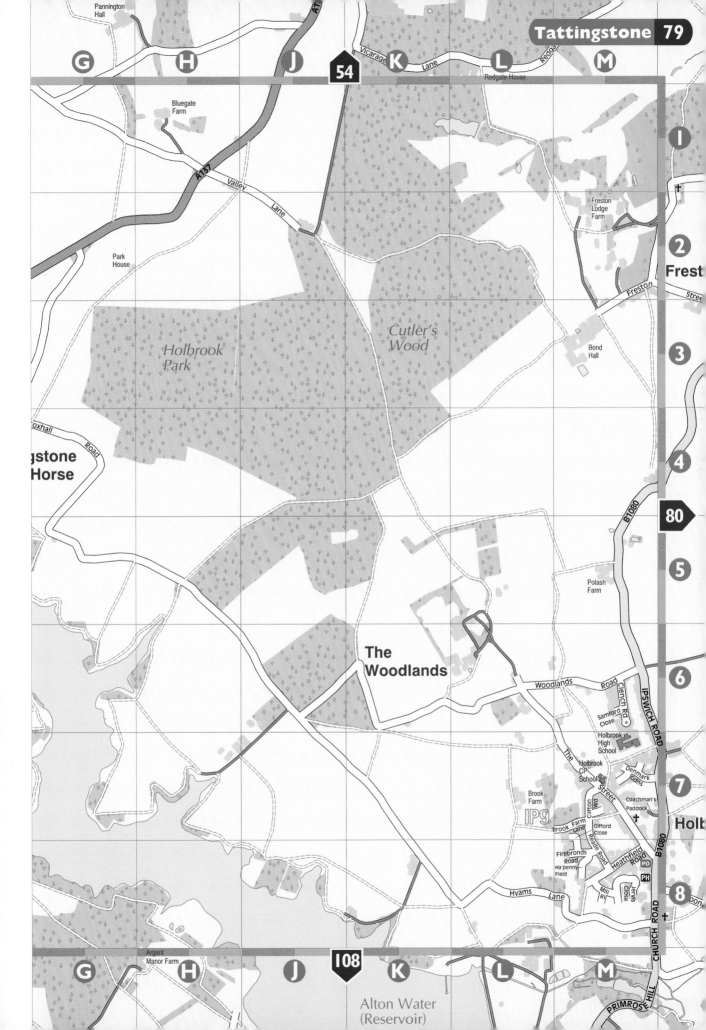

G H J **54** K L M

I

†

2
Frest

3

4

80

5

6

7

Holb

8

Pannington
Hall

Bluegate
Farm

A137 Valley Lane

Park
House

oxhall Road

gstone
Horse

Holbrook
Park

Cutler's
Wood

Vicarage Lane

Redgate House

Freston
Lodge
Farm

Bond
Hall

Freston

Street

B1080

Potash
Farm

The
Woodlands

Woodlands Road

Clench Rd

IPSWICH ROAD

Samford
Close

Holbrook
High
School

Holbrook
CP
School

Denmark
Gdns

Coachman's
Paddock

†

Brook
Farm

The Street

Clifton

Mill

Brook Farm Lane

IP9

Clifford
Close

Reade Road

Firebronds
Road
Ha'penny
Field

Heathfield Road

B1080

PO

PH

Mill
Rd

Jervis
Close

Hyams Lane

CHURCH HILL

†

Argent
Manor Farm

G H J **108** K L M

Alton Water
(Reservoir)

PRIMROSE HILL

A   B   C   **55**   D   E   F

I
2
3
4
79
5
6
7
8

River Orwell

FRESTON HILL

B1456

Freston Park

Freston

Street

B1456

Home Farm

Mannings Lane

Pratt's La

Suffolk Coast & Heaths Path

Suffolk Coast & Heaths Path

Cat House

MAIN ROAD

Ipswich High School for Girls

Woolverstone

PO

Woolverstone Park

Harkstead Lane

B1456

MAIN ROAD

Glebe Lane

Richardsons Lane

Freston Grove

Whitehouse Farm

Walnut Tree Farm

Bylam Lane

Clench Rd

IPSWICH ROAD

Harkstead Lane

Bylam Farm

Denmark

Coachman's Paddock

Holbrook

B1080

Heathfield Road

PO

PH

8

CHURCH ROAD

Fishponds Lane

Fir Tree Hill

Holbrook Gardens

New Road

Brick Kiln Road

Red House Farm

Ling's Lane

Grove Lane

A   B   C   **109**   D   E   F

Lovers Lane

HILL

Harkstead

I grid square represents 500 metres

The Vale Farm

Holbrook

Nacton

G **H** **J** **56** **K** **L** **M**

Goldsmith's Covert

Park Farm

The Street

Ipswich Road

Nacton Primary School

Church Road

Levington Road

Orwell Park School

Orwell Park House

Shore Lane

Suffolk Coast & Heaths Path

Broke Hall

I

2

3

Hall Point

River

Orwell

4

Suffolk Coast & Heaths Path

Pin Mill

PH

Suffolk Coast & Heaths Path

Clamp House

82

5

Orwell Rise

Pinmill Road

Wendy Close

Chelmondiston

Collimer Cl

Rectory Field

Hollow La

Woodlands

School

St Andrew's Dr

Church St

The Saplings

Hill Farm La

6

Ling's Lane

MAIN ROAD **B1456**

PO

B1456

Red House Farm

Wade's Lane

7

Pear Tree Farm

The Drift

8

Shotley Walk

G **H** **J** **110** **K** **L** **M**

B1456

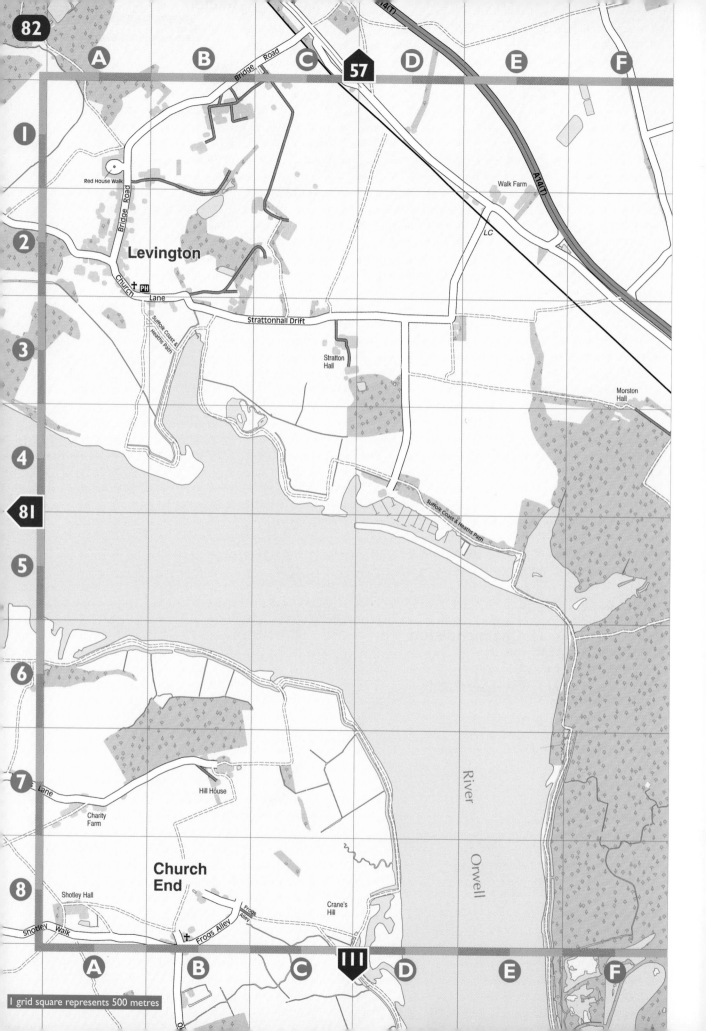

A B Bridge Road C 57 D E F

1

Red House Walk

2 Levington

Bridge Road

Church † PH Lane

Strattonhall Drift

3 Suffolk Coast & Heaths Path

Stratton Hall

Walk Farm

LC

A14(T)

Morston Hall

4

81

Suffolk Coast & Heaths Path

5

6

7 s Lane Hill House

Charity Farm

River

Church End

8 Shotley Hall

Shotley Walk Frogs Alley Frogs Alley Crane's Hill Orwell

A B C III D E F

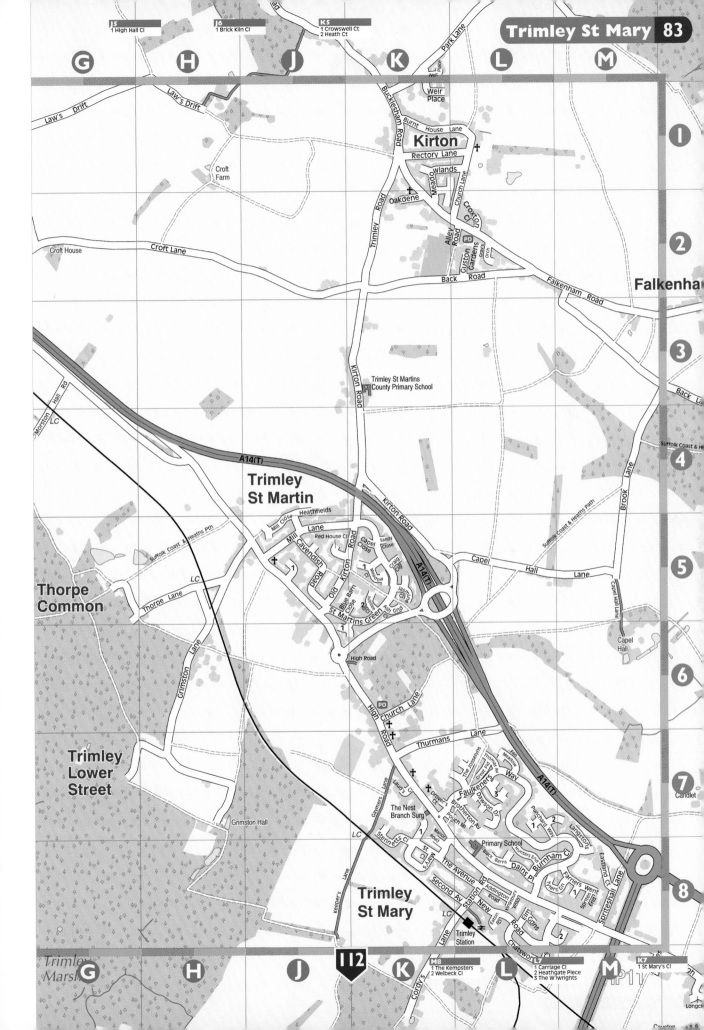

G H J K L M

1 High Hall Cl J5
1 Brick Kiln Cl J6
1 Crowswell Ct K5
2 Heath Ct

Law's Drift
Law's Drift

Croft Farm

Croft House
Croft Lane

Park Lane

Burnt House Lane
Kirton
Rectory Lane
Oakdene
Meadowlands
Church Lane
Croxton Cl
Alley Road
PO
Custon Gardens
Back Road
Falkenham Road

Falkenha

Back La

Morston Hall Rd
LC
A14(T)
Kirton Road

Trimley St Martins
County Primary School

Suffolk Coast & H

Brook Lane

Suffolk Coast & Heaths Path

**Trimley
St Martin**

Heathfields Lane
Mill Close
Red House Cl
Capel Close
Sandy Close
Cavendish Road
Old Kirton Road
Craig Cl
Kirton Road
Meadow
Blue Barn Cl
Jubilee
Jasmin Cl
St Martins Green
A14(T)
Capel Hall Lane

Capel Hall Lane

Capel Hall

**Thorpe
Common**

Thorpe Lane
LC
Grimston Lane

High Road
PO
Church Lane

Thurmans Lane

**Trimley
Lower
Street**

Grimston Hall
Keeper's Lane
Caymers Lane
LC
Laud's Cl
The Nest Branch Surg
Stennetts Cl
St Mary's
Drovers
Brotherton Av
Faulkeners
Dawson Dr
The Josselyns
Green Fld
Thomas Av
Fell Meadow
Way
A14(T)
Pritchard Way
Langstons
Candlet

Primary School
Hunters End
Black Barns
Mason Road
Dains Pl
Burnham Cl
Ferriers Went
Sprites End
Eastland Lane
Spriteshall Lane

The Avenue
Second Av
Station New Road
Addington Road
Kingsbury Road
Elm Gdns
Chatsworth
Cordy's Lane
**Trimley
St Mary**
LC
Trimley Station

Trimley Marsh

G H J I12 K L M P11

1 The Kempsters M8
2 Welbeck Cl
1 Carriage Cl
2 Heathgate Piece
3 The W'wrights
1 St Mary's Cl K7

Caysto
Longci

G H J 60 K L M

I
2
3
4
86
5
6
7
8

Oaster's Cn
Beard's Lane

Collier's End

Newland End

Cosh Farm

Harcamlow Way

Hampit Road

Clavering Farm

Harcamlow Way

Chardwell Farm

Bird Green

Thurrocks

Wood Hall

Ruttels

River Stort

Valance

Clavering Place Farm

urther
ord End

Valance Road

Roast Green

Stickling Green

Fore End

Chamberlaynes Farm

G H J 114 K L M

Deer's Green

Colvills Close

HIGH STREET

The bruce

CLATTERBURY LANE

B1038

Clavering

Steins WY

Stortford

PELHAM ROAD

A   B   C   D   E   F

61

I

Newland
End

Hobs
Aerie

2

3

Road

✝ **Arkesden**

PO
PH

The
Gap

85

Wicken Road

4

Wood

5

Severals
Farm

Poore

Street

Clatterbury Lane

CB11

Harcamlow Way

Harcamlow Way

**Wicken
Bonhunt**

Wicken
Hall ✝

B1038

6

B1038

B1038

Rickling Road

Harcamlow Way

7

PH

**Hill
Green**

CLATTERBURY LANE

8

✝

Coldhams
Farm

115

A   B   C   D   E   F

ROYSTON ROAD

B1039

B1039

M11

Long

Clanverend
Farm

Chinnel

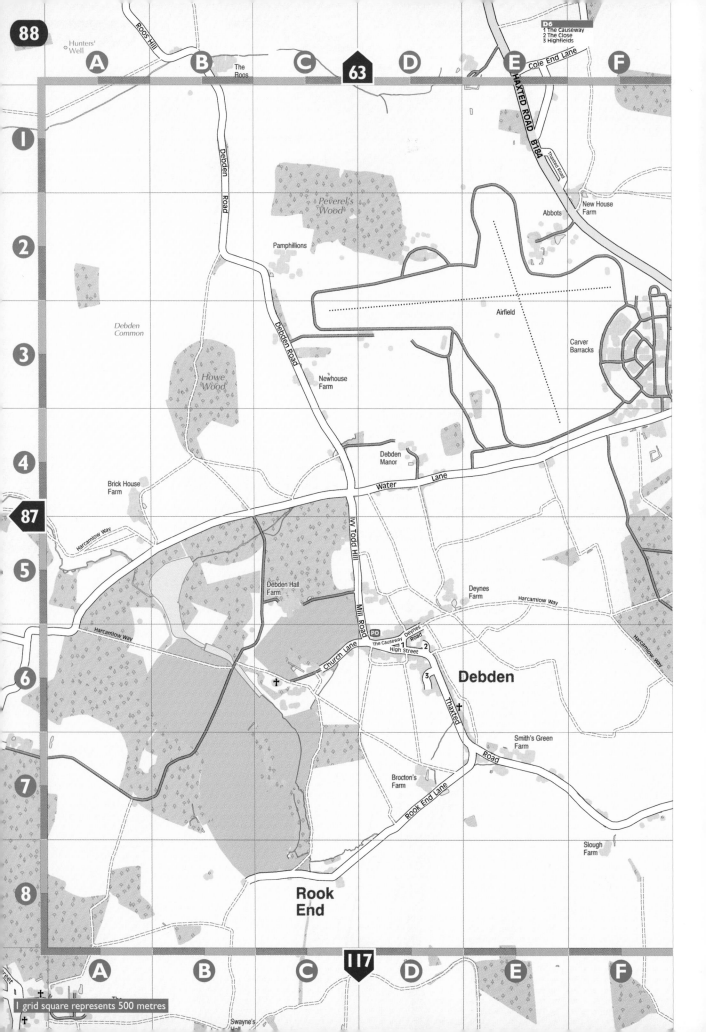

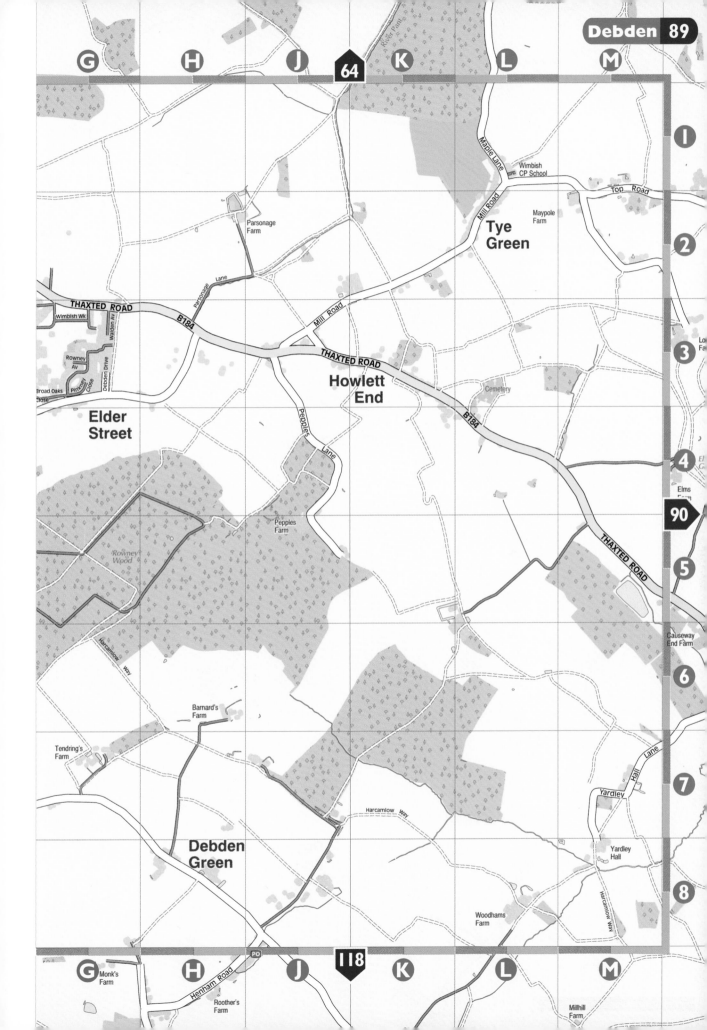

G H J **64** K L M

I

2

Top Road

Wimbish
CP School

Maple Lane

Mill Road

**Tye
Green**

Maypole
Farm

3

THAXTED ROAD

Wimbish Wk

B184

Parsonage Lane

Mill Road

THAXTED ROAD

Cemetery

Rowney
Av

Walden Av

Debden Drive

Pinkney Close

Broad Oaks
Close

**Howlett
End**

B184

4

Elms
Farm

**Elder
Street**

Pepples Lane

90

THAXTED ROAD

5

Rowney
Wood

Pepples
Farm

Causeway
End Farm

Harcamlow Way

6

Barnard's
Farm

Tendring's
Farm

7

Hall Lane

Yardley

Harcamlow Way

**Debden
Green**

Yardley
Hall

8

Woodhams
Farm

Harcamlow Way

G H J **118** K L M

Monk's
Farm

Hennam Road

PO

Roother's
Farm

Millhill
Farm

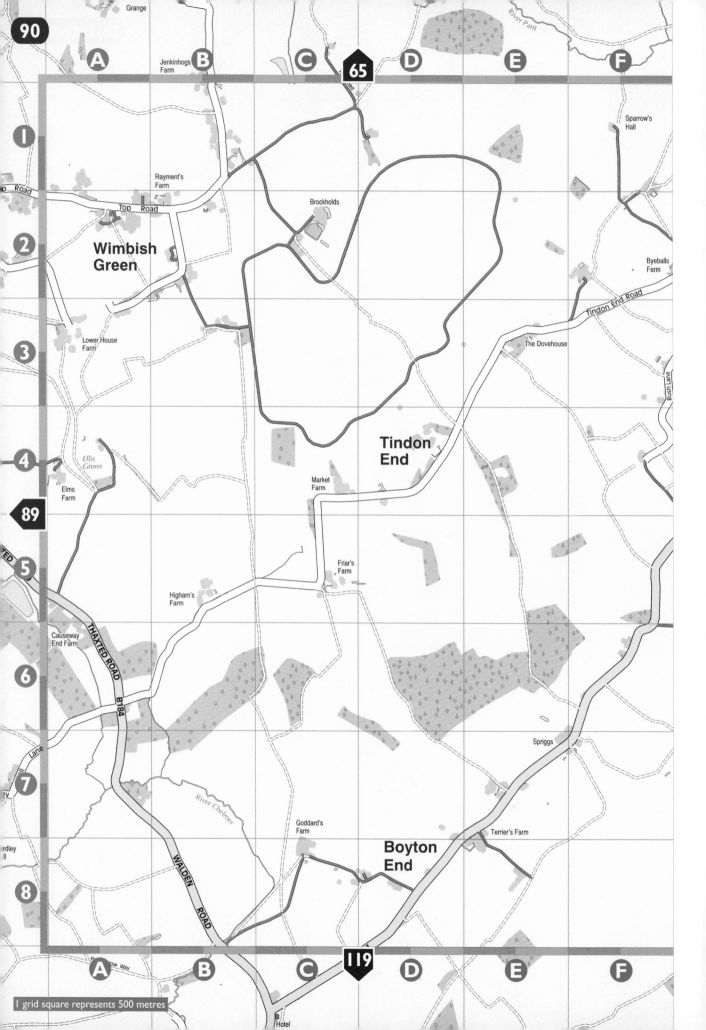

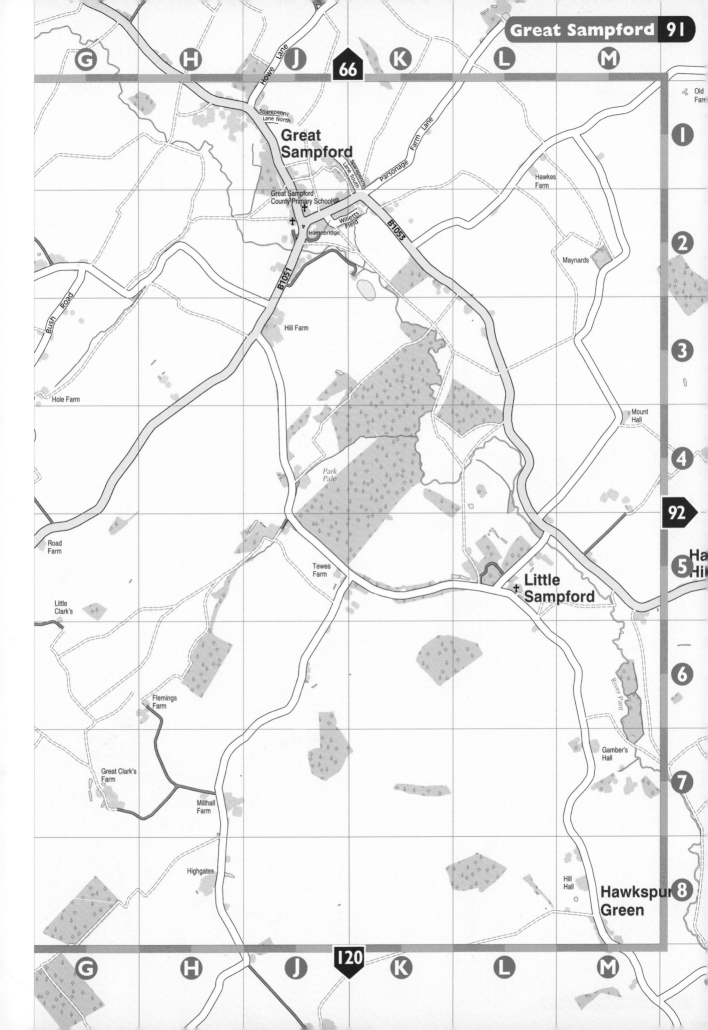

G H Howe Lane J 66 K L M

I

Sparepenny Lane North

Great Sampford

Sparepenny Lane South

Parsonage Farm Lane

Hawkes Farm

2

Great Sampford County Primary School

Willetts Field

Homebridge

B1053

B1051

Maynards

Hill Farm

3

Bush Road

Hole Farm

Mount Hall

4

Park Pale

92

Road Farm

Tewes Farm

Little Sampford

Ha Hi

5

Little Clark's

6

River Pant

Flemings Farm

Gamber's Hall

7

Great Clark's Farm

Millhall Farm

Highgates

Hill Hall

Hawkspur Green

8

G H J 120 K L M

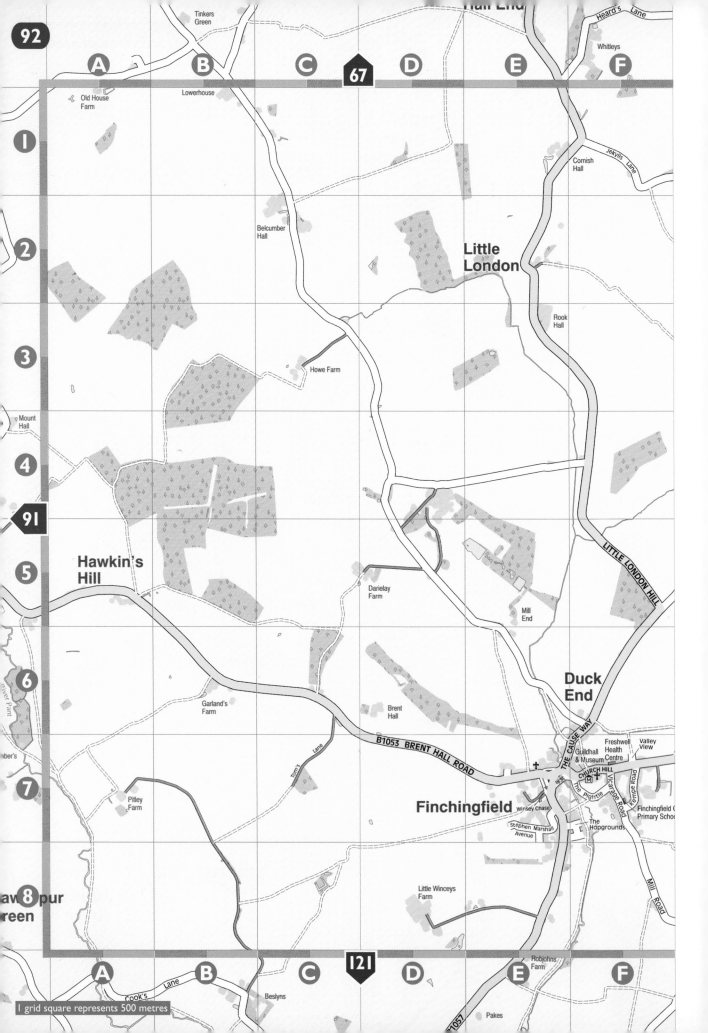

A B C 67 D E F

Tinkers
Green

Old House
Farm

Lowerhouse

Whitleys

Heard's Lane

I

Jekylls Lane

Cornish
Hall

Belcumber
Hall

**Little
London**

2

Rook
Hall

Mount
Hall

Howe Farm

3

4

LITTLE LONDON HILL

**Hawkin's
Hill**

5

Darielay
Farm

Mill
End

6

**Duck
End**

wer Pant

Garland's
Farm

Brent
Hall

THE CAUSEWAY

Freshwell
Health
Centre

Valley
View

B1053 BRENT HALL ROAD

Guildhall
& Museum

CHURCH HILL

Tom's Lane

Vicarage Road

ber's

7

Pitley
Farm

Winsey Chase

Finchingfield

The
Pightle

Finchingfield C
Primary Schoo

Stephen Marshall
Avenue

The
Hopgrounds

Mill Road

aw **8** pur
reen

Little Winceys
Farm

A B C 121 D E F

Robjohns
Farm

Cook's Lane

Beslyns

B1057

Pakes

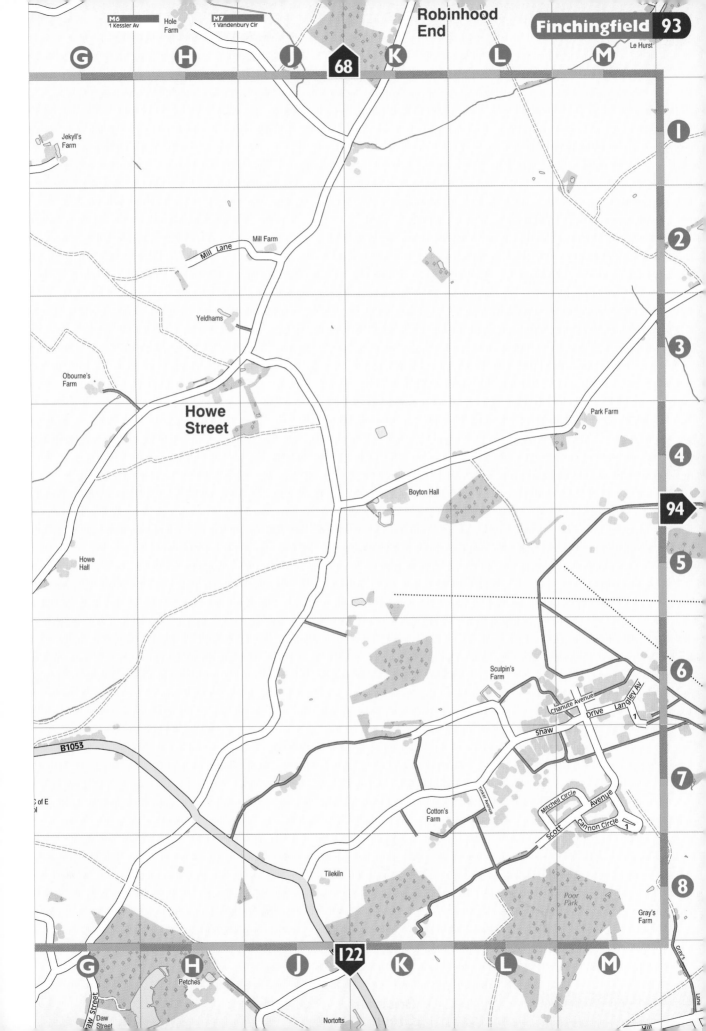

Robinhood
End

M6
1 Kessler Av

Hole
Farm

M7
1 Vandenbury Clr

68

G   H   J   K   L   M   Le Hurst

1
2
3
4
94
5
6
7
8

Jekyll's
Farm

Mill Farm

Mill Lane

Yeldhams

Park Farm

Obourne's
Farm

**Howe
Street**

Boyton Hall

Howe
Hall

Sculpin's
Farm

Chanute Avenue

Langley AV

Drive

Shaw

B1053

Mitchell Circle

Scott

Avenue

Cannon Circle

C of E
ol

Cotton's
Farm

Tinker Avenue

Tilekiln

Poor
Park

Gray's
Farm

122

G   H   J   K   L   M

Daw
Street

Petches

Nortofts

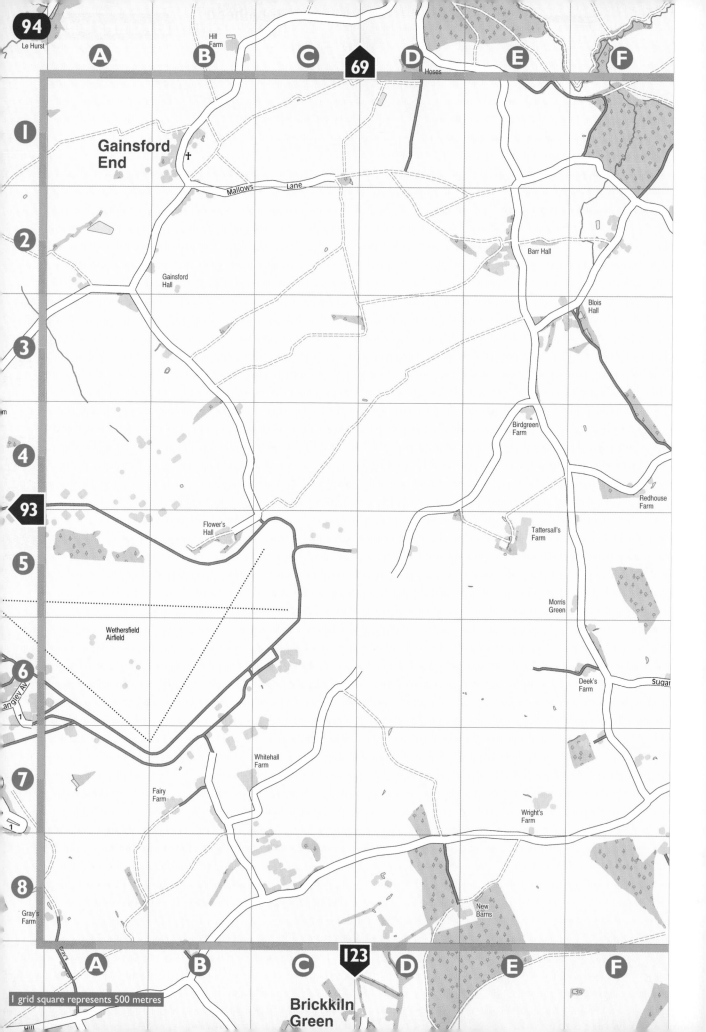

94
Le Hurst

A   B   **69**   D   E   F

1

Gainsford
End

Hill
Farm

Mallows   Lane

Hoses

2

Gainsford
Hall

Barr Hall

3

Blois
Hall

4

Birdgreen
Farm

93

Flower's
Hall

Tattersall's
Farm

Redhouse
Farm

5

Wethersfield
Airfield

Morris
Green

angley Av

6

7

Deek's
Farm

Sugar

7

Whitehall
Farm

Fairy
Farm

Wright's
Farm

1

8

Gray's
Farm

New
Barns

A   B   C   **123**   D   E   F

30

Gray's

1 grid square represents 500 metres

**Brickkiln
Green**

96

A5
1 Colne Rd
2 Hawkwood Rd
3 Jubilee Ct
4 Willow Mdw

A4
1 Brook Meadow
2 Spurgeon Cl

A3
1 Bewick Ct
2 Everitt Wy

A1
1 Bowmans Pk
2 Church La
3 Churchponds

A B C **71** D E F

Dannells Ash Farm

I

Hall Road

Nunnery Road

De Vere CP School

Bowmans Park

Park Vale Close

Priory Wood

Crown Street

Bayley Street

Castle Lane

St James's Street

Castle Hedingham

Nunnery Bridge

Queen St

New Park

Sheepcot Road

Doctors Surg

PO PH

Pottery La

Heddington Castle

Mary Lane

Pottery Farm

Sudbury Road

Chelmshoe House Farm

Monks Lodge

2

Hedingham County Secondary School

Christmas Field

Station Road

Hosden's Farm

St Giles C of E Primary School

St Giles Close

Monks Lodge Road

3

Sible Hedingham

Cygnet Court

Hopwell's Farm

Great Maplestead

Church Street

Brook Ter

Brook Meadow

Summerfields

Spring Ivy

4

Road

Brook Meadow

Swan Street

SWAN STREET

Spurgeon Close

Cambridge Avenue

Hilton House Surgery,

Alderford St

Spring Ivy

Purlshill

Barrett's Hall

95

Sparrow

Hilton Way

Swan Chase

A1017

Dyne's

Hall Road

5

Cobbs Fenn

Lamb Lane

POTTER STREET

6

Hull's Mill Farm

7

QUEEN ST

Wallace's Farm

River Colne

Bennett's Farm

A1124

HALSTEAD

ROAD

A1017

HEDINGHAM ROAD

Hepworth Hall

Doe's Corner

8

A1124

EDINGHAM RD

River Colne

Cutmaple

Brook Street Farm

I grid square represents 500 metres

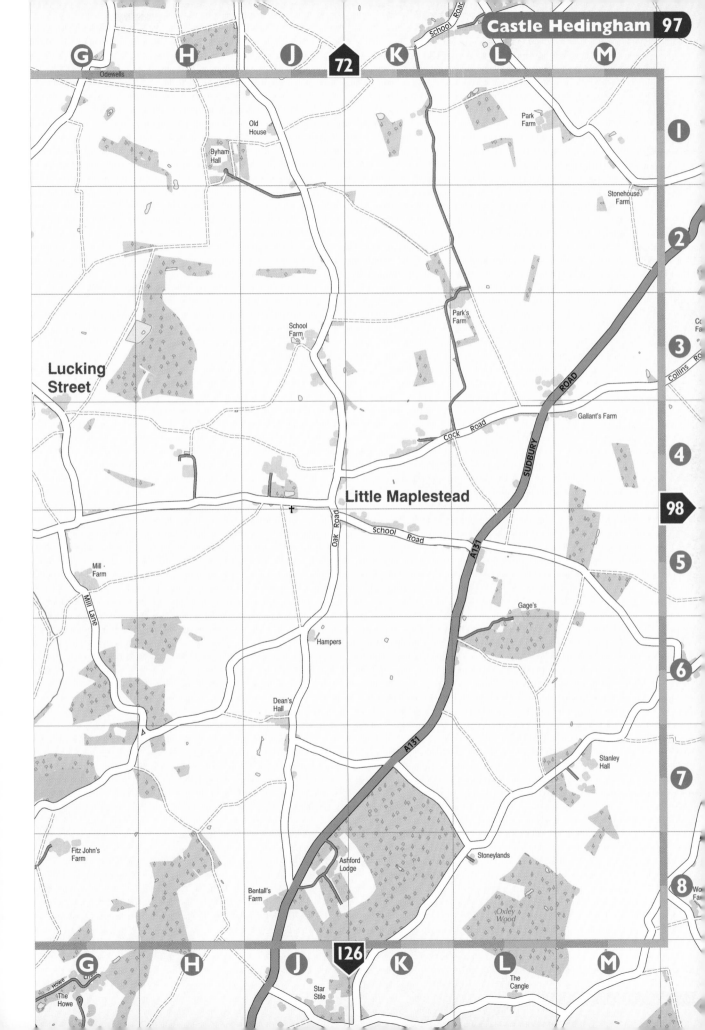

G H J **72** K L M

Odewells

Old House

Byham Hall

I

Park Farm

Stonehouse Farm

2

School Farm

Park's Farm

3

Lucking Street

Collins Ro

ROAD

SUDBURY

Gallant's Farm

4

Cock Road

Little Maplestead

98

Oak Road

School Road

A131

Mill Farm

5

Gage's

Mill Lane

Hampers

6

Dean's Hall

7

A131

Stanley Hall

Fitz John's Farm

Ashford Lodge

Stoneylands

8

Bentall's Farm

Oxley Wood

Wo Fa

G H **126** K L M

The Howe

Howe

Star Stile

The Cangle

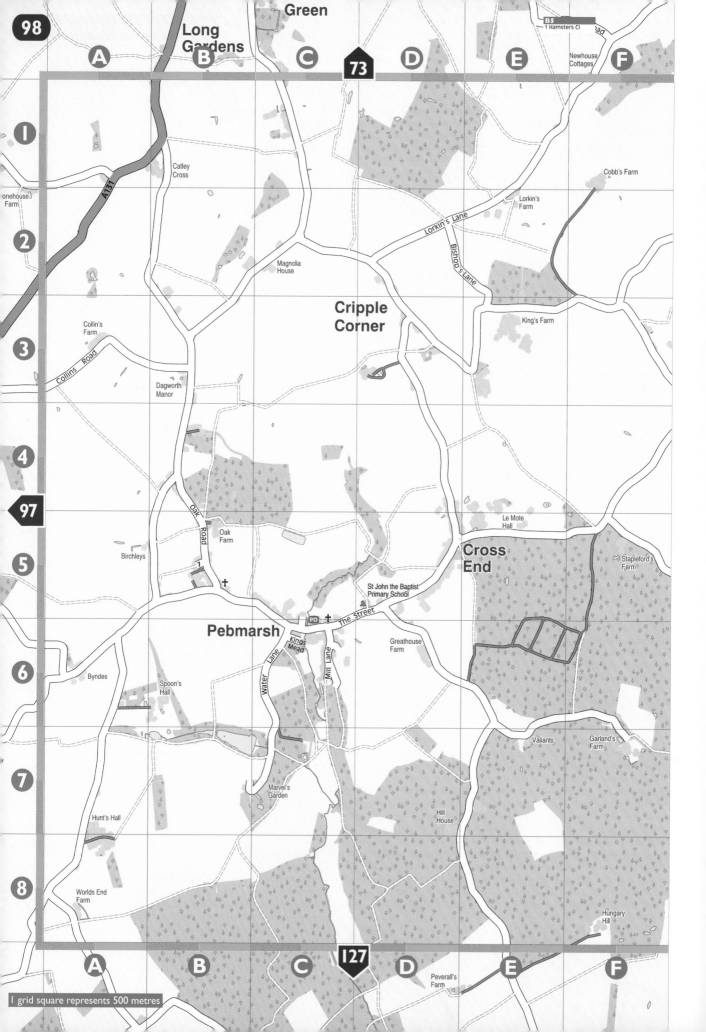

G H J **74** K L M

Ansell's Farm

Henny Back Road

Moat Lane

Lamarsh Road

Alphamstone Rd

Lamarsh

Bell Hill

Stour Valley Path

Stour Valley

River Stour

River

Alphamstone

Goulds Road

Shrub's Farm

Hewitts

Langley Hill

Springett's Hill

Hill Farm

Pebmarsh Road

Goulds

Clees Hall

Speck's Farm

Goulds Road

The Ferriers

100

Bure Stati

Colne Ro

Montague's Farm

Peyton Hall

Horne's Green

Baker's Hall

Fishpits

Butler's Farm

Ravensfield Farm

Pricketts Hall

Daw's Cross

Lower Jennies

Valley Green Farm

Cambridge Bro

Lamar

Craig

Mou

Baggarett's Farm

G H J **128** K L M

I

2

3

4

5

6

7

8

G H J K L M

Honey Tye

A134

High Road

Honey La

Edies Lane

PH
PO

Radleys Lane

Campion WY

New Black WY

Bramble WY

Kingsland

Red Barn Dr

Arger Fen

Hullback's Farm

Farthing Hall

Dead Lane
St Edmund WY

Guinea Wiggs Farm

Rickland Farm

Stour Valley Path

Wissington Grange

Radley's Farm

Campion Lane

Hill Farm

Nayland End Wood

Wissington Grove

Constable

Campions Hill

Malting Farm

Bures Road

Creem's

River Stour

Bures Road

Wissington

Bowdens

Bowdens Lane

Mill Hill

Church Road

Wormingford C of E Primary School

The Grange

Garnons Chase

Bottengoms

Stour Valley Pth

ningford

Colletts

Chase

School Lane

School Road

G H J K L M

130

Malting Farm

Cockrell's Farm

PO

I
2
3
102
5
6
7
8

A   B   C   D   E   F

1

Stoke-by-Nayland

Stoke-by-Nayland Primary School

Butt

School Street

PARK ST

PO

B1087

Poplar Farm

Stour Path

I

Hicks's Plantation

A134

2

Brunning's Farm

Harper's Hill

3

Gravel Hill

Shaddelows Farm

STOKE ROAD B1087

HARPER'S HILL A134

The Westerings

The Laburnum Wy

Willow Gv

Larch

Cemetery

Nayland CP School

Birch Path

Park's WW

Harper's Est

Cork Gv

BIRCH ST

Mill St

Fen St

4

Bear St

BEAR STREET

PH

High St

Church La

Nayland

Newlands La

Wiston   Road

Stour valley Pth

Court St

101

Horkesley_Road

Suffolk County

Essex County

5

Lane

Stour Valley Path

Water   Road

Thrift Farm

HORKESLEY HILL

Park Road

Burnt Dick Hill

6

Windyridge

Littlegarth School

Lower Dairy House

Nayland Road

Whitepark Farm

Kerseys

7

The Chantry

Ridgnalls

Boxted Church Road

8

Martins

NAYT ROAD

Holly Lodge Farm

Green Lane

Essex Way

Holly

Fishponds

Little Horkesley

A

B

C

131

D

A134

E

F

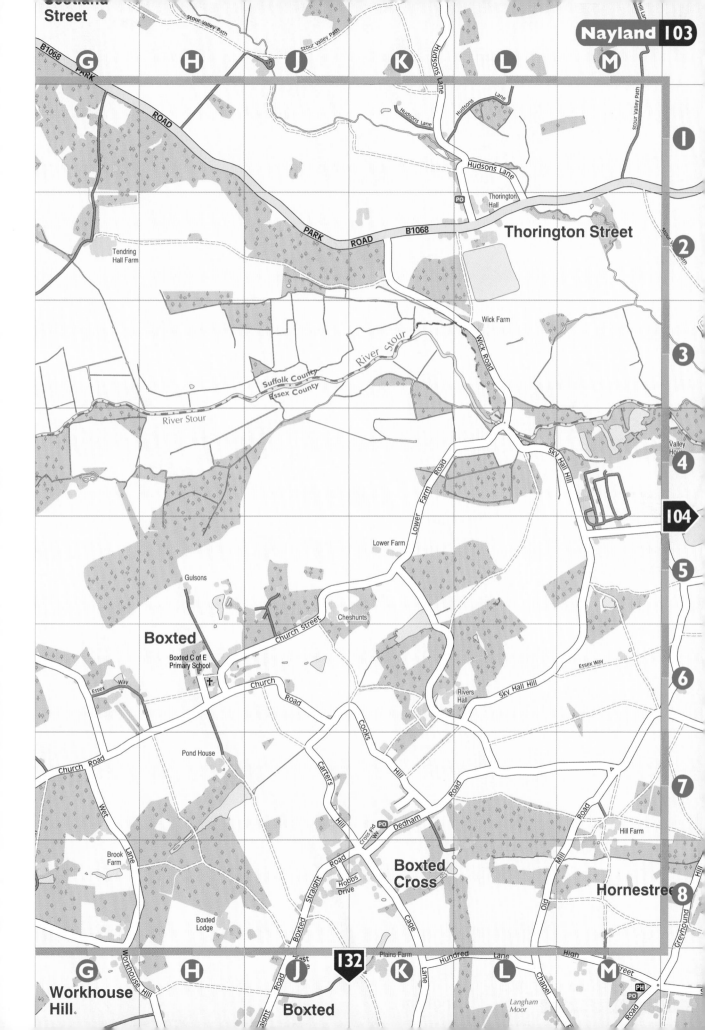

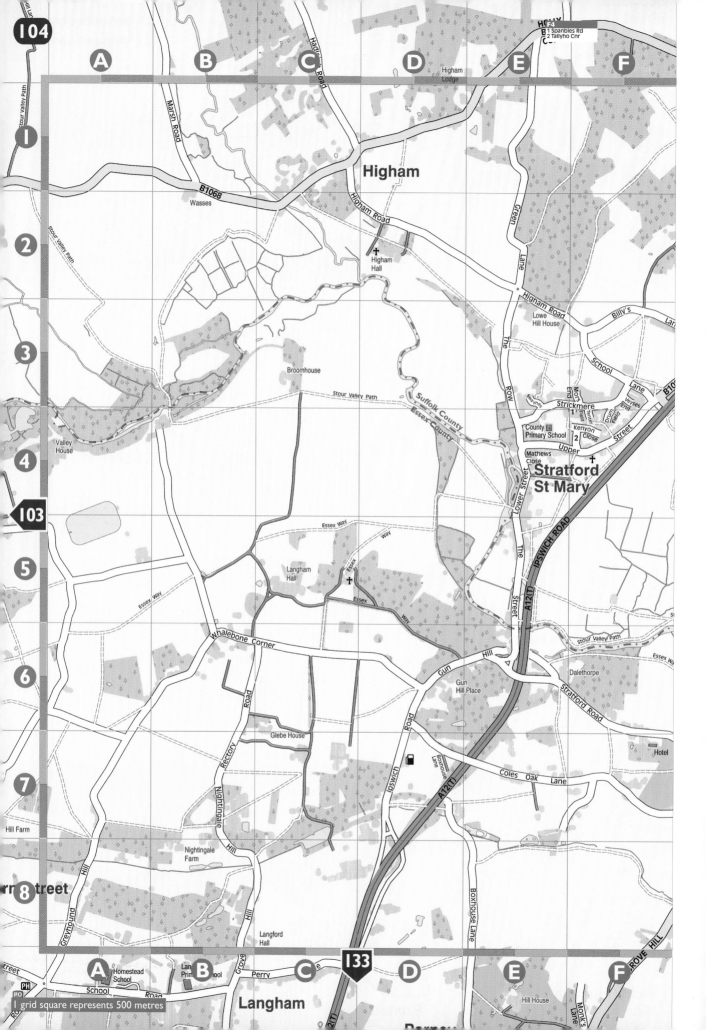

A B C D E F

1
2
3
4

103

5
6
7
8

Higham

Wasses

B1068

Higham Road

Higham Lodge

Higham Hall

Green Lane

Higham Road

Lowe Hill House

Billy's Lane

School Lane

The Row

Swaynes

Strickmere

Morks End

Veyses End

Drum Field

Kenyon Close

County Primary School

Mathews Close

Upper Street

Lower Street

Stratford St Mary

B1068

Broomhouse

Stour Valley Path

Suffolk County

Essex County

Essex Way

Way

Langham Hall

Essex Way

Essex Way

Whalebone Corner

Rectory Road

Nightingale Hill

Glebe House

Gun Hill

Gun Hill Place

Dalethorpe

Stratford Road

A12(T)

IPSWICH ROAD

The Street

Ipswich Road

Boxhouse Lane

A12(T)

Coles Oak Lane

Stour Valley Path

Essex Way

Hotel

Hill Farm

Nightingale Farm

Greyhound Hill

Langford Hall

PH
PO

Homestead School

School

Lang Prim School

Grove Road

Perry

A12(T)

Langham

Boxhouse Lane

Monk's Lane

Hill House

GROVE HILL

Marsh Road

Stour Valley Path

Valley House

A B C D E F

133

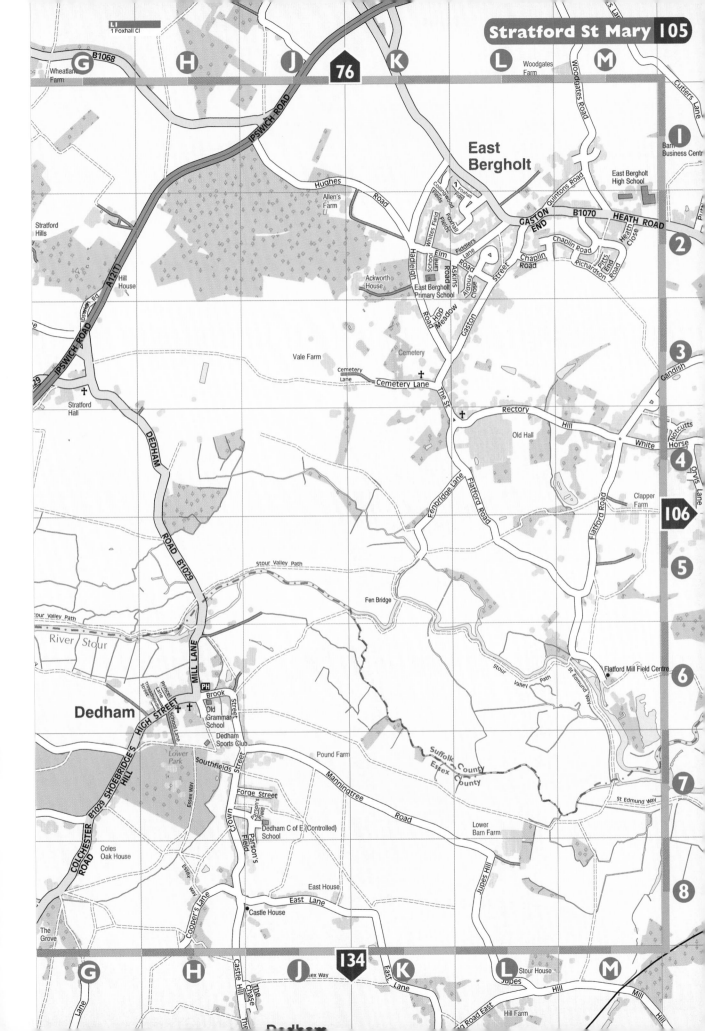

LI
1 Foxhall Cl

G B1068 H J 76 K L Woodgates Farm M

Wheatland Farm

IPSWICH ROAD

I
Barn Business Centre

East Bergholt

Hughes Road

Collingwood Field
Whites Field
Foxhall Fields
Fiddlers Lane

Quintons Road
East Bergholt High School

CASTON END B1070 HEATH ROAD 2

Allen's Farm

Stratford Hills

Hadleigh
School Lane
Elm Lane
Askins Road
Aldous Close
Caston Street
Chaplin Road
Chaplin Road
Richardson
Pitts End
Heath Close 2

A12(T) IPSWICH ROAD

Hill House

Ackworth House
East Bergholt Primary School
HOP MEADOW

B1029 IPSWICH ROAD

Vale Farm

Cemetery

Cemetery Lane
Cemetery Lane

The St

Gandish 3

Stratford Hall

DEDHAM ROAD B1029

Rectory
Old Hall

Hill
White Horse
Notcutts
Orvis Lane 4

Fenbridge Lane
Flatford Road

Clapper Farm

106

Stour Valley Path

Flatford Road

5

Fen Bridge

River Stour

MILL LANE

Stour Valley Path

St Edmund Way

Flatford Mill Field Centre 6

Dedham

Threadneedle Street
Princel Lane
HIGH STREET
PH
Brook Street
School Lane
Old Grammar School
Dedham Sports Club

Pound Farm

Suffolk County
Essex County

St Edmund Way 7

SHOEBRIDGE'S HILL
Lower Park
Southfields
Essex Way
Forge Street

Manningtree Road

Jupes Hill

Lower Barn Farm

COLCHESTER ROAD B1029

Coles Oak House

Crown Street
Parson's Field
Dedham C of E (Controlled) School

East House

The Grove

Cooper's Lane
Essex Way

East Lane

Castle House

8

G H J 134 K L Stour House M
Jupes Hill
Castle Hill
The Chase
Essex Way
East Lane
Hill Farm
Mill Hill
Road End East
Cutlers Lane

Dedham

108

A B C **79** D E F

White House Farm

Argent Manor Farm

Alton Water (Reservoir)

1

Bentley Lane

Holly Lane

Bentley Lane

Alton Hall Lane

Alton Water Sports Centre

2

Woodfield Lane

Catts Cl
Cattsfield

Larksfield Rd

Church Rd

HOLBROOK ROAD   B1080

Royal Hospital School

Wardma Infirmary

PRIMROSE HILL

Church Road

Hyams Lane

Ha'penny Field

Jervis Close

Mill Ri

PH

B1080

3

Lewis Lane

MANNINGTREE ROAD

PO

Findley Close

Church Road

Stutton

Stutton Primary School

Stutton Cl

Lower

Street

The Drift

Crepping Hall

Manor Lane

Lane

Upper Street

Hyam's Drive

Crowe Hall Lane

Lower Street

Stutton Gn

Suffolk Coast &

Heaths Path

Stutton House

4

Crepping Hall

Crowe Hall

107

5

Holbrook Bay

6

7

8

A B C **137** Jacq Bay D E F

Wall

Essex Way

Remembrance Wood

Lane

Nether Hall

1 grid square represents 500 metres

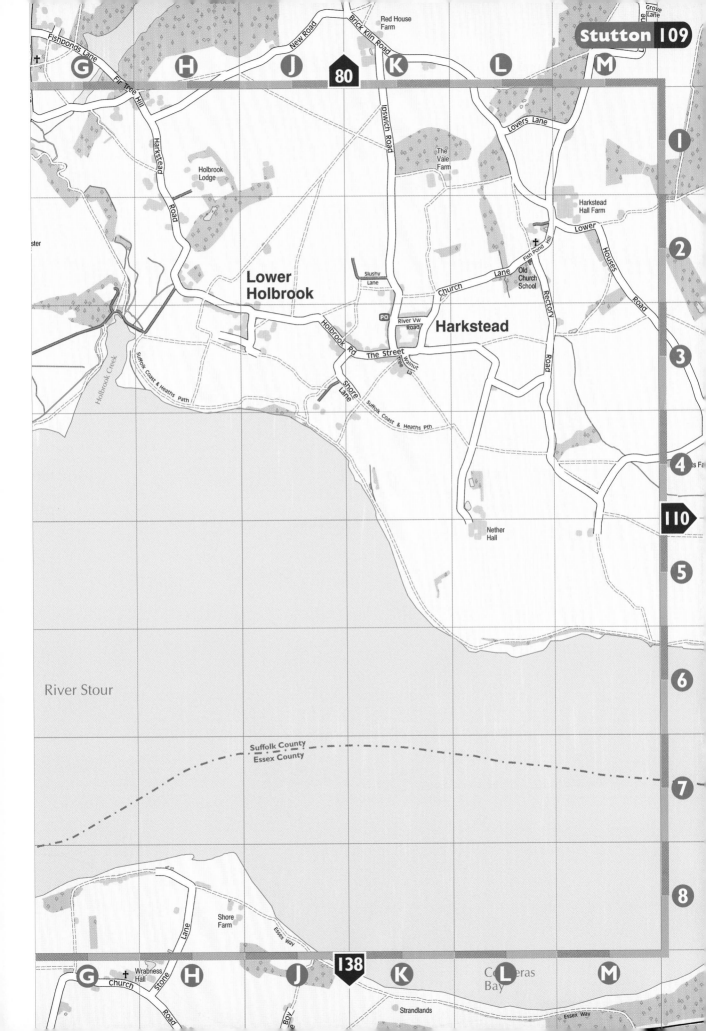

Grove
Lane

Fishponds Lane

New Road

Brick Kiln Road

Red House
Farm

G

Fir Tree Hill

H

J

80

K

Ipswich Road

L

Lovers Lane

M

I

Harkstead Road

Holbrook
Lodge

The Vale
Farm

Harkstead
Hall Farm

2

ster

Lower
Holbrook

Slushy
Lane

Fish Pond Hill

Church Lane

Old
Church
School

Lower Houses Road

3

Holbrook Creek

Suffolk Coast & Heaths Path

Holbrook Rd

PO

River VW
Road

The Street

Walnut Tree La.

Harkstead

Rectory Road

Harkstead
Hall Farm

4

as Fa

110

Holbrook Creek

Shore Lane

Suffolk Coast & Heaths Pth

Nether
Hall

5

River Stour

6

Suffolk County
Essex County

7

8

Shore
Farm

Essex Way

Stone Lane

Boy

e

G

Church

Wrabness
Hall

H

J

138

K

Colueras
Bay

M

Strandlands

Essex Way

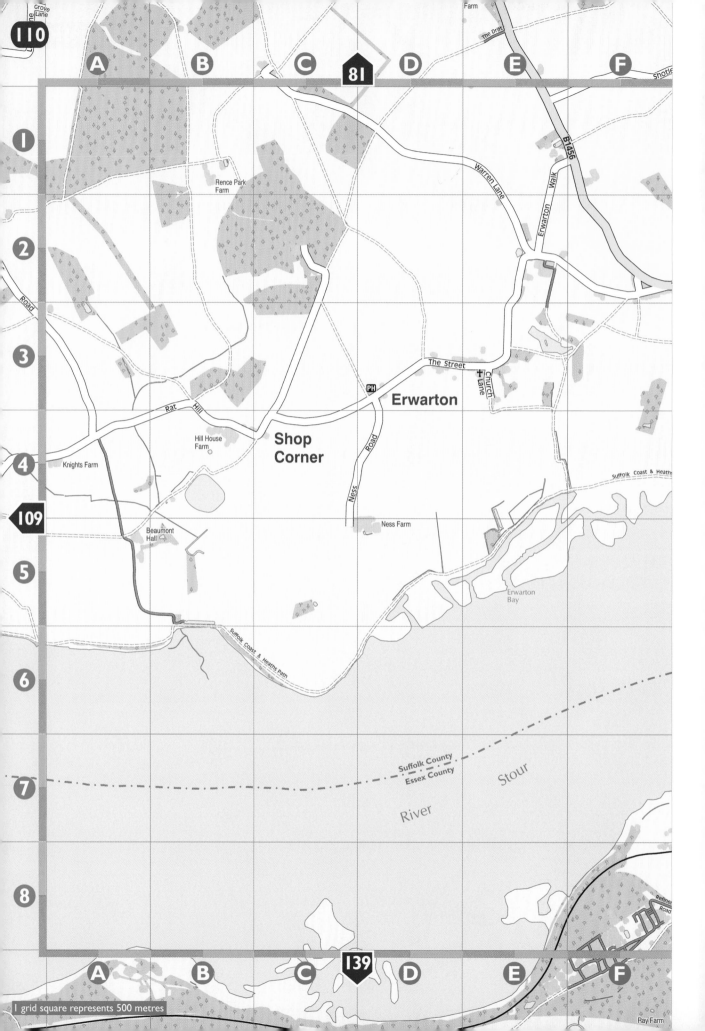

A B C D E F

81

I
2
3
4

109

5
6
7
8

Grove
Lane

Road

Farm

The Drift

B1456

Warren Lane

Erwarton Walk

Shotle

Rence Park
Farm

Knights Farm

Rat Hill

Hill House
Farm

PH

The Street

Church Lane

Erwarton

Shop
Corner

Ness Road

Ness Farm

Beaumont
Hall

Suffolk Coast & Heaths

Erwarton
Bay

Suffolk Coast & Heaths Path

Suffolk County
Essex County

River Stour

Refiner
Road

A B C D E F

139

Ray Farm

Church
d

Shotley Hall

Frogs
Alley

Crane's
Hill

G **H** **J** **82** **K** **L** **M**

Trimle Marsh

I

Shotley

Orwell View Road

Garden
Cl

The
Surgery

THE STREET

B1456

Kingsland

Queensland

Kingsland

Shotley
Primary
School

2

Over Hall

Shotley
Marshes

3

Path

Childer's Cl

Great Harlings

Tudor Cl

Gate Farm Rd

4

Link Rd

Kirkton Cl

Henley
Close

Blake Av

Kitchener Way

**Shotley
Gate**

Stourside

Lloyd Rd

Ganges Rd

PO

Ganges
Museum

Marina

I I2

Stourside

Lower

Harlings

5

Estuary Road

Estuary Crs

Bristol Hill

Caledonia
Rd

Battery
Lane

School
Rd

Shotley
Sailing Club

Qu Victoria Dr

King Edward VII Drive

6

8

9

Parkeston
Quay

Harwich Parkeston
Quay Station

LC

East Dock Road

East Dock Road

LC

THE QUAY

Hotel

King's
Head
St

WEST ST

GEORGE ST

PO

Guildhall

Harwich Town
Station

7

Car Ferry
Terminal

P

Station Road

Coller
Rd

Parkeston

Hamilton St

Tyler St

Parkeston
Road

Princes
St

Garland
Rd

PO

Pepys St

Coke St

Marta St

George
Street

Vansittart St

Canning St

Harbour
St

Harwich County
Primary School

Bath Side

Main Road

The Redoubt

8

West Dock Road

Refinery Road

Foster Road

Occupational
Health Centre

Edward
Street

Una Road

STATION ROAD

Matrix St

Adelaide St

Harwich
Industrial Estate

Ray Lane

Alexandra Rd

Alexandra

Kingsway Hall
Art and Theatre Way

G **H** **J** **I40** **K** **L** **M**

Harwich
Golf Club

Europa Way

Cemetery

Rawden Close

A120(T)

A120(T)

Dovercourt Station

Station Lane

Nelson
Road

HIGH ST

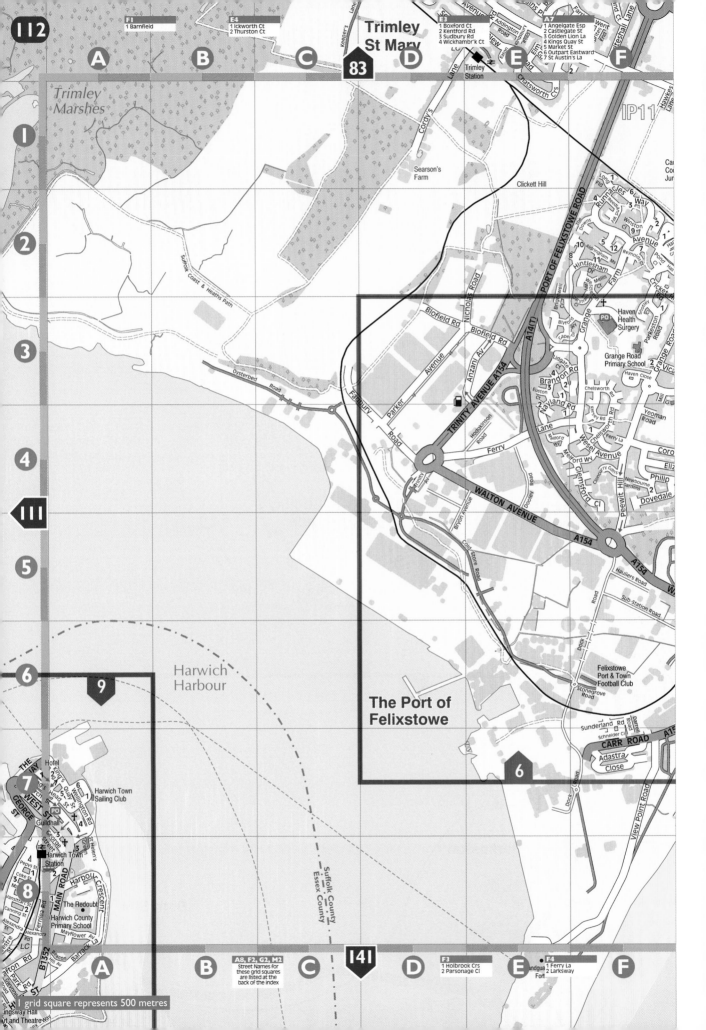

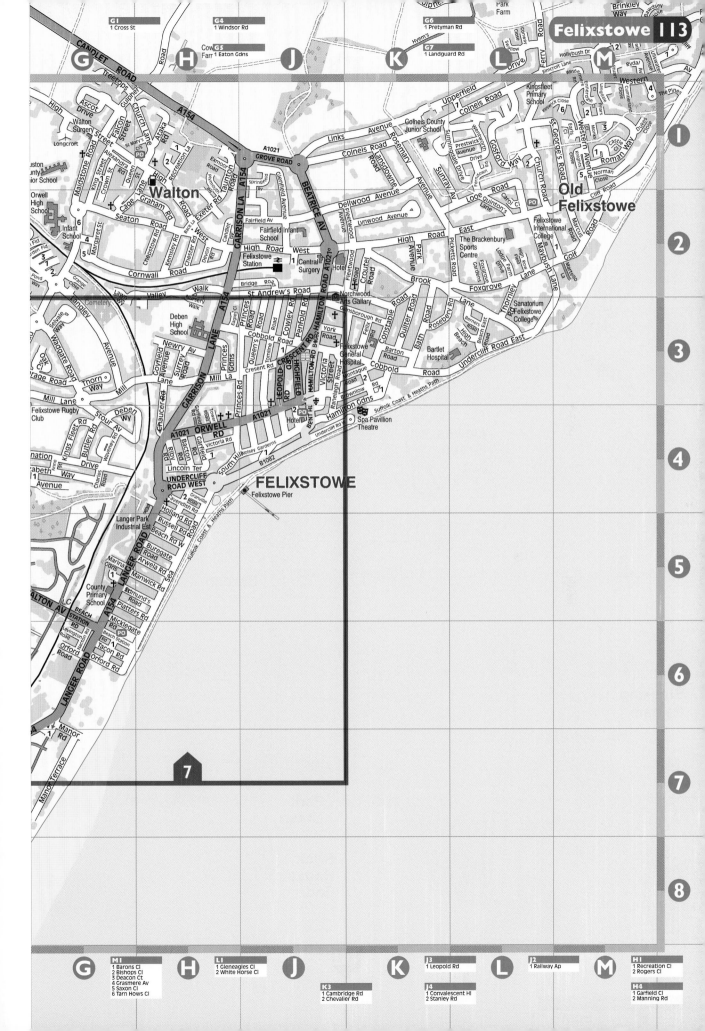

G
H
J
K
L
M

G1 1 Cross St
G4 1 Windsor Rd
Cow **G5**
Farr 1 Eaton Gdns
G6 1 Pretyman Rd
G7 1 Landguard Rd

I

2

3

4

5

6

7

8

CANDLET ROAD

Treetops

Gulpher

Park
Farm

Brinkley
Way

Bawdsey
Way

Hyem's

Conway
Swallow

Hollybush Dr

Elmcroft Lane

Ferry Road

Rydal
Ullswater Avenue
Close

The Pines

Western

AV

Ascot
Drive

High Street

Church Lane

A154

Upperfield

Colneis Road

Kingsfleet Primary
School

Keswick Close

Windermere Rd

Langstone Close

Cumberland
Close

Roman Way

Walton
Surgery

Falcon
Street

Alexandra Rd

St Mary's CfE
PO

Attoka
Rd

High

Recreation La

A1021

GROVE ROAD

Springs

Colneis County
Junior School

Rosemary

Wentworth

Prestworth
Avenue

St George's Road

Earls

Monks

Dukes
Close

Castle
Rise

Cliff Road

Norman
Close

Longcroft

King Street

Crown St

Queen
Rd

Exmoor
Rd

Glenfield Avenue

Links Avenue

Colneis Road

Lansdowne Road

Sunningdale Drive

Cosford Way

Carol Cl

Church Road

PO

Marcus Rd

Old
Felixstowe

Ruston
County
Junior School

Maidstone Road

Kemsley Rd

Chester Rd

Taunton Rd

Candlet

A1021

Deliwood Avenue

Fleetwood Avenue

Sunray Av

Looe
Road

Quinton's
Lane

Felixstowe
International
College

High Row
Field

Foxgrove
Gardens

Marybush Lane

Golf

Orwell
High School

6

Cage Lane

Graham Rd

Back La

Devon Rd

West

Fairfield Av

Fairfield Infant
School

High Road West

Lynwood Avenue

High Road

Park Avenue

The Brackenbury
Sports Centre

Picketts Road

Lodge Farm Drive

Thornley Road

Martello

Infant
School

Seaton Road

Chepstow Rd

Exeter Rd

Felixstowe Station

West

1 Central Surgery

Hotel

Fleetwood Road

Croutel Road

Brook

Foxgrove
Lane

Berners East

Beach East

Felixstowe
College

Garden Fld

5

Cornwall Road

Bridge Walk

St Andrew's Road

Norchwood
Arts Gallary

Gainsborough Rd

Constable Road

Quilter Road

Bath Road

Rosebery Rd

High
Beach

Sanatorium

7
3

Pond
Way

Grange
Rd

Nursery
Walk

York
Road

Felixstowe
General
Hospital

Felix
Road

Barton
Road

Cobbold Road

Undercliff Road East

Law

Valley Walk

A154

Deben High
School

Eagles Cl

Princes Road

Cobbold Road

Cowley Road

Penfold Road

CRESCENT RD

HAMILTON RD

B1082

Montague Rd

Bartlet
Hospital

Selvale Way

Wadgate Road

Newry Av

Surrey Road

Queen's Road

Cresent Road

Tomline

HIGHFIELD

Victoria Street

Ranelagh Road

Brownlow Rd

Suffolk, Coast & Heaths Path

Oak
Grove

Thorn
Way

Goyfield Avenue

Avenue

Garrison Lane

Princes Gdns

1

LEOPOLD RD

BENT HL

Spa Pavillion
Theatre

Garage Road

Mill Lane

Chaucer Rd

Princes Rd

Mill La

Garfield Rd

Tower
Hl

A1021

ORWELL RD

PO

Hamilton Gdns

Felixstowe Rugby
Club

Stour Av

Deben Wy

Garrison

A1021

Victoria Rd

1

Undercliff Rd

Kings Fleet Rd

Butley Rd

Waverley Rd

Lincoln Ter

Ribby
Rd

Batton
Rd

Garfield
Rd

South Hill

Wolsey Gardens

B1082

ation

Charles Road

Beach Rd

UNDERCLIFF
ROAD WEST

FELIXSTOWE

Elizabeth Way

Avenue

Cavendish Rd

2 Granville

Felixstowe Pier

Langer Park
Industrial Est

Holland Rd

Russell Rd

Beach Rd W

Suffolk, Coast & Heaths Path

LANGER ROAD

A154

Buregate Road

Marina
Gdns

Arwela Rd

Sea

WALTON AV

LC

County
Primary
School

Manwick Rd

Edmund's Road

Platters Rd

Beach
Station
PO

Micklegate Rd

Tacon Rd

Manor
Rd

Manor Terrace

Levington
Road

Nacton
Road

Orford Rd

Orford Road

G
M1
1 Barons Cl
2 Bishops Cl
3 Deacon Ct
4 Grasmere Av
5 Saxon Cl
6 Tarn Hows Cl

H
L1
1 Gleneagles Cl
2 White Horse Cl

J
K3
1 Cambridge Rd
2 Chevalier Rd

K
J3
1 Leopold Rd
J4
1 Convalescent Hl
2 Stanley Rd

L
J2
1 Railway Ap

M
H1
1 Recreation Cl
2 Rogers Cl
H4
1 Garfield Cl
2 Manning Rd

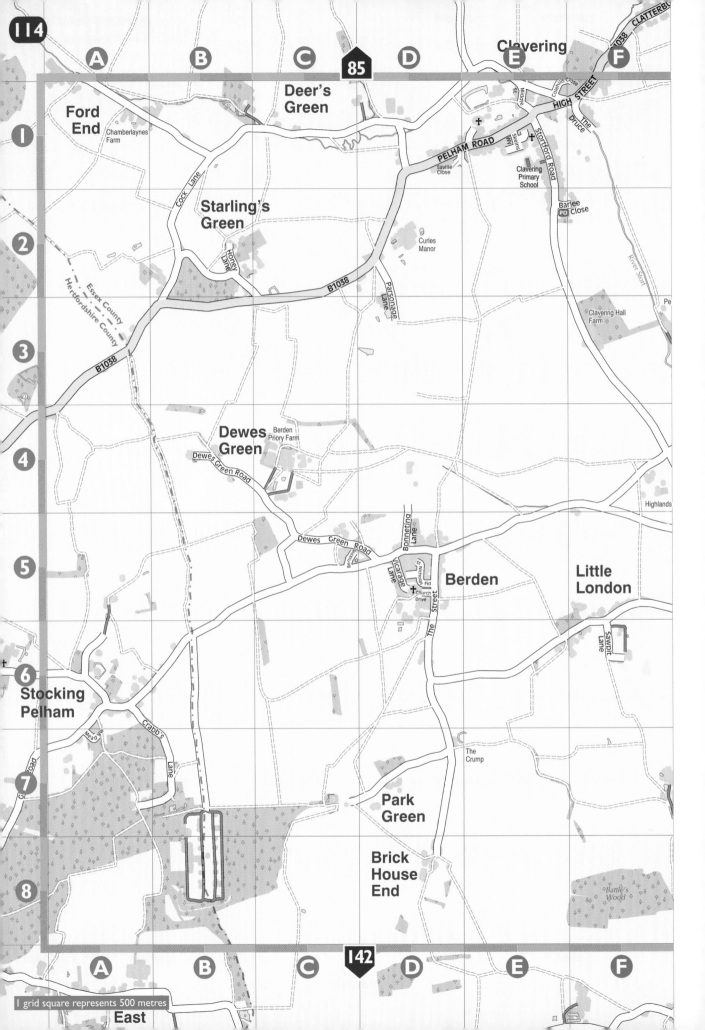

A   B   C   **85**   D   E   F

Clevering

CLATTERB

T1038

HIGH STREET

I Ford End

Chamberlaynes Farm

Cock Lane

Deer's Green

PELHAM ROAD

Saville Close

Middle St

Skeins WVI

Clavering Primary School

Stortford Road

The Druce

Barlee Close
PO

River Stort

Pe

2 **Starling's Green**

Honey Lane

B1038

Curles Manor

Parsonage Lane

3 Essex County

Hertfordshire County

B1038

Clavering Hall Farm

4 **Dewes Green**

Berden Priory Farm

Dewes Green Road

Highlands

5

Dewes   Green   Road

Berlands

Bonneting Lane

Vicarage Lane

St Nicholas Fld

The Street

Church Drive

Berden

Little London

Sawpit Lane

6 **Stocking Pelham**

Crabb's Lane

Mead

The Crump

7

Col Road

Park Green

8

Battle's Wood

Brick House End

A   B   **142**   C   D   E   F

East

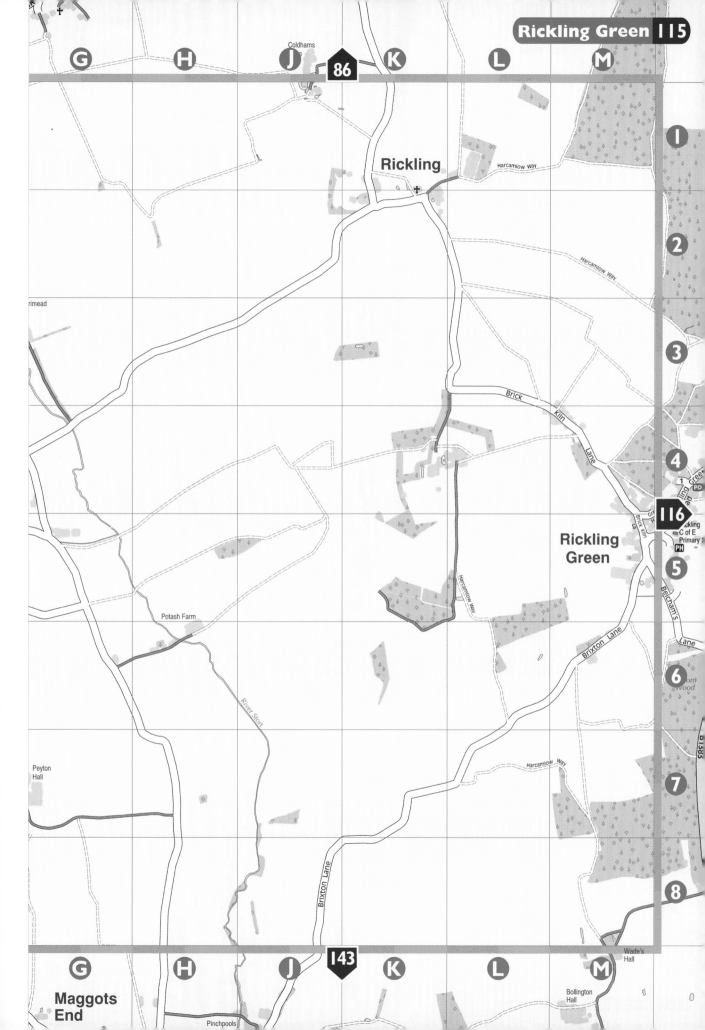

G   H   J   86   K   L   M

Coldhams

I

Rickling

Harcamlow Way

2

Harcamlow Way

rimead

3

Brick   Kiln   Lane

4

ckling Green   PO

116

**Rickling
Green**

Rickling
C of E
Primary

PH

5

Belcham's Lane

Potash Farm

Harcamlow Way

Brixton Lane

6

oni
Wood

River Stort

B 1383

Peyton
Hall

Harcamlow   Way

7

8

Wade's
Hall

**Maggots
End**

Bollington
Hall

Pinchpools

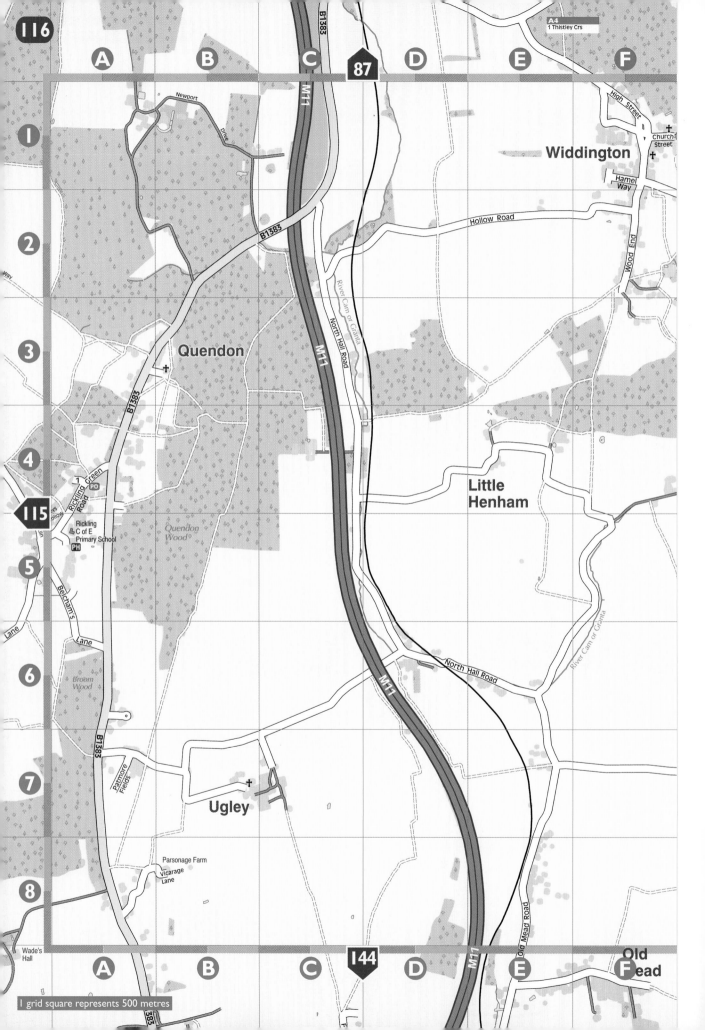

A B C D E F

87

1 Thistley Crs

Widddington

High Street

Church Street

Newport Drive

Hamel Way

Hollow Road

Wood End

B1383

Quendon

River Cam or Granta

North Hall Road

M11

Little Henham

Rickling Green Road

1 PO

115

Rickling C of E Primary School

PH

Quendon Wood

Belcham's Lane

Way

Lane

Lane

Broom Wood

North Hall Road

River Cam or Granta

B1383

Patmore Fields

Ugley

Parsonage Farm

Vicarage Lane

Old Mead Road

M11

Wade's Hall

A B C D E F

144

Old ₣ead

B1383

Rook
End

H8
1 Pimblett Rw

G H J 88 K L M

The
Hall

Swayne's
Hall

Mole Hall Lane

Mole
Hall

River Cam or Granta

Thistley
Hall

Cornells Lane

Cornells Lane

Prior's
Wood

Amberden
Hall

New Amberden
Hall

Staines
Farm

Henham Road

Chickney Road

118

Lovecotes Farm

Sibleys

Henham
Lodge

Chickney Road

Springate

Church Street

Chase

Highfields St

Wright's
Piece

The Chase

High

Starr Rd

Woodend
Green

PO

Hall Close

Crow Street

Carters La

Sages

School La

Vernon's Close

Henham & Ugley
CP School

Henham

Greenend Farm

Mill

B1051

I
2
3
4
5
6
7
8

G H J 145 K L M

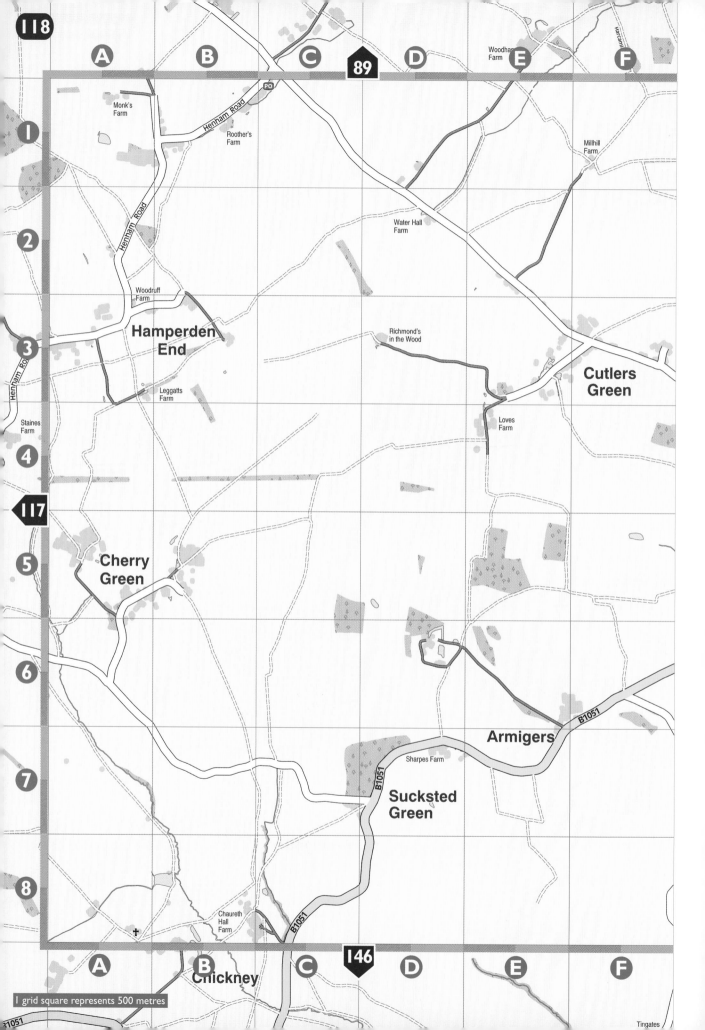

A   B   C   89   D   E   F

89

PO

Monk's Farm

Henham Road

Roother's Farm

Woodham Farm

Millhill Farm

1

Water Hall Farm

2

Henham Road

Woodruff Farm

Hamperden End

Richmond's in the Wood

Cutlers Green

3

Henham Rd

Leggatts Farm

Loves Farm

Staines Farm

4

117

5

Cherry Green

6

B1051

Armigers

Sharpes Farm

7

B1051

Sucksted Green

8

Chaureth Hall Farm

†

B1051

A   B   Chickney   C   146   D   E   F

146

Harcamlo

Tingates

B1051

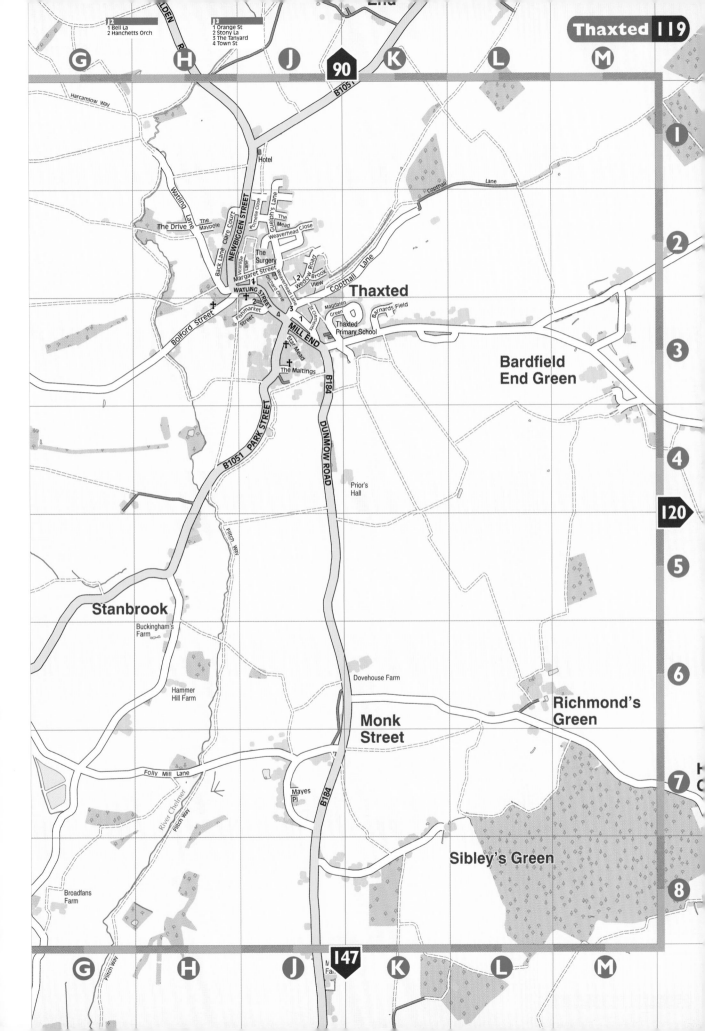

G   H   J   K   L   M

90
B105

1

2

3

4

120

5

6

7

8

J2
1 Bell La
2 Hanchetts Orch

J3
1 Orange St
2 Stony La
3 The Tanyard
4 Town St

Harcamlow Way

Hotel

Watling Lane

The Drive
The Maypole

NEWBIGGEN STREET

Back Lane
Clare Court
Rochelle Close
Guelph's Lane
The Mead
Weaverhead Close

The Surgery
Vicarage Lane
Margaret Street
Weaverhead Lane
Wedow Road
Brook View
Orchard Close

Copthall Lane
Copthall
Lane

WATLING STREET

Bolford Street

Fishmarket Street

MILL END

St Edmunds

Magdalen Green

Thaxted

Barnards Field

Thaxted Primary School

**Bardfield
End Green**

B1051 PARK STREET

Star Mead

The Maltings

B184

DUNMOW ROAD

Filtch Way

Prior's Hall

Stanbrook

Buckingham's Farm

Hammer Hill Farm

Dovehouse Farm

**Monk
Street**

**Richmond's
Green**

Folly Mill Lane

River Chelmer

Filtch Way

Mayes Pl

B184

Sibley's Green

Broadfans Farm

Filtch Way

147

G   H   J   K   L   M

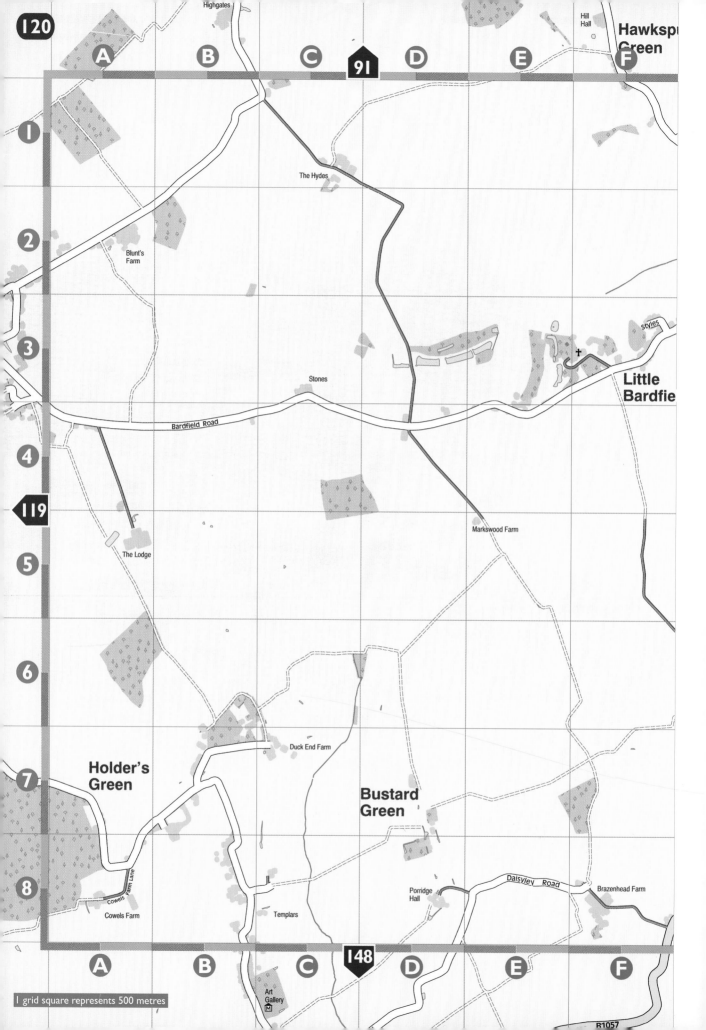

120

A B C 91 D E F

1

Highgates

Hill
Hall

Hawksp
Green

The Hydes

2

Blunt's
Farm

Styles

3

Stones

Little
Bardfie

†

Bardfield Road

4

119

Markswood Farm

The Lodge

5

6

7

Holder's
Green

Duck End Farm

Bustard
Green

Cowels Farm Lane

8

Cowels Farm

Templars

Porridge
Hall

Daisyley Road

Brazenhead Farm

A B C 148 D E F

I grid square represents 500 metres

Art
Gallery
Ⓜ

B1057

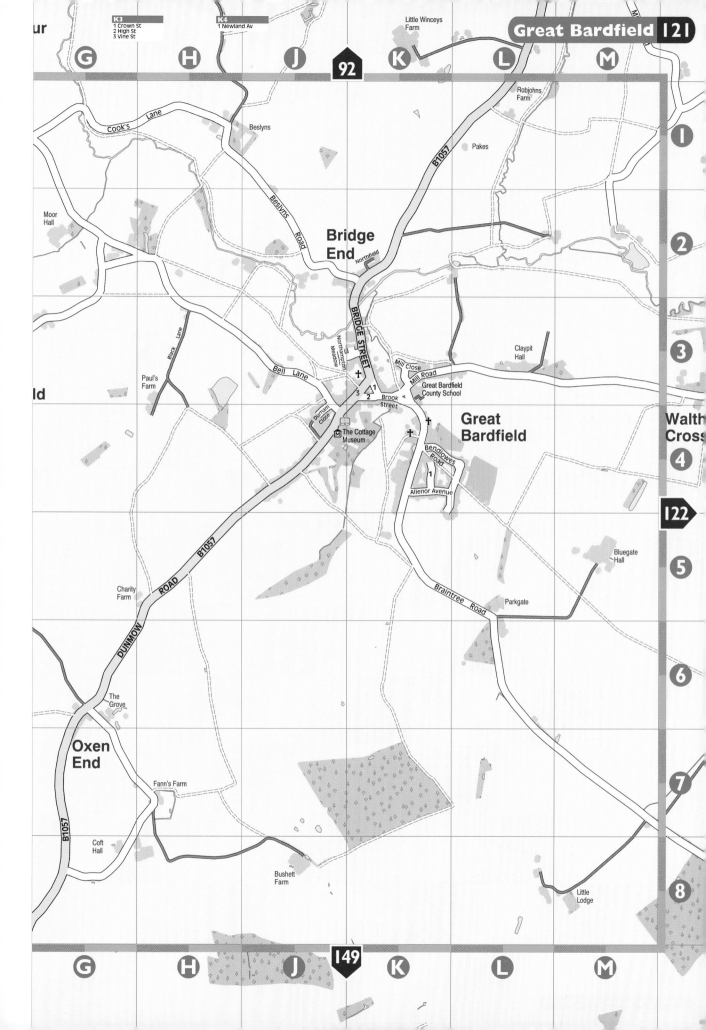

K3
1 Crown St
2 High St
3 Vine St

K4
1 Newland Av

G H J 92 K L M

ur

Cook's Lane

Beslyns

Moor Hall

Beslyns Road

B1057

Little Winceys Farm

Robjohns Farm

Pakes

Bridge End

Northfield

Walth Cross

1

2

3

4

122

5

6

7

8

BRIDGE STREET

Northampton Meadow

Bell Lane

Black Lane

Paul's Farm

Mill Close

Mill Road

Claypit Hall

Great Bardfield County School

Great Bardfield

Brook Street

3 7
2

Durham Close

The Cottage Museum

Bendlowes Road

1

Alienor Avenue

Charity Farm

DUNMOW ROAD B1057

Braintree Road

Parkgate

Bluegate Hall

The Grove

Oxen End

Fann's Farm

B1057

Coft Hall

Bushett Farm

Little Lodge

G H J 149 K L M

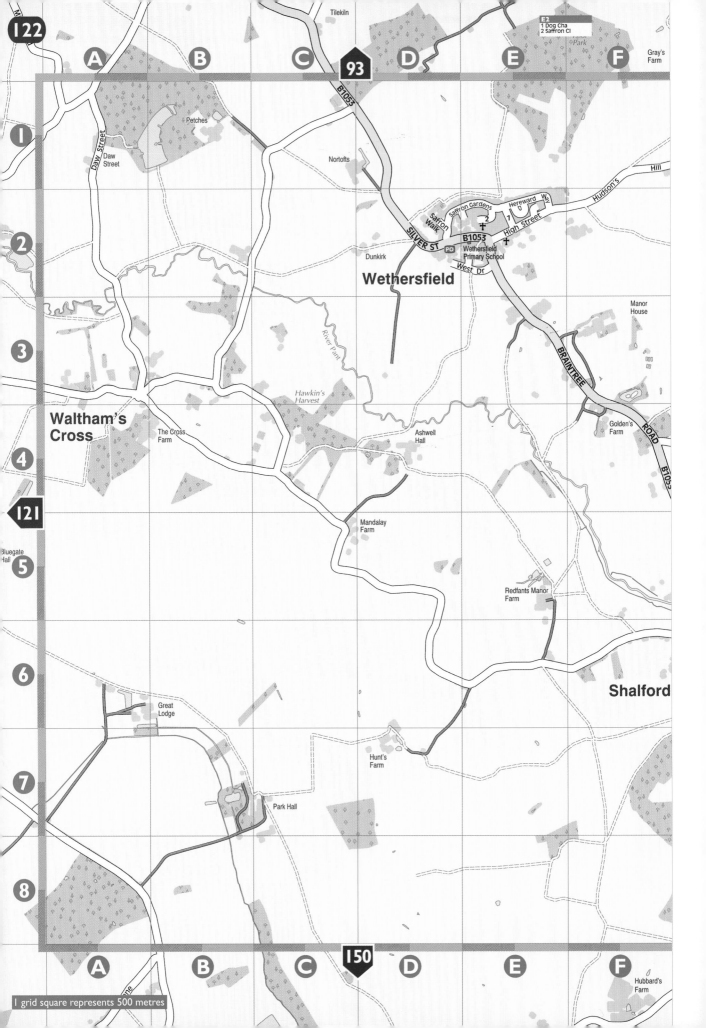

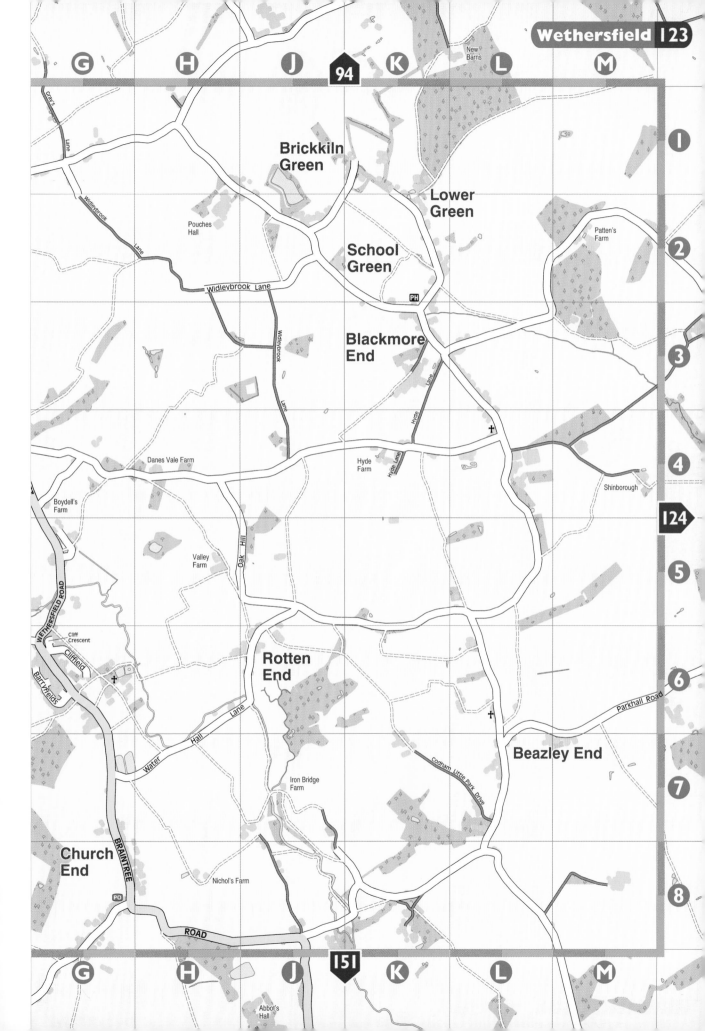

G   H   J   **94**   K   L   M

1

**Brickkiln
Green**

**Lower
Green**

Patten's
Farm

2

Pouches
Hall

Widleybrook Lane

**School
Green**

PH

3

**Blackmore
End**

4

Danes Vale Farm

Hyde
Farm

Shinborough

124

Boydell's
Farm

5

Valley
Farm

6

Cliff
Crescent

Clifffield

Parkhall Road

**Rotten
End**

Barryfields

**Beazley
End**

Codham Little Park Drive

7

Iron Bridge
Farm

8

**Church
End**

BRAINTREE

PO

Nichol's Farm

ROAD

G   H   J   **151**   K   L   M

Abbot's
Hall

124

A B C D E F

95

1

Hawkwoods

2

Liston Hall Farm

Baker's Farm

Bounce's Farm

3

123

inborough

4

Home Farm

Gosfield Lake Golf Club

St Margarets Preparatory School

Hall Drive

5

Church

Gosfield Lake

6

Parkhall Farm

Parkhall Road

Parkhall Road

Parkhall Road

Parkhall Wood

Ayleward's Farm

7

Harmas Farm

8

Bovingdon Wood

Gosfield Wood

A B C D E F

152

Fennes Road

A1017

1 grid square represents 500 metres

Iron Pear Tree Farm

Green

Farm

Listonhall Chase

A   B   C   97   D   E   F

I

2

HALSTEAD

3

Trinity Street

4

125

5

6

7

8

Greenstead
Gr 154

A   B   C   D   E   F

1 grid square represents 500 metres

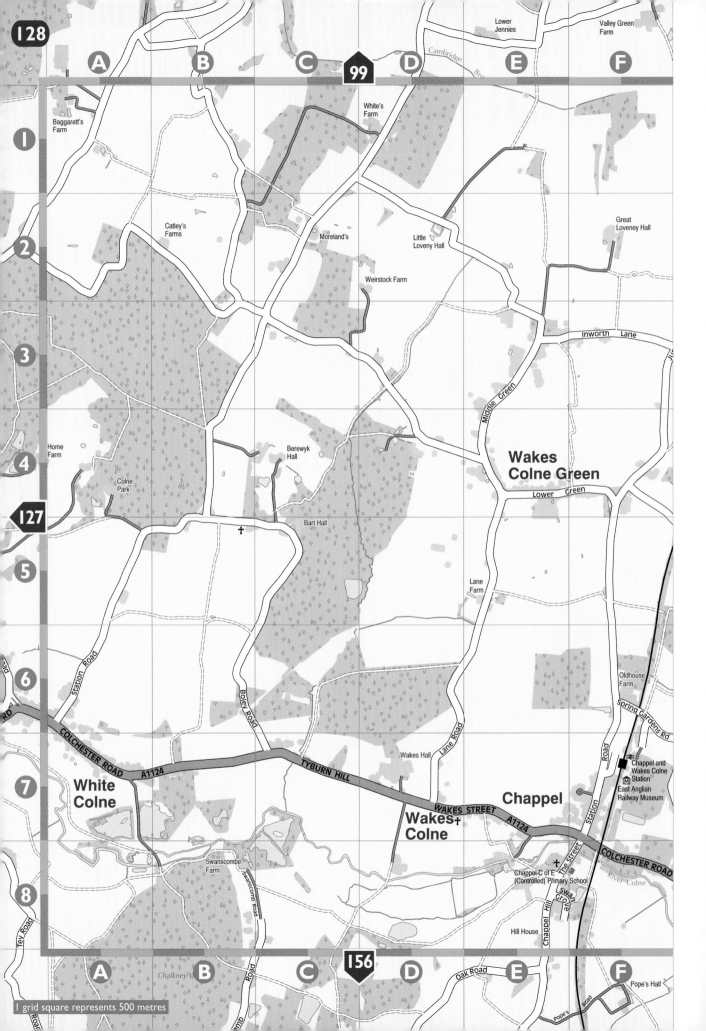

A B C **99** D E F

99

I

Baggarett's Farm

White's Farm

2

Catley's Farms

Moreland's

Little Loveny Hall

Weirstock Farm

Great Loveney Hall

Cambridge Brook

Lower Jennies

Valley Green Farm

Inworth Lane

3

Middle Green

4

Home Farm

Berewyk Hall

Wakes Colne Green

Colne Park

Bart Hall

Lower Green

5

Lane Farm

Station Road

6

Boley Road

Oldhouse Farm

Spring Gardens Rd

Wakes Hall

Lane Road

7

White Colne

COLCHESTER ROAD

A1124

TYBURN HILL

Wakes Hall

Wakes† Colne

WAKES STREET

A1124

Chappel

Station Road

Chappel and Wakes Colne Station

East Anglian Railway Museum

Tey Road

Swanscombe Farm

Swanscomb Road

Chappel C of E (Controlled) Primary School

The Street

Swan Grove

COLCHESTER ROAD

River Colne

Chappel Hill

8

Hill House

A B **156** C D E F

156

Chalkney Wd

Oak Road

Pope's Hall

Pope's Road

1 grid square represents 500 metres

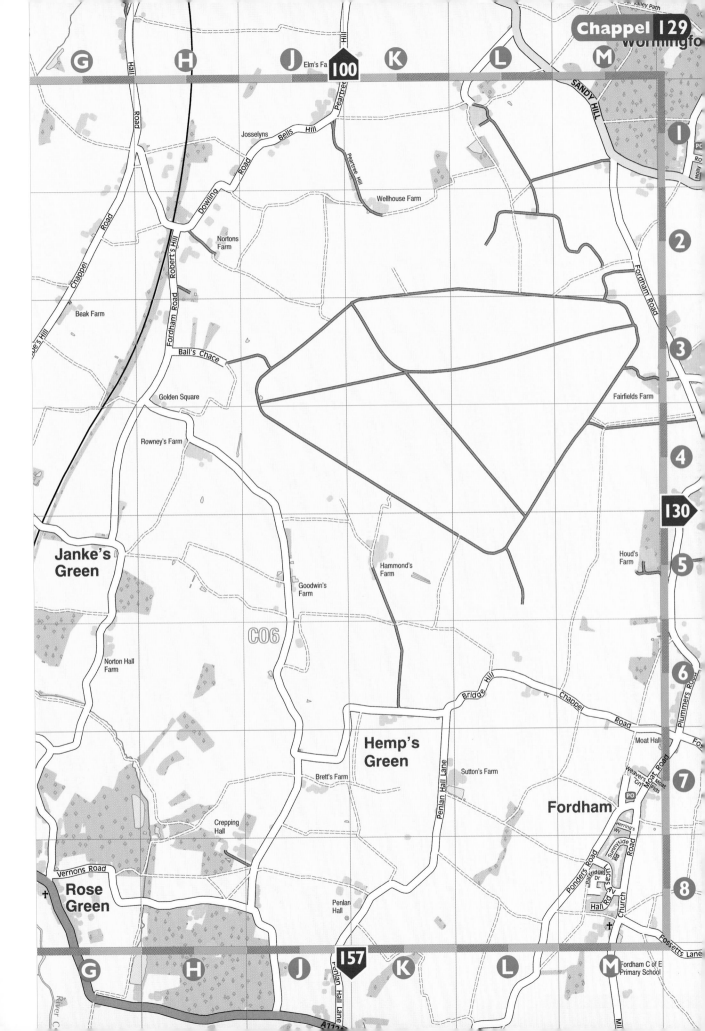

G   H   J   100   K   L   M

I

2

3

4

130

5

6

7

8

G   H   J   157   K   L   M

SANDY HILL

Josselyns   Bells Hill   Peartree Hill

Wellhouse Farm

Dowling Road

Robert's Hill

Chappel Road

Fordham Road

Beak Farm

Nortons Farm

Ball's Chace

Golden Square

Rowney's Farm

Fairfields Farm

Janke's Green

Houd's Farm

C06

Goodwin's Farm

Hammond's Farm

Norton Hall Farm

Plummers Road

Bridge Hill   Chappel Road

Moat Hall

Hemp's Green

Penlan Hall Lane

Brett's Farm

Sutton's Farm

Fordham

Crepping Hall

Ponders Road

Vernons Road

Rose Green

Penlan Hall

Fordham C of E Primary School

River C

A1124

Elm's Fa

Holly

Ro

PO

Weaver's Cnr

PO

Herring's Wy

Sunnyside Rd

Hall Rd

Church Road

Fossetts Lane

Mill

Valley Path

A
B
C
101
D
E
F

I

2

3

4

129

5

6

7

8

A
B
C
158
D
E
F

Valley Path
Primary School
The Grange
Garnons Chase
Lane
Lane
pol Road

Colletts
Chase
Stour Valley Pth
Malting Farm
Cockrell's Farm

PO
Robletts Way
Holly Oaks
MAIN
Little Horkesley Road
Cockrell's Rd
Holt's Road

Wood Hall
ROAD
Long's Farm
Holts
Workhouse Road
Vinesse Farm

Fordham Road
Jenkins Farm
Crabtree Lane
Vinesse Road

Fairfields Farm
Packards Lane

B1508

Houd's Fa
Highfield Farm
Rookery Farm

Plummers Road
Fordham Place
Pond Farm
COLCHESTER ROAD B1508

Moat Hall
Fossetts Lane
Coney Byes Farm
Nayland Road

PO
L Moat Fields

Hall Road
Hall Road

Essex Way

Fordham C of E
rimary School
Fossetts Lane
King's Farm
Essex Way
rmins Ct
Lexden
New

G
H
J
102
K
L
M
I

Wor
Hill

Fishponds
Hill

**Little
Horkesley**

London Road

Vinesse Road

Mount
Hall

Tog Lane

THE CAUSEWAY A134

AND ROAD A134

Holly Lodge
Farm

Essex Way

Lodge Farm

Enfield's
Farm

2

Boxted Road

Queen's

Redhouse Lane

Hea

3

Knowles's Farm

Breewood
Hall

School Lane

PO

Broad Lane

Essex Way

Redhouse
Farm

**Great
Horkesley**

Lincoln Lane

Sch

The
Badgers

Clevelands

Spratt's Marsh

4

**Westwood
Park**

Knight's Farm

Essex Way

132

Horkesley Road

5

London Road

Coach Road

Old House Road

Old House

A134

Ivy Lodge Road

Accommodation Road

Road

6

Tile House
Farm

Tile House Road

NAYLAND ROAD

Coach Road

Bishop
William
Ward School

Ramparts Cl

Coach Road

Manor
Close

Exeter
Close

Millers Cl

Malvern Way

Keelers

Sandon
Cl

Grantham Rd

Chilton
Close

Keelers
Way

Brick Kiln Road

Helm Cl

Blackbrook Rd

Kelso Cl

NAYLAND

Woodhouse Farm

Essex Way

Barnfield Rd

Green Lane

Terrace Hall Chase

7

Scarlet's
Farm

Manor
Farm

Essex Way

ROAD A134

Boxted Road

Severalls
Hospital

8

White Hart La

Manor Road

Ford Lane

Fords Lane

Howards
Croft

Defoe

Heathlands
Primary
School

Garthwood
Close

School Lane

Church Road

Church

Doctors
Surgery

Albany

Lodge Ct

Ormonde
Close

Coopers

Lorkin
Way

Hastings

Bray Co

Road

Bury Farm

159

A12

K

L

M

Leech's
Lane

Studd's
La

PO

Raven La

School

Mi

Link Rd

Braiswick La

Church Rd

Defoe

Colch

Cumford Cl

G

H

J

K

L

M

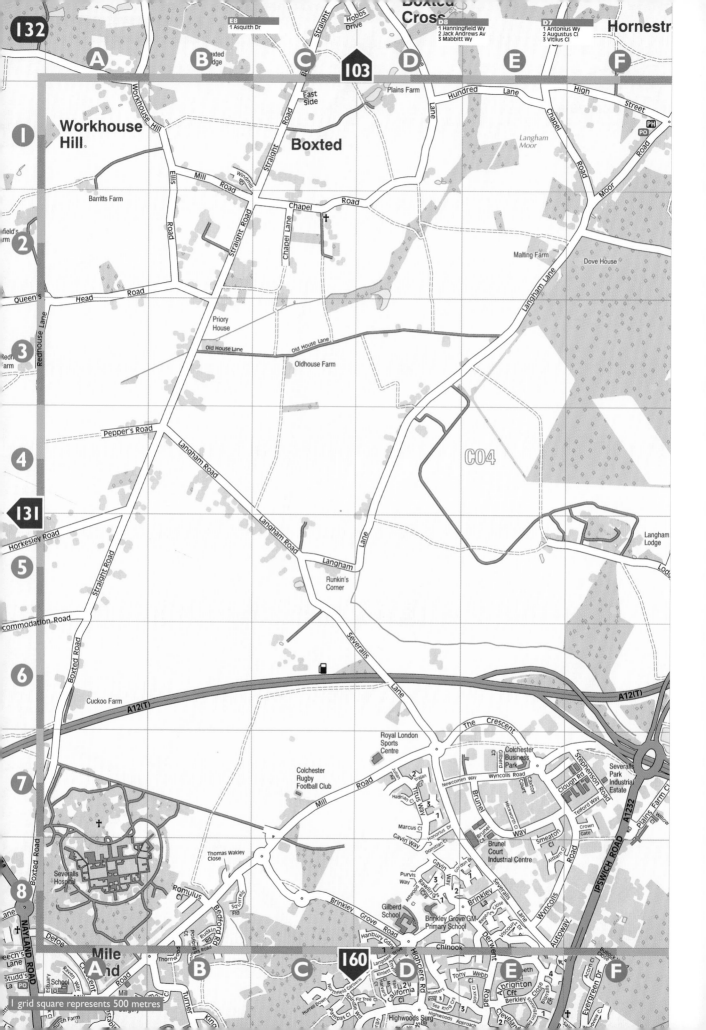

eet

G **H** **J** 104 **K** **L** **M**

Greyhound Hill

Hill

Boxhouse Lane

GROVE HILL

The Grove

Homestead School

Langham Primary School

Langford Hall

Perry Lane

Grove

Langham

School Road

Birchwood

Wick Road

A12(T) Road

Park Lane

Park Lane Farm

Birch Wood

Hart's Lane

Blue Barns Farm

Hart's Lane

Parney Heath

Hill House

Birchwood Road

Lamb Corner

Monk's Lane

B1029 ARDLEIGH ROAD

I

2

Malting Farm Lane

B1029

Malting Farm

3

Rookery Chase

Birchhall Corner

DEDHAM ROAD

Fen Lane

4

Ardle Heath

134

5

Do Su

St Marys C of E Primary School

Moorhouse Green

2

Close

A12(T)

Ipswich Road

Turnpike

Old Ipswich Road

Lane

Wick Lane

Wick Farm

Fountain Farm

Dead Lane

Gernon Rd

6

Lane

Old Ipswich Road

Hotel

Gatehouse Farm

Crown Lane

North

Lodge Lane

Guide Post Farm

Lodge Farm

Lodge Lane

A137 COLCHESTER ROAD

Green Lane

Green Lane

7

Marte Indus Estat

Martells Hall

Plains Farm

Harvey's Farm

Hillhouse Farm

Clover Way

Redbury Farm

Martells Industrial Estate

8

A120

Crown La South

Ardleigh Reservoir

G **H** m **J** 161 **K** **L** **M**

Fox

Mays Lane

H

Avenue Rd

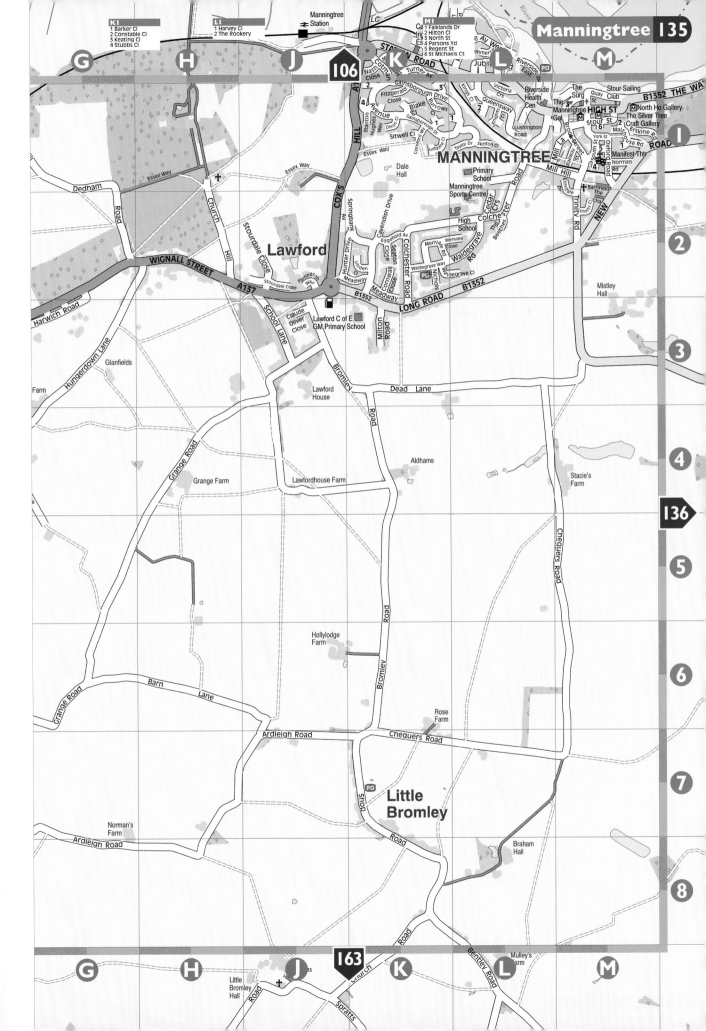

G **H** **J** **K** **L** **M**

K1
1 Barker Cl
2 Constable Cl
3 Keating Cl
4 Stubbs Cl

L1
1 Harvey Cl
2 The Rookery

M1
Ca 1 Falklands Dr
In 2 Hilton Cl
3 North St
ES 4 Parsons Yd
5 Regent St
6 St Michaels Ct

Manningtree
Station

MANNINGTREE

Dedham Road

Church Hill

WIGNALL STREET
A137

Harwich Road

Hungerdown Lane

Farm

Glanfields

Grange Road

Grange Farm

Barn Lane

Norman's Farm

Ardleigh Road

Lawford

Stourdale Close

Stourdale Close

School Lane

Claude Oliver Close

Lawford C of E
GM Primary School

Lawford House

Lawfordhouse Farm

Hollylodge Farm

Ardleigh Road

COX'S HILL

Essex Way

Essex Way

Springbank Av

Hunter Drive

Meadway

Linden Wa

B1352

Milton Road

Bromley Road

Bromley Road

Shop Road

Little Bromley

Dale Hall

Cavendish Drive

Nasty Cl

Corman Close

Fitzgerald Close

Stanton Hughes Way

Sitwell Cl

Edgefield Av

Seaton Close

Cornwall Meadway

Dixon Cl

Lydgate Wy

Cornfield Wy

Taylor Dr

Skelton Cl

Primary School

Manningtree Sports Centre

High School

Meriva

Merivale Close

Waldegrave Way

Nichols

PG

Waldegrave Cl

Colchester Road

Waldegrave Rd

Beeches Rd

Cedar Crs

Colchester Rd

LONG ROAD

B1352

Dead Lane

Aldhams

Rose Farm

Chequers Road

STATION ROAD

LC

Turner Av

Gainsborough Drive

Blake Burrows

Gainsborough Dr

Kings Av

Queensway

Victoria

Knowle

Lushington Road

Mill Hill

Mill Lane

Trinity Rd

Chapel La

Barnfield

Mistley Hall

Stacie's Farm

Chequers Road

M Falklands Dr

River

B1352 THE WA

Riverside Av

Jubilee

Riverside Health Cen

The Surg

Quay St

Stour Sailing Club

The Manningtree Gal

HIGH ST

M North Ho Gallery
The Silver Tree
2 Craft Gallery

Stour St

Brook Street

Oxford Road

Erskine Rd

ROAD

York St

Manifest Thtr

Norman Rd

NEW

Braham Hall

Mulley's Farm

136

I

2

3

4

5

6

7

8

G **H** **J** **K** **L** **M**

Little Bromley Hall

Church Road

Spratts

Bentley Road

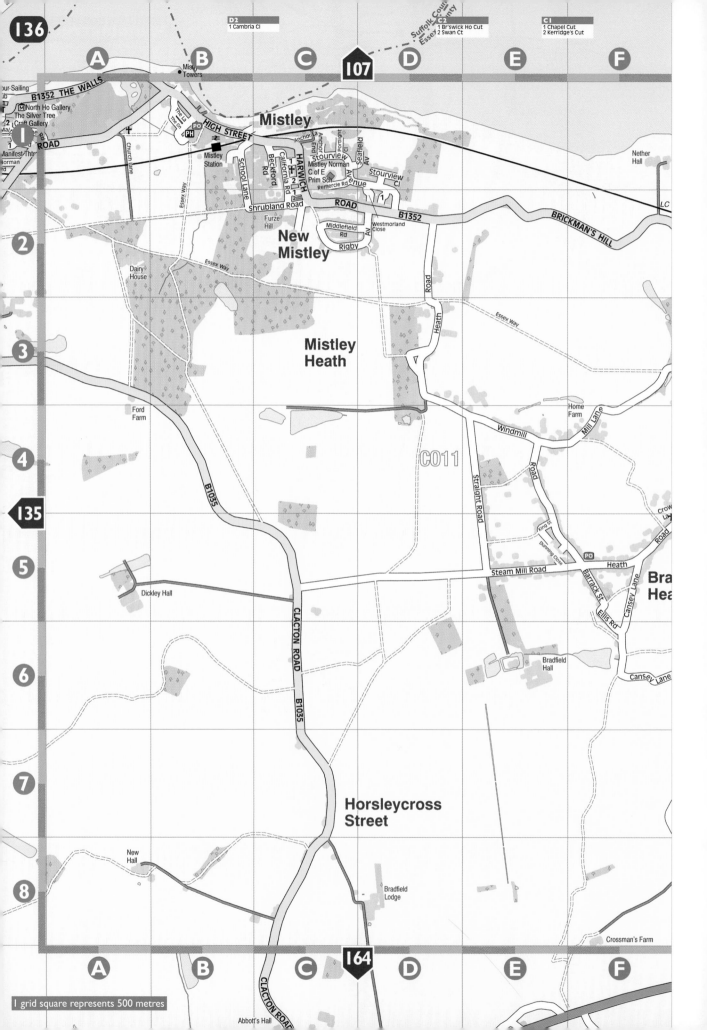

A   B   **107**   C   D   E   F

I

D2
1 Cambria Cl

Suffolk County
Essex County
1 Br'swick Ho Cut
2 Swan Ct

C1
1 Chapel Cut
2 Kerridge's Cut

Harbour-Sailing Club
B1352 THE WALLS
North Ho Gallery
The Silver Tree
Craft Gallery
Manifest Thtr
Norman

Misty Towers

Mistley
PO
PH
HIGH STREET
Church Lane
School Lane
Essex Way
Mistley Station
California Rd
Beckford Rd
HARWICH
Anchor La
Anchor End
Portlight
Mistley Norman C of E Prim Sch
Remercie Rd
Stourview Av
Seafield Av
Stourview Cl
AVENUE
1
Nether Hall

LC

New Mistley
Shrubland Road
Furze Hill
Middlefield Rd
Rigby Av
Westmorland Close
ROAD
B1352

BRICKMAN'S HILL

2

Dairy House
Essex Way

Heath   Road

Essex Way

3

Mistley Heath

Home Farm

Ford Farm

Windmill   Road
Mill Lane

C011

Straight Road

Crow
La

4

B1035

135

King St
Dunning Close
PO
Heath
Steam Mill Road
Barrack St
Cansey Lane
Road

**Bra
Hea**

5

Dickley Hall

Ellis Rd

CLACTON ROAD

Bradfield Hall

Cansey Lane

6

B1035

7

Horsleycross Street

New Hall

8

Bradfield Lodge

Crossman's Farm

A   B   **164**   C   D   E   F

CLACTON ROAD

Abbott's Hall

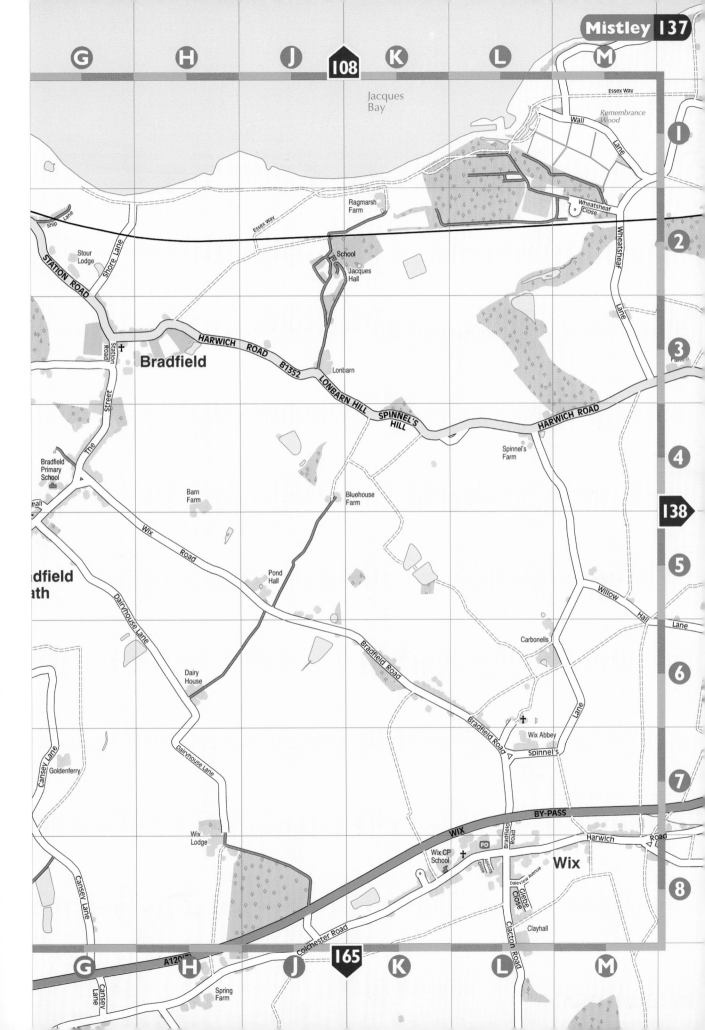

G   H   J   108   K   L   M

Jacques
Bay

Essex Way

Remembrance
Wood

Wall

Lane

1

Ship Lane

Essex Way

Ragmarsh
Farm

Wheatsheaf
Close

Wheatsheaf Lane

2

STATION ROAD

Stour
Lodge

Shore Lane

School

Jacques
Hall

HARWICH ROAD B1352

Bradfield

Station Road

Lonbarn

LONBARN HILL

Farm

3

The Street

SPINNEL'S HILL

HARWICH ROAD

Spinnel's
Farm

4

Bradfield
Primary
School

Barn
Farm

Bluehouse
Farm

138

radfield
ath

Wix   Road

Pond
Hall

Willow

Hall

Lane

5

Dairyhouse Lane

Carbonells

6

Dairy
House

Bradfield Road

Lane

Wix Abbey

Spinnel's

Cansey Lane

Goldenferry

Dairyhouse Lane

7

BY-PASS

Wix
Lodge

WIX

Bradfield Road

Harwich   Road

8

Wix CP
School

PO

Abbots Close

Wix

Daleview Avenue

Cansey Lane

Glebe Close

Clayhall

A120

Colchester Road

165

Clacton Road

G   H   J   165   K   L   M

Spring
Farm

Cansey
Lane

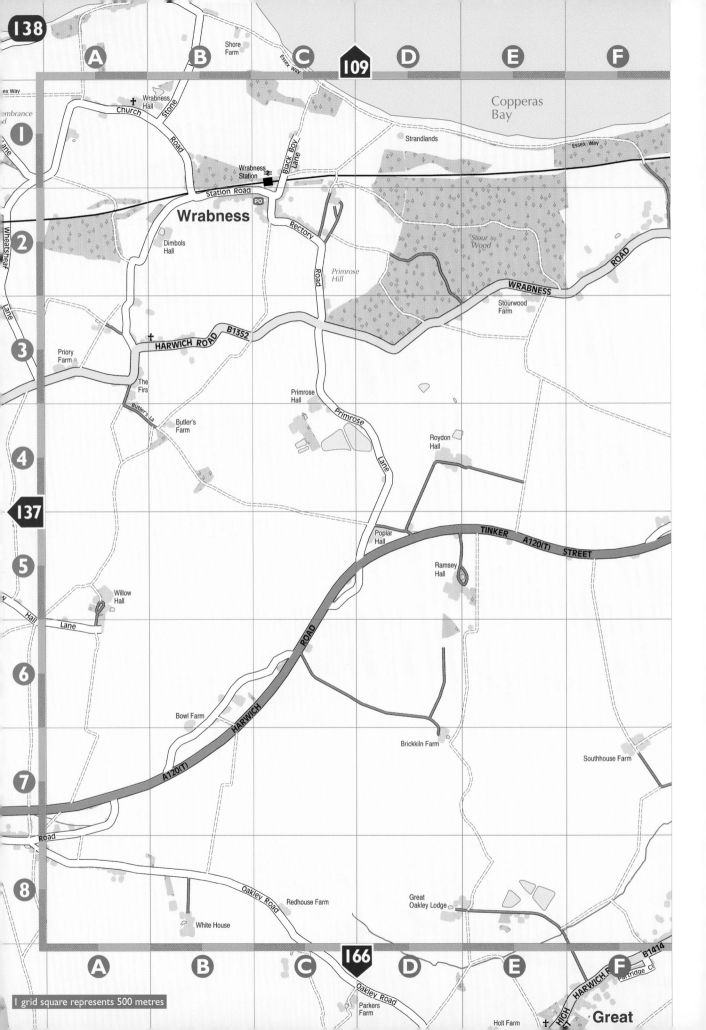

A B Shore Farm C   D E F

Copperas
Bay

Essex Way

1

embrance

Wrabness Hall
Church
Stone

Strandlands

Essex Way

Wrabness Station

Station Road

PO

Black Boy Lane

Wrabness

Wheatsheaf

Rectory Road

Stour Wood

WRABNESS ROAD

2

Dimbols Hall

Primrose Hill

Lane

Stourwood Farm

Priory Farm

HARWICH ROAD B1352

3

The Firs

Butler's La

Primrose Hall

Primrose Lane

Roydon Hall

Butler's Farm

4

Poplar Hall

TINKER A120(T) STREET

5

Willow Hall

Ramsey Hall

Hall

Lane

HARWICH ROAD

6

Bowl Farm

Brickkiln Farm

Southhouse Farm

A120(T)

7

Road

8

Oakley Road

Redhouse Farm

Great Oakley Lodge

White House

A B   D E F B1414

HIGH HARWICH Partridge cl

Oakley Road

Parkers Farm

Holt Farm **Great**

1 grid square represents 500 metres

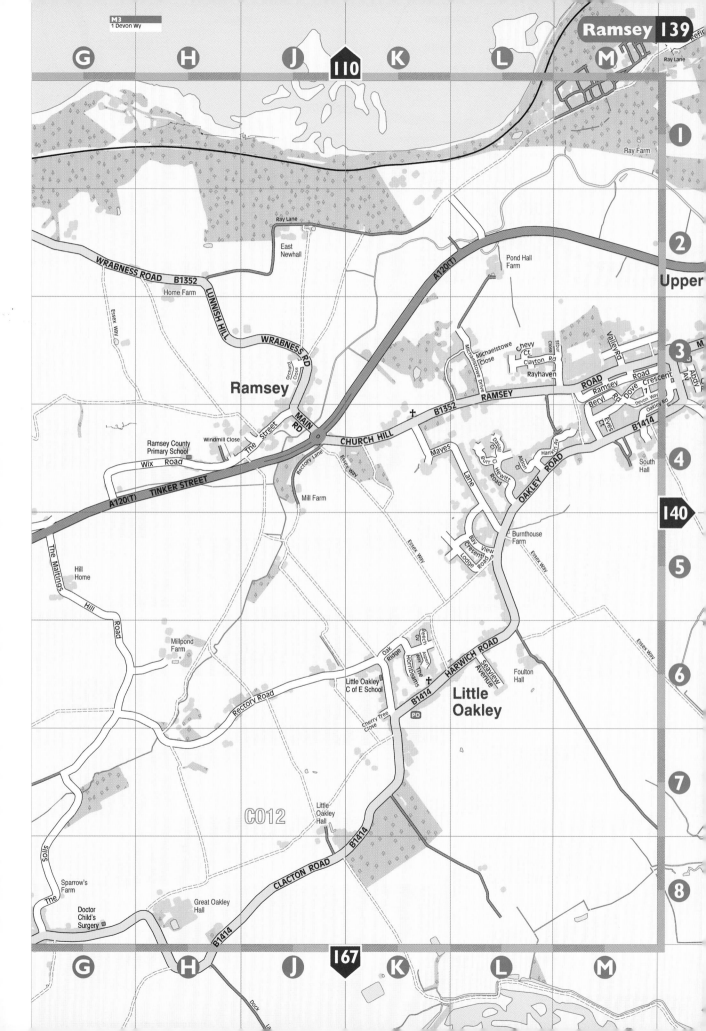

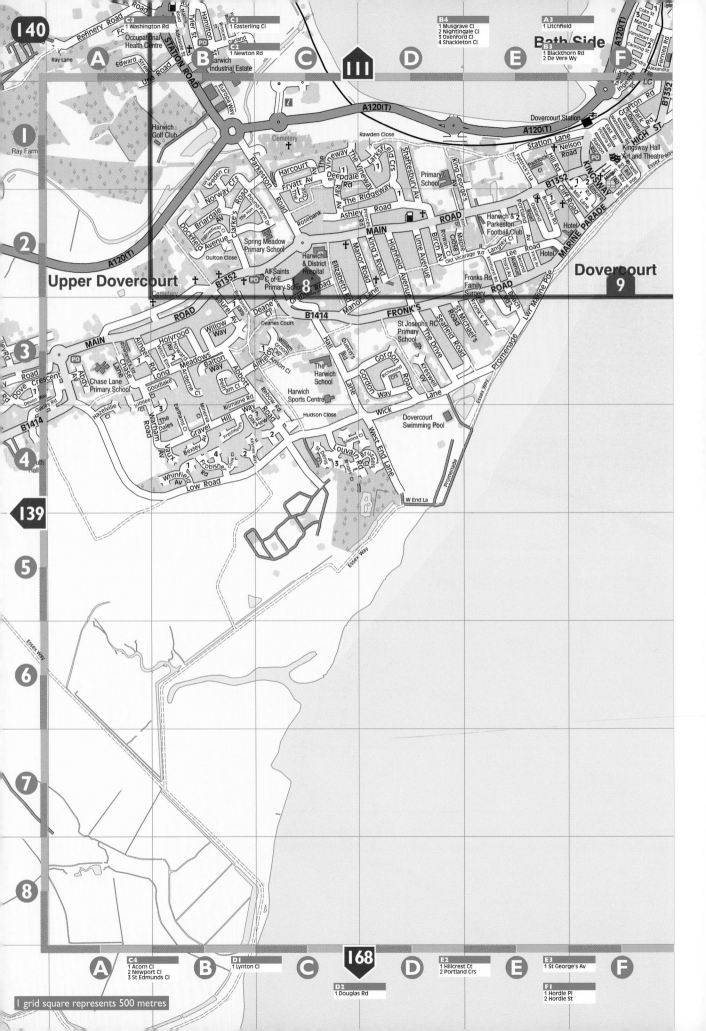

Refinery Road

Ray Lane

A

Edward Street

Occupational Health Centre

C3
1 Washington Rd

Tyler St

Hamilton

B

Princes

Garland

C1
1 Easterling Cl

C2
1 Newton Rd

C

D

Bath Side

B3
1 Blackthorn Rd
2 De Vere Wy

E

F

HIGH ST

Coke St
Maria St
Vansittart St
Canning St
Alexandra
Alexandra
LC

STATION ROAD

Harwich Industrial Estate

Europa Way

Uma Road

Harwich Golf Club

A120(T)

Cemetery

Rawden Close

Dovercourt Station

Station Lane

Nelson

PO

Kingsway Hall Art and Theatre

Essex

I

Ray Farm

Parkeston Road

Harcourt

The Vineway

Larksfield Crs

Shaftesbury Av

Primary School

King George's

King's

Road

Station Rd

Hill Rd

B1352

Cliff Road

MARINE PARADE

KINGSWAY

Kingsway Hall

Norway Crs

Weden Cl

Fryatt Av

Deepdale Rd

Ray Av

The Ridgeway

Road

Harwich & Parkeston Football Club

Portland

Brooklyn Rd

Oakland

Hotel

2

A120(T)

Briardale Avenue

Dockfield

Clarke's Road

Pound Farm Dr

Rosebank

Ashley Road

MAIN

King's Road

Highfield

Lime Avenue

Birch Av

Old Vicarage Rd

Langley Cl

Lee

Second Avenue

Hotel

Lwr Marine Pde

Dovercourt

Upper Dovercourt

Cemetery

B1352

PO

Spring Meadow Primary School

Oulton Close

All Saints C of E Primary School

Harwich & District Hospital

Elizabeth Rd

Manor Road

ROAD

Fronks Rd Family Surgery

Beach

8

9

ROAD

MAIN

Laurel Av

Deanes Court

B1414

FRONK'S

St Joseph's RC Primary School

St Michael's

Seafield Road

Promenade

Essex Way

3

PO

Chase Lane Primary School

Holyrood

Howard

Meadows

Willow Way

Balton Way

Abbott Road

Alfred

Anson Cl

Hall Lane

Queen's Rd

The Harwich School

Gordon Road

The Drive

Kreswell Gv

Gordon Way

Lane

Dove Crescent

B1414

Hazelville Cl

Jubilee

Long

Goodlake

The Dales

Minerva Cl

Kilmaine Rd

Rebow Road

Hudson Close

Harwich Sports Centre

WICK

Dovercourt Swimming Pool

4

South Hall

Warham Road

Vaux Av

Bexley

Gravel Hill Way

Frennhele's

Oak View

Vienna Cl

Louvain Rd

Brussels

West End Lane

Promenade

Whinfield Av

Low Road

Robishe Rd

Cook Cl

Denis

W End La

Essex Way

5

Essex Way

6

7

8

A

B

C

D

E

F

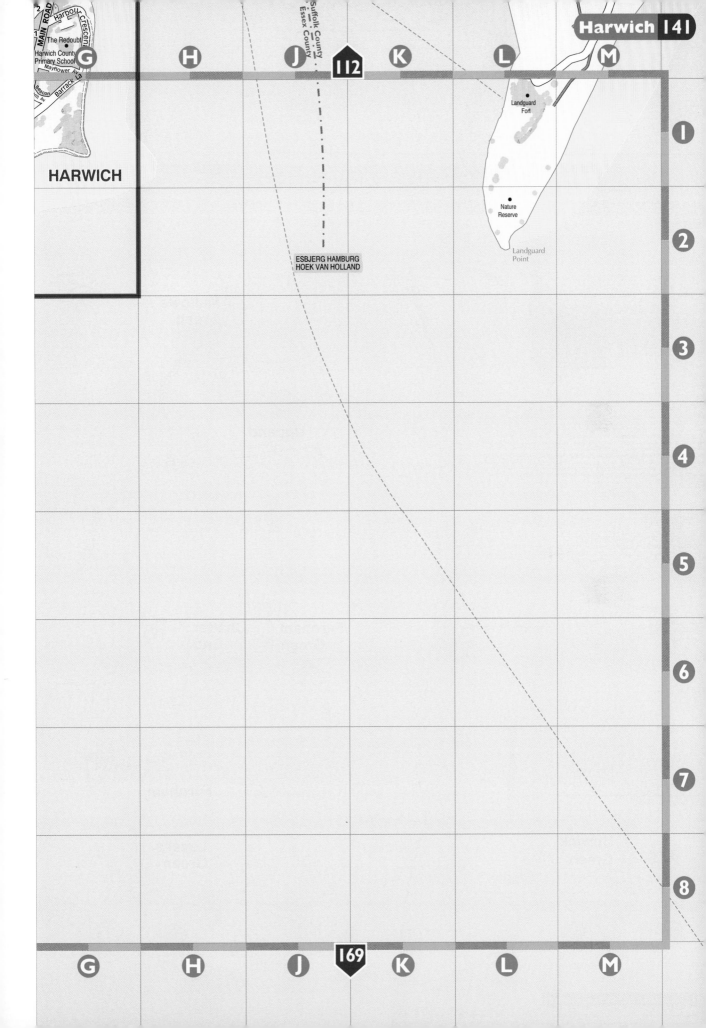

MAIN ROAD
Harbour Crescent
The Redoubt
Harwich County
Primary School
Mayflower Av
Beacon Hill Av
Barrack La

G

HARWICH

H

J

K

L

Landguard
Fort

M

1

Nature
Reserve

2

ESBJERG HAMBURG
HOEK VAN HOLLAND

Landguard
Point

3

4

Suffolk County
Essex County

5

6

7

8

G

H

J

K

L

M

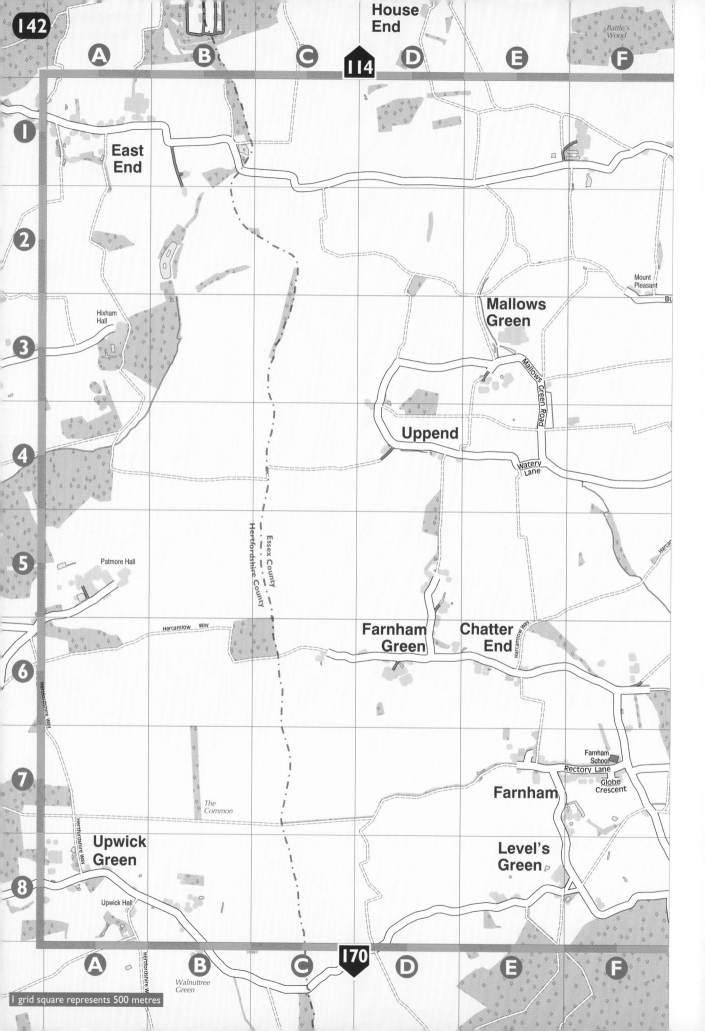

House
End

A   B   C   114   D   E   F

1   East
     End

2   Mount
                                                     Pleasant

                                          Mallows
                                          Green   Bu

3   Hixham
     Hall
                                                    Mallows Green Road

                                          Uppend

4   Watery
                                                    Lane

                         Essex County
                         Hertfordshire County

5   Patmore Hall

                                                              Harcamlow Way

     Harcamlow   Way   Harcam

6   Hertfordshire Way   Farnham   Chatter
                                          Green   End

                                                              Harcamlow Way

                                                    Farnham
                                                    School
7   The   Rectory Lane
                       Common   Globe
                                                    Crescent
                                          Farnham

8   Upwick   Level's
     Green   Green

     Hertfordshire Way

     Upwick Hall

A   B   C   170   D   E   F

Hertfordshire W

Walnuttree
Green

1 grid square represents 500 metres

G H J **115** K L M

1

2

3

4

144

5

6

7

8

Wade's Hall

Bollington Hall

Harcamlow Way

Maggots End

Pinchpools

Sheepcote Lane

...itt Lane

Stewarts Way

Mallers La

Anderson Close

Manuden House

Manuden

The Hall

Harcamlow Way

Harcamlow Way

The Street

Pinchpools Road

Dogden La

Mallows Green Road

Manuden CP School

Carrers Hill

River Stort

Parsonage Farm

...low Way

Bentfield Bury

Bentfield Green

Pennington Lane

Rainsford Road

...sdale Road

Gilbey Ct's

Primary School

Long Croft

Pasture Lodges

The Surge

Dove

Cross...

Bourne Brook

Waterside (School)

Hole Farm

Wetherfield

Bentfield End Causeway

Bentfield Gns

Bentfield

Bentfield Road

Cawkell Cl

STANSTED MOUNTFITCHET

Stansted Clinic

Greenfields

CHAPEL HL

St...

PO

Recreation Gnd

Mid...

Blythwood Gns

SILVER STREET

B138

Mill Side

Mill...

Broc...

Wood...

West Rd

Sto... Com...

Limekiln Lane

Hazel End

Mill Hill

Old Bell C...

Riverside Business Park

Stoney Common Rd

PINES HILL

B1383

West Rd

Fore...

Surrey County

Herts County

G H J **171** K L M

Gipsy Lane

ROAD

...thall Road

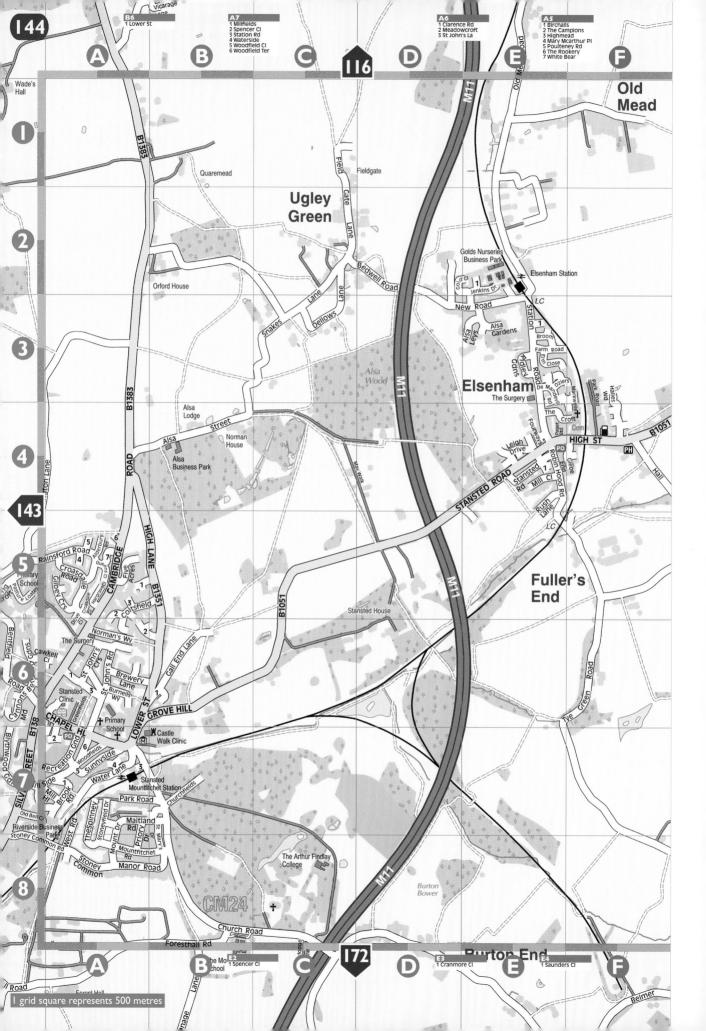

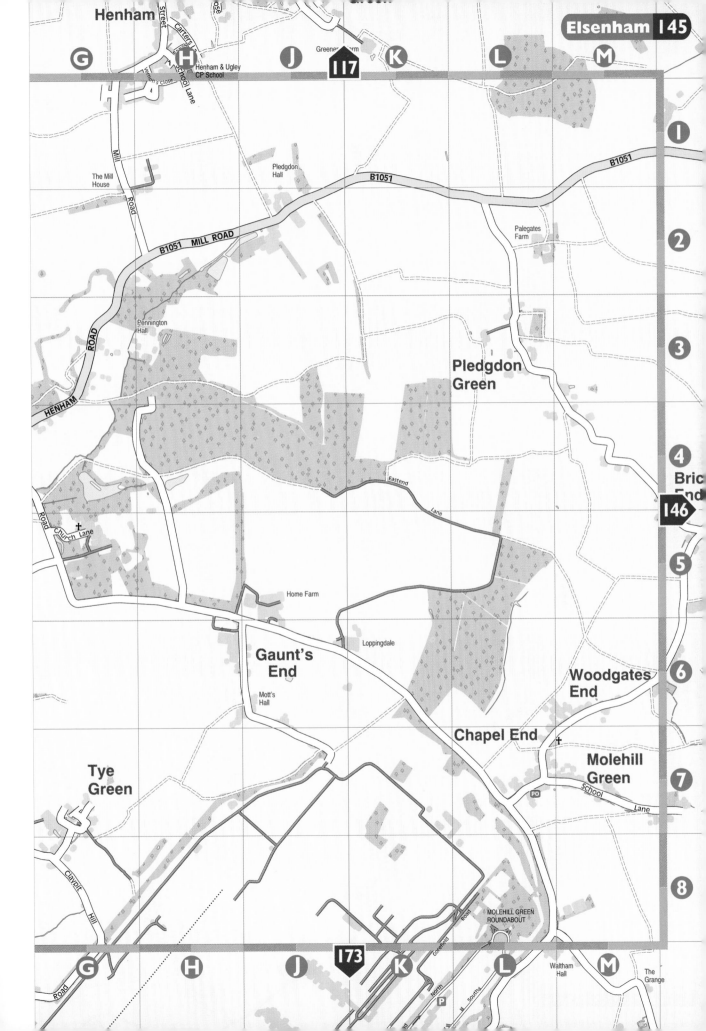

Henham

G   H   J   K   L   M

1

2

3

4

5

6

7

8

117

173

B1051

B1051 MILL ROAD

B1051

HENHAM   ROAD

MILL   Road

Street

Cartlers

School Lane

Vernon's Close

Henham & Ugley
CP School

The Mill
House

Pledgdon
Hall

Greener Farm

Palegates
Farm

Pledgdon
Green

Pennington
Hall

Eastend

Lane

146

Bric
End

Road
Church Lane

Home Farm

Loppingdale

Gaunt's
End

Mott's
Hall

Woodgates
End

Chapel End

Molehill
Green

School

Lane

Tye
Green

PO

Claypit Hill

Road

North

South

P

Corefield   Road

MOLEHILL GREEN
ROUNDABOUT

Waltham
Hall

The
Grange

G   H   J   K   L   M

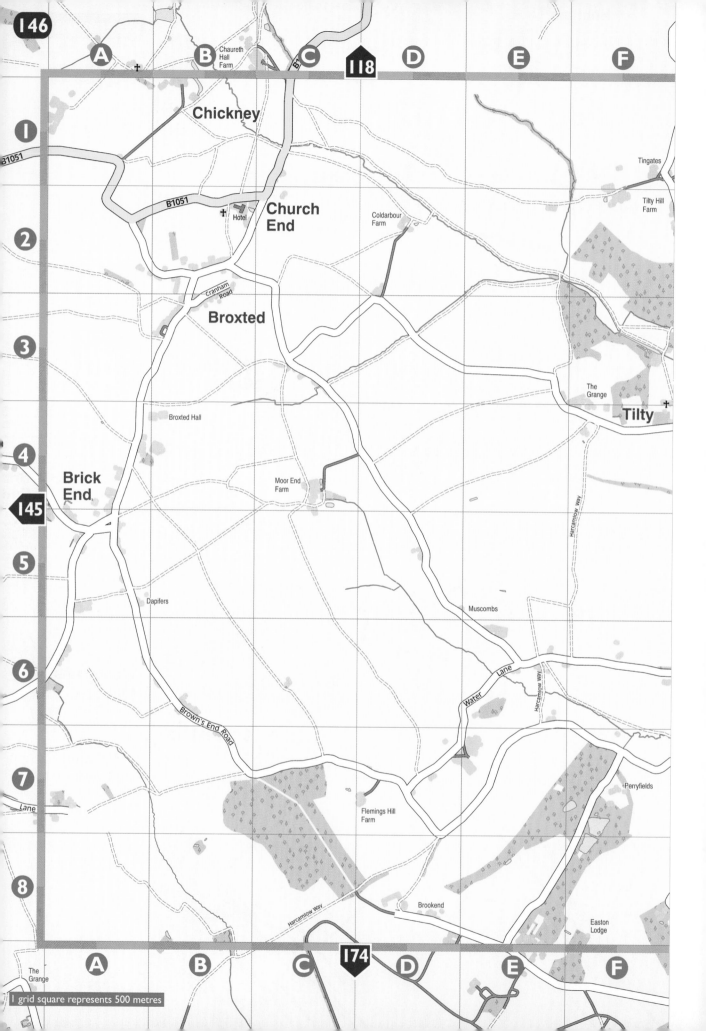

146

A
B   Chaureth
         Hall
         Farm
B1   C   118   D   E   F

Chickney

1
B1051

B1051   †
         Hotel   Church
                      End

2   Coldarbour
         Farm

Cranham
Road
Broxted

3   The
         Grange
Broxted Hall   Tilty

4
Brick
End   Moor End
         Farm
145

Brown's End Road

Dapifers

5

Muscombs

6   Water Lane   Harcamlow Way

7   Flemings Hill   Perryfields
Lane   Farm

Harcamlow Way   Brookend   Easton
                                     Lodge
8
The
Grange   A   B   C   174   D   E   F

1 grid square represents 500 metres

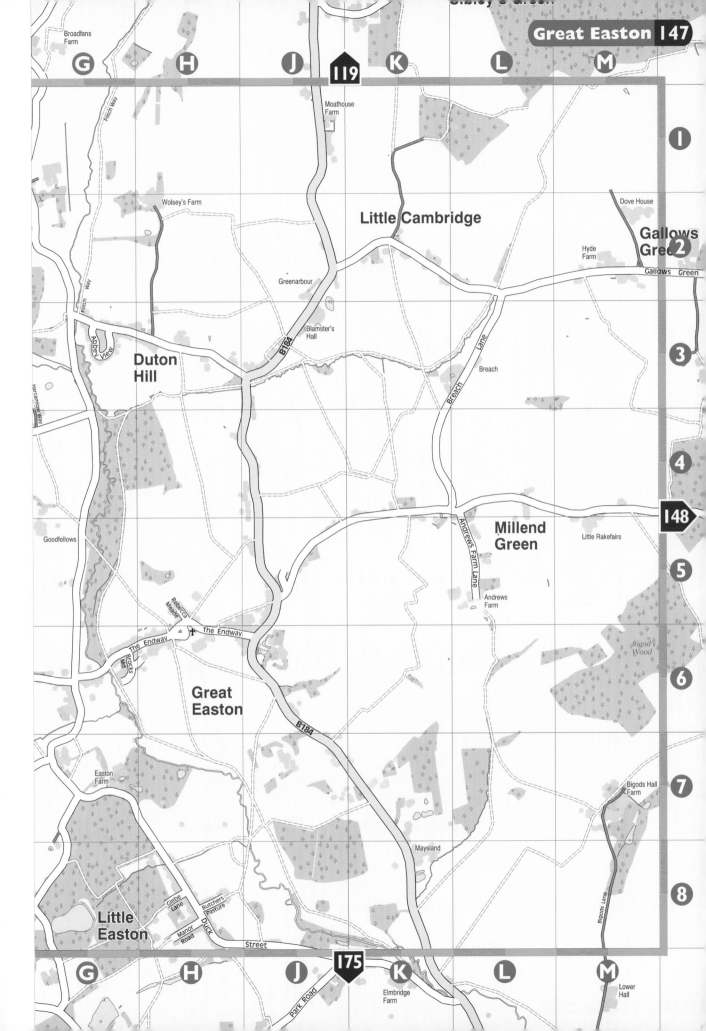

G H J **119** K L M

I **1**

Broadfans
Farm

Wolsey's Farm

Dove House

**Gallows
Green** **2**

Hyde
Farm

Gallows Green

Little Cambridge

Fitch Way

Greenarbour

Blamster's
Hall

B184

Breach
Lane

Breach **3**

Duton
Hill

Abbey View

Harcamlow Way

4

148

Goodfellows

**Millend
Green**

Andrews Farm Lane

Little Rakefairs

5

Andrews
Farm

Rebecca
Meade

The Endway

The Endway

Bigod's
Wood

6

The Endway

Brocks Md

**Great
Easton**

B184

7

Easton
Farm

Bigods Hall
Farm

Maysland

8

Glebe
Lane

Butchers
Pasture

**Little
Easton**

Manor
Road

Duck

Bigods Lane

Street

G H J **175** K L M

Park Road

Elmbridge
Farm

Lower
Hall

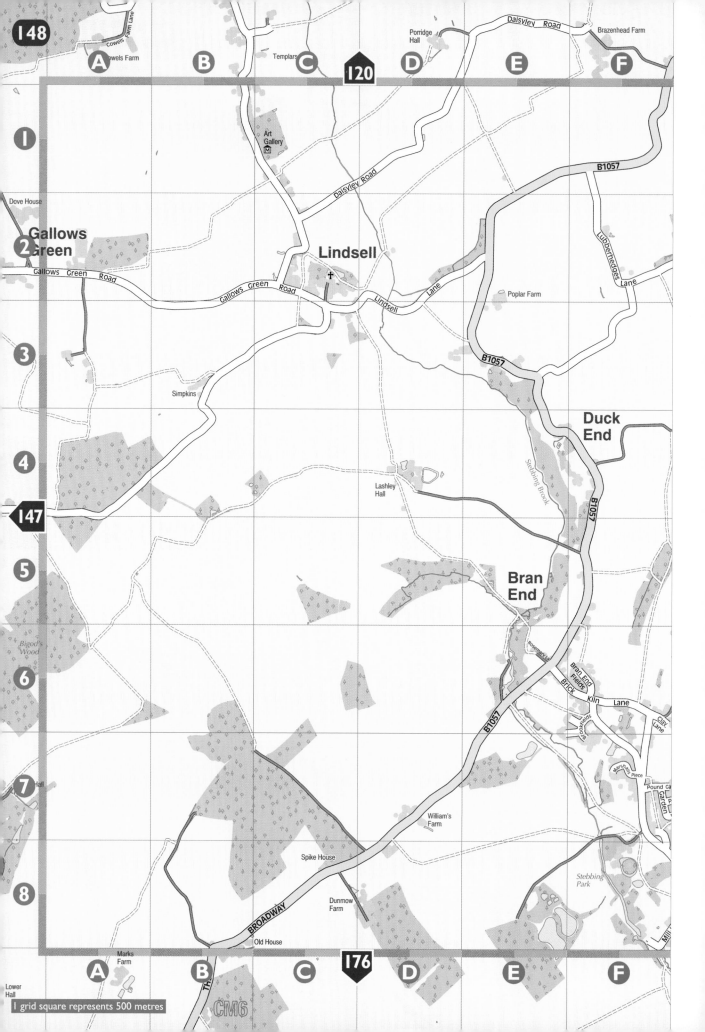

148

A   B   C   120   D   E   F

Cowels Farm

Farm Lane

Templars

Daisyley Road

Porridge Hall

Daisyley Road

Brazenhead Farm

B1057

I

Art Gallery M

Dove House

2 Gallows Green

Lindsell

Gallows Green Road

Gallows Green Road

Lindsell Lane

Poplar Farm

Lubberhedges Lane

3

Simpkins

B1057

147

Duck End

Lashley Hall

Stebbing Brook

B1057

4

5

Bran End

Bigod's Wood

6

Rosemary La

Bran End Fields

Brick Kiln Lane

Clay Lane

B1057

Brookfields

Marsh's Piece

Pound Ga

Gardens

7 Hall

William's Farm

Spike House

Stebbing Park

8

BROADWAY

Dunmow Farm

Old House

Marks Farm

A   B   Th   C   176   D   E   F

Lower Hall

CM6

MILL

I grid square represents 500 metres

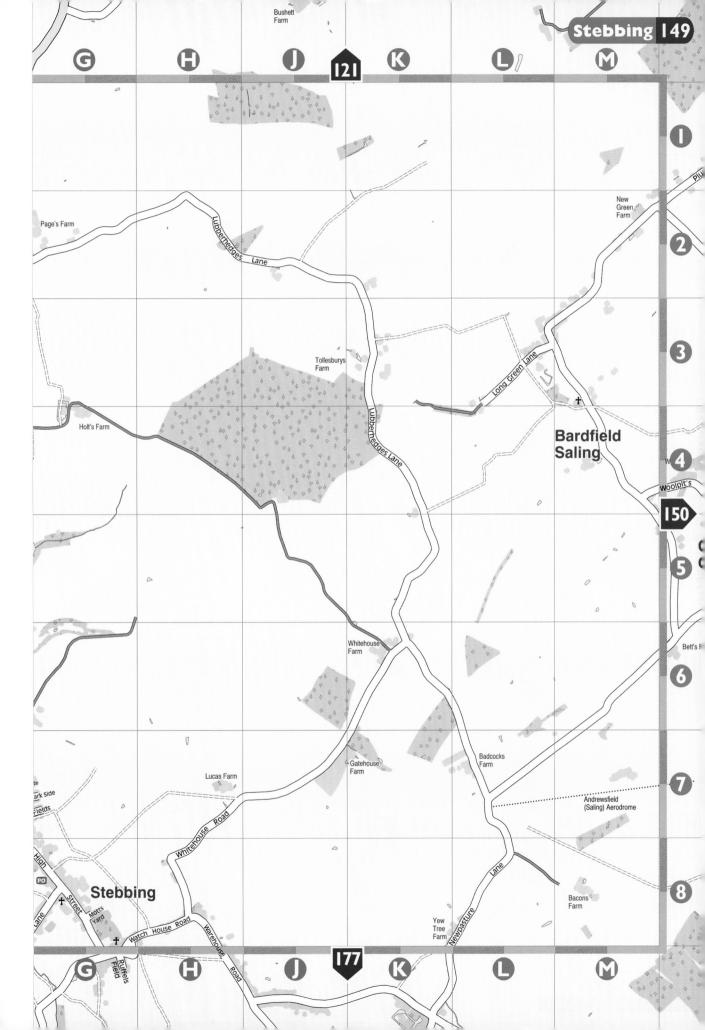

G H J 121 K L M

1

2

3

4

150

5

6

7

8

G H J 177 K L M

Bushett Farm

New Green Farm

Page's Farm

Lubberhedges Lane

Tollesburys Farm

Holt's Farm

Long Green Lane

Lubberhedges Lane

Bardfield Saling

Woolpit's

Bett's

Whitehouse Farm

Badcocks Farm

Lucas Farm

Gatehouse Farm

Andrewsfield (Saling) Aerodrome

Whitehouse Road

Stebbing

High

PO

Street

Motts Yard

Watch House Road

Warehouse Road

Ruffels Field

Newpasture Lane

Yew Tree Farm

Bacons Farm

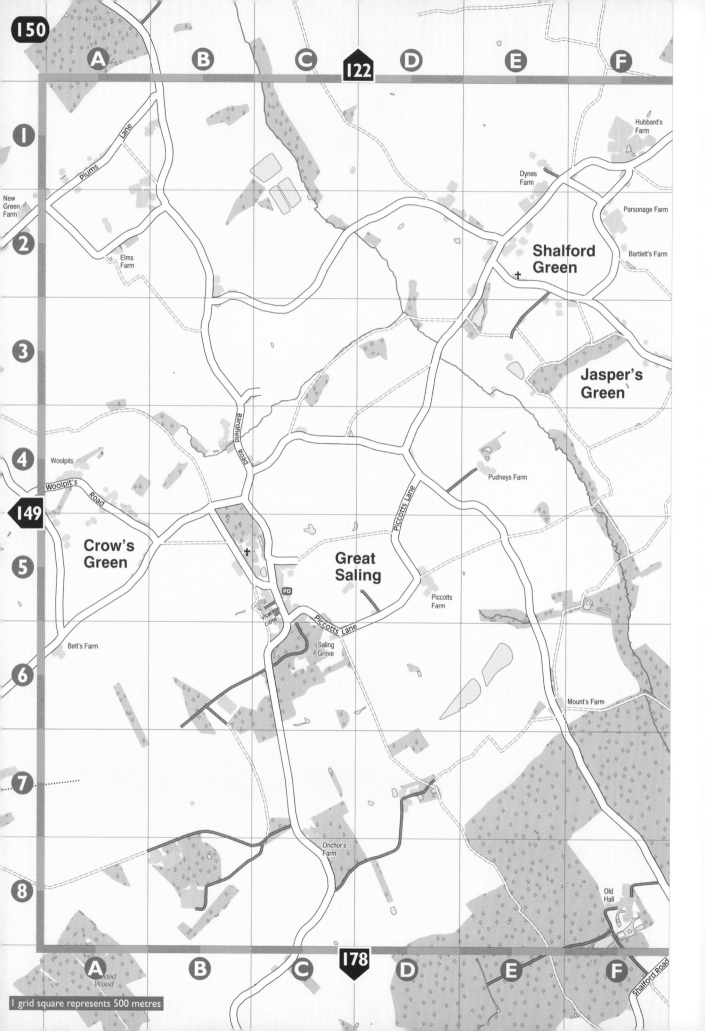

A   B   C   122   D   E   F

I

New
Green
Farm

Plums Lane

2   Elms
Farm

3

4   Woolpits

Woolpit's Road

149

5   Crow's
Green

Bardfield Road

†

PO

Vicarage
Close

Great
Saling

Bett's Farm

6   Saling
Grove

Piccotts Lane

Piccotts Lane

Piccotts
Farm

Pudneys Farm

Mount's Farm

Hubbard's
Farm

Dynes
Farm

Parsonage Farm

Shalford
Green   †

Bartlett's Farm

Jasper's
Green

7

8   Onchor's
Farm

Old
Hall

A   Axted
Wood   B   C   178   D   E   F   Shalford Road

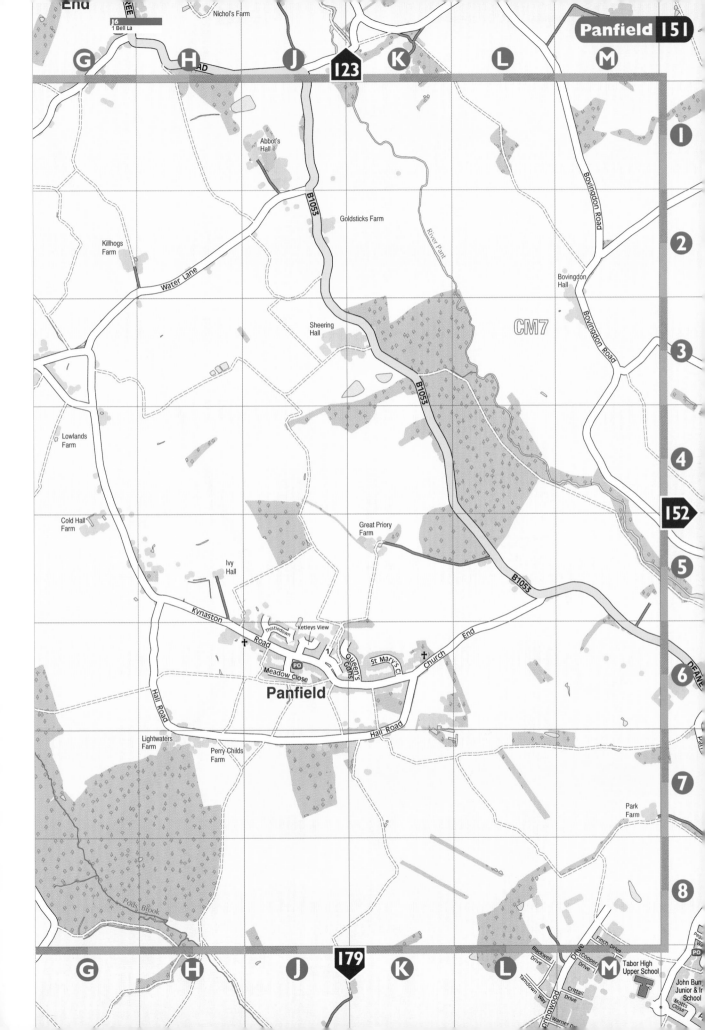

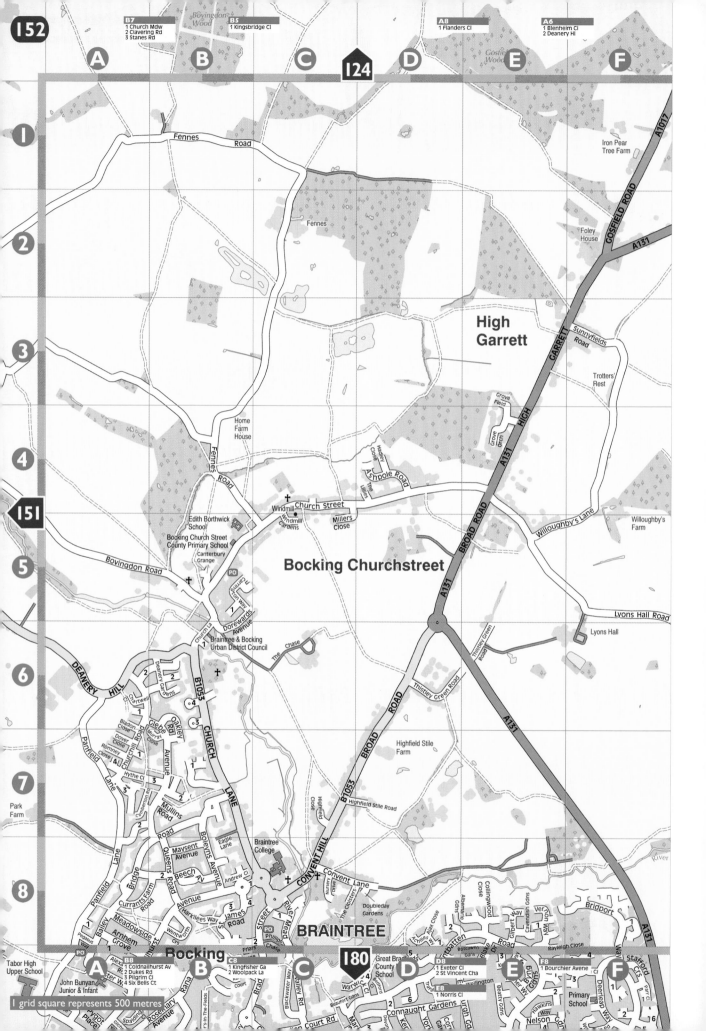

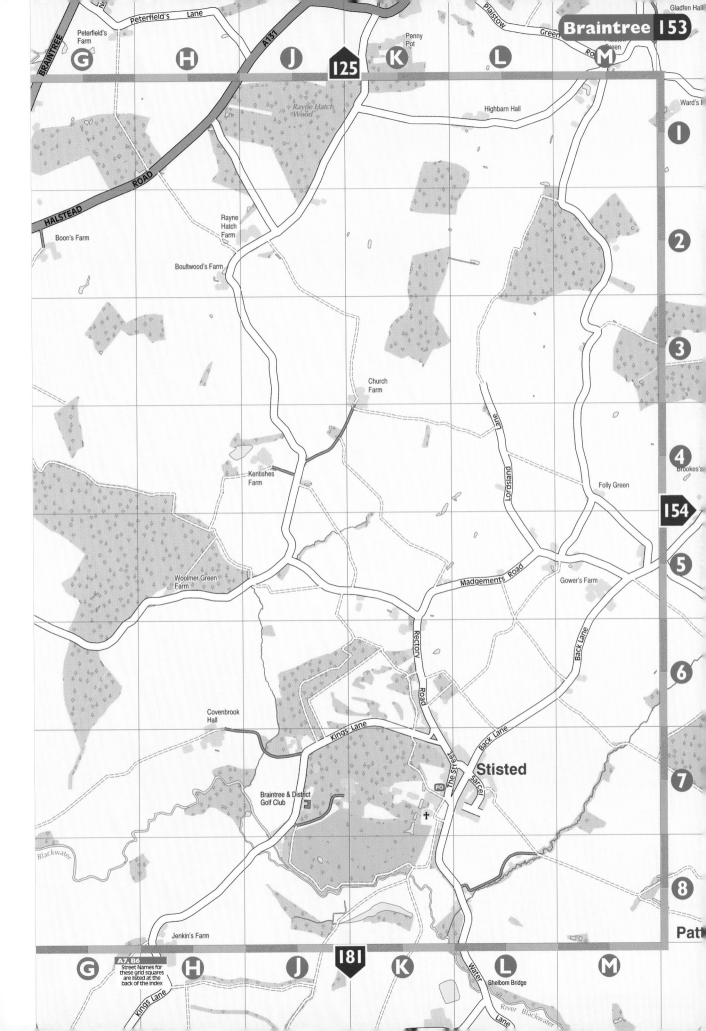

Gladfen Hall

Peterfield's Lane

Plaistow Green

Braintree

Peterfield's Farm

G **H** **J** **125** **K** **L** **M**

A131

Ward's

Penny Pot

Highbarn Hall

1

Rayne Hatch Wood

HALSTEAD ROAD

Boon's Farm

Rayne Hatch Farm

2

Boultwood's Farm

3

Church Farm

Brookes's

4

Kentishes Farm

Folly Green

Lordsland Lane

154

5

Woolmer Green Farm

Madgements Road

Gower's Farm

Rectory Road

Back Lane

6

Covenbrook Hall

Kings Lane

Back Lane

7

Braintree & District Golf Club

PO

The Street

Sarcel

Stisted

Blackwater

8

Jenkin's Farm

Pat

A7, B6
Street Names for these grid squares are listed at the back of the index

Kings Lane

Water

Shelborn Bridge

Lane

River Blackwater

A   B   C   D   E   F

Gladfen Hall

aistow
een

126

Gr**126**stead
Green

Nightingale
Hall

Ward's Farm

Burton's

Green

Road

PO

Whitings

1

2

Perces

Lodge
Farm

Burton
Green

Markshall Wood

Clavering's Farm

Mann's Farm

3

Nunty's Lane

Great Nunty's
Farm

Brookes's Farm

4

een

5

Nunty's Lane

Great
Monks
Wood

Bungate Wood

6

Woodhouse
Farm

Potash
Farm

7

Compasses Road

PH

Old Road

8

Pattiswick Hall

Doghouse Road

Church Road

Wells
m

Pattiswick

A   B   C   D   E   F

1 grid square represents 500 metres

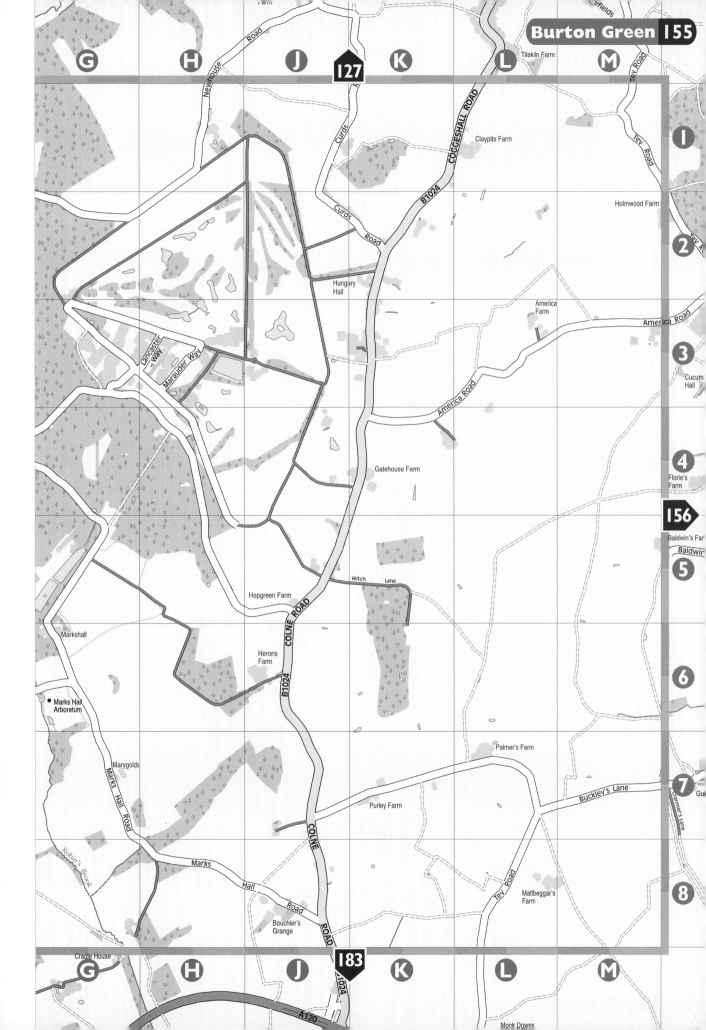

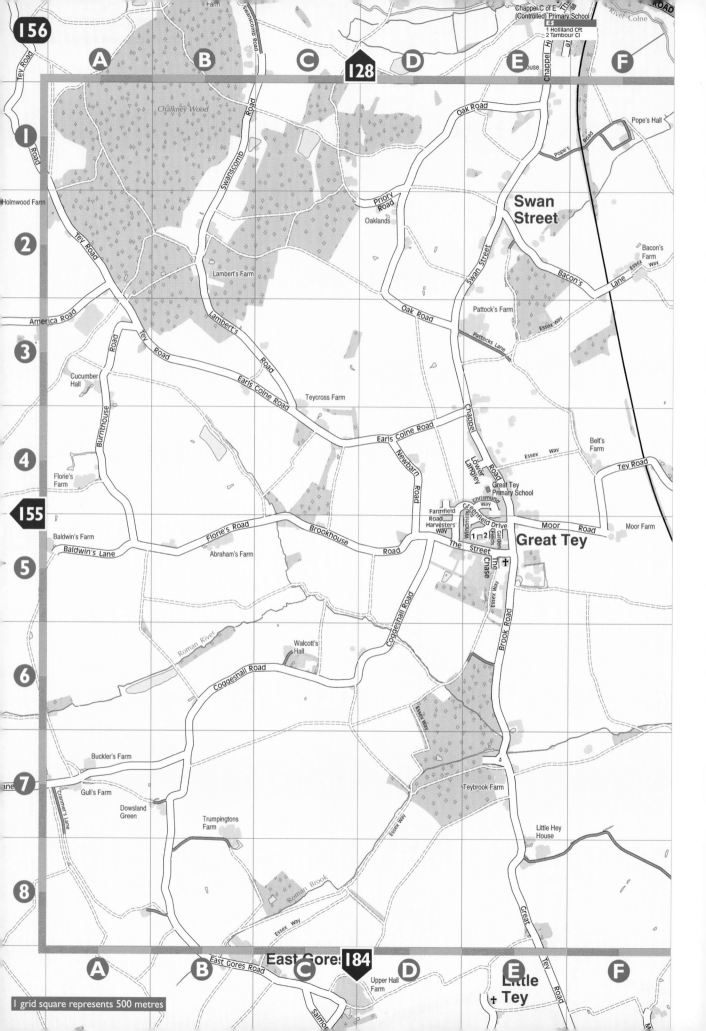

156

A   B   C   128   D   E   F

I

Chalkney Wood

Holmwood Farm

2   Lambert's Farm

America Road

3   Cucumber Hall

Tey Road
Swanscomb Road
Lambert's Road
Priory Road
Oaklands
Oak Road

Swan Street

Chappel C of E (Controlled) Primary School
E5
1 Holliland Cft
2 Tambour Cl

River Colne

ROAD

Pope's Hall

Bacon's Farm Way

Swan Street
Bacon's
Lane
Essex Way

Pattock's Farm
Pattocks Lane

Chappel Hill

Earls Colne Road
Teycross Farm

Earls Colne Road

Chappel Road
Lower Langley
Great Tey Primary School

Essex   Way
Belt's Farm

Tey Road

Burnthouse Road
Tey Road

4   Florie's Farm

155

Baldwin's Farm

Baldwin's Lane

5

Florie's Road
Abraham's Farm

Brookhouse
Road

Newbarn Road

Windmill Fields
Greenfield Drive
Chrismund Way
Farmfield Road
Harvesters' Way
The Street
1 2
Garden Fields

Great Tey

Moor Road
Moor Farm

The Chase
New Road

6

Roman River

Walcott's Hall

Coggeshall Road

Coggeshall Road

Brook Road

Essex Way

Buckler's Farm

7   Gull's Farm

Lane
Cramner's Lane

Dowsland Green

Trumpingtons Farm

Teybrook Farm

Essex Way

Little Hey House

8

Roman Brook

Essex Way

Great   Tey Road

A   B   C   184   D   E   F
East Gores Road   East Gores
Salmon
Upper Hall Farm
Little Tey

1 grid square represents 500 metres

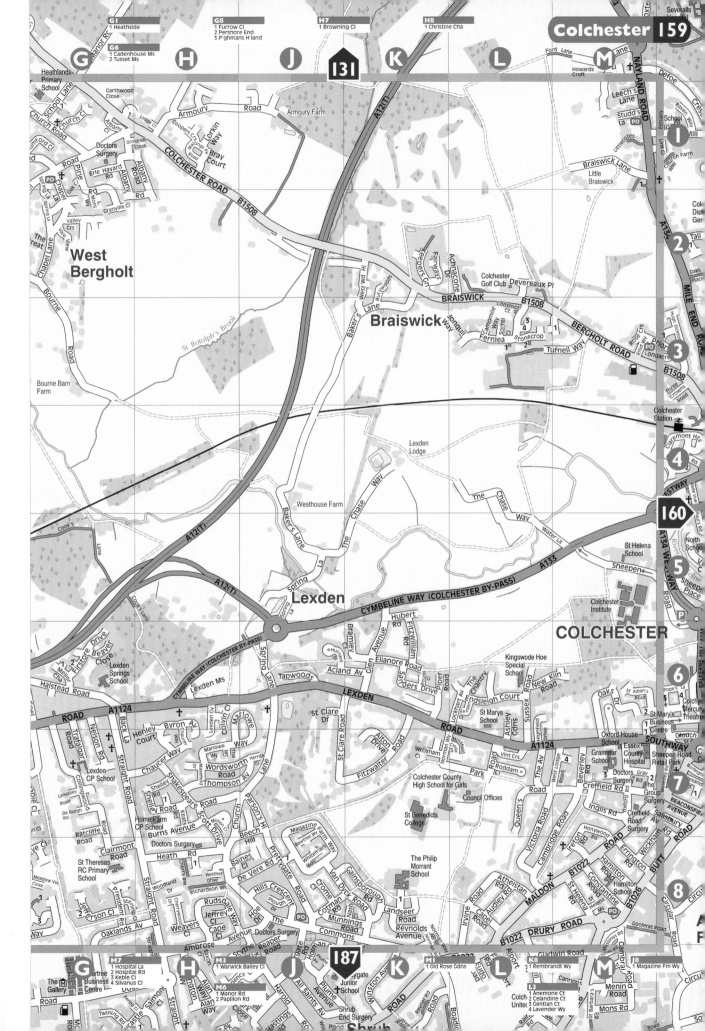

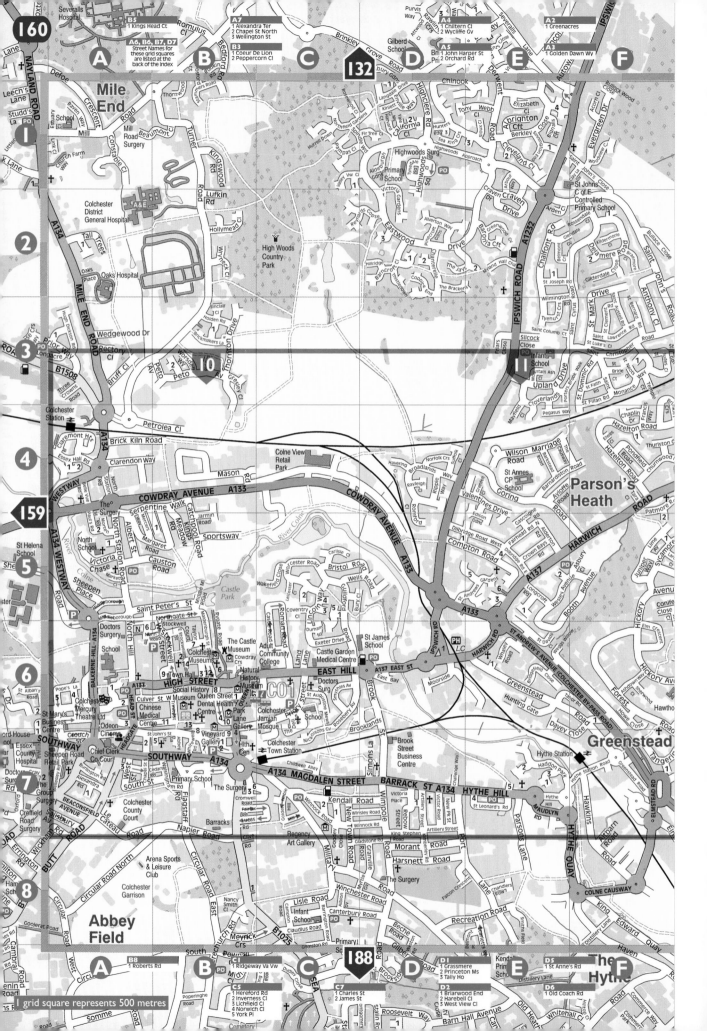

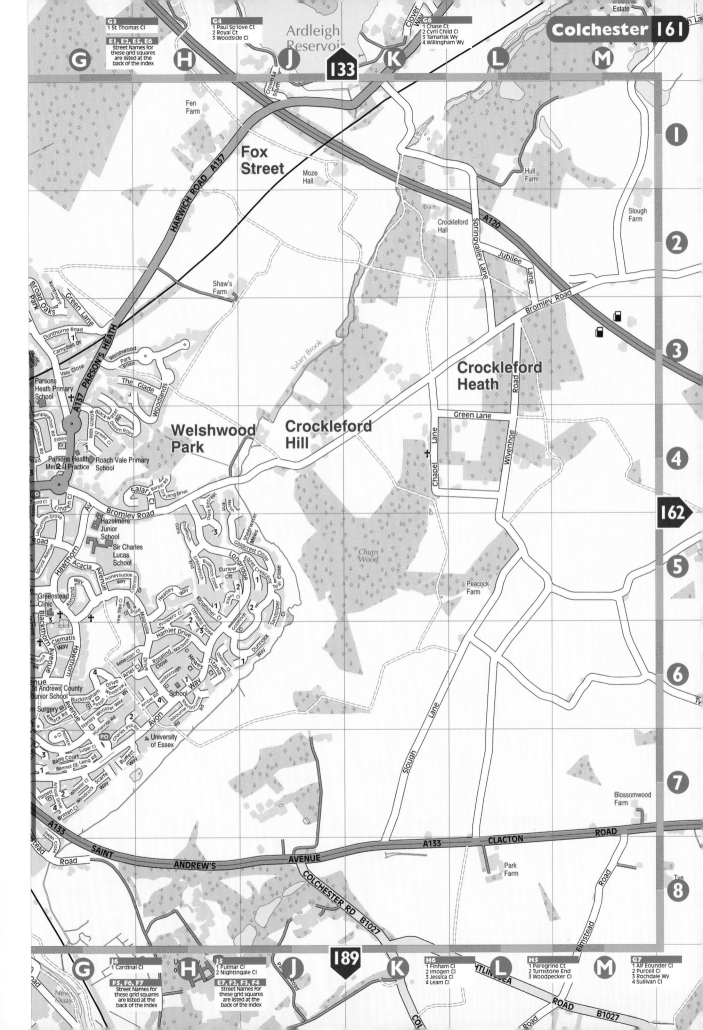

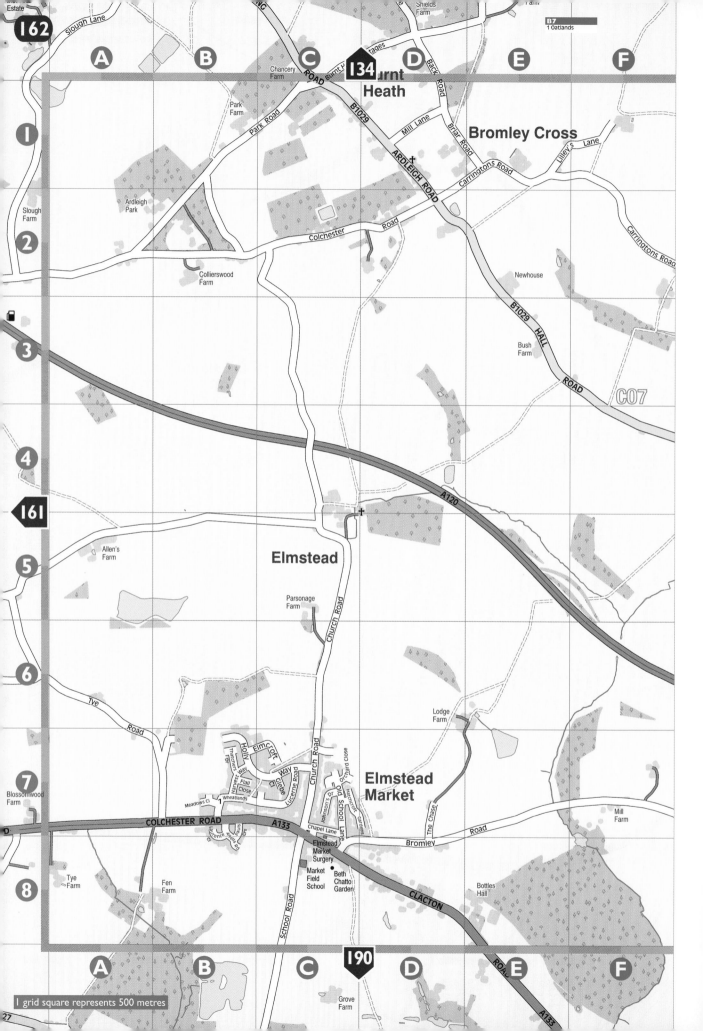

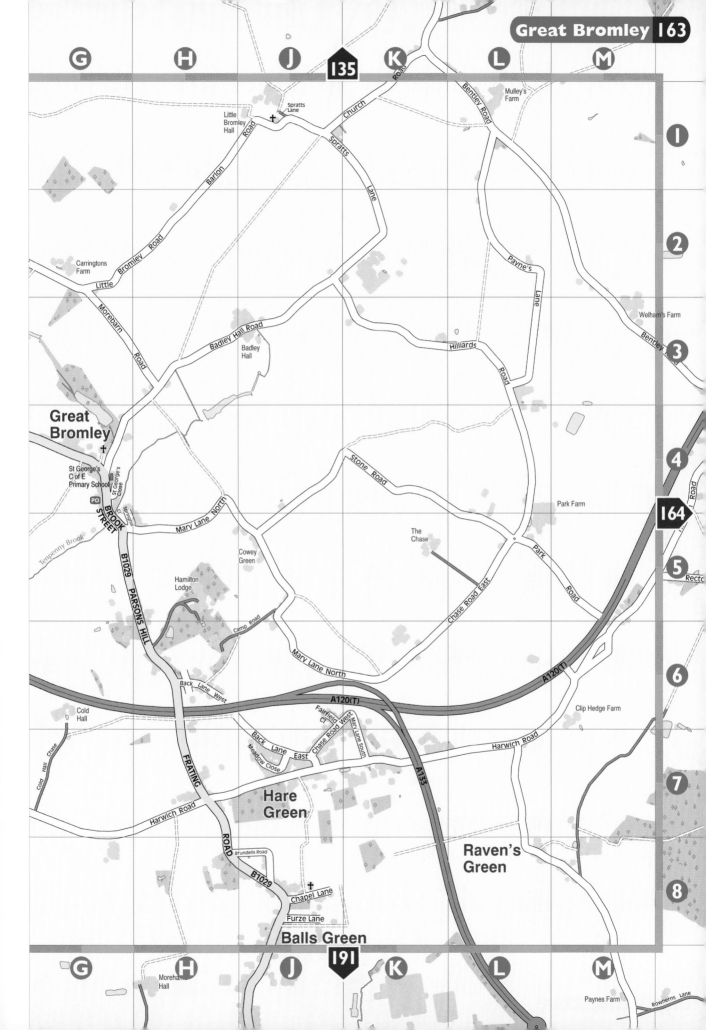

G   H   J   **135**   K   L   M

I

2

Mulley's Farm

Welham's Farm

3

Little Bromley Hall

Spratts Lane

Church Road

Bentley Road

Payne's Lane

Bentley

Barton Road

Carringtons Farm

Little Bromley Road

Morebarn Road

Badley Hall Road

Badley Hall

Spratts Lane

Hilliards Road

4

Great Bromley

St George's C of E Primary School

St George's Chase

Springall

BROOK STREET

PO

Tenpenny Brook

B1029

PARSONS HILL

Mary Lane North

Cowey Green

Hamilton Lodge

Camp Road

Stone Road

The Chase

Park Farm

Chase Road East

Park Road

164

Recto

5

6

Back Lane West

Mary Lane North

A120(T)

Clip Hedge Farm

Cold Hall

Cold Hall Chase

FRATING

Back Lane East

Meadow Close

Fairfield Cl

Chase Road West

Mary Lane South

A120(T)

Harwich Road

7

Hare Green

Harwich Road

A133

Raven's Green

ROAD

Brundells Road

B1029

Chapel Lane

Furze Lane

8

Balls Green

191

G   H   J   K   L   M

Morehams Hall

Paynes Farm

Rowhems Lane

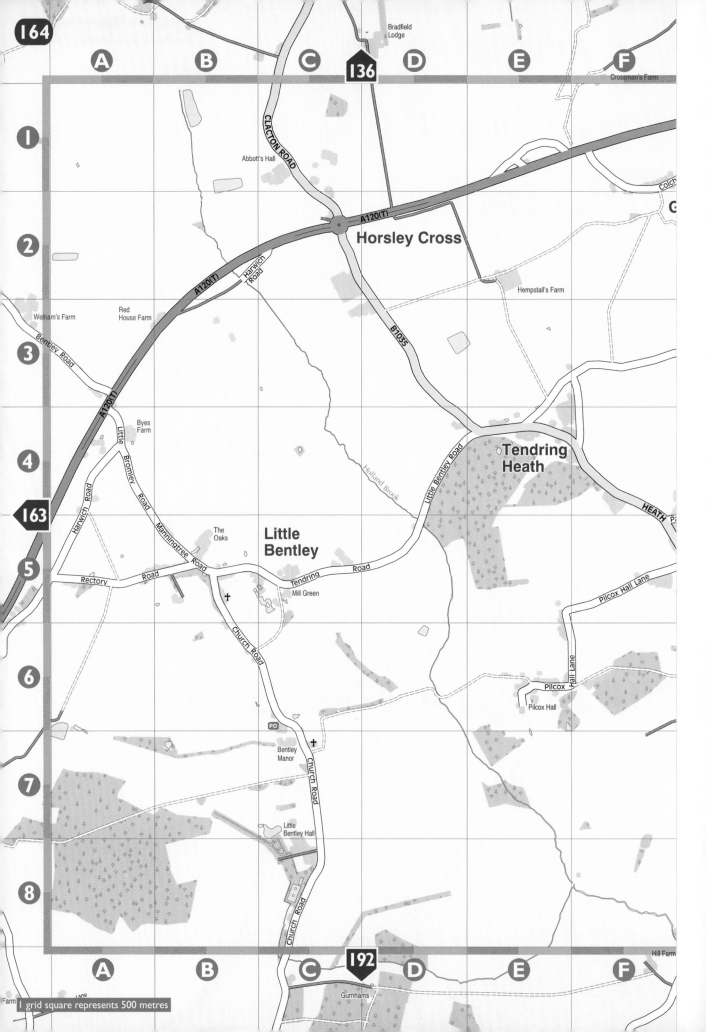

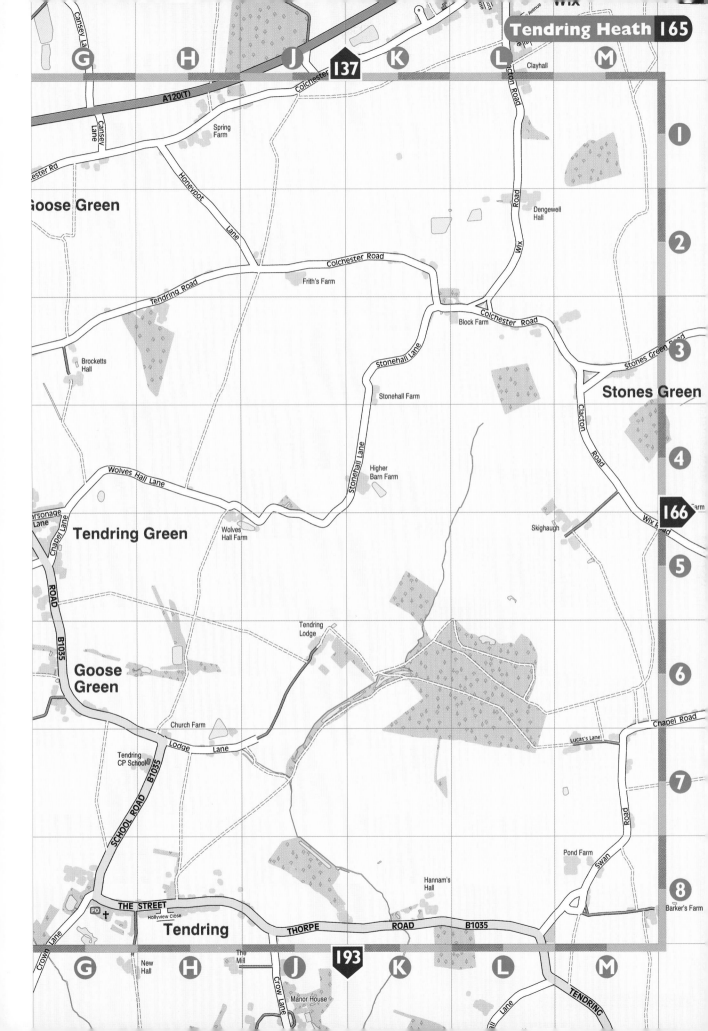

G H J **137** K L M

Cansey La

A120(T)

Colchester Road

Clayhall

WIX

Cansey Lane

I

Spring Farm

Honeypot Lane

Goose Green

Colchester Road

Wix Road

Dengewell Hall

2

Tendring Road

Frith's Farm

Colchester Road

Block Farm

Stones Green Road

3

Brocketts Hall

Stonehall Lane

Stonehall Farm

Clacton Road

Stones Green

4

Higher Barn Farm

Wolves Hall Lane

Stonehall Lane

Wix Road

166

Farm

Parsonage Lane

Chapel Lane

Tendring Green

Wolves Hall Farm

Skighaugh

5

ROAD

B1035

Tendring Lodge

6

Goose Green

Church Farm

Lodge Lane

Chapel Road

Lucas's Lane

Tendring CP School

B1035

SCHOOL ROAD

7

Swan Road

Pond Farm

8

Barker's Farm

THE STREET

Crown Lane

PO

Hollyview Close

Tendring

New Hall

The Mill

THORPE ROAD B1035

Hannam's Hall

Crow Lane

Manor House

TENDRING

all Lane

G H J **193** K L M

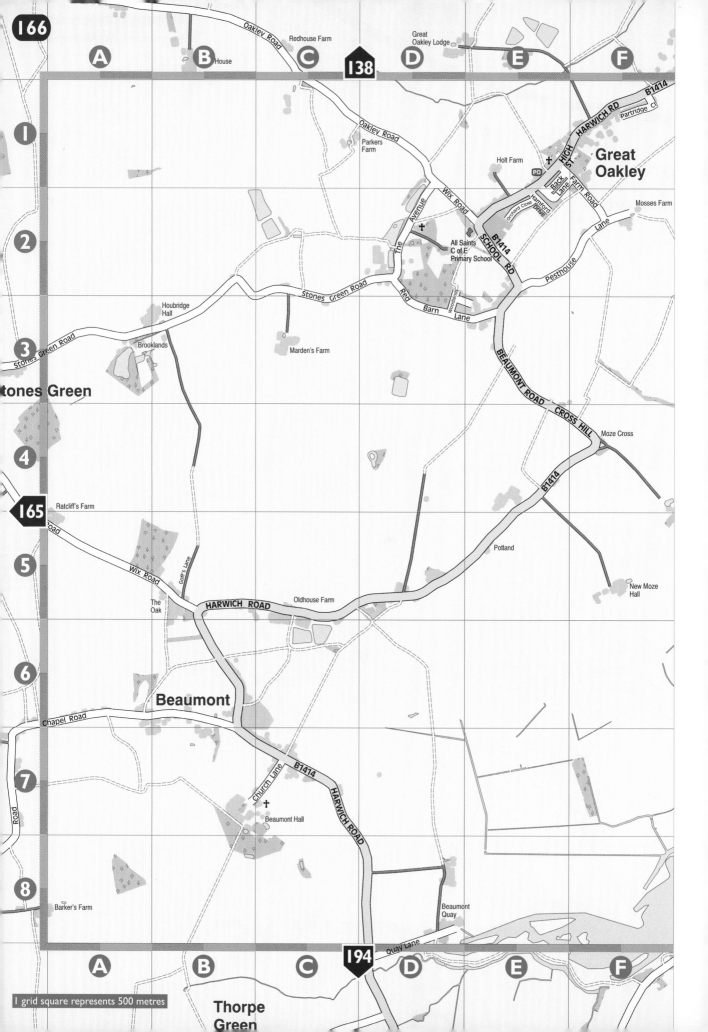

166

A   **B** House   **C**   **138**   **D**   **E**   **F**

Oakley Road
Redhouse Farm
Great Oakley Lodge

1

Oakley Road
Parkers Farm
Holt Farm
PO
†
Back Lane
HIGH ST
HARWICH RD
B1414
Partridge Cl
Great Oakley

The Avenue
Wix Road
Orchard Close
Hamford Drive
Farm Road
Mosses Farm

2
†
All Saints
C of E
Primary School
B1414
SCHOOL RD
Pesthouse

Houbridge Hall
Stones Green Road
Red Barn Lane
Woodlands

3
Brooklands
Stones Green Road
Marden's Farm
BEAUMONT ROAD
CROSS HILL

Stones Green
Moze Cross

4
B1414

165
Ratcliff's Farm
B1414

5
Wix Road
Goff's Lane
Potland
New Moze Hall

The Oak
HARWICH ROAD
Oldhouse Farm

6
Chapel Road
Beaumont

7
Road
Church Lane
B1414
HARWICH ROAD
†
Beaumont Hall

8
Barker's Farm
Beaumont Quay

A   **B**   **C**   **194**   **D**   **E**   **F**

I grid square represents 500 metres

Thorpe Green

The
Sparrow's
Farm

Doctor's
Q___ry

Great Oakley
Hall

CLACTON RO.

B1414

Dock
Lane

G
H
J
139
K
L
M

1

2

Oakley Creek

3

Pewit
Island

Old Moze
Hall

4

168

5

Hamford
Water

6

7

Skipper's
Island

Kirby Creek

8

White
Home

G
H
J
195
K
L
M

168

A   B   C   140   D   E   F

1

2

3

Pewit
Island

4

167

5

6

7   Horsey
     Island

8

Pennyhole
Bay

Stone
Marsh

CO13

Hedge-end
Island

Walton Channel

A   B   C   196   D   E   F

I grid square represents 500 metres

1

2

3

4

5

6

7

8

Nature
Reserve

The
Naze

Walton
Hall

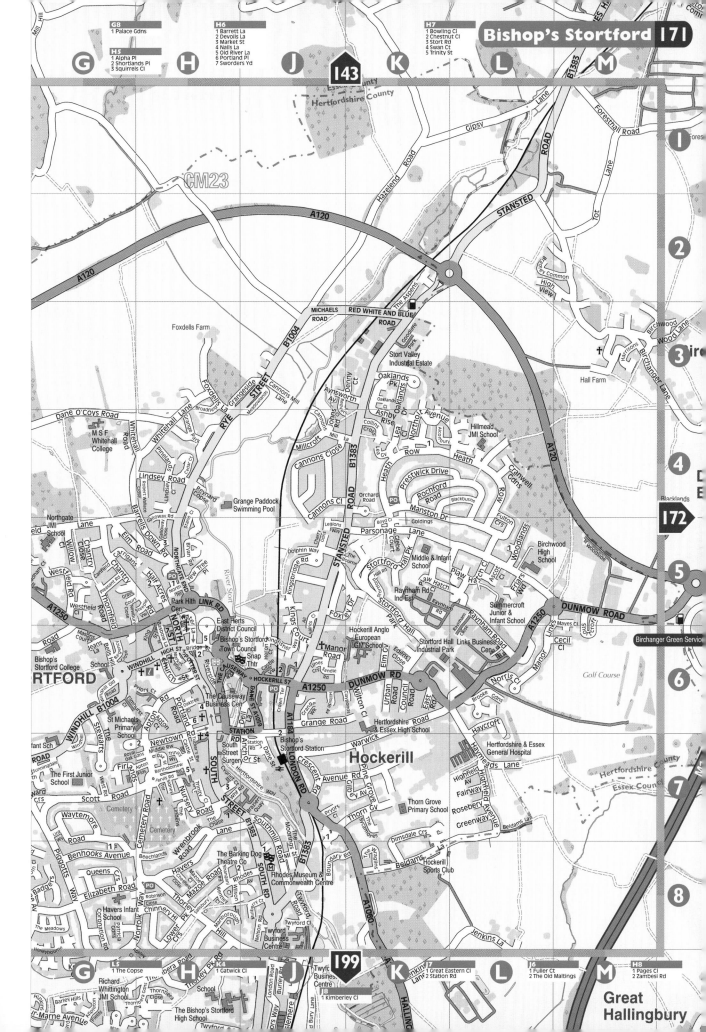

143

172

199

Great Hallingbury

172

A   B   Church Road   C   144   D   E   F   Burton End

Manor Road
SONEY
Common
College
Burton
Bower
M11
Belmer

Foresthall Rd
1   Forest Hall   CM24   †   Old Burylodge Lane
The Mountfitchet
School

Parsonage Lane   Sixth Avenue

Parsonage Farm   M11   Monks
Farm

2   Parsonage Farm
Indusrial Estate

Bury
Lodge   Bury Lodge Lane   Eleventh Avenue   Ninth Avenue
Second Av   First   Avenue   Tenth Av
Birchwood   Wood Lane   seventh   Third Av
3   Birchanger

P

Birchanger Lane

4   Duck
End   Round Coppice Road
Blacklands

171   M11

5   A120   Thremhall   Avenue   PRIORY WOOD
ROUNDABOUT   Bury Lodge Lane   Thremhall
Priory Farm

ROAD
Birchanger Green Service Area   A120   DUNMOW ROAD
6   Junction 8   Start
Hill   A120   Flitch Way

M11

rtfordshire County   Tilekiln
Green   Forest Way   Hatfield
Forest
7   Esse County   Harps Farm

Way

8   Bedlar's
Green   The Street   Beggar's Hall   Three Forest Wy   Harcamlow

Great   Church   Road   The Grove   Three Forests Way   Harcamlow Way   Three   Forest   Wy   Harcamlow Way
allingbury   A   B   C   200   D   E   F

I grid square represents 500 metres

Hallingbury

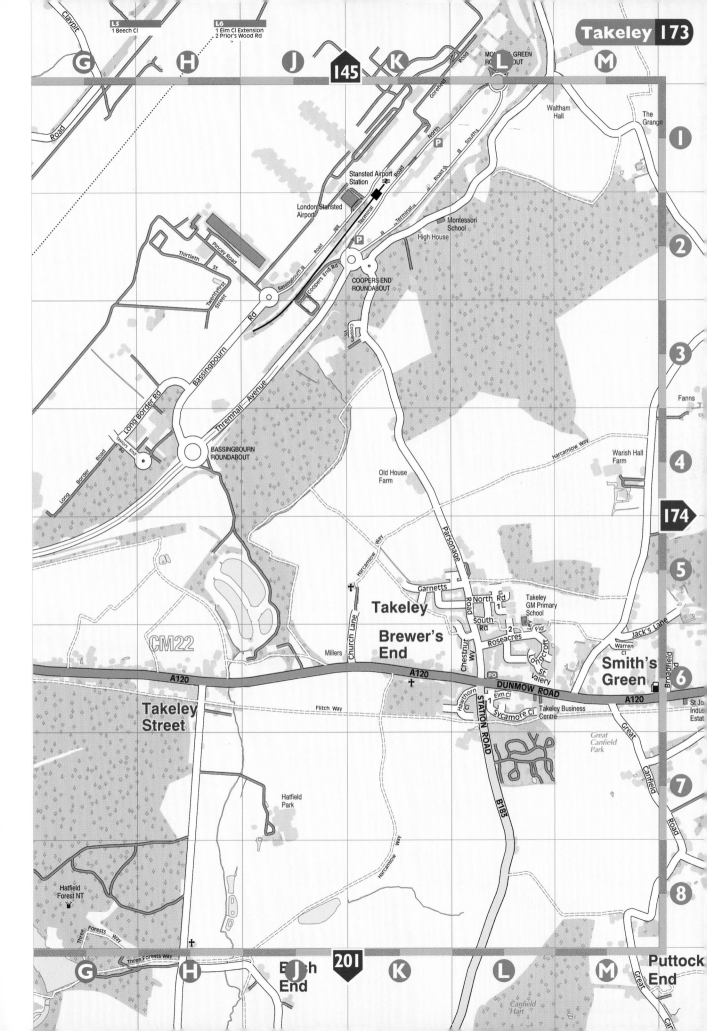

G   H   J   145   K   L   M

Claypit

Road

L5
1 Beech Cl

L6
1 Elm Cl Extension
2 Prior's Wood Rd

MOUNT GREEN
ROUNDABOUT

Gorefield Road

North Road

Waltham
Hall

The
Grange

I

P

2

London Stansted
Airport

Stansted Airport
Station

Montessori
School

Terminal Road

High House

Thirtleth
St

Pincey Road

Coopers End Rd

Bassingbourn Rd

Twentyfirst
street

COOPERS END
ROUNDABOUT

Road

3

Fanns

Coopers Vw

Bassingbourn Rd

Thremhall Avenue

Long Border Rd

Taylors End

Long Border Road

BASSINGBOURN
ROUNDABOUT

Harcamlow Way

Warish Hall
Farm

4

174

Old House
Farm

Harcamlow Way

Parsonage Road

5

CM22

Millers

Church Lane

Garnetts

North Rd

1

Takeley
GM Primary
School

Jack's Lane

Takeley

**Brewer's
End**

South
Rd

Roseacres

Fld

2

Longcroft

Warren
Cl

Broadfield Road

**Smith's
Green**

Chestnut Wy

St
Valery

PO

6

A120

A120

DUNMOW ROAD

A120

St Jo
Indus
Estat

**Takeley
Street**

Flitch Way

Hawthorn Way

Station Road

Elm Cl

Sycamore Cl

Takeley Business
Centre

Great
Canfield
Park

Great Canfield Road

7

Hatfield
Park

Harcamlow Way

B183

8

Hatfield
Forest NT

Three Forests Way

Three Forests Way

G   H   201   J   K   L   M

Canfield
Hart

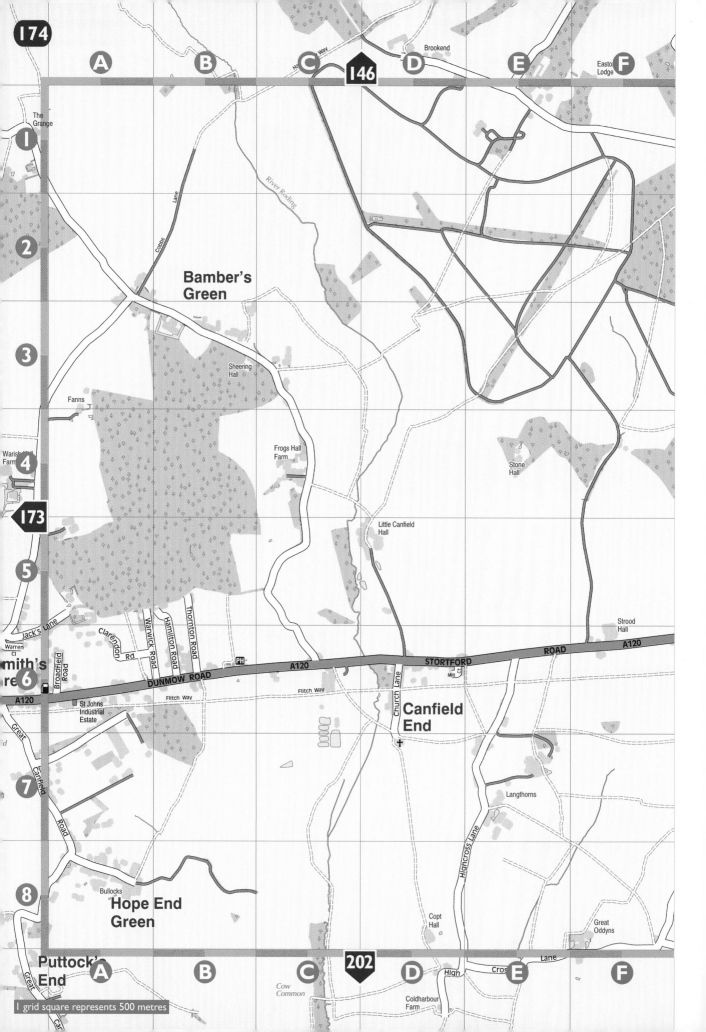

176

A   B   BROADWAY   C   D   E   F

Old House

F6
1 Moors La

B7
1 Chelmsford Rd

Stebbing
Park

148

Lower
Hall

1

Marks
Farm

Dunmow
Farm

CM6

Haydens

2

B1057

Crouches

Churchend

Tooley's
Farm

Brookend

Church
Gdns

CHURCH
END

St. Edmunds
Flds

3

RCH

St. Edmunds Flds

St. Edmunds
Flds

Merks
Hall

Homelye Farm

Throws

Counting
House
Lane

Millers
Cft

Windmill
Close

4

Ford Farm

Braintree
Road

Homelye Chase

A120

BRAINTREE   ROAD

175

Riverside

Braintree
Road

The
Dell

The Tenterfield

The Book
Gallery

5

New Street

Hasiers La

The Avenue

Oakcroft Avenue

Sunbank

A120

PH

1

Station Road

Station Yard
Ind Park

CHELMSFORD

Industrial Est

Ash Grove

Ongar Road
Trading
Est

Normansfield

Chelmsford Road
Industrial Est

Grange   Lane

The
Grange

St Mary's
Pl

The Street

Brook Street

6

Heywood
Lane

Lukin's

Lower Mill

Oak Ind Park

Flitch Way

ONGAR   ROAD

B184

B184

RD

A130

Langleys

Flitch Way

7

B184

Hoblongs
Industrial
Est

Flitch Way

Brook   Street

Brick
House

8

River Chelmer

Broadgroves

204

A   B   C   D   E   F

Barnston

Barnston Green

Rayfield Close

The
Chase

CHELMSF

Barnston
Lodge

Stebbing

PO

Street

Watch House Rd

Warehouse Road

Ruffels Field

Crofts Yard

G   H   J   **149**   K   L   M

Yew Tree Farm

Newpasture Lane

Bacon Farm

I

Cowlands Farm

Stebbing Green

2

Old Ryes

A120

3

Greenfields

Stebbingford Farm

Stebbing Road

A120

Bramble Lane

Seward's Hall

4

Prince's Halfyards

Blatches

178

Flitch Way

B1417

5

Felmoor Farm

Brook Farm

Little Dunmow

Flitch Way

Bourchiers

Station Road

Stebbing Road

W H G

6

Felsted CP School

Ravens Crs

Bayleys

Olney Vls

Hillside Road

Station Road

Chestnut Wk

Chaffix

Garnetts Lane

Players Ct

B1417

7

Algerton Cl

Road

Bury Farm

Felsted School

Gepps House Felsted School

Felsted School

Elwyn House Felsted School

Jollyboys Lane

The Orchard

Mill Road

The Surgery

Bury Flds

PO

Station Road

BRAINTREE

Follyfield Felsted School

8

Mrs Lipmans School

Riche Close

Felsted Preparatory School

Cromwell Pk

Felsted

B1417

Bakers Lane

Jollyboys

G   H   J   **205**   K   L   M

CHELMSFORD RO

Brockrum Close

Lane South

Jollyboys Lane

C G

Causeway

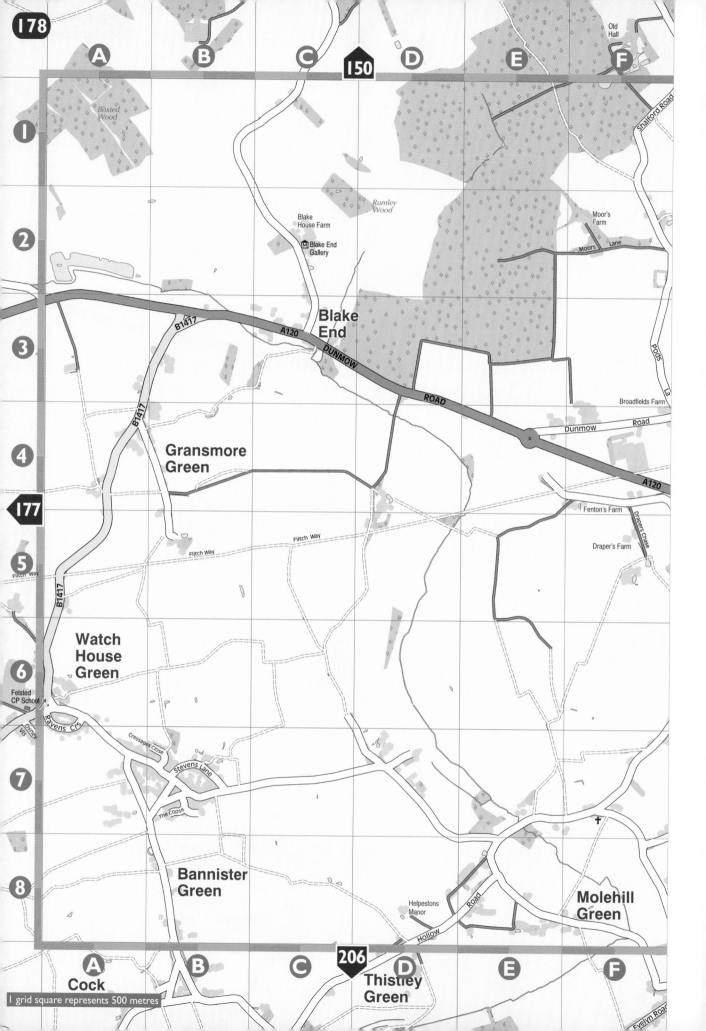

A **B** **C** 150 **D** **E** **F**

Old
Hall

1

Boxted
Wood

Shalford Road

Rumley
Wood

Moor's
Farm

2

Blake
House Farm

Moors Lane

M Blake End
Gallery

**Blake
End**

B1417

A120

DUNMOW

3

Pods La

ROAD

Broadfields Farm

Dunmow Road

B1417

**Gransmore
Green**

4

A120

Fenton's Farm

177

Draper's Chase

Flitch Way

Draper's Farm

5

Flitch Way

Flitch Way

B1417

**Watch
House
Green**

6

Felsted
CP School

Ravens Crs

Oxney Vis

Cressages Close

Stevens Lane

7

The Copse

8

**Bannister
Green**

Helpestons
Manor

✝

**Molehill
Green**

Hollow Road

A **B** **C** 206 **D** **E** **F**

Cock

**Thistley
Green**

Evelyn Road

G H J 151 K L M

180
151
207

H3
1 Blyth's Wy
2 Makemores
3 Philips Cl

H4
1 Symmons Cl

K6
1 Timbers Cl

K7
1 Cuckoo Wy
2 Elsham Dr
3 Highclere Rd
4 Penshurst Pl

Duckend Green

Pound Farmhouse

Rayne CP School

Shalford Road

Rayne

Rayne Lodge

RAYNE

B1256

Broomhills Industrial Estate

The Street

Enterprise Trading Estate

Cemetery

POD'S BROOK ROAD

Naylinghurst

Queenborough Lane

A120

A131

B1256

A131

180

Hill House Farm

Oaklands Close

Bartholomew Green

Mill Lane

Long Lane

School Road

Great Notley

Bridge End Lane

Queenborough Lane

London Road

Ludham Hall Lane

Row Green

White Court CP School

Pickpocket Lane

A131

Blackley's Farm

Cards Farm

Baker's Lane

I 2 3 4 5 6 7 8

Tabor High Upper School

John Bunyan & Inn

St Michaels Hospital

Willows Green

Young's

G H J 207 K L M

M6
1 Springmead
2 Thirlmere Cl

L8
1 Great Notley Av

L7
1 Crummock Cl
2 Grasmere Cl

L3
1 Birch Cl
2 Fresian Cl

K8
1 Elder Fld
2 Great Notley Av
3 Stanstrete Fld

L6
1 Clevedon Cl
2 Colville Cl
3 Framlingham Wy
4 Harnham Dr
5 Langdale

Blackley Lane

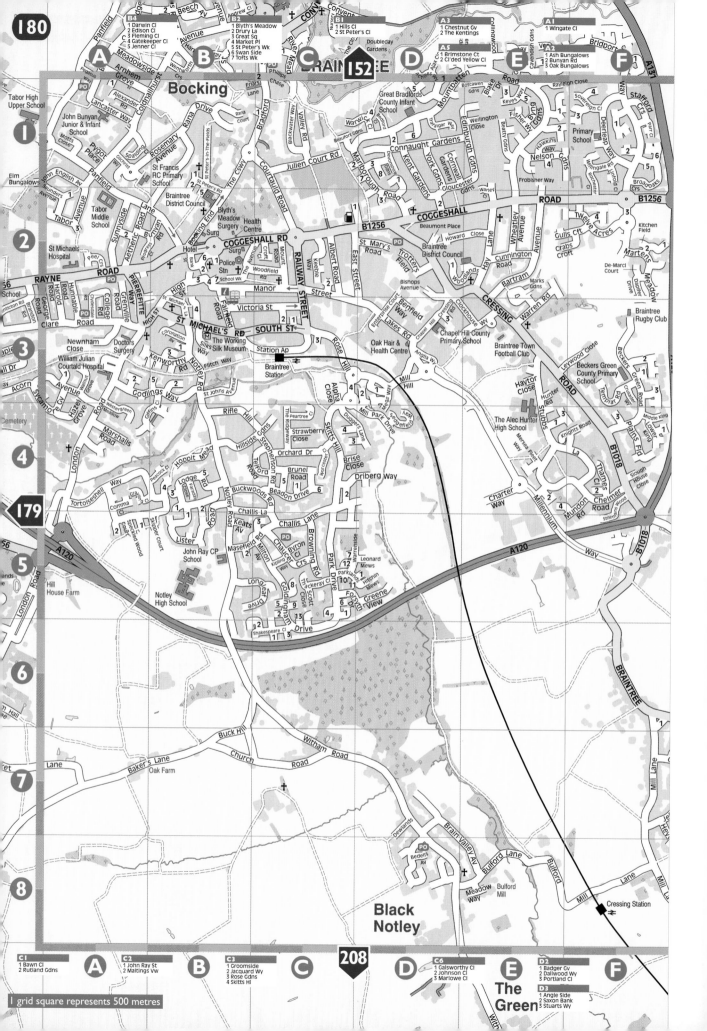

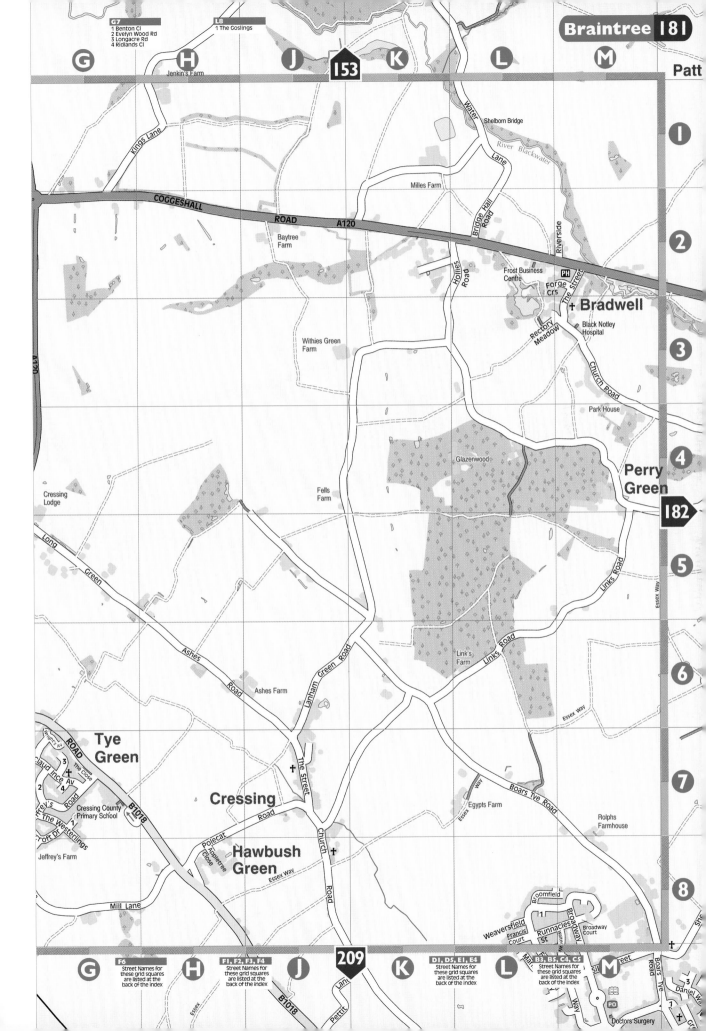

G7
1 Benton Cl
2 Evelyn Wood Rd
3 Longacre Rd
4 Ridlands Cl

LB
1 The Goslings

G **H** **J** 153 **K** **L** **M**

Jenkin's Farm

Kings Lane

Shelborn Bridge

Water Lane

River Blackwater

Milles Farm

Bridge Hall Road

Riverside

I

2

COGGESHALL ROAD A120

Baytree Farm

Hollies Road

Frost Business Centre

PH

Forge Crs

The Street

✝ **Bradwell**

Black Notley Hospital

3

Withies Green Farm

Rectory Meadow

Church Road

Park House

A120

Cressing Lodge

Fells Farm

Glazenwood

Perry Green

4

182

Long Green

Links Road

Essex Way

5

Ashes Road

Lanham Green Road

Link's Farm

Links Road

6

Ashes Farm

Essex Way

ROAD

Wright's Av

Tye Green

Claud Ince Av

The Close

The Street

Boars Tye Road

7

Egypts Farm

Essex Way

Rolphs Farmhouse

Jeffrey's

Road

B1018

Cressing County Primary School

The Westerlings

Croft Dr

Cressing

✝

Church Road

Broomfield

8

Jeffrey's Farm

Mill Lane

Polecat Close

Appletree Close

Hawbush Green

Essex Way

✝

Weaversfield

Francis Court

Runnacles St

Broadway

Broadway Court

Main

Meet

Boars Tye Road

Daniel W

PO

Doctors Surgery

✝

B1018

Pettit La

182

A   Pattiswick Hall

Pattiswick

Doghouse Road

Church Road

B

+

154

Hovells Farm

C

D

E

F

1

2

Holfield Grange

3

Coggeshall Road
Whiteshill Farm

Coggeshall Road   Coggeshall Road
COGGESHALL ROAD A120

Watery Lane

4

Perry Green

181

Fiveash Lane   Church Road

Bradwell
+ Hall

Essex Way

River Blackwater

Grigg's Farm   Coggeshall Town Football Club

5

Essex Way

Essex Way

Essex Way

Curd Hall Farm

6

Gosling's Farm

Herons Farm

Cuthedge Lane

Haywards

7

Woodhouse Farm

Allshot's Farm

8

Sheepcotes Lane

Sheepcotes Farm

SILVER
A   END

+

Boars Tye Road

3
Daniel

B

C

210

rey's Wood

D

E

F

ctors' Surgery   +   4

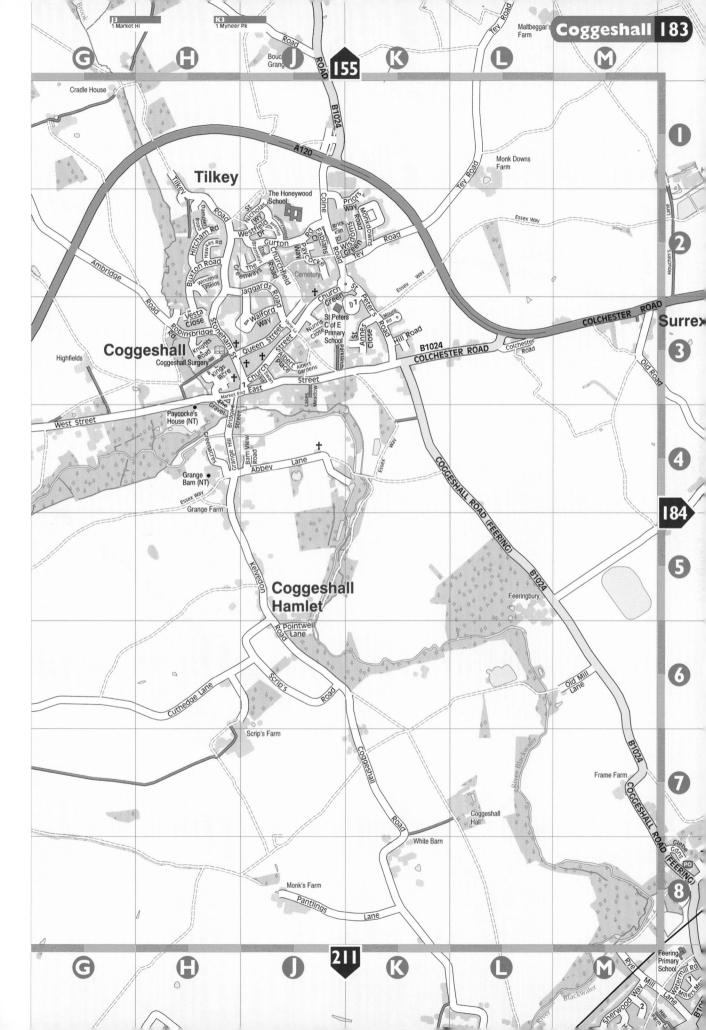

155

184

211

Tilkey

Coggeshall

Coggeshall Hamlet

Surrex

G H J K L M
I
2
3
4
5
6
7
8

Cradle House

A120

B1024

Tey Road

Maltbeggar's Farm

Monk Downs Farm

Essex Way

Houchin's Lane

COLCHESTER ROAD

Old Road

The Honeywood School

St Nicholas Wy

Westfield Dr

Hitcham Rd

Buxton Road

Tilkey Road

Ambridge Road

Hawkes Rd

Les Rd

Dunfield Road

Windmill Fields

Gurton Road

The Greenways

Brannies

Honeywood Avenue

Colne Rd

Churchfield Road

Paycocke Way

Fabians Rd

Brick Kiln Cl

Wisbons Rd

Monkdowns Road

Tey Road

Priors Way

Cemetery

Church Green

St Peter's Road

Essex Way

Essex Way

Jaggards Road

Walford Way

Lane L

Nunn's Close

St Peters C of E Primary School

St Annes Close

Hill Road

Mount Rd

parklands

B1024

COLCHESTER ROAD

Colchester Road

Vesta Close

Robinsbridge Rd

Stoneham St

Knights Road

Queen Street

Albert Street

Swan Street

Albert Place

Albert Gardens

Church Street

Kings Acre

Coggeshall Surgery

Highfields

East Street

Market End

Lakes Meadow

Essex Way

COGGESHALL ROAD (FEERING)

B1024

West Street

Paycocke's House (NT)

Gravel

Greenacres

Grange Hill

Bridge Street

Barn View Road

Abbey Lane

Grange Barn (NT)

Grange Farm

Essex Way

Feeringbury

Kelvedon Road

Pointwell Lane

Scrip's Road

Cuthedge Lane

Old Mill Lane

River Blackwater

Scrip's Farm

Coggeshall Road

Frame Farm

B1024

COGGESHALL ROAD (FEERING)

Coggeshall Hall

White Barn

Monk's Farm

Pantlings Lane

Glebe Gdns

PO

Feering Primary School

Sherwood Way

River Blackwater

Mill Lane

Waterfull Rd

Millers Me

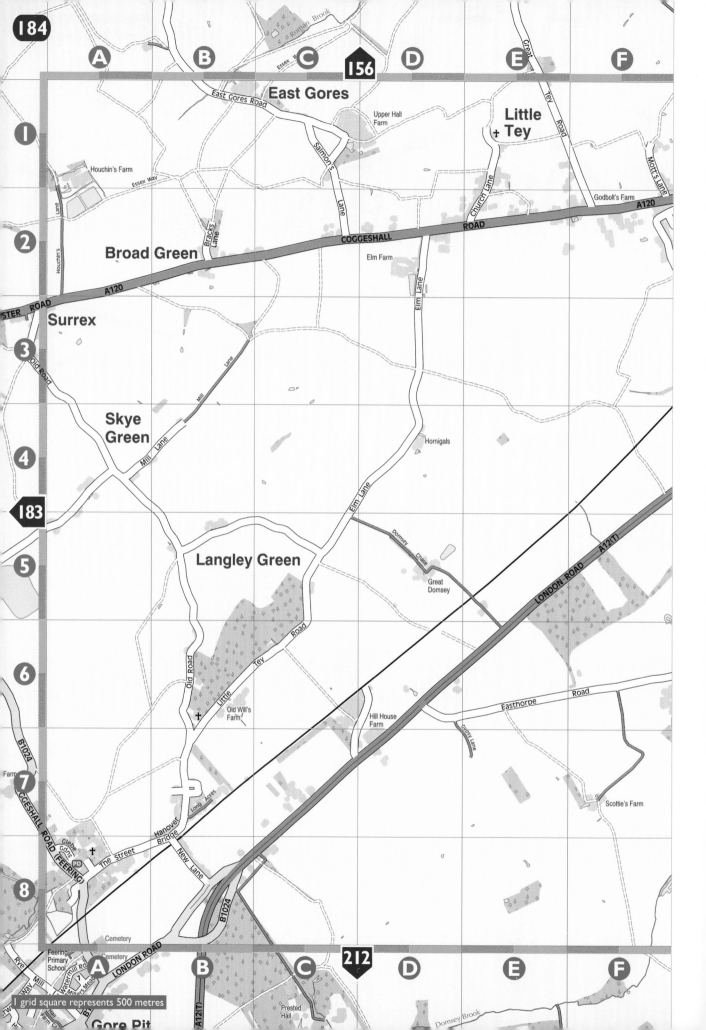

Ⓐ   Ⓑ   Ⓒ   **156**   Ⓓ   Ⓔ   Ⓕ

Ⓘ

Roman Brook

East Gores Road

East Gores

Upper Hall Farm

Little ✝ Tey

Houchin's Farm

Essex Way

Salmon's Lane

Godbolt's Farm

Mott's Lane

Church Lane

Ⓐ Lane

Bracks Lane

Ⓑ

Great Tey Road

2

Broad Green

A120

COGGESHALL ROAD

Elm Farm

A120

Houchin's

...STER ROAD

Surrex

3

Old Road

Mill Lane

Lane

Elm Lane

Skye Green

4

Hornigals

183

Elm Lane

Domsey Chase

5

Langley Green

Great Domsey

A12(T)

LONDON ROAD

Old Road

Little Tey Road

6

Eastthorpe Road

✝

Old Will's Farm

Hill House Farm

Gypsy Lane

B1024

Farm

7

Scottie's Farm

...GGESHALL ROAD (FEERING)

Long Acres Lane

Hanover Bridge

glebe Gdns

PO

✝

The Street

New Lane

8

B1024

Cemetery

Feering Primary School

WaterMill Rd

Miller's Mead

LONDON ROAD

New Mill

Rye...

Ⓐ   Ⓑ A12(T)   Ⓒ   **212**   Ⓓ   Ⓔ   Ⓕ

Prested Hall

Domsey Brook

Gore Pit

I grid square represents 500 metres

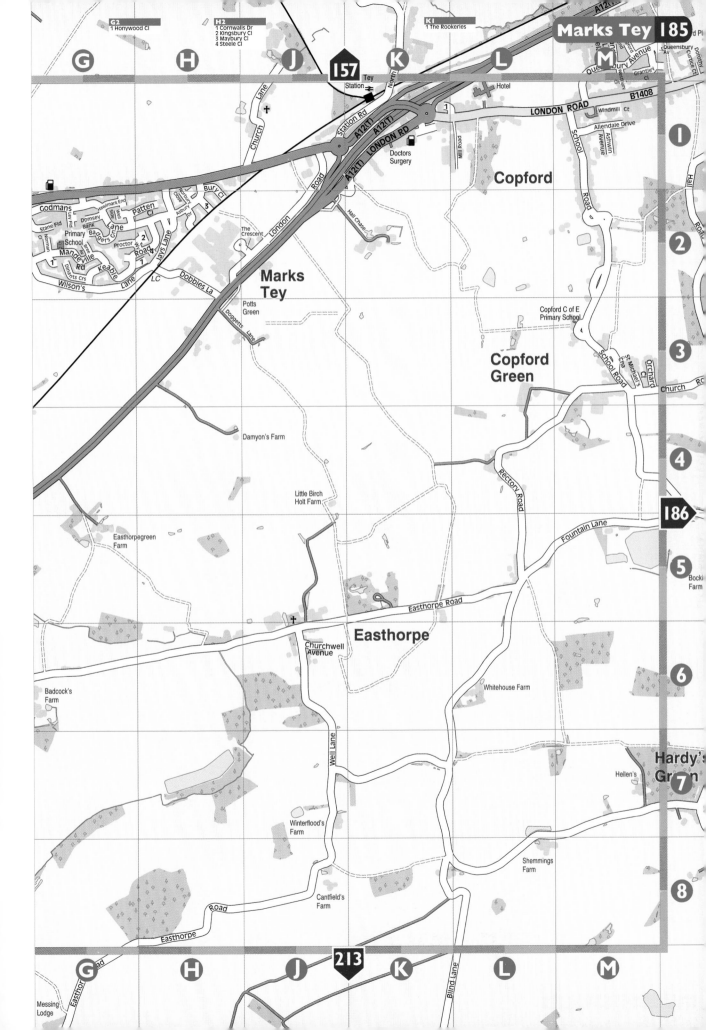

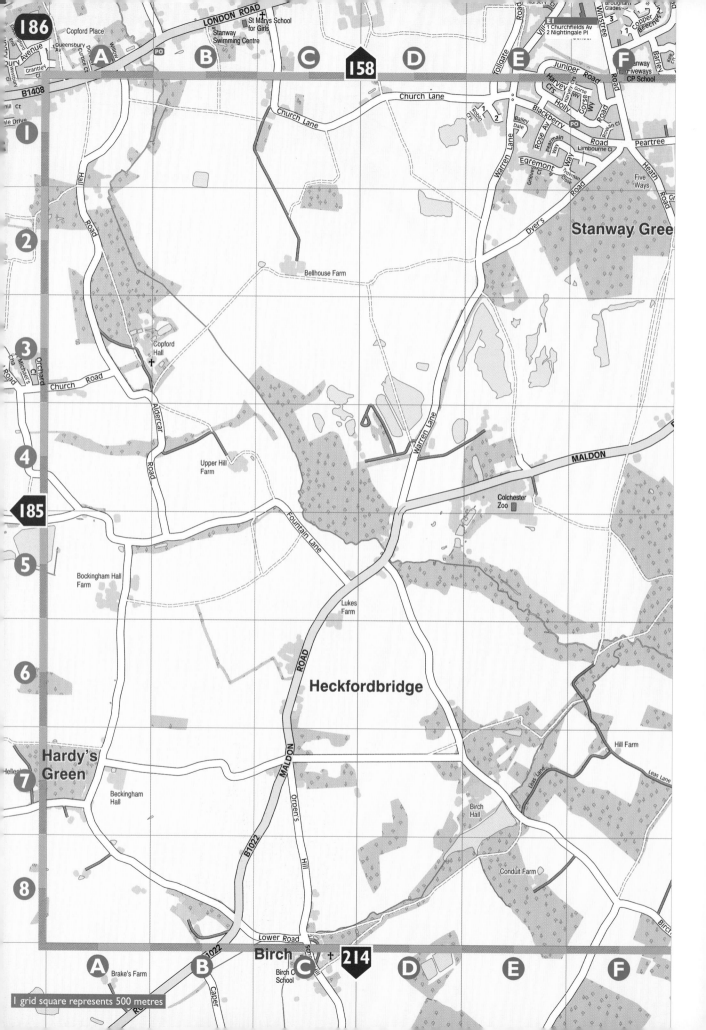

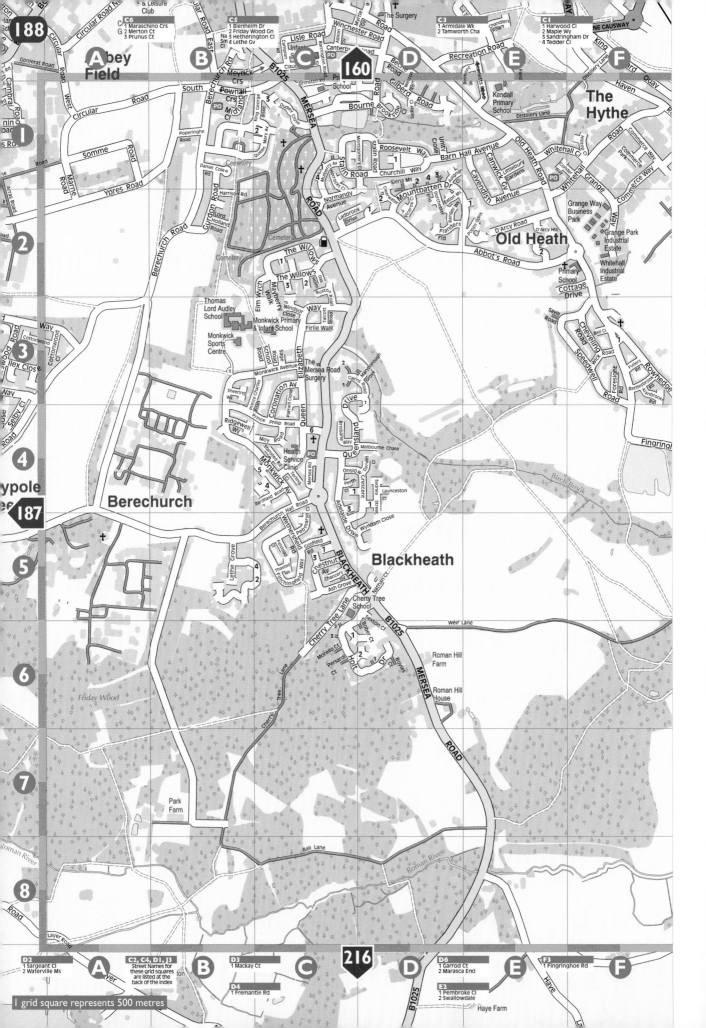

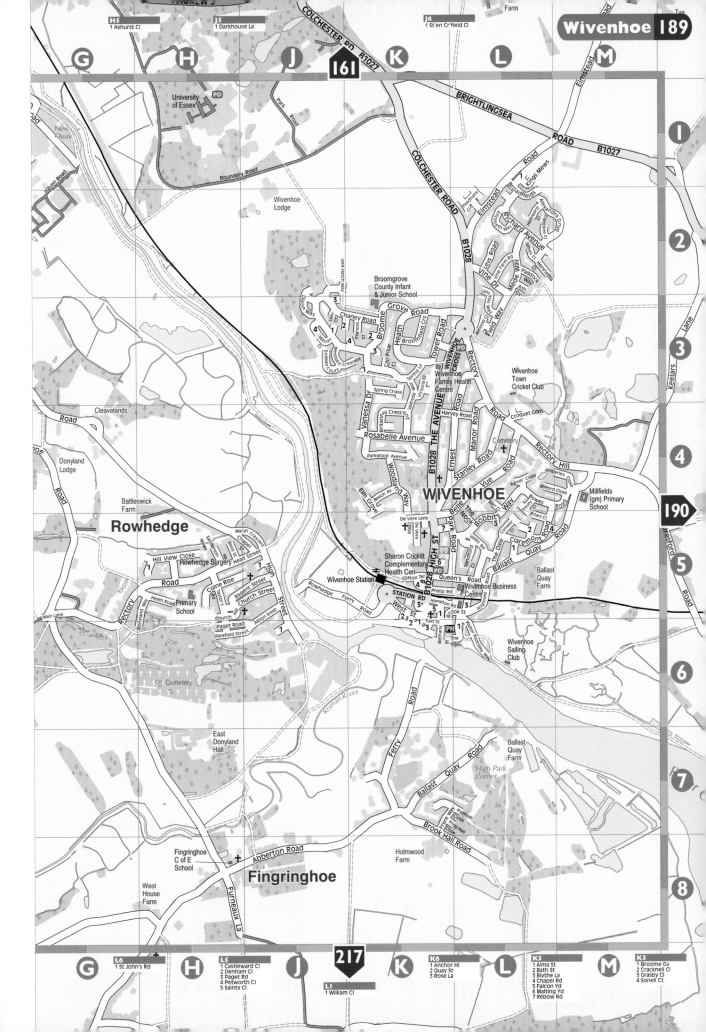

G H J K L M

161

190

217

WIVENHOE

Rowhedge

Fingringhoe

University of Essex

Wivenhoe Lodge

Broomgrove County Infant & Junior School

Wivenhoe Town Cricket Club

Millfields (gm) Primary School

Wivenhoe Family Health Centre

Wivenhoe Cross

Cleavelands

Donyland Lodge

Battleswick Farm

Rowhedge Surgery

Primary School

Sharon Crickitt Complementary Health Cen

Wivenhoe Station

Wivenhoe Business Centre

Wivenhoe Sailing Club

Ballast Quay Farm

The Folly

Roman River

East Donyland Hall

High Park Corner

Ballast Quay Farm

Fingringhoe C of E School

West House Farm

Holmwood Farm

BRIGHTLINGSEA ROAD B1027

COLCHESTER ROAD

B1028

Keelars Lane

Westord Road

G H J K L M

L6
1 St John's Rd

L5
1 Castleward Cl
2 Denham Cl
3 Paget Rd
4 Petworth Cl
5 Sainty Cl

L1
1 William Cl

K6
1 Anchor Hl
2 Quay St
3 Rose La

K5
1 Alma St
2 Bath St
3 Blythe La
4 Chapel Rd
5 Falcon Yd
6 Malting Yd
7 Rebow Rd

K3
1 Broome Gv
2 Cracknell Cl
3 Grasby Cl
4 Sonell Ct

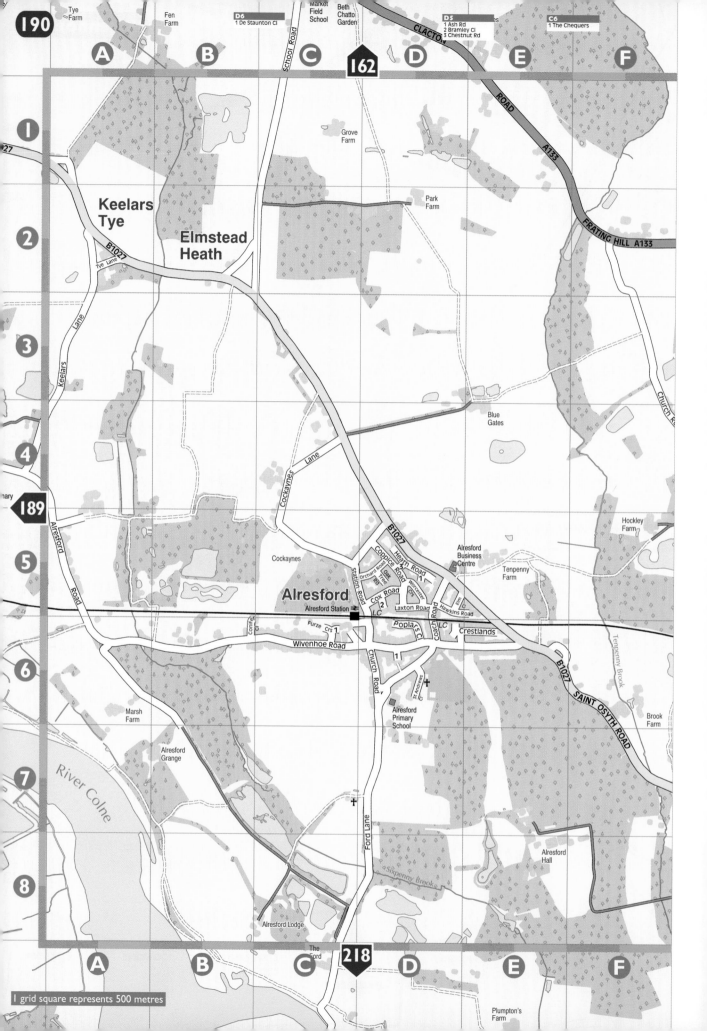

A B C D E F

162

D6
1 De Staunton Cl

CLACTON

D5
1 Ash Rd
2 Bramley Cl
3 Chestnut Rd

C6
1 The Chequers

Tye Farm

Fen Farm

Market Field School

Beth Chatto Garden

ROAD

1

Keelars Tye

Grove Farm

Park Farm

A133

B1027

2

Elmstead Heath

Tye Lane

FRATING HILL A133

Keelars Lane

3

Blue Gates

Church Rd

189

Cockaynes Lane

Hockley Farm

Alresford Road

4

Cockaynes

Alresford Business Centre

Tenpenny Farm

5

Alresford

Station Road

Orchard Road

Oak Tree Rd

Coppice Road

Heath Road

Worcester Crs

B1027

1

Alresford Station

Cox Road

Laxton Road

Elm Rd

Hawkins Road

LC

Conifers

Furze Crs 1

Poplar

Coach Road

Coach Rd

Crs

LC

Crestlands

Wivenhoe Road

Church Road

1

Tenpenny Brook

6

Marsh Farm

St Andrews Cl

B1027 SAINT OSYTH ROAD

Brook Farm

Alresford Primary School

Alresford Grange

River Colne

7

Ford Lane

Alresford Hall

Sixpenny Brook

8

Alresford Lodge

The Ford

218

Plumpton's Farm

A B C D E F

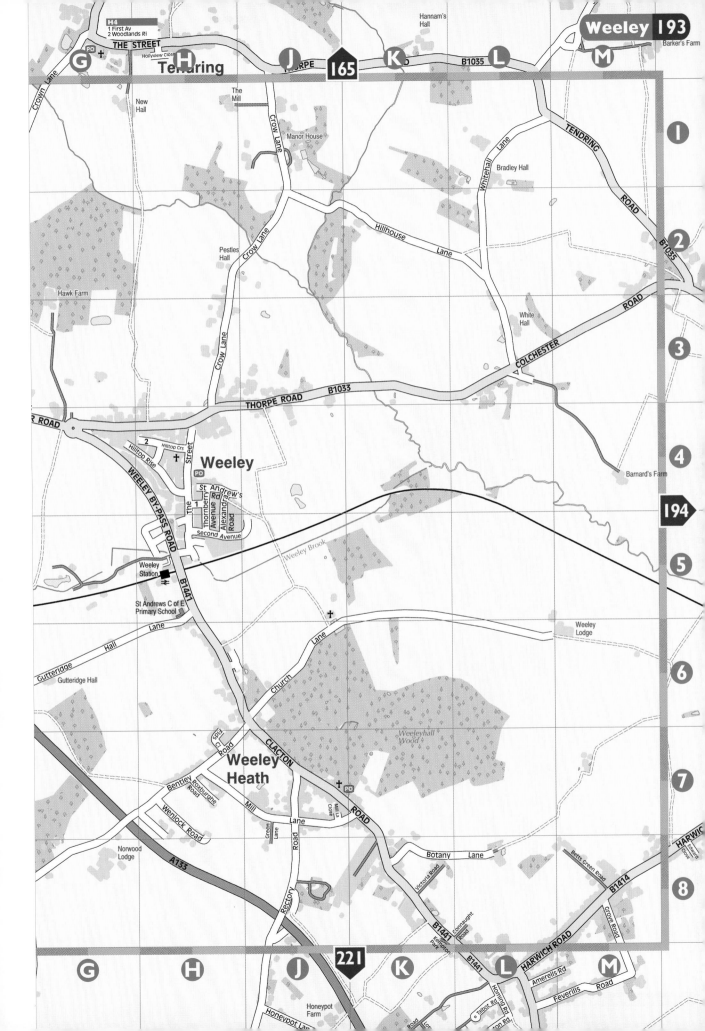

Barker's Farm

THE STREET

H4
1 First Av
2 Woodlands Ri

Hollyview Close

Tendring

THORPE

165

B1035

The Mill

New Hall

Manor House

Crow Lane

Hannam's Hall

Whitehall Lane

Bradley Hall

TENDRING ROAD

Pestles Hall

Crow Lane

Hillhouse Lane

White Hall

B1035

COLCHESTER ROAD

Hawk Farm

Crow Lane

THORPE ROAD   B1033

Barnard's Farm

R ROAD

Hilltop Rise

2   Hilltop Crs

The Street

Weeley

PO

St Andrew's Rd

Thornberry Avenue

Alexandra Road

Weeley Brook

194

WEELEY BY-PASS ROAD

Second Avenue

Weeley Station

B1441

St Andrews C of E Primary School

Hall   Lane

Gutteridge

Gutteridge Hall

Lane

Church

Lane

Weeley Lodge

CLACTON   ROAD

Weeleyhall Wood

Bentley Road

Roxburghe Road

Weeley Heath

Crds Cl

Cl Road

Mill   Lane

Mill Cl

PO

Wenlock Road

Green Lane

Botany   Lane

Victoria Road

Betts Green Road

HARWIC

Norwood Lodge

A133

Rectory Road

B1441

Connaught Road

Kempton Park

Edward Close

B1414

Grove Road

HARWICH ROAD

221

Amerells Rd

Feverills   Road

Honeypot Farm

Honeypot Lan

Talbot Rd

Horning Rd

ston Rd

G   H   J   K   L   M

A   B   C   D   E   F

Barker's Farm

C4
1 Beldams Cl

B6
1 Edward Rd

Beaumont
Quay

Quay Lane

**Thorpe
Green**

1
Golden Lane

Landermere
Hall

ROAD

2
B1035
Golden Lane

Valley Farm

Walton Road

Thorpe
Lodge

New
Hall

ROAD

Kentshill Farm

3
Vicarage Lane
St. Michael's Road
The Crs

B1033
New Town Road
Argyle Road

New Thorpe Av
Kenworth Grove
Spencer Road
Palmerston Road
Lonsdale Road

ROAD

B1414

College
Argyle Road

Rolph C of E Primary School

LANDERMERE

The Spennells
Rolph Lane
1

HIGH STREET

The Surgery
PO

Thorpe-le-Soken

Abbey
Abbey Crs
Oak Cl

4
Barnard's Farm

Mill Lane

ABBEY STREET

Byng Crs

Hall Lane

FRINTON

White Ldg Crs

The Grange Farm

ROAD
B1033

Thorpe
Cross

5

B1414

Thorpe
Hall

STATION ROAD

6
Malthouse

Thorpe-le-Soken Station
1

Thorpe Park Lane

Rice
Bridge
Industrial Est

Thorpe
Park

7
Woodlands

ROAD
B1414

Lodge Road

Holland Brook

HARWICH
Edward Close

8
B1414

Tan Lane

A   B   C   D   E   F

Clacton Grove

Little Clacton
Lodge

Lodge

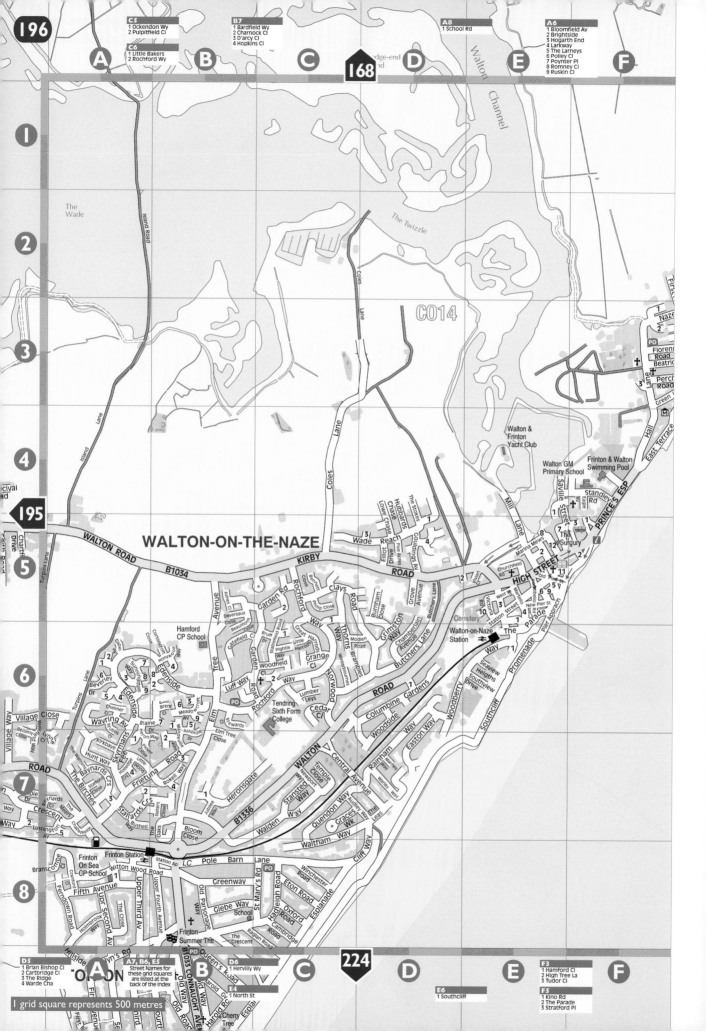

196

168

I
2
3

195

4
5
6
7
8

WALTON-ON-THE-NAZE

WALTON ROAD
B1034

KIRBY

ROAD

C014

The Wade

Island Road

The Twizzle

Coles Lane

Coles Lane

Walton Channel

Walton & Frinton Yacht Club

Walton GM Primary School

Frinton & Walton Swimming Pool

HIGH STREET

Walton-on-Naze Station

Tendring Sixth Form College

Hamford CP School

Frinton Station

Frinton On Sea CP School

Frinton Summer Thtr

Pole Barn Lane

B1336

WALTON

ROAD

Central Avenue

Promenade

PRINCE'S ESP

224

A   B   C   D   E   F

I grid square represents 500 metres

G3
1 Spendells Cl

The
Naze

Walton
Hall

Old Hall Lane

Sunny Point

Second Avenue
Third Av
Louise
Close
Park
Road

Greville
Cl

Cliff Parade

Road

The Frinton &
Walton Heritage Museum

I 1
2
3
4
5
6
7
8

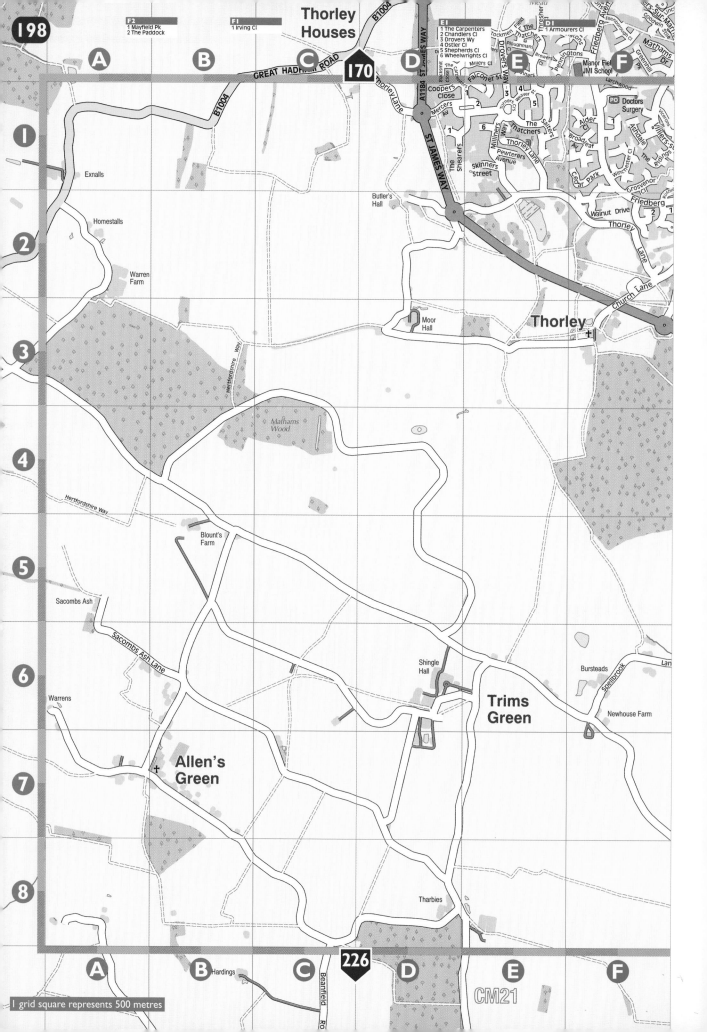

A B C 170 D E F

Thorley
Houses

GREAT HADHAM ROAD

B1004

B1004

ST JAMES WAY

A1184 ST JAMES WAY

Thorley Lane

Drovers Way

Falconer St

Coopers
Close

Mercers
Av

Millers Cl

The Carpenters

Buckknell

The Shearers

Millners
Way

Skinners
Street

Pewterers
Avenue

The
Thatchers

Ploughmans

Tockmen

Brewers

Penningtons

Salters

Thorley Lane

Cedar
Park

Broadleaf

Alder
Cl

Manor Field
JMI School

Larchwood

Greenhill

Friedberg Ave

Ellenborough Cl

Goodwin

Mathams
Dr

Villiers St

Vicrons
Cl

Ashdale

Winchester Cl

Grosvenor
Cl

Friedberg

The
Ridings

Rushleigh

PO Doctors
Surgery

Walnut Drive

Thorley
Lane

Church Lane

Exnalls

Homestalls

Warren
Farm

Butler's
Hall

Moor
Hall

Thorley

Hertfordshire Way

Mathams
Wood

Hertfordshire Way

Blount's
Farm

Sacombs Ash

Sacombs Ash Lane

Warrens

Shingle
Hall

Trims
Green

Bursteads

Spellbrook

Newhouse Farm

Lan

Allen's
Green

Tharbies

Hardings

Beanfield Ro

CM21

A   **B**   **C**   **D**   **E**   **F**

1

2

3

4

199

5

6

7

8

Bedlar's Green

Beggar's Hall

172

Church Road

The Street

The Grove

Three Forests Way

Harcamlow Way

Harcamlow Way

Three Forests Way

Hallingbury Street

Forest Lodge

Collin's Coppice

Hall Farm

Hallingbury Park

Howe Green House School

Morleys

Ladywell

Howe Green

Lodge Farm

Wall Wood

The Woods

New Barn Lane

Woodside Green

Three Forests Way

Forest Hall

Forest Farm

Monk's Wood

Goose Lane

Wright's Green

Forest Way

Ryes Lane

Little Hallingbury Park

Three Forests Way

Little Hallingbury Hall

8

Corringales

OLD STREET HILL

Town Farm

A   **B**   **C**   **228**   **D**   **E**   **F**

Stone Hall

Camp Farm

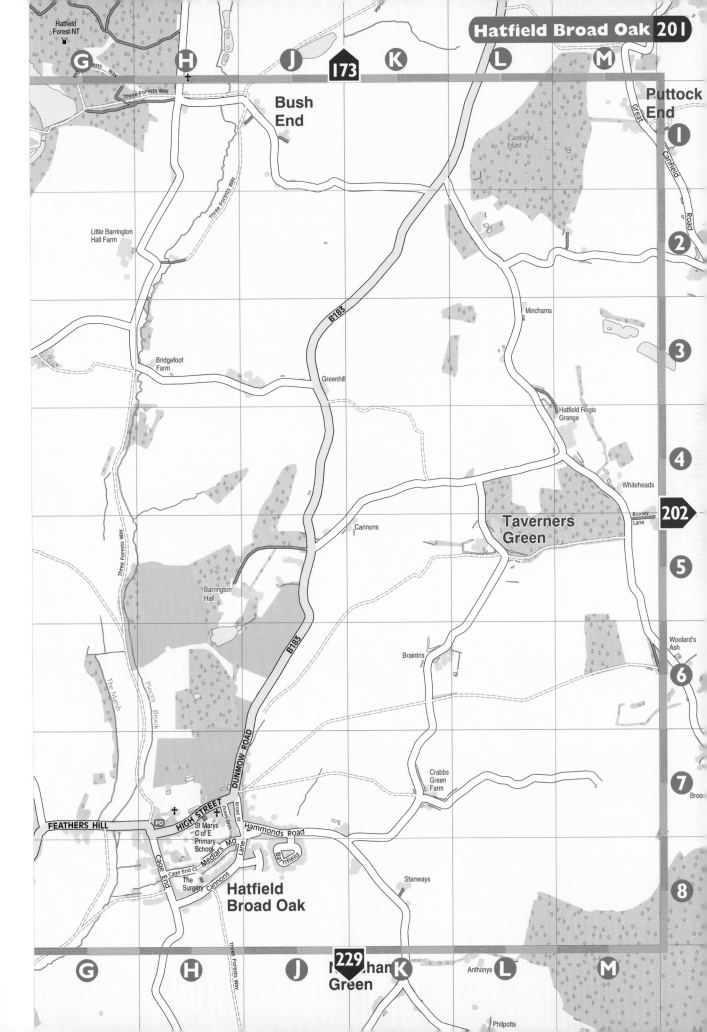

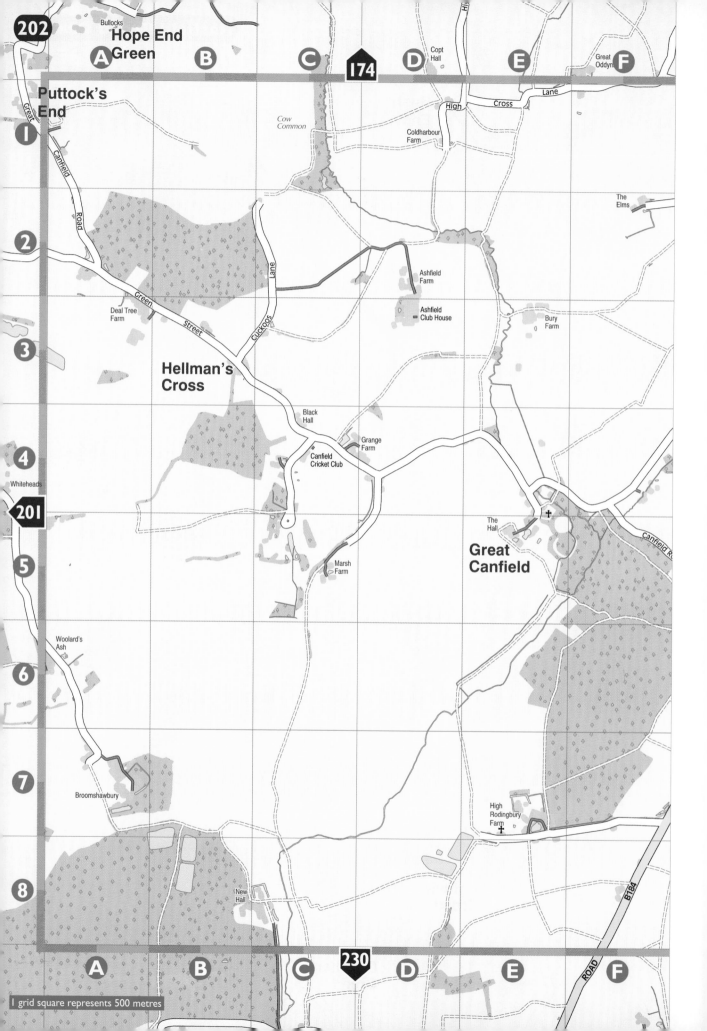

202

Hope End
Green

174

Copt
Hall

Great
Oddyn

Puttock's
End

High   Cross   Lane

Great

Cow
Common

The
Elms

Canfield   Road

Coldharbour
Farm

Ashfield
Farm

Ashfield
Club House

Bury
Farm

Deal Tree
Farm

Green   Street

Cuckoos   Lane

Hellman's
Cross

Black
Hall

Grange
Farm

Whiteheads

201

Canfield
Cricket Club

The
Hall

Great
Canfield

Canfield Rd

Marsh
Farm

Woolard's
Ash

Broomshawbury

High
Rodingbury
Farm

New
Hall

230

B184

ROAD

1 grid square represents 500 metres

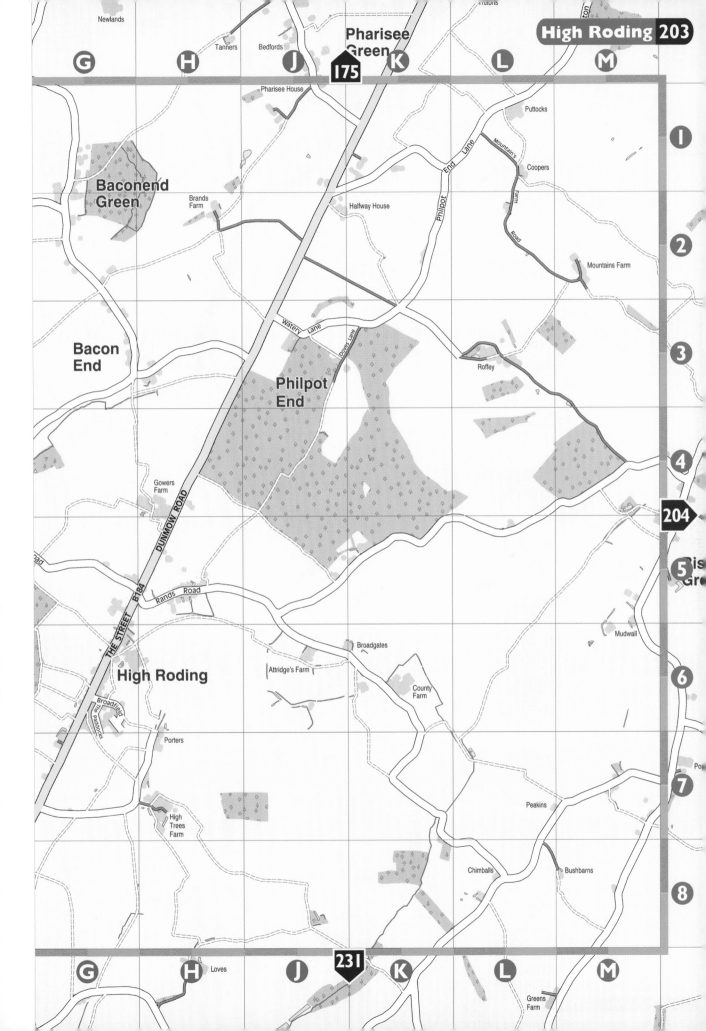

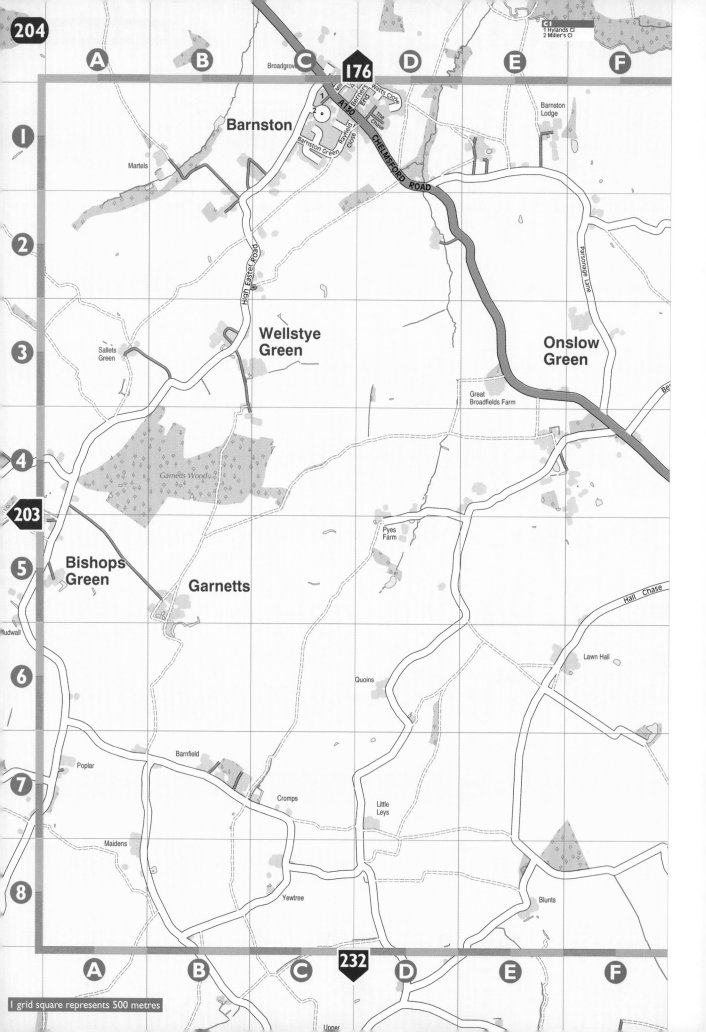

CI
1 Hylands CI
2 Miller's CI

A   B   C   176   D   E   F

Broadgrove

Barnston

Martels

Barnston Green

Barnston Lodge

CHELMSFORD ROAD

A130

Berners End

Watts Close

The Chase

Rayfield Close

High Easter Road

Parsonage Lane

Wellstye Green

Sallets Green

Onslow Green

Great Broadfields Farm

Garnetts Wood

203

Pyes Farm

Bishops Green

Garnetts

Hall Chase

Lawn Hall

Mudwall

Quoins

6

Poplar

Barnfield

Cromps

Little Leys

Maidens

Blunts

Yewtree

8

A   B   C   232   D   E   F

Upper

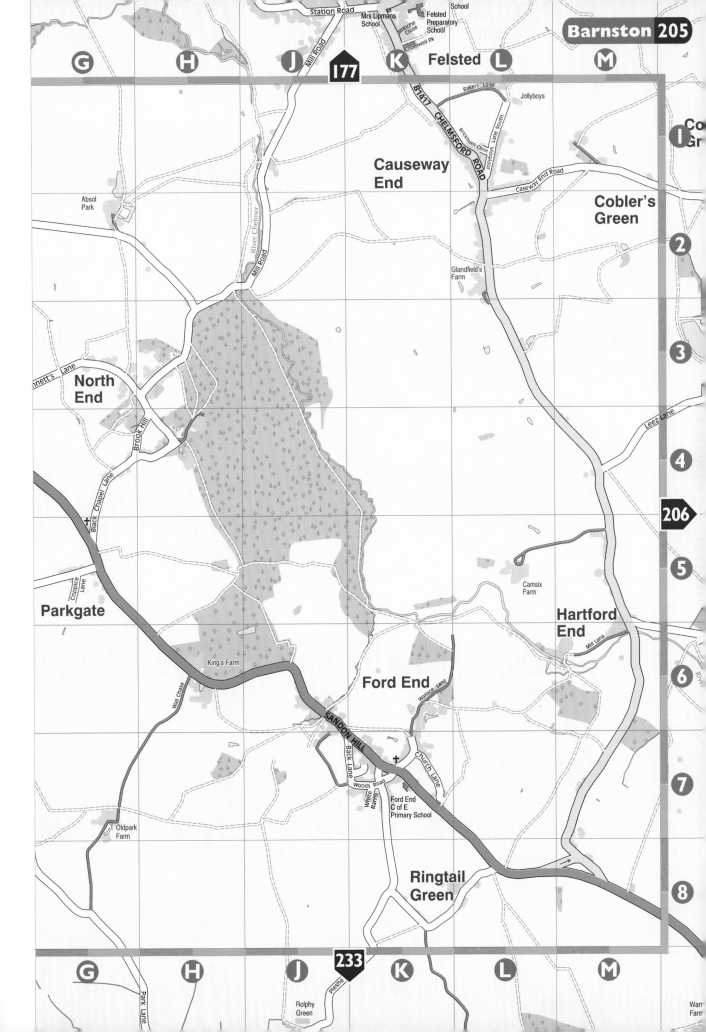

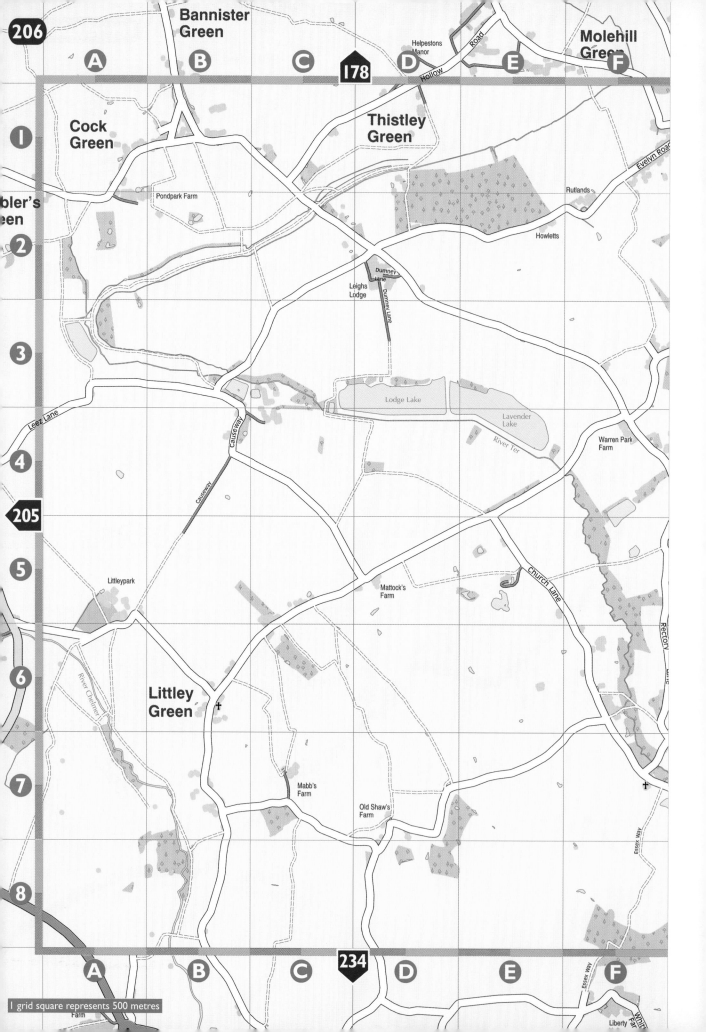

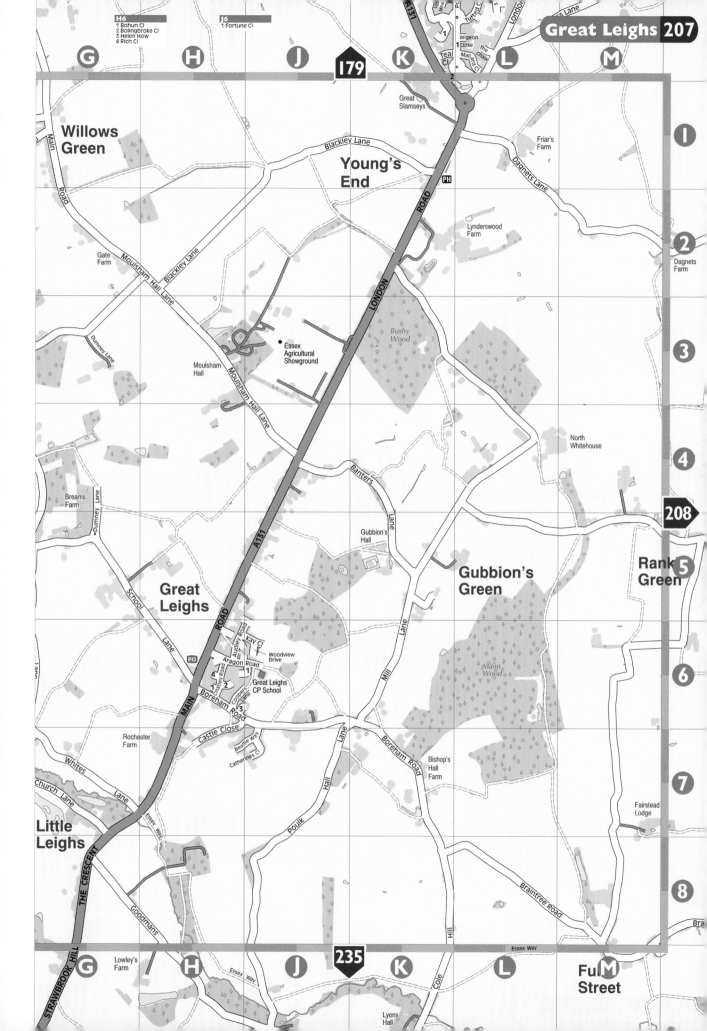

G H J 179 K L M

I

Willows
Green

Young's
End

Great
Slamseys

PH

Friar's
Farm

Dagnets Lane

2 Dagnets
Farm

Gate
Farm

Moulsham Hall Lane

Blackley Lane

Blackley Lane

LONDON ROAD

Lynderswood
Farm

3

Dumney Lane

Moulsham Hall

Moulsham Hall Lane

• Essex
Agricultural
Showground

Bushy
Wood

North
Whitehouse

4

Breams
Farm

Dumney Lane

Banters

Gubbion's
Hall

Mill Lane

Gubbion's
Green

Rank
Green 5

208

School Lane

A131 ROAD

Great
Leighs

Audley Road
Kay Cl
Aragon Road
Chatley Road
Coopers Lane
Woodview
Drive

Great Leighs
CP School

Mann
Wood

6

PO

MAIN ROAD

Boreham Road

Castle Close

Beadle Way
Catherines Cl

Boreham Road

Bishop's
Hall Farm

Poulk Hall Lane

7

Rochester
Farm

Whites Lane

Church Lane

Essex Way

Little
Leighs

THE CRESCENT

Goodmans

STRAWBROOK HILL

Lowley's
Farm

Fairstead
Lodge

Braintree Road

Essex Way

8

G H J 235 K Cole Hill L Fu M
Street

Lyons
Hall

H6
1 Bohun Cl
2 Bolingbroke Cl
3 Helen How
4 Rich Cl

J6
1 Fortune Cl

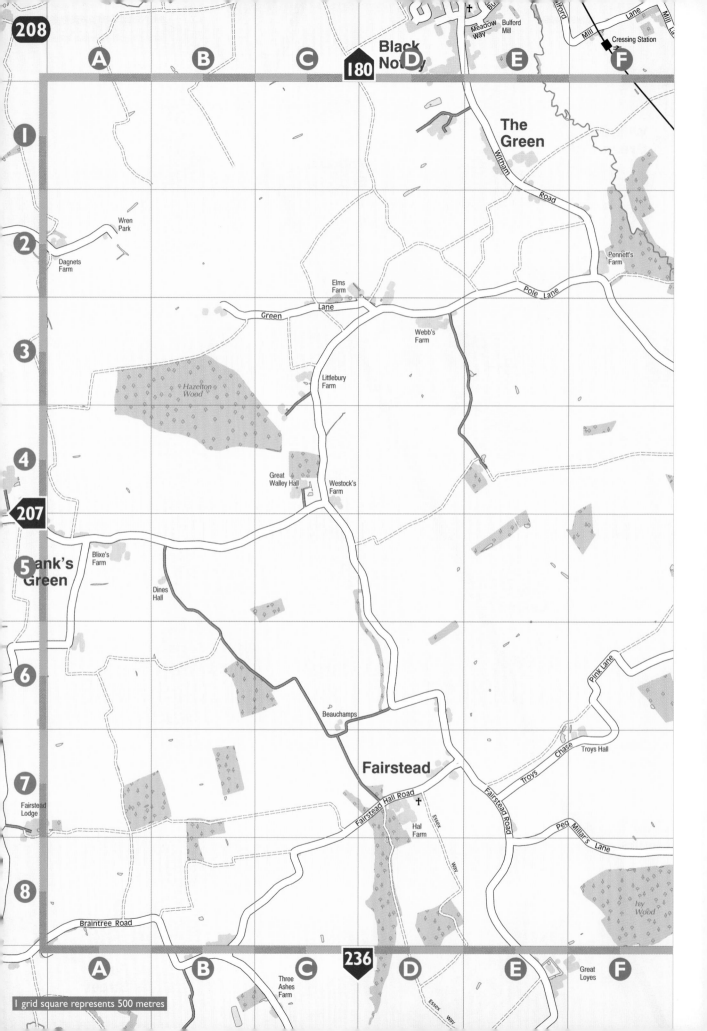

SILVER
END

182

Storey's Wood

A B C D E F

Doctors' Surgery

Daniel Way
Abraham

Valentine Way

Grooms Lane

School Road

Bowers Cl
Western Close

Western Lane

Boars Tye Road

Sheepcotes Lane

Primary School

Western Road

Park Gate Road

Porter's Farm

Parkgate Farm

Park Road

Sniveller's Lane

Ford Farm

Church Road

209

Rivenhall C of E
Primary School

PO

Tarecroft Wood

St Mary's Rd
Tusser Close

Beech Road

Hoo Hall

Rivenhall

Rickstones Road

Stovern's Hall

Oak Road

LC

Henry Dixon Road

Foxmead
Foxden

Southview School

Elm Hall County Primary School

Rickstones School

Elm Hall Farm

Conrad Road

Munro Road

Vigil Road

Blake Campbell Rd

Shaw Road

Hemingway Road

Bronte Road

Infant School

Rectory Lane

Forest Road

Cedar Drive
Elm Rise

Willow Rise

Poplar Close

Lime Cl

Rowan Way

CM8

Dorothy Sayers Drive

Laburnum Way

Yew Close

Ebenezer Close

Upper Acres

Cross Road

Junior School

LC

WITHAM

Oxlip Rd

Blackthorn

Glebe Crescent

Church St

St Nicholas Close

St Nicholas

Cemetery

Cress Road

Walnut Drive

Motts Lane

238

Oaks Golf Cl

Junr Cre

Waterside Business Park

A B C D E F

1 grid square represents 500 metres

K3
1 Croft Rd
2 Ratcliffe Ct

L2
1 Dowches Gdns
2 Mallard Cl

L3
1 Kingfisher Wy
2 Widgeon Pl

Monk's Farm

Pantlings   Lane

Felix Hall

Observer Way

Feering Primary School

Watermill Rd

Mill   Hall Farm Ct

Sherwood Way

Hunt Close

Driffield Close

Greenways

Barnfield

Worlds End

John Raven Court

River Blackwater

Kelvedon Station

Station Road

Feering

FEERING HILL

Leapingwells

Park Farm

Doucecroft School

Dowches Drive

Swan Street

Trews Gdns

Orchard Road

Tern Close

Heron Rd

Bittern Close

Avocet

Hollow   Road

Felix Place

Church Road

New Road

Rolley La

Glebe Road

Thorne Road

St Mary's Road

Kelvedon St Marys C of E Primary School

Canonium

Docwra Road

Curlew Close

Teal Way

Cemetery

LC

HIGH STREET

The Chase

B1024

Dunlin Court

KELVEDON

A12(T)

Church Street

Easterford Road

Riverside Way

Brockwell Lane

The Cloisters

Church Hall

Clark's Farm

LONDON ROAD

Maldon Road

B1024

Ewell   Hall   Chase

Ewell Hall

212

Highfields

Highfields Lane

Cranes   Lane

Crabb's Farm

Ashman's Farm

A12(T)

Hole Farm

River Blackwater

Durwards Hall

Brickhouse Farm

Kelvedon Hall Farm

Kelvedon Hall Lane

The Drive

Rivenhall End

M3
1 Gadwall Reach
2 Lapwing Dr

M1
1 Marshall Cl
2 Packe Cl

Hall Broad

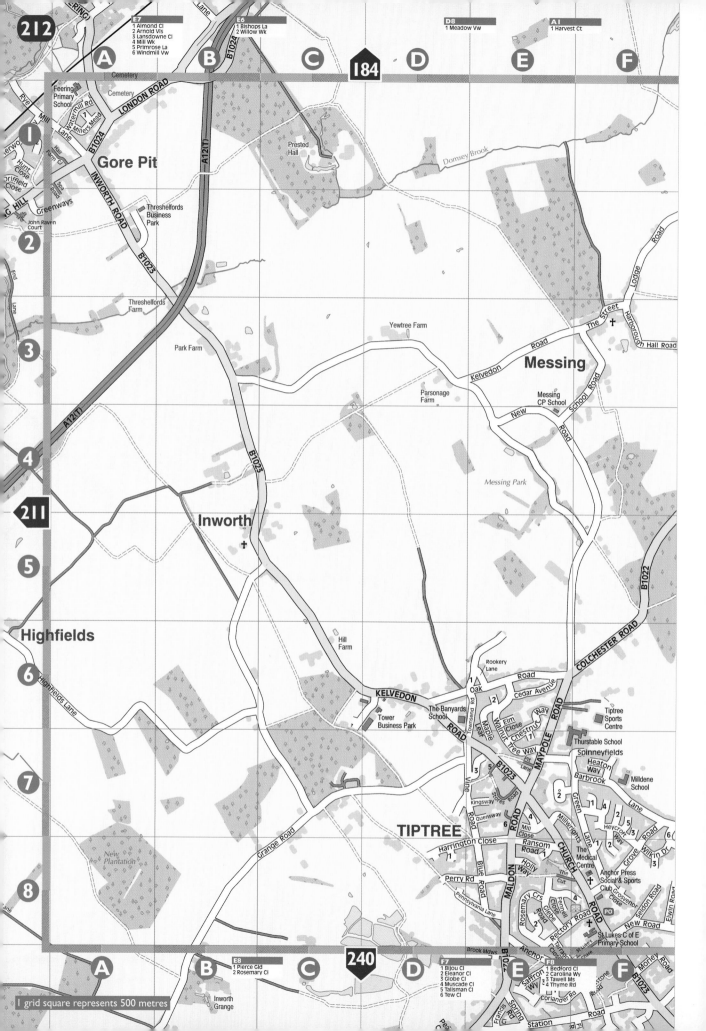

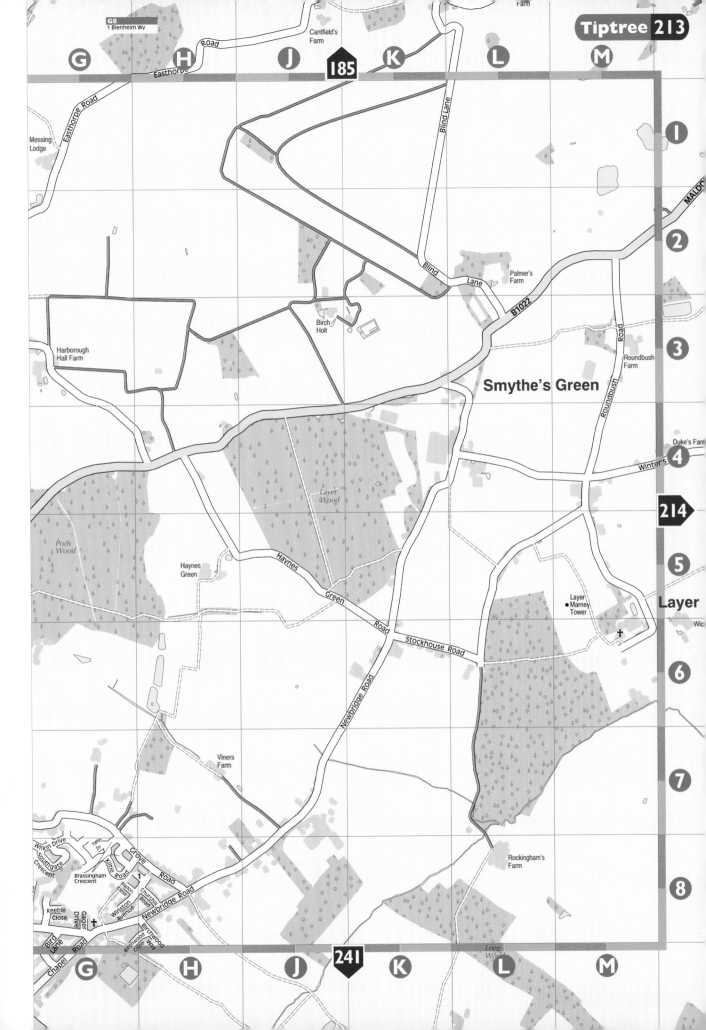

G8
1 Blenheim Wy

G H J K L M

I
2
MALD
3

185

Easthorpe Road
Road
Cantfield's Farm
Blind Lane
Blind
Lane
Palmer's Farm
B1022
Roundbush Farm
Messing Lodge
Easthorpe Road
Birch Holt
Smythe's Green
Roundbush Road
Duke's Farm
Harborough Hall Farm
4
Winter's
214
5
Layer
Layer Wood
Wic
Pods Wood
Layer Marney Tower
†
6
Haynes Green
Haynes Green Road
Stockhouse Road
Newbridge Road
7
Viners Farm
Rockingham's Farm
8
Wilkin Drive
Tiffin Dr
Southgate Crescent
Brassingham Crescent
Kittle Road
Grove Road
Rixton Close
Churchill Road
Winston Avenue
Keeble Close
Gager Drive
Newbridge Road
Bird Lane
Chapel Road
Birchwood Close
Birchwood Way
Long Wood
†
G H J K L M

241

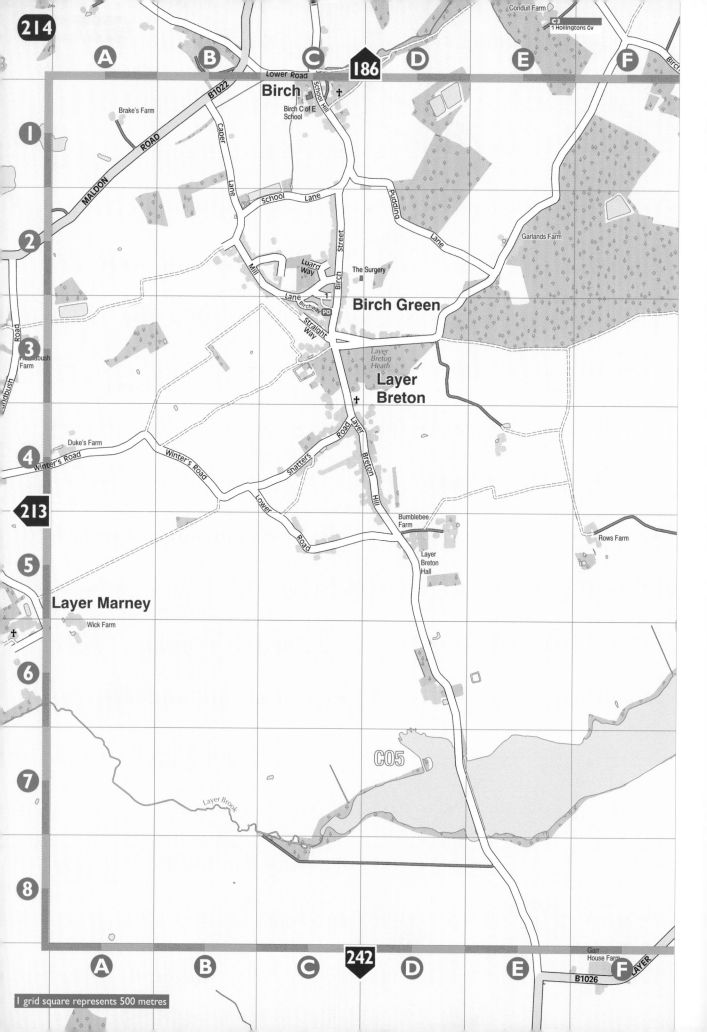

A   B   C   **186**   D   E   F

Conduit Farm

C3
1 Hollingtons Gv

Birch

Lower Road

B1022

Brake's Farm

MALDON ROAD

Birch C of E School

School Hill

1

Caper Lane

School Lane

Birch Street

Pudding Lane

Garlands Farm

2

Mill Lane

Luard Way

The Surgery

Birch Green

Road

Sandbush Farm

3

Birchway

PO

Straight Way

Layer Breton Heath

Layer Breton

213

Duke's Farm

Winter's Road

Winter's Road

Shatters Road

Lower Road

Layer Road

Layer Breton Hill

Bumblebee Farm

Rows Farm

4

5

Layer Marney

Wick Farm

Layer Breton Hall

6

C05

7

Layer Brook

Garr House Farm

8

A   B   C   **242**   D   E   F

LAYER

B1026

1 grid square represents 500 metres

Layer
de la Haye

G
H
J
K
L
M

I
2
3
4
216
5
6
7
8

Birch   Road
Malting
Green

CHURCH ROAD
Waterworks Close

Old Forge
Winstreet Cl
Green Acre Rd
Les Bois
Wood Fld
Hawfinch
Swallow Cl
Martin End
Yard
Great Ho
Farm Road

187

Abberton Road

Lo
House

Layer Road

WIGBOROUGH
ROAD
B1026

Layer
Hall

Rye Lane

Fields Farm
Road

Folly

Abberton Reservoir

Peldon
Lodge

Lodge
Lane

Peldon Road

Malting
Road

Peldon

Billets Farm

Harvey's Farm

Church
Road

Newports
Close

PO

ROAD

Stafford's Corner

School Lane

Moulsham's
Farm

243

Wigborough   Road

Lower   Road

Ne

Hyde Farm

G
H
J
K
L
M

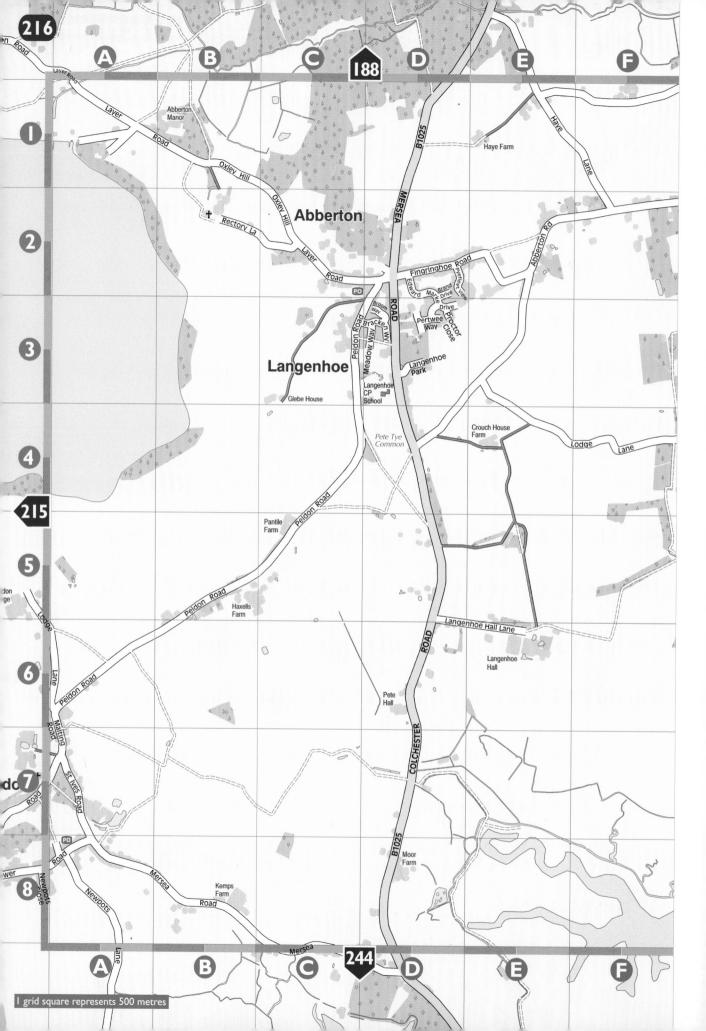

A   B   C   188   D   E   F

1

Layer Road

Layer   Road

Abberton Manor

Oxley Hill

2

Oxley Hill

† Rectory La   Abberton

Layer   Road

B1025

MERSEA

Haye Farm

Haye   Lane

Abberton Rd

Fingringhoe   Road

PO   Edward   Pertees View
Broom   Brand   Marke Drive
Way   Pertwee   Drive
Bracken Wy   Way   Proctor Close

3   Langenhoe   Peldon Road   ROAD

Langenhoe Park

Meadow Way

Glebe House   Langenhoe   Langenhoe
CP   School

4   Pete Tye   Crouch House
Common   Farm

Lodge   Lane

215

Peldon Road

Pantile
Farm

5   Peldon   Road   Haxells
Farm

Lodge   Lane

6   Peldon   Road

Langenhoe Hall Lane

Langenhoe
Hall

COLCHESTER   ROAD

Malting   Road

7   St Ives Road   Pete
Hall

Road   PO

Moor
Farm

B1025

8   Newpots Close   Mersea   Kemps
Farm

Newpots   Road

Lane   Mersea   Road

A   B   C   244   D   E   F

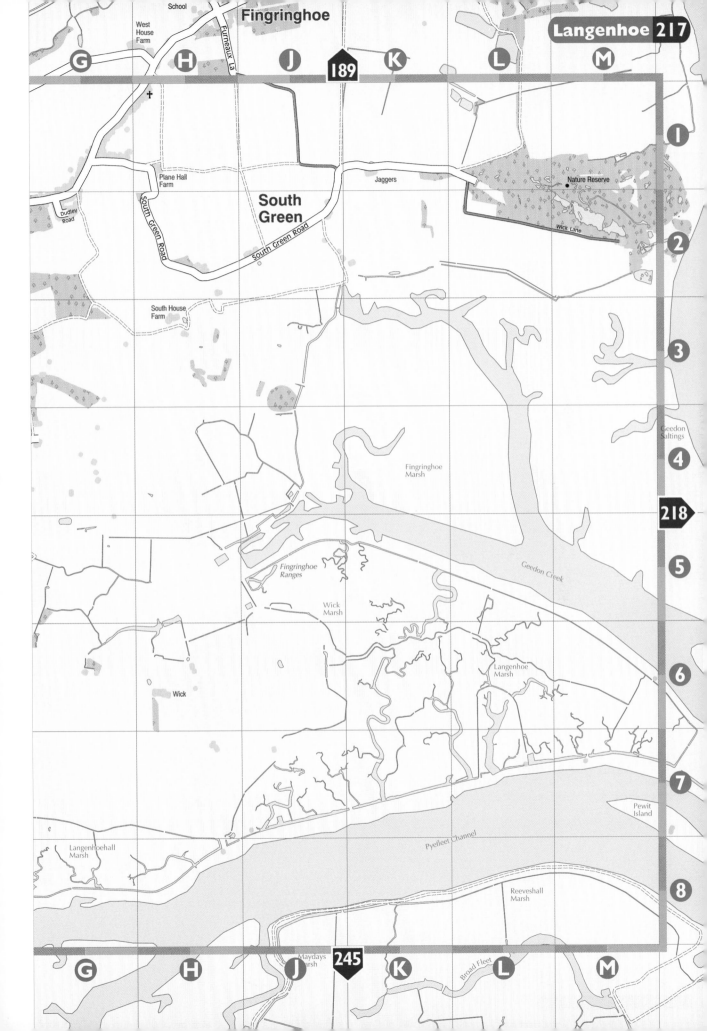

Fingringhoe

School

West
House
Farm

Furneaux La

189

Plane Hall
Farm

Dudtey
Road

South Green Road

South
Green

Jaggers

Wick Lane

Nature Reserve

South House
Farm

Geedon
Saltings

218

Fingringhoe
Marsh

Geedon Creek

Fingringhoe
Ranges

Wick
Marsh

Langenhoe
Marsh

Wick

Pewit
Island

Langenhoehall
Marsh

Pyefleet Channel

Reeveshall
Marsh

Maydays
Marsh

245

Broad Fleet

G H J K L M

I 2 3 4 5 6 7 8

A   B   C   D   E   F

Sixpenny Brook

Alresford Loc
The
Ford

Plumpton's
Farm

Alresford Creek

I

2

Aldboro
Point

Ford Lane

Moverons Lane

3

Moverons

Wapping Lane

BRIGHTLINGSE

Geedon
Saltings

†

River Colne

4

5

BRIGHTLING

Rat
Island

6

Elm Dr

Listor

Willd
Close

7

Pewit
Island

Promen

Western

8

Westmarsh
Point

A   B   C   D   E   F

1 grid square represents 500 metres

G4
1 Hythe Gv

G6
1 D'arcy Wy

H5
1 Hastings Pl
2 Winchelsea Pl

G5
1 Lodge Rd
2 Tudor Cl
3 The Woodlands

G **H** **J** **K** **L** **M**

191

B1027

CLACTON ROAD

Clover Drive

Hazel Close

B1027 CLACTON ROAD

220

Thors Farm

Gatehouse Farm

Greatmarsh Farm

Morses

Lowermarsh Farm

Lower Farm

Freelands

Eastman Point

Flag Creek

CHURCH

Samson's Road

Romney Close

St Andrew's Place

Fordwich Rd

Morses Lane

Folkards Lane

ROAD

The Colne Community School

Maltings

sarre Way

Samsons Close

Bateman Road

Churchill Cl

Camperwell Close

Barn Road

SEA

Red Lane

Dover Road

Dover Rd

Regent Cl

Bellfield Av

Stoney Lane

Robinson Road

ROAD

Deal Way

Love Lane

Sandwich Road

Cinque Road

Kent Road

Port Lane

Farm Walk

Manor House Way

Pertwee Close

B1029

Seaview Road

North Road

Brightlingsea United Football Club

Stanley Av

Chapel Road

Granville Way

Marennes Crescent

Dean Street

Upper Park Rd

Well Street

Pyefleet Close

Chestnut Drive

Spring Chase

Spring Road

Queen St

Springfields

Bayard Av

George Av

Beaumont Avenue

Whitehorse Rd

Greenhurst Road

Creekhurst Close

Park

Ash Cl

Cedar Av

Blanton Way

Walnut Way

Birch

Beacon Cl

Junior Sch

Infant School

Ladysmith Av

Edward Avenue

Richard Av

Elizabeth Wy

Albert Rd

Margaret Close

Chapel Rd

Link Rd

Hurst Close

Fair Close

Colne Medical Cen

Marsh Park

Western Rd

Eastern Rd

The Surgery

York Rd

Victoria Place

Anne Cl

Charles St

Tom May Ct

High Street

Hurst Green

Mill Street

STATION RD

Duke St

Nelson Street

NEW STREET

Sydney St

Tower Street

Lime Street

Tower St

Back Waterside Lane

Colne Road

B1029

Ophir Rd

WATERSIDE

Way

Prom

Oyster Tank Road

Sailing Club

University Yacht Club

Colne Yacht Club

Brightlingsea Creek

St Osyth Stone Point

Cindery Island

Brightlingsea Creek

St Osyth

East Essex Aviation Society & Museum

247

J7
1 Kirkhurst Cl

J6
1 Hill House Ct

H8
1 Copperas Rd
2 Francis St

H7
1 George Cut
2 Hall Cut
3 Thomas St
4 Wellington St
5 Windsor Ct

H6
1 Recreation Wy

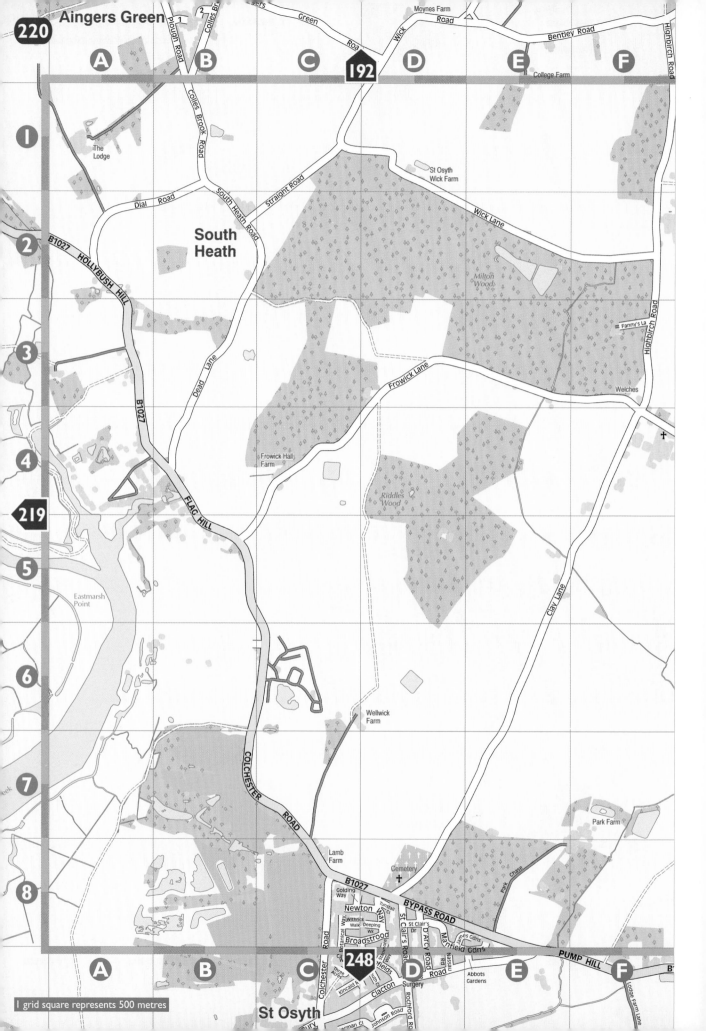

K7
1 Ashstead Cl
2 Bisley Cl
3 Holmwood Cl
4 Mychett Cl
5 Warnham Cl

L7
1 Caterham Cl
2 Cottage Gn
3 Daniell Cl
4 Deben Wk
5 Minsmere Dr
6 Smythe Cl

L8
1 Banister Cl
2 Woolwich Rd

Victoria Road
Green Roy

HARWICH ROAD
B1441
Connaught Road
Kempton Park
Amerells Rd
Feverills Road
Talbot Rd
Thorrington Rd
Henning Rd
Lotts Rd
Bateman's Road

THE STREET

High Birch
Maldon Wood
Ampers Wick

Honeypot Farm
Honeypot Lane
Rectory

193

B1441

Row Heath

Rectory Road

C016

Elm Road
Galloway Dr
PO

Little Clacton

Engaines Primary Sch

Barrington
Clapgate
Peartree Wy
St Osyth Drive
East
St Osyth Rd

Bertram Avenue
Alan Dr
Christopher Drive

Sunnyside Way
St Leys Dr
Hazelwood Crs
Stonehall

Heath Road
Hartleywood Farm

St Osyth Heath

Dead Lane

St Osyth Rd West
St

Osyth Road

B1442
LONDON

222

B1441

Bovill's Hall

Picker's Ditch

ROAD

High Grove

Hartley Wood

Long Grove

A133

Little Clacton Road

Rookwood Cl
Raycliff
Cswy Reach
Sheriffs Wy
Marion Av
Friars Cl
Way
Abbotts

Elm Farm

Brockham Wk
Ottershaw
Cranleigh
Ripley

Abinger
Dorking
Chipstead
Wk
Crescent
Edson Cl
Reigate Rd
Redgate
Mersham
Woolner Road
Dutterphine Rd
Sillett Cl
Middleton

Constable
Avenue
Cann Hall
Primary School
Sheppard Cl
Corman Rd
Ladbrooke Road
Westcote
Thorpe Cl
Munnings Dr
Crome Road

Bright Cl
Burrows
Blake Dr
Hunt

Purley Way
Cottage Gv
Bocking's Grove

Earls Hall

Bocking's Elm

St John's Rd
PO

B1027
ST JOHN'S ROAD
Orchard
Spring Cl
Land Cl
Autumn Way
Peter Bruff
Gilders
Finer Cl
Podham Way

Hendon Cl
Hanwell Cl
Stanmore Rd
Neasden Av

12

Critchfield

Great Clacton

8

Waterworks Dr

Duchess Farm

Hall Drive

B1027

Clare Way
Hatfield
Hadleigh Rd
Dedham Av
Nayland
Drive
Boxted Lane

Parry Drive
Kingsman
Hudson Cl
Young Cl

Wistaria Pl
Marigold
Fuchsia Wk
Camellia
Either Rd
Douglas

Coppins Green CP School

249

Bluehouse
Av
Battisford Dr
Snape Cl
Ongar
Levenham Way
Mendlesham Way
Polstead Way
Ravenscroft School

Hyacinth
Clematis Rd
Chrysthemum
Dahlia Cl
Ruston Dr
Stambridge Rd
Road
Coppins
M8
1 Kilburn Gdns
M7
1 Dupont Cl
Colbayns High School
Pathfields
Thomas
Melbourne
St Marks Rd
St Magdalen
LONDON

Waterworks Dr
School

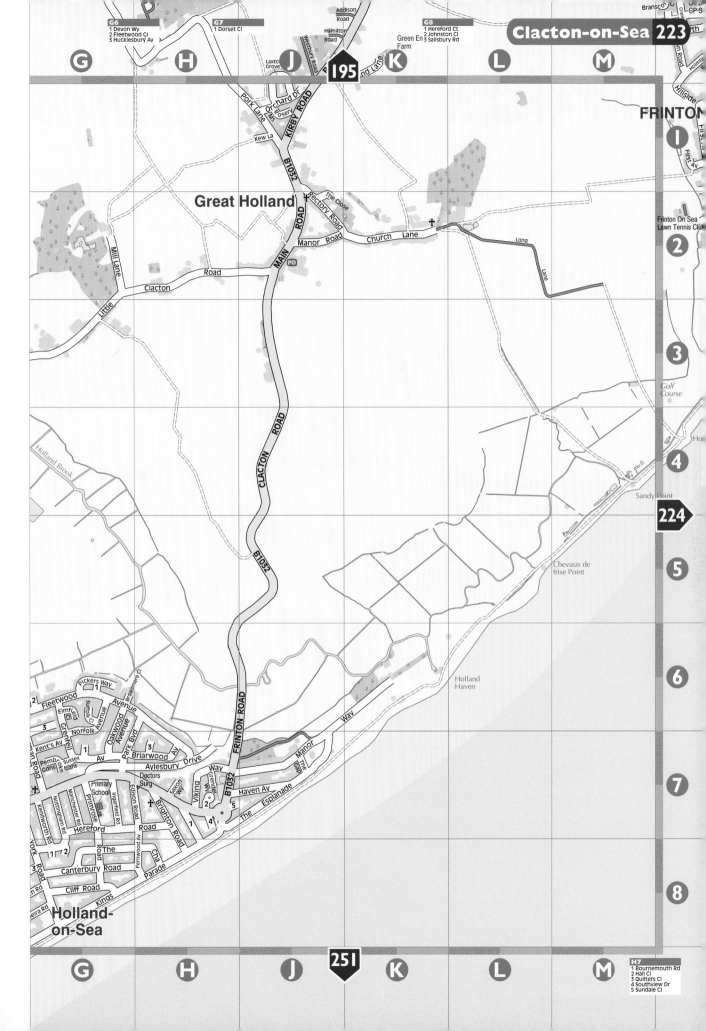

G6
1 Devon Wy
2 Fleetwood Cl
3 Hucklesbury Av

G7
1 Dorset Cl

G8
1 Hereford Ct
2 Johnston Cl
3 Salisbury Rd

FRINTON

G H J **195** K L M

I

2 Frinton On Sea
Lawn Tennis Club

Addison
Road

Hamilton
Road

Green En
Farm

Laxto
Grove

Orchard Dr
osery

Pork Lane

Kew La

Westbury Road

nd Lane

KIRBY ROAD

B1032

Great Holland

The Close

Rectory Road

Manor   Road   Church   Lane

MAIN   ROAD

PO

Long   Lane

3

Golf
Course

4

Sandy Point

224

5

Chevaux de
frise Point

6

Holland
Haven

Mill Lane

Little   Clacton   Road

Holland Brook

CLACTON   ROAD

B1032

FRINTON ROAD

Manor   Way

The Gap

Pickers Way

Fleetwood

Broadmere Cl

Elmf
eld

Grenfell

Suffolk

Norfolk

Avenue

Oakwood Avenue

Park Blvd

Av

Briarwood

Drive

Kent's Av

Pemb
Gdns

oke

Sussex

Icans

Aylesbury

Way

Grendel

Viking

Way

Doctors
Surg

B1032

Haven Av

The   Esplanade

Primary
School

Primrose

Inparfield Rd

Edison Rd

Brighton Road

Kenilworth Rd

Manchester Rd

Nottingham Rd

Hereford

Road

York

Road

The

Fernwood Av

Cha

Parade

Canterbury   Road

Cliff   Road

Kings

eira Rd

**Holland-
on-Sea**

7

8

G H J **251** K L M

H7
1 Bournemouth Rd
2 Hall Cl
3 Quilters Cl
4 Southview Dr
5 Sundale Cl

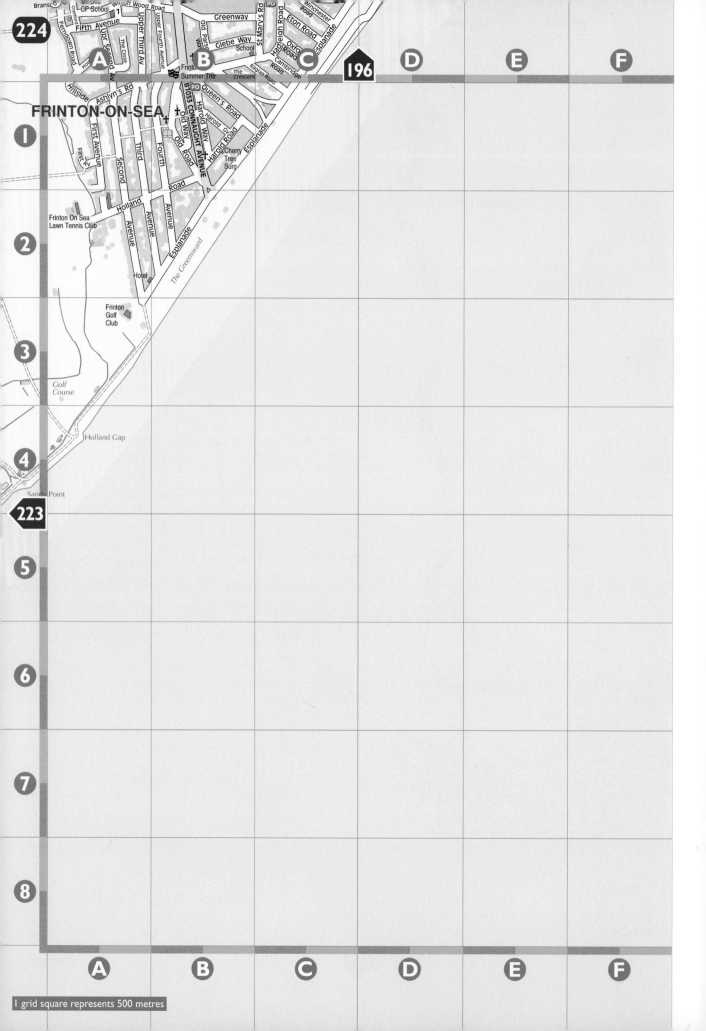

A B C 196 D E F

FRINTON-ON-SEA

Brans... GP School Witton Wood Road
Ferndown Road Fifth Avenue Upr Second Av Old Parso... Greenway
Camford The Close Glebe Way School St Mary's Rd Winchester
Upper Third Av Upper Fourth Avenue Frinton Eton Road
Hillside Ashlyn's Rd Summer Thtr The Crescent Oxfo... Esplanade
First Avenue B1033 CONNAUGHT AVENUE Queen's Road Cambridge Road
Harold Way Harold CVd Raglan Road

I
First Av Third Fourth Old Way Harold Road Esplanade
Second Avenue Road Cherry Tree Surg

2
Frinton On Sea Holland Avenue Avenue Esplanade
Lawn Tennis Club Avenue Avenue The Greensward
Hotel

Frinton Golf Club

3
Golf Course

Holland Gap

4
Sandy Point

5

6

7

8

A B C D E F

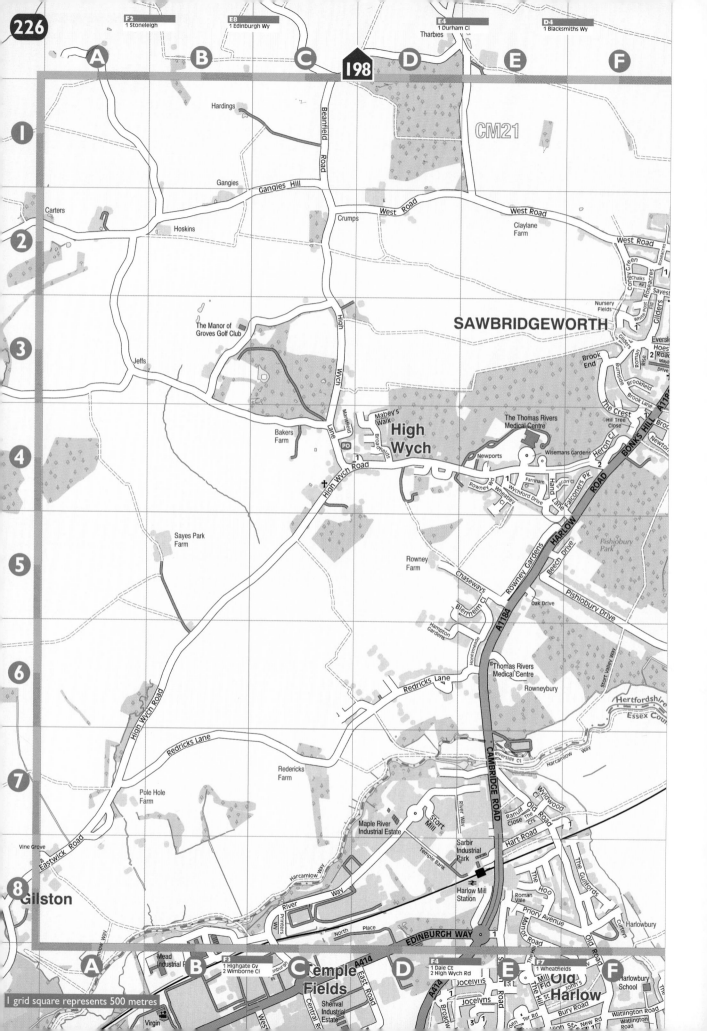

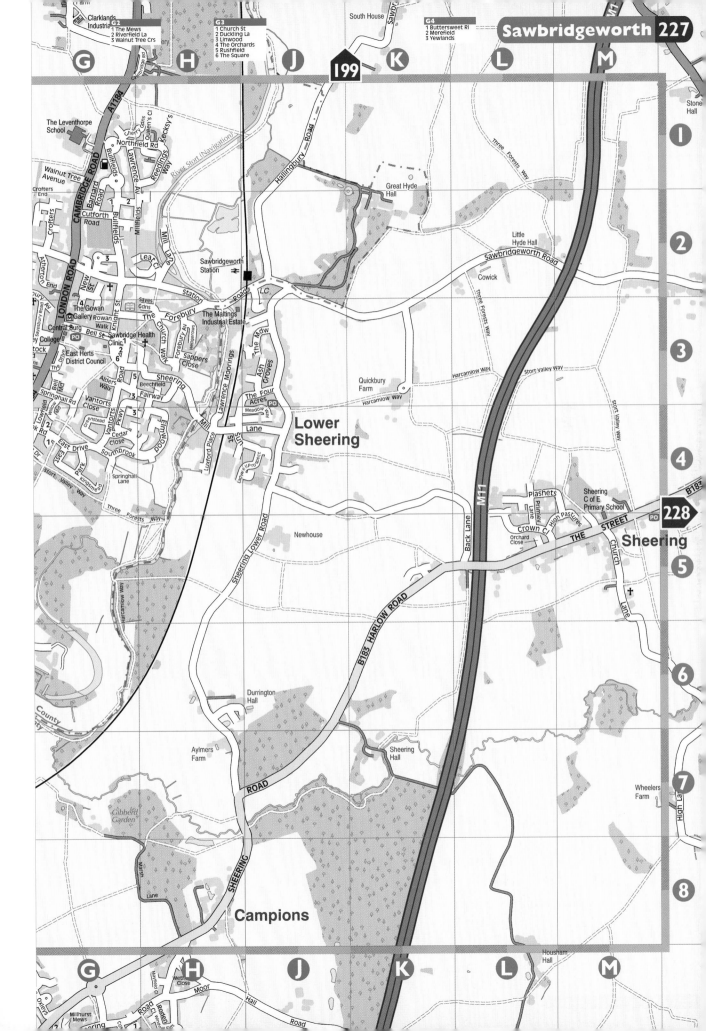

G H J 199 K L M

I
2
3
4
228
5
6
7
8

G2
1 The Mews
2 Riverfield La
3 Walnut Tree Crs

G3
1 Church St
2 Duckling La
3 Linwood
4 The Orchards
5 Rushfield
6 The Square

G4
1 Buttersweet Ri
2 Merefield
3 Yewlands

Clarklands
Industrial
The Leventhorpe
School
Walnut Tree
Avenue
Crofters
End
Crofters
Atherton's End
Aylesbury Av
Central Surg
College
East Herts
District Council
Springhall Rd
Vantorts
Close
East Drive
Park
Kingsme
Three Forests Way
Harcamlow Way
Gibberd
Garden
Marsh
Cambridge Rd
A1184
CAMBRIDGE ROAD
LONDON ROAD
Northfield Rd
Lawrence Av
Bullfields
Barnard Road
Cutforth Road
Mill Lane
Queen's Cl
Reedings
Kecksy's
New St
Knight St
Bell St
The Gowan Gallery
Rowan Walk
Sawbridge Health Clinic
PO
Church Walk
Forebury Av
Hedgerows
Sappers Close
The Forebury
The Maltings Industrial Estate
Sheering
Beechfield
Fairway
Vantorts Close
Cedar Close
Elmwood
Southbrook
Springhall Lane
Orenstead
Mill Road
Lawrence Moorings
Luxford Place
Ash Groves
The Mdw
The Four Acres
Meadow
PO
Ladywell Prospect
Sun St
River Stort (Navigation)
Mill Lane
Sawbridgeworth Station
Station Road
LC
Saves Gdns
Hallingbury Road
South House
Sawbr
Stone Hall
Great Hyde Hall
Little Hyde Hall
Sawbridgeworth Road
Cowick
Three Forests Way
Three Forests Way
Harcamlow Way
Harcamlow Way
Stort Valley Way
Stort Valley Way
Quickbury Farm
M11
Lower Sheering
Sheering Lower Road
Newhouse
B183 HARLOW ROAD
Durrington Hall
Aylmers Farm
ROAD
SHEERING
SHEERING
Lane
Back Lane
Plashets
Primley Lane
Crown C
Orchard Close
High Pastures
Sheering C of E Primary School
THE STREET
PO
B18
Sheering
Church Lane
Sheering Hall
Wheelers Farm
High La
Housham Hall
Millhurst Mews
Weth Close
Moor
Hall
Road
Campions

G H J K L M

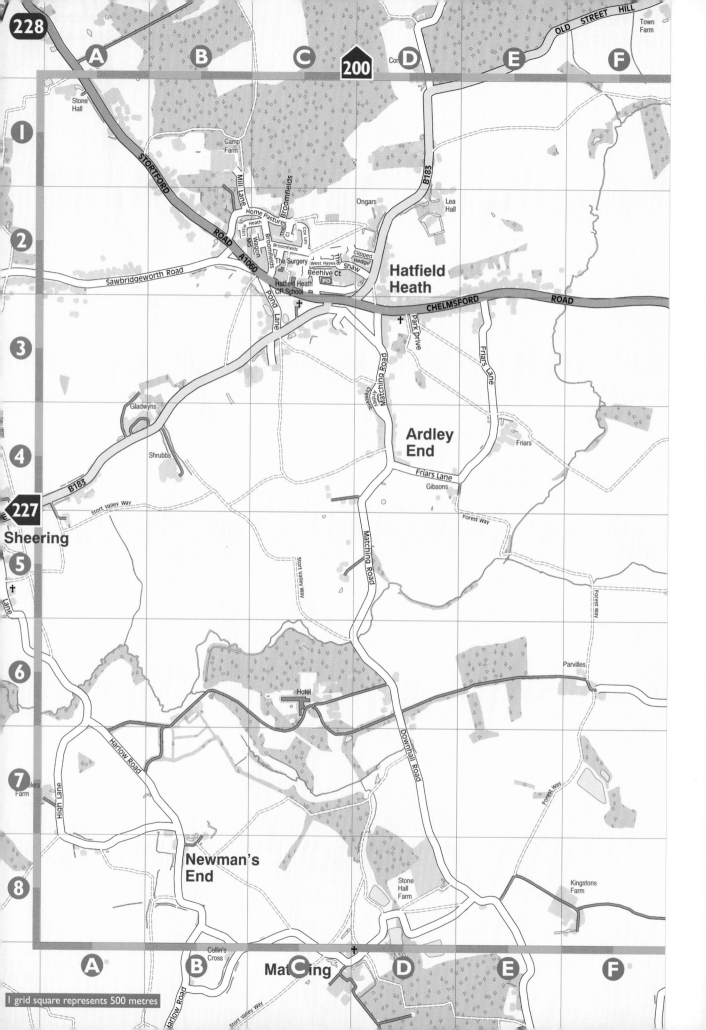

200

227

Sheering

Hatfield Heath

Ardley End

Newman's End

Mat**C**ing

Stone Hall

Camp Farm

STORTFORD

Mill Lane

Home Pastures

Broomfields

Heath Cl

Wagon

The Cl

Cox Ley

Broomfields

ROAD

A1060

The Surgery

West Hayes

Beehive Ct

PO

Hatfield Heath CP School

Sawbridgeworth Road

Pond Lane

Shaw

Clipped Hedge

Ongars

Lea Hall

B183

Cor

CHELMSFORD ROAD

Park Drive

Friar's Lane

Ardley Crescent

Matching Road

Gladwyns

Shrubbs

B183

Stort Valley Way

Stort Valley Way

Stort Valley Way

Friars

Friars Lane

Gibsons

Forest Way

Forest Way

Forest Way

Parvilles

Hotel

Downhall Road

Harlow Road

High Lane

elers Farm

Collin's Cross

Harlow Road

Stone Hall Farm

Kingstons Farm

OLD STREET HILL

Town Farm

I 2 3 4 5 6 7 8

A B C D E F

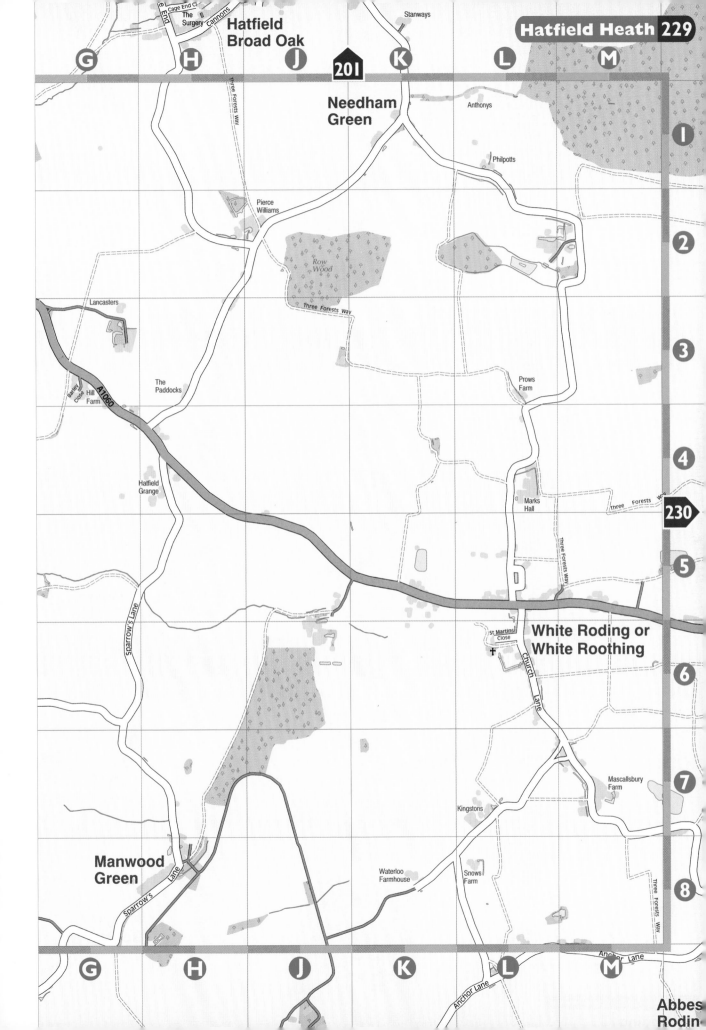

G H J 201 K L M

Cage End Cl
The
Surgery
Cannons
Hatfield Broad Oak

Stanways

Anthonys

I

Needham Green

Philpotts

Pierce Williams

2

Row Wood

Three Forests Way

Lancasters

3

Prows Farm

The Paddocks

A1060

Barley Close Hill Farm

4

Hatfield Grange

Marks Hall

Three Forests Way

230

Three Forests Way

5

Sparrow's Lane

St Martins Close

White Roding or White Roothing

Church Lane

6

Mascallsbury Farm

7

Kingstons

Manwood Green

Sparrow's Lane

Waterloo Farmhouse

Snows Farm

Three Forests Way

8

G H J K L M

Anchor Lane

Anchor Lane

Abbes Rodin

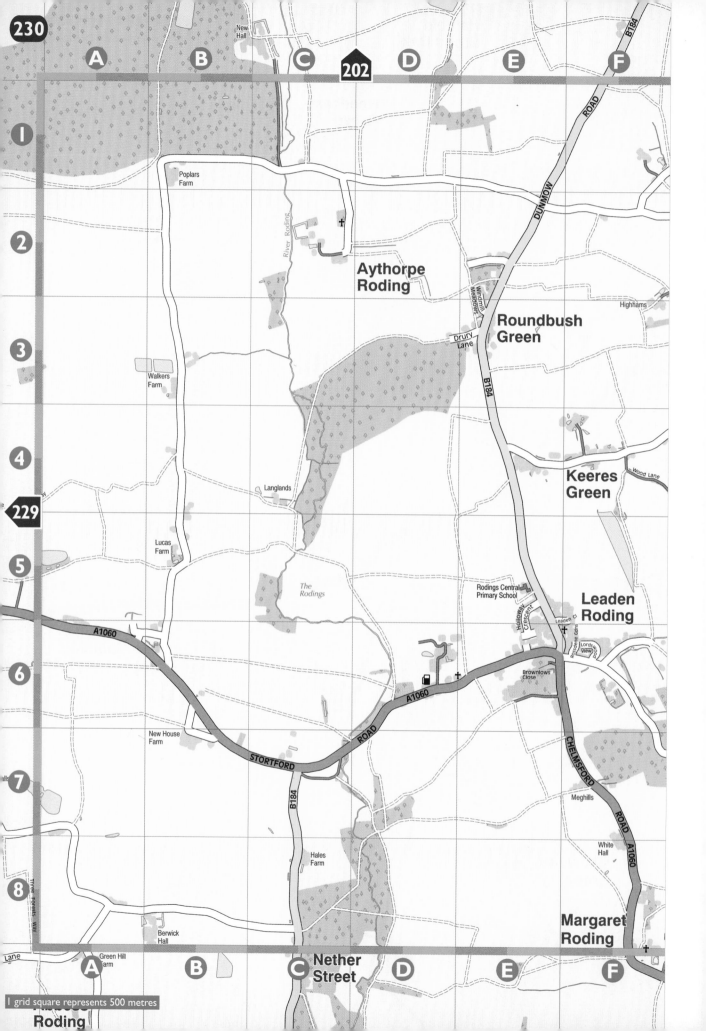

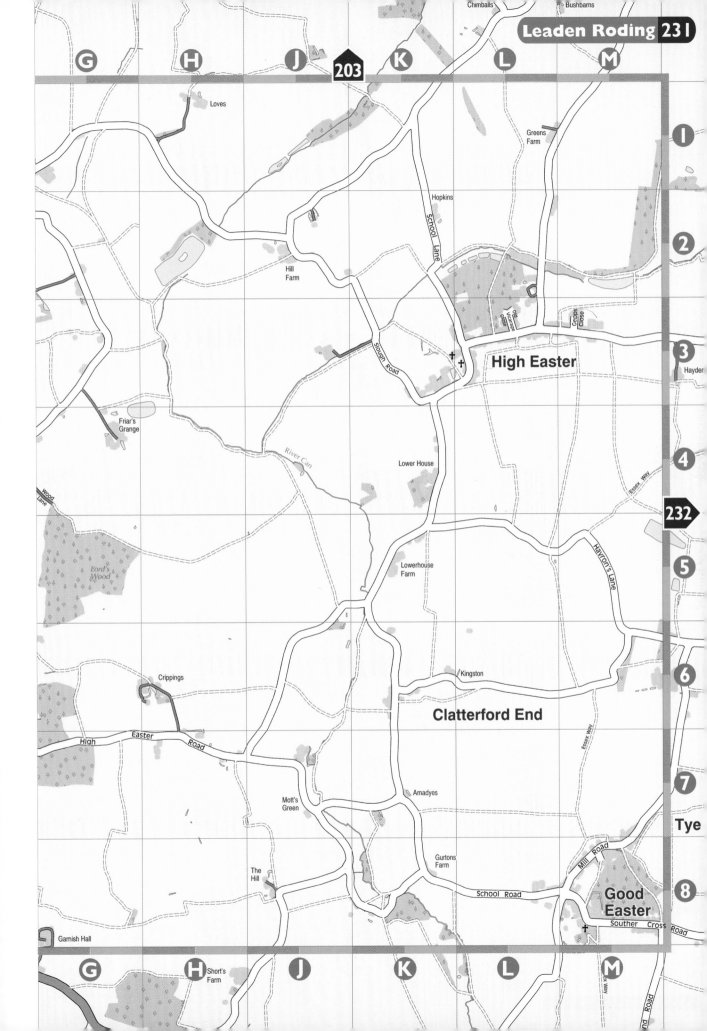

Chimballs

Bushbarns

G   H   J   **203**   K   L   M

Loves

Greens
Farm

I

Hopkins

School Lane

2

Hill
Farm

Old
Vicarage
Green

Gepps
Close

High Easter

3

Hayder

Friar's
Grange

River Can

Lower House

4

Wood
Lane

Essex Way

232

Lord's
Wood

Lowerhouse
Farm

Havron's Lane

5

Crippings

Kingston

Essex Way

6

Clatterford End

High   Easter   Road

7

Mott's
Green

Amadyes

Tye

Mill Road

Gurtons
Farm

The
Hill

School   Road

**Good
Easter**

8

Souther   Cross   Road

Garnish Hall

G   H   J   K   L   M

Short's
Farm

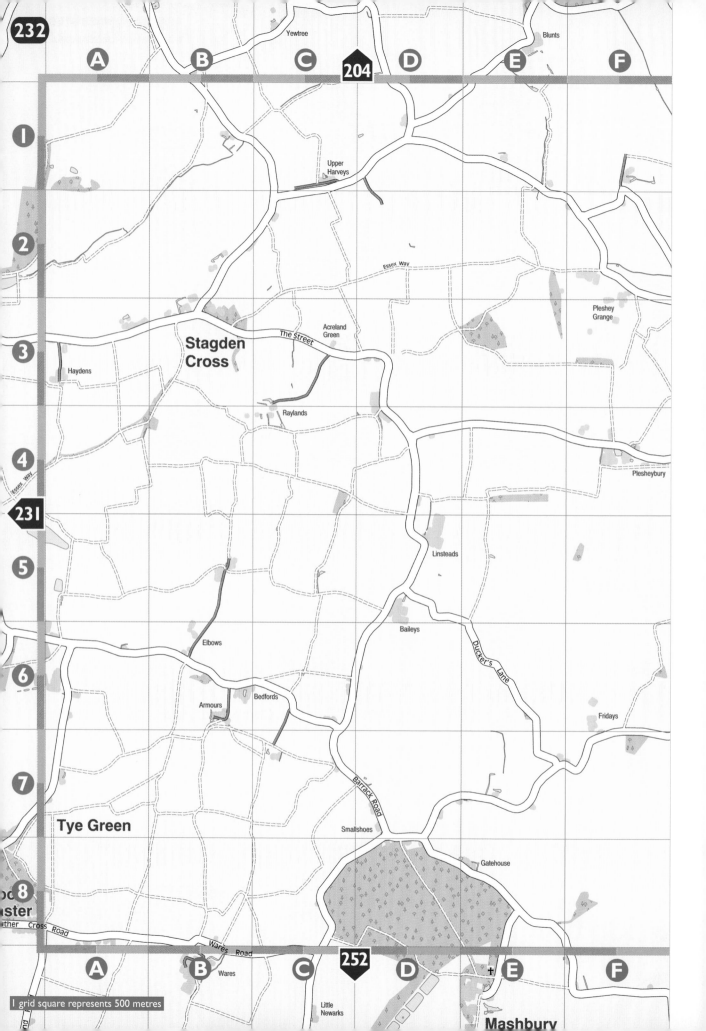

A B C **204** D E F

I

Yewtree

Blunts

Upper
Harveys

2

Essex Way

Pleshey
Grange

3

The street

Acreland
Green

**Stagden
Cross**

Haydens

Raylands

4

Essex Way

Plesheybury

231

5

Linsteads

Baileys

Ducker's Lane

6

Elbows

Bedfords

Fridays

Armours

7

Barrack Road

Tye Green

Smallshoes

Gatehouse

8

ster

ther Cross Road

Wares Road

A B C **252** D †E F

Wares

Little
Newarks

Mashbury

Ringtail
Green

G   H   J   205   K   L   M

I

Park Lane

Rolphy
Green

Pleshey Road

Park
Farm

2

Croft Lane

Grange Road

Pleshey

Oak
Hall

3

Woolmers
Mead

Vicarage Road

Back Lane

Essex Way

Pump
Lane

Waltham
Bury

4

Essex Way

234

Bury Lane

Fitzjohn's
Farm

5

Barrack La

High
Houses

Great
Waltha

6

Humphrey's Farm Lane

Bards
Hall

Mashbury Road

Israel's Farm

Humphrey's
Farm

Breeds

7

Fanner's
Green

8

G   H   J   253   K   L   M

Beadle's
Hall

Wal
Farm

Dyers

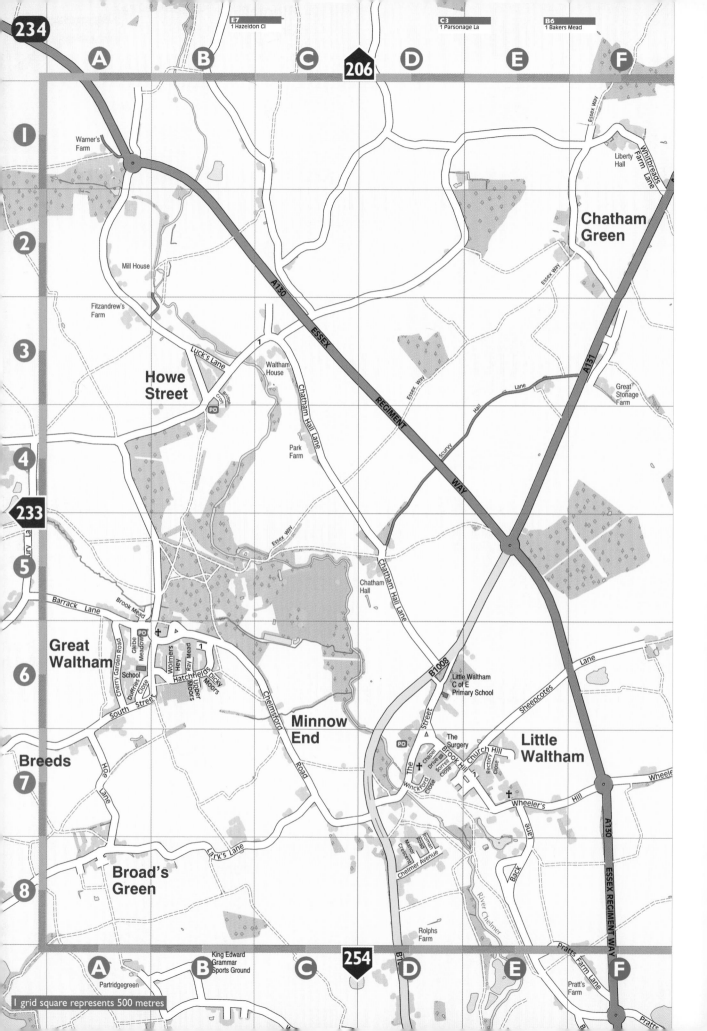

G H J 207 K L M

THE CRESC

A131 STRAWBROOK HILL

Goodmans Lane

Lowley's Farm

Essex Way

Essex Way

Fuller Street

Lyons Hall

Cole Hill

River Ter

Sandy Wood

Boreham Road

Daisleys Lane

Leylar Farm

Lyonshall Wood

White House Farm

Wakering's Farm

Long's Farm

Longs Lane

Noake's Farm

Boreham Road

Bird's Farm

Sheepcotes Farm

Alstead's Farm

Drakes Lane

Drakes Lane

Drake's Farm

Drakes Lane Industrial Estate

Lawns Farm

Boreham Road

Russell Green

Leighs Road

's Hill

Power's Farm

Domsey Lane

Peverel's Farm

Bre Ha

255

G H J K L M

Boreham Airfield

I

2

3

4

236

5

6

7

8

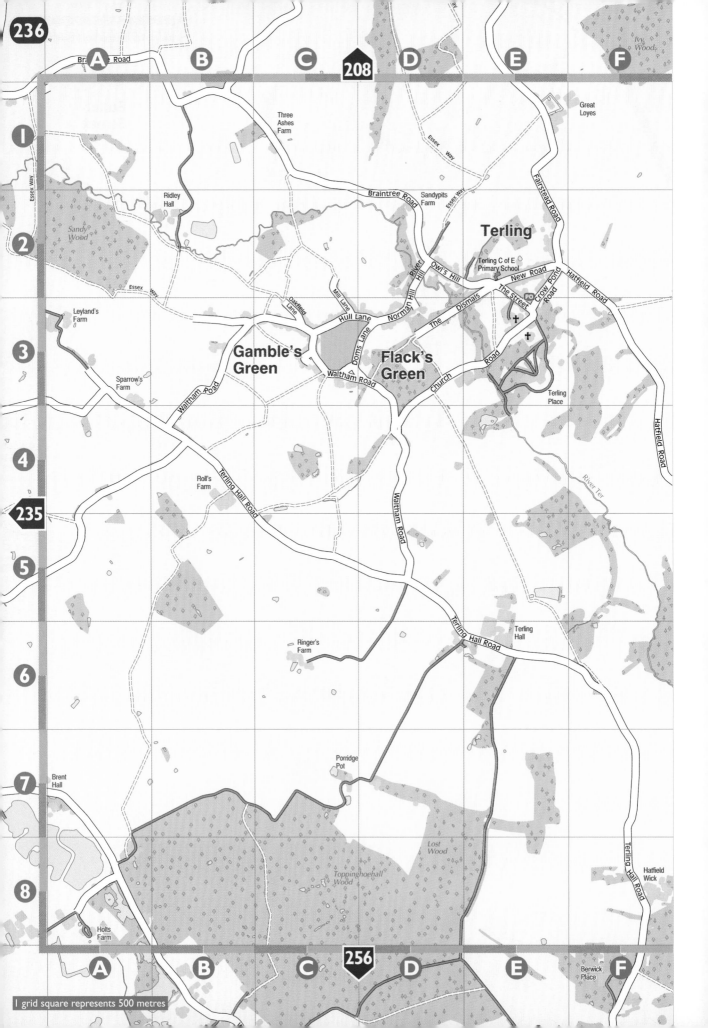

Ⓐ   Ⓑ   Ⓒ   Ⓓ   Ⓔ   Ⓕ

Ⓘ

Great
Loyes

Ivy
Wood

Essex Way

Three
Ashes
Farm

Ⓘ

Essex Way

Ridley
Hall

Braintree Road

Sandypits
Farm

Essex Way

Fairstead Road

Terling

Ⓑ

Sandy
Wood

Terling C of E
Primary School

New Road

Hatfield Road

Essex Way

Oakfield
Lane

Hull Lane

Mill Lane

Norman Hill

Owl's Hill

River

The Street

Crow Pond Road

PO

✝

✝

Gamble's
Green

Leyland's
Farm

Doms Lane

The Dismals

Ⓑ

Sparrow's
Farm

Flack's
Green

Church Road

Terling
Place

Waltham Road

Waltham Road

Ⓐ

Roll's
Farm

Terling Hall Road

River Ter

Hatfield Road

Ⓔ

Ringer's
Farm

Terling Hall Road

Terling
Hall

Ⓕ

Porridge
Pot

Ⓖ

Brent
Hall

Lost
Wood

Terling Hall Road

Ⓗ

Toppinghoehall
Wood

Hatfield
Wick

Holts
Farm

Berwick
Place

Ⓐ   Ⓑ   Ⓒ   Ⓓ   Ⓔ   Ⓕ

1 grid square represents 500 metres

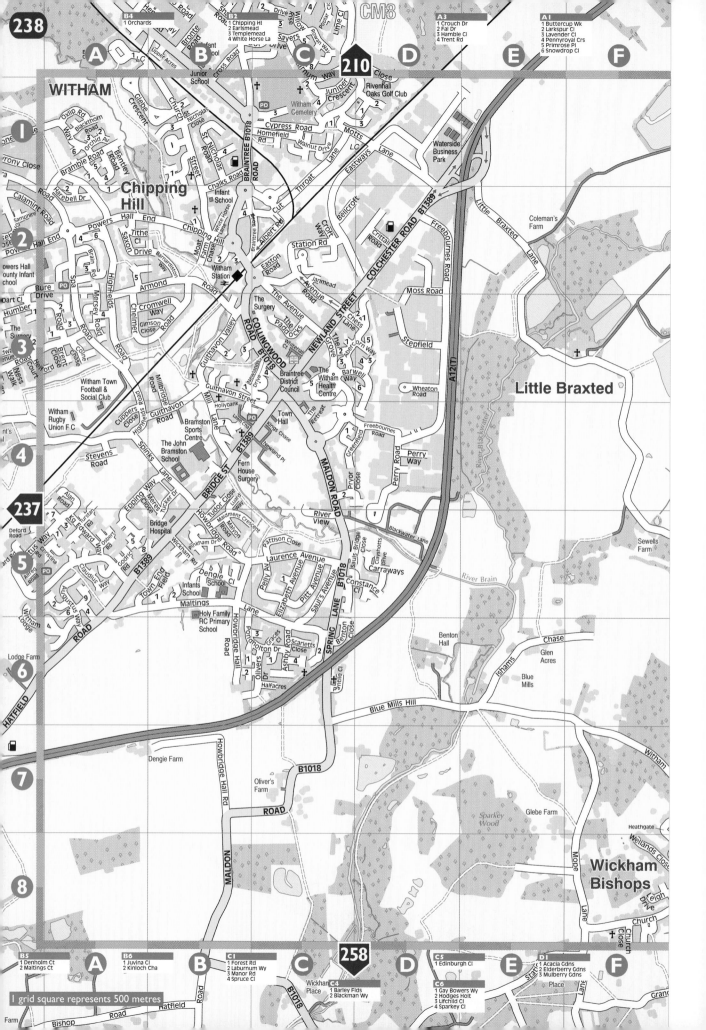

G H J **211** K L M

I

2

3

Braxted Park House

The Avenue

Hall Broad Farm

Church Chase

Great Braxted Hall

Noak's Cross

Sextons Lane

Tiptree Road

PH

Great Braxted

4

Bung Row

PO

Braxted Lane

240

5

Broomfield's Farm

Lea Lane

Threadgold's Farm

Hale's Farm

Rookery Lane

Kings Rd

Brickspring

Eaton Way

6

Gre Tot

Spring

Mill

Road

Chapel Road

Mount Pleasa Est

Mount

Green Man Lane

Chantry Wood

Carters Lane

Braxted Road

Road

Maclarens Hill

Beacon Hill

Road

Mountains

Mountains

COLCHESTER ROAD

Mount Lodge Chase

7

Beacon Hill

Goat Lodge Road

To Hi

Beacon Road

The Surgery

Finch's

Birch Rise

Road

Wellands Road

The Tiptree

The Street

Arbour Lane

Beech Green

Poney Chase

PO

Holt Dr

Kelvedon

B1022

Beckingham Road

8

Blacksmiths Lane

Byron Dr

Roots Lane

Longmead

School Road

Great Totham Road

PH

Maypole

Walden

Great Totham County Primary School

House Warren

Forrester Park Golf & Tennis Club

ROAD

To Hi

Gre Totham

Crabb's Farm

Lane

Prince

Catchpole Lane

Morr

Hefor Way

MALDON ROAD

seagers

ullways

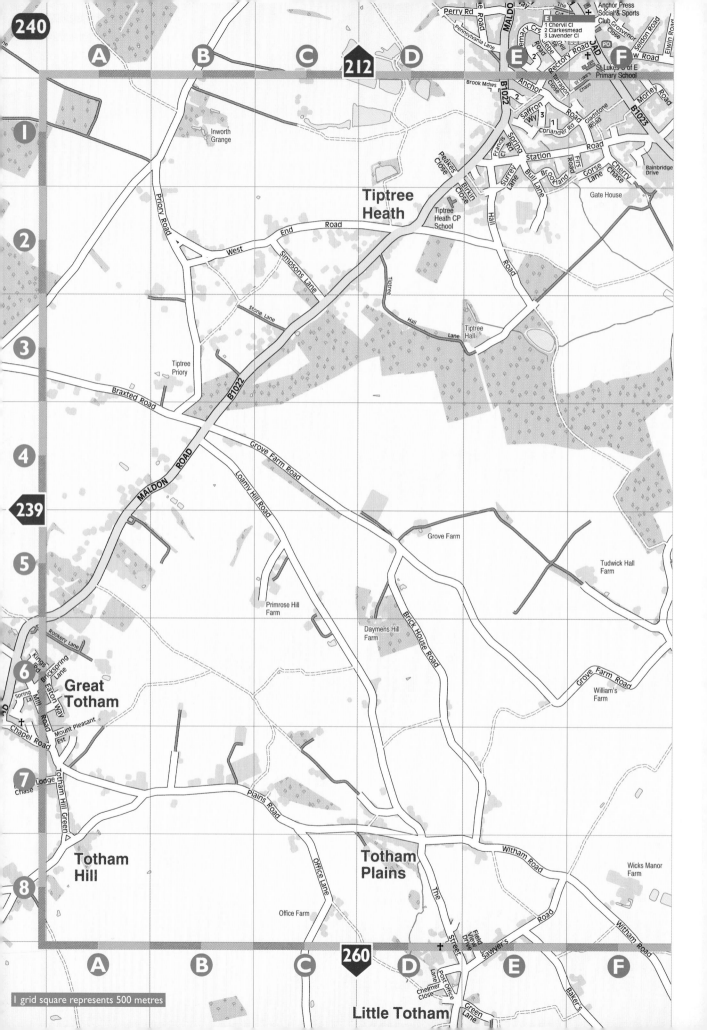

G H J 213 K L M

I

2

3

4

242

5

6

7

8

Paternoster Heath

FACTORY HILL

Tudwick Road

Chapel Road

Bird Lane

Keeble Close

Brassingham Crescent

Winston Avenue

Churchill Road

Newbridge Road

Birchwood Way

Birchwood Close

Laver Brook

Brook Close

Strawberry La

D'ARCY ROAD

Knight Cl

PO

The Folly

Brook Road

Hawthorn Road

Blackthorn Way

Stockhouse Cl

Barnhall Road

Gobolt's Farm

Park Lane

Park Farm

Long Wood

Barn Hall Farm

Barnhall Road

Tolleshunt Knights

B1023

Top Road

Oxley Green

OXLEY HILL

Blind Lane

Honeypot Lane

Rectory Road

High Hall

Green Lane

Tuckett's Farm

Lower Farm

B1023

KELVEDON ROAD

Pointers Farm

Home Farm

Tudwick Road

D'Arcy Gate

Limesbrook

G H 261 J K L M

Frame Farm

Chase Jl

The

Renters Farm

PO

NORTH STREET

SOUTH STREET

Tolleshunt D'Arcy

Salter's Meadow

Festival Gdns

CHURCH ST

Tolleshunt Darcy C of E Primary School

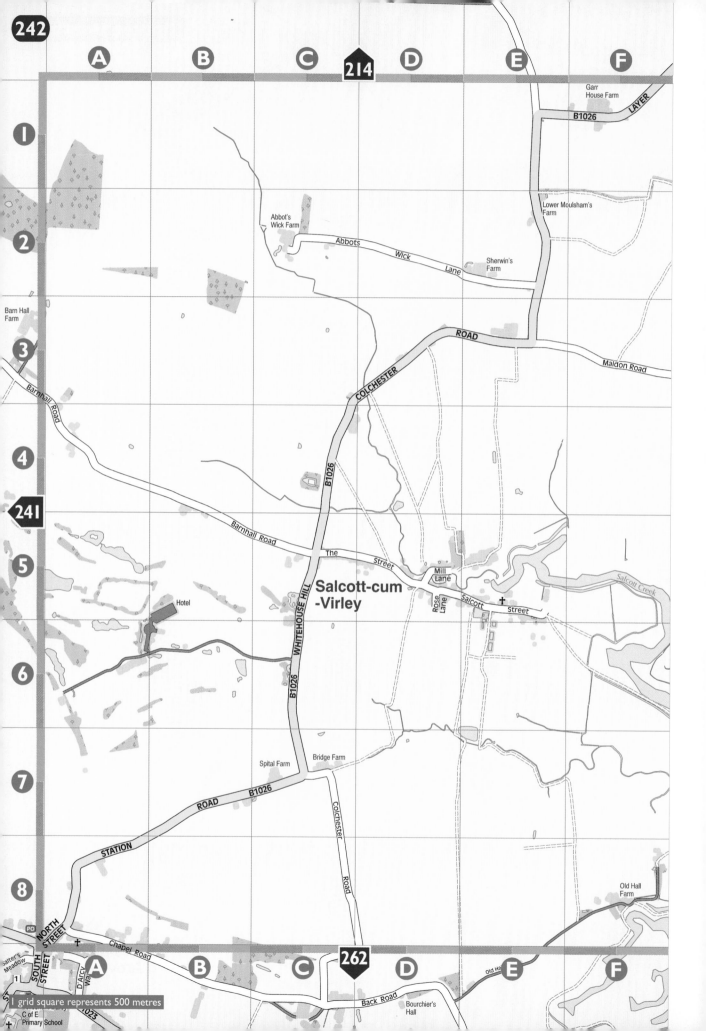

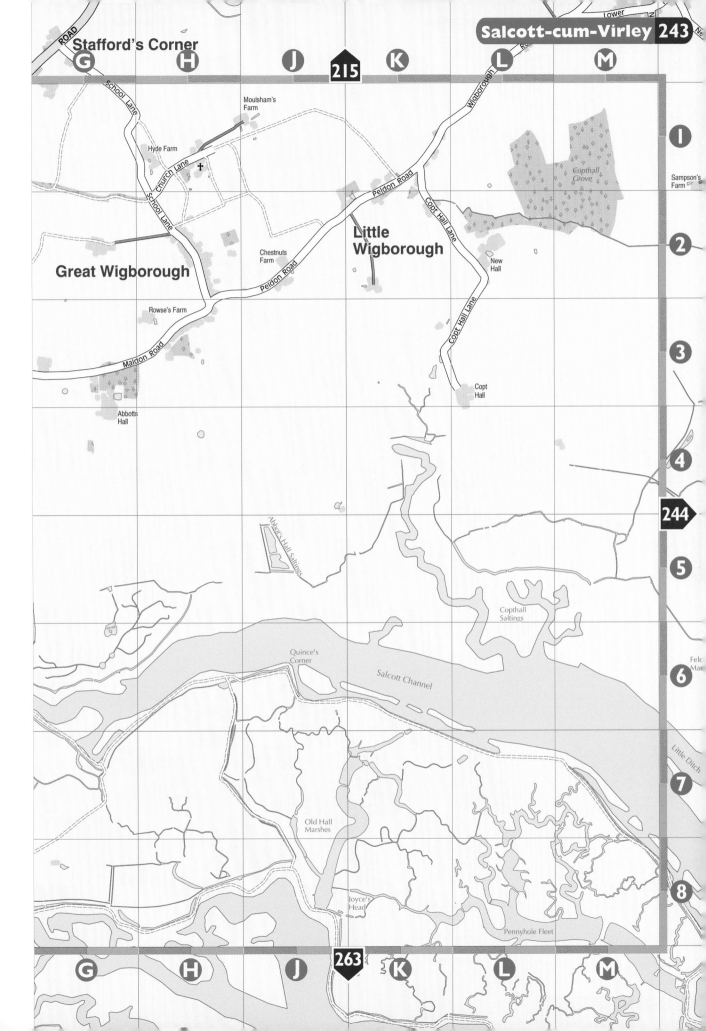

Stafford's Corner

G **H** **J** 215 **K** **L** **M**

ROAD

School Lane

Moulsham's Farm

Hyde Farm

Church Lane

Peldon Road

Wigborough Road

I

Copthall Grove

Sampson's Farm

2

Little Wigborough

Chestnuts Farm

Copt Hall Lane

New Hall

Great Wigborough

School Lane

Peldon Road

Rowse's Farm

Maldon Road

Copt Hall Lane

Copt Hall

3

Abbotts Hall

4

Abbot's Hall Saltings

244

5

Copthall Saltings

Quince's Corner

Salcott Channel

6

Feld Mai

Little Ditch

7

Old Hall Marshes

Joyce's Head

8

Pennyhole Fleet

G **H** **J** 263 **K** **L** **M**

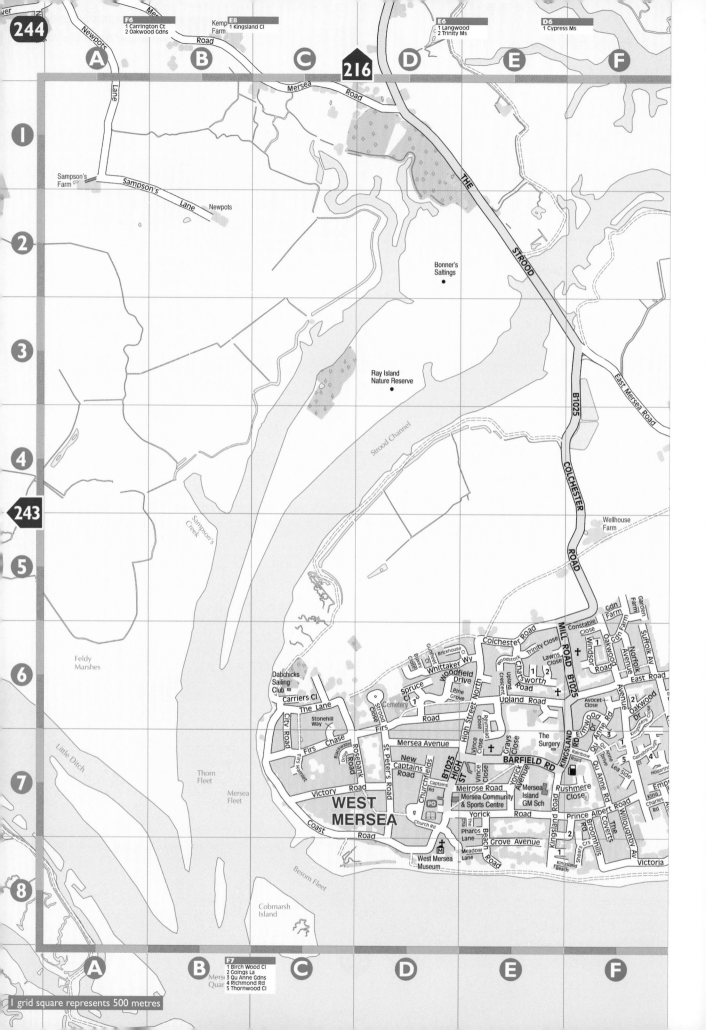

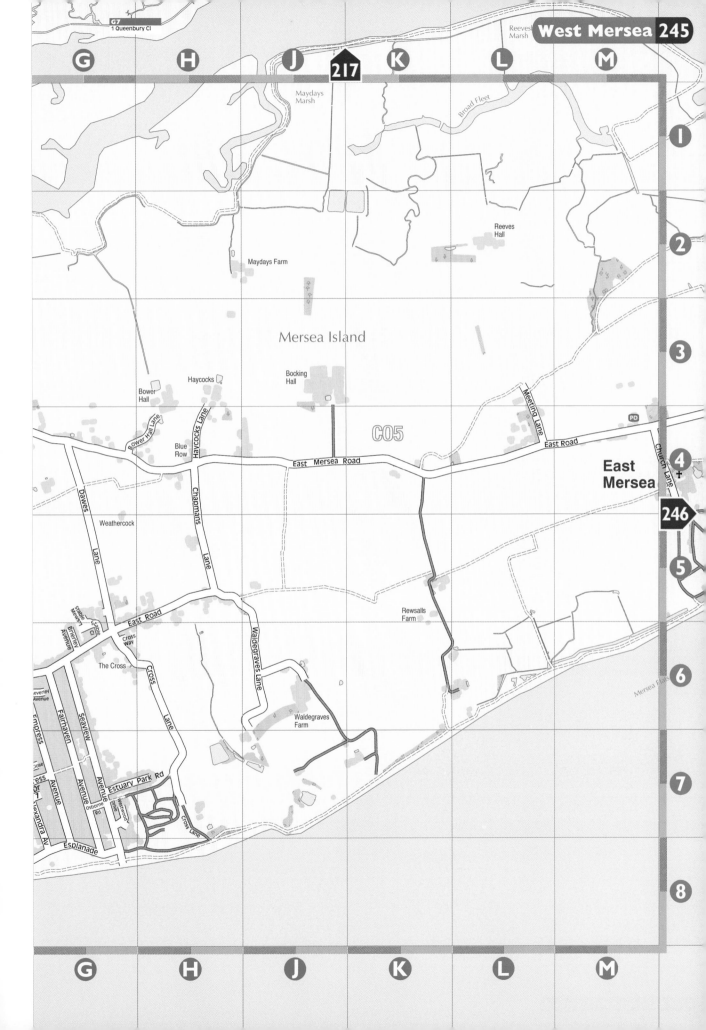

G7
1 Queenbury Cl

G · H · J · 217 · K · L · M

1

2

3

4

5

6

7

8

Reeves Marsh

Maydays Marsh

Broad Fleet

Reeves Hall

Mersea Island

Maydays Farm

Bower Hall

Haycocks

Bocking Hall

Meeting Lane

East Road

PD

East Mersea

246

Bower Hall Lane

Haycocks Lane

Blue Row

East Mersea Road

C05

Church Lane

Dawes Lane

Weathercock

Chapmans Lane

East Road

Stable Mews

Brierley Avenue

Cross Way

The Cross

Cross Lane

Waldegraves Lane

Rewsalls Farm

Mersea Flats

Beverley Avenue

Fairhaven Avenue

Seaview Avenue

Empress Avenue

Avenue

Alexandra Av

Avenue

Estuary Park Rd

Osborne Rd

Westwood Drive

Waldegraves Farm

Cross Lane

Esplanade

G · H · J · K · L · M

A   B   C   218   D   E   F

I

2

3

PO

4
 as
ersea

245

5

6

7

8

A   B   C   D   E   F

Promenade
Western
Westmarsh
Point

Ivy House
Nature
Reserve

Mersea
Stone

Ivy Lane

East Road

North
Barn

Broman's
Farm

Broman's   Lane

East Road
Fen Farm

Cudmore Grove
Country Park

Shop Lane

Church Lane

Mersea Flats

1 grid square represents 500 metres

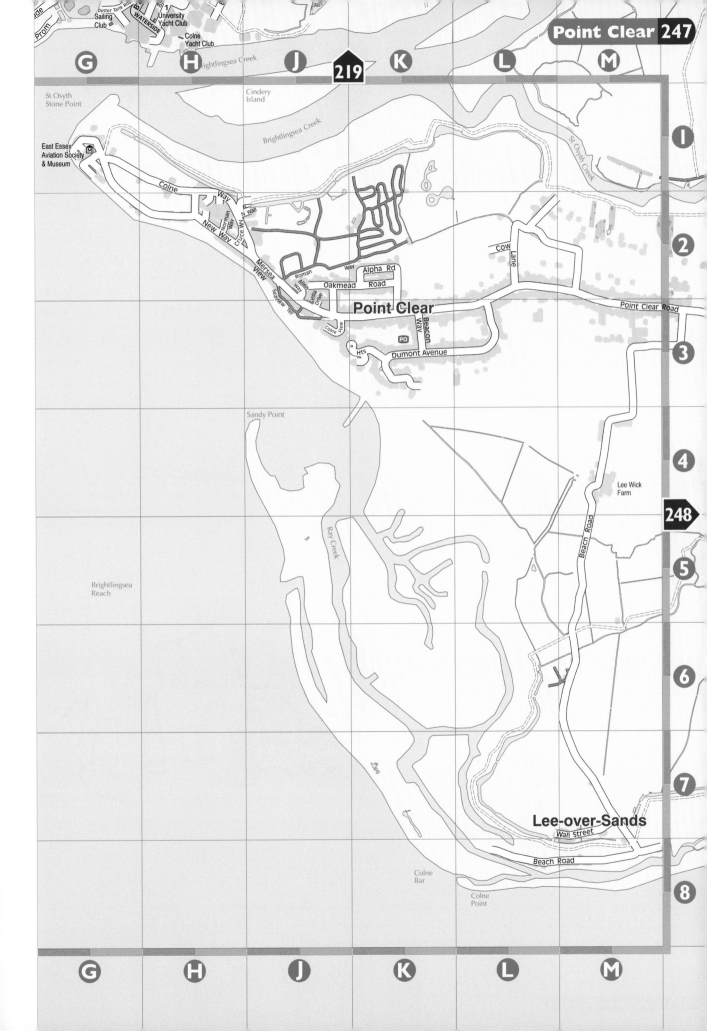

University
Yacht Club

Colne
Yacht Club

Brightlingsea Creek

219

St Osyth
Stone Point

Cindery
Island

Brightlingsea Creek

St Osyth Creek

East Essex
Aviation Society
& Museum

Colne Way

New Way

Norman Way

Cruce W

N Wall

Cow Lane

Mersea View

Roman Way

Allen Way

Oakmead

Alpha Rd

Road

Point Clear

Point Clear Road

Seaview Ter

Lydia Drive

Colne Way

Beacon Way

PO

Hts

Dumont Avenue

Sandy Point

Lee Wick
Farm

248

Brightlingsea
Reach

Ray Creek

Beach Road

Lee-over-Sands

Wall Street

Beach Road

Colne
Bar

Colne
Point

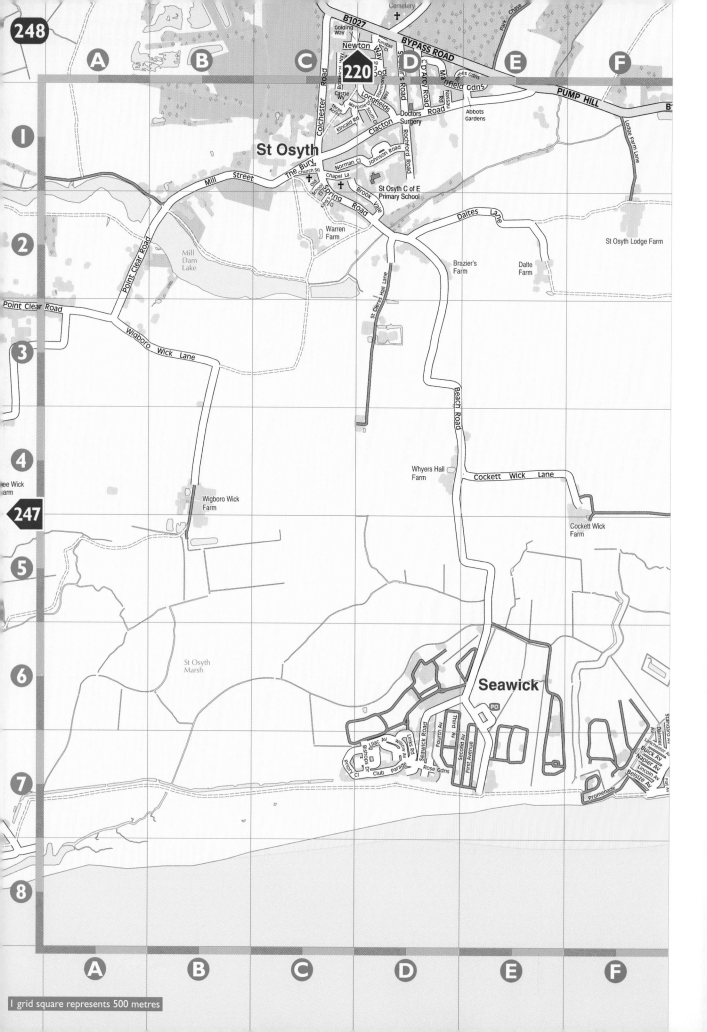

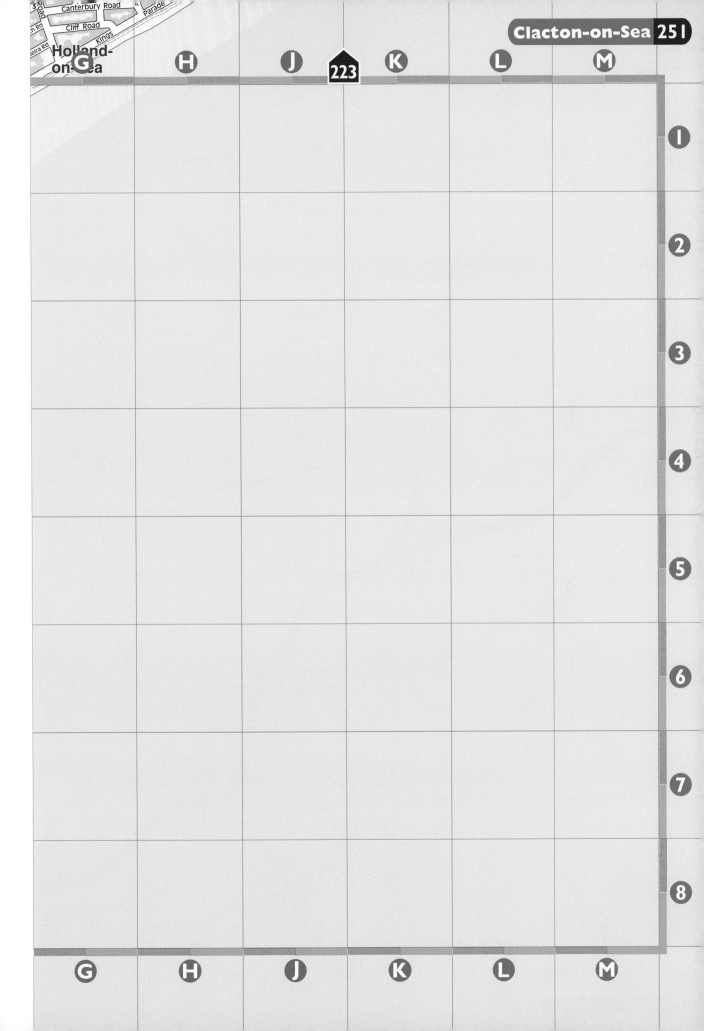

Canterbury Road

Cliff Road

Kings

Holland-
on-Sea

Parade

G **H** **J** 223 **K** **L** **M**

1

2

3

4

5

6

7

8

Canterbury Road

Cliff Road

Parade

G **H** **J** **K** **L** **M**

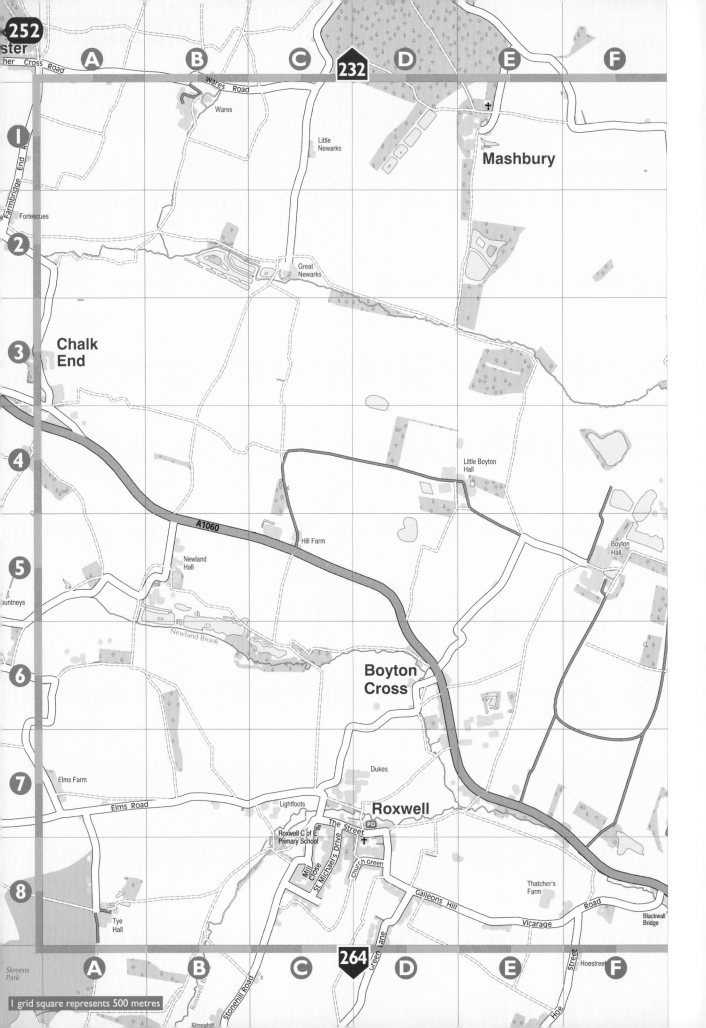

252

ster

her Cross Road

A · B · C · **232** · D · E · F

Wares Road

Wares

Little Newarks

Mashbury

I

Farmbridge End R

Fortescues

2

Great Newarks

3 Chalk End

4 A1060

Hill Farm

Little Boyton Hall

Boyton Hall

5

Newland Hall

ountneys

Newland Brook

6 Boyton Cross

7 Elms Farm

Elms Road

Dukes

Lightfoots

Roxwell

PO

Roxwell C of E Primary School

Mill Close

St Michael's Drive

The Street

Church Green

Green Lane

Galleons Hill

Thatcher's Farm

8

Tye Hall

Roxwell B

Stonehill Road

Vicarage Road

Hoe Street

Blackwall Bridge

Hoestreet

Skreens Park

A · B · C · **264** · D · E · F

1 grid square represents 500 metres

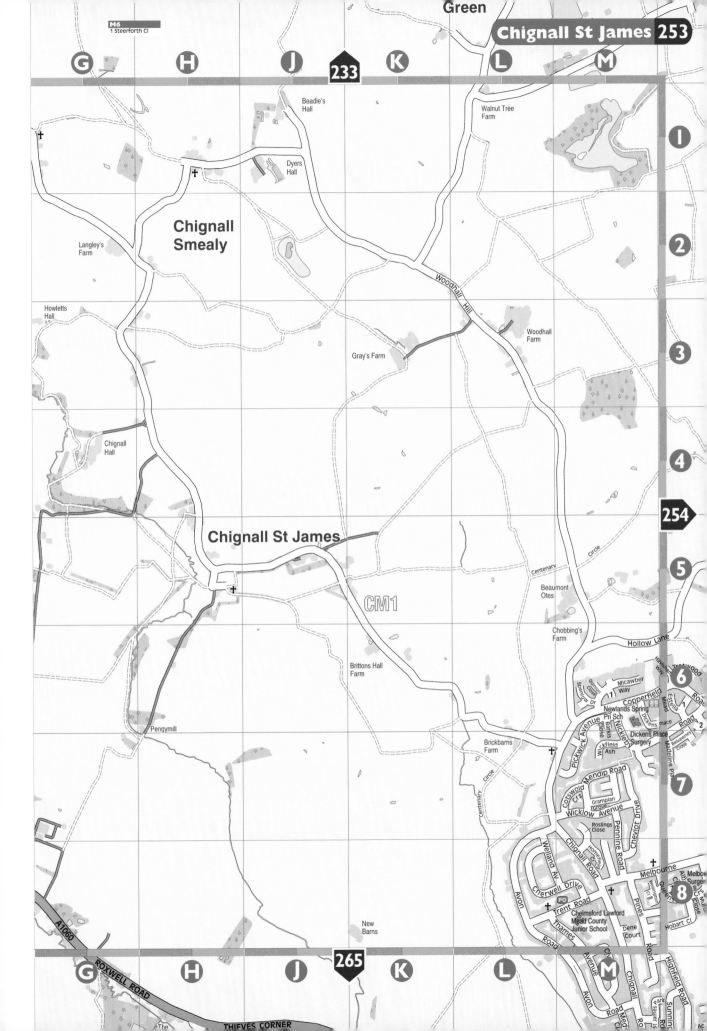

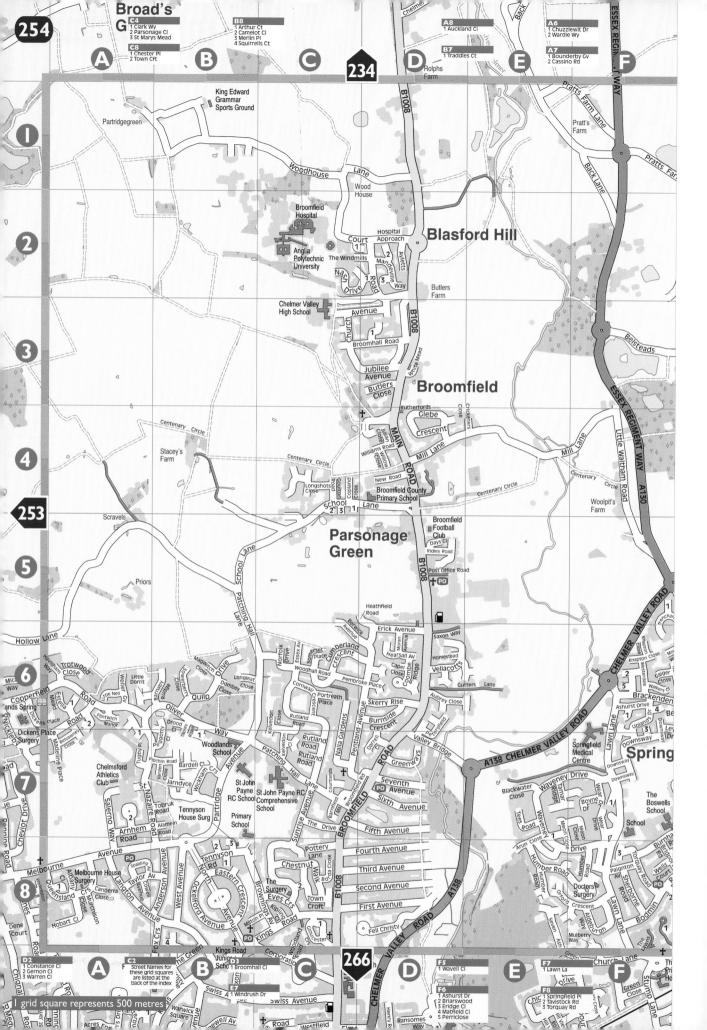

Broad's

G
C4
1 Clark Wy
2 Parsonage Cl
3 St Marys Mead

C8
1 Chester Pl
2 Town Cft

B8
1 Arthur Ct
2 Camelot Cl
3 Merlin Pl
4 Squirrells Ct

A8
1 Auckland Cl

B7
1 Traddles Ct

A6
1 Chuzzlewit Dr
2 Wardle Wy

A7
1 Bounderby Gv
2 Cassino Rd

A   B   C   234   D   E   F

I

Partridgegreen

King Edward
Grammar
Sports Ground

Woodhouse   Lane

Rolphs
Farm

Pratt's
Farm Lane

Pratt's
Farm

2

Wood
House

Broomfield
Hospital

Court

Hospital
Approach

Blasford Hill

Anglia
Polytechnic
University

The Windmills

Nash   Drive   Road

Mandeville Way

Ayletts

Butlers
Farm

Chelmer Valley
High School

Church   Avenue

Broomhall Road

B1008

White Mead

Belsteads

3

Jubilee
Avenue

Butlers
Close

Broomfield

Rutherfords

Glebe

Cricketers Close

Mill Lane

Centenary   Circle

Crescent

Stacey's
Farm

Centenary   Circle

Williams Road
Willow Close
Julian Close

MAIN   ROAD

Mill Lane

Centenary   Circle

Woolpit's
Farm

4

Scravels

Longshots
Close

Goulands Road
Copland Close

New Road

Broomfield County
Primary School

School   Lane

253

Parsonage
Green

Broomfield
Football
Club
Days Cl

Ridley Road

B1008

Post Office Road

PO

5

Priors

Patching   Hall   Lane

School   Lane

Heathfield
Road

Hollow Lane

Trotwood
Close

Little
Dorrit

Madwitch   Drive

Longleat
Close

Dombey
Close

Norfolk   Drive

Essex Av
Somerset Cl

Woodhall Road

Berwick
Avenue

Erick Avenue

Meon Avenue

Cumberland   Crescent

Hearsall Av

Capel
Close

Saxon Way

Homestead

Vellacotts

Gutters   Lane

Knapton Close

Brackenden

6

Copperfield
and Spring

Havisham   Way

Estella   Mead

Road

Little Nell

Weller Cl

Quilp

Flintwick   Manor

Oliver   Way

Swerrsert

Barnaby
Rudge

Cornwall Crescent

Portreath
Place

Skerry Rise

Coombe Ridge

Aubrey Close

Ashurst Drive

Upland's

Walkers

Gaiger
Close

Dickens Place
Surgery

Madeline Place

Belvawney
Close

Drood
Rapley Cl

Kelvedon
Close

Rutland
Road

Pembroke Place

Burnside
Crescent

Bekersfield

Valley Bridge

Springfield
Medical
Centre

Spring

7

Chelmsford
Athletics
Club

Cheviot Drive

St Nazaire Road

Tobruk
Road

Partridge   Avenue

Pipchin Road

Garden
Cres

Bardell Cl

Wickham Cres

Woodlands
School

Jarndyce

St John
Payne
RC School

Patching   Hall   Lane

St John Payne RC
Comprehensive
School

Rutland
Road

Nalla Gardens

Pentland Avenue

Courtlands

Broomfield Rd

Dynes Cl

Greenways

A138 CHELMER VALLEY ROAD

Downsway

Waveney Drive

Tamar
Ridge

Boyne
Dr

The
Boswells
School

8

Melbourne   Avenue

Salerno   Way

Arnhem
Road

Alamein
Road

Tennyson
House Surg

Primary
School

Eastern Crescent

North Ockerford Avenue

Tennyson
Rd

Sunrise Avenue

The Drive

Chestnut
Walk

Pottery
Lane

The
Surgery
Eves Crs

Town
Cft

B1008

Seventh
PO   Avenue

Sixth   Avenue

Fifth   Avenue

Fourth   Avenue

Third   Avenue

Second   Avenue

First   Avenue

BROOMFIELD   ROAD

Fell Christy

A138

Blackwater
Close

Tees
Road

Humber Road

Arun Close

Meon Close

West
Drive

Decoy
Way

Paignton
Av

Doctors'
Surgery

Sherborne
Way

Lawn Lane

Burnham Rd

Wells
Court

PO

Mulberry
Way

Melbourne
Surgery

Albany
Crs

Queensland
Close

Hobart Cl

Anderson Avenue

West Avenue

Canberra
Close

Milton Pl

Taylor Close

Spalding Av

Brownings Av

Kings   Road

Chestnut
Walk

Woodland Close

Gloucester
Rd

Ada Close

Corporation   Road

Fox Crs

The Green

Warwick
Square

Newell Av

Swiss A Windrush Dr

Swiss   Avenue

Westfield

Kings Road
Junior Sch

266

Boxton Cl

Henry Rd

Ransomes
Way

CHELMER VALLEY ROAD

Church Lane

Stump Lane

Green
Close

A   B   C   266   D   E   F

D2
1 Constance Cl
2 Gernon Cl
3 Warren Cl

C2
Street Names for
these grid squares
are listed at the
back of the index

D
1 Broomhall Cl

F5
1 Wavell Cl

F7
1 Lawn La

F6
1 Ashurst Dr
2 Briarswood
3 Eridge Cl
4 Matfield Cl
5 Perriclose

F8
1 Springfield Pl
2 Tavistock Rd
3 Torquay Rd

1 grid square represents 500 metres

235

256

267

G5
1 Saddle Ri

G6
1 Forsythia Cl
2 Montgomery Cl
3 Snowdrop Cl
4 Tulip Cl

G7
1 Sidmouth Rd

H8
1 Dahlia Cl
2 Lavender Ct
3 Wallasea Gdns

H7
1 Bouchers Mead
2 Camellia Ct
3 Heather Ct
4 Wallflower Ct

H6
1 Hunters Wy
2 Vermeer Ride

H5
1 Goldenacres

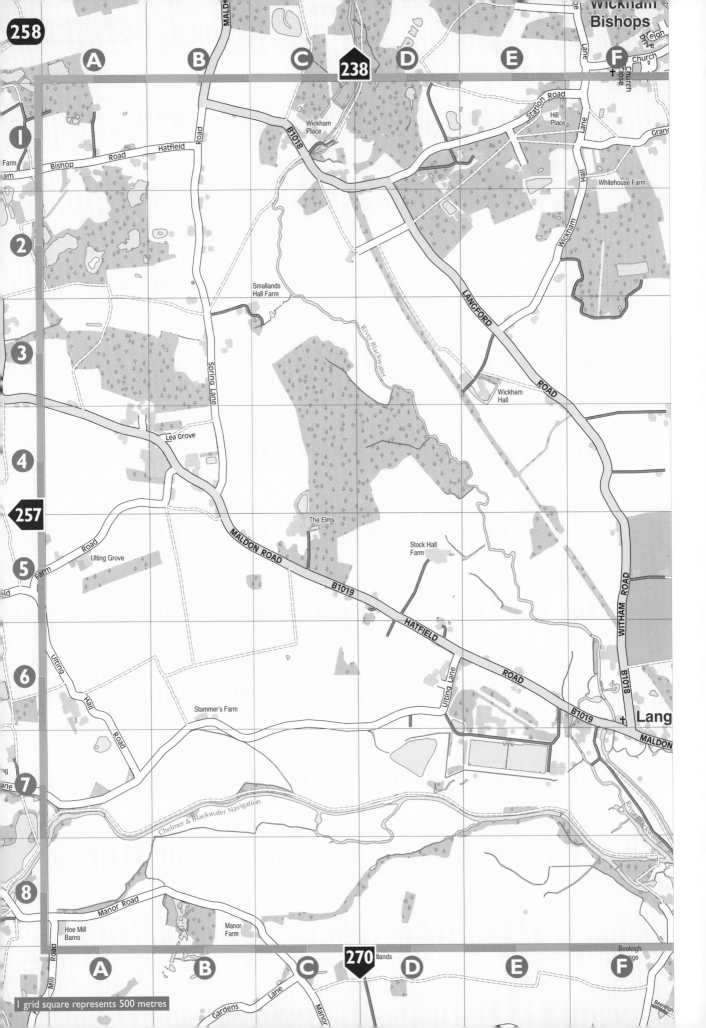

258

A B C **238** D E F

I

Wickham
Bishops

Wickham Place

Hatfield Road

Bishop Road

Farm

2

Smallands
Hall Farm

Whitehouse Farm

Hill Place

Station Road

Wickham Hall Lane

Grange

River Blackwater

LANGFORD

ROAD

3

Spring Lane

Lea Grove

Wickham Hall

257

4

The Elms

Road

Ulting Grove

Stock Hall Farm

MALDON ROAD

B1019

5

Farm

Ulting Hall Road

HATFIELD

ROAD

WITHAM ROAD

B1018

6

Stammer's Farm

Ulting Lane

B1019

Lang

MALDON

7

Chelmer & Blackwater Navigation

River Blackwater

8

Manor Road

Hoe Mill Barns

Manor Farm

Beeleigh

A B **270** lands C D E F

Mill Road

Gardens Lane

Manor

Beeleigh

1 grid square represents 500 metres

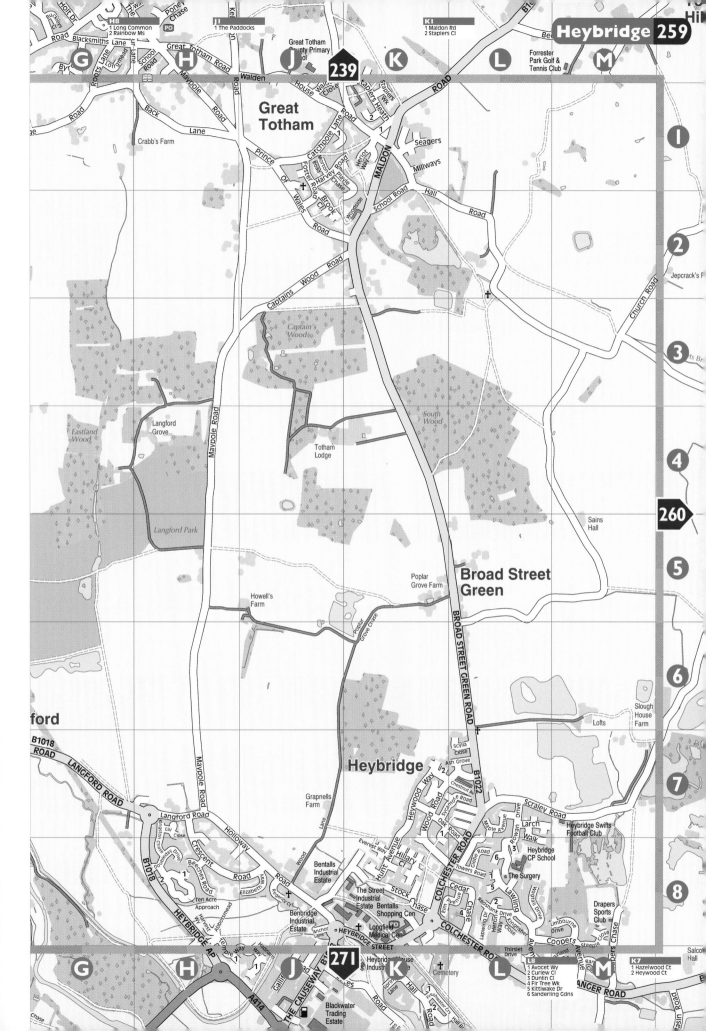

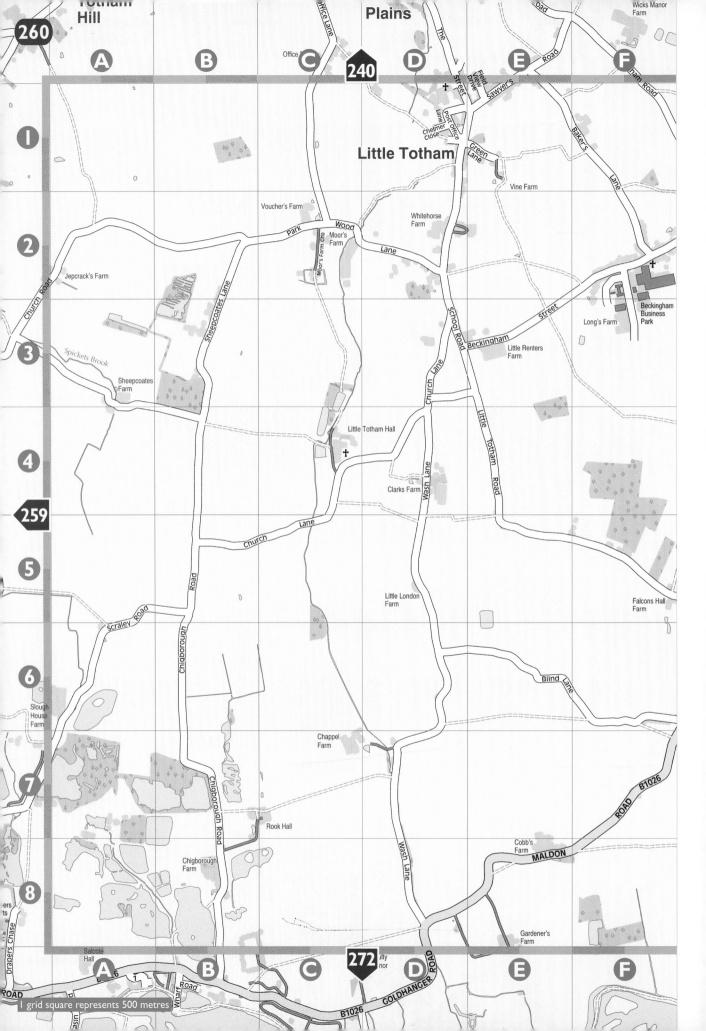

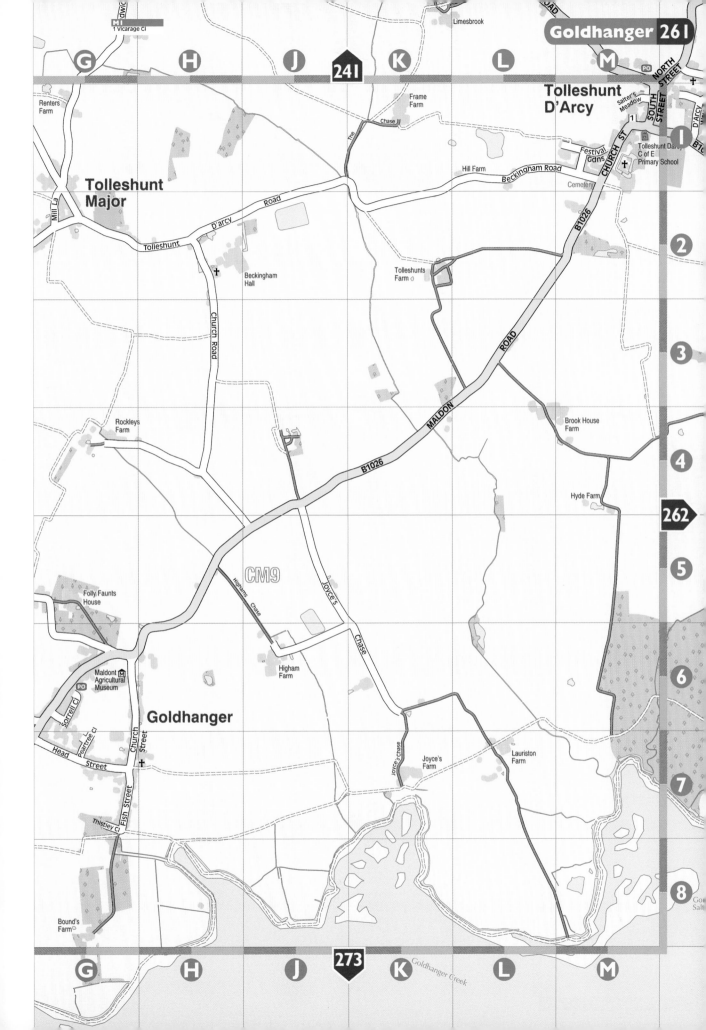

G H J **241** K L M

Limesbrook

Renters Farm

Frame Farm

Chase

Tolleshunt D'Arcy

Salter's Meadow

PO

NORTH STREET

SOUTH STREET

1

Festival Gdns

CHURCH ST

Tolleshunt Darcy C of E Primary School

D'Arcy Road

Tolleshunt Major

Mill La

Hill Farm

Beckingham Road

Cemetery

B1026

I

Tolleshunt

D'Arcy Road

Church Road

Beckingham Hall

Tolleshunts Farm

2

ROAD

3

MALDON

Rockleys Farm

Brook House Farm

4

B1026

Hyde Farm

262

CM9

Highams Chase

Joyce's Chase

5

Folly Faunts House

6

Maldont Agricultural Museum

PO

Sorrell Cl

Peartree Cl

Higham Farm

Goldhanger

Head Street

Church Street

Joyce's Chase

Joyce's Farm

Lauriston Farm

7

Fish Street

Thistley Cl

8

Bound's Farm

Goldhanger Salt

G H J **273** K Goldhanger Creek L M

G   H   J   **243**   K   L   M

Joyce's Head

Pennyhole Fleet

Old Hall Creek

Tollesbury Fleet

North Channel

Woodrolfe Creek

Great Cob Island

South Channel

Shingle Point

Thurstable Close
Thurstable Way
Road
Woodrolfe Road
Tollesbury Sailing Club
Woodrolfe Park

Orchard Close
Crescent Rd
Kings Wk
Mell
Darnet Rd
Woodrolfe Farm Lane

Tollesbury Wick Marshes

Mell Road
Monk Walk
Wycke Lane

Mell Farm

Mill Creek

Mill Point

1
2
3
4
5
6
7
8

G   H   J   K   L   M

Tolwell Creek

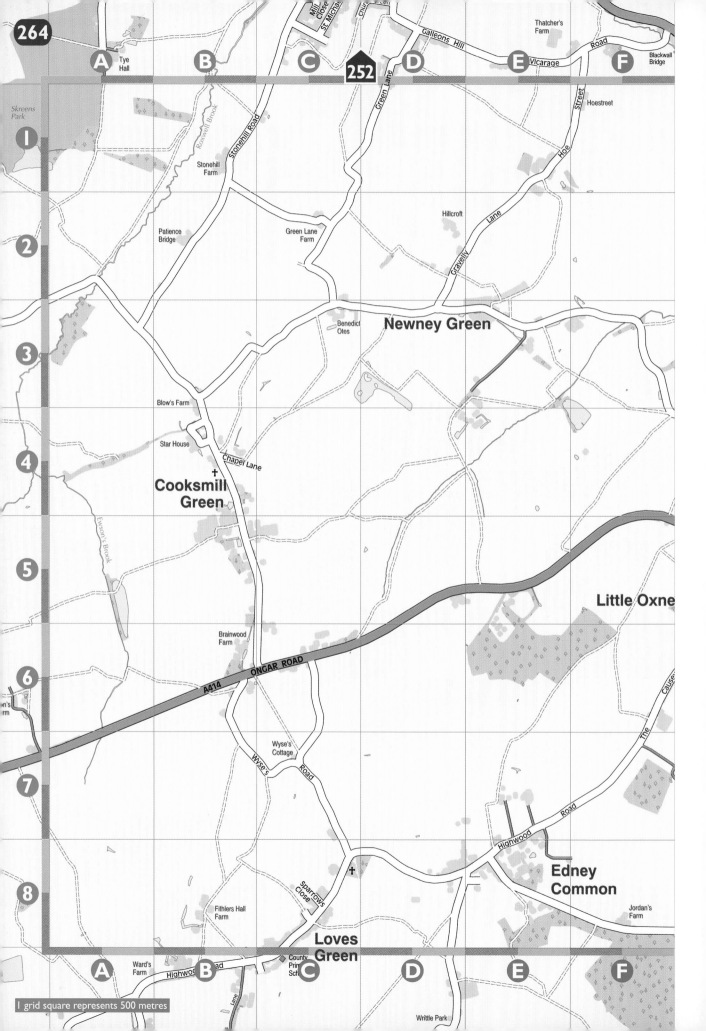

266

H4
1 Mansfields

H5
1 The Shrubberies

J4
1 Blackthorn Cl

M1
1 Skreens Ct

K5
1 Lucerne Wy

K4
1 Comyns Pl
2 Ongark Rd
3 Romans Pl
4 St John's Gn

Great Oxney Green

Writtle

ey Green

ROXWELL ROAD

THIEVES CORNER

Roxwell Road

ROXWELL ROAD A1060

The Hickerage

Reed's Farm

Warren Farm

River Can

Cow Watering Lane

Lordship Road

Lawford Lane

Roxwell Avenue

Beach's Drive

Cliveden Close

Sunningdale Rd

Writtle College

Fox Burrows Lane

Sturgeons Farm

Benedict Dr

Abbess

St Catherin Rd

St Peter

Fore

The Writtle Surgery

Mayfield Road

Bruce Road

Wykeham Road

Hylands School

Hatfield GV

Exmoor Close

Sherwood Drive

Rothbury

Stansted

Victoria Road

Back Road

St John's Road

The Green

Lawford Lane

Melba Court

Westlands County Secondary School

Milburn

Harewood Road

Fosters Cl

East View

Ongar Road

Redwood Dr

Daws Close

Longmeads

Purcell Close

Little Meadow

Chancery Place

Church Lane

Bridge Street

Romans Way

Chelmsford Road

Longacre

Hanbury Road

Tower Road

Great Godfreys

Checkers Road

Home Mead

Millfields

Sawney Brook

Well Field

Laurence Croft

The Coverts

Nicholas Cl

Loves Walk

The Priory

Penrose Mead

Russell W

Widfor Industr Estate

Highwood Rd

Brandocks

Long Rollestons

Little Lewis

The Ryle

Further Meadow

Lodge Road

Lodge Road

Paradise Road

Oxney Mead

A414

Ongar Road

Junior School

County Junior School

Margaretting Road

Pound Fields

Rectory Road

Shakeston Cl

Buglers Rise

Hunt's Close

Hunt's Drive

Shakestones

Centenary Circle

New Rollestons Farm

A414

Widforo

Roper's Farm

Lee Farm

Montpelier's Farm

Bumpstead's Farm

Hylands Park

Nathan's Lane

Margaretting Road

Southw Farm

Hyland House & Park

Elm Farm

Melbourne

Cherwell Drive

Trent Road

Chelmsford Mead Cou Junior Sch

Avon Road

Thames Road

Clyde Crs

Chignall Road

Highfield Road

Dene Court

Hobart Cl

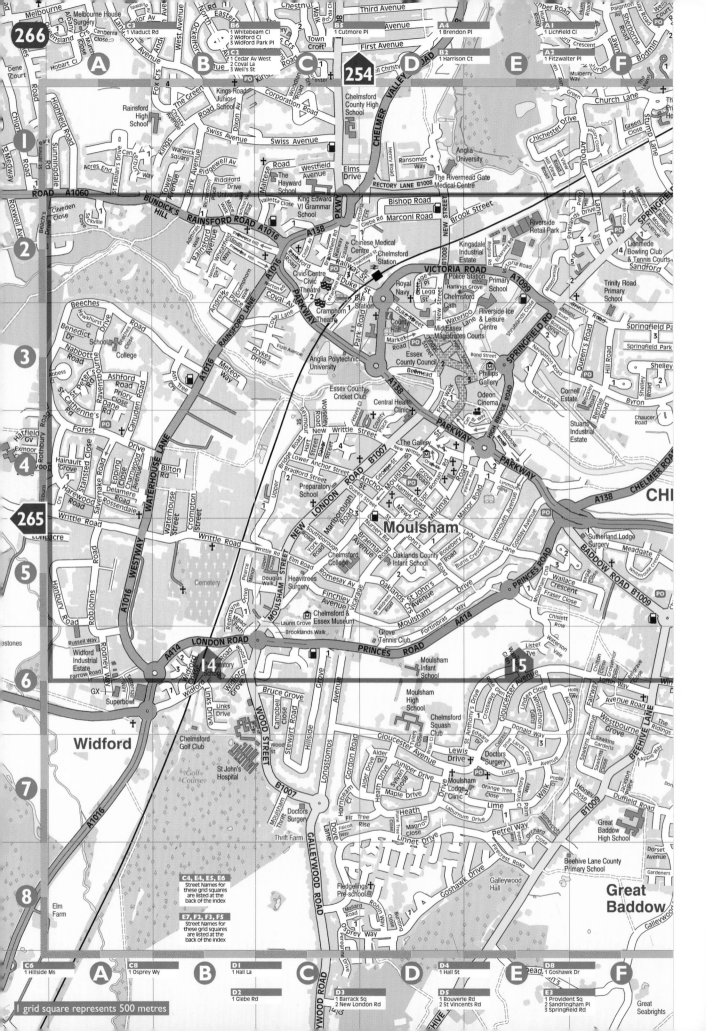

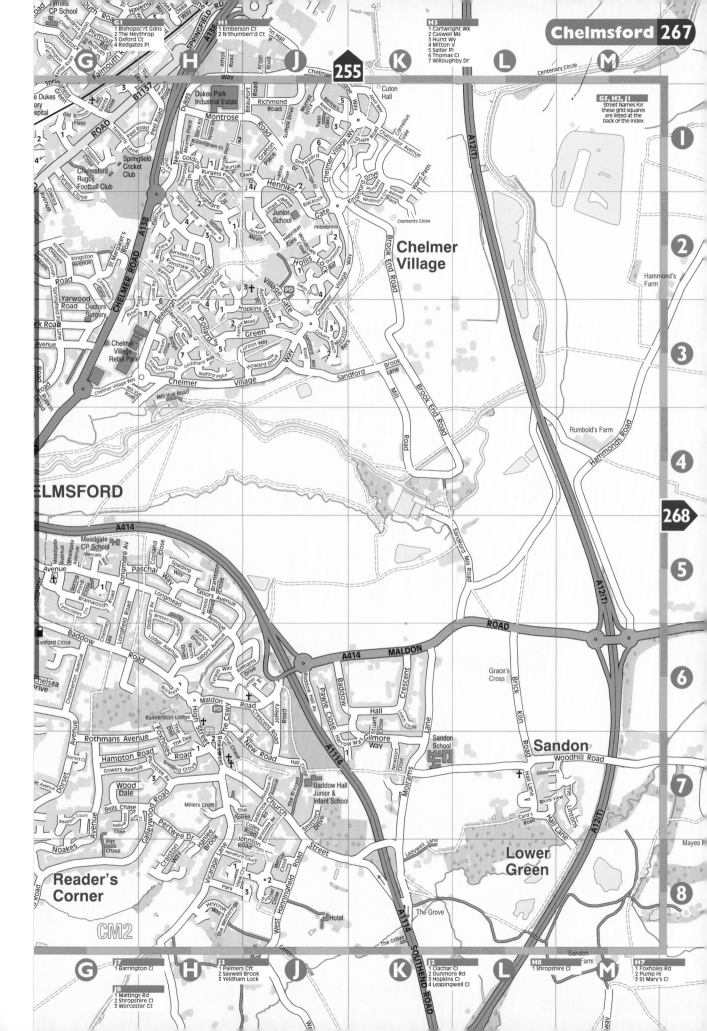

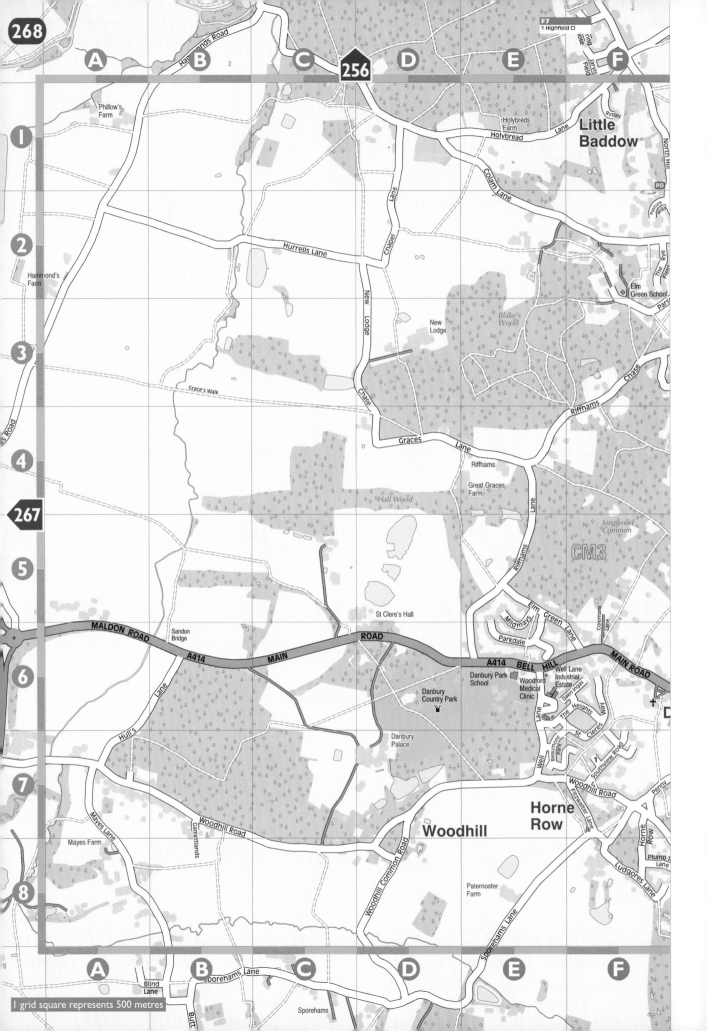

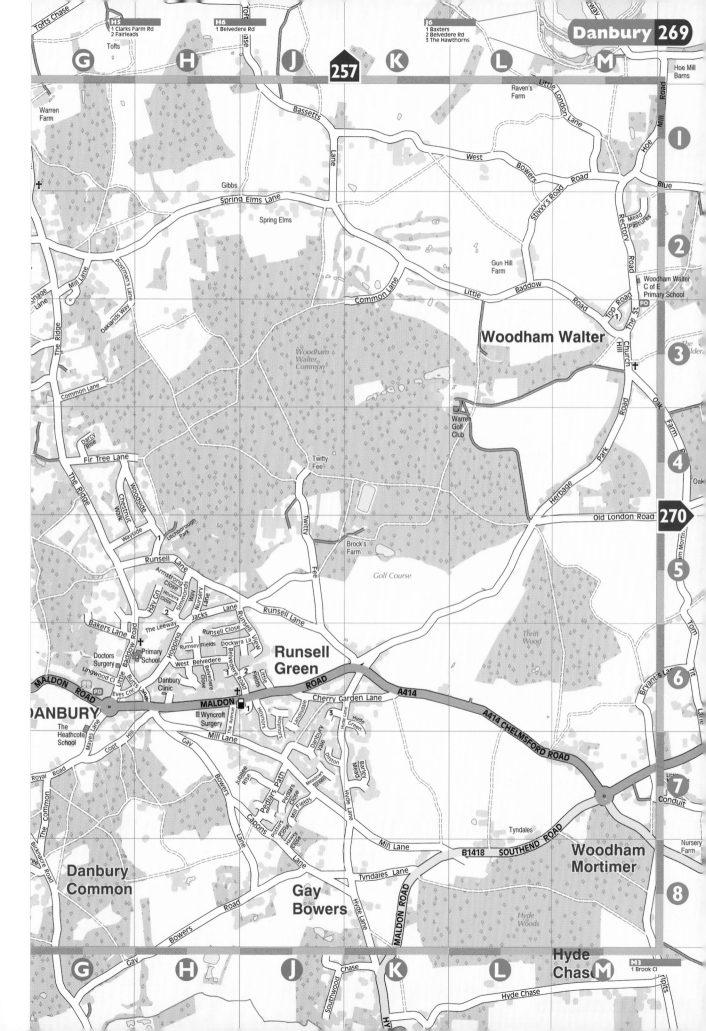

A B 258 C D E F

Hoe Mill Barns

Manor Road

Manor Farm

Woodlands

Beeleigh Grange Farm

1

Hoe Mill Road

Gardens

Hop Lane

Manor Road

Cut-A-Thwart Lane

Cut-A-Thwart Lane

Beeleigh Turning

Blue Mill Lane

Abbey

Mead Pastures

Rector Road

Whitehouse Farm

Curling Tye Lane

Beeleigh Farms

2

Woodham Walter C of E Primary School

PO

The St

Curling Tye Green

Cemetery

The Wilderness

Curling Tye Lane

Brook Farm

3

Hill

Road

Oak Farm Road

London Road

4

Oak Farm

Wood Corner

Old London Road

Woodham Mortimer Road

Lodge Farm

Wycke Hill

5

Spital Rd

Tom

A414 SPITAL ROAD

6

Bryant's Lane

Tit Lane

A414

Limebrook Farm

Hall Farm

MALDON ROAD

Brookhead Farm

Little Meadows

Rectory Lane

Lodge Road

7

Conduit Lane

Post Office Lane

Hill Farm

Nursery Farm

BURNHAM

Elms Farm

Hazeleigh

8

Marplits

Little Grange

ROAD

B1010

Lodge Road

Cemetery

HI, J5, L1
Street Names for these grid squares are listed at the back of the index

A B C D E F

Hazeleigh

1 grid square represents 500 metres

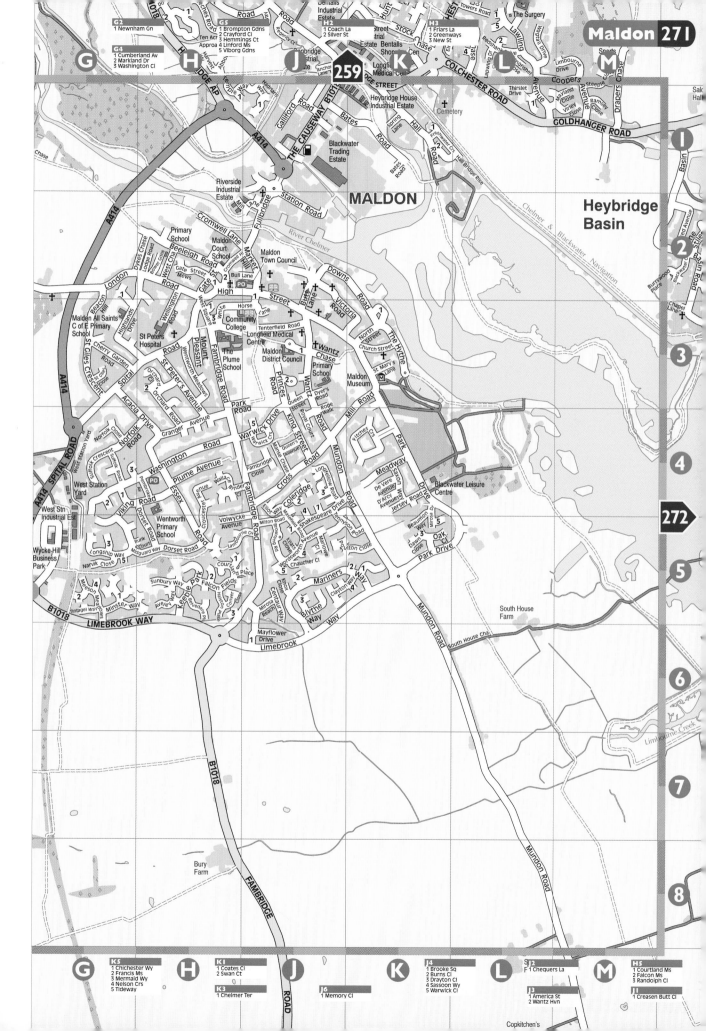

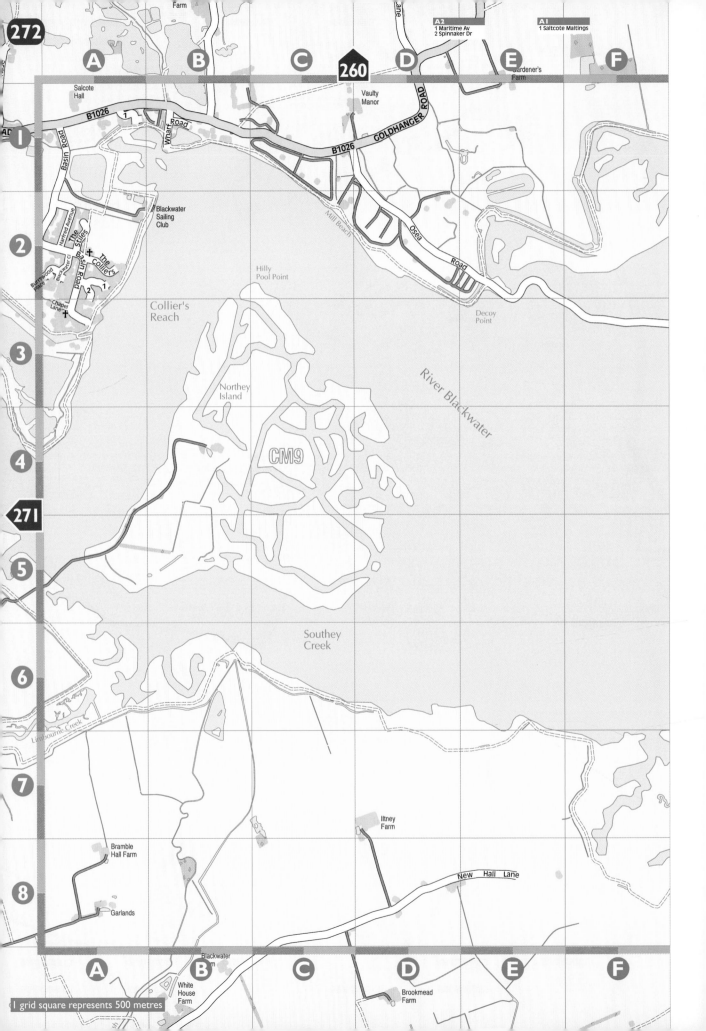

260

271

A1
1 Saltcote Maltings

A2
1 Maritime Av
2 Spinnaker Dr

Salcote
Hall

B1026

Wharf Road

Vaulty
Manor

B1026 GOLDHANGER ROAD

Gardener's
Farm

Blackwater
Sailing
Club

Harford Avenue

Burrswood
Place

Blackwater Cl

Basin Road

Chapel
Lane

The
Stiles

The
Collier's

Mill Beach

Osea Road

Decoy
Point

Collier's
Reach

Hilly
Pool Point

Northey
Island

CM9

River Blackwater

Southey
Creek

Limbourne Creek

Iltney
Farm

Bramble
Hall Farm

New Hall Lane

Garlands

Blackwater
Farm

White
House
Farm

Brookmead
Farm

Bound
Farm

G

H

J

261

K

L

M

Go
Salt

1

Goldhanger Creek

2

The Stumble

3

The Chase

West Point

CM9

Osea
Island

East Point

4

Osea
Farm

5

6

Cooper's
Creek

Mundon
Stone Point

Steeple
Creek

7

8

Canney
Road

G

H

J

K

L

M

Lawling Cre

St Peter's Way

land Creek

Canney Road

Abberton 216 C2
Abbey Field 160 A8
Aingers Green 192 A4
Aldham 157 K5
Allen's Green 198 B7
Alphamstone 99 H2
Alresford 190 C5
Ardleigh 134 B6
Ardleigh Heath 134 A5
Ardley End 228 D4
Arkesden 86 A3
Armigers 118 E7
Ashdon 40 C5
Ashen 45 M4
Audley End 62 D5
Audley End 72 A5
Aythorpe Roding 230 D2
Bacon End 203 G3
Baconend Green 203 G1
Ballingdon 4 A9
Balls Green 163 J8
Bamber's Green 174 B2
Bannister Green 178 B8
Bardfield End Green 119 L3
Bardfield Saling 149 M4
Barley 58 C3
Barnston 204 B1
Bartholomew Green 179 G6
Bartlow 20 C6
Bath Side 9 J4
Baythorne End 45 G3
Beacon End 158 F7
Beacon Hill 33 M2
Beacon Hill 239 K7
Beaumont 166 B6
Beazley End 123 L7
Bedlar's Green 172 C8
Belchamp Otten 47 L5
Belchamp St Paul 47 H4
Belchamp Walter 48 C7
Belstead 53 L6
Bentfield Bury 143 K5
Bentfield Green 143 L5
Bentley 78 A6
Berden 114 D5
Berechurch 188 A4
Birch 214 C1
Birchanger 172 A3
Birch Green 214 C3
Birchhall Corner 133 L3
Birdbrook 44 C6
Bird Green 85 G6
Bishops Green 204 A5
Bishop's Stortford 170 E6
Blackheath 188 D5
Blackmore End 123 K4
Black Notley 180 D8
Blacksmith's Corner 53 L7
Blake End 178 C3
Blasford Hill 254 D2
Bocking 180 B1
Bocking Churchstreet .. 152 C5
Bocking's Elm 221 J8
Boreham 256 A5
Borley 49 H2
Borley Green 48 F3
Boxted 103 H6
Boxted 132 C1
Boxted Cross 103 K8
Boyton Cross 252 D6
Boyton End 24 F8
Boyton End 90 D8
Bradfield 137 H3
Bradfield Heath 136 F5
Bradwell 181 M3
Braintree 152 C6
Braiswick 159 K3
Bramford 30 C3
Bran End 148 E5
Brantham 106 F4
Breeds 233 M7
Brewer's End 173 K6
Brick End 146 A4
Brick House End 114 D8
Brickkiln Green 123 J1
Bridge End 121 J2
Bridge Green 60 D7
Brightlingsea 218 F5
Brightwell 57 L2
Broad Green 59 K2
Broad Green 184 A2
Broad's Green 234 A8
Broad Street Green 259 L5
Brockley Green 25 G2
Broke Hall 55 L2
Bromley Cross 162 E1
Broomfield 254 D3
Broxted 146 B3
Brundon 49 L4
Bucklesham 57 K5
Building End 59 J6
Bulmer 49 H8
Bulmer Tye 73 H2
Bures 100 B5
Bures Green 100 C2
Burnt Heath 134 D8
Burrsville Park 222 C6
Burton End 172 L1
Burton Green 154 D3
Bury Green 170 A6
Bush End 201 J1
Bustard Green 120 D7
Calford Green 24 B6
California 32 D7
Campions 227 H8
Camps End 41 J4
Canfield End 174 D6
Capel St Mary 77 H4
Cardinal's Green 21 K3
Castle Camps 42 A2
Castle Hedingham 96 A1
Castle Hill 31 J2
Catmere End 61 J1
Cattawade 106 F6
Causeway End 205 K1
Cavendish 27 M3
Chalk End 252 A3
Chantry 54 A2

Chapel End 145 L7
Chappel 128 E7
Chatham Green 234 F2
Chatter End 142 D6
Chattisham 52 C4
Chelmer Village 267 K2
Chelmondiston 81 H6
Chelmsford 15 M6
Cherry Green 118 A5
Chickney 146 B1
Chignall Smealy 253 H2
Chignall St James 253 H5
Chilton 5 K4
Chilton Street 26 A3
Chipping Hill 238 A2
Chitts Hills 158 F5
Chrishall 59 M1
Church End 40 B6
Church End 82 B8
Church End 123 G8
Church End 146 C2
Churchend 176 A2
Church Street 47 K2
Clacton-on-Sea 13 J7
Clare 26 E5
Clatterford End 231 K6
Clavering 85 L8
Cobbs Fenn 95 M6
Cobler's Green 205 M2
Cock Green 206 A1
Coggeshall 183 G3
Coggeshall Hamlet 183 J5
Cokenach 58 A8
Colchester 10 A6
Cole End 63 M7
Coles Green 52 D5
Colne Engaine 127 J4
Cook's Green 222 D3
Cooksmill Green 264 B4
Cooper's End 60 C8
Copdock 53 H6
Copford 185 L1
Copford Green 185 L3
Cornard Tye 51 G6
Cornish Hall End 67 K8
Countess Cross 127 M3
Cradle End 170 B5
Craig's End 68 E6
Crawley End 35 M8
Cressing 181 H7
Cripple Corner 98 C3
Crockleford Heath 161 L3
Crockleford Hill 161 J4
Cross End 98 D6
Crow's Green 150 A5
Curling Tye Green 270 C2
Cutlers Green 118 F3
Danbury 268 F6
Danbury Common 269 G8
Debden 88 D6
Debden Green 89 H8
Dedham 105 G6
Dedham Heath 134 C1
Deer's Green 114 C1
Delvin End 95 H2
Dewes Green 114 B4
Dorking Tye 75 L7
Dovercourt 9 H8
Duck End 92 E6
Duck End 148 F4
Duck End 172 A4
Duckend Green 179 G2
Duddenhoe End 60 C7
Duton Hill 147 G3
Duxford 16 E5
Earls Colne 127 L6
East Bergholt 105 L1
East End 106 F3
East End 142 A1
East Gores 184 C1
Easthorpe 185 K6
East Mersea 245 M4
Edney Common 264 E8
Eight Ash Green 158 D5
Elder Street 89 G4
Elmdon 60 C1
Elmstead 162 C5
Elmstead Heath 190 B2
Elmstead Market 162 D7
Elsenham 144 D3
Erwarton 110 D3
Fairstead 208 D7
Falkenham 83 M2
Fanner's Green 233 K8
Farnham 142 E7
Farnham Green 142 D6
Faulkbourne 209 K6
Feering 211 L2
Felixstowe 7 L4
Felsted 177 K8
Finchingfield 92 D7
Fingringhoe 189 J8
Flack's Green 236 D3
Flint Cross 34 E3
Ford End 114 A1
Ford End 205 M6
Fordham 129 L7
Fordham Heath 158 C4
Fordstreet 157 L2
Forry's Green 95 J7
Foxash Estate 134 E4
Foxearth 28 E7
Fox Street 161 J1
Frating 191 G4
Frating Green 191 J2
Freston 80 A2
Frinkle Green 44 C8
Frinton-on-Sea 223 M1
Frogs' Green 64 B5
Fuller's End 144 E5
Fuller Street 235 M1
Further Ford End 84 F7
Gainsborough 55 K5
Gainsford End 94 A1
Gallows Green 147 M2
Gallows Green 157 L4
Gamble's Green 236 B3
Garnetts 204 B5

Gaston Green 199 K6
Gaunt's End 145 J6
Gay Bowers 269 J8
Gestingthorpe 72 A4
Gipsy Row 76 F3
Glemsford 28 E1
Good Easter 231 M8
Goose Green 164 F2
Goose Green 165 G6
Gore Pit 212 A1
Gosfield 125 G6
Gransmore Green 178 B4
Grass Green 69 K4
Great Baddow 266 F8
Great Bardfield 121 L4
Great Bentley 191 M5
Great Braxted 239 L4
Great Bromley 163 G4
Great Canfield 202 E5
Great Chesterford 38 A3
Great Chishill 59 G3
Great Clacton 12 D2
Great Cornard 50 F8
Great Dunmow 175 L6
Great Easton 147 H6
Great Hallingbury 199 M1
Great Henny 73 L5
Great Holland 223 H2
Great Horkesley 131 J4
Great Leighs 207 H5
Great Maplestead 96 E3
Great Notley 179 K6
Great Oakley 166 F1
Great Oxney Green 265 H4
Great Saling 150 C5
Great Sampford 91 J1
Great Tey 156 E5
Great Totham 240 A6
Great Totham 259 J1
Great Waldingfield 51 H1
Great Waltham 234 A6
Great Wenham 76 D4
Great Wigborough 243 G2
Great Yeldham 70 C3
Greenstead 11 M8
Greenstead Green 126 C8
Green Street 170 A4
The Green 208 E1
Greenwich 54 F4
Gubbion's Green 207 L5
Hadstock 19 L7
Hallingbury Street 200 D1
Halstead 125 M3
Hamperden End 118 A3
Hanchet End 22 D4
Hardy's Green 185 M7
Hare Green 163 J7
Harkstead 109 K3
Hartford End 205 M5
Harwich 9 H6
Hatfield Broad Oak 201 H8
Hatfield Heath 228 D2
Hatfield Peverel 237 K8
Haverhill 22 F5
Hawbush Green 181 H8
Hawkin's Hill 92 A5
Hawkspur Green 91 M8
Hazel End 143 J7
Hazel Stub 22 E6
The Heath 78 D7
Heckfordbridge 186 C6
Helions Bumpstead 42 D5
Hellman's Cross 202 B3
Hemp's Green 129 K7
Hempstead 66 B4
Henham 117 G8
Henny Street 74 B4
Heybridge 259 K7
Heybridge Basin 271 M2
Heydon 35 J8
Higham 104 D1
High Easter 231 L3
Highfields 211 M6
High Garrett 152 E3
High Houses 233 M6
High Roding 203 G6
Highstreet Green 95 J3
High Wych 226 D4
Hill Green 86 A7
Hintlesham 52 B1
Hinxton 17 J5
Hockerill 171 K7
Holbrook 80 A7
Holder's Green 120 A7
Holland-on-Sea 223 G8
Holton St Mary 76 C7
Honey Tye 101 M1
Hope End Green 174 A8
Horne Row 268 E7
Hornestreet 103 M8
Horseheath 21 K2
Horsley Cross 164 C5
Horsleycross Street ... 136 C7
Howe Green 200 A3
Howe Street 93 H4
Howe Street 234 A3
Howlett End 89 J3
Hurst Green 219 J7
The Hythe 188 F1
Ickleton 37 J2
Inworth 212 B6
Ipswich 3 H8
Janke's Green 129 G5
Jasper's Green 150 F3
Jaywick 249 H5
Kedington 24 D3
Keelars Tye 190 A2
Keeres Green 230 F4
Kelvedon 211 L6
Kesgrave 33 L5
Kirby Cross 195 K6
Kirby-le-Soken 195 L4
Kirton 83 K1
Knowl Green 47 H6
Lamarsh 99 L1
Lamb Corner 133 M1
Langenhoe 216 C3

Langford 258 F6
Langham 133 H1
Langley 84 E3
Langley Green 184 B5
Latchmore Bank 199 J3
Lattinford Hill 76 F7
Lawford 135 J2
Layer Breton 214 D3
Layer de la Haye 187 H8
Layer Marney 214 A5
Leaden Roding 230 F5
Lee-over-Sands 247 L7
Level's Green 142 E8
Levington 82 A2
Lexden 159 J5
Lindsell 148 C2
Linton 20 A2
Liston 29 J7
Liston Garden 29 G6
Little Baddow 268 F1
Little Bardfield 120 F3
Little Bealings 33 M1
Little Bentley 164 C5
Little Braxted 238 E3
Little Bromley 135 K7
Littlebury 62 A1
Littlebury Green 61 J4
Little Cambridge 147 K2
Little Chesterford 38 A5
Little Chishill 59 G6
Little Clacton 221 M2
Little Cornard 75 G2
Little Dunmow 177 G6
Little Easton 147 G8
Little Henham 116 E4
Little Horkesley 131 G1
Little Leighs 207 G7
Little Linton 19 J2
Little London 92 D2
Little London 114 F5
Little Maplestead 97 J4
Little Oakley 139 L6
Little Oxney Green 264 F5
Little Sampford 91 L5
Little Tey 184 E1
Little Totham 260 C1
Little Waltham 234 E7
Little Wenham 77 G2
Little Wigborough 243 K2
Little Wratting 23 M2
Little Yeldham 71 G1
Littley Green 206 B6
Long Gardens 73 H8
Long Melford 29 M6
Loves Green 264 C8
Lower Green 84 A6
Lower Green 123 K2
Lower Green 267 L8
Lower Holbrook 109 J2
Lower Sheering 227 J4
Lower Street 108 D4
Lucking Street 97 G3
Mace Green 52 F6
Maggots End 143 G1
Maidenhall 54 D3
Maldon 271 K2
Mallows Green 142 E3
Manningtree 135 K1
Manuden 143 H3
Manwood Green 229 G6
Maple End 64 F6
Margaret Roding 230 F8
Marks Tey 185 J2
Mashbury 252 E1
Maypole Green 187 M4
Meadowend 45 L8
Meesden 84 B8
Messing 212 E3
Middleton 74 A1
Mile End 160 A1
Millend Green 147 L5
Mill Green 21 L6
Minnow End 234 C6
Mistley 136 C1
Mistley Heath 136 C3
Molehill Green 145 M7
Molehill Green 178 F8
Monk Street 119 K6
Mott's Green 199 M7
Moulsham 15 G7
Mount Bures 100 A7
Mount Pleasant 256 F4
Mowden 256 F4
Nacton 56 D3
Nayland 102 D4
Needham Green 229 J1
New England 44 B3
Newman's End 228 B8
Newman's Green 50 C1
New Mistley 136 C2
Newney Green 264 D3
Newport 87 J5
Newton 51 K7
North End 71 H2
North End 205 J4
Northend 62 C1
Nosterfield End 22 B8
Nounsley 257 J3
Old Felixstowe 113 M2
Old Heath 188 E2
Old Mead 144 F1
Olmstead Green 42 A6
Onslow Green 204 E3
Ovington 46 D4
Oxen End 121 G7
Oxley Green 241 J4
Pale Green 42 F4
Panfield 151 J6
Pannel's Ash 46 A4
Parkeston 8 A1
Parkgate 205 G6
Park Green 114 D7
Parney Heath 133 K1
Parsonage Green 254 C5
Paternoster Heath 241 J2
Pattiswick 154 A8

Pebmarsh 98 B6
Peldon 215 M7
Pentlow 28 A7
Pentlow Street 28 C5
Perry Green 181 M4
Pharisee Green 175 J8
Philpot End 203 J3
Playford 33 K1
Pledgdon Green 145 L3
Pleshey 233 G3
Point Clear 247 K3
Pond Street 60 B6
The Port of Felixstowe .. 6 A8
Potash 78 A6
Powers Hall End 237 L2
Priory Heath 55 M4
Puttock End 47 M7
Puttock's End 201 M1
Quendon 116 B3
Racecourse 55 H3
Radwinter 65 G6
Radwinter End 65 J1
Ramsey 139 H3
Rank's Green 207 M5
Raven's Green 163 L8
Raydon 76 A3
Rayne 179 G3
Reader's Corner 267 G8
Richmond's Green 119 M6
Rickling 115 K1
Rickling Green 115 M5
Ridgewell 45 J7
Ringtail Green 205 K8
Rivenhall 210 D6
Rivenhall End 211 G7
Roast Green 85 H7
Robinhood End 68 D8
Rodbridge Corner 49 L1
Rook End 88 C8
Roost End 44 C1
Rose Green 129 G8
Rose Hill 3 M9
Rotten End 123 J6
Roundbush Green 230 E3
Row Green 179 M7
Row Heath 221 J2
Rowhedge 189 G5
Roxwell 252 D7
Runsell Green 269 J6
Rush Green 249 K2
Rushley Green 71 H7
Rushmere St Andrew 32 F5
Rushmere Street 33 H4
Sackers Green 75 J1
Saffron Walden 63 J4
St Osyth 248 C1
St Osyth Heath 221 G4
Salcott-cum-Virley ... 242 C5
Sandon 267 L7
Sawbridgeworth 226 D3
School Green 123 K2
Seawick 248 E6
Seven Star Green 158 B5
Sewards End 64 A4
Shaftenhoe End 58 D5
Shalford 122 F6
Shalford Green 150 E2
Sheering 227 M5
Shop Corner 110 C4
Shotley 111 G2
Shotley Gate 111 K4
Shrub End 187 K1
Shudy Camps 21 K7
Sible Hedingham 96 A3
Sibley's Green 119 K8
Silver End 210 A1
Skye Green 184 A4
Smith's End 58 C5
Smith's Green 43 H8
Smith's Green 173 M6
Smythe's Green 213 L3
Southey Green 95 L8
South Green 217 J2
South Heath 220 B2
Spellbrook 199 G6
Springfield 254 F7
Springwell 38 C6
Sproughton 30 D7
Stafford's Corner 215 G8
Stagden Cross 232 B3
Stambourne 68 E3
Stambourne Green 68 C4
Stanbrook 119 G6
Stansted Mountfitchet .. 143 L6
Stanway 158 B8
Stanway Green 186 F2
Starling's Green 114 B2
Start Hill 172 G6
Stebbing 149 G8
Stebbing Green 177 M2
Steeple Bumpstead 43 K5
Steventon End 40 E3
Stickling Green 85 M7
Stisted 153 L7
Stocking Green 64 D4
Stoke 2 E9
Stoke by Clare 45 L2
Stoke Park 54 B4
Stones Green 165 M3
Stratford St Mary 104 E4
Strethall 61 G1
Sturmer 44 A1
Stutton 108 B3
Sucksted Green 118 D7
Sudbury 4 F3
Surrex 184 A3
Swan Street 156 E2
Takeley 173 K5
Takeley Street 173 H6
Tattingstone 78 E6
Tattingstone White Horse .. 78 F4
Taverners Green 201 L5
Temple End 48 D2
Tendring 165 H8
Tendring Green 165 G6
Tendring Heath 164 E4
Terling 236 E2
Thaxted 119 K2

Thistley Green ... 206 D1	Toppesfield ... 69 K6	Upwick Green ... 142 A8	Wethersfield ... 122 D2	Wivenhoe ... 189 K4
Thorington Street ... 103 L2	Totham Hill ... 240 A8	Wakes Colne ... 128 D7	Wherstead ... 54 D7	Wix ... 137 L8
Thorley ... 198 E3	Totham Plains ... 240 D8	Wakes Colne Green ... 128 E4	Whiteash Green ... 125 H2	Wixoe ... 44 F2
Thorley Houses ... 170 C8	Trimley Lower Street ... 83 G7	Waltham's Cross ... 122 A4	White Colne ... 128 A7	Woodend Green ... 117 K8
Thorley Street ... 199 G2	Trimley St Martin ... 83 J4	Walton ... 113 H2	White House ... 31 G3	Woodgates End ... 145 M6
Thorpe Common ... 83 G5	Trimley St Mary ... 83 K8	Walton-on-the-Naze ... 196 A5	White Notley ... 209 G4	Woodham Mortimer ... 269 M8
Thorpe Green ... 194 B1	Trims Green ... 198 E6	Warren Heath ... 56 B4	White Roding or	Woodham Walter ... 269 L3
Thorpe-le-Soken ... 194 C4	Twinstead ... 73 L7	Washbrook ... 53 G4	White Roothing ... 229 L6	Woodhill ... 268 D7
Thorrington ... 191 K8	Twinstead Green ... 73 J8	Washbrook Street ... 53 G3	Whittlesford ... 16 E1	The Woodlands ... 79 K6
Tilbury Green ... 45 M7	Tye Green ... 89 L2	Watch House Green ... 178 A6	Whitton ... 30 F2	Woodside Green ... 200 B4
Tilbury Juxta Claire ... 46 D8	Tye Green ... 145 G7	Water End ... 40 D7	Wicken Bonhunt ... 86 D5	Woolverstone ... 80 C4
Tilekiln Green ... 172 B7	Tye Green ... 181 G7	Weeley ... 193 H4	Wickham Bishops ... 238 F8	Workhouse Green ... 75 G6
Tilkey ... 183 H1	Tye Green ... 232 A7	Weeley Heath ... 193 H7	Wickham St Paul ... 72 E8	Workhouse Hill ... 132 A1
Tilty ... 146 F4	Ugley ... 116 B7	Wellstye Green ... 204 C3	Widdington ... 116 E1	Wormingford ... 100 F8
Tindon End ... 90 D4	Ugley Green ... 144 C2	Welshwood Park ... 161 H4	Widford ... 266 A7	Wrabness ... 138 B2
Tiptree ... 212 D7	Ulting Wick ... 257 L6	Wendens Ambo ... 62 A8	Wiggens Green ... 43 G4	Wright's Green ... 199 M6
Tiptree Heath ... 240 D2	Uppend ... 142 D4	West Bergholt ... 159 G2	Willows Green ... 207 G1	Writtle ... 265 J5
Tollesbury ... 262 E4	Upper Dovercourt ... 140 A2	Westbourne ... 31 G4	Wimbish ... 64 E7	Young's End ... 207 J1
Tolleshunt D'Arcy ... 261 L1	Upper Green ... 84 F3	Westerfield ... 32 A1	Wimbish Green ... 90 A2	
Tolleshunt Knights ... 241 J3	Upper Street ... 108 A4	West Mersea ... 244 C7	Witham ... 238 A1	
Tolleshunt Major ... 261 G1	Upsher Green ... 51 K1	Westwood Park ... 131 G4	Withersfield ... 22 F1	

USING THE STREET INDEX

Street names are listed alphabetically. Each street name is followed by its postal town or area locality, the Postcode District, the page number, and the reference to the square in which the name is found.

Example: **Abbey Meadow** HSTD CO9 .... 95 M3 1

Some entries are followed by a number in a blue box. This number indicates the location of the street within the referenced grid square. The full street name is listed at the side of the map page.

GENERAL ABBREVIATIONS

ACC ...ACCESS	CUTT ...CUTTINGS	HOL ...HOLLOW	NW ...NORTH WEST	SKWY ...SKYWAY
ALY ...ALLEY	CV ...COVE	HOSP ...HOSPITAL	O/P ...OVERPASS	SMT ...SUMMIT
AP ...APPROACH	CYN ...CANYON	HRB ...HARBOUR	OFF ...OFFICE	SOC ...SOCIETY
AR ...ARCADE	DEPT ...DEPARTMENT	HTH ...HEATH	ORCH ...ORCHARD	SP ...SPUR
ASS ...ASSOCIATION	DL ...DALE	HTS ...HEIGHTS	OV ...OVAL	SPR ...SPRING
AV ...AVENUE	DM ...DAM	HVN ...HAVEN	PAL ...PALACE	SQ ...SQUARE
BCH ...BEACH	DR ...DRIVE	HWY ...HIGHWAY	PAS ...PASSAGE	ST ...STREET
BLDS ...BUILDINGS	DRO ...DROVE	IMP ...IMPERIAL	PAV ...PAVILION	STN ...STATION
BND ...BEND	DRY ...DRIVEWAY	IN ...INLET	PDE ...PARADE	STR ...STREAM
BNK ...BANK	DWGS ...DWELLINGS	IND EST ...INDUSTRIAL ESTATE	PH ...PUBLIC HOUSE	STRD ...STRAND
BR ...BRIDGE	E ...EAST	INF ...INFIRMARY	PK ...PARK	SW ...SOUTH WEST
BRK ...BROOK	EMB ...EMBANKMENT	INFO ...INFORMATION	PKWY ...PARKWAY	TDG ...TRADING
BTM ...BOTTOM	EMBY ...EMBASSY	INT ...INTERCHANGE	PL ...PLACE	TER ...TERRACE
BUS ...BUSINESS	ESP ...ESPLANADE	IS ...ISLAND	PLN ...PLAIN	THWY ...THROUGHWAY
BVD ...BOULEVARD	EST ...ESTATE	JCT ...JUNCTION	PLNS ...PLAINS	TNL ...TUNNEL
BY ...BYPASS	EX ...EXCHANGE	JTY ...JETTY	PLZ ...PLAZA	TOLL ...TOLLWAY
CATH ...CATHEDRAL	EXPY ...EXPRESSWAY	KG ...KING	POL ...POLICE STATION	TPK ...TURNPIKE
CEM ...CEMETERY	EXT ...EXTENSION	KNL ...KNOLL	PR ...PRINCE	TR ...TRACK
CEN ...CENTRE	F/O ...FLYOVER	L ...LAKE	PREC ...PRECINCT	TRL ...TRAIL
CFT ...CROFT	FC ...FOOTBALL CLUB	LA ...LANE	PREP ...PREPARATORY	TWR ...TOWER
CH ...CHURCH	FK ...FORK	LDG ...LODGE	PRIM ...PRIMARY	U/P ...UNDERPASS
CHA ...CHASE	FLD ...FIELD	LGT ...LIGHT	PROM ...PROMENADE	UNI ...UNIVERSITY
CHYD ...CHURCHYARD	FLDS ...FIELDS	LK ...LOCK	PRS ...PRINCESS	UPR ...UPPER
CIR ...CIRCLE	FLS ...FALLS	LKS ...LAKES	PRT ...PORT	V ...VALE
CIRC ...CIRCUS	FLS ...FLATS	LNDG ...LANDING	PT ...POINT	VA ...VALLEY
CL ...CLOSE	FM ...FARM	LTL ...LITTLE	PTH ...PATH	VIAD ...VIADUCT
CLFS ...CLIFFS	FT ...FORT	LWR ...LOWER	PZ ...PIAZZA	VIL ...VILLA
CMP ...CAMP	FWY ...FREEWAY	MAG ...MAGISTRATE	QD ...QUADRANT	VIS ...VISTA
CNR ...CORNER	FY ...FERRY	MAN ...MANSIONS	QU ...QUEEN	VLG ...VILLAGE
CO. ...COUNTY	GA ...GATE	MD ...MEAD	QY ...QUAY	VLS ...VILLAS
COLL ...COLLEGE	GAL ...GALLERY	MDW ...MEADOWS	R ...RIVER	VW ...VIEW
COM ...COMMON	GDN ...GARDEN	MEM ...MEMORIAL	RBT ...ROUNDABOUT	W ...WEST
COMM ...COMMISSION	GDNS ...GARDENS	MKT ...MARKET	RD ...ROAD	WD ...WOOD
CON ...CONVENT	GLD ...GLADE	MKTS ...MARKETS	RDG ...RIDGE	WHF ...WHARF
COT ...COTTAGE	GLN ...GLEN	ML ...MALL	REP ...REPUBLIC	WK ...WALK
COTS ...COTTAGES	GN ...GREEN	ML ...MILL	RES ...RESERVOIR	WKS ...WALKS
CP ...CAPE	GND ...GROUND	MNR ...MANOR	RFC ...RUGBY FOOTBALL CLUB	WLS ...WELLS
CPS ...COPSE	GRA ...GRANGE	MS ...MEWS	RI ...RISE	WY ...WAY
CR ...CREEK	GRG ...GARAGE	MSN ...MISSION	RP ...RAMP	YD ...YARD
CREM ...CREMATORIUM	GT ...GREAT	MT ...MOUNT	RW ...ROW	YHA ...YOUTH HOSTEL
CRS ...CRESCENT	GTWY ...GATEWAY	MTN ...MOUNTAIN	S ...SOUTH	
CSWY ...CAUSEWAY	GV ...GROVE	MTS ...MOUNTAINS	SCH ...SCHOOL	
CT ...COURT	HGR ...HIGHER	MUS ...MUSEUM	SE ...SOUTH EAST	
CTRL ...CENTRAL	HL ...HILL	MWY ...MOTORWAY	SER ...SERVICE AREA	
CTS ...COURTS	HLS ...HILLS	N ...NORTH	SH ...SHORE	
CTYD ...COURTYARD	HO ...HOUSE	NE ...NORTH EAST	SHOP ...SHOPPING	

POSTCODE TOWNS AND AREA ABBREVIATIONS

BOC ...Burnham-on-Crouch	COLN ...Colchester north	HLWE ...Harlow east	MGTR ...Manningtree	SAFWN ...Saffron Walden north
BRTR ...Braintree	COLS ...Colchester south	HSTD ...Halstead	MHAD ...Much Hadham	SAFWS ...Saffron Walden south
BSF ...Bishop's Stortford	COLW ...Colchester west	HVHL ...Haverhill	NHMKT ...Needham Market	SBW ...Sawbridgeworth
BUNT ...Buntingford	COS ...Clacton-on-Sea	ING ...Ingatestone	RBSF ...Rural Bishop's Stortford	STDN ...Standon
BURES ...Bures	FOS ...Frinton-on-Sea	IP ...Ipswich	RCHLM ...Rural Chelmsford	STSD ...Stansted
CBE/LIN ...Cambridge east/Linton	FRAM/WMKT ...Framlingham/ Wickham Market	IPNE ...Ipswich northeast	RCOLE ...Rural Colchester east	SUD ...Sudbury
CBS ...Cambridge south	FX ...Felixstowe	IPSE ...Ipswich southeast	RCOLW ...Rural Colchester west	WDBR ...Woodbridge
CHLM/GWD ...Chelmsford/Galleywood	GTDUN ...Great Dunmow	K/T/MI ...Kelvedon/Tiptree/ Mersea Island	RCOS ...Rural Clacton-on-Sea	WIT ...Witham
CHLM/WR ...Chelmsford/Writtle	HADL ...Hadleigh	KESG ...Kesgrave	RIPS/CAP ...Rural Ipswich south/ Capel St Mary	WOTN ...Walton-on-the-Naze
CHONG ...Chipping Ongar	HAR ...Harwich	KIR/NAC ...Kirton/Nacton	RIPW ...Rural Ipswich west	
CHTY ...Chantry	HLW ...Harlow	MAL ...Maldon	ROY ...Royston	
COL ...Colchester				

Index - streets

Abb - Ald

A

Abberton Rd COLS CO2 ... 187 K8	Abbotts Ct HVHL CB9 ... 24 A8	Acres End CHLM/WR CM1 ... 266 A1	Ainger Rd HAR CO12 ... 140 A3	RCOLE CO7 ... 219 J7
K/T/MI CO5 ... 189 J8	Abbotts Rd HVHL CB9 ... 23 J4	Acton CI RIPW IP8 ... 30 C3	Aingers Green Rd RCOLE CO7 ... 192 B8	WIT CM8 ... 238 C2
Abbess CI CHLM/WR CM1 ... 14 A4	Abbotts Wy BSF CM23 ... 199 G2	SUD CO10 ... 4 E4	Ainslie Rd IP IP1 ... 2 B4	Albert St COL CO1 ... 10 B4
Abbey Crs RCOS CO16 ... 194 C4	Abdy Av HAR CO12 ... 140 A3	Acton Gdns RIPW IP8 ... 30 C2	Aisne Rd COLS CO2 ... 187 M1	HAR CO12 ... 9 K5
Abbey Gate St COLS CO2 ... 10 C8	Abell Wy CHLM/GWD CM2 ... 267 K1	Acton La SUD CO10 ... 4 C6	Aisthorpe RIPS/CAP IP9 ... 77 H4 1	Albion Gv COLS CO2 ... 160 C8
Abbey La RCOLW CO6 ... 183 L4	Abels Rd HSTD CO9 ... 125 M5	SUD CO10 ... 5 G1	Ajax CI BRTR CM7 ... 152 D8	Albion HI IPNE IP4 ... 3 L3
SAFWN CB10 ... 62 F4	Abercorn Wy IPNE IP4 ... 32 D4	SUD CO10 ... 50 B1	Alamein Rd CHLM/WR CM1 ... 254 B7	Albion St K/T/MI CO5 ... 189 J6
Abbey Meadow HSTD CO9 ... 95 M3 1	Aberdeen Wy IPNE IP4 ... 32 D4	Acton Rd RIPW IP8 ... 30 C3	COLS CO2 ... 187 L3	Albrighton Cft COLN CO4 ... 160 E1
Abbey Rd SUD CO10 ... 4 C2	Aberfoyle CI IPNE IP4 ... 32 E4 1	Adair Rd IP IP1 ... 2 B4	Alanbrooke Rd COLS CO2 ... 188 F3	Alconbury BSF CM23 ... 171 K4
Abbey St RCOS CO16 ... 194 C4	Abinger CI RCOS CO16 ... 221 L2	Adams CI CHTY IP2 ... 54 E2 1	Alan Dr RCOS CO16 ... 221 M4	Aldeburgh CI HVHL CB9 ... 23 G7
SAFWN CB10 ... 37 J1	Abraham Dr WIT CM8 ... 210 A1	Adams Ct SAFWS CB11 ... 62 E5	Alan Rd IPSE IP3 ... 3 M8	RCOS CO16 ... 249 K1 1
Abbey Turning MAL CM9 ... 270 F2	Abram's La ROY SG8 ... 35 L8	Adams PI KESG IP5 ... 33 L6	WIT CM8 ... 238 A4	Aldeburgh Gdns COLN CO4 ... 160 D1
Abbey Vw GTDUN CM6 ... 147 G3	Acacia Av COLN CO4 ... 161 G5	Adastral CI FX IP11 ... 6 E9	Alan Wy COLW CO3 ... 187 H1	Alderbury Wy CHLM/WR CM1 ... 254 F8
Abbotsbury CI CHTY IP2 ... 54 C4	Acacia CI IPSE IP3 ... 56 A4	Addington Rd FX IP11 ... 83 L8	Albany CI CHLM/WR CM1 ... 254 A8	Alder CI BSF CM23 ... 144 A5
Abbots CI COS CO15 ... 222 A1	Acacia Dr MAL CM9 ... 271 G3	Addison Rd FOS CO13 ... 195 J8	RCOLW CO6 ... 159 G1	Aldercar Rd RCOLW CO6 ... 186 B4
MGTR CO11 ... 137 L8	Acacia Gdns WIT CM8 ... 238 D1 1	SUD CO10 ... 5 H3	Albany Gdns East COS CO15 ... 13 L4	Alder Dr CHLM/GWD CM2 ... 266 D7
Abbots Gdns RCOS CO16 ... 248 E1	Accommodation Rd	Adelaide Dr COLS CO2 ... 188 C4	Albany Gdns West COS CO15 ... 13 K4	Alderford St HSTD CO9 ... 96 A5
Abbots La COLW CO3 ... 158 C6	RCOLW CO6 ... 131 M6	Adelaide Rd IPNE IP4 ... 32 F7	The Albany IPNE IP4 ... 3 J1	Alderlee CHTY IP2 ... 54 B5
Abbotsmead MAL CM9 ... 259 H8	Acer Gv RIPW IP8 ... 53 L4	Adelaide St HAR CO12 ... 8 A5	Albany Rd RCOLW CO6 ... 159 H1	Alderman Rd IP IP1 ... 2 C6
Abbot's Rd COLS CO2 ... 188 E2	Achnacone Dr COLN CO4 ... 159 L2	Admirals Wk CHLM/WR CM1 ... 14 C1	Albemarle Gdns BRTR CM7 ... 152 E8	Alde Rd HVHL CB9 ... 23 J5
Abbots Wick La K/T/MI CO5 ... 242 C2	Acland Av COLW CO3 ... 159 J6	Aetheric Rd BRTR CM7 ... 180 A2	Albemarle St HAR CO12 ... 9 K4	Alders Wk SBW CM21 ... 227 G3
Abbott Rd HAR CO12 ... 140 B3	Acorn Av BRTR CM7 ... 179 M3	Affleck Rd COLN CO4 ... 161 G6	Alberta CI KESG IP5 ... 33 J4 1	Alderton CI GTDUN CM6 ... 177 L7
Abbotts CI CHLM/WR CM1 ... 15 L2 1	HSTD CO9 ... 125 M4	Agar Road Ap WOTN CO14 ... 196 E5 1	Albert Gdns COS CO15 ... 13 K5	Alderton Rd COLN CO4 ... 11 K4
	Acorn CI HAR CO12 ... 140 C4 1	Agate CI IP IP1 ... 30 F4	RCOLW CO6 ... 183 J3	Aldon CI HAR CO12 ... 139 L4
	RCOLE CO7 ... 160 F1	Agate Rd COS CO15 ... 12 F8	Albertine CI COLW CO3 ... 158 E7	
	RIPW IP8 ... 53 L3	Agincourt Rd COS CO15 ... 12 C4	Albert PI RCOLW CO6 ... 183 J3	
			Albert Rd BRTR CM7 ... 180 C2	

Aldous Cl RCOLE CO7 .... 105 L2
Aldridge Cl CHLM/GWD CM2 .... 267 J1
Aldringham Ms FX IP11 .... 112 F2
Alexander Dr SUD CO10 .... 51 H2
Alexander Rd BRTR CM7 .... 180 A1
Alexandra Av K/T/MI CO5 .... 244 F7
Alexandra Dr RCOLE CO7 .... 189 L2
Alexandra Rd COLW CO3 .... 10 A8
  COS CO15 .... 12 F6
  FX IP11 .... 113 G1
  HAR CO12 .... 9 H1
  HSTD CO9 .... 95 M4
  IPNE IP4 .... 3 K4
  RCOS CO16 .... 193 H5
  SUD CO10 .... 5 G6
Alexandra St HAR CO12 .... 9 K5
Alexandra Ter COLW CO3 .... 10 A9
Alfells Rd RCOLE CO7 .... 162 B7
Alfred Ter WOTN CO14 .... 196 E5 2
Alfreg Rd WIT CM8 .... 237 M5
Alienor Av BRTR CM7 .... 121 K4
Allectus Wy WIT CM8 .... 237 M5
Allenby Rd CHTY IP2 .... 31 H7
Allendale Dr RCOLW CO6 .... 185 M1
Allens Cl RCHLM CM3 .... 256 B4
Alleyne Wy RCOS CO16 .... 247 J2
Alley Rd KIR/NAC IP10 .... 83 K2
Allfields Rd COLN CO4 .... 140 B3
Allington Cl IPNE IP4 .... 3 M3
Allington Wk HVHL CB9 .... 23 G5
All Saints Av COLW CO3 .... 187 J1
All Saints Cl BSF CM23 .... 171 J5
  CHLM/WR CM1 .... 267 G1
All Saints' Rd IP IP1 .... 2 A2
Alma Cl IPNE IP4 .... 32 C4
Alma Dr CHLM/WR CM1 .... 14 E3
Alma St RCOLE CO7 .... 189 K5 1
Almond Cl COS CO15 .... 12 A6
  K/T/MI CO5 .... 212 E7 1
  RCOLE CO7 .... 189 L3
Almondhayes CHTY IP2 .... 54 D2
Almond Wy COLN CO4 .... 161 G5
Alpe St IP IP1 .... 2 C3
Alpha Cl BRTR CM7 .... 180 C3
Alphamstone Rd BURES CO8 .... 99 K1
Alpha Pl BSF CM23 .... 171 H5 1
Alpha Rd RCOS CO16 .... 247 K2
Alport Av COLS CO2 .... 187 L1
Alresford Rd RCOLE CO7 .... 190 A5
Alsa Gdns RBSF CM22 .... 144 E3
Alsa Leys RBSF CM22 .... 144 E3
Alsa St STSD CM24 .... 144 B4
Alston Cl SUD CO10 .... 51 K7
Alston Rd IPSE IP3 .... 3 M9
Altbarn Cl COLN CO4 .... 132 E8
Altbarn Rd COLS CO2 .... 160 F8
Alton Dr COLW CO3 .... 159 K7
Alton Hall La RIPS/CAP IP9 .... 108 B1
Alton Park La COS CO15 .... 249 J4
Alton Park Rd COS CO15 .... 12 D7
Alton Rd COS CO15 .... 12 F8
Alverton Cl BRTR CM7 .... 179 K6
Alverton Wy COLN CO4 .... 160 D2
Alvis Av COS CO15 .... 249 G7
Alyssum Cl CHLM/WR CM1 .... 255 H7
Amberley Cl RCOLE CO7 .... 189 L4
Ambleside Ct COS CO15 .... 13 K6
Ambridge Rd RCOLW CO6 .... 183 G2
Ambrose Av COLW CO3 .... 187 H1
Amcotes Pl CHLM/GWD CM2 .... 15 K8
Amerells Rd RCOS CO16 .... 221 L1
America Rd RCOLW CO6 .... 155 K4
America St MAL CM9 .... 271 J3 1
Amos Hl SUD CO10 .... 73 K5
Amoss Rd CHLM/GWD CM2 .... 267 H5
Ancaster Rd CHTY IP2 .... 2 C9
Anchor End MGTR CO11 .... 136 C1
Anchor Hl RCOLE CO7 .... 189 K6 1
  MGTR CO11 .... 136 C1
Anchor La MAL CM9 .... 259 J8
Anchor Rd COS CO15 .... 12 D6
  K/T/MI CO5 .... 240 E1
Anchor St BSF CM23 .... 171 J7
  CHLM/GWD CM2 .... 15 G6
Anderson Av CHLM/WR CM1 .... 254 B8
Anderson Cl BSF CM23 .... 143 H3
Andrews Farm La GTDUN CM6 .... 147 L5
Andrews Pl CHLM/WR CM1 .... 14 D3
Andros Cl IPSE IP3 .... 55 J5 1
Anemone Cl COLN CO4 .... 159 L3 1
Angelgate Esp HAR CO12 .... 9 L3 1
Angel La GTDUN CM6 .... 175 M5
  IPNE IP4 .... 3 H7
  SUD CO10 .... 28 D1
Angel Rd RIPW IP8 .... 30 C3
Anglesea Rd IP IP1 .... 2 C3
  RCOLE CO7 .... 189 L5
Anglesey Cl BSF CM23 .... 170 E6
Angle Side BRTR CM7 .... 180 D3 1
Anglia Cl COLS CO2 .... 187 K2
Anglia Wy BRTR CM7 .... 180 D3
Angus Cl IPNE IP4 .... 32 D4
Anita Cl East CHTY IP2 .... 31 G8
Anita Cl West CHTY IP2 .... 31 G8
Anjou Gn CHLM/WR CM1 .... 255 J6
Annbrook Rd CHTY IP2 .... 54 A4
Ann Coles Cl HVHL CB9 .... 43 L7
Anne Cl RCOLE CO7 .... 219 H7
Anne St FX IP11 .... 7 G4
Ann St IP IP1 .... 2 C3
Ann Suckling Rd HVHL CB9 .... 23 J3
Ansar Rd SAFWS CB11 .... 63 G6 1
Anson Cl HAR CO12 .... 140 C3
Anson Wy BRTR CM7 .... 180 E1 1
Antonia Cl COLN CO4 .... 160 F2
Antonia Cl HVHL CB9 .... 24 A6
Antonius Wy COLN CO4 .... 132 D7 1
Antrim Rd IP IP1 .... 30 F4
Anvil Wy CHLM/WR CM1 .... 255 G6
Anzani Av FX IP11 .... 6 C2
Anzio Crs COLS CO2 .... 187 L3
Appleby Rd RIPW IP8 .... 53 L4
Appleton Flds BSF CM23 .... 199 G1
Appletree Cl BRTR CM7 .... 181 H8
Apple Wy CHLM/GWD CM2 .... 266 E7

The Approach COS CO15 .... 249 J5 1
Apsley Cl BSF CM23 .... 199 G1
Apton Cl BSF CM23 .... 171 H6
Apton Flds BSF CM23 .... 171 H7
Apton Rd BSF CM23 .... 171 H6
Aragon Cl COS CO15 .... 249 H5
Aragon Rd CHLM CM3 .... 207 H6
Arakan Cl COLS CO2 .... 187 K4
Arbour La CHLM/WR CM1 .... 266 F1
  WIT CM8 .... 239 G8
Arbour Wy COLN CO4 .... 160 E1
Arcade St IP IP1 .... 2 E5
Archangel Gdns CHTY IP2 .... 54 A1 1
Archery Flds COS CO15 .... 13 K2
Arden Cl COLN CO4 .... 160 E2
Arderne Ct HAR CO12 .... 140 B3
Ardleigh Rd MGTR CO11 .... 135 G8
  RCOLE CO7 .... 133 M2
  RCOLE CO7 .... 162 D1
Ardley Crs RBSF CM22 .... 228 D3
Argents La COLW CO3 .... 158 D3
Argyle Rd RCOS CO16 .... 194 C3
Argyle St IPNE IP4 .... 3 H5
Ariel Cl COLN CO4 .... 161 G6
Arkle Ct KESG IP5 .... 33 M6
Arkwright Rd FX IP11 .... 31 G7
Armidale Wk COLS CO2 .... 188 C3 1
Armiger Wy WIT CM8 .... 238 D3 1
Armonde Rd RCHLM CM3 .... 256 A4 1
Armourers Ct BSF CM23 .... 198 D1 1
Armoury Rd RCOLW CO6 .... 159 H1
Arms La HVHL CB9 .... 24 D4
Armstrong Cl RCHLM CM3 .... 269 H5
Armstrong Wy HSTD CO9 .... 70 C3 1
Arnhem Gv BRTR CM7 .... 152 A8
Arnhem Rd CHLM/WR CM1 .... 254 A7
Arnold Cl IP IP1 .... 31 H2
Arnold Rd COS CO15 .... 12 C9
Arnold Vls K/T/MI CO5 .... 212 E7 2
Arnstones Cl COLN CO4 .... 11 K5
Arras Rd COLS CO2 .... 187 M1
Arrendene Rd HVHL CB9 .... 23 H4
Arrow Rd COLN CO4 .... 161 H6
Arthur Ct CHLM/WR CM1 .... 254 B8 1
Arthur St COL CO1 .... 10 D8
Arthy Cl RCHLM CM3 .... 257 J1 1
Artillery St COL CO1 .... 11 H9
Arun Cl CHLM/WR CM1 .... 254 E8
Arundel Wy IPSE IP3 .... 56 A2
Arwela Rd FX IP11 .... 7 J5
Asbury Cl COLN CO4 .... 11 L5
Asbury Dr RCOLW CO6 .... 185 H2
Ascham La CBS CB2 .... 16 D1
Ascot Cl BSF CM23 .... 171 L5
Ascot Dr FX IP11 .... 113 G1
  IPSE IP3 .... 55 K2
Ash Bungalows BRTR CM7 .... 180 A2 1
Ashby Rd BSF CM23 .... 171 K4
Ashby Rd WIT CM8 .... 238 O6
Ash Cl COS CO15 .... 12 A6
  RCHLM CM3 .... 257 J1
  RCOLE CO7 .... 219 G6
Ashcroft Rd IP IP1 .... 31 H4
Ashdale Rd KESG IP5 .... 33 M5
Ashdale St BSF CM23 .... 198 F1
Ashdon Rd SAFWN CB10 .... 39 M8
  SAFWN CB10 .... 63 G3
  SAFWN CB10 .... 64 F1
Ashdown Rd COLN CO4 .... 11 M7
Ashdown Wy COLN CO4 .... 11 M7
  IPSE IP3 .... 55 M2
Ashen Cl SUD CO10 .... 45 M4
Ashen Hl SUD CO10 .... 45 L3
Ashen La SUD CO10 .... 45 L2
Ashen Rd HSTD CO9 .... 45 K5
  SUD CO10 .... 26 D7
  SUD CO10 .... 46 C4
Ashes Cl FOS CO13 .... 196 B5
Ashes Rd BRTR CM7 .... 181 H6
Ash Fall WIT CM8 .... 210 C8 1
Ashfield Farm Rd MAL CM9 .... 257 M5
Ashford Rd CHLM/WR CM1 .... 14 B4
Ash Gn SAFWN CB10 .... 37 M4
Ash Ground Cl FX IP11 .... 83 K5
  MGTR CO11 .... 106 F5
Ash Gv CHLM/GWD CM2 .... 266 E6
  COLS CO2 .... 188 C5
  GTDUN CM6 .... 175 M6
  HVHL CB9 .... 23 G4
  MAL CM9 .... 259 K7
  RCOLE CO7 .... 189 L2
  RIPS/CAP IP9 .... 77 J4
  SUD CO10 .... 50 D8
Ash Groves SBW CM21 .... 227 J3
Ashlea Cl HVHL CB9 .... 23 K7 1
Ashlea Rd HVHL CB9 .... 23 K7
Ashley Gdns COLW CO3 .... 159 L7
Ashley Rd HAR CO12 .... 8 D8
Ashley St CHTY IP2 .... 2 F9
Ashlong Gv HSTD CO9 .... 126 A2
Ashlyn's Rd FOS CO13 .... 224 A1
Ashmere Gv IPNE IP4 .... 3 L4
Ashmere Ri SUD CO10 .... 5 G5
Ashmole Dr FOS CO13 .... 196 B7
Ashpole Rd BRTR CM7 .... 152 D4
Ash Ri COLW CO3 .... 187 H2
Ashwin Av RCOLW CO6 .... 185 M1
Askins Rd RCOLE CO7 .... 105 L2
Aspen Cl HVHL CB9 .... 23 G4
The Aspens BSF CM23 .... 171 K3
Aspen Wy COLN CO4 .... 11 M4
Aspin Ms SAFWN CB10 .... 63 G2 1
Asquith Dr COLN CO4 .... 132 B1 1
Assington Rd SUD CO10 .... 51 L8
Aster Cl BSF CM23 .... 170 F7
  CHLM/WR CM1 .... 255 H7

  COS CO15 .... 12 A4
Aster Rd CHTY IP2 .... 54 A1
Astley Rd COS CO15 .... 12 C5
Ataka Rd FX IP11 .... 113 H1
Athelstan Rd RCOLW CO6 .... 159 L8
Atherton End SBW CM21 .... 227 G2
Atherton Rd CHTY IP2 .... 53 M3
Atlas Ct RCOLW CO6 .... 127 J6
Atlas Rd RCOLW CO6 .... 127 H6
Atterton Rd HVHL CB9 .... 22 F4
Attwood Cl COLN CO4 .... 132 D8
Aubrey Cl CHLM/WR CM1 .... 254 D6
Auckland Cl CHLM/WR CM1 .... 254 A8 1
Audley End Rd SAFWS CB11 .... 62 C4
Audley Rd COLW CO3 .... 159 L8
  RCHLM CM3 .... 207 H6
  SAFWS CB11 .... 62 F4
Audley Wy CBE/LIN CB1 .... 21 J2
  FOS CO13 .... 196 C7
Audrey Gdns BSF CM23 .... 199 H2
Augustus Cl COLN CO4 .... 132 D7 2
  HVHL CB9 .... 23 H7 1
Augustus Wy WIT CM8 .... 238 A5
Austen Cl BRTR CM7 .... 180 C5 1
Austin Av COS CO15 .... 249 G7
Austin St CHTY IP2 .... 2 F8
Auton Cft SAFWS CB11 .... 62 F6 1
Autoway COLN CO4 .... 160 E1
Autumn Cl RCOS CO16 .... 12 A1
Aveley Wy MAL CM9 .... 271 H5
Aveline Rd RCOLE CO7 .... 133 M6
Avenue Rd BSF CM23 .... 171 J7
  CHLM/GWD CM2 .... 266 F6
  WIT CM8 .... 238 C2
The Avenue BRTR CM7 .... 180 B2
  COLW CO3 .... 159 L7
  COS CO15 .... 222 D6
  FX IP11 .... 83 K8
  GTDUN CM6 .... 176 A5
  HAR CO12 .... 166 D2
  IP IP1 .... 31 L4
  RCHLM CM3 .... 269 H7
  RCOLW CO6 .... 158 F2
  RIPW IP8 .... 53 H6
  WIT CM8 .... 238 C2
Avignon Cl COLS CO2 .... 188 D1
Avocet Cl FOS CO13 .... 196 A7 1
  K/T/MI CO5 .... 211 M3
  K/T/MI CO5 .... 244 F6
Avocet Wy MAL CM9 .... 259 L8 1
Avondale Rd COS CO15 .... 13 J5
  IPSE IP3 .... 55 J3
Avon Rd CHLM/GWD CM2 .... 265 M1
Avon Wy COLN CO4 .... 161 H6
Aylesbury Dr COS CO15 .... 223 H7
Ayletts CHLM/GWD CM2 .... 254 D2
Ayloffe Rd COLN CO4 .... 11 K3
Aynsworth Av BSF CM23 .... 171 J3
Ayr Rd IPNE IP4 .... 32 D4

B

Back Hamlet IPSE IP3 .... 3 J7
Back Hl CBE/LIN CB1 .... 19 K7
Back La BRTR CM7 .... 153 L7
  COLW CO3 .... 159 G6
  FX IP11 .... 113 G6
  GTDUN CM6 .... 119 H2
  HAR CO12 .... 166 E2
  RBSF CM22 .... 199 K6
  RBSF CM22 .... 227 L5
  RCHLM CM3 .... 205 J7
  RCHLM CM3 .... 233 G3
  RCHLM CM3 .... 234 E8
  RIPS/CAP IP9 .... 78 E7
  RIPW IP8 .... 53 G5
  SAFWN CB10 .... 37 J2
  WIT CM8 .... 259 H1
Back La East RCOLE CO7 .... 163 J7
Back La West RCOLE CO7 .... 163 H6
Back Rd CBE/LIN CB1 .... 19 K1
  CHLM/WR CM1 .... 265 H1
  KIR/NAC IP10 .... 83 K2
  MAL CM9 .... 262 D1
  RCOLE CO7 .... 134 C2
Back Waterside La RCOLE CO7 .... 219 H8
Bacon's La RCOLW CO6 .... 156 E2
Bacton Rd FX IP11 .... 7 J3
Baddow Hall Av
  CHLM/GWD CM2 .... 267 J6
Baddow Hall Crs
  CHLM/GWD CM2 .... 267 J6
Baddow Place Av
  CHLM/GWD CM2 .... 267 J7
Baddow Rd CHLM/GWD CM2 .... 15 J5
Baden Powell Dr COLW CO3 .... 187 J2
Bader Cl IPSE IP3 .... 55 L3
Badger Gv BRTR CM7 .... 180 D2 1
Badgers BSF CM23 .... 171 G8
Badgers Bank CHTY IP2 .... 54 A4
Badgers Gn RCOLW CO6 .... 185 G2
Badgers Gv RCOLW CO6 .... 131 K4
Badley Hall Rd RCOLE CO7 .... 163 H3
Badleys Cl SUD CO10 .... 51 H2
Badminton Rd COS CO15 .... 249 J6
Badshah Av IPSE IP3 .... 55 K2
Bagshaw Rd HAR CO12 .... 9 J7
Bailey Bridge Rd BRTR CM7 .... 152 A8
Bailey Cl CHTY IP2 .... 31 G7
  HVHL CB9 .... 23 M6
Bailey Dl COLN CO4 .... 186 E1 1
Bailey La SUD CO10 .... 26 E4
Bainbridge Dr K/T/MI CO5 .... 240 F1
Baines Cl COLN CO4 .... 159 H8
Baird Cl CHTY IP2 .... 31 H6
Baker Av RCHLM CM3 .... 257 J2
Baker Rd RIPS/CAP IP9 .... 111 J5 1
Baker's La BRTR CM7 .... 179 L8
  CBE/LIN CB1 .... 19 M3
  COLN CO4 .... 159 K3
  COLW CO3 .... 159 A4
  GTDUN CM6 .... 205 L1
  MAL CM9 .... 260 E1
  RCHLM CM3 .... 269 G6
  ROY SG8 .... 58 B2

Bakers Md RCHLM CM3 .... 234 B6 1
Baker's Rd SUD CO10 .... 47 H4
Baker St CHLM/GWD CM2 .... 14 F5
Baldry Cl RIPW IP8 .... 53 L4
Baldwin's La RCOLW CO6 .... 156 A5
Balfe Ct COLW CO3 .... 187 G1
Balingdon La CBE/LIN CB1 .... 19 M2
Balkerne Gdns COLW CO3 .... 10 B7
Balkerne Hl COLW CO3 .... 10 A7
Ballast Quay Rd K/T/MI CO5 .... 189 K7
  RCOLE CO7 .... 189 L5
Ballater Cl IP IP1 .... 31 G1
Ballingdon Hl SUD CO10 .... 49 L8
Ballingdon St SUD CO10 .... 4 A8
Ball La COLS CO2 .... 188 C8
Ball's Chace RCOLW CO6 .... 129 H3
Balmoral Av COS CO15 .... 12 O6
Balsham Rd CBE/LIN CB1 .... 19 M2
Balton Wy HAR CO12 .... 140 B3
Banham Dr SUD CO10 .... 4 F4
Banister Cl RCOS CO16 .... 12 B1
Bankart La CHLM/GWD CM2 .... 267 H1
Bank Rd IPNE IP4 .... 3 K4
Bank St BRTR CM7 .... 180 B2
Banters La RCHLM CM3 .... 207 J4
Bantocks Rd SUD CO10 .... 51 G2
Bantoft Ter IPSE IP3 .... 55 L3
Banyard Cl KESG IP5 .... 33 M6 1
Barbel Rd COLN CO4 .... 161 H4
Barbour Gdns COLS CO2 .... 187 H3
Barbrook La K/T/MI CO5 .... 212 F7
Barclay Cl CHLM/WR CM1 .... 267 H7
Bardell Cl CHLM/WR CM1 .... 254 B7
Bardfield Rd BRTR CM7 .... 150 B4
  COLS CO2 .... 188 C4
  GTDUN CM6 .... 120 B4
Barfield Wy FOS CO13 .... 196 B7 1
Barfield Rd K/T/MI CO5 .... 244 E7
Bargate La RCOLE CO7 .... 134 C2
Barker Cl CHTY IP2 .... 30 F8
  HVHL CB9 .... 43 K7 1
  MGTR CO11 .... 135 K1 1
Barker Rd SUD CO10 .... 4 D1
Barkis Cl CHLM/WR CM1 .... 253 M6
Barkstead Rd COLN CO4 .... 11 K2
Barkway Hl ROY SG8 .... 58 A7
Barlee Cl SAFWS CB11 .... 114 E2
Barley Cl RBSF CM22 .... 229 G3
Barley La SAFWS CB11 .... 62 F4 1
Barley Flds WIT CM8 .... 238 C4 1
Barley Hills BSF CM23 .... 199 G1
Barley Md RCHLM CM3 .... 269 K7
Barley Rd ROY SG8 .... 34 C7
  ROY SG8 .... 58 E3
Barley Wy CBE/LIN CB1 .... 19 M3
  COLW CO3 .... 158 F8
Barlon Rd MGTR CO11 .... 163 H1
Barlow's Reach
  CHLM/GWD CM2 .... 267 J1
Barnaby Rudge CHLM/WR CM1 .... 254 B6
Barnard Cl SAFWS CB11 .... 87 H5 1
Barnardiston Wy WIT CM8 .... 238 D3
Barnard Rd SBW CM21 .... 227 G2
Barnards Fld GTDUN CM6 .... 119 K3
Barncroft Cl COLN CO4 .... 160 D2
Barnfield FX IP11 .... 112 F1 1
  K/T/MI CO5 .... 211 M2
  MGTR CO11 .... 135 M1
  RBSF CM22 .... 201 J8
  RIPS/CAP IP9 .... 77 K4
Barnfield Ms CHLM/WR CM1 .... 254 C7
Barnfield Rd RCOLW CO6 .... 131 L7
Barn Flds COLW CO3 .... 158 F7
Barn Gn CHLM/WR CM1 .... 255 G6
Barn Hall Av COLS CO2 .... 188 D1
Barnhall Rd MAL CM9 .... 241 K3
Barnham Pl KESG IP5 .... 33 H7
Barn La MGTR CO11 .... 135 H6
Barn Md BRTR CM7 .... 180 F3 1
Barnston Gn GTDUN CM6 .... 204 C1
Barn View Rd RCOLW CO6 .... 183 J4
Baronia Cft COLN CO4 .... 160 E2
Barons Cl FX IP11 .... 113 M1 1
The Barons BSF CM23 .... 170 F8
Baronsdale Cl IP IP1 .... 31 K4
Baronswood Wy COLS CO2 .... 187 M3
Barrack La HAR CO12 .... 9 L6
  IP IP1 .... 2 D4
  RCHLM CM3 .... 234 A5
Barrack Rd CHLM/WR CM1 .... 232 C7
Barrack Sq CHLM/GWD CM2 .... 15 H4
Barrack St COL CO1 .... 11 G8
  MGTR CO11 .... 136 F5
Barr Cl RCOLE CO7 .... 189 L4
Barrel Cl RCOLE CO7 .... 191 J2
Barrells Down Rd BSF CM23 .... 171 G4
Barrett La BSF CM23 .... 171 H6 1
Barrington Cl
  CHLM/GWD CM2 .... 267 J7 1
  RCOS CO16 .... 221 L3
Barrington Gdns COS CO15 .... 222 E8
Barrington Rd COLS CO2 .... 160 C8
Barryfields BRTR CM7 .... 123 G8
Barsey Cl HVHL CB9 .... 22 E4
Bartholomew Cl SAFWN CB10 .... 38 A3 1
Bartholomew Rd BSF CM23 .... 171 H7
Bartholomew St IPNE IP4 .... 3 L5
Bartlow Rd CBE/LIN CB1 .... 19 M3
  CBE/LIN CB1 .... 41 L1
Barton Cl CHTY IP2 .... 54 A3 1
Barton Dr HVHL CB9 .... 24 D3
Barton Gv HVHL CB9 .... 24 D3
Barton Rd FX IP11 .... 113 K3
Bartram Av BRTR CM7 .... 180 E2 1
Barwell Wy WIT CM8 .... 238 C3
Basbow La BSF CM23 .... 171 H5
Basin Rd MAL CM9 .... 272 A1
Bassetts La MAL CM9 .... 269 J3
Bassingbourn Rd STSD CM24 .... 173 H3
Bassingbourn Rbt RBSF CM22 .... 173 H4
Bateman Rd COLS CO2 .... 219 G5
Bateman's Rd RCOS CO16 .... 221 K1
Bates Rd MAL CM9 .... 271 J1
Bath Rd FX IP11 .... 113 K3

Bath St CHTY IP2 .... 54 F2
  RCOLE CO7 .... 189 K5 2
Bathurst Cl COLS CO2 .... 188 C4 1
Battery La RIPS/CAP IP9 .... 111 K5
Battisford Dr RCOS CO16 .... 249 J1
Battles La COS CO15 .... 249 H7
Battlesbrook Rd COLS CO2 .... 188 F3
Bawdsey Cl RCOS CO16 .... 249 K1
Bawn Cl BRTR CM7 .... 180 C1 1
Bawtree Crs CBE/LIN CB1 .... 20 A2
Bawtree Wy COLW CO3 .... 159 J8
Baxters RCHLM CM3 .... 269 J6 1
Bayard Av RCOLE CO7 .... 219 H6
Bayley St HSTD CO9 .... 96 B1
Baynards Crs FOS CO13 .... 196 A7
Bay Rd HAR CO12 .... 9 J7
Bay View Crs HAR CO12 .... 139 L5
Beach Crs COS CO15 .... 249 H7
Beachcroft Av FOS CO13 .... 195 M7 1
Beach Rd COS CO15 .... 13 H7
  HAR CO12 .... 9 H7
  K/T/MI CO5 .... 244 E7
  RCOS CO16 .... 247 L8
Beach Rd East FX IP11 .... 113 L3
Beach Rd West FX IP11 .... 7 J5
Beach's Dr CHLM/WR CM1 .... 265 M2
Beach Station Rd FX IP11 .... 7 H7
Beach Wy COS CO15 .... 249 H7
Beacon Cl RCOLE CO7 .... 219 G7
Beacon Fld FX IP11 .... 113 G2 1
Beacon Hts RCOS CO16 .... 247 K3
Beacon Hl MAL CM9 .... 271 G3
  WIT CM8 .... 239 J7
Beacon Hill Av HAR CO12 .... 9 K6
Beaconsfield Av COLW CO3 .... 10 A9
Beaconsfield Cl SUD CO10 .... 4 C4
Beaconsfield Rd COS CO15 .... 13 G6
  IP IP1 .... 31 H6
  SUD CO10 .... 4 C5
Beacon Wy COLW CO3 .... 158 E7
  RCOS CO16 .... 247 K3
The Beadles RBSF CM22 .... 199 K5 1
Beadle Wy RCHLM CM3 .... 207 H7
Beadon Dr BRTR CM7 .... 180 C4
Beanfield Rd SBW CM21 .... 226 C1
Beard's La SAFWS CB11 .... 85 J1
Beardsley Dr CHLM/WR CM1 .... 255 G6
Bear St RCOLW CO6 .... 102 B4
Beatrice Av FX IP11 .... 113 J1
Beatrice Cl IPSE IP3 .... 55 J2
Beatrice Rd COS CO15 .... 12 E8
  WOTN CO14 .... 196 F3
Beatty Gdns BRTR CM7 .... 180 E1
Beatty Rd IPSE IP3 .... 55 K3
  SUD CO10 .... 5 G2
Beaufort Gdns BRTR CM7 .... 180 C1
Beaufort Rd CHLM/GWD CM2 .... 267 J1
Beaufort St IP IP1 .... 2 B3
Beaulieu Bvd CHLM/WR CM1 .... 255 H6
Beaumont Cl COS CO15 .... 12 C5
  RCOLE CO7 .... 219 J6
Beaumont Cl COLN CO4 .... 160 A1
  FOS CO13 .... 196 B6
Beaumont Ct HVHL CB9 .... 23 K7
Beaumont Hl GTDUN CM6 .... 175 M3
Beaumont Pk RCHLM CM3 .... 268 C7
Beaumont Pl BRTR CM7 .... 180 D2
Beaumont Rd HAR CO12 .... 166 E3
Beaumont V HVHL CB9 .... 23 K7
Beaumont Wy MAL CM9 .... 271 K5
Beaver Cl COLW CO3 .... 159 G6
Beche Rd COLS CO2 .... 160 D8
Becker Rd COLW CO3 .... 187 G1
Beckers Green Rd BRTR CM7 .... 180 F3
Beckford Rd MGTR CO11 .... 136 C1
Beckingham Rd MAL CM9 .... 239 L8
  MAL CM9 .... 261 L1
Beckingham St MAL CM9 .... 260 E3
Beck Rd SAFWN CB10 .... 62 E1
Becontree Cl COS CO15 .... 222 B5
Bedells Av BRTR CM7 .... 180 D8
Bedford Cl BRTR CM7 .... 180 D1
  K/T/MI CO5 .... 212 F1 1
Bedford Rd COLN CO4 .... 132 B8
  COS CO15 .... 222 F8
Bedford St IP IP1 .... 2 D4
Bedwell Rd RBSF CM22 .... 144 D2
Beech Av BRTR CM7 .... 152 B8
  HSTD CO9 .... 95 M4
  RCOLE CO7 .... 189 K4
Beech Cl RBSF CM22 .... 173 L5 1
  RIPW IP8 .... 30 C7
Beechcroft Rd IP IP1 .... 31 H3
Beech Dr SBW CM21 .... 226 E5
Beeches Cl CHLM/WR CM1 .... 14 B3
  SAFWS CB11 .... 62 E6
Beeches Rd CHLM/WR CM1 .... 14 A3
  MAL CM9 .... 259 H8
The Beeches IPSE IP3 .... 3 L8
  MGTR CO11 .... 135 L2
Beechfield SBW CM21 .... 227 H3
Beech Gn WIT CM8 .... 239 H8
Beech Gv HAR CO12 .... 139 K6
  HSTD CO9 .... 95 M4
  HVHL CB9 .... 23 G4
  IPSE IP3 .... 55 H2
Beech Hl COLW CO3 .... 159 J8
Beechlands BSF CM23 .... 171 H8
Beech Ri RCHLM CM3 .... 257 J1
Beech Rd KESG IP5 .... 33 H6
  SUD CO10 .... 5 K9
  WIT CM8 .... 210 D6
Beech Wy CBE/LIN CB1 .... 19 L3
Beechwood Cl COLS CO2 .... 187 M3
Beehive Ct RBSF CM22 .... 228 C2
Beeleigh Cha MAL CM9 .... 270 F1
Beeleigh Cl COLS CO2 .... 188 C4 2
Beeleigh Link CHLM/GWD CM2 .... 267 H3
Beeleigh Rd MAL CM9 .... 271 H2
Begonia Cl CHLM/WR CM1 .... 255 H7
Belcham Gn HSTD CO9 .... 46 D7
Belchamp's La SAFWS CB11 .... 116 A5
Beldams Cl RCOS CO16 .... 194 C4 1
Beldams La BSF CM23 .... 171 L7
Belgrave Cl IPNE IP4 .... 32 A4
Bellamy Cr FOS CO13 .... 195 M7
Bell Cl CHTY IP2 .... 2 F8
  COLS CO2 .... 188 F3

Bellcroft WIT CM8......................238 C2
Belle Vue CHLM/GWD CM2 .....14 E6
Belle Vue Rd COL CO1.............10 A3
  IPNE IP4.................................3 K4
  RCOLE CO7.........................189 K5
  SUD CO10............................4 E6
Bellfield Av RCOLE CO7...........219 H5
Bellfield Cl RCOLE CO7............219 J6
Bellfiled Cl RCOLE CO7............219 J6
Bell HI BURES CO8..................99 L1
  RCHLM CM3.......................268 E6
Bell La BRTR CM7..................121 J3
  BRTR CM7..........................151 J6 1
  CHTY IP2.............................2 F8
  GTDUN CM6........................119 J2 1
  KESG IP5............................33 K5
Bellmead CHLM/GWD CM2........15 G4
Bell Md SBW CM21..................227 G3
Bells Cha CHLM/GWD CM2........267 G7
Bells Cl SAFWS CB11................62 F5
Bells HI BSF CM23...................171 G6
  BURES CO8.........................129 J1
Bells Rd SUD CO10..................48 B7
Bell St CHLM/GWD CM2.............267 H7
  SBW CM21..........................227 G3
Belmer Rd STSD CM24...............172 F1
Belmonde Dr CHLM/WR CM1......254 F6
Belmont Cl CHLM/WR CM1..........255 G6
Belmont Crs COLN CO4..............160 E2
Belmont HI SAFWS CB11.............87 J4
Belmont Pl COL CO1...................188 E1
Belmont Rd RIPW IP8.................53 L4
Belsize Av COS CO15.................248 F7
Belstead Av CHTY IP2.................54 D2
Belstead Rd CHTY IP2.................54 B4
Belsteads Farm La
  CHLM/WR CM1....................254 F3
Belvawney Cl CHLM/WR CM1.......254 A7
Belvedere Cl RCHLM CM3...........269 H6
Belvedere Pl MAL CM9...............271 H5
Belvedere PI IPNE IP4.................3 K1
  RCHLM CM3.......................269 J6 2
  RCHLM CM3.......................269 H6 1
Bembridge Cl COS CO15............222 B5
Bemerton Gdns FOS CO13..........195 L7
Benacre Rd IPSE IP3..................55 J3
Bendlowes Rd BRTR CM7...........121 K4
Benedict Dr CHLM/WR CM1.........14 A3
Benezet St IP IP1.......................2 C3
Benfield Wy BRTR CM7...............180 D3
Benhooks Av BSF CM23...............171 G8
Bennet Ct COLN CO4..................161 G7
Bennett Cl BRTR CM7.................180 C5 2
  WOTN CO14.......................196 C5
Bennett Rd IP IP1......................30 F5
Bennett's La GTDUN CM6............204 F3
Bennett Wy RCHLM CM3.............257 J1
Benskins Cl BSF CM23...............114 C5
Bentall Cl HSTD CO9..................126 B5 1
Bentfield End Cswy STSD CM24...143 M3
Bentfield Gdns STSD CM24..........143 M6
Bentfield Rd STSD CM24.............143 M6
Bent Fld FX IP11........................7 M3
Bent La IPNE IP4........................33 G6
Bentley Av COS CO15................249 G2
Bentley Cl BSF CM23.................171 H8
Bentley La RIPS/CAP IP9...........107 M1
  RIPW IP8...........................53 L8
Bentley Rd MGTR CO11..............163 L1
  RCOS CO16........................192 E8
  WIT CM8............................238 A1
Benton Cl BRTR CM7..................181 G7 1
  WIT CM8............................238 C6
Berbice La GTDUN CM6..............175 L3
Berechurch Hall Rd COLS CO2....187 L4
  COLS CO2..........................188 C5
Berechurch Rd COLS CO2...........187 M4
Bergholt Rd COLN CO4...............159 M3
  MGTR CO11.......................106 D6
Beridge Rd HSTD CO9................125 M3
Berkeley Cl IPNE IP4...................32 A4
Berkeley Rd COS CO15................13 G3
Berkley Dr CHLM/GWD CM2.........267 H3
Berkley Cl COLN CO4..................160 E1
Bermuda Rd KIR/NAC IP10...........56 A6
Bernard Cl FOS CO13.................196 A7 2
Bernard Crs IPSE IP3.................55 K3
Berners End GTDUN CM6............204 C1
Berners St IP IP1.......................2 D4
Bernside BRTR CM7...................180 B3 1
Berrimans Cl COLN CO4..............11 M8 1
Berry Cl IPSE IP3.......................56 B4
Bertram Av RCOS CO16..............221 M4
Beryl Rd HAR CO12.....................139 M4
Beslyns Rd BRTR CM7...............121 J2
Bethany St RCOLE CO7...............189 K6
Betjeman Cl BRTR CM7..............180 C5 3
Betts Green Rd RCOS CO16.........193 M8
Beverley Av K/T/MI CO5..............244 F6
Beverley Dr FOS CO13...............196 A6
Beverley Rd COLW CO3.............159 M7
  IPNE IP4..............................3 L1
Bevington Ms WIT CM8..............238 D3 2
Bewick Ct HSTD CO9.................96 A3 1
Bexhill Cl COS CO15..................249 L5
Bexley Av HAR CO12.................140 B4
Bibb Wy IP IP1...........................2 B6
Bicknacre Rd RCHLM CM3..........268 F6
The Biggen CBS CB2...................17 G5
Bignalls Cft COLN CO4...............160 E1
Bigods La CHLM/GWD CM6..........147 M8
Bijou Cl K/T/MI CO5...................212 F7 1
Bilberry End CBE/LIN CB1............19 L6
Bildeston Gdns IP IP1.................31 M4 1
Billy's La RCOLE CO7.................104 F3
Bilsdale Cl COLN CO4.................160 E1 1
Bilton Rd CHLM/WR CM1.............14 C6
Binley Rd CHLM/GWD CM2...........267 G3
Birchalls STSD CM24..................144 A5 1
Birchanger La BSF CM23............171 M3
Birch Av HAR CO12......................8 F1
  RCOLE CO7........................192 A5
Birch Cl BRTR CM7....................179 L3 1
  COS CO15..........................12 A5
  RCOLE CO7........................219 G2
Birchcroft Rd IP IP1....................31 K3
Birch Dr MGTR CO11..................106 F4

The Birches FOS CO13...............196 A7
Birch Fall RCOLW CO6.................102 B4
Birch HI WIT CM8........................239 G7
Birch Rd COLS CO2.....................186 F8
Birch St COLS CO2.....................214 C2
  RCOLW CO6.......................102 C4
Birchway COLS CO2...................214 C3
Birchwood BSF CM23.................171 M3
Birchwood Cl K/T/MI CO5...........241 G1
Birch Wood Cl K/T/MI CO5..........244 F7 1
Birchwood Dr KESG IP5..............33 G4 1
Birchwood Rd COLN CO4............133 J1
  RCOLE CO7........................133 K2
Birchwood Wy K/T/MI CO5..........213 H8
  RCOLE CO7........................133 K2
Birdbrook Rd HSTD CO9.............68 C2
Birdbush Av SAFWS CB11............62 F6
Bird La K/T/MI CO5....................241 G1
Birds Cl SAFWN CB10.................37 H2
Birkdale Ri RCHLM CM3..............257 K1
Birkfield Cl CHTY IP2..................2 A9
Birkfield Dr CHTY IP2..................54 A4
Birkin Cl K/T/MI CO5...................240 D1
Biscay Cl HVHL CB9...................23 L6
Bishop Rd CHLM/WR CM1............15 G1
  COLS CO2..........................187 J2
Bishops Av BRTR CM7................180 D2
  BSF CM23.........................199 H2
Bishops Cl FX IP11.....................113 M1 2
Bishopscourt Gdns
  CHLM/WR CM1....................267 G1 1
Bishops Dr RCOS CO16..............248 D7
Bishop's HI IPSE IP3...................3 K8
Bishop's La HSTD CO9................98 D2
  K/T/MI CO5........................212 E6 1
Bishops Park WY BSF CM23.........170 D6
Bisley Cl RCOS CO16..................221 K7 2
Bittern Cl CHTY IP2.....................54 A2 1
  K/T/MI CO5........................211 M3
Bixley Dr IPNE IP4.......................33 G8
Bixley La IPNE IP4.......................33 H8
Bixley Rd IPSE IP3......................55 M2
Black Barns FX IP11....................83 L8
Blackberry Rd COLW CO3...........186 E1
Black Boy La MGTR CO11...........138 C1
Blackbrook Rd RCOLW CO6..........131 L6
Blackbushe BSF CM23................171 L4
Black Chapel La GTDUN CM6.......205 G6
Blackdown Av KESG IP5...............33 H7
Blackfriars SUD CO10...................4 B8
Blackheath COLS CO2.................188 C5
Black Horse La IP IP1...................2 E5
Blackhouse La SUD CO10.............74 D2
Blacklands Cl SAFWS CB11..........62 E6
Black La BRTR CM7....................121 H3
Blackley La RCHLM CM3.............207 H2
Blacklock CHLM/GWD CM2..........267 J2
Blackman Wy WIT CM8...............238 C4 2
Blackmore Cl HVHL CB9..............23 H4
Blacksmith Cl CHLM/WR CM1......255 G6
Blacksmiths Cl BSF CM23...........170 D8
Blacksmiths HI SUD CO10.............45 K1
Blacksmiths La CBE/LIN CB1........21 L8
  HAR CO12..........................55 J5
  SUD CO10..........................73 H3
  WIT CM8............................239 G8
Blacksmiths Wy SBW CM21.........226 D4 1
Blackthorn Av COLN CO4............161 G6
Blackthorn Cl CHLM/WR CM1......265 J4 1
  IPSE IP3.............................56 A4 1
Blackthorn Rd HAR CO12............140 B3 1
  WIT CM8............................238 A1
Blackthorn Wy MAL CM9.............241 J3
Blackwall Br CHLM/WR CM1.........252 F8
Blackwater Av COLN CO4.............161 G4
Blackwater Cl CHLM/WR CM1.......254 E7
  MAL CM9............................272 A2
Blackwater Dr K/T/MI CO5............244 C7
Blackwater La WIT CM8...............238 D5
Blackwater Wy BRTR CM7...........180 C1
Bladen Dr IPNE IP4......................33 H8
Bladon Cl BRTR CM7..................152 A6
  K/T/MI CO5........................213 G8
Bladon Wy HVHL CB9.................23 K4
Blaine Dr FOS CO13...................196 A6
Blair Cl BSF CM23......................170 E6
  IPNE IP4..............................33 G8
Blake Av RIPS/CAP IP9...............111 J4
Blake Cl MGTR CO11..................135 K1
Blake Dr BRTR CM7....................180 E1
  RCOS CO16........................221M7
Blakeland HI CBS CB2.................16 F5
Blake Rd IP IP1..........................31 H2
  WIT CM8............................210 B8
Blamsters Crs HSTD CO9............125M5
Blanchard Cl FOS CO13..............195 J6
Blanche St IPNE IP4.....................3 H5
Blandford Rd IPSE IP3.................55 K5
Blenheim Cl BRTR CM7...............152 A6 1
  HVHL CB9.........................23 K4
  MGTR CO11.......................106 F4
  SBW CM21.........................226 D5
Blenheim Ct BSF CM23...............170 D8
Blenheim Dr COLS CO2...............188 C5 1
Blenheim Rd COS CO15...............12 C8
  IP IP1................................2 A2
Blenheim Wy K/T/MI CO5............213 G8 1
Blickling Cl CHTY IP2..................54 D3 1
Blind La K/T/MI CO5....................213 K2
  MAL CM9............................241 K4
  MAL CM9............................260 E6
Blofield Rd IP IP11........................6 C1
Blois Rd HVHL CB9......................43 M5
Bloom Cl FOS CO13...................196 M7
Bloomfield Av RCOS CO13...........196 A6 1
Bloomfield St IPNE IP4.................32 D7
Blue Barn Cl FX IP11...................83 J5
Bluebell Av RCOS CO16..............12 A3
Bluebell Cl CHTY IP2...................54 A1
  WIT CM8............................238 A2 1
Bluegate La RIPS/CAP IP9............77 J6
Bluehouse Av RCOS CO16............249 J1
Blue Mill La MAL CM9.................269M1
Blue Mills HI WIT CM8................238 D6
Blue Rd K/T/MI CO5....................212 E8
Bluestem Rd IP IP3.....................55 M1 1
Blunts Hall Rd WIT CM8..............237 L4
Blyford Rd RCOS CO16...............249 J1
Blyford Wy FX IP11.....................6 D1

Blyth Cl CHTY IP2.......................54 C4
Blythe La RCOLE CO7.................189 K5 3
Blythe Wy MAL CM9...................271 J5
Blyth's Meadow BRTR CM7.........180 B2 1
Blyth's Wy BRTR CM7.................179 H3 1
Blythwood Gdns STSD CM24........143 M7
Boadicea Wy COLS CO2..............187 L1
Boars Tye Rd WIT CM8...............181 L7
Bobbits La RIPS/CAP IP9.............54 A5
Bobbits Wy RCOLE CO7..............189 L5
Bober Ct COLS CO2....................188 D6
Bocking End BRTR CM7..............180 B2
Bocking's Gv RCOS CO16............221 K8
Bodiam Cl BRTR CM7.................159 K6
  RCOLE CO7........................190 D5 2
Bodiam Rd IPSE IP3...................55 M1 1
Bodmin Cl KESG IP5...................33 J7
Bodmin Rd CHLM/WR CM1..........254 F8
Bogmoor Rd ROY SG8.................58 B7
Bohun Cl RCHLM CM3................207 H6 1
Bois Hall Gdns HSTD CO9...........126 B3 1
Boley Dr COS CO15.....................13 K3
Boleyns Av BRTR CM7................152 B7
Boleyn Wy COS CO15..................249 H5
  HVHL CB9.........................22 F6
  RCHLM CM3.......................256 B4
Boley Rd RCOLW CO6.................128 B6
Bolford St GTDUN CM6...............119 H3
Bolingbroke Cl RCHLM CM3.........207 H6 2
Bolton La IPNE IP4......................3 G4
  IPNE IP4..............................3 H6
Bond St CHLM/GWD CM2.............15 J3
Bonham Cl COS CO15.................13 J1
Bonington Cha CHLM/WR CM1 .....255 G7
Bonks HI SBW CM21...................226 F4
Bonneting La BSF CM23..............114 D5
Bonnington Rd IPSE IP3..............55 H4 1
Boone Pl WIT CM8......................238 C3 1
Booth Av COLN CO4....................11 K6
Borda Cl CHLM/WR CM1.............254 C8
Boreham Rd RCHLM CM3............235 K2
Borley Rd SUD CO10...................49 K1
Borough La SAFWS CB11............62 F5
Borradale Ct HVHL CB9...............43 K7
Borrowdale Av IPNE IP4..............31 M4
Boscawen Gdns BRTR CM7..........180 D1
Boss Hall Rd IP IP1.....................31 G6
Bostock Rd CHTY IP2..................54 E4
Boston Rd IPNE IP4......................3 M3
Boswells Dr CHLM/GWD CM2.......15 K3
Botanical Wy RCOS CO16............248 C1
Botany La RCOS CO16................193 K8
Bouchers Md CHLM/WR CM1 ....255 H7 1
Boundary Rd BSF CM23..............171 J8
  COLN CO4..........................189 H1
  HVHL CB9.........................23 M8
Bounderby Gv
  CHLM/WR CM1....................254 A7 1
Bounstead HI COLS CO2.............187 L8
Bounstead Rd COLS CO2.............187 M6
Bourchier Avene BRTR CM7.........152 F8 1
Bourchier Wy HSTD CO9.............125 M5
Bournebridge HI HSTD CO9..........125 L5
Bourne Cl HSTD CO9..................125 M5
Bourne HI CHTY IP2....................54 E5
Bournemouth Rd COS CO15........223 H7 1
Bourne Rd COLS CO2..................188 C1
  HVHL CB9.........................23 K5
  RCOLW CO6.......................159 G2
The Bourne BSF CM23................171 K5
Bouverie Rd CHLM/GWD CM2.......15 H7
Bovingdon Rd BRTR CM7............151 M1
Bowdens La RCOLW CO6............101 H6
Bower Gdns MAL CM9.................271 H2
Bower Hall Dr HVHL CB9..............43 K7
Bower Hall La K/T/MI CO5............245 G4
Bowers Cl WIT CM8....................210 A2
Bowes Rd RCOLE CO7.................189 L4
Bowland Dr RIPW IP8..................53 L4
Bowling Cl BSF CM23..................171 H7 1
Bowmans Pk HSTD CO9..............96 A1 1
Bowsers La SAFWN CB10.............39 K3
Bowthorpe Cl IP IP1.....................2 F3
Boxford Cl FX IP11......................112 F1 1
Boxhouse La RCOLE CO7.............104 D7
Boxley La RBSF CM22.................201 M5
Box Mill La HSTD CO9.................126 A2
Boxted Av RCOS CO16.................249 K1
Boxted Church Rd RCOLW CO6.....102 E8
Boxted Cl COLN CO4..................131 M8
  RCOLW CO6.......................131 L2
Boxted Straight Rd COLN CO4......103 J8
Boyd Cl BSF CM23......................171 K5
Boydlands RIPS/CAP IP9.............77 J4
Boyles Ct COLS CO2...................188 D6
Boyne Dr CHLM/WR CM1.............254 F7
Boyton Cl HVHL CB9...................23 J3
Boyton Rd IPSE IP3....................55 K5
Boytons Acre SAFWS CB11..........62 F5
Boyton's La SAFWN CB10............66 B3
Brackenbury Cl IP IP1..................2 C1
Brackenden Cl CHLM/WR CM1......254 F6
Brackenhayes Cl CHTY IP2...........54 D2
The Brackens COLN CO4.............160 D2
Bracken Wy K/T/MI CO5..............216 C3
Brackley Cl FX IP11....................112 F2 1
Bracks La RCOLW CO6................184 B2
Bradfield Rd MGTR CO11............137 L8
Bradford St BRTR CM7................180 C1
  CHLM/GWD CM2................14 E6
Brading Av COS CO15.................222 C6
Bradley Cl GTDUN CM6...............175 L3 1
Bradley Common BSF CM23.........171 L2
Bradley Ms SAFWN CB10............63 H3 1
Bradley St CHTY IP2...................2 E9
Braemar Av CHLM/GWD CM2........14 F7
Braemore Cl COLN CO4...............160 F2
Brain Rd WIT CM8......................238 A2
Braintree Rd BRTR CM7..............121 K5
  BRTR CM7..........................123 G7
  BRTR CM7..........................180 F6
  GTDUN CM6.......................176 A5
  HSTD CO9.........................125 G8
  RCHLM CM3.......................207 L8
  WIT CM8............................238 D2
Brain Valley Av BRTR CM7..........180 D7
Braiswick COLN CO4...................159 H3
Braiswick La COLN CO4..............159M1
Braithwaite Dr SUD CO10............51 H2 1

Bramble Cl HVHL CB9.................22 F4 1
Bramble Dr IPSE IP3....................56 A4
Bramble La GTDUN CM6.............177 G4
Bramble Rd WIT CM8..................238 A1
Brambles WOTN CO14.................196 C6
The Brambles BSF CM23.............170 E7
  COLW CO3.........................187 H2
Bramblewood RIPW IP8..............53 L3 1
Bramford La IP IP1......................2 A3
Bramford Rd IP IP1.....................30 E5
Bramhall Cl CHTY IP2..................53 M4
Bramley Cl BRTR CM7.................180 C4 1
  COLW CO3........................159 K6
  RCOLE CO7........................190 D5 2
Bramley Rd HVHL CB9.................22 E5
The Bramleys RCOLW CO6...........183 J2
Bramston Cl CHLM/GWD CM2......267 H5
Bramwoods Rd
  CHLM/GWD CM2................267 G6
Brand Cl BRTR CM7....................152 B6 1
Brand Dr K/T/MI CO5...................216 D2
Brandeston Cl SUD CO10.............51 G2 1
Brandon Rd BRTR CM7................179M3
  FX IP11..............................6 D2
Brands Cl SUD CO10...................50 E8
Bran End Flds GTDUN CM6...........148 F6
Bransby Gdns IPNE IP4................3 J3
Branscombe Cl FOS CO13...........195M8
Branston Rd COS CO15................12 B5
Brantham HI MGTR CO11.............106 E5
Brassingham Crs K/T/MI CO5........213 G8
Brantham Hl MGTR CO11.............106 E5
Braxted La WIT CM8...................239 J7
Braxted Rd WIT CM8...................239 J7
Bray Ct RCOLW CO6...................159 H1
Braziers Quay BSF CM23............171 J7
Brazier's Wood Rd IPSE IP3..........55 K5
Breachfield Rd COLS CO2............187 L3
Breach La GTDUN CM6................147 K3
Brecon Cl CHTY IP2....................54 D3
Bredfield Cl FX IP11....................112 F2 2
Bree Av RCOLW CO6...................185 G2
Brendon Dr KESG IP5..................33 H7
Brendon Pl CHLM/WR CM1...........14 A6 1
Brent Cl FOS CO13.....................196 B6
  WIT CM8............................238 A3
Brent Hall Rd BRTR CM7.............92 D7
Brentwood Rd COS CO15............222 E7
Bretten Cl RCOS CO16................249 J1 1
Brettenham Crs IP IP1.................31M4
Brewers Cl BSF CM23.................170 E8
Brewery La STSD CM24...............144 A6
Brian Bishop Cl WOTN CO14........196 D5 1
Brian Cl CHLM/GWD CM2............266 D7
Briardale Av HAR CO12................8 A8
Briarfields FOS CO13..................195 L5
Briarhayes Cl CHTY IP2...............54 D2
Briar Rd RCOLE CO7...................162 D1
Briarswood CHLM/WR CM1..........254 F6 2
Briarwood Av COS CO15..............223 G7
Briarwood End COLN CO4............160 D2 1
Brickbarn Cl GTDUN CM6............205 L1
Brickhouse La K/T/MI CO5............244 D6
Brick House La RCHLM CM3.........256 A6
Brickhouse Rd RCOLW CO6..........127 J2
Brick Kiln Cl FX IP11...................83 J6 1
  RCOLW CO6.......................183 J2
Brick Kiln La GTDUN CM6............148 E6
  RCOLE CO7........................191 G8
  SAFWN CB11......................115M5
Brick Kiln Rd CHLM/GWD CM2.....267 L6
  COL CO1............................10 B2
  RCOLW CO6.......................131 K7
  RIPS/CAP IP9.....................80 D8
Brick Kiln Wy BRTR CM7.............180 F3 2
Brickmakers La COLN CO4...........160 B3
Brickman's HI MGTR CO11...........136 E2
Brickspring La MAL CM9..............239M6
Brick St COLW CO3.....................158 D4
Bridewell St SUD CO10...............26 E5
Bridgebrook Cl COLN CO4............11M2
Bridge Cft RCHLM CM3...............234 B3
Bridge End La BRTR CM7.............179 L5
Bridgefield Cl COL CO1................11 K7
Bridge Hall Rd BRTR CM7............181 L2
Bridge HI RCOLW CO6.................129 L6
Bridge Rd FX IP11.......................113 J2
  KIR/NAC IP10.....................57 H8
Bridge St BRTR CM7...................171 H6
  BSF CM23..........................100 B5
  BURES CO8........................99 M7
  CHLM/WR CM1...................265 K4
  HSTD CO9.........................70 C4 1
  IP IP1................................2 F8
  RCOLW CO6.......................183 H4
  SAFWN CB10......................62 E3
  WIT CM8............................238 B4
Bridgwater Rd CHTY IP2.............53M3
Bridport Av IPSE IP3...................55M2
Bridport Rd CHLM/WR CM1..........254 F8
Bridport Wy BRTR CM7...............152 F8
Brierley Av K/T/MI CO5.................245 G6
Bright Cl RCOS CO16..................221M7
Brighton Rd COS CO15................223 H7
Brightside FOS CO13..................196 A6 2
Brightwell Cl FX IP11....................6 D1
Brimstone Ct BRTR CM7..............180 A5 1
Brindley Rd COS CO15................222 D5
The Bringey CHLM/GWD CM2.......267 J2
Brinkley Crs COLN CO4................11M2
Brinkley Grove Rd COLN CO4.......132 C8
Brinkley La COLN CO4.................132 E8
Brinkman Rd CBE/LIN CB1...........19M2
Brisbane Rd IPNE IP4...................32 F7
Brisbane Wy COLS CO2...............188 C4
Brise Cl BRTR CM7.....................180 C4
Bristol Cl WIT CM8.....................210 A2 1
Bristol HI RIPS/CAP IP9...............111 K5 2
Bristol Rd COL CO1.....................10 F5
  IPNE IP4..............................32 C8
Bristowe Av BRTR CM7...............180 D7
Britannia Crs RCOLE CO7............189 K4
Britannia Rd IPNE IP4..................32 D7
Brittany Wy COLS CO2.................188 D1 1
Britten Cl COLN CO4...................161 G2
Britten Crs CHLM/GWD CM2.........267 H5

Brixton Cl COS CO15...................249 L5
Brixton La BSF CM23..................115 J8
  RBSF CM22.......................115M6
Broadcroft Crs HVHL CB9............23 G5
Broadfield BSF CM23..................171 H3
  GTDUN CM6.......................203 G8
Broadfield Rd RBSF CM22...........174 A6
Broadfields RCOLE CO7...............189 L1
  SBW CM21.........................226 D4
Broadlands Wy COLN CO4...........11 H3
  IPNE IP4............................33 H8
Broad La RCOLW CO6.................131 L3
Broadleaf Av BSF CM23..............198 E1
Broad Meadow RIPW IP8..............53 L3 2
Broadmead Rd COLN CO4............161 G4
Broadmere Cl COS CO15.............223 G6
Broadmere Rd IP IP1...................31 G5
Broad Oaks Cl SAFWN CB10........88 F3
Broadoaks Crs BRTR CM7...........180 F1
Broad Oaks Pk COLN CO4...........161 G2
Broad Rd BRTR CM7...................152 D7
  HSTD CO9.........................72 D6
Broad St HVHL CB9....................23 H5
  RBSF CM22.......................201 H7
Broad Street Green Rd
  MAL CM9...........................259 L5
Broadstrood RCOS CO16.............220 C8
Broadwater Gdns
  RIPS/CAP IP9.....................111 J5 2
Broadway COS CO15...................249 J7
  WIT CM8............................181M8
Broadway Ct WIT CM8................181M8
The Broadway GTDUN CM6..........176 B5
Brock Cl WIT CM8.......................238 A3 1
Brockham Cl RCOS CO16.............221 K7
Brockley Crs IP IP1.....................30 F7
Brockley Rd CHLM/GWD CM2.......15 L4
Brocks Md GTDUN CM6...............147 G6
Brockwell La K/T/MI CO5.............211 L4
Broke Av RIPW IP8......................30 D3
Broke Hall Gdns IPSE IP3.............55M1
Broman's La K/T/MI CO5..............246 C3
Bromeswell Rd IPNE IP4..............32 A4
Bromley Cl CHTY IP2..................54 E2 2
Bromley La SAFWS CB11............87 K4
Bromley Rd COLN CO4................161 G4
  MGTR CO11.......................135 K6
  RCOLE CO7........................162 D8
  RCOLE CO7........................191 J1
Brompton Gdns MAL CM9............271 G5 1
Bronte Cl BRTR CM7...................180 C5 3
Bronte Rd WIT CM8....................210 B8
Brook Cl BRTR CM7....................179 L3 1
  K/T/MI CO5........................241 H2
  MAL CM9...........................259 J2
  MAL CM9...........................269 M3 1
Brooke Av SAFWN CB10..............63 G2
Brooke Gdns BSF CM23..............171 L6
Brook End SBW CM21.................226 F3
Brook End Rd
  CHLM/GWD CM2................267 J1 1
Brooke Sq MAL CM9...................271 J4 1
Brook Farm Cl HSTD CO9............126 C4
Brook Farm La RIPS/CAP IP9.......79 L7
Brookfield Rd IP IP1....................31 H5
Brookfields GTDUN CM6..............148 F5
  SBW CM21.........................226 F3
Brook Hall Rd K/T/MI CO5............189 K7
Brookhampton St SAFWN CB10....17 J8
Brook HI GTDUN CM6..................205 H4
  RCHLM CM3.......................234 D7
Brookhill Wy IPNE IP4.................56 H7
Brookhouse Rd RCOLW CO6.........156 C5
Brookhurst Cl CHLM/GWD CM2.....15M1
Brookland K/T/MI CO5..................240 E1
Brooklands COL CO1...................10 F8
  COS CO15..........................249 G7
Brooklands Gdns COS CO15.........249 G7
Brooklands Ri MGTR CO11...........106 F5
Brooklands Rd MGTR CO11..........106 E6
Brooklands Wk CHLM/GWD CM2...14 E8
Brook La CHLM/GWD CM2............267 K3
  FX IP11.............................113 K2
  KIR/NAC IP10.....................83M4
  NHMKT IP6........................33 J1
  RIPS/CAP IP9.....................77 G3
  SBW CM21.........................226 F3
Brooklyn Rd HAR CO12................9 H8
Brook Md RCHLM CM3.................234 A5
Brook Meadow HSTD CO9............95 M4 1
  HSTD CO9.........................96 A4 1
Brook Mdw K/T/MI CO5................240 E1
Brook Rd K/T/MI CO5...................241 H2
  RCOLW CO6.......................156 F6
  RCOLW CO6.......................157 K8
  SBW CM21.........................226 F4
  STSD CM24........................144 A7
Brook Service Rd HVHL CB9.........23 J5
Brooks Hall Rd IP IP1...................2 A2
Brookside Cl COLS CO2...............188 D1
Brooksies SAFWS CB11..............60 B7
Brook St BRTR CM7....................121 K3
  CHLM/WR CM1...................15 H1
  COL CO1............................11 G7
  GTDUN CM6.......................176 F6
  MGTR CO11.......................135M1
  RCOLE CO7........................105 H6
  RCOLE CO7........................163 G4
  RCOLE CO7........................189 K5
  RCOLW CO6.......................127 G4
Brook Ter HSTD CO9...................96 A4
Brook V RCOS CO16...................248 C1
Brook Vw CHLM/GWD CM2...........267 L2
Brookview CHTY IP2...................54 A5
Brook Vw GTDUN CM6.................119 J2
Broom Crs IPSE IP3....................55 H4
Broome Gv RCOLE CO7...............189 K3 1
Broom Farm Rd RBSF CM22.........144 E3
Broom Fld FX IP11......................113 G2 1
Broomfield WIT CM8...................181 L8
Broomfield Common RIPW IP8......30 D7
Broomfield Crs RCOLE CO7..........189 K3
Broomfields RBSF CM22..............228 C2
Broomhall Cl CHLM/WR CM1........254 D3 1
Broomhall Rd CHLM/WR CM1........254 C3
Broomhayes CHTY IP2.................54 C3
Broom Hill Rd IP IP1...................2 A1

Broomhills Rd K/T/MI CO5 .... 244 F7
Broom Knoll MGTR CO11 .... 106 E3
Broom St SUD CO10 .... 50 D8
Broom Wy K/T/MI CO5 .... 216 D3
  RIPS/CAP IP9 .... 77 J3
Brotherton Av FX IP11 .... 83 K7
Broton Dr HSTD CO9 .... 126 B4
Brougham Glades COLW CO3 ... 158 F8
Broughton Cl COLS CO2 .... 187 L2
Broughton Rd IP IP1 .... 2 D2
Browning Cl COLW CO3 .... 159 H7 1
Browning Rd BRTR CM7 .... 180 C8
  IP IP1 .... 31 H2
  MAL CM9 .... 271 J3
  MGTR CO11 .... 106 E6 1
Brownings Av CHLM/WR CM1 ... 254 C8
Brownlows Cl GTDUN CM6 .... 230 E6
Brownsea Wy COLW CO3 .... 187 J1
Browns Gv KESG IP5 .... 33 M6 2
Bruce Gv CHLM/GWD CM2 .... 266 C6
Bruce Rd CHLM/WR CM1 .... 265 K4
Bruff Cl COLN CO4 .... 10 B1
Bruff Dr FOS CO13 .... 196 C6
Bruges Rd HAR CO12 .... 140 C4
Brundells Rd RCOLE CO7 .... 163 H8
Brundon La SUD CO10 .... 4 A2
Brunel Ct COLN CO4 .... 132 E7
Brunel Rd BRTR CM7 .... 180 C4
  CHTY IP2 .... 31 G7
  COS CO15 .... 222 D5
Brunel Wy COLN CO4 .... 132 E7
Brunswick House Cut
  MGTR CO11 .... 136 C2 1
Brunswick Rd IPNE IP4 .... 3 L2
Brunwin Rd BRTR CM7 .... 179 H3
Brussels Cl HAR CO12 .... 140 D4
Bryan Rd BSF CM23 .... 171 H5
Bryant's La MAL CM9 .... 269 M6
Brybank Rd HVHL CB9 .... 22 E4
Bryony Cl HVHL CB9 .... 23 G4
Buchan Cl BRTR CM7 .... 180 C5 5
Buckenhoe Rd SAFWN CB10 .... 63 G2 2
Buckfast Av FOS CO13 .... 195 M7
Buckfast Cl CHTY IP2 .... 54 C3 1
Buck Hi BRTR CM7 .... 180 B7
Buckingham Ct
  CHLM/GWD CM2 .... 267 H1
Buckingham Dr COLN CO4 .... 161 G6
Buckingham Rd HVHL CB9 .... 23 G2 1
Bucklesham Rd IPSE IP3 .... 56 B4
  KIR/NAC IP10 .... 83 K1
Buckleys CHLM/GWD CM2 .... 267 H6
Buckleys Cl WIT CM8 .... 239 G8
Buckley's La RCOLW CO6 .... 155 M7
Buck's Horns La RIPW IP8 .... 53 K6
Buckwoods Rd BRTR CM7 .... 180 B4
Buddleia Cl CHTY IP2 .... 54 A1
Buddleia Ct RCOLE CO7 .... 189 J3 1
Bude Cl KESG IP5 .... 33 J7 1
Buffett Wy COLW CO3 .... 161 G7
Buglers Ri CHLM/WR CM1 .... 265 K5
Buick Av COS CO15 .... 248 F7
Building End Rd ROY SG8 .... 59 H6
Bulford La BRTR CM7 .... 180 B4
Bulford Mill La BRTR CM7 .... 180 B8
Bullace Cl COLN CO4 .... 160 F2
Bullen Cl BRTR CM7 .... 30 C3
Bullen La RIPW IP8 .... 30 C3
Bullfields SAFWN CB11 .... 87 J5
  SBW CM21 .... 227 G2
Bullfinch Cl COLN CO4 .... 161 H5
Bull Hill Rd COS CO15 .... 13 H2
Bull La K/T/MI CO5 .... 240 E1
  MAL CM9 .... 271 H2
  SAFWN CB11 .... 84 D3
Bullocks La SUD CO10 .... 4 D7
Bullock Wood Cl RCOLE CO7 ... 166 F7
Bulmer Rd SUD CO10 .... 49 L7
Bulmer St SUD CO10 .... 72 F1
Bulstrode Rd CHTY IP2 .... 3 G8
Bulwer Rd IP IP1 .... 2 A4
Bumfords La RCHLM CM3 .... 257 J6
Bumpstead Rd HVHL CB9 .... 43 K1
  HVHL CB9 .... 43 K1
Bundick's La CHLM/WR CM1 ... 14 B1
Bung Rw WIT CM8 .... 239 K4
Bunting Cl CHLM/GWD CM2 ... 266 D8
Bunting Rd CHTY IP2 .... 53 M2
Buntry La SUD CO10 .... 25 G1
Bunyan Cl IP IP1 .... 31 J2
Bunyan Rd BRTR CM7 .... 180 A2 2
Bure Dr WIT CM8 .... 237 M2
Bures Rd RCOLW CO6 .... 101 H5
  SUD CO10 .... 50 C8
Burgate Cl RCOS CO16 .... 249 J1
Burgess Fld CHLM/GWD CM2 ... 267 H1
Burghley Av BSF CM23 .... 170 E6
Burghley Cl BRTR CM7 .... 179 K7
  CHTY IP2 .... 54 C3 2
Burke Cl IP IP1 .... 31 H2
Burke Rd IP IP1 .... 31 H2
Burkitts La SUD CO10 .... 4 C6
Burley Rd BSF CM23 .... 199 J1
Burlington Rd COLW CO3 .... 10 A8
  IP IP1 .... 2 C5
Burmanny Cl COS CO15 .... 12 B6
Burma Rd CBS CB2 .... 16 C4
Burnell Ga CHLM/WR CM1 .... 255 J6
Burnells Wy STSD CM24 .... 144 A6
Burnham Cl FX IP11 .... 83 L8
  IPNE IP4 .... 3 M3
  WOTN CO14 .... 196 D6
Burnham Rd CHLM/WR CM1 ... 254 F8
  MAL CM9 .... 270 B8
Burnsall Cl SAFWN CB11 .... 63 H5 1
Burns Av COLW CO3 .... 159 H8
Burns Cl MAL CM9 .... 271 J4 2
Burns Crs CHLM/GWD CM2 ... 15 H7
Burnside SBW CM21 .... 226 F3
Burnside Crs CHLM/WR CM1 ... 254 D6
Burns Rd IP IP1 .... 31 G2
Burnt Dick Hi COLN CO4 .... 102 F6
Burnt Heath Cottages
  RCOLE CO7 .... 134 C8
Burnt House La KIR/NAC IP10 ... 83 K1
Burnthouse Rd RCOLW CO6 ... 156 A4

Burr Cl HAR CO12 .... 139 L4
Burrell Rd CHTY IP2 .... 2 D8
Burroughs Piece Rd SUD CO10 ... 4 E6
Burrows Cl RCOS CO11 .... 135 K1
  RCOS CO16 .... 221 M7
Burrows Rd RCOLW CO6 .... 127 K7
Burrs Rd COS CO15 .... 13 H1
Burrswood Pl MAL CM9 .... 271 M2
Burstall Cft RCOS CO16 .... 249 K1 2
Burton Cl HVHL CB9 .... 23 G6
Burton End HVHL CB9 .... 22 F6
Burton Pl CHLM/GWD CM2 ... 267 H1
Bury Cl COL CO1 .... 10 F5
  RCOLW CO6 .... 185 H2
Bury Flds GTDUN CM6 .... 177 J8
Bury La RCHLM CM3 .... 233 M5
  RCHLM CM3 .... 237 H8
  ROY SG8 .... 59 M4
Bury Lodge La RBSF CM22 .... 172 E5
  STSD CM24 .... 172 C2
Bury Rd IP IP1 .... 30 F1
The Bury RCOS CO16 .... 248 C1
Bury to Clare Wk SUD CO10 ... 26 E2
Burywoods RCOL CO4 .... 159 K3
Bushell Wy FOS CO13 .... 196 A7
Bushey Cl RIPS/CAP IP9 .... 77 J4
Bushey Ley BRTR CM7 .... 180 F2 1
Bush Gv SUD CO10 .... 49 L7
Bush La SAFWN CB10 .... 90 F3
Bushman Gdns RIPW IP8 .... 30 C3 1
Bush Rd SAFWN CB10 .... 91 G3
Bustler's Ri CBS CB2 .... 16 E5
Butcher Rw SAFWN CB11 .... 62 F3 1
Butcher's Hi SAFWN CB10 .... 37 J1
Butchers La RIPS/CAP IP9 .... 77 K4
  WOTN CO14 .... 196 D6
Butchers Pasture GTDUN CM6 ... 147 H8
Butler Cl SAFWS CB11 .... 63 G4
Butler Rd HSTD CO9 .... 125 M3
Butlers CHLM/WR CM1 .... 254 D3
Butler's La MGTR CO11 .... 138 A4
  SAFWN CB10 .... 39 L7
Butler Smith Gdns KESG IP5 ... 33 L6 1
Butlers Wy HSTD CO9 .... 70 C4
Butley Cl CHTY IP2 .... 54 B5
Butley Rd FX IP11 .... 7 H3
Buttercup Cl RIPW IP8 .... 53 L4
Buttercup Wk WIT CM8 .... 238 A1 1
Butterfield Rd RCHLM CM3 .... 256 A5
Butterfly Gdns IPNE IP4 .... 33 G8
Butter Market IP IP1 .... 2 F5
Buttersweet Ri SBW CM21 ... 227 G4 1
Butt La GTDUN CM6 .... 142 F3
  MAL CM9 .... 271 J3
Buttleys La GTDUN CM6 .... 175 H5
Butt Rd COLS CO2 .... 159 M8
  SUD CO10 .... 5 J8
Butts La RCHLM CM3 .... 269 G6
Buxey Cl K/T/MI CO5 .... 244 D6
Buxton Rd COLS CO2 .... 188 C2
  RCOLW CO6 .... 183 H2
Byfield Rd SUD CO10 .... 5 H3
Bylam La RIPS/CAP IP9 .... 80 E6
Byland Cl CHTY IP2 .... 54 C3
Bylands Cl BSF CM23 .... 170 F7
Byng Crs RCOS CO16 .... 194 D4
Byng Gdns BRTR CM7 .... 180 E1
Bypass Rd RCOS CO16 .... 220 D8
Byrd's Farm La SAFWN CB10 ... 63 G2 3
Byron Av COLW CO3 .... 159 H6
Byron Cl BRTR CM7 .... 180 C5
Byron Dr WIT CM8 .... 239 G8
Byron Rd CHLM/GWD CM2 ... 15 M4
  IP IP1 .... 31 G1
Byrony Cl WIT CM8 .... 237 M1

C

Cadenhouse Ms COLW CO3 .... 159 G6 1
Cage End RBSF CM22 .... 201 H8
Cage End Cl RBSF CM22 .... 201 H8
Cage La COLN CO4 .... 103 K8
  FX IP11 .... 113 G2
Cairns Rd COLS CO2 .... 188 C3
Caithness Cl IPNE IP4 .... 32 D5
Calamint Rd WIT CM8 .... 237M2
Caledonia Rd RIPS/CAP IP9 ... 111 K5
California Cl COLN CO4 .... 160 D1
California Rd MGTR CO11 .... 136 C1
Callis St SUD CO10 .... 26 D5
Calverley Cl BSF CM23 .... 199 G2
Camberley La IPNE IP4 .... 32 F6
Camberton Rd BRTR CM7 .... 152 A7
Camborne Cl KESG IP5 .... 33 K8
Cambrai Rd COLS CO2 .... 159 M8
Cambria Cl MGTR CO11 .... 136 D2 1
Cambridge Av COLW CO3 .... 96 A5
Cambridge Cl HVHL CB9 .... 23 G4
Cambridge Dr CHTY IP2 .... 54 A4
Cambridge Rd CBE/LIN CB1 ... 19 K3
  COLW CO3 .... 159 L8
  COS CO15 .... 12 C4
  FOS CO13 .... 196 C8
  FX IP11 .... 113 K3 1
  HLW CM20 .... 226 E7
  KESG IP5 .... 33 J3
  ROY SG8 .... 58 A4
  ROY SG8 .... 58 C2
  SAFWN CB11 .... 62 B1
  SBW CM21 .... 199 G8
  STSD CM24 .... 144 A5
Cambridge Wy BURES CO8 ... 100 B5
  HVHL CB9 .... 23 G4 1
Camden Rd IPSE IP3 .... 55 K1
Camellia Av RCOS CO16 .... 12 A3
Camellia Cl CHLM/WR CM1 ... 255 H7 2
Camellia Crs RCOS CO16 .... 12 A3
Camelot Cl CHLM/WR CM1 ... 254 B8 2
Camoise Cft RCOLW CO6 .... 69 K6 1
Camomile Wy COLN CO4 .... 159 L3
Campbell Cl CHLM/GWD CM2 ... 266 C6
Campbell Dr COLN CO4 .... 161 G3
Campbell Rd IPSE IP3 .... 55 L4
  WIT CM8 .... 210 B8

Campernell Cl RCOLE CO7 .... 219 H5
Campion La RCOLW CO6 .... 101 M2
Campion Rd CHTY IP2 .... 54 B1
  COLS CO2 .... 160 C8
Campions Hi RCOLW CO6 .... 101 M4
Campion Wy WIT CM8 .... 238 A2 2
Camp Rd RCOLE CO7 .... 163 H6
Canford Rd CBE/LIN CB1 .... 20 D6
  HVHL CB9 .... 23 H6
  HVHL CB9 .... 42 B4
Camulodunum Wy COLS CO2 ... 187 L4
Camulus Cl COLS CO2 .... 187 J3 1
Cam Wy WIT CM8 .... 237 M3 1
Camwood Gdns IPSE IP3 .... 55 K1 1
Canberra Cl CHLM/WR CM1 ... 254 A8
  COS CO2 .... 188 C4 3
  IPNE IP4 .... 32 F7 1
Can Bridge Wy CHLM/GWD CM2 ... 15 J5
Candlet Gv FX IP11 .... 113 H2
Candytuft Rd CHLM/WR CM1 ... 255 H7
Canfield BSF CM23 .... 171 G6
Canfield Rd GTDUN CM6 .... 202 F5
Canford Rd CHLM/GWD CM2 ... 267 G6
Canhams Rd SUD CO10 .... 50 D8
Canham St IP IP1 .... 2 D5
Canney Rd BOC CM0 .... 273 L8
Canning St HAR CO12 .... 9 K5
Cannon Cir BRTR CM7 .... 93 M7
Cannon Rd COL CO1 .... 11 H9 1
Cannons Cl BSF CM23 .... 171 J5
  COLS CO2 .... 187 M1
Cannons La RBSF CM22 .... 201 H8
Cannons Md STSD CM24 .... 143 M6
Cannons Mill La BSF CM23 ... 171 J4
Cannon St COL CO1 .... 11 H9
Canon Cl HVHL CB9 .... 23 H4
Canonium Ms K/T/MI CO5 ... 211 L3
Cansey La RCHLM CM3 .... 269 G4
Canterbury Cl CHTY IP2 .... 54 B5
Canterbury Gra BRTR CM7 ... 152 B5
Canterbury Rd COLS CO2 .... 160 C8
  COS CO15 .... 223 G8
Canterbury Wy CHLM/WR CM1 ... 14 B3
Canuden Rd CHLM/WR CM1 ... 14 B5
Canvey Wk CHLM/WR CM1 ... 255 G7
Canwick Gv COLS CO2 .... 188 E1
Cape Cl COLW CO3 .... 159 H8
Capel Cl BRTR CM7 .... 179 H3
  CHLM/WR CM1 .... 254 D6
  FX IP11 .... 83 K5
Capel Dr FX IP11 .... 6 D1
Capel Hall La FX IP11 .... 83 L5
Capel Pk FOS CO13 .... 196 A6
Capel Rd BRTR CM7 .... 179 H3
  COLW CO3 .... 159 L8
Caper La COLS CO2 .... 214 B1
Capons La RCHLM CM3 .... 269 J7
Cap Pillar Cl RCOLE CO7 .... 189 K3
Captains Rd K/T/MI CO5 .... 244 D7
Captains Wood Rd MAL CM9 ... 259 J3
Carbonels SUD CO10 .... 51 G2
Cardew Drift KESG IP5 .... 33 M5
Cardiff Av CHTY IP2 .... 54 D4
Cardigan St IP IP1 .... 2 E7
Cardinal Cl COLN CO4 .... 161 J6 1
Cardinal St IP IP1 .... 2 E7
Cardinal Wy HVHL CB9 .... 23 H4 1
Card's Rd CHLM/GWD CM2 ... 267 L2
Carisbrooke Av COS CO15 ... 222 C5
Carlisle Cl COL CO1 .... 10 F4
Carlton Cl HSTD CO9 .... 70 C3 2
  HVHL CB9 .... 23 H4 2
  KESG IP5 .... 33 J6
Carlton Wy IPNE IP4 .... 32 A5
Carlyle Cl IP IP1 .... 31 H1
Carmarthen Cl CHTY IP2 .... 54 C4
Carmel St SAFWN CB10 .... 37 M3
Carmen St SAFWN CB10 .... 37 M2
Carnarvon Rd COS CO15 .... 13 G6
Carnation Cl CHLM/WR CM1 ... 255 H8
Carnation Dr SAFWN CB10 ... 63 H3
Carolbrook Rd CHTY IP2 .... 54 A4
Carol Cl FX IP11 .... 113 L2
Carolina Wy K/T/MI CO5 .... 212 F8 2
Caroline Cl IP IP1 .... 189 L2
The Carpenters BSF CM23 ... 198 E1 1
Carraways WIT CM8 .... 238 D5
Carriage Cl FX IP11 .... 83 L7 1
Carriage Dr CHLM/WR CM1 ... 255 G6
Carriers Cl K/T/MI CO5 .... 244 C6
Carrigans BSF CM23 .... 171 G6
Carrington Ct K/T/MI CO5 ... 244 B6 1
Carringtons Rd RCOLE CO7 ... 162 D1
Carrington Wy BRTR CM7 ... 152 B5
Carr Rd FX IP11 .... 6 E9
Carrs Rd COS CO15 .... 12 C5
Carr St IPNE IP4 .... 3 G6
Carsey Hi CBE/LIN CB1 .... 21 K7
Carshalton End COLW CO3 ... 187 H1
Carsons Dr SUD CO10 .... 50 B8
Cartbridge Cl WOTN CO14 ... 196 D5 2
Carter Cl CBS CB2 .... 17 G5
Carters Cft SAFWN CB10 .... 40 D4
Carters Hi BSF CM23 .... 143 J4
  COLN CO4 .... 103 J7
Carters La RBSF CM22 .... 117 H8
  WIT CM8 .... 239 H7
Carters Leys BSF CM23 .... 170 F5
Cartwright Wk
  CHLM/GWD CM2 .... 267 H3 2
Case La RIPS/CAP IP9 .... 79 M7
Cassino Rd CHLM/WR CM1 ... 254 A7 2
  COLS CO2 .... 187 L2
Castle Av HVHL CB9 .... 23 G6
Castle Cl FX IP11 .... 113 M1
  HSTD CO9 .... 96 B1 1
  RCHLM CM3 .... 207 H7
Castle Cross SAFWN CB10 ... 63 G2
Castlegate St HAR CO12 .... 9 L2
Castle Hi HVHL CB9 .... 134 B1
Castle La HSTD CO9 .... 96 B1
  HVHL CB9 .... 23 G5
Castle Meadow HSTD CO9 ... 95 M3
Castle Rd COL CO1 .... 10 E5
  COS CO15 .... 12 E6

IP IP1 .... 31 G4
Castle St BSF CM23 .... 171 H7
  SAFWN CB10 .... 62 F3
Castle Vw BSF CM23 .... 171 J6
Castle Wk HVHL CB9 .... 23 G5 1
Castle Wy RCOS CO16 .... 248 C1
Castleward Cl RCOLE CO7 .... 189 L5 1
Caswell Ms CHLM/GWD CM2 ... 267 H3 2
Catchpole La MAL CM9 .... 259 J1
Catchpool Rd COL CO1 .... 10 C3
Caterham Cl RCOS CO16 .... 221 L7 1
Catesbray RIPS/CAP IP9 .... 77 H4
Catherine Cl COS CO15 .... 13 J1
Catherine Hunt Wy COLS CO2 ... 187 K3
Catherines Cl RCHLM CM3 ... 207 H7
Catkin Cl HVHL CB9 .... 22 F4
Catons La SAFWN CB10 .... 62 D2
Cat's La SUD CO10 .... 5 H7
Cattawade St MGTR CO11 ... 106 C3
Cattermole Cl RCOS CO16 ... 249 K2
Catts Cl RIPS/CAP IP9 .... 108 B3
Cattsfield RIPS/CAP IP9 .... 108 B3
Cauldwell Av IPNE IP4 .... 3 M4
Cauldwell Hall Rd IPNE IP4 ... 32 C6
Causeway End MGTR CO11 ... 106 D8 1
Causeway End Rd GTDUN CM6 ... 205 L2
Causeway Reach RCOS CO16 ... 222 A6
The Causeway BRTR CM7 ... 92 E7
  BRTR CM7 .... 180 B2
  BSF CM23 .... 171 H6
  CHLM/GWD CM2 .... 267 H7
  CHLM/WR CM1 .... 264 F7
  COLN CO4 .... 11 K2
  GTDUN CM6 .... 175 M3
  HSTD CO9 .... 45 H5
  HSTD CO9 .... 69 K7
  HSTD CO9 .... 126 A4 1
  HVHL CB9 .... 23 G6 1
  MAL CM9 .... 257 M7
  MAL CM9 .... 271 J1
  RCOLW CO6 .... 131 K4
  SAFWS CB11 .... 84 E2
  SAFWN CB11 .... 88 D6 1
Causton Rd COL CO1 .... 10 B4
Caustons Cl SUD CO10 .... 50 E8 1
Cavan Rd IP IP1 .... 30 F3
Cavendish Av COLS CO2 .... 188 E1
Cavendish Dr MGTR CO11 ... 135 K2
Cavendish Gdns BRTR CM7 ... 152 E8
  CHLM/GWD CM2 .... 267 G2
Cavendish La SUD CO10 .... 28 B1
Cavendish Rd FX IP11 .... 7 J4
  SUD CO10 .... 26 F6
Cavendish St IPSE IP3 .... 3 L8
Cavendish Wy SUD CO10 .... 4 E6
Cawell Cl STSD CM24 .... 143 M6
Cawkwell Cl CHLM/GWD CM2 ... 267 H1
Caxton Ct COLN CO4 .... 132 E7
Cecil Cl BSF CM23 .... 171 M6
Cecil Rd IP IP1 .... 30 F3
Cedar Av CHLM/WR CM1 .... 14 F2
  K/T/MI CO5 .... 212 E6
  KESG IP5 .... 33 J7
  RCOLE CO7 .... 218 F6
Cedar Av West CHLM/WR CM1 ... 14 E1
Cedar Cha MAL CM9 .... 259 L8
Cedar Cl FOS CO13 .... 196 C6
  MGTR CO11 .... 106 F4
  SBW CM21 .... 227 G4
Cedar Crs MGTR CO11 .... 135 L2
Cedarcroft Rd IP IP1 .... 31 H3
Cedar Dr WIT CM8 .... 210 C8
Cedar Pk BSF CM23 .... 198 F1
Cedars La RIPS/CAP IP9 .... 77 H4
Cedars Rd COLS CO2 .... 10 B8
Cedar Wy RCOLE CO7 .... 192 A5
Celandine Cl COLN CO4 .... 159 L3 2
Cemetery La IPNE IP4 .... 3 K1
  RCOLE CO7 .... 105 J3
Cemetery Rd BSF CM23 .... 171 H6
  IPNE IP4 .... 3 H4
Centaur Wy MAL CM9 .... 271 J5
Centenary Cl COLW CO3 .... 158 E6
Centenary Cir CHLM/WR CM1 ... 254 B4
  RCHLM CM3 .... 255 J4
Centenary Wy RCOS CO16 ... 222 A4
Central Av FOS CO13 .... 196 C7
  IPSE IP3 .... 55 M5
The Centre HSTD CO9 .... 126 A3
Centurion Wy COLS CO2 .... 187 J3
Chadburn Rd SUD CO10 .... 29 M5
Chadfont Cl COS CO15 .... 13 L2
Chalfont Rd COS CO15 .... 160 E2
Chalkers Cl RIPS/CAP IP9 .... 77 J4
Chalklands CBE/LIN CB1 .... 19 L2
  SAFWN CB10 .... 63 G2 4
Chalkners Cl RIPS/CAP IP9 ... 77 J4
Chalks Av SBW CM21 .... 226 F2
Chalks Rd WIT CM8 .... 238 B2
Chalkstone Wy HVHL CB9 ... 23 L7
Chalky La ROY SG8 .... 59 M3
Chalky Rd CBE/LIN CB1 .... 18 D2
Challenge Wy COL CO1 .... 11 H9
Challis La BRTR CM7 .... 180 C5
Chalon St IP IP1 .... 2 D6
Chamberlain Av WOTN CO14 ... 196 D6
Chamberlain Wy RIPW IP8 ... 53 L3
Chancellor Av CHLM/GWD CM2 ... 267 K1
Chancery Gv COLS CO2 .... 188 C5
Chancery Pl CHLM/WR CM1 ... 265 K4
Chandlers Cl BSF CM23 .... 198 E1 2
  RCOS CO16 .... 249 K2
Chandlers Rw COL CO1 .... 160 B4
Chaney Rd RCOS CO16 .... 189 J3
Chanterelle COLN CO4 .... 160 D2
Chantry Cl BSF CM23 .... 171 G6
  COS CO15 .... 222 A6
Chantry Gn CHTY IP2 .... 53 M2
Chantry La RCHLM CM3 .... 256 C2
Chantry Rd CHLM/GWD CM2 ... 171 G6
The Chantry COLW CO3 .... 159 L6
Chanute Ay BRTR CM7 .... 93 L6
Chapel Cl RIPS/CAP IP9 .... 77 J4
  SUD CO10 .... 51 G2 2
Chapel Cft RCOLE CO7 .... 134 A6

Chapel Cut MGTR CO11 .... 136 C1 1
Chapel Dr RCHLM CM3 .... 234 D7
Chapel End Wy HSTD CO9 ... 68 D3
Chapel Fld RIPW IP8 .... 30 C3
Chapelfields FOS CO13 .... 196 A7
Chapel HI BRTR CM7 .... 180 D3
  HSTD CO9 .... 125 M3
  SUD CO10 .... 71 M1
Chapel La CHLM/WR CM1 ... 264 B4
  COLN CO4 .... 132 C2
  FOS CO13 .... 195 J7
  MAL CM9 .... 272 A3
  RCHLM CM3 .... 268 D2
  RCOLE CO7 .... 161 K4
  RCOLE CO7 .... 162 C7
  RCOLE CO7 .... 163 J8
  RCOLE CO7 .... 191 J8
  RCOLW CO6 .... 159 G2
  RCOS CO16 .... 165 G5
  RCOS CO16 .... 248 C1
  RIPW IP8 .... 53 L6
  RIPW IP8 .... 53 J4
  SAFWS CB11 .... 87 J1 1
  SUD CO10 .... 74 E4
Chapel Rd COLN CO4 .... 132 C2
  COLW CO3 .... 158 E7
  HSTD CO9 .... 45 K6
  K/T/MI CO5 .... 241 G1
  MAL CM9 .... 239 M7
  MAL CM9 .... 262 A1
  RCOLE CO7 .... 189 K5 1
  RCOLE CO7 .... 219 J6
  RCOLW CO6 .... 158 F2
  RCOS CO16 .... 165 M6
Chapel St CBS CB2 .... 16 F4
  HSTD CO9 .... 45 H6
  HSTD CO9 .... 126 A3
  HVHL CB9 .... 43 L6
  K/T/MI CO5 .... 189 H5
Chapel St North COLS CO2 ... 10 B8
Chapel St South COLS CO2 ... 10 B8
Chaplains Cl HVHL CB9 .... 23 H4 3
Chaplin Dr COLN CO4 .... 11 M2
Chaplin Rd RCOLE CO7 .... 105 L2
Chaplins FOS CO13 .... 196 B6 1
Chaplin Wk SUD CO10 .... 50 F8
Chapman Rd COS CO15 .... 13 G6
Chapmans La K/T/MI CO5 ... 245 H4
Chappel HI RCOLW CO6 .... 128 E8
Chappel Rd RCOLW CO6 .... 129 M6
  RCOLW CO6 .... 129 G2
  RCOLW CO6 .... 156 E3
Chapple Dr HVHL CB9 .... 23 H4 4
Charlecote Rd BRTR CM7 ... 179 L6
Charles Pell Rd COLN CO4 ... 161 G7
Charles Rd FX IP11 .... 7 H4
  RCOLE CO7 .... 219 H7
Charles St COL CO1 .... 10 F9
  IP IP1 .... 2 E4
Charlotte Dr FOS CO13 .... 196 A7 3
Charlotte's RIPW IP8 .... 52 D5
Charlotte Wy WIT CM8 .... 238 D3 3
Charlton Av FX IP11 .... 31 H3
Charnock Cl FOS CO13 .... 196 B7 2
Charnwood Av CHLM/WR CM1 ... 14 B6
The Charters GTDUN CM6 ... 175 M3
Charter Wy BRTR CM7 .... 180 E4
Chartfield Dr FOS CO13 .... 195 M5
Chartwell Cl BRTR CM7 .... 152 A4
  IPNE IP4 .... 32 D1 1
Chase Cl HVHL CB9 .... 23 J4
Chase Ct COLN CO4 .... 11 M8
  COLN CO4 .... 161 G6 1
Chase La HAR CO12 .... 140 A3
Chase Rd East RCOLE CO7 ... 163 L6
The Chase BRTR CM7 .... 152 C6
  BRTR CM7 .... 179 L8
  BSF CM23 .... 171 H7
  CHLM/GWD CM2 .... 267 H7
  COL CO1 .... 11 L7 1
  COS CO15 .... 223 G8
  GTDUN CM6 .... 204 D1
  HVHL CB9 .... 43 K6
  K/T/MI CO5 .... 211 L3
  K/T/MI CO5 .... 244 E7
  MAL CM9 .... 261 K1
  MAL CM9 .... 262 F4
  MAL CM9 .... 273 H3
  MGTR CO11 .... 107 H4
  MGTR CO11 .... 135 M2
  RBSF CM22 .... 117 H7
  RCHLM CM3 .... 256 A6
  RCOLE CO7 .... 134 C1
  RCOLE CO7 .... 162 D7
  RCOLW CO6 .... 156 E6
  SUD CO10 .... 28 E7
Chaseways SBW CM21 .... 226 D5
The Chase Wy COLW CO3 ... 159 L4
Chaters HI SAFWN CB10 .... 63 G3
Chatham Hall La RCHLM CM3 ... 234 C3
Chatley Rd RCHLM CM3 .... 207 H6
Chatsworth Av BRTR CM7 ... 179 K6
Chatsworth Cl BSF CM23 ... 170 E6
Chatsworth Crs CHTY IP2 ... 54 C3
  FX IP11 .... 83 L8
Chatsworth Dr IPNE IP4 .... 33 G8
Chatsworth Gdns COS CO15 ... 12 C8
Chatsworth Rd K/T/MI CO5 ... 244 E6
Chattisham Rd RIPW IP8 .... 52 D5
Chaucer Cl COS CO15 .... 249 J4
  MAL CM9 .... 271 J5
Chaucer Crs BRTR CM7 .... 180 C5
Chaucer Rd CHLM/GWD CM2 ... 15 M5
  FX IP11 .... 7 J3
  IP IP1 .... 31 H2
  SUD CO10 .... 4 A1
Chaucer Wy COLW CO3 .... 159 H6
Chauntry Rd HVHL CB9 .... 23 H6
Chelmer Av RCHLM CM3 .... 234 D8
Chelmer Dr FOS CO13 .... 196 A4
  MAL CM9 .... 260 D1
Chelmer Lea CHLM/GWD CM2 ... 267 G6
Chelmer Pl CHLM/WR CM1 ... 15 K2
Chelmer Rd BRTR CM7 .... 180 F4
  CHLM/GWD CM2 .... 15 M6
  HVHL CB9 .... 23 K5
  WIT CM8 .... 238 A3

Chelmer Ter MAL CM9 .... 271 K3 1
Chelmerton Av
  CHLM/GWD CM2 .... 267 G6
Chelmer Valley Rd
  CHLM/WR CM1 .... 266 D1
Chelmer Village Wy
  CHLM/GWD CM2 .... 267 G3
Chelmsford Rd CHLM/WR CM1 .. 265 L4
  COS CO4 .... 222 E7
  GTDUN CM6 .... 176 B7 1
  MAL CM9 .... 269 L6
  RBSF CM22 .... 228 D3
  RCHLM CM3 .... 234 C8
Chelsea Cl IP IP1 .... 31 H4
Chelsea Ct SUD CO10 .... 4 F6
Chelsea Rd SUD CO10 .... 4 F6
Chelsworth Av IPNE IP4 .... 31 M4
  SUD CO10 .... 5 K8
Chelsworth Rd FX IP11 .... 6 E3
Cheltenham Av IP IP1 .... 31 K4
Chelwater CHLM/GWD CM2 ...... 15 M8
Chepstow Rd FX IP11 .... 113 H2
  IP IP1 .... 31 K1 1
Chequers BSF CM23 .... 170 E5 1
Chequers La GTDUN CM6 .... 175 M5
  MAL CM9 .... 271 J2 1
Chequers Rd CHLM/WR CM1 .... 265 H4
  MGTR CO11 .... 135 K7
The Chequers RCOLE CO7 .... 190 G6 1
Cheriton Rd BRTR CM7 .... 180 E4 1
Cherry Blossom Cl RIPW IP8 .... 53 K3
Cherry Cha K/T/MI CO5 .... 240 F1
Cherry Cl CBE/LIN CB1 .... 19 K2
Cherrygarden La
  CHLM/GWD CM2 .... 14 D7
Cherry Garden La RCHLM CM3 .. 269 J6
  SAFWS CB11 .... 87 H5
  RCHLM CM3 .... 234 A6
Cherry Garden Rd MAL CM9 ..... 271 G3
Cherry Gdns BSF CM23 .... 171 J5
  SBW CM21 .... 227 G1
Cherry Gardens La IPNE IP4 .... 32 D6
Cherry La HSTD CO9 .... 70 C5
Cherry Rw COLW CO3 .... 159 H8
Cherry Tree Av COS CO15 .... 12 B9
Cherry Tree Cl HAR CO12 .... 139 K6
Cherry Tree La COLS CO2 .... 188 C7
Cherrytree Ri WIT CM8 .... 210 C8 2
Cherrytree Rd SUD CO10 .... 5 J7
Cherrywood Dr COLW CO3 ...... 159 H8
Cherrywoods RCOLE CO7 .... 191 M5
Chervil Cl K/T/MI CO5 .... 240 E1 1
Cherwell Dr CHLM/WR CM1 ..... 253 L8
Chesapeake Cl RIPS/CAP IP9 ... 81 H6
Chesapeake Rd IPSE IP3 .... 55 J5 2
Chesfield Cl BSF CM23 .... 171 H8
Chesham Rd CHTY IP2 .... 2 D9
Chessington Gdns IP IP1 .... 31 H5 1
Chess La WIT CM8 .... 238 C3
Chesterfield Dr IP IP1 .... 31 H3
Chester Pl CHLM/WR CM1 .... 254 C8 1
Chester Rd FX IP11 .... 113 H2
Chesterton Cl CHTY IP2 .... 54 B4
Chestnut Av COLS CO2 .... 188 C5
  COS CO15 .... 12 A7
  COS CO15 .... 249 J3
  FOS CO13 .... 195 L7
  HSTD CO9 .... 125 G5
  MAL CM9 .... 259 L7
  RCHLM CM3 .... 257 J2
  SAFWS CB11 .... 61 L4
Chestnut Cl BSF CM23 .... 171 H7 2
  HVHL CB9 .... 23 H5
  KESG IP5 .... 33 G4
  SUD CO10 .... 51 G2
Chestnut Ct SAFWS CB11 .... 87 L5 2
Chestnut Dr BRTR CM7 .... 180 A3 1
Chestnut Gv RCOLE CO7 .... 190 D5 3
The Chestnuts CHTY IP2 .... 53 L3
Chestnut Wk CHLM/WR CM1 .... 254 C8
  GTDUN CM6 .... 177 L7
  RCHLM CM3 .... 269 G4
Chestnut Wy K/T/MI CO5 .... 212 E7
  RBSF CM22 .... 173 L6
  RCOLE CO7 .... 219 G6
Chevalier Rd FX IP11 .... 113 K3 2
Chevallier St IP IP1 .... 2 A4
Cheveling Rd COLS CO2 .... 188 F3
Cheviot Dr CHLM/WR CM1 ...... 253 M8
Chevy Ct HAR CO12 .... 139 L3
Cheyne Ct SUD CO10 .... 4 C7
Chichester Dr CHLM/WR CM1 ... 266 E1
Chichester Rd SAFWS CB11 .... 63 G5
Chickney Wy MAL CM9 .... 271 K5 1
Chickney Rd RBSF CM22 .... 117 L7
Chigborough Rd MAL CM9 .... 260 B6
Chignall Rd CHLM/WR CM1 ..... 265 M1
Chilburn Rd COS CO15 .... 222 B6
Childers Rd RIPS/CAP IP9 .... 111 J4
Childers Fld FX IP11 .... 112 F2 3
Childwell Aly COL CO1 .... 10 E8
Chiltern Cl COL CO1 .... 10 A3
Chilton Cl CHLM/GWD CM2 ..... 15 L9
  RCOLW CO6 .... 131 K6
Chilton Ct SUD CO10 .... 5 G7
Chilton Lodge Rd SUD CO10 .... 5 G7
Chilton Rd IPSE IP3 .... 55 L1
Chimswell Wy HVHL CB9 .... 22 F5
Chingford Av COS CO15 .... 222 B6
Chinnel La SAFWS CB11 .... 61 M8
Chinnery Hi BSF CM23 .... 171 H8
Chinook COLN CO4 .... 160 D1
Chippetts La COLW CO3 .... 157 L6
Chippingdell WIT CM8 .... 238 D1
Chipping Hi HSTD CO9 .... 96 A1
  WIT CM8 .... 238 B2 1
Chipstead Wk RCOS CO16 ...... 221 L7
Chishill Rd ROY SG8 .... 58 C3
  ROY SG8 .... 59 H2
Chislett Rw CHLM/GWD CM2 ... 15 K8
Chittock Cl RCOS CO16 .... 249 K2
Chitts Hi COLW CO3 .... 158 F6
Chivers Rd HVHL CB9 .... 22 F6
Choats Wd RCOLW CO6 .... 158 B4
Chrismund Wy RCOLW CO6 ..... 156 E4
Christchurch St IPNE IP4 .... 3 H3
Christina Rd WIT CM8 .... 237 M5
Christine Cha COLW CO3 .... 159 H8 1

Christmas Fld HSTD CO9 .... 95 M3
Christopher Dr RCOS CO16 ..... 221 M4
Christopher La SUD CO10 .... 4 C7
Church Av CHLM/WR CM1 .... 266 B1
Church Cha WIT CM8 .... 239 H2
Church Cl KESG IP5 .... 33 K5 1
  RCOLW CO6 .... 159 G1
  SUD CO10 .... 27 M3 1
  WIT CM8 .... 238 F8
Church Crs COS CO15 .... 13 H7
  RIPW IP8 .... 30 C7
Church Dr BSF CM23 .... 114 D5
  GTDUN CM6 .... 175 M3
  ROY SG8 .... 58 C4
Church End BRTR CM7 .... 151 K6
Church Farm Wy COLN CO4 ..... 160 A1
Churchfield ROY SG8 .... 58 C4
Church Fld SAFWS CB11 .... 63 G6 2
Church Field Rd SUD CO10 ...... 5 J2
  WOTN CO14 .... 196 E5
Churchfield Rd RCOLW CO6 ..... 183 J2
Church Flds HSTD CO9 .... 70 B3
  K/T/MI CO5 .... 244 D7
  STSD CM24 .... 144 B7
Churchfields AV COS CO15 ...... 186 E1 1
Churchfields Dr HVHL CB9 ...... 43 K7
Church Gdns CHLM/WR CM1 ... 175 M3
Church Gn CHLM/WR CM1 ...... 252 D8
  HSTD CO9 .... 70 F1 1
  RCOLW CO6 .... 183 J3
  RIPW IP8 .... 30 D4
  WIT CM8 .... 17 K8
Church Gv RCOLW CO6 .... 157 K5
Church Hi BRTR CM7 .... 92 F7
  HAR CO12 .... 139 J4
  HVHL CB9 .... 42 E5
  K/T/MI CO5 .... 189 H5
  MAL CM9 .... 269 M3
  MGTR CO11 .... 135 H2
  RCHLM CM3 .... 234 E7
  RCOLW CO6 .... 127 L7
  SAFWS CB10 .... 40 C5
  WIT CM8 .... 209 H5
Churchill AV HSTD CO9 .... 126 C2
  HVHL CB9 .... 23 K4
  IPNE IP4 .... 32 D8
Churchill Cl RCOLE CO7 .... 219 H5
Churchill Dr SUD CO10 .... 4 C1
Churchill Ri CHLM/WR CM1 ..... 255 G6
Churchill Rd BRTR CM7 .... 152 A7
  COS CO15 .... 213 H8
Churchill Wy COLS CO2 .... 188 D1
Church La BRTR CM7 .... 152 B6
  BSF CM23 .... 198 F3
  CBE/LIN CB1 .... 19 L3
  CBE/LIN CB1 .... 41 M2
  CHLM/WR CM1 .... 265 K4
  CHLM/WR CM1 .... 266 F1
  COLW CO3 .... 159 H7
  COLW CO3 .... 186 C1
  FOS CO13 .... 223 K2
  FX IP11 .... 83 K6
  FX IP11 .... 113 G1
  GTDUN CM6 .... 174 D6
  GTDUN CM6 .... 229 L6
  HAR CO12 .... 9 L3 2
  HSTD CO9 .... 45 K7
  HSTD CO9 .... 69 K6
  HSTD CO9 .... 96 A1 2
  K/T/MI CO5 .... 243 H2
  K/T/MI CO5 .... 245 M4
  KIR/NAC IP10 .... 57 J4
  KIR/NAC IP10 .... 82 A2
  KIR/NAC IP10 .... 83 L2
  MAL CM9 .... 260 B5
  MAL CM9 .... 260 D3
  MGTR CO11 .... 107 G4
  MGTR CO11 .... 136 A1
  NHMKT IP6 .... 32 B1
  NHMKT IP6 .... 33 K1
  RBSF CM22 .... 145 G6
  RBSF CM22 .... 173 K6
  RBSF CM22 .... 227 M5
  RCHLM CM3 .... 205 K7
  RCHLM CM3 .... 206 E5
  RCOLW CO6 .... 102 D4
  RCOLW CO6 .... 184 E2
  RCOLW CO6 .... 185 J1
  RCOS CO16 .... 166 C7
  RCOS CO16 .... 193 J6
  RIPS/CAP IP9 .... 109 K2
  RIPS/CAP IP9 .... 110 E3
  RIPW IP8 .... 30 D8
  RIPW IP8 .... 52 F5
  SAFWS CB11 .... 88 C6
  SUD CO10 .... 73 M5
Church Md WIT CM8 .... 209 H4
Church Mdw BRTR CM7 .... 152 B7 1
Church Pk SUD CO10 .... 45 L2
Church Pth CBE/LIN CB1 .... 19 K7
Churchponds HSTD CO9 .... 96 A1 3
Church Rd BRTR CM7 .... 154 B8
  BRTR CM7 .... 180 B7
  BRTR CM7 .... 181 J7
  BRTR CM7 .... 181 M3
  CBE/LIN CB1 .... 21 L8
  COLN CO4 .... 103 J6
  COLS CO2 .... 215 H1
  COS CO15 .... 13 J7
  FX IP11 .... 113 L1
  HSTD CO9 .... 68 F3
  HSTD CO9 .... 70 B3
  HSTD CO9 .... 72 D6
  HSTD CO9 .... 124 F6
  HSTD CO9 .... 126 C6
  K/T/MI CO5 .... 211 L3
  K/T/MI CO5 .... 212 E8
  K/T/MI CO5 .... 215 M8
  K/T/MI CO5 .... 244 D7
  KIR/NAC IP10 .... 81 K1
  MAL CM9 .... 257 L7
  MAL CM9 .... 259 M3
  MAL CM9 .... 261 H3
  MGTR CO11 .... 138 A1
  RBSF CM22 .... 172 C8
  RBSF CM22 .... 199 L3

RCHLM CM3 .... 236 D3
RCHLM CM3 .... 256 A5
RCHLM CM3 .... 257 J2
RCOLE CO7 .... 162 C7
RCOLE CO7 .... 164 B6
RCOLE CO7 .... 190 D6
RCOLE CO7 .... 190 F3
RCOLE CO7 .... 191 J8
RCOLW CO6 .... 103 G7
RCOLW CO6 .... 129 M8
RCOLW CO6 .... 186 A3
RIPS/CAP IP9 .... 78 D7
RIPS/CAP IP9 .... 78 A6
RIPS/CAP IP9 .... 108 C3
RIPS/CAP IP9 .... 109 G1
ROY SG8 .... 59 M2
SAFWN CB10 .... 66 B5
STSD CM24 .... 144 B8
SUD CO10 .... 49 G8
SUD CO10 .... 50 C8
SUD CO10 .... 51 K7
SUD CO10 .... 73 J7
SUD CO10 .... 73 H2
WIT CM8 .... 210 D4
WIT CM8 .... 238 F8
WOTN CO14 .... 196 E5 3
Church Sq BURES CO8 .... 100 B4 1
  RCOS CO16 .... 248 C1
Church St BRTR CM7 .... 152 C4
  BSF CM23 .... 171 H6
  CHLM/GWD CM2 .... 267 J2 1
  CHLM/WR CM1 .... 15 H3 1
  COLN CO4 .... 103 J6
  COLW CO3 .... 10 B7
  GTDUN CM6 .... 175 M3
  HAR CO12 .... 9 K3
  HSTD CO9 .... 72 A5
  HSTD CO9 .... 95 M4
  HSTD CO9 .... 96 F4
  HVHL CB9 .... 22 E1
  HVHL CB9 .... 43 K6
  K/T/MI CO5 .... 189 H5
  K/T/MI CO5 .... 211 K3
  MAL CM9 .... 261 G7
  MAL CM9 .... 261 M1
  MAL CM9 .... 262 F4
  MAL CM9 .... 271 K3
  RBSF CM22 .... 228 C2
  RCOLW CO6 .... 127 J4
  RCOLW CO6 .... 183 J3
  RIPS/CAP IP9 .... 81 G6
  SAFWN CB10 .... 37 J1
  SAFWN CB10 .... 37 M3
  SAFWS CB11 .... 62 A8
  SAFWS CB11 .... 87 J4
  SAFWS CB11 .... 116 F1
  SBW CM21 .... 227 G3 1
  SUD CO10 .... 4 B8
  SUD CO10 .... 26 D5
  SUD CO10 .... 47 K3
  WIT CM8 .... 238 B1
Church Vw RCOLE CO7 .... 134 A6 1
Church Wk COLW CO3 .... 10 B7
  HVHL CB9 .... 44 A1
  SAFWS CB11 .... 62 B1
  SBW CM21 .... 227 H3
  SUD CO10 .... 4 C5
  SUD CO10 .... 29 M3
Churchwell Av K/T/MI CO5 ...... 185 J6
Churnwood Rd COLN CO4 .... 11 M3
Chuzzlewit Dr
  CHLM/WR CM1 .... 254 A6 1
Cinque Port Rd RCOLE CO7 .... 219 H6
Circular Rd East COLS CO2 ..... 160 B8
Circular Rd North COLS CO2 ... 160 A8
Circular Rd South COLS CO2 ... 188 A1
Circular Rd West COLS CO2 .... 160 A8
City Rd K/T/MI CO5 .... 244 O6
Civic Dr IP IP1 .... 2 D5
Clachar Cl CHLM/GWD CM2 ... 267 J2 1
Clacton Rd FOS CO13 .... 223 J4
  HAR CO12 .... 139 J8
  MGTR CO11 .... 136 B4
  RCOLE CO7 .... 161 L8
  RCOLE CO7 .... 162 D8
  RCOLE CO7 .... 191 J8
  RCOS CO16 .... 193 J7
  RCOS CO16 .... 248 E1
Claire Rd COS CO15 .... 195 K7
Clairmont Cl BRTR CM7 .... 180 B3 2
Clairmont Rd RCOLW CO6 ...... 159 G8
Clapgate Dr RCOS CO16 .... 221 L3
Clapgate La IPSE IP3 .... 55 J2
Clapton Hall La GTDUN CM6 ... 175 M8
Clara Reeve Cl COLW CO3 ...... 187 H1
Clare Cl HSTD CO9 .... 126 A6
Clare Ct GTDUN CM6 .... 119 H2
Claremont Hts K/T/MI CO5 ..... 10 A2 1
Claremont Rd RCOLE CO7 ...... 189 L5
Clarence Cl CHLM/GWD CM2 .. 267 J1 2
Clarence Rd IPSE IP3 .... 55 K4
  STSD CM24 .... 144 A6 1
  SUD CO10 .... 4 C4
  SUD CO10 .... 26 D4
Clarendon Pk COS CO15 .... 13 L2
Clarendon Rd HVHL CB9 .... 23 H6
  RBSF CM22 .... 174 A6
Clarendon Wy COL CO1 .... 10 B3
Clare Rd BRTR CM7 .... 179 M3
  IPNE IP4 .... 32 B5
  K/T/MI CO5 .... 211 K4
Clare Wy RCOS CO16 .... 221 K8
Clarkesmead K/T/MI CO5 .... 240 E1 2
  RCOLE CO7 .... 134 B3
  RCOLW CO6 .... 155 L1
  RCOLW CO6 .... 182 C3
Clarke's Rd HAR CO12 .... 8 A4
Clarks Farm Rd RCHLM CM3 ... 269 H5 1
Clarkson St IP IP1 .... 2 A4
Clarks Wood Dr BRTR CM7 ..... 180 F2 2
Clark Wy CHLM/WR CM1 .... 254 C4 1
Clatterbury La SAFWS CB11 ... 86 A6
Claude Ince Av BRTR CM7 ...... 180 F7
Claude St IP IP1 .... 2 E4
Claudian Cl HVHL CB9 .... 23 M6
Claudius Rd COLS CO2 .... 160 C8
Claudius Wy WIT CM8 .... 238 A5
Clavering Rd BRTR CM7 .... 152 B7 2

Claverton Wy IPNE IP4 .... 32 F8 1
  IPNE IP4 .... 55 M1 2
  IPNE IP4 .... 56 A1 1
Claydon Cl CBE/LIN CB1 .... 42 A1
Clayhall Rd COS CO15 .... 13 J2
Clay Hi SUD CO10 .... 73 L5
Clayhive Dr HVHL CB9 .... 23 H6 1
Clay La COLN CO4 .... 160 F1
  RCOS CO16 .... 220 E5
Clay Lane Gv COLN CO4 .... 160 F1
Claypit Hi RBSF CM22 .... 145 G8
Clay Pit Piece SAFWS CB11 .... 63 G7
Claypits Av BURES CO8 .... 100 B5
Claypits La SUD CO10 .... 28 F7
Claypits Rd RCHLM CM3 .... 256 B4
Clay Pits Wy BRTR CM7 .... 180 F2 3
Clayponds BSF CM23 .... 171 J6
Clayshotts Dr WIT CM8 .... 238 D5
Clays Rd WOTN CO14 .... 196 C5
Clayton Rd HAR CO12 .... 139 L3
Clayton Wy MAL CM9 .... 271 J5
Claywall Br HVHL CB9 .... 43 K6
Clearwater COLS CO2 .... 188 D1
Clematis Wy COLN CO4 .... 161 G6
Clements Cl CHLM/GWD CM2 .. 267 K2
  HVHL CB9 .... 23 H6
Clements Dr HVHL CB9 .... 23 H6
Clement's La HVHL CB9 .... 23 H6
Clench Cl IPNE IP4 .... 3 H5
Clench Rd RIPS/CAP IP9 .... 79 M6
Clermont Av SUD CO10 .... 4 C1
Clevedon Cl BRTR CM7 .... 179 L6 1
Cleveland Cl COLN CO4 .... 160 E1
Cleves Ct RCHLM CM3 .... 256 A4 2
Cleves Rd HVHL CB9 .... 22 F6
Clicket Hi BURES CO8 .... 100 D5
Cliff Crs BRTR CM7 .... 123 G6
Cliffield BRTR CM7 .... 123 G6
Cliff La IPSE IP3 .... 55 H2
Clifford Rd IPNE IP4 .... 3 G1
Cliff Pde WOTN CO14 .... 197 G3
Cliff Rd COS CO15 .... 223 H8
  FX IP11 .... 113 M2
  HAR CO12 .... 9 H8
  IPSE IP3 .... 55 G2
Cliff Wy FOS CO13 .... 196 C8
Clifton Wy CHTY IP2 .... 53 M3
Clifton Wd RIPS/CAP IP9 .... 79 M7
Clipped Hedge RBSF CM22 ..... 228 C2
Clive Av IP IP1 .... 31 K3
Cliveden Cl CHLM/WR CM1 .... 14 A1
Clive Rd COLS CO2 .... 160 B8
Clockhouse Wy BRTR CM7 ..... 180 D3
Cloes La RCOS CO16 .... 249 K1
The Cloisters BRTR CM7 .... 152 C8
  K/T/MI CO5 .... 211 K4
Cloncurry Gdns FX IP11 .... 6 E4
Clopton Dr SUD CO10 .... 29 L7
The Close BRTR CM7 .... 181 G7
  COS CO15 .... 249 J6
  FOS CO13 .... 196 A8
  FOS CO13 .... 223 J2
  HAR CO12 .... 8 C7
  RBSF CM22 .... 228 C2
  RIPS/CAP IP9 .... 78 F6
  SAFWS CB11 .... 88 D2 2
  SUD CO10 .... 4 F4
Clouded Yellow Cl BRTR CM7 .. 180 A5 2
Clough Rd COLN CO4 .... 132 E7
Clovelly Cl IPNE IP4 .... 56 B1
Clover Av BSF CM23 .... 170 D7
Clover Cl CBE/LIN CB1 .... 19 M3 1
  SUD CO10 .... 28 A4
Clover Dr RCOLE CO7 .... 191 J8
Clover Fld HVHL CB9 .... 22 E5
Cloverlands COLN CO4 .... 11 K2
Clovers WIT CM8 .... 125 M4 1
Clover Wy RCOLE CO7 .... 133 K8
Cluanie Orch SUD CO10 .... 28 A4
Club Pde RCOS CO16 .... 248 D7
Clyde Crs CHLM/WR CM1 .... 265 M1
Clydesdale Rd BRTR CM7 ...... 154 B1
Coach House Wy WIT CM8 ...... 238 B3 1
Coach La MAL CM9 .... 271 H2 1
Coachman's Paddock
  RIPS/CAP IP9 .... 79 M7
Coach Rd RCOLE CO7 .... 190 D6
  RCOLW CO6 .... 131 G6
  SAFWN CB10 .... 66 A3
Coan Av COS CO15 .... 249 M4
Coast Rd K/T/MI CO5 .... 244 C7
Coates Cl MAL CM9 .... 271 K1 1
Coats Hutton Rd COLS CO2 .... 187 K2
Cobbold Ms IPNE IP4 .... 3 G4
Cobbold Rd FX IP11 .... 7 K1
  FX IP11 .... 113 K3
Cobbold St IPNE IP4 .... 3 G4
Cobbs La RBSF CM22 .... 174 B2
Cobbs PI CHLM/WR CM1 .... 15 L1
Cobden PI IPNE IP4 .... 3 H5
Cobham Rd IPSE IP3 .... 55 L2
Cock And Bell La SUD CO10 ... 29 L5
Cockaynes La RCOLE CO7 ...... 190 C4
Cockett Wick La RCOS CO16 ... 248 E4
Cock La SAFWS CB11 .... 114 B2
Cockrell's Rd RCOLW CO6 ...... 130 C1
Cock Rd HSTD CO9 .... 97 K4
Codham Little Park Dr
  BRTR CM7 .... 123 K7
Cody Rd IPSE IP3 .... 55 L4
Coeur De Lion COLN CO4 .... 160 B3 1
Coggeshall Rd BRTR CM7 ...... 180 B2
  K/T/MI CO5 .... 183 K7
  RCOLE CO7 .... 134 B3
  RCOLW CO6 .... 155 L1
  RCOLW CO6 .... 182 C3
Coggeshall Road (Feering)
  K/T/MI CO5 .... 183 K4
Coggeshall Wy HSTD CO9 ...... 126 C3 1

HAR CO12 .... 165 J2
HSTD CO9 .... 126 B4
IPNE IP4 .... 32 A4
MAL CM9 .... 239 M8
MAL CM9 .... 242 C7
MAL CM9 .... 242 D3
MAL CM9 .... 259 K8
MGTR CO11 .... 135 K2
RCOLE CO7 .... 105 G8
RCOLE CO7 .... 133 L7
RCOLE CO7 .... 162 A7
RCOLE CO7 .... 189 K1
RCOLE CO7 .... 192 A2
RCOLW CO6 .... 128 A6
RCOLW CO6 .... 183 L3
RCOS CO16 .... 192 F4
WIT CM8 .... 238 D2
Cold Hall Cha RCOLE CO7 ...... 163 G7
Coldnailhurst Av BRTR CM7 .... 152 B8 1
Cold Store Rd FX IP11 .... 6 B5
Cole End La SAFWN CB10 ...... 63 L8
Cole Hi RCHLM CM3 .... 235 K1
Colehills Cl SAFWS CB11 .... 114 E1
Colemans Ct RCHLM CM3 ...... 268 F6
Cole Ness Rd IPSE IP3 .... 55 J5
Coleridge Rd IP IP1 .... 31 H2
  MAL CM9 .... 271 J4
Coles Cl CBE/LIN CB1 .... 19 L3
  WOTN CO14 .... 196 L2
Coles Oak La RCOLE CO7 .... 104 E7
College Cl BSF CM23 .... 170 F6
College Rd BRTR CM7 .... 180 A2
  COS CO15 .... 13 J5
College St IPSE IP3 .... 2 F7
Coller Rd HAR CO12 .... 8 A4
Colles Brook Rd RCOLE CO7 ... 192 B8
Colletts Cha RCOLW CO6 .... 130 B1
Colley Rd CHLM/GWD CM2 ..... 267 J7
The Colliers MAL CM9 .... 272 A2
Collimer Cl RIPS/CAP IP9 ...... 81 G5
Collindale Gdns COS CO15 ..... 222 E8
Collingwood Av IPSE IP3 .... 55 K2 1
Collingwood Cl BRTR CM7 ...... 152 E8
Collingwood Flds RCOLE CO7 .. 105 K1
Collingwood Rd COLW CO3 ..... 159 G2
  WIT CM8 .... 249 M4
Collins Cl BRTR CM7 .... 180 B3 3
Collins Cross BSF CM23 .... 171 J4
Collinson's CHTY IP2 .... 30 E8
Collins Rd HSTD CO9 .... 98 A3
Colne Bank Av COLW CO3 ...... 10 A4
Colne Cha WIT CM8 .... 238 A3
Colneford Hi RCOLW CO6 ...... 127 M7
Colneis Rd FX IP11 .... 113 J1
Colne Park Rd RCOLW CO6 .... 127 M5
Colne Ri K/T/MI CO5 .... 189 H5
Colne Rd BURES CO8 .... 100 A5
  COS CO15 .... 13 G7
  HSTD CO9 .... 96 A5 1
  HSTD CO9 .... 126 B3
  RCOLE CO7 .... 219 G2
  RCOLW CO6 .... 155 J6
  RCOLW CO6 .... 183 L1
Colne Springs HSTD CO9 .... 45 K6
Colne Valley Cl HSTD CO9 ...... 125 M3
Colne Valley Rd HVHL CB9 ..... 23 J6
Colne Vw RCOS CO16 .... 247 J3
Colne Wy RCOS CO16 .... 247 H1
Colneys Cl SUD CO10 .... 4 B2
Colthorpe Rd COS CO15 .... 222 B5
Colts Cft ROY SG8 .... 59 G3
Coltsfield STSD CM24 .... 144 A6
Coltsfoot Cl COLN CO4 .... 159 L3
Coltsfoot Rd CHTY IP2 .... 54 A1
The Colts BSF CM23 .... 199 G2
Columbia Cl KESG IP5 .... 33 J6
Columbine Gdns CHTY IP2 ..... 31 G8
  FOS CO13 .... 196 B6
Columbine Ms COLW CO3 ...... 158 E6 1
The Columbines SUD CO10 .... 28 A3
Colville Cl BRTR CM7 .... 179 L6 2
Colvin Cl COLW CO3 .... 159 H7
Colyers Reach CHLM/GWD CM2 267 J3
Comma Cl BRTR CM7 .... 180 A4
Commerce Pk COLS CO2 .... 188 F1
Commerce Wy COLS CO2 .... 188 F1
  MGTR CO11 .... 106 E8
Commercial Rd IP IP1 .... 2 D8
Common Hi SAFWN CB10 .... 62 F3
Common La MAL CM9 .... 269 K8
  RCHLM CM3 .... 269 G8
  ROY SG8 .... 59 K6
The Commons COLW CO3 ...... 159 J8
Common St SUD CO10 .... 26 D5
The Common RCHLM CM3 ...... 269 G7
Compasses Rd BRTR CM7 ...... 154 B8
Compton Rd COLN CO4 .... 11 J5
Comyns PI CHLM/WR CM1 ..... 265 K4 1
Conan Doyle Cl BRTR CM7 ..... 180 C5 6
Conder Wy COLS CO2 .... 188 E1
Conduit La MAL CM9 .... 270 A7
Coney Gn SBW CM21 .... 226 F2
Congreve Rd IP IP1 .... 31 K3
Conies Rd HSTD CO9 .... 125 M6
  RCOLE CO7 .... 190 B6
Conifer Cl COLN CO4 .... 11 M5
  RCOLE CO7 .... 190 B6
Coniston Cl BRTR CM7 .... 179 L2
Coniston Rd IPSE IP3 .... 55 K3
Connaught Av FOS CO13 .... 224 B1
Connaught Cl COS CO15 .... 13 M5
Connaught Gdns BRTR CM7 ... 180 A2
Connaught Gdns East COS CO15 .. 13 L4
Connaught Gdns West 13 L4
Connaught Rd HVHL CB9 .... 23 G6
  IP IP1 .... 30 F3
  RCOS CO16 .... 193 K8
Conquerors Cl RCHLM CM3 .... 257 K2 1
Conrad Rd WIT CM8 .... 210 B8
Constable Av RCOS CO16 .... 221 L7
Constable Cl COLN CO4 .... 160 A1
  K/T/MI CO5 .... 244 F6
  MGTR CO11 .... 135 K1 2
Constable Rd FX IP11 .... 113 K3
  HVHL CB9 .... 22 F4
  IPNE IP4 .... 3 H3

SUD CO10 .... 4 D4
Constance Cl CHLM/WR CM1 .. 254 D2 1
WIT CM8 .... 238 C5
Constantine Rd COLW CO3 ..159 M8
IP IP1 .... 2 C7
WIT CM8 .... 238 A5 2
Constitution HI IP IP1 .... 2 D1
SUD CO10 .... 4 E5
Convalescent HI FX IP11 ...... 7 L4
Convent Rd BRTR CM7 .... 152 C8
Convent La BRTR CM7 .... 152 C8
Conway Cl CHTY IP2 .... 54 D3
HSTD CO9 .... 125 M5
RCOLE CO7 .... 189 L5
Conyer Cl MAL CM9 .... 271 H5
Cook Cl HAR CO12 .... 140 B4
Cook Pl CHLM/GWD CM2 ..... 267 H2
Cooks Cl HSTD CO9 .... 126 B5
Cooks HI COLN CO4 .... 103 K6
Cook's La BRTR CM7 .... 121 G1
COLW CO3 .... 159 G5
Coolyne Wy COS CO15 .... 222 D6
Coombe Ri CHLM/WR CM1 .... 254 D6
Coombers RIPS/CAP IP9 ...... 77 H4
Coopers Av MAL CM9 .... 259 L8
Coopers Cl BSF CM23 .... 198 D1
Coopers Crs RCOLW CO6 ...... 159 H1
Coopers End Rd RBSF CM22 ... 173 J2
Coopers End Rbt RBSF CM22 .. 173 K2
Coopers La COS CO15 .... 12 A5
RCHLM CM3 .... 207 H6
RCOLE CO7 .... 105 H8
Coopers Vls RBSF CM22 ...... 173 K3
Copeland Cl CHLM/GWD CM2 .. 267 H5
CHLM/WR CM1 .... 254 C4
Copleston End RCOLW CO6 .... 157 M8
Coppins Cl CHLM/WR CM1 .... 267 G1
Coppins Rd COS CO15 .... 12 A4
Coprolite St IPSE IP3 .... 9 J7
The Copse BSF CM23 .... 171 L5 1
GTDUN CM6 .... 178 B7
Copthall La GTDUN CM6 ...... 119 J2
Copt Hall La K/T/MI CO5 ..... 243 K2
Copt HI RCHLM CM3 .... 269 G7
Copy HI HVHL CB9 .... 43 G2
Coral Dr IP IP1 .... 30 F4
Coralin Wk COLW CO3 .... 158 E7
Cordell Pl SUD CO10 .... 29 M5
Cordell Rd SUD CO10 .... 29 L5
Corder Rd IPNE IP4 .... 3 H1
Cordwinders RCOLE CO7 ..... 106 A4
Cordy's La FX IP11 .... 112 D7
Cornard Rd SUD CO10 .... 4 E7
Cornel Cl WIT CM8 .... 237 M1
Cornelius V CHLM/GWD CM2 .. 267 K5
Cornells La SAFWS CB11 ..... 117 G2
Corner Pk SAFWN CB10 ...... 63 G2
Cornerth Crs SUD CO10 ...... 5 J9
Cornflower Cl CHTY IP2 ..... 54 A1
COLW CO3 .... 158 E6
Cornflower Dr CHLM/WR CM1 .. 255 H8
Cornflower Rd COS CO15 ..... 249 L6
Cornford Wy MGTR CO11 .... 135 K1
Cornish Cl CBE/LIN CB1 ..... 21 J2
Cornish Hall End Rd BRTR CM7 . 67 M6
HSTD CO9 .... 68 C4
Cornwall Cl MGTR CO11 ..... 135 K2
Cornwall Crs CHLM/WR CM1 .. 254 C6
Cornwall Gdns BRTR CM7 .... 180 C1
Cornwallis Pl SAFWN CB10 ... 63 G2 5
SAFWN CB10 .... 63 G3 1
Cornwallis Rd HVHL CB9 ..... 23 H6
Cornwall Rd FX IP11 .... 113 G2
Cornwalls Dr RCOLW CO6 .... 185 H2 1
Coronation Av IP IP1 .... 31 K4
COLS CO2 .... 188 C4
Coronation Dr FX IP11 .... 6 F3
Coronation Ri SUD CO10 ..... 51 H1
Coronation Rd BSF CM23 .... 171 G8
COS CO15 .... 12 B5
IPNE IP4 .... 32 D8
Corporation Av CHTY IP2 .... 54 C5
Corporation Rd CHLM/WR CM1 . 266 C1
Cortoncroft Cl FOS CO13 .... 196 B6
Corton Rd IPSE IP3 .... 55 K4
Cotman Av MGTR CO11 ...... 106 D8
Cotman Rd COLW CO3 .... 159 J8
IPSE IP3 .... 55 J4
RCOS CO16 .... 221 M7
Cotswold Av IP IP1 .... 31 K4
Cotswold Cl COLN CO4 ...... 160 E1 2
Cotswold Crs CHLM/WR CM1 . 253 M7
Cotswold Dr SUD CO10 ...... 29 L2
Cotswold Rd COS CO15 ..... 13 G2
Cottage Dr COLS CO2 .... 188 E2
Cottage Gn RCOS CO16 ...... 221 L7 2
Cottage Gv RCOS CO16 ...... 221 L7
Cottage Pl CHLM/WR CM1 .... 15 H2
Cottage Wk RCOS CO16 ...... 221 K7
Cottingham Rd RIPW IP8 ..... 53 K4
Cottonwood Cl COLS CO2 ..... 187 M3
Coulsdon Cl RCOS CO16 ..... 221 L7
Council Rd BSF CM23 .... 171 K6
Counting House La
    GTDUN CM6 .... 175 M4
County Pl CHLM/GWD CM2 .... 15 G5
Coupals Cl HVHL CB9 .... 23 L7
Coupals Rd HVHL CB9 .... 23 L7
Courtauld Cl HSTD CO9 ...... 126 B4
Courtauld Rd BRTR CM7 ..... 180 C1
Courtenay Cl SUD CO10 ...... 4 B1
Courtland Ms MAL CM9 ...... 271 H5 1

Courtland Pl MAL CM9 .... 271 H5
Courtlands CHLM/WR CM1 .... 254 C7
Court Rd CHLM/WR CM1 ..... 254 C2
Court St RCOLW CO6 .... 102 C4
Coval Av CHLM/WR CM1 ..... 14 E2
Coval La CHLM/WR CM1 ..... 14 E3
Coventry Cl COL CO1 .... 10 E5
Covert Cl HVHL CB9 .... 23 J4
The Coverts CHLM/WR CM1 .. 265 K4
K/T/MI CO5 .... 244 F7
Cowdray Av COL CO1 .... 10 C3
Cowdray Crs COL CO1 ...... 10 D6 1
Cowell Av CHLM/WR CM1 .... 254 A8
Cowell St CHTY IP2 .... 54 E2
Cowels Farm La GTDUN CM6 . 120 A8
Cow La RCOS CO16 .... 247 L2
    SAFWN CB10 .... 38 B2
Cowley Rd FX IP11 .... 7 H4
Cowpar Ms BRTR CM7 .... 180 C5 7
Cowper St IPNE IP4 .... 32 D7
Cowslip Cl CHTY IP2 .... 31 G8
Cowslip Ct COLW CO3 ...... 158 E6
Cow Watering La
    CHLM/WR CM1 .... 265 H2
Coxhall La RIPS/CAP IP9 .... 78 F4
Cox La IPNE IP4 .... 3 G6
Cox Ley RBSF CM22 .... 228 C2
Cox Rd RCOLE CO7 .... 190 D5
Cox's HI MGTR CO11 .... 135 J2
Coytes Gdns IP IP1 .... 2 E6
Crabbe St IPNE IP4 .... 32 C7
Crabb's HI RCHLM CM3 ...... 257 H4
Crabb's La BUNT SG8 .... 114 A6
Crabs Cft BRTR CM7 .... 180 E2
Crabtree FOS CO13 .... 195 L5 1
Crabtree Cft CBE/LIN CB1 ... 19 K2
Crabtree La RCOLW CO6 .... 130 E3
Cracknell Cl RCOLE CO7 ..... 189 K3 2
Craig Cl FX IP11 .... 83 K5
Craigfield Av COS CO15 ..... 222 B7
Craig's La BURES CO8 .... 100 A7
Craiston Wy CHLM/GWD CM2 . 267 H8
Cramphorn Wk CHLM/WR CM1 . 14 D2
Cranborne Cha IPNE IP4 .... 32 C4
Cranbrook La SUD CO10 .... 29 H4
Cranes La K/T/MI CO5 ...... 211 H4
Cranford Cl FOS CO13 ...... 196 A4
Cranham Rd GTDUN CM6 .... 146 B3
Cranleigh Cl RCOS CO16 .... 221 K7
Cranmer's La RCOLW CO6 ... 156 A7
Cranmore Cl RBSF CM22 .... 144 E3 1
Cranwell Crs IPSE IP3 ...... 55 L4
Cranwell Gdns BSF CM23 ... 171 L4
Cranwell Gv KESG IP5 ...... 33 L6
Craven Dr COLN CO4 .... 160 E2
Crawford La KESG IP5 ...... 33 L6 2
Crawley End ROY SG8 ...... 59 M1
Crayfields GTDUN CM6 ..... 175 M4
Crayford Cl MAL CM9 ...... 271 G5 2
Creasen Butt Cl MAL CM9 ... 271 J1 1
Credon Cl COS CO15 .... 222 B6
Credon Dr COS CO15 .... 222 B6
Creekhurst Cl RCOLE CO7 ... 219 J7
Creffield Rd COLW CO3 ..... 159 M7
Crepping Hall Dr RIPS/CAP IP9 . 108 B3
Crescent Rd BSF CM23 ..... 171 J7
    CHLM/GWD CM2 .... 267 J6
    FX IP11 .... 7 L2
    IP IP1 .... 2 C4
    MAL CM9 .... 259 H8
    WOTN CO14 .... 196 E5 4
The Crescent COLN CO4 .... 132 E6
    COS CO15 .... 222 D6
    FOS CO13 .... 196 B8
    HLWE CM17 .... 226 E7
    RCHLM CM3 .... 207 G8
    RCOLW CO6 .... 130 F8
    RCOLW CO6 .... 131 K4
    RCOLW CO6 .... 185 J2
    RCOS CO16 .... 194 B3
Cressages Cl GTDUN CM6 ... 178 A7
Cress Cft BRTR CM7 .... 180 F4 1
Cressing Rd BRTR CM7 ..... 180 D3
    WIT CM8 .... 209 M5
Crestlands RCOLE CO7 ..... 190 D6
The Crest SBW CM21 .... 226 F3
Cricketers Cl CHLM/WR CM1 . 254 D3
Cricketfield La BSF CM23 .. 170 F5
Cricket Hill Rd FX IP11 .... 112 F2
Crispin Cl HVHL CB9 .... 22 F6
Crittall Cl WIT CM8 .... 210 A1 1
Crittall Rd WIT CM8 .... 238 D2
Croasdaile Cl STSD CM24 ... 144 A5
Croasdale Cl STSD CM24 ... 144 A5
Crocus Cl CHTY IP2 .... 54 A1
Crocus Flds SAFWN CB10 ... 63 G2
Crocus Wy CHLM/WR CM1 ... 255 G6
Croft Cl BRTR CM7 .... 180 C2
Croft Cl CHLM/WR CM1 ..... 255 G6
Crofters SBW CM21 .... 227 G2
Crofters End SBW CM21 .... 227 G1
Croft La HVHL CB9 .... 23 K7
    KIR/NAC IP10 .... 83 H2
    RCHLM CM3 .... 233 H2
Crofton Rd IPNE IP4 .... 32 D6
Croft Rd COS CO15 .... 12 D4
    K/T/MI CO5 .... 211 K3 1
    SUD CO10 .... 4 C5
Croft St CHTY IP2 .... 54 E2
The Croft BURES CO8 ...... 100 B4
    HSTD CO9 .... 70 C3 3
    RBSF CM22 .... 144 E4
    RCOLW CO6 .... 127 J7
    SUD CO10 .... 28 D1
Croft Wy WIT CM8 .... 238 C2
Cromarty Rd IPNE IP4 ..... 32 C5
Crome Cl COLW CO3 .... 159 J8
Crome Rd COS CO16 .... 221 M7
Cromer Rd IP IP1 .... 31 H5
Crompton Rd CHTY IP2 .... 31 G6
Crompton St CHLM/WR CM1 . 14 C7
Cromwell Cl BSF CM23 ..... 170 D6
Cromwell HI MAL CM9 ..... 271 H2
Cromwell La MAL CM9 ..... 271 H2
Cromwell Pk GTDUN CM6 ... 177 K8
Cromwell Rd COLS CO2 .... 10 D9

SAFWS CB11 .... 63 G6
Cromwell Sq IP IP1 .... 2 E6
Cromwell Wy WIT CM8 ..... 238 A3
Croquet Gdns RCOLE CO7 ... 189 L4
Cross Cl HVHL CB9 .... 23 J4
Crossfield Rd COS CO15 .... 12 F5
Cross Field Wy COLN CO4 ... 103 K8
Crossfield Wy FOS CO13 .... 195 K7
Crossgate Fld FX IP11 ...... 113 G2 3
Cross HI HAR CO12 .... 166 E4
Cross La K/T/MI CO5 .... 245 H6
Crossley Av COS CO15 ..... 249 G6
Crossley Gdns IP IP1 ...... 30 E3
Cross Rd MAL CM9 .... 271 J4
    WIT CM8 .... 238 B1
Cross St FX IP11 .... 113 G1 1
    SAFWN CB10 .... 62 F4 2
    SUD CO10 .... 4 B8
Crosstree Wk COLS CO2 .... 188 C2 1
Cross Wy K/T/MI CO5 ...... 245 G6
Crossways CBE/LIN CB1 .... 19 M3
    CHLM/GWD CM2 .... 266 E6
    COS CO15 .... 249 H5
    RCOLW CO6 .... 127 H4 1
Crotchets Cl RIPS/CAP IP9 .. 77 J4
Crouch Dr WIT CM8 .... 238 A3 1
Crouchman's Farm Rd
    MAL CM9 .... 257 L7
Crouch St COLW CO3 ...... 10 A8
Crowe Hall La RIPS/CAP IP9 . 108 C3
Croutel Rd FX IP11 .... 113 K2
Crowhall La RCOLW CO3 .... 10 A7
Crowhurst Rd COLN CO4 ... 131 M1
Crowland Cl CHTY IP2 ..... 54 C3
Crowland Rd HVHL CB9 .... 23 H5
Crow La RCOS CO16 .... 193 H3
Crown Bays Rd COLN CO4 .. 11 K4
Crown Cl RBSF CM22 ...... 227 L5
Crown Ga COLN CO4 .... 132 F7
Crown La RCOLE CO7 ...... 192 F2
Crown La North RCOLE CO7 . 133 G6
Crown La South RCOLE CO7 . 161 J1
Crown Meadow BRTR CM7 .. 180 F1 1
Crown Rd COS CO15 .... 12 B9
Crown St BRTR CM7 .... 121 K3 1
    FX IP11 .... 113 G2
    HSTD CO9 .... 96 A1
    IP IP1 .... 2 E4
    RCOLE CO7 .... 105 H7
Crown Ter BSF CM23 ...... 171 J6
Crow Pond Rd RCHLM CM3 . 236 E3
Crow St RBSF CM22 .... 117 H8
Crowswell Ct FX IP11 ..... 83 K5 1
Croxton Cl KIR/NAC IP10 .. 83 L2
Crozier Av BSF CM23 ...... 170 E5
Cruce Wy RCOS CO16 ..... 247 H2
Crummock Cl BRTR CM7 ... 179 L7 1
Crunch Cft HVHL CB9 ..... 24 A8
Crusader Wy BRTR CM7 .... 180 F3
Cuckfield Av IPSE IP3 ..... 56 A2
Cuckoo Hl BURES CO8 .... 100 B4
    HSTD CO9 .... 95 K5
Cuckoos La GTDUN CM6 ... 202 B3
Cuckoo Wy BRTR CM7 ..... 179 K7 1
Cullingham Rd IP IP1 ..... 2 A5
Culver St East COL CO1 .... 10 D7
Culver St West COL CO1 ... 10 B7
Cumberland Av MAL CM9 .. 271 G4 1
Cumberland Cl BRTR CM7 .. 180 D1 1
    FX IP11 .... 113 M1
Cumberland Crs
    CHLM/WR CM1 .... 254 C6
Cumberland St IP IP1 ..... 2 C3
Cunnington Rd BRTR CM7 .. 180 E2
Cunobelin Wy COLS CO2 ... 187 M3
Cuppers Cl WIT CM8 ...... 238 A4
Curds Rd RCOLW CO6 ..... 155 J2
Curlew Cl COS CO15 ...... 222 B7
    K/T/MI CO5 .... 211 M3
    MAL CM9 .... 259 L8 2
Curlew Cft COLN CO4 ..... 161 H5
Curlew Rd CHTY IP2 ...... 53 M2
Curling Tye La MAL CM9 ... 270 B2
Currants Farm Rd BRTR CM7 . 152 A8
Curriers' La IP IP1 .... 2 D6
Curteys HLWE CM17 ...... 226 F8
Curtis Cl RCOS CO16 ...... 249 K2
    RIPW IP8 .... 53 L4 1
Curzon Rd SUD CO10 ..... 5 J5
Curzon Wy CHLM/GWD CM2 . 267 J3
Cusak Rd CHLM/GWD CM2 .. 267 H3
Cut-a-thwart La MAL CM9 .. 270 D2
Cutforth Rd SBW CM21 .... 227 G2
Cut Hedge BRTR CM7 ..... 179 L7
Cuthedge La RCOLW CO6 .. 182 D6
Cutlers La RCOLE CO7 ..... 76 F8
Cutler St IP IP1 .... 2 E7
Cutmore Pl CHLM/GWD CM2 . 14 D8
Cuton Hall La CHLM/GWD CM2 . 255 J8
The Cut K/T/MI CO5 .... 212 E8
Cut Throat La WIT CM8 .... 238 C2
Cutting Dr HSTD CO9 ..... 126 A4
Cygnet Ct BSF CM23 ...... 171 H7
    HSTD CO9 .... 96 A4
Cymbeline Way
    (Colchester By-Pass)
    COLW CO3 .... 159 H6
Cypress Cl COS CO15 ..... 222 A6
Cypress Ct GTDUN CM6 ... 175 K4
Cypress Dr CHLM/GWD CM2 . 266 E7
Cypress Gv COLN CO4 .... 161 G6
Cypress Ms K/T/MI CO5 ... 244 D6 1
Cypress Rd WIT CM8 ...... 238 C1
Cyril Child Cl COLN CO4 ... 161 G6 2

D

Daen Ingas RCHLM CM3 .... 268 E6
Daffodil Cl CHTY IP2 .... 54 A2
Daffodil Wy CHLM/WR CM1 .. 255 G6
Dagnets La BRTR CM7 ..... 207 L1
Dahlia Cl CHLM/WR CM1 .... 255 H8 1
    COS CO15 .... 12 A3
Daimler Av COS CO15 ..... 248 F6
Daimler Rd IP IP1 .... 30 E3
Dains Pl FX IP11 .... 83 L8

SAFWS CB11 .... 63 G6
Dairyhouse La MGTR CO11 .. 137 G5
Daisleys La RCHLM CM3 .... 235 J3
Daisy Green Rd COLW CO3 .. 157 M5
Daisyley Rd GTDUN CM6 ... 148 C2
Dale Cl COLW CO3 .... 158 D6
Dale Hall La IP IP1 .... 31 K3
Dale Rd IP IP1 .... 31 J4
The Dales HAR CO12 ...... 140 B4
Dales Vw RIPW IP8 .... 53 G5
Dales View Rd IP IP1 ...... 31 J5
The Dale RCOLE CO7 ...... 189 L5
Daleview Av MGTR CO11 ... 137 L8
Dallwood Wy BRTR CM7 ... 180 D2 2
Dalrymple Cl CHLM/GWD CM2 . 15 M1
Daltes La RCOS CO16 ..... 248 D2
Dalton Gdns BSF CM23 .... 199 G2
Dalton Rd IP IP1 .... 2 C5
Damant's Farm La FOS CO13 . 194 F5
Damases La RCHLM CM3 ... 256 D3
Damask Rd COLW CO3 ..... 158 E6
Dampier Rd RCOLW CO6 ... 183 H2
Danbury V RCHLM CM3 .... 269 J7
Dancing Dicks La WIT CM8 . 237 J3
Dandalan Cl IP IP1 .... 30 F6
Dane Acres BSF CM23 ..... 170 F5
Dane Cl HVHL CB9 .... 24 C3
Dane Common HVHL CB9 .. 24 C3
Dane O'coys Rd BSF CM23 . 170 F5
Dane Pk COS CO15 .... 170 F5
Dane Rd CHLM/WR CM1 ... 14 B4
Danes Ct SUD CO10 ...... 74 D1
Dane St BSF CM23 .... 171 J7
Daniel Cole Rd COLS CO2 .. 188 B1
Daniell Cl RCOS CO16 ..... 221 L7 3
Daniell Dr COLS CO2 ...... 187 K3
Daniel Wy WIT CM8 .... 210 A1
Daphne Cl BRTR CM7 ..... 179 L6
Dapifer Dr BRTR CM7 ..... 180 F2 2
D'arcy Av MAL CM9 .... 271 K4
Darcy Ri RCHLM CM3 ..... 269 G4
D'arcy Rd COLS CO2 ...... 188 E2
    K/T/MI CO5 .... 241 H2
    RCOLE CO7 .... 219 G1 1
D'arcy Wy MAL CM9 .... 262 A1
Darkhouse La K/T/MI CO5 .. 189 J5 1
Darnel Wy COLW CO3 ..... 158 D6
Darnet Rd MAL CM9 .... 263 G4
Darrell Cl CHLM/WR CM1 .. 254 D7
Darsham Cl FX IP11 .... 6 E8
Darsham Cl FX IP11 .... 6 E1
Dart Cl WIT CM8 .... 237 M3
Dartmouth Rd CHLM/WR CM1 . 255 G7
Darwin Cl BRTR CM7 ...... 180 B4 1
    COLS CO2 .... 188 C4
Darwin Rd IPNE IP4 .... 3 M6
Dash End HVHL CB9 .... 24 D3
Dash End La HVHL CB9 .... 24 D3
Dashwood Cl RIPW IP8 .... 53 M4
Daundy Cl CHTY IP2 ...... 30 F8
Davall Cl HAR CO12 .... 139 L4
Davey Cl COL CO1 .... 11 K8
    IPSE IP3 .... 55 H4
Davidson Cl SUD CO10 .... 74 E1
Davy Rd COS CO15 .... 222 E5
Dawes Cl RIPS/CAP IP9 ... 77 H4
Dawes La K/T/MI CO5 ..... 245 G4
Dawlish Rd COS CO15 ..... 249 L5
Dawn Cl MAL CM9 .... 271 K5
Dawnford Cl COLW CO3 ... 158 E6 2
Daws Cl CHLM/WR CM1 ... 265 H4
Dawson Cl SAFWN CB10 .. 63 H3 2
Dawson Drift KESG IP5 ... 33 L6 3
Dawson Dr FX IP11 .... 83 L7
Daw St BRTR CM7 .... 122 A1
    HSTD CO9 .... 44 D8
Days Cl CHLM/WR CM1 ... 254 D5
Days Gn RIPS/CAP IP9 .... 77 H4
Days Rd RIPS/CAP IP9 .... 77 H3
Dazeley's La RCOLE CO7 ... 106 B5
Deacon Cl FX IP11 .... 113 M1 3
Dead La BURES CO8 ...... 101 G3
    MGTR CO11 .... 135 K3
    RCOLE CO7 .... 133 L5
    RCOS CO16 .... 220 B3
    RCOS CO16 .... 221 K4
Deal Cl BRTR CM7 .... 152 A7 1
    COS CO15 .... 249 L5
Deal Wy RCOLE CO7 ..... 219 G4
Deanery Gdns BRTR CM7 .. 152 B6
Deanery HI BRTR CM7 .... 152 A6 2
Deane's Cl FX IP11 .... 113 M1 2
Deanes Ct HAR CO12 .... 140 C3
Deanhill Av COS CO15 .... 13 M2
Dean Rd CBE/LIN CB1 .... 20 D6
Dean Rogers Pl BRTR CM7 . 152 B6 2
Deans Cl HVHL CB9 ...... 23 H4
Dean St RCOLE CO7 ..... 219 G6
Debden Dr SAFWN CB10 .. 89 G3
Debden Rd SAFWS CB11 .. 62 F5
    SAFWS CB11 .... 63 G7
    SAFWS CB11 .... 87 J5
Deben Dr SUD CO10 ...... 5 G4
Deben Cl COLN CO4 ...... 161 G4
    HVHL CB9 .... 24 C3
    IP IP1 .... 31 H4
Deben Valley Dr KESG IP5 . 33 L6
Deben Wk RCOS CO16 .... 221 L7 4
Deben Wy FX IP11 .... 7 H3
De Bohun Ct SAFWN CB10 . 63 G3
Dedham Av RCOS CO16 ... 249 K1
Dedham Meade RCOLE CO7 . 134 B2
Dedham Rd COLN CO4 .... 103 K4
    MGTR CO11 .... 135 G1
    RCOLE CO7 .... 105 H4
Deepdale Rd HAR CO12 ... 8 D7
Deeping Wk RCOS CO16 ... 220 D8
Deerleap Wy BRTR CM7 ... 180 F1
Defoe Crs COLN CO4 ..... 132 A8
Defoe Rd IP IP1 .... 31 J1
Deford Rd WIT CM8 ...... 237 M5
De Greys Cl SUD CO10 ... 50 E8
Delamere Rd CHLM/WR CM1 . 14 B6

COLN CO4 .... 160 F2
Dell La BSF CM23 .... 171 J6
    RBSF CM22 .... 199 J5
Dellows La RBSF CM22 .... 144 C3
The Dell CHLM/GWD CM2 .. 267 H6
    COL CO1 .... 10 E8
    GTDUN CM6 .... 178 A4
Dellwood Av FX IP11 ...... 113 J2
Delvyn's La HSTD CO9 .... 71 L7
De Mandeville Rd RBSF CM22 . 144 E3
De-marci Ct BRTR CM7 .... 180 F2
Dene Ct CHLM/WR CM1 .... 253 M8
Dengie Cl WIT CM8 .... 238 B5
Denham Cl RCOLE CO7 .... 189 L5 2
Denholm Ct WIT CM8 ..... 238 B5 1
Denmark Gdns RIPS/CAP IP9 . 79 M7
Denny Ct BSF CM23 ...... 171 K3
Denton Cl FX IP11 .... 53 M3
Derby Cl IPNE IP4 .... 32 C8
Derby Rd IPSE IP3 .... 55 J1
Dereham Av IPSE IP3 .... 55 H2
Dereham Cl COLS CO2 ... 187 L2
Derwent Gdns COS CO15 . 222 E7
Derwent Rd COLN CO4 ... 132 E8
    IPSE IP3 .... 55 H2
Derwent Wy BRTR CM7 ... 179 L7
De Staunton Cl RCOLE CO7 . 190 D6 1
Devereaux Cl FOS CO13 .. 196 B5
Devereaux Pl COLN CO4 .. 159 L2
De Vere Av MAL CM9 ..... 271 K4
De Vere Cl RCHLM CM3 ... 257 K2
    RCOLE CO7 .... 189 K5
De Vere La RCOLE CO7 ... 189 K5
De Vere Rd COLW CO3 .... 159 H8
    RCOLW CO6 .... 127 H6
De Veres Rd HSTD CO9 ... 125 M4 2
De Vigier Av SAFWN CB10 . 63 J3
Devlin Rd RIPW IP8 ...... 53 K4
Devoils La BSF CM23 ..... 171 H6 2
Devon Rd COLS CO2 ...... 187 K2
    FX IP11 .... 113 H2
Devonshire Gdns BRTR CM7 . 180 D1
Devonshire Rd IPSE IP3 .. 3 L7
Devon Wy COS CO15 ..... 223 G6 1
    HAR CO12 .... 139 M3 1
Dewar La KESG IP5 .... 33 L6
Dewes Green Rd BSF CM23 . 114 B4
Dewlands BRTR CM7 ..... 180 D8
Deynes Rd SAFWS CB11 .. 88 D6
Dial La IP IP1 .... 2 F5
Dial Rd RCOLE CO7 ...... 220 A2
Diamond Cl IP IP1 .... 30 E4
Diana Wy COS CO15 ..... 12 B8
Dickens Cl BRTR CM7 .... 180 C5 3
Dickens Pl CHLM/WR CM1 . 253 M6
Dickens Rd CHTY IP2 .... 31 G7
Dickinson Ter KESG IP5 .. 33 M6 3
Dicky Moors RCHLM CM3 . 234 B6
Didsbury Cl CHTY IP2 .... 53 M3
Digby Rd IPNE IP4 .... 32 E6
Dilbridge Rd East COLN CO4 . 11 J4
Dilbridge Rd West COLN CO4 . 11 H4
Dillwyn St IP IP1 .... 2 B5
Dillwyn St West IP IP1 ... 2 B5
Dilston RCHLM CM3 ...... 269 J7
Dimsdale Crs BSF CM23 .. 171 K8
Dinants Crs RCOLW CO6 .. 185 G2
Dinsdale Cl COLN CO4 ... 11 K5
The Dismals RCHLM CM3 . 236 D3
Distillery La COLS CO2 ... 188 E1
Ditchingham Gv IPNE IP4 . 33 G7
Dixon Av CHLM/WR CM1 .. 266 B1
    RCOS CO16 .... 221 L7
Dixon Cl MGTR CO11 .... 135 K1
Dixon Wy RCOLE CO7 .... 189 J2
Dobbies La RCOLW CO6 .. 185 H2
Dockfield Av HAR CO12 ... 8 A8
Dock La HAR CO12 .... 167 J1
Dock St CHTY IP2 .... 2 F8
Dockwra La RCHLM CM3 .. 269 H6
Doctor's La SUD CO10 ... 45 M3
Doctor Watson's La KESG IP5 . 33 J4
Docwra Rd K/T/MI CO5 ... 211 L3
Doddenhill Cl SAFWN CB10 . 63 G2 6
Dodmans RIPS/CAP IP9 ... 77 J4 1
Dodson V KESG IP5 ...... 33 L6
Dog Cha BRTR CM7 ...... 122 E2 4
Dogden La BSF CM23 .... 143 G3
Doggetts La RCOLW CO6 . 185 H3
Doghouse Rd BRTR CM7 .. 154 A8
Dogs Head St IPNE IP4 ... 2 F6
Dolby Ri CHLM/GWD CM2 . 267 H3
Dolphin Cl CBE/LIN CB1 .. 19 M3 2
Dolphin Wy BSF CM23 ... 171 J5
Dombey Cl CHLM/WR CM1 . 254 B6
Dombey Rd CHTY IP2 .... 31 G8
Domitian Cl COLN CO4 ... 132 D8
Domsey Bank RCOLW CO6 . 185 G2
Domsey Cha K/T/MI CO5 . 184 D5
Domsey La RCHLM CM3 .. 255 G2
Doms La RCHLM CM3 .... 236 C3
Donald Wy CHLM/GWD CM2 . 266 E6
Donard Dr RCOLW CO6 ... 158 F1
Don Ct WIT CM8 .... 237 M3
Donegal Rd IP IP1 .... 30 F3
Donne Dr COS CO15 ..... 249 J5
Donyland Wy K/T/MI CO5 . 189 H6
Dooley Rd HSTD CO9 .... 125 M4
Dorchester End COLS CO2 . 188 D2
Dorchester Rd IP IP1 .... 55 M2
Dorewards Av BRTR CM7 . 152 B6
Dorking Crs COLN CO4 ... 221 L7
Dorothy Sayers Dr WIT CM8 . 210 B8
Dorset Av CHLM/GWD CM2 . 266 F7
Dorset Cl CHLM/GWD CM2 . 267 G2
    COS CO15 .... 223 G2 1
    IPNE IP4 .... 32 B4
Dorset Rd MAL CM9 ...... 271 H4
Dorvis La SAFWN CB10 ... 40 D4
Doubleday Dr MAL CM9 ... 259 H8
Doubleday Gdns BRTR CM7 . 152 D8
Douglas Gv WIT CM8 ..... 237 M3 2
Douglas Rd COS CO15 ... 12 B4
    HAR CO12 .... 8 E7
Douglas Wk CHLM/GWD CM2 . 14 D8
Dove Cl BSF CM23 .... 199 G3
    STSD CM24 .... 144 A6

Dove Crs HAR CO12 .... 139 M3
Dovedale FX IP11 .... 6 F4
Dovedale Gdns COS CO15 .... 222 E7
Dove House Rd HVHL CB9 .... 23 J5 1
Dove La CHLM/GWD CM2 .... 266 C7
 COS CO15 .... 249 M5 1
Dover Cl IPSE IP3 .... 55 K1
Dover Rd IPSE IP3 .... 55 K1
 RCOLE CO7 .... 219 H5
Doves La GTDUN CM6 .... 203 J3
Dove St IPNE IP4 .... 3 J5
Dowches Dr K/T/MI CO5 .... 211 L2
Dowches Gdns K/T/MI CO5 .... 211 L2 1
Dowling Rd BURES CO8 .... 129 H2
Downhall Rd RBSF CM22 .... 228 D7
Downing Cl CHTY IP2 .... 54 B3
Downside Cl CHTY IP2 .... 54 B5
Downs Crs GTDUN CM6 .... 175 J3
 HVHL CB9 .... 23 H5
Downs Rd MAL CM9 .... 271 J3
The Downs FX IP11 .... 112 F2
 GTDUN CM6 .... 175 M4
Downsway CHLM/WR CM1 .... 254 F6
Downton Dr HVHL CB9 .... 23 G5
Dragon's Gn SAFWN CB10 .... 63 M4 1
Drake Av IPSE IP3 .... 55 K3
Drake Gdns BRTR CM7 .... 180 E1 2
Drake Rd SUD CO10 .... 5 H2
Drakes Ap COS CO15 .... 249 J4
Drake Sq North IPSE IP3 .... 55 K3
Drake Sq South IPSE IP3 .... 55 K3
Drakes La RCHLM CM3 .... 235 H6
Drapers Cha BRTR CM7 .... 178 F4
 MAL CM9 .... 271 M1
Drapers La HVHL CB9 .... 42 D3
Drapery Common COLS CO10 .... 28 D1
Drayman's Cl BSF CM23 .... 170 D8
The Drays SAFWN CB10 .... 29 K8
Drayton Cl MAL CM9 .... 271 J4 3
The Dreys SAFWN CB10 .... 63 M5
Driberg Wy BRTR CM7 .... 180 C4
Driffield Cl K/T/MI CO5 .... 211 M1
The Drift IPNE IP4 .... 32 C7
 IPSE IP3 .... 55 L4
 RIPS/CAP IP9 .... 81 L8
 RIPS/CAP IP9 .... 108 E3
 SUD CO10 .... 50 B5
The Driftway IPNE IP4 .... 32 D7
The Drive CHLM/WR CM1 .... 254 C6
 COS CO15 .... 222 D6
 GTDUN CM6 .... 119 H2
 HAR CO12 .... 140 D3
 SBW CM21 .... 227 G3
 WIT CM8 .... 211 G7
Drood Cl CHLM/WR CM1 .... 254 B6
Drover's Ct FX IP11 .... 85 K7
Drovers Wy BSF CM23 .... 198 E1 3
The Druce SAFWN CB11 .... 114 F1
Drum Fld RCOLE CO7 .... 104 F4
Drury La BRTR CM7 .... 180 B2 2
 GTDUN CM6 .... 230 D3
 HSTD CO9 .... 45 J7
Drury Rd COLS CO2 .... 159 L8
Dryden Cl MAL CM9 .... 271 J5 1
Dryden Rd IP IP1 .... 31 J2
Du Cane Pl WIT CM8 .... 238 C3 2
Duchess Cl BSF CM23 .... 170 D6 1
Duckamere RIPW IP8 .... 30 C4
Ducker's La CHLM/WR CM1 .... 232 E6
Duckling La SBW CM21 .... 227 G3 2
Duck St GTDUN CM6 .... 147 H8
 SAFWN CB11 .... 62 A8
Duddery Hl HVHL CB9 .... 23 H6
Duddery Rd HVHL CB9 .... 23 J6
Dudley Cl COLS CO2 .... 188 C1
 RCHLM CM3 .... 256 A4
Dudley Rd COS CO15 .... 12 D5
 K/T/MI CO5 .... 217 G2
 RCOLW CO6 .... 127 H4
Duffield Rd CHLM/GWD CM2 .... 266 F7
Duffries Cl RCHLM CM3 .... 234 A6
Dugard Av COLW CO3 .... 187 G1
Duggers La BRTR CM7 .... 180 C4
Dugmore Av FOS CO13 .... 195 L5
Dukes Cl FX IP11 .... 113 M1
Dukes La CHLM/GWD CM2 .... 267 H1
Dukes Orch RBSF CM22 .... 201 H7
Dukes Ride BSF CM23 .... 170 E6
Dukes Rd BRTR CM7 .... 152 B8 2
Duke St CHLM/WR CM1 .... 14 F2
 IPSE IP3 .... 3 J8
 RCOLE CO7 .... 219 G4
Dulwich Rd COS CO15 .... 222 F8
 COS CO15 .... 250 E1
Dumbarton Rd IPNE IP4 .... 32 D5
Dumney La RCHLM CM3 .... 206 D2
Dumont Av RCOS CO16 .... 247 K3
Duncan Ri HSTD CO9 .... 70 B3 1
Duncan Rd COLS CO2 .... 187 K1
Dunlin Cl MAL CM9 .... 259 L8 3
Dunlin Ct K/T/MI CO5 .... 211 L3
Dunlin Rd CHTY IP2 .... 54 A3
Dunlop Rd CHTY IP2 .... 31 H7
Dunmore Rd
 CHLM/GWD CM2 .... 267 J2 2
Dunmow Rd BRTR CM7 .... 121 G8
 BRTR CM7 .... 178 E4
 BRTR CM7 .... 178 C3
 BSF CM23 .... 171 G6
 GTDUN CM6 .... 119 J4
 GTDUN CM6 .... 203 H5
 RBSF CM22 .... 172 C6
Dunning Cl MGTR CO11 .... 136 E5
Dunnock Wy COLN CO4 .... 161 J6
Dunoon Cl BRTR CM7 .... 180 F1 2
Dunsey Wood Cl HVHL CB9 .... 22 F4
Dunster Dr HVHL CB9 .... 23 G6
Dunthorne Rd COLN CO4 .... 161 G3
Dunthorpe Rd RCOS CO16 .... 221 M7 1
Dupont Cl RCOS CO16 .... 221 M7 1
Durham Dr BRTR CM7 .... 121 J4
 SBW CM21 .... 226 E4
Durham Sq COL CO1 .... 10 F6
Duxford Rd SAFWN CB10 .... 17 H8
 SAFWN CB10 .... 17 J6
Dyers La SUD CO10 .... 75 L2
Dyer's Rd COLW CO3 .... 186 E2
 HSTD CO9 .... 69 G4

MAL CM9 .... 271 J3
Dykes Cha MAL CM9 .... 271 G2
Dyke St IP IP1 .... 2 E3
Dyne's Hall Rd HSTD CO9 .... 96 E5

E

Eagle Av WOTN CO14 .... 196 F4
Eagle La BRTR CM7 .... 152 B8
Eagles Cl FX IP11 .... 7 K1
Eagle St IPNE IP4 .... 3 G6
Earlhams Cl HAR CO12 .... 140 B3
 FX IP11 .... 113 M1
Earls Cl BSF CM23 .... 170 F7
Earls Colne Rd RCOLW CO6 .... 156 B3
Earlsfield Dr CHLM/GWD CM2 .... 267 H2
Earls Hall Dr RCOS CO16 .... 249 G1
Earlsmead WIT CM8 .... 238 B2 2
East Bay COL CO1 .... 11 G7
Eastby Cl SAFWN CB11 .... 63 H5
Eastcliff Av COS CO15 .... 13 M3
East Dock Rd HAR CO12 .... 8 B3
East Dr SBW CM21 .... 227 G4
East End La RCOLE CO7 .... 106 C2
Easterford Rd K/T/MI CO5 .... 211 L3
Easterling Cl HAR CO12 .... 8 D7
Eastern Av HVHL CB9 .... 23 H5
Eastern Cl IPNE IP4 .... 56 B1 1
Eastern Crs CHLM/WR CM1 .... 254 B8
Eastern Rd RCOLE CO7 .... 219 G7
Eastgate St HAR CO12 .... 9 K2
East Gores Rd RCOLW CO6 .... 184 B1
East Hl COL CO1 .... 10 F6
Easthorpe Rd K/T/MI CO5 .... 185 H8
 K/T/MI CO5 .... 213 G1
Eastland Ct FX IP11 .... 83 M8
East La RCOLE CO7 .... 105 J8
East Lawn IPNE IP4 .... 32 E5
East Mersea Rd K/T/MI CO5 .... 244 F3
East Mill Gn RIPS/CAP IP9 .... 78 A7
Easton Rd WIT CM8 .... 238 C2
Easton Wy FOS CO13 .... 196 D7
East Pk SBW CM21 .... 227 G4
East Rd BSF CM23 .... 171 K6
 K/T/MI CO5 .... 244 F6
East Side COLN CO4 .... 132 C1
East Stockwell St COL CO1 .... 10 C6
East St BRTR CM7 .... 180 C2
 COL CO1 .... 11 G6
 HAR CO12 .... 9 J6
 MAL CM9 .... 262 F4
 RCOLE CO7 .... 189 K6
 RCOLW CO6 .... 183 J3
 SAFWN CB10 .... 63 G4
 SUD CO10 .... 4 E5
East Ter WOTN CO14 .... 196 F4
East View Cl SAFWN CB10 .... 65 H6
Eastways WIT CM8 .... 238 C4
Eastwood Dr COLN CO4 .... 160 D2
Eaton Cl FX IP11 .... 83 L8
Eaton Gdns FX IP11 .... 7 H6
Eaton Ms COLS CO2 .... 188 D2
Eaton Wy MAL CM9 .... 239 M6
Ebenezer Cl WIT CM8 .... 210 A8
Ebony Cl COLS CO2 .... 187 M3
Eccles Rd CHTY IP2 .... 53 M3
Eckersley Rd CHLM/WR CM1 .... 15 J2
Eden Cl WIT CM8 .... 238 A2 3
Eden Rd HVHL CB9 .... 23 J6
 IPNE IP4 .... 32 D8 2
Edens Cl BSF CM23 .... 171 K6
Edenside FOS CO13 .... 196 B6
Edgefield Av MGTR CO11 .... 135 K2
Edgeworth Rd CHTY IP2 .... 54 A3 2
Edgware Rd COS CO15 .... 12 C2
Edgworth Rd SUD CO10 .... 4 D8
Edinburgh Cl WIT CM8 .... 238 C5 1
Edinburgh Gdns BRTR CM7 .... 180 D1
Edinburgh Wy HLWE CM17 .... 226 E8 1
Edison Cl COS CO15 .... 223 G7
Edison Gdns COLN CO4 .... 11 J3
Edison Rd COS CO15 .... 223 G7
Edith Cavell Wy HVHL CB9 .... 43 K7
Edith Rd COS CO15 .... 12 F8
 FOS CO13 .... 195 M5
Edmonton Cl KESG IP5 .... 33 J6
Edmonton Rd KESG IP5 .... 33 J5
Edmund Cl HVHL CB9 .... 23 H5 1
Edmund Gn HSTD CO9 .... 125 G5 1
Edmund St WIT CM8 .... 238 A5 3
Edward Av RCOLE CO7 .... 219 H6
Edward Cl IP IP1 .... 31 H5
 RCOS CO16 .... 194 A8
Edward Dr CHLM/GWD CM2 .... 266 E6
Edward Marke Dr K/T/MI CO5 .... 216 D2
Edward Rd RCOS CO16 .... 194 B6 1
Edward St COS CO15 .... 111 G8
Egerton Green Rd COLS CO2 .... 187 J2
Egglestone Cl CHTY IP2 .... 54 B4
Eggshell La HSTD CO9 .... 68 A2 3
Egremont St SUD CO10 .... 28 D2
Egremont Wy COLW CO3 .... 186 E1
Egret Crs COLN CO4 .... 161 J5
Ehringshausen Wy HVHL CB9 .... 23 H6
Eight Acre La COLS CO2 .... 187 L3
Elderberry Gdns WIT CM8 .... 238 D1 2
Elder Fld BRTR CM7 .... 179 K8 1
Eldon Cl COS CO15 .... 161 G4
Eldred Av COLS CO2 .... 187 K2
Eldred Dr SUD CO10 .... 74 E1
Eleanor Cl K/T/MI CO5 .... 212 F7 2
Elgin Av CHLM/WR CM1 .... 14 E3
Elianore Rd COLW CO3 .... 159 K6
Eliot Wy MAL CM9 .... 271 J4
Elizabeth Av WIT CM8 .... 238 C6
Elizabeth Cl COLN CO4 .... 160 E1
 SAFWN CB10 .... 63 H3
Elizabeth Rd BSF CM23 .... 171 G6
 HAR CO12 .... 8 D9
Elizabeth Wy FX IP11 .... 6 F4
 HSTD CO9 .... 126 A3 2

MAL CM9 .... 259 J8
RCHLM CM3 .... 257 J1 2
RCOLE CO7 .... 189 L2
RCOLE CO7 .... 219 H7
SAFWN CB10 .... 63 H3
SUD CO10 .... 49 L8
Ellenborough Cl BSF CM23 .... 170 F8
Ellenbrook Rd CHTY IP2 .... 53 M4
 RIPW IP8 .... 54 A5
Ellen Wy BRTR CM7 .... 179 L6
Elliots Dr WOTN CO14 .... 196 D5
Elliott St IP IP1 .... 2 B5
Ellis Rd COLN CO4 .... 132 B1
 COS CO15 .... 12 F8
 MGTR CO11 .... 136 F5
 MAL CM9 .... 259 K8
Elmbrook Dr BSF CM23 .... 199 G1 1
Elm Bungalows BRTR CM7 .... 179 M1
Elm Cl CHLM/GWD CM2 .... 267 G2
 HSTD CO9 .... 95 M3 2
 HVHL CB9 .... 23 H5
 K/T/MI CO5 .... 212 E6
 MGTR CO11 .... 106 F4
 RBSF CM22 .... 144 E3
 RBSF CM22 .... 173 L6
 RCOLE CO7 .... 190 D5
Elm Close Extension
 .... 173 L6 1
Elm Ct HVHL CB9 .... 24 A8
 SAFWN CB11 .... 60 D1
Elm Crs COLN CO4 .... 11 M6
Elmcroft RCOLE CO7 .... 162 B7
Elmcroft Rd IP IP1 .... 31 J3
Elmdale Dr MGTR CO11 .... 135 M1
Elmden Ct COS CO15 .... 12 F1
Elm Dr HAR CO12 .... 8 F8
 HSTD CO9 .... 126 B4
 RCOLE CO7 .... 218 F6
Elmers La KESG IP5 .... 33 M6
Elmfield Cl COS CO15 .... 223 G6
Elm Gdns FX IP11 .... 83 L8
Elm Green La RCHLM CM3 .... 268 E5
Elm Gv BSF CM23 .... 171 K6
 COS CO15 .... 222 A7
 FOS CO13 .... 195 L7
 RCOLE CO7 .... 189 K4
 RCOLW CO6 .... 102 B4
 SAFWN CB10 .... 62 F4 3
Elm Ri WIT CM8 .... 210 B8
Elm Rd BSF CM23 .... 171 G6
 CHLM/GWD CM2 .... 14 E7
 KESG IP5 .... 33 H6
 RCOLE CO7 .... 105 K2
 RCOS CO16 .... 221 L2
 SUD CO10 .... 5 G7
Elms Cl CBS CB2 .... 16 F4
Elms Dr CHLM/WR CM1 .... 266 C1
Elms Hall Rd RCOLW CO6 .... 156 D5
Elms Rd CHLM/WR CM1 .... 252 A7
Elmstead Rd COLS CO2 .... 11 M9 1
 RCOLE CO7 .... 189 L2
The Elms SAFWN CB10 .... 38 A2
Elm St IP IP1 .... 2 E5
Elm Tree Av FOS CO13 .... 196 B6
Elm Tree Cl FOS CO13 .... 196 B7
Elm Wk RCHLM CM3 .... 179 H3
Elm Wy RCHLM CM3 .... 256 A4
Elmwood SBW CM21 .... 227 H4
Elmwood Av COLS CO2 .... 187 K3
Elmwood Dr K/T/MI CO5 .... 244 D6
Elm Wych COLS CO2 .... 188 C3
Elsham Dr BRTR CM7 .... 179 K7 2
Elsmere Rd IP IP1 .... 31 L5
Elthorne Pk COS CO15 .... 222 A7
Elton Pk CHTY IP2 .... 30 F7
Elwes Cl COLN CO4 .... 11 L2
Elwin Rd K/T/MI CO5 .... 212 F8
Ely Rd IPNE IP4 .... 32 B4
Elysian Gdns MAL CM9 .... 262 E4
Emberson Ct
 CHLM/GWD CM2 .... 267 H1 1
Emblems GTDUN CM6 .... 175 L3
Emerald Cl KESG IP5 .... 33 L5
Emlen St IP IP1 .... 2 B5
Emmanuel Cl CHTY IP2 .... 54 B3
Empire Rd HAR CO12 .... 9 J7
Empress Av K/T/MI CO5 .... 244 F6
Empress Dr K/T/MI CO5 .... 244 F7
Emson's Cl CBE/LIN CB1 .... 19 M3
Endean Ct RCOLE CO7 .... 189 J3
Endeavour Cl MAL CM9 .... 262 F3
Endsleigh Cl COS CO15 .... 159 L6
The Endway GTDUN CM6 .... 147 G6
 HVHL CB9 .... 43 L5
Engleric ROY SG8 .... 59 M1
Enid Wy COLN CO4 .... 159 M3
Ennerdale Av BRTR CM7 .... 179 L7
Enterprise Cl BRTR CM7 .... 180 D3
Enville Wy COLN CO4 .... 160 D1
Epping Cl CHLM/WR CM1 .... 14 B6
 COS CO15 .... 222 B5
Epping Wy WIT CM8 .... 238 A5
Epsom Cl COS CO15 .... 222 B5
Epsom Dr IP IP1 .... 31 K1
Erbury Pl SUD CO10 .... 26 D1
Erick Av CHLM/WR CM1 .... 254 D6
Eridge Cl CHLM/WR CM1 .... 255 G8
Eriswell Rd HVHL CB9 .... 23 K5
Erle Havard Rd RCOLW CO6 .... 159 G1
Ernest Rd RCOLE CO7 .... 189 L4
Ernleigh Rd IPNE IP4 .... 220 F3
Errington Rd COLW CO3 .... 159 M8
Erskine Rd MGTR CO11 .... 135 M1
Erwarton Wk RIPS/CAP IP9 .... 110 E2
Esplanade FOS CO13 .... 196 C8
The Esplanade COS CO15 .... 223 J7
Essex Av CHLM/WR CM1 .... 254 C6
 COS CO15 .... 249 G7
 SUD CO10 .... 4 F1

Essex Hall Rd COL CO1 .... 10 A2
Essex Hl SAFWN CB11 .... 60 C2
Essex Regiment Wy
 RCHLM CM3 .... 234 D3
 MAL CM9 .... 271 H4
Essex Rd BRTR CM7 .... 180 D1 2
 COLN CO4 .... 104 C5
 HAR CO12 .... 140 E3
 IPSE IP3 .... 56 A4
 MGTR CO11 .... 136 B2
 RCOLW CO6 .... 102 F8
 RCOLW CO6 .... 157 G2
 WIT CM8 .... 181 L7
Essex Yeomanry Wy COLW CO3 .... 158 D6
Estella Md CHLM/WR CM1 .... 254 A6
Estuary Cl COLN CO4 .... 160 A1
Estuary Crs COS CO15 .... 12 D6
 RIPS/CAP IP9 .... 111 K5
Estuary Ms MAL CM9 .... 262 F3 1
Estuary Park Rd K/T/MI CO5 .... 245 G6
Estuary Rd RIPS/CAP IP9 .... 111 J5
Eton Rd COS CO15 .... 13 G4
 FOS CO13 .... 196 C8
Eudo Rd COLS CO2 .... 187 L1
Europa Wy HAR CO12 .... 8 B6
 IP IP1 .... 30 E5
Eustace Rd IP IP1 .... 31 G5
Euston Av IPNE IP4 .... 33 H7
Euston St IP IP1 .... 6 D2
Evabrook Cl CHTY IP2 .... 54 A4 1
Evelyn Rd RCHLM CM3 .... 206 F1
Evelyn Wood Rd BRTR CM7 .... 181 G7 2
Everest Wy MAL CM9 .... 259 K8
Evergreen Dr RCOLE CO7 .... 160 F1
Everitt Rd SAFWN CB10 .... 63 H3
Everitt Wy HSTD CO9 .... 96 A3 2
Everton Crs IP IP1 .... 31 H4
Eves Cnr RCHLM CM3 .... 269 G6
Eves Ct HAR CO12 .... 139 M4
Eves Crs CHLM/WR CM1 .... 254 C8
Evesham Cl CHTY IP2 .... 54 C3
Ewan Cl COLS CO2 .... 158 E7
Ewan Wy COLW CO3 .... 158 E7
Ewell Hall Cha K/T/MI CO5 .... 211 L4
Exeter Cl BRTR CM7 .... 152 D8 1
 RCOLW CO6 .... 131 K6
Exeter Dr COL CO1 .... 10 F6
Exeter Rd CHLM/WR CM1 .... 255 G8
 FX IP11 .... 113 H2
 IPSE IP3 .... 55 K1
Exmoor Cl CHLM/WR CM1 .... 265 M4
Exmoor Rd FX IP11 .... 113 H1

F

Fabians Cl RCOLW CO6 .... 183 J2
Factory Cl K/T/MI CO5 .... 241 G2
Factory La MGTR CO11 .... 106 E6
Factory La East HSTD CO9 .... 126 A4
Factory La West HSTD CO9 .... 126 A4
Fagbury Rd FX IP11 .... 112 C3
Fairbairn Av KESG IP5 .... 33 M6
Fair Cl RCOLE CO7 .... 219 J7
Fairclough Av RCOS CO16 .... 249 K2
Fairfax Md CHLM/GWD CM2 .... 267 H3
Fairfax Rd COLS CO2 .... 10 D9
Fairfield Av FX IP11 .... 113 J2
Fairfield Gdns COLN CO4 .... 11 J5 1
Fairfield Rd BRTR CM7 .... 180 B3
 CHLM/WR CM1 .... 14 F2
 COS CO15 .... 12 F5
 IPSE IP3 .... 55 J3
Fairfield Wy CBE/LIN CB1 .... 19 M2
Fairhaven Av K/T/MI CO5 .... 245 G6
Fairhead Rd North COLN CO4 .... 11 J4
Fairhead Rd South COLN CO4 .... 11 J4
Fairleads RCHLM CM3 .... 269 H5 2
Fair Leas SAFWN CB10 .... 63 G7
Fairlop Cl COS CO15 .... 222 B5
Fairstead Hall Rd RCHLM CM3 .... 208 C2
Fairstead Rd RCHLM CM3 .... 208 E7
Fairway BSF CM23 .... 171 L2
 CHLM/GWD CM2 .... 266 F6
 SBW CM21 .... 227 H3
Fairways COLN CO4 .... 159 K2
The Fairways IPNE IP4 .... 33 G8
Fairycroft Rd SAFWN CB10 .... 62 F4
Fairy Hall La BRTR CM7 .... 179 J4
Falcon Cl HVHL CB9 .... 23 L5
 SBW CM21 .... 226 E4
Falcon Crs COL CO1 .... 160 D8
Falconer Rd HVHL CB9 .... 23 L7
Falconers Pk SBW CM21 .... 226 F4
Falconer St BSF CM23 .... 170 E8
Falcon Flds MAL CM9 .... 271 H5
Falcon Ms MAL CM9 .... 271 H5 2
Falcon St FX IP11 .... 113 G2
 IP IP1 .... 2 E6
Falcon Wy CHLM/GWD CM2 .... 266 C2
 COS CO15 .... 222 B7
Falcon Yd RCOLE CO7 .... 189 K5 5
Fal Dr WIT CM8 .... 238 A3 2
Falkenham Rd KIR/NAC IP10 .... 83 L2
Falkland Cl RCHLM CM3 .... 256 A5
Falklands Dr MGTR CO11 .... 135 M1 1
Falklands Rd HVHL CB9 .... 23 J3
Fallowden La HVHL CB9 .... 40 A5
Fallowfield Cl HAR CO12 .... 8 A3
Fallowfield Rd COLS CO2 .... 187 L3
Falmouth Cl KESG IP5 .... 33 K7
Falmouth Rd CHLM/WR CM1 .... 255 G8
Fambridge Cha WIT CM8 .... 209 H3
Fambridge Rd MAL CM9 .... 271 J4
 MAL CM9 .... 271 H3
Fanny's La HSTD CO9 .... 220 F3
Faraday Cl BRTR CM7 .... 180 B4
Faraday Rd IPSE IP3 .... 3 M7
Farmadine SAFWS CB11 .... 63 G4
Farmadine Gv SAFWS CB11 .... 63 G4
Farmers Wy RCOS CO16 .... 249 K2
Farmfield Rd RCOLW CO6 .... 156 D4
Farmleigh Av COS CO15 .... 222 B5
Farm Rd HAR CO12 .... 166 E1

Farm Wk RCOLE CO7 .... 219 G5
Farnham Cl SBW CM21 .... 226 E4
Farriers End COLW CO3 .... 158 F8 1
Farriers Went FX IP11 .... 83 M8
Farrington Cl COL CO1 .... 11 K8
Farthing Cl BRTR CM7 .... 180 F1 3
Farthing Rd IP IP1 .... 30 E6
Farthings Went RIPS/CAP IP9 .... 77 K3 1
Fastnet Cl HVHL CB9 .... 23 M5
Faulkbourne Rd WIT CM8 .... 237 L1
Faulkeners Wy FX IP11 .... 83 L7
Fawkner Cl CHLM/GWD CM2 .... 267 H3
Fawley Cl IPSE IP4 .... 32 E6
Feathers Fld FX IP11 .... 112 F2 4
Feathers Hl RBSF CM22 .... 201 H3
Feedhams Cl RCOLE CO7 .... 189 L2
Feering Hl K/T/MI CO5 .... 211 M2
Felaw St CHTY IP2 .... 3 G8
Felix Cl KESG IP5 .... 33 K6
Felix Rd FX IP11 .... 113 K3
 IPSE IP3 .... 55 L3
Felixstowe Cl RCOS CO16 .... 249 J1 2
Felixstowe Rd IPSE IP3 .... 55 J1
 KIR/NAC IP10 .... 56 C5
Fellbrigg Av KESG IP5 .... 33 H7 1
Fell Christy CHLM/WR CM1 .... 254 D8
Fell Rd HSTD CO9 .... 44 D4
Felstead Cl COLS CO2 .... 188 C5
Fen Br RCOLE CO7 .... 105 K5
Fen La RCOLE CO7 .... 133 M4
Fen Meadow FX IP11 .... 83 L7
Fenn Cl RCOLE CO7 .... 191 J2
Fennel Cl K/T/MI CO5 .... 212 E8
Fennels Cl HVHL CB9 .... 23 J6
Fennes Rd BRTR CM7 .... 152 B4
Fenno Cl COLW CO3 .... 187 G1
Fen St RCOLW CO6 .... 102 D4
Fenton Rd HVHL CB9 .... 23 K5
Fentons Wy KESG IP5 .... 33 L6
Fen Vw RIPW IP8 .... 53 G5
Ferguson Cl SAFWN CB11 .... 63 J3 1
Ferndale Cl COS CO15 .... 222 B6
Ferndale Rd HAR CO12 .... 9 K5
Ferndown Rd FOS CO13 .... 196 A8
 FX IP11 .... 113 L1
Ferndown Wy RCHLM CM3 .... 257 K1
Fern Gv HVHL CB9 .... 23 G5
Fernhayes Cl CHTY IP2 .... 54 C2
Fernlea COLN CO4 .... 159 L3
Fernlea Rd HAR CO12 .... 9 K6
Fern Wy COS CO15 .... 249 H6
Fernwood Av COS CO15 .... 223 H8
Ferry La FX IP11 .... 6 E3
Ferry Rd K/T/MI CO5 .... 189 K7
Festival Gdns MAL CM9 .... 261 M1
Feverills Rd RCOS CO16 .... 221 L1
Fiat Av COS CO15 .... 248 F7
Fiddlers Folly RCOLW CO6 .... 158 A4
Fiddlers Hl COLW CO3 .... 158 A3
Fiddlers La RCOLE CO7 .... 105 L2
Field Cl CBE/LIN CB1 .... 19 K3
Field Dr RCOLE CO7 .... 191 M4
Field Gate La RBSF CM22 .... 144 C3
Fields Cl RCOS CO16 .... 193 M6
Fields Farm Rd COLS CO2 .... 215 K1
Field Vw KIR/NAC IP10 .... 57 J5
Field View Dr MAL CM9 .... 240 B8
Field Wy RCOLE CO7 .... 189 L3
Fife Rd IPNE IP4 .... 32 D4
Fifth Av CHLM/WR CM1 .... 254 D8
 FOS CO13 .... 196 A8
 HSTD CO9 .... 126 D4
Finbars Wk IPNE IP4 .... 3 L6
Finborough Cl KESG IP5 .... 33 H7
Fincham's Cl CBE/LIN CB1 .... 19 M3
Finchdale COS CO15 .... 222 F7 1
Finch Dr RCOLE CO7 .... 191 M4
Finch Hl SUD CO10 .... 49 J6
Finchingfield Rd HSTD CO9 .... 68 D7
 HVHL CB9 .... 43 L7
Finchingfield Wy COLS CO2 .... 188 C5
Finchley Av CHLM/GWD CM2 .... 14 F8
Finchley Rd IPNE IP4 .... 3 J4
Finch's WIT CM8 .... 239 H7
Findley Cl RIPS/CAP IP9 .... 108 B3
Finer Cl RCOS CO16 .... 12 B2
Fingringhoe Rd COLS CO2 .... 188 F3 1
 K/T/MI CO5 .... 216 D2
Finham Cl COLN CO4 .... 161 H6 1
Finney's Drift KIR/NAC IP10 .... 56 B8
Fircroft Rd IP IP1 .... 31 J3
Firebronds Rd RIPS/CAP IP9 .... 79 M8
Firecrest Rd CHLM/GWD CM2 .... 266 B8
Firlands BSF CM23 .... 171 G7
Firlie Wk COLS CO2 .... 188 C3
Firmins Ct RCOLW CO6 .... 158 F5
Firs Cha K/T/MI CO5 .... 244 C7
Firs Dr CHLM/WR CM1 .... 265 K4
Firs Hamlet K/T/MI CO5 .... 244 C7
Firs Rd K/T/MI CO5 .... 240 F1
 K/T/MI CO5 .... 244 D7
First Av CHLM/WR CM1 .... 254 D8
 COS CO15 .... 13 M4
 FOS CO13 .... 224 A1
 HAR CO12 .... 9 H9
 HSTD CO9 .... 126 D4
 RCOS CO16 .... 193 H4 1
 RCOS CO16 .... 248 E7
 SUD CO10 .... 7 L5
 WOTN CO14 .... 196 F4
The Firs CBS CB2 .... 16 F3
Firstore Dr COLW CO3 .... 159 G6
Fir Tree Cl COLN CO4 .... 160 D1
Fir Tree Hl RIPS/CAP IP9 .... 80 A8
Fir Tree La RCHLM CM3 .... 269 G4
Fir Tree Ri CHLM/GWD CM2 .... 266 C7
 RIPW IP8 .... 53 L3
Fir Tree Wk MAL CM9 .... 259 L8 4
Fir Wy COS CO15 .... 249 H6
Firwood's Rd HSTD CO9 .... 126 A5
Fishbane Cl COS CO15 .... 249 H6
Fisher Cl HVHL CB9 .... 23 M6 1
Fisher's La RCOLE CO7 .... 106 E2
Fisher Wy BRTR CM7 .... 180 E1
Fishmarket St GTDUN CM6 .... 119 H3
Fish Pond Hl RIPS/CAP IP9 .... 109 L2
Fishponds Hl RCOLW CO6 .... 102 A8

Fishponds La RIPS/CAP IP9 80 A8
Fish St MAL CM9 261 G7
Fisin Wk COLW CO3 187 G2
Fitches Crs MAL CM9 271 K4
Fitzgerald Cl MGTR CO11 135 K1
Fitzgerald Rd RIPW IP8 30 C4
Fitzgilbert Rd COLS CO2 187 L1
Fitzmaurice Rd IPSE IP3 55 K2 2
Fitzpiers SAFWN CB10 63 G3
Fitzroy St IP IP1 2 F4
Fitzwalter La RCHLM CM3 268 F7
Fitzwalter Pl CHLM/WR CM1 14 A1
Fitzwalter Rd COLW CO3 159 K7
RCHLM CM3 256 B5
Fitzwilliam Cl CHTY IP2 54 B3
Fitzwilliam Rd COLW CO3 159 K6
Five Acres STSD CM24 144 A5
WOTN CO14 196 D5
Fiveash La BRTR CM7 182 A4
Flag Hl RCOS CO16 220 B4
Flagstaff Rd COLS CO2 10 C9
Flail Cl RCOLE CO7 162 B7
Flanders Cl BRTR CM7 152 A8 1
Flanders Fld COLS CO2 188 D2
Flatford Dr RCOS CO16 249 K1
Flatford Rd RCOLE CO7 105 L4
Flavian Cl HVHL CB9 23 M6
Flaxfields CBE/LIN CB1 19 L2
Flax La SUD CO10 28 E1
Fleetwood Av COS CO15 223 G6
FX IP11 113 J2
Fleetwood Cl COS CO15 223 G6 2
Fleetwood Rd FX IP11 113 K2
Fleming Cl BRTR CM7 180 B4 3
Fletcher Rd IPSE IP3 55 J5
Fletchers La KESG IP5 33 M5
Flindell Dr RIPW IP8 30 C3
Flint Cl CHTY IP2 54 D3
Flintwich Mnr CHLM/WR CM1 254 A6
Flitch La GTDUN CM6 176 A6
Flitch Wy BRTR CM7 178 C5
GTDUN CM6 147 G3
RBSF CM22 172 F6
RBSF CM22 174 B6
Flixton Cl RCOS CO16 249 J1 3
Flora Rd WIT CM8 237 M1
Florence Rd WOTN CO14 196 F3
Florie's Rd RCOLW CO6 156 B5
Flowers Wy COS CO15 249 J6
Flowmere Rd ROY SG8 35 J8
Foden Av IP IP1 30 E3
Folkards La RCOLE CO7 219 H5
Folly La RIPW IP8 77 M1
Folly Mill La GTDUN CM6 119 H7
Folly Rd SUD CO10 51 H2
The Folly COLS CO2 187 J7
K/T/MI CO5 241 H3
RCOLE CO7 189 K6
Fonnereau Rd IP IP1 2 E3
Fordham Pl IPNE IP4 33 H8 1
Fordham Rd RCOLW CO6 129 H3
Ford La COLN CO4 131 L8
RCOLE CO7 190 D8
Ford Rd COS CO15 12 D6
Fords La COLN CO4 131 M8
Fordson Rd CHLM/GWD CM2 255 K7
Ford St RCOLW CO6 157 J1
Fordstreet Hl RCOLW CO6 157 L3
Fordwater Cl HSTD CO9 44 D2
Fordwich Rd RCOLE CO7 219 G4
Forebury Av SBW CM21 227 H3
The Forebury SBW CM21 227 H3
Fore Fld BRTR CM7 180 F2 4
Forefield Gn CHLM/WR CM1 255 H6
Fore Hamlet IPSE IP3 3 J7
Foresight Rd COLS CO2 188 F3
Forest Dr CHLM/WR CM1 14 A5
Forest Gld HVHL CB9 23 H3
Foresthall Rd STSD CM24 171 M1
Forest Park Av COS CO15 222 A6
Fore St IPNE IP4 3 H7
IPNE IP4 3 G6
Forest Rd COLN CO4 11 L6
WIT CM8 238 C1 1
Forfar Cl IPNE IP4 32 D4
Forge Cl KIR/NAC IP10 57 J4 2
Forge Crs BRTR CM7 181 L2
Forge St RCOLE CO7 105 H7
Forsyth Dr BRTR CM7 180 C5
Forsythia Cl CHLM/WR CM1 255 G6 1
Forties Cl HVHL CB9 23 M5
Fortinbras Wy CHLM/GWD CM2 15 G9
Fortune Cl RCHLM CM3 207 J6 1
Fossetts La RCOLW CO6 129 M8
Foster Rd HAR CO12 111 G8
MAL CM9 259 J1
Fosters Cl CHLM/WR CM1 265 H4
Foundation St IPNE IP4 3 G7
Foundry La IPSE IP3 2 F7
RCOLW CO6 127 K7
RCOLW CO6 157 M8
Fountain La K/T/MI CO5 185 M5
Fountains Rd CHTY IP2 54 B4
Four Acres SAFWN CB10 37 M2
SAFWS CB11 63 G4
The Four Acres SBW CM21 227 J3
Four Ash Hl HSTD CO9 45 G4
Fourth Av CHLM/WR CM1 254 C8
COS CO15 250 E1
FOS CO13 224 B1
HSTD CO9 126 D4
RCOS CO16 248 D7
Fourways RBSF CM22 144 E4
Fowe's La SUD CO10 47 K6
Fowlmere Rd ROY SG8 35 G1
Foxburrow Cl HVHL CB9 23 H4
Fox Burrows La CHLM/WR CM1 265 K3
Fox Crs CHLM/WR CM1 266 B1
Foxdells La BSF CM23 171 H3
Foxden WIT CM8 210 F7
Foxes La RCOLW CO6 157 M5
SUD CO10 45 M4
Foxes Rd SUD CO10 45 M4
Foxglove Cl BSF CM23 170 E7
COS CO15 222 B6
WIT CM8 237 M2
Foxglove Crs IPSE IP3 56 A4
Foxglove Wy CHLM/WR CM1 255 H7
Foxgrove Gdns FX IP11 113 L2
Foxgrove La FX IP11 113 L2
Foxhall Cl RCOLE CO7 105 L1 1
Foxhall Flds RCOLE CO7 105 L1
Foxhall Rd IPNE IP4 3 L7
IPNE IP4 56 A1
IPSE IP3 32 C8
Foxholes Rd
CHLM/GWD CM2 267 H7 1
Foxley Dr BSF CM23 171 J5
Foxmead WIT CM8 210 F7
Foxtail Rd IPSE IP3 55 M5
Foxwood Cl RCOLE CO7 134 D3
Foxwood Crs IPNE IP4 33 H8
Frambury La SAFWS CB11 87 H5
Framlingham Wy BRTR CM7 179 L6 3
Frampton Rd IPSE IP3 55 J5
Frances Cl RCOLE CO7 189 K3
Frances Ga CHLM/WR CM1 255 J6
Franciscan Wy IP IP1 2 E6
Francis Cl HVHL CB9 23 H5
K/T/MI CO5 240 E1
Francis Ct WIT CM8 181 L8
Francis Ms MAL CM9 271 K5 2
Francis Rd BRTR CM7 179 M3
SUD CO10 4 D7
Francis St RCOLE CO7 219 H8 2
Francis Wy COLN CO4 11 M2
WIT CM8 209 L1
Frank Clater Cl COLN CO4 11 J5
Franklin Rd IPSE IP3 55 K3
Fraser Cl CHLM/GWD CM2 15 K8
Fraser Rd IP IP1 31 H6
RIPW IP8 30 D2
Frating Abbey Farm Rd
RCOLE CO7 191 L7
Frating Hl RCOLE CO7 190 F2
Frating Rd RCOLE CO7 134 B8
Freebournes Rd WIT CM8 238 D4
Freehold Rd IPNE IP4 32 C7
Freeland Rd COS CO15 12 E9
Freelands RCOLE CO7 219 L7
Freewood La SAFWS CB11 60 C2
Fremantle Rd COLS CO2 188 D4 1
Frensham Cl COLW CO3 158 F6 1
Frere Wy K/T/MI CO5 189 K7
Freshfields HAR CO12 140 B4
Freshwater Crs MAL CM9 271 K1
Freshwater Wy COS CO15 222 B5
Freshwell Gdns SAFWN CB10 62 E3 1
Freshwell St SAFWN CB10 62 F3 2
Fresian Cl BRTR CM7 179 L3 2
Freston Hl RIPS/CAP IP9 80 A1
Freston St RIPS/CAP IP9 79 M2
Friar Cl HVHL CB9 23 H4
Friars RIPS/CAP IP9 77 K5
Friars Bridge Rd IP IP1 2 D6
Friars Cl FX IP11 113 M1
HSTD CO9 95 L3
RCOLE CO7 189 L5
RCOS CO16 222 A7
Friars La BRTR CM7 180 B1
MAL CM9 271 H3 1
RBSF CM22 228 D4
Friars St IP IP1 2 E6
SUD CO10 4 C7
Friars Wk CHLM/GWD CM2 15 H5
Friars Wd BSF CM23 171 L5
Friday Wood Gn COLS CO2 188 C5 2
Friedberg Av BSF CM23 170 F8
Friends Fld BURES CO8 100 B4
Friends Wk KESG IP5 33 M5
SAFWS CB11 62 F6
Frietuna Rd FOS CO13 196 A7
Frinton Rd COS CO15 223 H7
FOS CO13 195 L7
RCOS CO16 194 D4
Fritton Cl CHTY IP2 54 C4
Frobisher Dr COS CO15 249 H4
Frobisher Rd HAR CO12 140 B4
IPSE IP3 55 G4
Frobisher Wy BRTR CM7 180 E1
Frogge St SAFWN CB10 37 K3
Frog Hall Cl K/T/MI CO5 189 K7
Frogs Aly RIPS/CAP IP9 82 B8
Fronk's Av HAR CO12 140 E3
Fronk's Rd HAR CO12 140 D3
Front Rd IPSE IP3 55 M5
Frowick La RCOS CO16 220 D3
Fryatt Av HAR CO12 8 C7
Fryth Cl HVHL CB9 23 J4
Fuchsia La IPNE IP4 32 C8
Fulcher Av CHLM/GWD CM2 267 H2
Fulfen Wy SAFWS CB11 62 F6
Fullbridge MAL CM9 271 J2
Fuller Ct BSF CM23 171 J6 1
Fuller's Cl K/T/MI CO5 211 K3
Fullers Rd COLS CO2 188 F3
Fulmar Cl COLN CO4 161 J5 1
Fulton Crs BSF CM23 171 L4
Furneaux La K/T/MI CO5 189 H8
Furness Cl CHTY IP2 54 B5
The Furrells CBE/LIN CB1 19 L3
Furriers Cl BSF CM23 170 E8
Furrow Cl COLW CO3 159 G8 1
Further Meadow
CHLM/WR CM1 265 J5
Further St SUD CO10 75 M1
Furze Crs RCOLE CO7 190 C6
Furze La RCOLE CO7 163 J8
Fynn Valley Wk NHMKT IP6 33 H1

G

Gablefields CHLM/GWD CM2 267 L7
Gaces Acre SAFWS CB11 87 J4
Gadwall Reach K/T/MI CO5 211 M3 1
Gager Dr K/T/MI CO5 213 G8
Gage's Rd SUD CO10 47 G6
Gaiger Cl CHLM/WR CM1 254 F6
Gainsborough Cl K/T/MI CO5 244 F7
RCOS CO16 221 L7
Gainsborough Crs
CHLM/GWD CM2 267 G2
Gainsborough Dr MGTR CO11 135 K1
Gainsborough La IPSE IP3 55 H5
Gainsborough Rd COLW CO3 159 K8
FX IP11 7 M1
HVHL CB9 22 F4
IPNE IP4 3 G1
SUD CO10 4 C5
Gainsborough St SUD CO10 4 C7
Gainsford Av COS CO15 13 M3
Gainsford End Rd HSTD CO9 69 K7
Gall End La STSD CM24 144 B6
Galleons Hill Vicarage Rd
CHLM/WR CM1 252 D8
Galliford Rd MAL CM9 271 J1
Galloway Cl BSF CM23 171 H5
Galloway Dr RCOS CO16 221 L2
Galloway Rd BSF CM23 171 H5
Gallows Green Rd GTDUN CM6 147 M2
Gallows Hl SAFWS CB11 62 E6
Galsworthy Cl BRTR CM7 180 C6 1
Galway Av IP IP1 31 G4
Gandish Rd RCOLE CO7 106 A3
Ganges Rd RIPS/CAP IP9 111 J5
Gangies Hl SBW CM21 226 C2
Gannet Cl HVHL CB9 23 L5
Gannet Rd CHTY IP2 54 A2
Ganwick Cl HVHL CB9 23 H3
Gaol La SUD CO10 4 D6
The Gap COS CO15 223 J7
SAFWS CB11 86 B4
Garden Cl RIPS/CAP IP9 111 G2
Gardeners CHLM/GWD CM2 266 F8
Gardeners Rd HSTD CO9 126 B4
Garden Farm K/T/MI CO5 244 F5
Garden Fld FX IP11 112 F2
RCHLM CM3 257 H1
Garden Flds GTDUN CM6 148 F7
RCOLW CO6 156 E5
Garden Rd COS CO15 249 J6
FOS CO13 196 B6
Garfield Cl FX IP11 7 K3
Garfield Rd FX IP11 7 K3
Garland Rd HAR CO12 8 B5
Garnetts RBSF CM22 173 K5
Garnetts La GTDUN CM6 177 L7
Garnons Cha RCOLW CO6 101 J8
Garrettlands CHLM/GWD CM2 268 B7
Garrick Wy IP IP1 31 J2
Garrison La FX IP11 7 J3
SUD CO10 51 G2
Garrod Ct COLS CO2 188 D6 1
Garrods RIPS/CAP IP9 77 K4
Garthwood Cl RCOLW CO6 159 G1
Gascoigne Rd COLN CO4 11 J4
Gaston End RCOLE CO7 105 L2
Gaston St RCOLE CO7 105 L3
Gatacre Rd IP IP1 2 A3
Gate Farm Rd RIPS/CAP IP9 111 K4
Gatefield Cl FOS CO13 196 B6
Gatekeeper Cl BRTR CM7 180 B4 4
Gate St MAL CM9 271 H2
Gate Street Ms MAL CM9 271 H2
Gatwick Cl BSF CM23 171 K4 1
Gauden Rd BRTR CM7 152 B6 3
Gavin Wy COLN CO4 132 D8
Gay Bowers La RCHLM CM3 269 H7
Gay Bowers Wy WIT CM8 238 C6 1
Gaye St IP IP1 2 C4
Gaymers La FX IP11 83 K7
Gazelle Ct COLN CO4 160 E1 3
Generals Ms FX IP11 112 F2 5
Genesta Cl MAL CM9 262 F3
Geneva Rd IP IP1 2 D4
Gentian Ct COLN CO4 159 L3 3
Geoff Seaden Cl COL CO1 11 K8
George Av RCOLE CO7 219 H6
George Cl COS CO15 12 B7
George Cut RCOLE CO7 219 H7 1
George Frost Cl IPNE IP4 3 G2
George Gent Cl HVHL CB9 43 K7 2
George La SUD CO10 28 D2
George Rd BRTR CM7 179 M3
George St CHLM/GWD CM2 15 G6
COL CO1 10 C6
HAR CO12 9 L4
RIPW IP8 52 B2
Gepps Cl CHLM/WR CM1 231 M3
Geralds Av IPNE IP4 32 C8
Gerard Av BSF CM23 199 G1
Gerard Rd RCOS CO16 221 L7
Gernon Cl CHLM/WR CM1 254 D2 2
Gernon Rd RCOLE CO7 134 A6
Gestingthorpe Rd SUD CO10 48 B8
Gibbons Ct GTDUN CM6 175 M4 1
Gibbons St IP IP1 2 B5
Gibbs Fld BSF CM23 170 F8
Gibson Cl SAFWN CB10 62 F4
Gibson Gdns SAFWN CB10 62 F4
Gibson Rd HSTD CO9 95 M5
Gibson Wy SAFWN CB10 62 F4
Giffins Cl BRTR CM7 180 A4
Gifford Cl RIPS/CAP IP9 79 M7
Giffords Pl IPNE IP4 33 H7
Gilberd Ct COLN CO4 132 E7
Gilberd Rd COLS CO2 188 D1
Gilbert Rd SUD CO10 26 D4
Gilbert Wy BRTR CM7 152 E8
Gilbey Av BSF CM23 171 K7
Gilbey Crs STSD CM24 144 A5
Gilbey Gn SAFWS CB11 87 H4
Gilchrist Wy BRTR CM7 180 A1
Gilderdale Cl COLN CO4 160 F2
Gilders SBW CM21 226 F3
Gilders Wy RCOS CO16 12 B1
Gill Cl MAL CM9 259 H7
Gilmore Wy CHLM/GWD CM2 267 K7
Gilpin Wy BRTR CM7 179 L6
Gilwell Park Cl COLW CO3 187 J1
Gimson Cl WIT CM8 238 A3
Gippeswyk Av CHTY IP2 2 B9
Gippeswyk Rd CHTY IP2 2 C9
Gipping Cl HVHL CB9 23 G7
Gippingstone Rd RIPW IP8 30 C4
Gipping Valley River Pth
RIPW IP8 30 C2
Gipping Wy RIPW IP8 30 C3
RIPW IP8 30 D7
Gipsy La BSF CM23 171 L1
Girling St SUD CO10 4 D5
Girton Rd HVHL CB9 23 K6
Girton Wy CHTY IP2 54 B4
The Glade COLN CO4 161 G3
Gladeview COS CO15 222 B6
Gladiator Wy COLS CO2 187 J3
Gladstone Ct CHLM/GWD CM2 15 H6 1
Gladstone Rd COL CO1 160 C8
IPSE IP3 3 L7
K/T/MI CO5 240 F1
Gladwin Rd COLS CO2 187 L1
Glamorgan Rd CHTY IP2 54 D4
Glanville Pl KESG IP5 33 K7
Glastonbury Cl CHTY IP2 54 B4
Glebe Av BRTR CM7 152 A6
Glebe Cl MGTR CO11 137 L8
RCOLE CO7 162 C7
RIPS/CAP IP9 78 E6
RIPW IP8 30 D7
Glebe Ct BSF CM23 171 K5
Glebe Crs CBS CB2 17 K1
CHLM/WR CM1 254 D4
WIT CM8 238 A1
Glebe End RBSF CM22 144 F4
RIPS/CAP IP9 77 K3
Glebefield Rd RCHLM CM3 257 K1 1
Glebe Gdns K/T/MI CO5 184 A8
Glebelands RCOLW CO6 131 K4
Glebe La GTDUN CM6 147 H8
RIPS/CAP IP9 80 C5
Glebe Meadow RCHLM CM3 234 A6
Glebe Rd CHLM/WR CM1 15 G1
COLS CO2 187 L3
K/T/MI CO5 211 K3
K/T/MI CO5 212 E8
MAL CM9 259 L8
The Glebe HVHL CB9 23 J4
SAFWS CB11 63 G6
Glebe Wy COS CO15 249 J6
FOS CO13 196 B8
Glemham Dr IPNE IP4 56 B1
Glemsford Cl FX IP11 6 E4
Glen Av COLW CO3 159 K6
Glenavon Rd IPNE IP4 32 F6
Glencoe Rd IPNE IP4 32 E4
Glendale Gv COLN CO4 160 E2
Gleneagles Cl FX IP11 113 L1 1
Gleneagles Dr IPNE IP4 32 F8
Gleneagles Wy RCHLM CM3 257 K1
Glenfield Av FX IP11 113 J1
Glenhurst Av IPNE IP4 32 D5
Glenside SUD CO10 5 H9
Glentress Cl COLN CO4 160 F2 1
Glisson Sq COLS CO2 187 K1
Globe Cl K/T/MI CO5 212 F7 3
Globe Crs BSF CM23 142 F7
Gloucester Av CHLM/GWD CM2 266 D7
COLS CO2 187 K2 1
MAL CM9 271 H5
Gloucester Crs CHLM/WR CM1 254 C8
Gloucester Gdns BRTR CM7 180 D2
Gloucester Rd HVHL CB9 23 G6
IPSE IP3 55 J3
Gloucester Wy SUD CO10 4 A1
Goat Lodge Rd MAL CM9 239 J8
Godbold Cl KESG IP5 33 M6 4
Goddard Rd IP IP1 30 E2
Goddard Rd East IP IP1 30 F2
Goddard Wy CHLM/GWD CM2 267 H3
SAFWN CB10 63 G2
Godfrey Wy GTDUN CM6 175 M3
Godlings Wy BRTR CM7 180 A3
Godmans La RCOLW CO6 185 G2
Godric Rd WIT CM8 238 A5
Godwin Cl HSTD CO9 125 M4
Goff's La RCOS CO16 166 B5
Goings La K/T/MI CO5 244 F7 2
Gold Cl RBSF CM22 144 D2
Goldcrest Cl COLN CO4 161 H5
Goldcrest Rd CHTY IP2 53 M2 1
Goldenacres CHLM/WR CM1 255 H5 1
Golden Dawn Wy COLN CO4 160 A3 1
Golden La RCOS CO16 194 B2
SAFWN CB10 65 H3
Golden Lion La HAR CO12 9 L3 3
Golden Noble Hl COLS CO2 10 E9
Goldfinch Cl COLN CO4 161 H6
Goldhanger Rd MAL CM9 271 L1
Goldingham Dr BRTR CM7 180 C5
Goldings BSF CM23 171 K5
Goldings Cl HVHL CB9 23 J3
Golding Thoroughfare
CHLM/GWD CM2 267 H2 1
Golding Wy RCOS CO16 220 C8
SUD CO10 28 D1
Goldlay Av CHLM/GWD CM2 15 J7
Goldlay Gdns CHLM/GWD CM2 15 J6
Goldlay Rd CHLM/GWD CM2 15 J6
Goldsmith Rd IP IP1 31 G1
Gold St SAFWN CB10 62 F4
Golf Green Rd COS CO15 249 J5
Golf Rd FX IP11 113 M2
Goodchild Wy HSTD CO9 70 C3 4
Goodey Cl COL CO1 160 C8
Goodlake Cl HAR CO12 140 A3
Goodliffe Pk BSF CM23 171 K3
Goodmans La RCHLM CM3 207 G8
Goodwins Cl SAFWS CB11 62 A2 1
Goodwin Stile BSF CM23 170 F8
Goodwood Cl IP IP1 31 K1
Goojerat Rd COLS CO2 159 M8
Goose La RBSF CM22 199 M6
Gordon Dr COLN CO4 132 D8
Gordon Rd CHLM/GWD CM2 266 C7
HAR CO12 140 D3
IPNE IP4 32 C6
Gordon Wy HAR CO12 140 D3
Gorefield Rd RBSF CM22 173 K1
Gore La BRTR CM7 179 H3
Gore Rd BRTR CM7 179 J3
Goring Rd COLN CO4 11 J3
IPNE IP4 32 D7
Gorsehayes CHTY IP2 54 D2
Gorse La COS CO15 222 C5
K/T/MI CO5 240 F1
Gorse Rd IPSE IP3 55 K3
Gorse Wy COLW CO3 186 F1
COS CO15 249 H6
Gosbecks Rd COLS CO2 187 J2
Gosbecks Vw COLS CO2 187 J3
Gosfield Rd BRTR CM7 152 F2
COLS CO2 188 C5
Gosford Cl SUD CO10 26 D5
Gosford Wy FX IP11 113 L1
Goshawk Dr
CHLM/GWD CM2 266 D8 1
The Goslings WIT CM8 181 L8 1
Gouldings Av WOTN CO14 196 D5
Goulds Rd BURES CO8 99 G4
Goulton Rd CHLM/WR CM1 254 C4
Gowers Av CHLM/GWD CM2 267 G7
Gower St CHTY IP2 2 F8
Goyfield Av FX IP11 7 J2
Grace Gdns BSF CM23 199 H1
Graces Cl WIT CM8 238 C6
Graces La RCHLM CM3 268 D4
Graces Wk FOS CO13 196 C7
RCHLM CM3 268 B3
Grafton Pl CHLM/GWD CM2 267 J1
Grafton Rd HAR CO12 9 K6
Grafton Wy IP IP1 2 E7
Graham Av IP IP1 2 C1
Graham Rd FX IP11 113 H2
IP IP1 2 C2
Grailands BSF CM23 170 F5
Grammar School Pl SUD CO10 4 C7 1
Grampian Gv CHLM/WR CM1 253 M7
The Granary SUD CO10 26 D7
Grange Cl FOS CO13 196 C6
FX IP11 113 G2
HSTD CO9 126 A6
Grange Farm Av FX IP11 6 E1
Grange Hl RCOLW CO6 183 H4
Grange La GTDUN CM6 176 D6
Grange Pk BSF CM23 171 H4
Granger Av MAL CM9 271 H4
Grange Rd BSF CM23 171 J6
FX IP11 6 F3
HAR CO12 140 C3
IPNE IP4 3 K6
K/T/MI CO5 212 C8
MGTR CO11 135 G6
RCHLM CM3 233 G3
RCOLW CO6 131 K6
ROY SG8 35 M1
SAFWN CB10 36 C5
WIT CM8 258 F1
Grangeside BSF CM23 171 H3
Grange Wk BSF CM23 171 J6
Grange Wy COLS CO2 188 F1
Granta Cl SAFWN CB10 37 M4
Granta Leys CBE/LIN CB1 19 K2
Granta V CBE/LIN CB1 19 M3
Grantchester Pl KESG IP5 33 J5 1
Grantham Crs CHTY IP2 2 B9
Grantham Rd RCOLW CO6 131 K7
Grantley Cl RCOLW CO6 157 M8
Granville Cl RCOLW CO6 159 G2
Granville Rd COL CO1 160 D8
COS CO15 13 H6
FX IP11 7 K4
Granville St IP IP1 2 C4
Granville Wy RCOLE CO7 219 J6
Grasby Cl RCOLE CO7 189 K3 3
Grasmere Av FX IP11 113 M1 4
Grasmere Cl BRTR CM7 179 L7 2
IPSE IP3 55 K4 1
Grasmere Gdns FOS CO13 196 B6 2
Grassfields FOS CO13 196 A7 4
Grassmere COLN CO4 160 D1 1
Gravel Hl RCOLW CO6 102 C3
Gravel Hill Wy HAR CO12 140 B4
Gravelly La CHLM/WR CM1 264 D2
Gravel Pit La MGTR CO11 107 G3
Gravelpit La MGTR CO11 107 G2
The Gravel RCOLW CO6 183 H3
Grayling Cl BRTR CM7 180 A4
Grayling Dr COLN CO4 161 H4
Gray Rd COLW CO3 159 M7
Grays Cl K/T/MI CO5 244 E7
Grays Ct BSF CM23 171 G5
Gray's La BRTR CM7 123 G1
Grays Md HSTD CO9 95 M3 3
Gray's Orch KIR/NAC IP10 83 L2
Great Bentley Rd RCOLE CO7 191 J5
Great Canfield Rd RBSF CM22 173 M6
Great Cob CHLM/WR CM1 255 G8
Great Colman St IPNE IP4 2 F5
Great Eastern Cl BSF CM23 171 J7 1
Great Eastern Rd SUD CO10 4 E7
Great Fld FX IP11 83 L7
Great Gipping St IP IP1 2 D6
Great Godfreys CHLM/WR CM1 265 H4
Great Hadham Rd BSF CM23 170 E8
Great Harlings RIPS/CAP IP9 111 J4
Great Harrods FOS CO13 196 C6
Great Holland Common Rd
COS CO15 222 F3
Great House Farm Rd
COLS CO2 187 J8
Great Notley Av BRTR CM7 179 L8 1
BRTR CM7 179 K8 2
Great Oak Ct HSTD CO9 70 C4
Great Sq BRTR CM7 180 B2 3
Great Tey Rd RCOLW CO6 156 E8
Great Totham Rd WIT CM8 239 H8
Great Tufts RIPS/CAP IP9 77 K4
Great Whip St CHTY IP2 2 F8
Great Yeldham Rd HSTD CO9 69 K7
Grebe Cl CHTY IP2 54 A3
Green Acre SUD CO10 51 G2
Greenacres CBS CB2 16 F4
COLN CO4 160 A2 1
COS CO15 13 K2
RCOLW CO6 183 H4
Green Acres Rd COLS CO2 187 H8
Greenbury Cl ROY SG8 58 B4 1
Green Cl CHLM/WR CM1 266 F1
RCHLM CM3 257 L2
Green Crs KIR/NAC IP10 57 J5
Green End La FOS CO13 195 J8
Greene Vw BRTR CM7 180 D5
Green Farm Rd RCOLW CO6 127 K3
Greenfield WIT CM8 238 C4
Greenfield Dr RCOLW CO6 156 D4
Greenfields HSTD CO9 125 G6
STSD CM24 144 A6
Greenfields Wy HVHL CB9 23 G7

Greenfinch Av CHTY IP2 53 M2
Greenfinch End COLN CO4 161 H5
Greenford Rd COS CO15 12 B6
Greenhill Pk BSF CM23 170 F8
Greenhurst Rd RCOLE CO7 219 J7
Green La CBE/LIN CB1 19 L3
CHLM/WR CM1 264 D1
COLN CO4 161 G2
GTDUN CM6 175 L4
K/T/MI CO5 212 F7
K/T/MI CO5 241 G4
MAL CM9 260 E1
NHMKT IP6 32 E1
RCOLE CO7 104 E2
RCOLE CO7 133 M7
RCOLE CO7 161 L4
RCOLW CO6 102 F8
RCOLW CO6 131 L7
RCOLW CO6 157 K5
RCOS CO16 193 J8
RIPS/CAP IP9 78 E6
SUD CO10 25 J1
WIT CM8 208 C3
WOTN CO14 196 F3
Green Man La WIT CM8 239 H7
Greensmill MGTR CO11 106 D8 2
Greenspire Gv RIPW IP8 53 K3 1
Greenstead SBW CM21 227 G4
Greenstead Rd COL CO1 11 J6
COLS CO2 11 L8
The Greens IPNE IP4 56 B1
Green St CBS CB2 16 F4
GTDUN CM6 202 A2
The Green BSF CM23 199 H2 1
CHLM/WR CM1 265 K4
CHLM/WR CM1 266 B1
COS CO15 249 K3
MGTR CO11 136 B1
Greenview Pk COS CO15 222 C6
Greenway BSF CM23 171 L7
FOS CO13 196 B8
Green Wy RCOLW CO6 127 J3
Greenway Gdns BRTR CM7 179 M6
Greenways CHLM/WR CM1 254 D7
HSTD CO9 125 G6 1
K/T/MI CO5 211 M2
MAL CM9 271 H3 2
SAFWS CB11 63 G6
Greenways Cl IP IP1 2 D1
The Greenways RCOLW CO6 183 J2
The Greenway COS CO15 222 D6
Greenwich Cl IPSE IP3 55 G3
Greenwich Rd IPSE IP3 54 F3
Greenwood Cl HVHL CB9 23 G6 2
Greenwood Gv COLN CO4 160 E2
Gregory St SUD CO10 4 C6
Grendel Wy COS CO15 223 H7
Grenfell Av COS CO15 223 G6
Grenfell Cl COLN CO4 11 J3
Grenville Rd BRTR CM7 180 A2
SUD CO10 4 F1
Gresley Cl COLN CO4 10 D1
Greville Cl WOTN CO14 197 G3
Grey Friars Rd IP IP1 2 E7
Greyhound Hl COLN CO4 133 G1
Greyhound Rd SUD CO10 28 D2
Greys Cl SUD CO10 27 L4
Greys Hollow SAFWS CB11 115 M5
Greystones Cl COLW CO3 187 J2
Grieves Ct COLW CO3 186 E1
Grimston La FX IP11 83 H6
Grimston Rd COLS CO2 188 C1
Grimston Wy WOTN CO14 196 D6
Grimwade Cl MGTR CO11 106 F6
Grimwade St IPNE IP4 3 H7
The Grindle RIPW IP8 30 B6
Grinstead La RBSF CM22 199 L7
The Grip CBE/LIN CB1 19 K4
Groom Pk COS CO15 12 E3
Groomside BRTR CM7 180 C3 1
Grooms La WIT CM8 210 A1
Grosvenor Cl BSF CM23 198 F2
CHLM/GWD CM2 15 L9
IPNE IP4 32 A5 1
K/T/MI CO5 212 F8
Grosvenor Rd SUD CO10 49 M3
Grove Av K/T/MI CO5 244 E8
WOTN CO14 196 D5
Grove Farm Rd WIT CM8 240 B4
Grove Fld BRTR CM7 152 E3
The Grove, Henley Rd IP IP1 31 L3
Grove Hl COLN CO4 133 H1
RCOLE CO7 133 M1
RIPW IP8 53 L6
STSD CM24 144 A6
Grove La IPNE IP4 3 K6
RIPS/CAP IP9 80 F8
Grove Orch BRTR CM7 152 E4
Grove Rd CHLM/GWD CM2 15 H6
FX IP11 113 J1
K/T/MI CO5 212 F8
MGTR CO11 106 F5
RCOS CO16 193 M8
RIPS/CAP IP9 78 A7
The Grove CBE/LIN CB1 19 K2
CHLM/GWD CM2 267 K8
COS CO15 13 G7
RBSF CM22 200 B1
STDN SG11 170 A6
WIT CM8 238 C3
Gryme's Dyke Wy COLW CO3 186 F2
Guelph's La GTDUN CM6 119 J2
Guernsey Wy BRTR CM7 179 M3
Guildford Rd COL CO1 10 F5
Guildhall Wy SAFWN CB10 40 C6
The Guilfords HLWE CM17 226 F8
Guinea Cl BRTR CM7 180 F1 4
Guithavon Ri WIT CM8 238 B3 2
Guithavon Rd WIT CM8 238 B4
Guithavon St WIT CM8 238 B3
Guithavon Va WIT CM8 238 B3
Gulls Cft BRTR CM7 180 E2
Gull's La RCOLE CO7 134 C2
Gulpher Rd FX IP11 113 G1
Gunfleet Cl K/T/MI CO5 244 D6
Gun Hl COLN CO4 104 D6
Gurdon Rd COLS CO2 188 B2
Gurlings Cl HVHL CB9 23 J3
Gurney Benham Cl COLS CO2 187 K1 1
Gurton Rd RCOLW CO6 183 J2
Guston Gdns KIR/NAC IP10 83 L2
Gutteridge Hall La RCOS CO16 193 G6
Gutters La CHLM/WR CM1 254 D6
Guy Cook Cl SUD CO10 50 E8
Gwendoline Rd IPNE IP4 56 A1
Gwyn Cl RCHLM CM3 256 A4 3
Gwynne Rd HAR CO12 9 K6
Gymnasium St IP IP1 2 C4
Gypsy La K/T/MI CO5 184 D6

H

Haddon Pk COL CO1 11 K8
Hadham Ct BSF CM23 170 F5
Hadham Gv BSF CM23 170 E5
Hadham Rd BSF CM23 170 F5
Hadleigh Rd FOS CO13 196 C8
RCOLE CO7 105 K2
RCOS CO16 221 K8
RIPW IP8 53 L1
Hadley Cl BRTR CM7 152 D4
Hadrian Cl COLN CO4 132 D7
HVHL CB9 23 M6 2
Hadrians Cl WIT CM8 238 A5 4
Hadrians Wy MAL CM9 259 J8
Hadstock Rd CBE/LIN CB1 19 K4
Haggars La RCOLE CO7 191 H2
Haglemere Dr IPNE IP4 3 K3
Haig Ct CHLM/GWD CM2 14 E6
Hailes Wd RBSF CM22 144 F3
Hainault Gv CHLM/WR CM1 14 A5
Hale Cl CHTY IP2 53 M3
Halesowen Cl CHTY IP2 54 B5 1
Half Acres BSF CM23 171 H5
Halfacres WIT CM8 238 C6
Halford Ct RIPW IP8 53 L3
Halifax Rd CHTY IP2 54 D3
Hall Bridge Ri MAL CM9 271 L1
Hall Cha GTDUN CM6 204 F5
RCOLW CO6 185 K2
Hall Cl CHLM/GWD CM2 267 J7
COS CO15 223 H7 2
Hallcroft Cha COLN CO4 160 E1 4
Hall Cut RCOLE CO7 219 H7 2
Hall Dr HSTD CO9 124 F5
Hall Farm Cl K/T/MI CO5 212 A1
Hall Fld FX IP11 112 F2
Hallingbury Cl RBSF CM22 199 K4
Hallingbury Rd BSF CM23 171 K8
BSF CM23 199 K1
SBW CM21 227 J1
Halliwell Rd IPNE IP4 32 D7
Hall La CHLM/GWD CM2 267 L7
CHLM/WR CM1 266 D1 1
HAR CO12 140 C3
HSTD CO9 45 K7
RCOS CO16 194 C5
ROY SG8 59 H3
WOTN CO14 196 F4
Hall Pond Wy FX IP11 112 F2
Hall Ri SUD CO10 49 L8
Hall Rd BRTR CM7 151 H6
BURES CO8 100 A8
HVHL CB9 24 D2
K/T/MI CO5 240 E2
KIR/NAC IP10 57 G1
MAL CM9 259 K2
MAL CM9 262 F4
MAL CM9 271 K1
RBSF CM22 144 F4
RCOLE CO7 162 E3
RCOLW CO6 129 M8
RCOLW CO6 130 F8
RCOLW CO6 186 A1
SUD CO10 48 C7
SUD CO10 49 J3
Hall St CHLM/GWD CM2 15 H5
SUD CO10 29 L6
Hall View Rd RCOLE CO7 192 A6
Hall Wk RIPW IP8 30 B3
Halstead Rd BRTR CM7 153 G2
COLW CO3 158 D6
FOS CO13 195 L5
HSTD CO9 96 C7
HSTD CO9 125 G6
RCOLW CO6 127 H6
RCOLW CO6 157 J1
Halston Pl MAL CM9 271 H5
Halton Crs IPSE IP3 55 L4 1
Hamble Cl WIT CM8 238 A3 3
Hamel Wy SAFWS CB11 116 F1
Hamford Cl WOTN CO14 196 F3 1
Hamford Dr HAR CO12 166 E2
Hamilton Gdns FX IP11 7 M3
Hamilton Ms SAFWS CB11 63 H3 3
Hamilton Rd COLW CO3 159 M8
FOS CO13 195 J8
FX IP11 7 M2
FX IP11 113 J2
IPSE IP3 55 K2
RBSF CM22 174 B5
RCOLE CO7 189 K5
SUD CO10 4 D7
Hamilton St FX IP11 113 G2 4
HAR CO12 8 B4
Hamlet Ct BURES CO8 100 A5 1
Hamlet Dr COLN CO4 161 H6
Hamlet Rd CHLM/GWD CM2 15 G6
HVHL CB9 23 J6
Hammonds Rd
CHLM/GWD CM2 267 M4
RBSF CM22 201 J7
Hampit Rd SAFWS CB11 85 M3
Hampstead Av COS CO15 12 C2
Hampton Gdns SBW CM21 226 D6
Hampton Rd CHLM/GWD CM2 267 G7
IP IP1 31 H6
Hamsters Cl HSTD CO9 98 B5 1
Hanaper Dr ROY SG8 58 B4
Hanbury Gdns COLN CO4 132 D8
Hanbury Rd CHLM/WR CM1 14 A8
Hance La BRTR CM7 179 H3
Hanchetts Orch GTDUN CM6 119 J2 2
Handford Cut IP IP1 2 B5
Handford Rd IP IP1 2 B5
Hand La SBW CM21 226 E4
Hankin Av HAR CO12 139 L4
Hanlee Brook CHLM/GWD CM2 267 H8
Hanningfield Wy COLN CO4 132 D8 1
Hanover Br K/T/MI CO5 184 B8
Hanwell Cl RCOS CO16 12 C1
Ha'penny Fld RIPS/CAP IP9 79 M8
Harborough Hall Rd
K/T/MI CO5 212 F3
Harbour Crs HAR CO12 9 L4
HAR CO12 9 M5
HAR CO12 9 L4
Harcamlow Wy GTDUN CM6 119 G1
GTDUN CM6 146 E6
GTDUN CM6 146 C8
RBSF CM22 115 L5
RBSF CM22 145 G2
RBSF CM22 172 E8
ROY SG8 59 K1
SAFWN CB10 39 J8
SAFWS CB11 87 L2
Harcourt Av HAR CO12 8 C7
Hardings Cl RCOLW CO6 157 K5
Hardwick Cl IPNE IP4 33 G8
Hardwick Rd HVHL CB9 23 K5
Hardy Cl BRTR CM7 180 C5 9
MGTR CO11 106 E6
Hardy Crs IP IP1 31 H1
Harebell Cl COLN CO4 160 D2 2
Harebell Dr WIT CM8 238 A2
Harebell Rd CHTY IP2 54 B1
Harefield SUD CO10 29 M3
Harefield Ri CBE/LIN CB1 20 A3
Harewood Rd CHLM/WR CM1 14 A6
Harfred Av MAL CM9 272 A2
Hargrave Cl STSD CM24 144 A5
Harkilees Wy BRTR CM7 152 B8
Harkstead La RIPS/CAP IP9 80 C4
Harkstead Rd RIPS/CAP IP9 109 H1
Harlings Gv CHLM/WR CM1 15 H2
Harlow Rd HLWE CM17 227 K6
SBW CM21 226 E5
Harness Cl CHLM/WR CM1 255 G6
Harnham Dr BRTR CM7 179 L6 4
Harold Cl HSTD CO9 126 B4
Harold Gv FOS CO13 224 B1
Harold Rd BRTR CM7 180 A2
COS CO15 13 H6
FOS CO13 224 B1
Harold Wy FOS CO13 224 B1
Harpclose Rd SUD CO10 4 E4
Harper's Hl RCOLW CO6 102 A3
Harper's Hill Est RCOLW CO6 102 B4
Harpur's Rd SUD CO10 28 D1
Harrington Cl K/T/MI CO5 212 D8
Harrison Ct CHLM/WR CM1 14 C1
Harrison Dr BRTR CM7 180 C4 2
Harrison Gv KESG IP5 33 L5
Harrison Rd COLS CO2 188 B2
Harrisons BSF CM23 171 M3
Harrow Cl IPNE IP4 32 C8
Harrow Hl HSTD CO9 69 H7
Harrow Rd COS CO15 13 G4
HVHL CB9 23 G6
Harrow Wy CHLM/GWD CM2 267 J7
Harsnett Rd COL CO1 160 D8
Hart Cl HVHL CB9 23 H3
Hartest Wy SUD CO10 5 K9
Hartley Cl CHLM/GWD CM2 267 J1
Hartley St CHTY IP2 54 E2
Hart Rd HLWE CM17 226 E8
Hart's La RCOLE CO7 133 H4
Hart St CHLM/GWD CM2 14 E5
Harvard Ct COLN CO4 160 D1
Harvest Ct K/T/MI CO5 212 A1 1
Harvest End COLW CO3 158 F8
Harvesters' Wy RCOLW CO6 259 H5
Harvest Wy MAL CM9 259 H8
RCOLE CO7 162 B7
Harvey Cl MGTR CO11 135 L1 1
Harvey Crs COLW CO3 158 E8
Harvey Rd COLS CO2 187 K3
MAL CM9 259 J1
RCOLE CO7 189 K4
Harvey St HSTD CO9 126 B3
Harvey Wy SAFWN CB10 63 H3
SAFWN CB10 66 B4
Harwich Rd COLN CO4 11 K4
HAR CO12 139 K6
MGTR CO11 136 C1
RCOLE CO7 134 A5 1
RCOLE CO7 163 H7
RCOLE CO7 191 L2
RCOS CO16 221 L1
Harwood Cl COLS CO2 188 C1 1
Haselfoot Rd RCHLM CM3 256 B5
Haselmere Gdns FOS CO13 196 B6 3
Haskell Ms BRTR CM7 180 C5 10
Haslemere BSF CM23 199 J1
Hasler Rd MAL CM9 262 F3
Haslers La GTDUN CM6 175 M5
Hastings Av COS CO15 249 M5
Hastings Pl RCOLE CO7 219 H5 1
Hastings Rd COLW CO3 187 J1
Hatchcroft Gdns RCOLE CO7 162 C7
Hatchfields RCHLM CM3 234 B6
Hatch Gn RBSF CM22 199 K5
Hatfield Gv CHLM/WR CM1 265 M4
Hatfield Rd IPSE IP3 55 J1
MAL CM9 258 D6
RCHLM CM3 236 E2
WIT CM8 237 M7
Haubourdin Ct HSTD CO9 126 C3 2
Haughley Dr IPNE IP4 33 H7 2
Haven Av COS CO15 223 H7
Haven Cl FX IP11 6 F2
Havengore CHLM/WR CM1 255 G8
Haven Rd COLS CO2 188 F1
The Havens KIR/NAC IP10 56 A6
The Haven HAR CO12 8 B8
Haverhill Rd CBE/LIN CB1 21 J2
HVHL CB9 23 K3
HVHL CB9 24 C3
HVHL CB9 42 E5
HVHL CB9 43 K4
Havering Cl COLN CO4 11 G3
COS CO15 222 A6
Havers La BSF CM23 171 H8
Havisham Wy CHLM/WR CM1 253 M6
Hawbridge RIPS/CAP IP9 77 J3
Hawes St CHTY IP2 54 F2
Hawfinch Rd COLS CO2 187 J8
Hawkendon Rd RCOS CO16 249 J1
Hawke Rd IPSE IP3 55 G4
Hawkes La FX IP11 112 F1
Hawkes Rd RCOLW CO6 183 H2
Hawkesway COS CO15 222 B7
Hawkhurst Cl CHLM/WR CM1 14 A3
Hawkins Rd COLS CO2 11 L9
RCOLE CO7 190 D5
SUD CO10 5 G1
Hawkins Wy BRTR CM7 180 E1
Hawks Cl RCHLM CM3 269 J8
Hawkwood Rd HSTD CO9 95 M5
HSTD CO9 96 A5 2
Hawlmark End RCOLW CO6 185 G2
Hawthorn Av COLN CO4 161 G5
Hawthorn Cl
CHLM/GWD CM2 266 E7 1
HSTD CO9 126 C3 3
RBSF CM22 173 L6
Hawthorn Dr CHTY IP2 54 B2
Hawthorn Ri BSF CM23 199 H2
Hawthorn Rd COS CO15 222 A6
HVHL CB9 22 F4
HVHL CB9 23 G4 2
MAL CM9 241 J3
RCHLM CM3 237 J8
SUD CO10 5 J7
Hawthorns HSTD CO9 95 M3 4
The Hawthorns RCHLM CM3 269 J6 3
Haycocks La K/T/MI CO5 245 H4
Haycocks Rd HVHL CB9 22 E4
Haycroft BSF CM23 171 L7
Haye La K/T/MI CO5 216 E1
Hayes Cl CHLM/GWD CM2 15 G6
Hayes Rd COS CO15 12 F7
Hay Gn RCHLM CM3 269 H5
Hayhill Rd IPNE IP4 3 J3
Hayhouse Rd RCOLW CO6 127 J8
Hay La BRTR CM7 180 E2
Hayley Bell Gdns BSF CM23 199 H2
Hayman Rd IPSE IP3 55 H4
Haymeads La BSF CM23 171 L7
Haynes Green Rd K/T/MI CO5 213 J5
Hayron's La CHLM/WR CM1 231 M5
Haytor Cl BRTR CM7 180 E3
The Haywain COLW CO3 158 F8 2
Haywards Flds KESG IP5 33 M5 1
Hazel Cl HVHL CB9 23 G6
RCOLE CO7 191 J8
Hazelcroft Rd IP IP1 31 K3
Hazeldon Cl RCHLM CM3 234 E7 1
Hazel Dr IPSE IP3 56 A4
Hazeleigh Hall La MAL CM9 270 E8
Hazelend Rd BSF CM23 171 K2
Hazel Gv BRTR CM7 180 A4
Hazell Av COLS CO2 187 J2
Hazelton Rd COLN CO4 11 L2
Hazelville Cl HAR CO12 140 A4
Hazelwood Ct MAL CM9 259 K7 1
Hazelwood Crs RCOS CO16 221 L4
Hazlemere Rd COS CO15 250 E1
Hazlitt Rd IP IP1 31 J2 1
Headgate COLS CO2 10 B8
Headingham Cl CHTY IP2 54 C3 3
Headland Av HVHL CB9 23 G6
Head St COL CO1 10 B7
HSTD CO9 126 B3
K/T/MI CO5 189 H5
MAL CM9 261 G7
Heard's La BRTR CM7 67 M8
BRTR CM7 67 L7
Hearsall Av CHLM/WR CM1 254 D6
Heath Cl RCOLE CO7 105 M2
Heath Ct FX IP11 83 K5 2
Heath Dr CHLM/GWD CM2 266 D7
Heather Av IPSE IP3 55 L2
Heather Cl BSF CM23 170 F7
COLS CO2 187 H7
COS CO15 222 D6
Heather Ct CHLM/WR CM1 255 H7 3
Heathercroft Rd IP IP1 31 J1
Heather Dr COLW CO3 159 H8
Heatherhayes CHTY IP2 54 C2
Heathfield Rd CHLM/WR CM1 254 D5
RIPS/CAP IP9 79 M8
Heathfields COLW CO3 158 D5
FX IP11 83 J4
Heathgate WIT CM8 238 F7
Heathgate Piece FX IP11 83 L7 2
Heathlands RCOLE CO7 191 J8
Heathlands Pk IPNE IP4 56 A1
Heath La IPNE IP4 32 E8
Heath Rd COLW CO3 158 B4
COLW CO3 159 H8
COLW CO3 186 F1
IPNE IP4 32 E6
K/T/MI CO5 189 H5
MGTR CO11 136 F5
MGTR CO11 136 D3
RCOLE CO7 105 M2
RCOLE CO7 189 K3
RCOLE CO7 190 D5
RCOS CO16 164 F4
RCOS CO16 221 G4
Heath Rw BSF CM23 171 K4
Heathside RCOLW CO6 159 G1 1
The Heath COLS CO2 187 J7
RCOLE CO7 134 B1
SUD CO10 51 G1
Heath Vw KESG IP5 33 J7
Heath Wy SUD CO10 51 G1
Heatley Wy COLN CO4 161 H5
Heaton Wy K/T/MI CO5 212 F7
Heckford's Rd RCOLE CO7 192 A3
Heckworth Cl COLN CO4 132 E7
Hedge Dr COLS CO2 187 K3
Hedgelands COLW CO3 157 M8
Hedgerows SBW CM21 227 H3
Hedingham Rd HSTD CO9 72 C6
HSTD CO9 125 G5
SUD CO10 72 E5
The Heights RCHLM CM3 268 E6
Helena Rd IPSE IP3 3 J9
Helen How RCHLM CM3 207 H6 3
Helford Ct WIT CM8 237 M3
Helions Bumpstead Rd
HVHL CB9 23 J8
HVHL CB9 43 H1
Helions Park Av HVHL CB9 23 J6
Helions Park Gdns HVHL CB9 23 J6
Helions Park Gv HVHL CB9 23 J6 1
Helions Rd HVHL CB9 43 J7
Helions Service Rd HVHL CB9 23 J6
Helions Wk HVHL CB9 23 J6
Helm Cl RCOLW CO6 131 L6
Helston Cl KESG IP5 33 K7
Helston Rd CHLM/WR CM1 255 G8
Hemingway Rd WIT CM8 210 A8
Hemmings Ct MAL CM9 271 G5 3
Hempstead Rd HVHL CB9 22 E4
Henderson Cl HVHL CB9 22 E4
RIPW IP8 30 C4 1
Hendon Cl RCOS CO16 12 C1
Hengrave Cl CHTY IP2 54 C3
Henham Rd RBSF CM22 145 G4
SAFWS CB11 117 M3
Henley Av IP IP1 31 K2
Henley Ct COLW CO3 159 G7
Henley Rd IP IP1 31 L3
Henniker Ga CHLM/GWD CM2 267 J2
Henniker Rd IP IP1 30 F5
Henny Back Rd BURES CO8 99 G1
Henny Rd BURES CO8 74 D7
Henrietta Cl RCOLE CO7 189 L2
Henry Cl COS CO15 12 B8
Henry Dixon Rd WIT CM8 210 F7
Henry Rd CHLM/WR CM1 266 D1
IPSE IP3 55 K4
Henslow Rd IPNE IP4 32 D8
Henstead Gdns IPSE IP3 55 J3
Herald Cl BSF CM23 170 F7
Herbage Park Rd MAL CM9 269 L4
Herbert Rd COS CO15 12 E5
Hereford Ct CHLM/GWD CM2 267 H8
COS CO15 223 G8 1
Hereford Rd COL CO1 10 F6
COS CO15 223 G7
Hereward Cl RCOLE CO7 189 L2
Hereward Wy BRTR CM7 122 E2
Heriot Wy MAL CM9 259 K1
Hermitage Mdw SUD CO10 26 E4
Heron Cl SBW CM21 226 F4
Heron Ct BSF CM23 171 J6
Heron Gld COS CO15 222 B6
Heron Rd CHTY IP2 54 A2
K/T/MI CO5 211 M2
Heronsgate FOS CO13 196 B7
Heron Wy FOS CO13 196 A6
MAL CM9 259 L8
Herrick Cl COLW CO3 159 J7
Herring's Wy RCOLW CO6 129 M7
Hertford La ROY SG8 35 M8
SAFWS CB11 60 B1
Hertford Rd SUD CO10 26 D4
Hertfordshire Wy STDN SG11 170 A1
Hervey Cl RIPS/CAP IP9 111 J4
Hervey St IPNE IP4 3 H3
Hervilly Wy WOTN CO14 196 D6 1
Hetherington Cl COLS CO2 188 C5 3
Hewes Cl COLN CO4 161 H6
Hewitt Rd HAR CO12 139 L4
Hexham Cl CHTY IP2 54 C3 4
Heybridge Ap MAL CM9 259 H8
Heybridge St MAL CM9 259 J8
Heycroft Dr BRTR CM7 180 F7
Heycroft Wy CHLM/GWD CM2 267 H8
K/T/MI CO5 212 F7
RCOLW CO6 102 B4
Heydon La ROY SG8 35 K8
SAFWS CB11 60 B1
Heydon Rd ROY SG8 59 G3
The Heythrop
CHLM/WR CM1 267 G1 2
Heywood Cl CHTY IP2 54 A4 2
Heywood Ct MAL CM9 259 K7 2
Heywood La GTDUN CM6 175 M6
Heywood Wy MAL CM9 259 K7
Hibbard Rd RIPW IP8 30 E3
Hickford Hl SUD CO10 26 F7
Hickory Av COLN CO4 11 M6
Hicks Wy HVHL CB9 24 A8 1
Hidcote Wy BRTR CM7 179 K6
Higham Rd RCOLE CO7 104 C2
Highams Cha MAL CM9 261 H5
High Beach FX IP11 113 L3
Highbirch Rd RCOS CO16 192 F8
High Bridge Rd CHLM/GWD CM2 15 J5
Highbury Wy SUD CO10 5 K9
Highclere Rd BRTR CM7 179 K7 3
COLN CO4 160 D1
High Cl ROY SG8 35 J8
Highcross La GTDUN CM6 174 E8
High Cross La GTDUN CM6 202 D1
High Cross La East GTDUN CM6 175 G8
High Easter Rd GTDUN CM6 204 B3
GTDUN CM6 231 G7
Highfield SUD CO10 26 E6
Highfield Ap IP IP1 31 H4 1
Highfield Av BSF CM23 171 L7
HAR CO12 8 E8
Highfield Cl BRTR CM7 152 C7
CBS CB2 16 F5
RCHLM CM3 268 F7 1
Highfield Dr COLW CO3 159 L7
Highfield Rd CHLM/WR CM1 266 A1
FX IP11 7 M2
IP IP1 31 G3
SUD CO10 5 G3
High Flds GTDUN CM6 175 M5
Highfields HSTD CO9 70 C3
HSTD CO9 126 A5
RBSF CM22 117 H7
RIPS/CAP IP9 78 A7
SAFWN CB10 63 G3
SAFWS CB11 88 D6 3
Highfields La K/T/MI CO5 211 M6
Highfields Rd WIT CM8 238 A2
Highfield Stile Rd BRTR CM7 152 C7
High Garrett BRTR CM7 152 E4
Highgate Gv SBW CM21 226 F3 1
High Hall Cl FX IP11 83 J5 1
Highland Rd BSF CM23 199 H2

Highlands HSTD CO9 .... 125 G4
Highlands Dr MAL CM9 .... 271 G3
High La RBSF CM22 .... 228 A7
STSD CM24 .... 144 A5
Highmead STSD CM24 .... 144 A5 3
High Meadow GTDUN CM6 .... 175 L5
High Pastures RBSF CM22 .... 227 L5
High Rd COLS CO2 .... 187 H8
FX IP11 .... 83 K6
High Rd East FX IP11 .... 113 K2
High Rd West FX IP11 .... 113 H1
High Row Fld FX IP11 .... 113 L2
High Stile GTDUN CM6 .... 175 L5
High St BRTR CM7 .... 121 K3 2
BRTR CM7 .... 122 E2
BRTR CM7 .... 180 B2
BSF CM23 .... 171 H6
BURES CO8 .... 100 B4
CBE/LIN CB1 .... 19 K3
CBE/LIN CB1 .... 42 A2
CHLM/GWD CM2 .... 267 H6
CHLM/WR CM1 .... 15 H3
COL CO1 .... 10 B7
COLN CO4 .... 132 F1
COS CO15 .... 13 H7
FX IP11 .... 113 G1
GTDUN CM6 .... 148 F8
GTDUN CM6 .... 175 M5
HAR CO12 .... 9 J7
HAR CO12 .... 166 E1
HSTD CO9 .... 70 C4
HSTD CO9 .... 126 A3
HVHL CB9 .... 23 J6
IP IP1 .... 2 E4
K/T/MI CO5 .... 189 J5
K/T/MI CO5 .... 211 L3
K/T/MI CO5 .... 244 D7
MAL CM9 .... 262 E4
MAL CM9 .... 271 H7
MGTR CO11 .... 135 M1
RBSF CM22 .... 117 H8
RBSF CM22 .... 201 H7
RCOLE CO7 .... 105 G2
RCOLE CO7 .... 189 K6
RCOLE CO7 .... 219 H7
RCOLW CO6 .... 102 D4
RCOLW CO6 .... 127 J7
RCOS CO16 .... 194 B3
RIPW IP8 .... 30 C7
ROY SG8 .... 58 B3
ROY SG8 .... 59 M2
SAFWN CB10 .... 17 J6
SAFWN CB10 .... 38 A3
SAFWN CB10 .... 62 F4
SAFWN CB10 .... 66 A4
SAFWS CB11 .... 62 B1
SAFWS CB11 .... 87 J5
SAFWS CB11 .... 88 D6
SAFWS CB11 .... 114 E1
SAFWS CB11 .... 116 F1
SUD CO10 .... 26 D6
SUD CO10 .... 27 M4
SUD CO10 .... 29 M2
WOTN CO14 .... 196 E5
High St North K/T/MI CO5 .... 244 E7
High Tree La WOTN CO14 .... 196 F3 2
High Vw BSF CM23 .... 171 L2
High View Av COS CO15 .... 222 A7
High View Cl COS CO15 .... 222 A7
Highview Cl RCOLW CO6 .... 4 C1
High View Rd IP IP1 .... 30 F5
Highwood La SUD CO10 .... 51 M4
Highwoods Ap COLN CO4 .... 160 D1
Highwoods Sq COLN CO4 .... 160 D2
High Wych La SBW CM21 .... 226 C3
High Wych Rd HLW CM20 .... 226 A7
SBW CM21 .... 226 F4 2
Hildabrook Cl CHTY IP2 .... 54 A4 3
Hillary Cl CHLM/WR CM1 .... 266 F1
IPNE IP4 .... 32 C8
MAL CM9 .... 259 K8
Hill Cl SUD CO10 .... 29 M5
Hill Crs CHLM/GWD CM2 .... 15 L4
HVHL CB9 .... 23 J4
Hillcrest COS CO15 .... 222 B7
FOS CO13 .... 195 M5
Hillcrest Av RIPW IP8 .... 30 D3
Hillcrest Ct HAR CO12 .... 9 H8
Hillcrest Rd SUD CO10 .... 4 D1
Hill Farm La RIPS/CAP IP9 .... 81 H6
Hill Farm Rd CBS CB2 .... 16 D1
NHMKT IP6 .... 33 K1
Hill House Ct RCOLE CO7 .... 219 J6 1
Hillhouse La RCOS CO16 .... 193 K2
Hill House Rd IPNE IP4 .... 3 K7
Hilliards Rd RCOLE CO7 .... 163 L3
Hillie Bunnies RCOLW CO6 .... 127 K6
Hill La HVHL CB9 .... 44 B1
Hillman Av COS CO15 .... 249 G7
Hillridge COLN CO4 .... 160 D2
Hill Rd CHLM/GWD CM2 .... 15 L4
COS CO15 .... 222 A7
HAR CO12 .... 9 H7
HAR CO12 .... 139 G6
RCOLW CO6 .... 183 K3
SAFWN CB10 .... 65 M5
Hills Cl BRTR CM7 .... 180 B1 1
Hills Crs COLW CO3 .... 159 J8
Hillside FOS CO13 .... 224 A1
Hillside Av BSF CM23 .... 171 J6
Hillside Crs COS CO15 .... 222 E8
IPSE IP3 .... 55 K2
Hillside Gdns BRTR CM7 .... 180 B4
Hillside Gv CHLM/GWD CM2 .... 266 C5
Hillside Ms CHLM/GWD CM2 .... 14 F9
Hillside Rd GTDUN CM6 .... 177 H7
SUD CO10 .... 5 G6
Hills Rd HSTD CO9 .... 95 M5
Hill St SAFWN CB10 .... 62 F4
Hilltop Cl COLS CO2 .... 188 C1
Hilltop Crs RCOS CO16 .... 193 H4
Hill Top La SAFWS CB11 .... 62 F6
Hill Tree Cl SBW CM21 .... 226 F4
Hill View Cl K/T/MI CO5 .... 189 H5
Hill View Rd CHLM/WR CM1 .... 266 E1
Hillway CBE/LIN CB1 .... 19 L3
Hilton Cl MGTR CO11 .... 135 M1 2

Hilton Rd IPSE IP3 .... 55 L4
Hilton Wy HSTD CO9 .... 96 A5
Hines Cl RCOLW CO6 .... 157 K5
Hintesham Cl IPNE IP4 .... 33 H8 2
Hintlesham Dr FX IP11 .... 112 F2
Hinxton Rd CBS CB2 .... 17 G5
Hipkins BSF CM23 .... 199 G1
Histon Cl KESG IP5 .... 33 H6 1
Hitcham Rd RCOLW CO6 .... 183 H2
Hitchcock Pl SUD CO10 .... 4 D2
Hitch Common Rd
SAFWS CB11 .... 87 H5 2
Hitchin Ms BRTR CM7 .... 180 D5
Hitherwood Rd COLS CO2 .... 187 L3
Hobart Cl CHLM/WR CM1 .... 254 A8
Hobbs Cl RCOLW CO6 .... 103 J8
Hobbs Dr COLN CO4 .... 28 F2
Hockerill St BSF CM23 .... 171 J6
Hockney Gdns IPSE IP3 .... 55 J5
Hodges Holt WIT CM8 .... 238 C6 2
Hoe Dr COLW CO3 .... 159 J8
Hoe La RCHLM CM3 .... 234 A7
COS CO15 .... 28 B5
Hoe Mill Rd MAL CM9 .... 269 M1
Hoestock Rd SBW CM21 .... 226 F3
Hoe St CHLM/WR CM1 .... 264 E1
Hogarth Cl K/T/MI CO5 .... 244 F7
Hogarth End FOS CO13 .... 196 A6 3
Hogarth Rd IPSE IP3 .... 55 H4
Hogarth Sq IPSE IP3 .... 55 H4
Hog's La ROY SG8 .... 59 M2
Holborough Cl COLN CO4 .... 161 H6
Holbrook Cl RCOS CO16 .... 249 K1
SUD CO10 .... 51 G2
Holbrook Crs FX IP11 .... 6 F1
Holbrook Rd HVHL CB9 .... 23 G7
IPSE IP3 .... 55 G4
RIPS/CAP IP9 .... 108 C3
RIPS/CAP IP9 .... 109 J3
Holcombe Crs CHTY IP2 .... 53 M3
Holden Rd COLN CO4 .... 160 B3
Holdsworth Cl SUD CO10 .... 28 D2 1
Holkham Cl IPNE IP4 .... 33 H8 3
Holland Pk COS CO15 .... 13 K3
Holland Rd COS CO15 .... 13 H7
COS CO15 .... 13 J5
FOS CO13 .... 195 K8
FOS CO13 .... 224 A2
FX IP11 .... 7 J5
IPNE IP4 .... 3 M4
RCOS CO16 .... 222 C3
Hollands Rd HVHL CB9 .... 23 J7
Holledge Crs FOS CO13 .... 196 A7
Hollies Rd BRTR CM7 .... 181 L2
Holliland Cft RCOLW CO6 .... 156 E5 1
Hollingtons Gv COLS CO2 .... 214 C3 1
Hollis Lock CHLM/GWD CM2 .... 267 J2
Holliwel Cl COLW CO3 .... 158 F7
Holloway Crs GTDUN CM6 .... 230 E6
Holloway Rd MAL CM9 .... 259 H7
Hollow Hl HVHL CB9 .... 22 D1
Hollow La BURES CO8 .... 100 B2
RCHLM CM3 .... 253 M6
RIPS/CAP IP9 .... 81 H6
Hollow Rd GTDUN CM6 .... 178 D8
K/T/MI CO5 .... 211 H3
RIPW IP8 .... 52 F5
ROY SG8 .... 59 M4
SAFWS CB11 .... 60 D1
SAFWS CB11 .... 116 E2
SUD CO10 .... 46 A3
Hollybank WIT CM8 .... 238 B4
Hollybush Hl RCOLE CO7 .... 220 A2
Hollybush Wy CBE/LIN CB1 .... 20 A2
Holly Cl COLS CO2 .... 187 L3
Hollycroft Cl IP IP1 .... 31 J2
Hollyhock Rd SAFWN CB10 .... 63 G3
Holly La KESG IP5 .... 33 G3
RCOLW CO6 .... 131 L1
RIPS/CAP IP9 .... 108 A2
RIPW IP8 .... 53 L5
Hollymead Cl COLN CO4 .... 160 B2
Holly Oaks RCOLW CO6 .... 130 A1
Holly Rd COLW CO3 .... 186 E1
IP IP1 .... 2 D2
KESG IP5 .... 33 H6
Hollytree Ct COLS CO2 .... 187 L2
Hollyview Cl RCOS CO16 .... 165 H8
Holly Wy CHLM/GWD CM2 .... 266 E6
K/T/MI CO5 .... 212 E8
Hollywood Cl CHLM/GWD CM2 .... 267 G7
Holman Crs COLW CO3 .... 186 C1
Holman Rd HSTD CO9 .... 126 A4 2
Holmans RCHLM CM3 .... 256 A5
Holmbrook Wy FOS CO13 .... 196 A8
Holmes Rd HSTD CO9 .... 126 A5
Holmwood Rd RCOS CO16 .... 221 K7 3
Holt Dr COLS CO2 .... 188 C6
WIT CM8 .... 239 G8
Holt's Rd RCOLW CO6 .... 130 D2
Holybread La RCHLM CM3 .... 268 E1
Holyrood HAR CO12 .... 140 B3
Holyrood Cl CHTY IP2 .... 54 B4
Holywells Cl IPSE IP3 .... 3 K9
Holy Wells Rd IPSE IP3 .... 55 G2
Homebridge SAFWN CB10 .... 91 J2
Home Cl HVHL CB9 .... 43 L6
Home Farm La RCOLE CO7 .... 134 C5
Homefield RIPS/CAP IP9 .... 77 K4
Homefield Cl CHLM/WR CM1 .... 253 M8
Homefield Rd COLS CO2 .... 187 L4
HVHL CB9 .... 23 G8
WIT CM8 .... 238 C1
Homefield Wy BRTR CM7 .... 180 F6 1
RCOLW CO6 .... 127 K6
Homelye Cha GTDUN CM6 .... 176 D4
Home Md CHLM/WR CM1 .... 265 J4
Home Pastures RBSF CM22 .... 228 B2
Homer Cl IP IP1 .... 31 H1
Homerton Cl COS CO15 .... 222 B5
Homestead CHLM/WR CM1 .... 254 D6
Homing Rd RCOS CO16 .... 221 L1
Honeybourne BSF CM23 .... 199 G4
Honey Cl CHLM/GWD CM2 .... 266 F7
Honey La RCOLW CO6 .... 101 L1
SAFWS CB11 .... 114 B2
Honeymeade HLW CM20 .... 226 E6

Honeypot La MAL CM9 .... 241 K4
MGTR CO11 .... 165 H1
Honeypots CHLM/GWD CM2 .... 266 E7
Honeysuckle Cl BSF CM23 .... 170 E7
Honeysuckle Gdns CHTY IP2 .... 54 A1 2
Honeysuckle Wy COLN CO4 .... 161 G5
RCOLE CO7 .... 191 J8 1
WIT CM8 .... 237 M1
Honywood Av RCOLW CO6 .... 183 J2
Honywood Cl HSTD CO9 .... 126 B2 1
Honywood Rd COLW CO3 .... 159 M7
Honywood Wy FOS CO13 .... 196 B6
Hood Gdns BRTR CM7 .... 180 E1 3
Hood Rd IPSE IP3 .... 55 G4
The Hoo HLWE CM17 .... 226 E8
Hop Gardens La MAL CM9 .... 270 B1
The Hopgrounds BRTR CM7 .... 92 F7
Hopkins Cl CHLM/GWD CM2 .... 267 J2 3
FOS CO13 .... 196 B7 4
Hopkins Md CHLM/GWD CM2 .... 267 H3
Hopkirk Cl RCHLM CM3 .... 269 H5
Hop Meadow RCOLE CO7 .... 105 K3
Hopping Jacks La RCHLM CM3 .... 269 H6
Hopton Ri HVHL CB9 .... 22 E5
Hordle Pl HAR CO12 .... 9 J7 1
Hordle St HAR CO12 .... 9 J7 2
Horkesley Hl RCOLW CO6 .... 102 C5
Horkesley Rd RCOLW CO6 .... 102 C5
RCOLW CO6 .... 131 M5
Horley Cl RCOS CO16 .... 221 L7
Hornbeam Cl CHLM/GWD CM2 .... 266 C7
COLS CO2 .... 187 M3
The Hornbeams HAR CO12 .... 139 K6
Horne Rw RCHLM CM3 .... 268 F8
Horner Pl WIT CM8 .... 238 C3 3
Horn Hl HSTD CO9 .... 95 L8
Horn La CBE/LIN CB1 .... 19 K3
Horrocks Cl COLS CO2 .... 188 C1
Horseheath Gn CBE/LIN CB1 .... 21 L4
Horseheath Rd CBE/LIN CB1 .... 19 M3
COS CO15 .... 22 C1
Horseshoe Cl SAFWS CB11 .... 60 D1
Horseshoe La HVHL CB9 .... 23 G6 3
Horsey Rd FOS CO13 .... 195 L5
Horsham Av IPSE IP3 .... 55 M2
Horsham Cl HVHL CB9 .... 22 E4 1
Hospital Ap CHLM/WR CM1 .... 254 D2
Hospital La COLW CO3 .... 159 M7 1
Hospital Rd COLW CO3 .... 159 M7 2
Houchin's La RCOLW CO6 .... 184 A2
Houghton Rd K/T/MI CO5 .... 33 H8 4
Howard Av HAR CO12 .... 140 B3
Howard Cl BRTR CM7 .... 180 D2
Howard Dr CHLM/GWD CM2 .... 267 J3
Howard Rd COS CO15 .... 250 E1
SAFWN CB10 .... 63 G3
Howards RCHLM CM3 .... 256 A5 1
Howards Cft COLN CO4 .... 131 M8
Howard's La CBE/LIN CB1 .... 21 J3
Howard St IPNE IP4 .... 32 D6
Howard Vyse Ct COS CO15 .... 12 F1
Howbridge Hall Rd WIT CM8 .... 238 B5
Howbridge Rd WIT CM8 .... 238 B5
Howe Av IPSE IP3 .... 55 L2
Howe Cha HSTD CO9 .... 126 A1
Howe Cl COLN CO4 .... 11 L7
Howe La SAFWN CB10 .... 91 J1
Howe Rd HVHL CB9 .... 23 G4
Hoxter Wy SUD CO10 .... 4 D1
Hoxton Cl COS CO15 .... 12 C3
Hoynors RCHLM CM3 .... 269 J6
Hubbards Cha WOTN CO14 .... 196 D4
Hubert Rd COLW CO3 .... 159 K5
Hucklesbury Av COS CO15 .... 223 G6 3
Hudson Cl HAR CO12 .... 140 C4
HVHL CB9 .... 23 L7 1
COS CO15 .... 12 A2
Hudson's Hl BRTR CM7 .... 122 F2
Hudsons La RCOLW CO6 .... 103 L1
Hugh Dickson Rd COLN CO4 .... 160 A3
Hughes Rd RCOLE CO7 .... 105 J1
Hull La RCHLM CM3 .... 236 C3
Hull's La CHLM/GWD CM2 .... 268 A7
Hulton Cl RCHLM CM3 .... 256 A5
Humber Av COS CO15 .... 249 G7
Humber Doucy La IPNE IP4 .... 32 C3
Humber Rd CHLM/WR CM1 .... 254 E8
WIT CM8 .... 237 M3
Humphrey's Farm La
RCHLM CM3 .... 233 L6
Humphry Rd SUD CO10 .... 4 D4
Hundon Rd HVHL CB9 .... 24 E3
Hundred La COLN CO4 .... 132 D1
Hungerdown La MGTR CO11 .... 135 G3
RCOLE CO7 .... 134 E6
Hunnable Rd BRTR CM7 .... 180 A2
Hunt Av MAL CM9 .... 259 K8
Hunt Cl K/T/MI CO5 .... 211 M1
Hunt Dr RCOS CO16 .... 12 C1
Hunter Dr MGTR CO11 .... 135 K2
Hunter Rd BRTR CM7 .... 180 E3
Hunter's Cha RCOLW CO6 .... 134 A3
Hunters End FX IP11 .... 83 L8
Hunters Rdg COLN CO4 .... 160 L1
Hunters Wy CHLM/GWD CM2 .... 255 H6 1
SAFWS CB11 .... 62 F6
Huntingdon Wy COS CO15 .... 222 A7
Hunting Ga COL CO1 .... 11 K7
Hunt's Cl CHLM/WR CM1 .... 265 K5
Hunt's Farm Cl MAL CM9 .... 262 F3
Hunts Hl SUD CO10 .... 28 D1
Hunts La SAFWN CB10 .... 17 K6
Hunts Rd CBS CB2 .... 16 F5
Hunt Wy FOS CO13 .... 196 A7
Hunwicke Rd COLN CO4 .... 161 G7
Hurdle Makers Hl RIPW IP8 .... 52 F1
Hurnard Dr COLW CO3 .... 159 J6
Hurrell Down COLN CO4 .... 160 C1
RCHLM CM3 .... 256 B4 1
Hurrells La RCHLM CM3 .... 268 C2

Hurst Cl RCOLE CO7 .... 219 J7
Hurst Wy CHLM/GWD CM2 .... 267 H3 3
Hutland Rd IPNE IP4 .... 3 M3
Huxtables La COLW CO3 .... 158 C4
Hyacinth Cl MAL CM9 .... 263 G4
RCOS CO16 .... 12 A3
Hyams La RIPS/CAP IP9 .... 79 L8
RIPS/CAP IP9 .... 108 B4
Hyde Gn RCHLM CM3 .... 269 K6
Hyde La BRTR CM7 .... 123 K4
Hyde Rd SUD CO10 .... 4 D7
Hydewood Rd HSTD CO9 .... 70 D2
Hylands Cl GTDUN CM6 .... 204 C1 1
Hyll Cl RCOLW CO6 .... 37 M2
Hyntle Cl CHTY IP2 .... 31 G8
Hythe Cl BRTR CM7 .... 152 A7
COS CO15 .... 249 M5
Hythe Gv RCOLE CO7 .... 219 G4 1
Hythe Hl COL CO1 .... 11 K9
Hythe Quay COL CO1 .... 11 K9
Hythe Station Rd COLS CO2 .... 11 L8
The Hythe MAL CM9 .... 271 K3

I

Iceni Wy COLS CO2 .... 187 K2
Ickleton Rd CBS CB2 .... 16 F5
SAFWN CB10 .... 17 J8
SAFWS CB11 .... 60 C1
Icknield Cl SAFWN CB10 .... 37 J2 1
Icknield Wy ROY SG8 .... 59 M2
SAFWS CB11 .... 60 C1
Icknield Way Pth ROY SG8 .... 34 B6
SAFWS CB11 .... 37 K5
Ickworth Ct FX IP11 .... 6 D3
Ickworth Crs IPNE IP4 .... 33 H8
Ilex Cl COLS CO2 .... 187 M3
Imogen Cl COLN CO4 .... 161 H6 2
Imperial Cl COLS CO2 .... 187 L4
Imphal Cl COLS CO2 .... 187 L4
Ingarfield Rd COS CO15 .... 223 G7
Ingelrica Av RCHLM CM3 .... 257 K2 2
Ingestre St HAR CO12 .... 9 K6
Ingham Rd HVHL CB9 .... 23 K5
Inglenook COS CO15 .... 222 D6
Ingleside Ct SAFWS CB11 .... 62 F4 4
Inglis Rd COLW CO3 .... 159 M7
Ingram Ms BRTR CM7 .... 180 D5 1
Ingram's Piece RCOLE CO7 .... 134 A6 2
Ingram's Well Rd SUD CO10 .... 4 F7
Inkerpole Pl CHLM/GWD CM2 .... 267 H1
Innham Hl HSTD CO9 .... 95 L7
Inverness Cl COL CO1 .... 10 E5
Inverness Rd IPNE IP4 .... 32 C3
Inworth La RCOLW CO6 .... 128 F3
Inworth Rd K/T/MI CO5 .... 212 A1
Inworth Wk COLS CO2 .... 188 C4 4
Ipswich Rd COL CO1 .... 11 H6
COLN CO4 .... 11 J1
COLN CO4 .... 104 D7
COLN CO4 .... 132 F8
COS CO15 .... 222 F7
KIR/NAC IP10 .... 56 B7
MGTR CO11 .... 106 F4
RCOLE CO7 .... 105 G3
RIPS/CAP IP9 .... 79 M6
Ireland Rd IPSE IP3 .... 55 H4
Ireton Rd COLW CO3 .... 159 M8
Iris Cl CHLM/WR CM1 .... 255 H8
CHTY IP2 .... 31 H8
Irlam Rd COS CO15 .... 12 B2
Iron Latch La COLW CO3 .... 158 E5
Irongate Cl COLW CO3 .... 159 L8
Irving Cl BSF CM23 .... 198 F1 1
Isbourne Rd COLN CO4 .... 161 H6
Ishams Cha WIT CM8 .... 238 E6
Island La FOS CO13 .... 196 A4
Island Rd FOS CO13 .... 196 A2
Ivry St IP IP1 .... 2 D2
Ivy La K/T/MI CO5 .... 246 D2
Ivy Lodge Rd RCOLW CO6 .... 131 L5
Ivy Todd Hl SAFWS CB11 .... 88 C5
Ixworth Rd HVHL CB9 .... 23 G7

J

Jacaranda Cl CHLM/WR CM1 .... 255 H7
Jack Andrews Av COLN CO4 .... 132 D8 2
Jack Hatch Wy RCOLE CO7 .... 189 J2
Jack's La RBSF CM22 .... 173 M6
Jackson Pl CHLM/GWD CM2 .... 266 F7
Jackson Rd COS CO15 .... 12 F8
Jackson's La SAFWN CB10 .... 37 M2
Jackson's Sq SAFWN CB10 .... 37 M2
Jacquard Wy BRTR CM7 .... 180 C3 2
Jaggards Rd RCOLW CO6 .... 183 J2
James Boden Cl FX IP11 .... 113 G2 5
James Carter Rd COLW CO3 .... 187 G2
James Cl RCOLE CO7 .... 189 L2
James Gdns RCOS CO16 .... 220 D8
Jameson Rd COS CO15 .... 12 B5
James Rd COS CO15 .... 12 B8
James St COL CO1 .... 10 F9
Janebrook Rd CHTY IP2 .... 54 A3 3
Janmead WIT CM8 .... 238 C2
Janus Cl HVHL CB9 .... 23 M7 2
Jarmin Rd COL CO1 .... 10 C4
Jarndyce CHLM/WR CM1 .... 254 B7
Jarvis Fld RCHLM CM3 .... 256 F8
Jarvis Rd CHLM/GWD CM2 .... 267 H3
Jasmine Cl BSF CM23 .... 170 E7
Jasmine Cl CHTY IP2 .... 54 B2 1
COLN CO4 .... 11 M5
FX IP11 .... 83 K5
Jasmine Wy COS CO15 .... 249 J6
Jay Cl HVHL CB9 .... 23 L6
Jays La RCOLW CO6 .... 185 H2
The Jays COLN CO4 .... 160 D2
Jaywick Cl RCOS CO16 .... 249 J3
Jaywick Rd HVHL CB9 .... 23 J5
Jeans La BRTR CM7 .... 171 G6
Jefferies Rd IPNE IP4 .... 3 J5
Jefferson Cl COLW CO3 .... 159 G8
Jeffery Rd CHLM/GWD CM2 .... 267 J6
Jeffrey Cl COLW CO3 .... 159 H8
Jeffrey's Rd BRTR CM7 .... 180 F7

Jekylls La BRTR CM7 .... 92 F1
Jellicoe Wy BRTR CM7 .... 180 E1 4
Jenkins Dr RBSF CM22 .... 144 E2
Jenkins La BSF CM23 .... 171 L8
Jenner Cl BRTR CM7 .... 180 B4 5
Jenner Md CHLM/GWD CM2 .... 267 J2
Jermyns Cl RIPS/CAP IP9 .... 77 K3 2
Jersey Rd MAL CM9 .... 271 K4
Jersey Wy BRTR CM7 .... 179 M3
Jervis Cl RIPS/CAP IP9 .... 79 M8
Jervis Rd BSF CM23 .... 171 H7
Jessica Cl COLN CO4 .... 161 H6 3
Jewell Vw KESG IP5 .... 33 M6
Jimmy's La MGTR CO11 .... 107 H3
Joes Rd SUD CO10 .... 51 G6
John English Av BRTR CM7 .... 179 M1
John Kent Av COLS CO2 .... 187 K3
John Harper St COL CO1 .... 10 B4 1
John Raven Ct K/T/MI CO5 .... 211 M2
John Ray St BRTR CM7 .... 180 C2 1
Johnson Cl BRTR CM7 .... 180 C6 2
CHTY IP2 .... 54 E2
Johnson Rd CHLM/GWD CM2 .... 267 H8
RCOS CO16 .... 248 D1
Johnson's Dr RCOLE CO7 .... 162 C7
Johns Rd BSF CM23 .... 171 J4
Johnston Cl COS CO15 .... 223 G8 2
HSTD CO9 .... 126 B5
Johnston Wy MAL CM9 .... 271 J5 2
John St RCOLE CO7 .... 219 H7
John Tibauld Ct HVHL CB9 .... 43 K7 3
Joiner's Ct CBE/LIN CB1 .... 19 K3
Joiner's Rd CBE/LIN CB1 .... 19 K3
Jollyboys La North GTDUN CM6 .... 177 L7
Jollyboys La South GTDUN CM6 .... 205 L1
Jonquil Wy COLN CO4 .... 159 K3
Joseph Gdns WIT CM8 .... 210 A1 2
Josselin Cl RCOLW CO6 .... 127 K6
The Josselyns FX IP11 .... 83 L7
Joyce's Cha MAL CM9 .... 261 J5
Jubilee Av CHLM/WR CM1 .... 254 D3
COS CO15 .... 222 A6
Jubilee Cl FX IP11 .... 83 K5
HAR CO12 .... 140 A4
Jubilee Ct GTDUN CM6 .... 175 L4
HSTD CO9 .... 96 A5 3
Jubilee End MGTR CO11 .... 106 E8
Jubilee La RCOLE CO7 .... 161 L2
Jubilee Ri RCHLM CM3 .... 269 H7
Jubilee Rd SUD CO10 .... 4 E4
Jubilee Wy FOS CO13 .... 196 B2
Julian Av COLN CO4 .... 132 D7
Julian Cl CHLM/WR CM1 .... 254 D4
HVHL CB9 .... 23 M6
Julien Court Rd BRTR CM7 .... 180 C1
June Av IP IP1 .... 31 K3
Juniper Cl HSTD CO9 .... 126 B3
Juniper Ct GTDUN CM6 .... 175 K4 1
Juniper Crs WIT CM8 .... 238 C1
Juniper Dr CHLM/GWD CM2 .... 266 D7
Juniper Rd COLW CO3 .... 158 E8
RCHLM CM3 .... 256 A5
Juniper Wy COLN CO4 .... 11 M5
Jupes Hl RCOLE CO7 .... 105 L8
RCOLW CO6 .... 128 F3
Jupiter Cl HVHL CB9 .... 23 L7 2
Jupiter Rd IPNE IP4 .... 32 D6
Justinian Cl HVHL CB9 .... 23 M6
Juvina Cl WIT CM8 .... 238 B6 1

K

Kale Cft COLW CO3 .... 158 F8
Karen Cl IP IP1 .... 31 K4
Kate's La SAFWN CB10 .... 40 E5
Kay Cl RCHLM CM3 .... 207 J6
Keable Rd RCOLW CO6 .... 185 G2
Keating Cl MGTR CO11 .... 135 K1 3
Keats Av BRTR CM7 .... 180 B5
Keats Cl MAL CM9 .... 271 J5
Keats Crs IP IP1 .... 31 H2 1
Keats Rd COLW CO3 .... 159 H7
Keble Cl COLW CO3 .... 159 M7 3
Kecksy's SBW CM21 .... 227 H1
Kedington Hl SUD CO10 .... 74 D3
Keeble Cl K/T/MI CO5 .... 213 G8
Keeble Ct RCOLE CO7 .... 192 A6
Keeble Pk MAL CM9 .... 271 H5
Keeble Wy BRTR CM7 .... 180 C2
Keelars La RCOLE CO7 .... 190 A3
Keelers Wy RCOLW CO6 .... 131 K6
Keepers Gn COLN CO4 .... 159 K2
Keeper's La FX IP11 .... 83 J8
Keith Cl COS CO15 .... 222 D5
Kelly Rd CHTY IP2 .... 31 G8
Kelso Cl RCOLW CO6 .... 131 L7
Kelvedon Cl CHLM/WR CM1 .... 254 C7
Kelvedon Dr IPNE IP4 .... 33 H8
Kelvedon Hall La K/T/MI CO5 .... 211 M8
Kelvedon Rd K/T/MI CO5 .... 212 D6
MAL CM9 .... 241 L7
RCOLW CO6 .... 183 J5
WIT CM8 .... 239 H8
Kelvin Rd IP IP1 .... 31 H4
Kemball St IPNE IP4 .... 32 C5
Kempe Rd BRTR CM7 .... 92 F7
Kempson Dr SUD CO10 .... 50 E8
The Kempsters FX IP11 .... 83 M8 1
Kempton Cl IP IP1 .... 31 J2
Kempton Pk RCOS CO16 .... 193 K8
Kempton Rd IP IP1 .... 31 J2
Kemsley Rd FX IP11 .... 113 H2
RCOLW CO6 .... 127 J7
Kendall Rd COL CO1 .... 10 F9
Kenilworth Gv RCOS CO16 .... 194 C3
Kenilworth Rd RCOS CO15 .... 223 G7
Kennedy Cl IPNE IP4 .... 32 C7
Kennedy Wy COS CO15 .... 13 K1
Kennels Rd KIR/NAC IP10 .... 57 G3
Kensington Rd IP IP1 .... 31 J5
Kent Cl RCOLE CO7 .... 219 H6
Kent Crs BSF CM23 .... 199 G1
Kentford Rd FX IP11 .... 6 E2
Kent Gdns BRTR CM7 .... 180 D1
The Kentings BRTR CM7 .... 180 A3 2
Kentmere COLN CO4 .... 161 G2

Kent's Av COS CO15 .... 223 G7
Kents Grass MAL CM9 .... 262 F3
Kents Yd SAFWS CB11 .... 62 B1 1
Kentwell Cl IPNE IP4 .... 56 B1
Kenwood Gdns CBE/LIN CB1 .... 20 A3
Kenworthy Rd BRTR CM7 .... 180 A3
Kenyon Cl RCOLE CO7 .... 104 F4
Kenyon Dr SUD CO10 .... 51 H2
Kenyon St CHTY IP2 .... 2 F9
Kerby Ri CHLM/GWD CM2 .... 267 H3
Kerridge's Cut MGTR CO11 .... 136 C1 2
Kerry Av IP IP1 .... 30 F3
Kerry Ct COL CO1 .... 11 J6
Kersey Av SUD CO10 .... 5 K8
Kersey Dr RCOS CO16 .... 221 K8
Kersey Rd FX IP11 .... 6 E3
Kessler Av BRTR CM7 .... 93 M6 1
Kesteven Rd CHTY IP2 .... 2 B9
Kestrel Gdns BSF CM23 .... 170 E7
Kestrel Ri HSTD CO9 .... 126 B4
Kestrel Rd CHTY IP2 .... 53 M2
Kestrel Wy COS CO15 .... 222 B7
Keswick Av COS CO15 .... 222 E7
Keswick Cl FX IP11 .... 113 L1
Ketleys Vw BRTR CM7 .... 151 J6
Kettlebaston Wy IP IP1 .... 31 M4 2
Kew La FOS CO13 .... 223 J1
Keyes Wy BRTR CM7 .... 180 C1
Keymer Wy COLW CO3 .... 187 H1 1
Keynes Wy HAR CO12 .... 140 B4
Key Rd COS CO15 .... 12 E5
Key St IPSE IP3 .... 3 G7
Khartoum Rd IPNE IP4 .... 3 M3
Kidder Rd BRTR CM7 .... 179 H4
Kilburn Gdns RCOS CO16 .... 12 C1
Kildare Av IP IP1 .... 30 F3
Kildermorie Cl COLN CO4 .... 160 F2
Kilmaine Rd HAR CO12 .... 140 B4
Kiln Barn Av COS CO15 .... 222 B6
Kiln Dr SUD CO10 .... 5 H8
Kiln Fld FX IP11 .... 112 F2 6
Kiltie Rd K/T/MI CO5 .... 213 G8
Kincaid Rd RCOS CO16 .... 248 C1
Kimberley Cl BSF CM23 .... 171 J8 1
King Charles Rd K/T/MI CO5 .... 244 F7
King Coel Rd COLW CO3 .... 158 F6
King Edward Quay COLS CO2 .... 160 F8
King Edward Rd IPSE IP3 .... 55 K2
King Edward Vii Dr
  RIPS/CAP IP9 .... 111 K5
King Edward Wy WIT CM8 .... 238 A5
Kingfisher Av CHTY IP2 .... 53 M2
Kingfisher Cl COLN CO4 .... 161 H5
  HVHL CB9 .... 23 L5 1
  MAL CM9 .... 259 L8
Kingfisher Ga BRTR CM7 .... 152 C8 1
Kingfisher Mdw HSTD CO9 .... 126 B4 1
Kingfishers COS CO15 .... 222 B7
Kingfisher Wy BSF CM23 .... 171 J6
  K/T/MI CO5 .... 211 L3 1
King George Rd COLS CO2 .... 188 C1
King George's Av HAR CO12 .... 8 F7
King Harold Rd COLW CO3 .... 187 J1
Kings Acre RCOLW CO6 .... 183 H3
Kings Av COS CO15 .... 222 B8
  IPNE IP4 .... 3 J6
Kingsbridge Cl BRTR CM7 .... 152 B5 1
Kingsbridge Rd BSF CM23 .... 171 J5
Kingsbury Cl RCOLW CO6 .... 185 H2 2
Kingsbury Rd FX IP11 .... 83 L8
Kings Cha WIT CM8 .... 238 C4
Kings Cl MGTR CO11 .... 135 L1
  RCOS CO16 .... 248 C2
Kings Ct BSF CM23 .... 171 J5
Kingsfield Av IP IP1 .... 31 M4
Kings Fleet Rd FX IP11 .... 7 G8
Kingsford Dr CHLM/GWD CM2 .... 267 K2
Kingsgate Dr IPNE IP4 .... 32 B5
Kings Head Ct COL CO1 .... 10 B4
King's Head St HAR CO12 .... 9 K3
King's Hl HVHL CB9 .... 24 C4
  SUD CO10 .... 5 G8
Kingsland RIPS/CAP IP9 .... 111 G3
Kingsland Beach K/T/MI CO5 .... 244 E8
Kingsland Cl K/T/MI CO5 .... 244 E8 1
Kingsland Rd K/T/MI CO5 .... 244 E8
Kings La BRTR CM7 .... 181 G1
Kingsley Cl IP IP1 .... 31 J2
Kingsman Dr RCOS CO16 .... 12 A2
Kingsmead SBW CM21 .... 227 G4
Kings Meadow HVHL CB9 .... 24 C3
  SUD CO10 .... 5 G8
Kings Meadow Rd COL CO1 .... 10 C4
Kingsmere Cl K/T/MI CO5 .... 244 F7
Kings Ms RCOLE CO7 .... 189 L1
Kings Pde COS CO15 .... 223 G8
  COS CO15 .... 250 F1
King's Quay St HAR CO12 .... 9 L2
Kings Rd BRTR CM7 .... 152 A7 2
  CHLM/WR CM1 .... 266 B1
  COS CO15 .... 249 M4
  HAR CO12 .... 8 E9
  HSTD CO9 .... 126 A4
  MAL CM9 .... 239 M6
King Stephen Rd COL CO1 .... 11 G8
Kingston Av CHLM/GWD CM2 .... 267 G2
Kingston Cha MAL CM9 .... 259 H7
Kingston Crs CHLM/GWD CM2 .... 267 G2
Kingston Rd IP IP1 .... 31 H5
King St BSF CM23 .... 171 H6
  FX IP11 .... 113 G2
  HSTD CO9 .... 96 B1 2
  IP IP1 .... 2 E5
  MAL CM9 .... 271 J4
  MGTR CO11 .... 136 E5
  SUD CO10 .... 5 G7
Kings Wk MAL CM9 .... 263 G4
King's Wy IPSE IP3 .... 55 K3
Kingsway CBS CB2 .... 16 A4
  HAR CO12 .... 9 J7
  K/T/MI CO5 .... 212 E2
Kingswood Rd COLN CO4 .... 160 B1
Kingwell Av COS CO15 .... 12 F2
Kinlett Cl COLS CO2 .... 160 C1
Kinloch Cha WIT CM8 .... 238 B6 2
Kino Rd WOTN CO14 .... 196 F5 1
Kinross Rd IPNE IP4 .... 32 D4

Kintbury CBS CB2 .... 16 F5
Kipling Cl CHLM/WR CM1 .... 254 C8
Kipling Rd IP IP1 .... 31 H2
Kipling Wy BRTR CM7 .... 180 C5
Kirby Cl IPNE IP4 .... 32 C8
Kirby Hall Rd HSTD CO9 .... 70 F8
Kirby Rd FOS CO13 .... 195 J8
  FOS CO13 .... 196 C5
  FOS CO13 .... 223 J1
Kirby St IPNE IP4 .... 32 C6
Kirkbaye FOS CO13 .... 196 A7
Kirkham Cl CHTY IP2 .... 54 C7
Kirkhurst Cl RCOLE CO7 .... 219 J7 1
Kirk Pl CHLM/GWD CM2 .... 267 H2 2
Kirkton Cl RIPS/CAP IP9 .... 111 J4
Kirton Rd KIR/NAC IP10 .... 83 K3
Kitchener Rd IP IP1 .... 31 H5
Kitchener Wy RIPS/CAP IP9 .... 111 J5
Kitchen Fld BRTR CM7 .... 180 F2
Kitchen Hl SUD CO10 .... 49 K7
Kittiwake Cl CHTY IP2 .... 54 A7
Kittiwake Dr MAL CM9 .... 259 L8 5
Knapton Cl CHLM/WR CM1 .... 254 F6
Knightsbridge Cl COLS CO2 .... 187 L2 1
Knights Cl BSF CM23 .... 170 D5
  FX IP11 .... 113 M1
  K/T/MI CO5 .... 241 H2
  MGTR CO11 .... 135 L1
Knightsdale Rd IP IP1 .... 31 J4
Knights La KESG IP5 .... 33 M6
Knights Rd BRTR CM7 .... 180 E4
  RCOLW CO6 .... 183 H3
Knight St SBW CM21 .... 227 G3
Knights Wy GTDUN CM6 .... 175 M4
Knole La SAFWS CB11 .... 60 C6
Knowles Cl MAL CM9 .... 271 J5
Knox Cl MAL CM9 .... 271 J5
Knox Gdns COS CO15 .... 12 F2
Knox Rd COS CO15 .... 12 E1
Knutsford Cl RIPW IP8 .... 53 L4
Kohima Rd COLS CO2 .... 187 K4
Kreswell Gv HAR CO12 .... 140 D3
Kynaston Pl WIT CM8 .... 238 D3 4
Kynaston Rd BRTR CM7 .... 151 H5

L

Laburnum RCHLM CM3 .... 257 J2
Laburnum Cl COS CO15 .... 12 A6
  IPSE IP3 .... 56 A3 1
  RCOLE CO7 .... 192 A5 1
  RIPW IP8 .... 53 L3 3
Laburnum Crs FOS CO13 .... 195 M7
Laburnum Dr CHLM/GWD CM2 .... 266 D7
Laburnum Gdns KESG IP5 .... 33 G4 2
Laburnum Gv COLN CO4 .... 161 G5
Laburnum Wy RCOLW CO6 .... 102 B4
  WIT CM8 .... 238 C1 2
Lacey St IPNE IP4 .... 3 J4
Lacey's Wy CBS CB2 .... 16 F4
Lacon Rd RIPW IP8 .... 30 C3
Ladbrook Dr COLS CO2 .... 188 C2
Ladbrooke Rd RCOS CO16 .... 221 M7
Ladell Cl COLW CO3 .... 187 G2
Lady La CHLM/GWD CM2 .... 15 J7
  IP IP1 .... 2 D5
Ladysmith Av RCOLE CO7 .... 219 G6
Ladywell Cl CHLM/GWD CM2 .... 267 M8
Ladywell Prospect SBW CM21 .... 227 H4
Ladywood Rd IPNE IP4 .... 32 E6
Laing Cl COLN CO4 .... 161 G7
Lake Av COS CO15 .... 12 A5
Lakeside Rd CHTY IP2 .... 54 A3
Lakes Meadow RCOLW CO6 .... 183 J4
Lakes Rd BRTR CM7 .... 180 D3
Lake Wk COS CO15 .... 12 A5
Lake Wy COS CO15 .... 249 H6
Lakforth SUD CO10 .... 29 M5
Lakin Cl CHLM/GWD CM2 .... 267 J2
Lamarsh Hl BURES CO8 .... 74 D6
  BURES CO8 .... 100 A4
Lamarsh Rd BURES CO8 .... 99 J2
Lambert Cross SAFWN CB10 .... 63 G2
Lamberts La KESG IP5 .... 32 E3
Lambert's Rd RCOLW CO6 .... 156 B3
Lamb La HSTD CO9 .... 95 M6
Lambourne Cl COLW CO3 .... 186 F1
  COS CO15 .... 222 B6
Lambourne Gv MAL CM9 .... 271 H5
Lambourne Rd IP IP1 .... 31 K1
Lammas Wy RCOLE CO7 .... 189 L2
Lanark Rd IPNE IP4 .... 32 D4
Lancaster Gdns East COS CO15 .... 13 K4
Lancaster Gdns West COS CO15 .... 13 K5
Lancaster Rd IPNE IP4 .... 3 J5
  SUD CO10 .... 49 M3
Lancaster Wy BRTR CM7 .... 180 A1
  BSF CM23 .... 170 D5
  RCOLW CO6 .... 155 H3
Lanchester Av COS CO15 .... 248 F7
Lancing Av IPNE IP4 .... 32 C5
Land Cl RCOS CO16 .... 12 A1
Landermere Rd RCOS CO16 .... 194 C4
Landguard Rd FX IP11 .... 7 G9
Landisdale RCHLM CM3 .... 269 J6
Land La COL CO1 .... 10 E6
Landscape Vw SAFWS CB11 .... 62 F7
Landsdown Rd SUD CO10 .... 5 G3
Landseer Cl IPSE IP3 .... 55 K9
Landseer Rd COLW CO3 .... 159 K8
  IPSE IP3 .... 55 G3
Lanercost Wy CHTY IP2 .... 54 C4
Lane Rd RCOLW CO6 .... 128 D7
The Lane K/T/MI CO5 .... 244 C6
  MGTR CO11 .... 136 B1
Langdale BRTR CM7 .... 179 L6 5
Langdale Cl IP IP1 .... 113 M1
Langdale Dr COLN CO4 .... 160 D1
Langdale Gdns CHLM/GWD CM2 .... 15 H7
Langenhoe Hall La K/T/MI CO5 .... 216 D6
Langenhoe Pk K/T/MI CO5 .... 216 D3
Langer Rd FX IP11 .... 7 H6
Langford Rd MAL CM9 .... 259 H7
  WIT CM8 .... 258 E2
Langham Dr RCOS CO16 .... 249 K1
Langham La COLN CO4 .... 132 C5

Langham Rd COLN CO4 .... 132 C5
Langham Wy HVHL CB9 .... 22 D4
Langley Cl BRTR CM7 .... 93 M6
  FX IP11 .... 7 G1
Langley Hl HAR CO12 .... 9 G9
Langley Hi BURES CO8 .... 99 L2
Langstons FX IP11 .... 83 M7
Langton Av CHLM/WR CM1 .... 254 A8
Langwood K/T/MI CO5 .... 244 E6 1
Lanham Green Rd BRTR CM7 .... 181 J6
Lansdowne Cl K/T/MI CO5 .... 212 E7 3
Lansdowne Rd FX IP11 .... 113 K1
  IPNE IP4 .... 32 C8 1
Lanvalley Rd COLW CO3 .... 159 G7
Lapwing Dr K/T/MI CO5 .... 211 M3 2
  MAL CM9 .... 259 L8
Lapwing Rd CHTY IP2 .... 53 M2 2
Larch Cl COS CO15 .... 11 M4
Larchcroft Cl IP IP1 .... 31 K3
Larchcroft Rd IP IP1 .... 31 J3
The Larches RCHLM CM3 .... 256 A5 2
Larch Gv CHLM/GWD CM2 .... 266 E7
  RCOLW CO6 .... 102 B4
  WIT CM8 .... 210 C8 3
Larch Wk MAL CM9 .... 259 L7
Larchwood BSF CM23 .... 170 F8
Larchwood Cl CHTY IP2 .... 30 E8
Larkfield Rd RCOLE CO7 .... 191 M4
Larkhill Wy FX IP11 .... 112 F2 7
Lark Ri SUD CO10 .... 49 M8 1
Larks Cl HVHL CB9 .... 23 L6
Larksfield Crs BRTR CM7 .... 8 E7
Larksfield Rd RIPS/CAP IP9 .... 108 C2
Lark's La RCHLM CM3 .... 234 B8
Larkspur Cl BSF CM23 .... 170 F7
  WIT CM8 .... 238 A1 2
Larkspur Rd CHTY IP2 .... 54 B2
Larksway BSF CM23 .... 170 E2
  FX IP11 .... 6 F4
Larkway FOS CO13 .... 196 A6 4
The Larneys RCOS CO16 .... 196 A6 5
Latchmore Bank RBSF CM22 .... 199 K3
Lathcoates Crs
  CHLM/GWD CM2 .... 267 G6
Lattice Av IPNE IP4 .... 32 C7
Laud's Cl FX IP11 .... 83 K7
Launceston Cl COLS CO2 .... 188 D4
Laurel Av HAR CO12 .... 8 B9
  KESG IP5 .... 33 J6
Laurel Cl COS CO15 .... 222 D6
  HVHL CB9 .... 22 F4
Laurel Dr GTDUN CM6 .... 175 K4 2
  SUD CO10 .... 29 L6
Laurel Gv CHLM/GWD CM2 .... 14 D8
Laurelhayes CHTY IP2 .... 54 C2
Laurence Av WIT CM8 .... 238 C5
Laurence Cl RCOLE CO7 .... 162 B7
Laurence Cft CHLM/WR CM1 .... 265 K4
Lavender Cl BSF CM23 .... 170 F7
  K/T/MI CO5 .... 240 E1 3
  WIT CM8 .... 238 A1 3
Lavender Ct CHLM/WR CM1 .... 255 H8 2
Lavender Hl CHTY IP2 .... 54 B1
Lavender Wk COS CO15 .... 249 J6
Lavender Wy COLN CO4 .... 159 L3 4
Lavenham Cl RCOS CO16 .... 249 K1
Lavenham Rd CHTY IP2 .... 31 G8
Lawford Av MAL CM9 .... 259 L8
Lawling Av MAL CM9 .... 259 L8
Lawn Cha WIT CM8 .... 238 B4
Lawn La CHLM/WR CM1 .... 254 F7 1
Lawns Cl K/T/MI CO5 .... 244 E6
The Lawns CHLM/WR CM1 .... 254 F6
  IPNE IP4 .... 32 E5
Lawn Wy FX IP11 .... 113 G9
Lawrence Av SBW CM21 .... 227 G1
Lawrence Moorings SBW CM21 .... 227 H4
Laws Cl SAFWS CB11 .... 62 F6
Law's Drift KIR/NAC IP10 .... 83 G1
Lawshall's Hl RCOLW CO6 .... 127 M5
Laxton Cl FOS CO13 .... 195 J8
Laxton Rd RCOLE CO7 .... 190 D5
Layer Breton Hl COLS CO2 .... 214 C4
Layer Rd COLS CO2 .... 187 K3
  HVHL CB9 .... 23 G6
  K/T/MI CO5 .... 216 A1
  K/T/MI CO5 .... 242 F1
Layzell Cft SUD CO10 .... 74 E1
Leach Cl CHLM/GWD CM2 .... 267 K6
Lea Cl BRTR CM7 .... 180 F4 2
  BSF CM23 .... 171 K4
Leaden Cl GTDUN CM6 .... 230 E5
Lea Gv BSF CM23 .... 171 K4
  MAL CM9 .... 258 B4
Lea La WIT CM8 .... 239 H4
Leam Cl COLN CO4 .... 161 H6 4
Leapingwell Cl
  CHLM/GWD CM2 .... 267 J2 4
Lea Side K/T/MI CO5 .... 244 F7
Leas La COLS CO2 .... 186 E7
Leas Rd COLS CO2 .... 187 L4
  COS CO15 .... 12 C8
The Leas FOS CO13 .... 196 C5
Leat Cl SBW CM21 .... 227 H2
Leather La HSTD CO9 .... 70 C4
  HVHL CB9 .... 23 G6
Le Cateau Rd COLS CO2 .... 10 A9
Ledo Rd CBS CB2 .... 16 B3
Leech's La COLN CO4 .... 159 M1
Lee Rd HAR CO12 .... 9 G9
  IPSE IP3 .... 55 H2
The Leeway RCHLM CM3 .... 269 H6
Leez Rd RCHLM CM3 .... 205 M4
Leggatt Dr RIPW IP8 .... 30 C5
Legg St CHLM/WR CM1 .... 15 H2
Legions Wy BSF CM23 .... 171 J5
Leicester Cl CHTY IP2 .... 54 B4
  COL CO1 .... 10 E5
Leicester Ct WIT CM8 .... 209 M2 1
Leigh Dr RBSF CM22 .... 144 E4
  WIT CM8 .... 238 F8
Leighton Av IPSE IP3 .... 55 J5
Leighton Sq IPSE IP3 .... 55 J5
Leiston Rd HVHL CB9 .... 23 H6
Lely Rd IPSE IP3 .... 55 H5
Lemons Hl RIPS/CAP IP9 .... 78 F6

Leonard Ms BRTR CM7 .... 180 D5
Leopold Gdns IPNE IP4 .... 32 C5
Leopold Rd FX IP11 .... 7 L3
  IPNE IP4 .... 32 C6
Les Bois COLS CO2 .... 187 J8
Leslie Rd BSF CM23 .... 55 L4
Lethe Gv COLS CO2 .... 188 C5 4
Letton Cl RIPS/CAP IP9 .... 77 J4
Levens Wy BRTR CM7 .... 179 L7
Levington La KIR/NAC IP10 .... 57 J5
Levington Rd FX IP11 .... 7 G7
  IPSE IP3 .... 55 J1
  KIR/NAC IP10 .... 81 L1
Lewes Cl IPSE IP3 .... 56 A2
Lewin Pl RCHLM CM3 .... 256 A5
Lewis Dr CHLM/GWD CM2 .... 266 D7
Lewis La RIPS/CAP IP9 .... 107 M3
Lexden Cl COS CO15 .... 159 L6
Lexden Gv COLW CO3 .... 159 H7
Lexden Ms COLW CO3 .... 159 H6
Lexden Rd COLW CO3 .... 159 J6
  RCOLW CO6 .... 158 F1
Leybourne Dr CHLM/WR CM1 .... 254 F6
Leyburne Rd RCOS CO16 .... 196 C6
Ley Fld RBSF CM22 .... 173 L6
  RCOLE CO7 .... 185 G2
Leyfields BRTR CM7 .... 179 H4
Leys Dr RCOS CO16 .... 225 L4
Leyside BRTR CM7 .... 179 G3
Leys Rd RCOLE CO7 .... 189 L2
The Leys CHLM/GWD CM2 .... 255 H8
The Ley BRTR CM7 .... 180 F4 3
Leyton Ct COS CO15 .... 222 B6
Leywood Cl BRTR CM7 .... 180 E3
Lichfield Cl CHLM/WR CM1 .... 266 A1 1
  COL CO1 .... 10 F5
Lidgate Ct FX IP11 .... 6 D2
Lifchild Cl WIT CM8 .... 238 C6 3
Lilac Av RCOS CO16 .... 248 D7
Lilac Cl CHLM/GWD CM2 .... 266 E7 2
Lilac Ct RCOLW CO6 .... 189 J3
Lilley's La RCOLE CO7 .... 162 E1
The Lillies BRTR CM7 .... 152 D4
Lily Cl CHLM/WR CM1 .... 255 H7
Limbourne Dr MAL CM9 .... 259 L8
Lime Av COLN CO4 .... 11 M4
  HAR CO12 .... 8 B9
Limebrook Wy MAL CM9 .... 271 J8
Lime Cl COS CO15 .... 12 A6
  WIT CM8 .... 210 C8
Limecroft Cl IP IP1 .... 31 J2 2
Limefields SAFWN CB10 .... 62 F1 1
Lime Gv SUD CO10 .... 49 L8
Limekiln La STSD CM24 .... 143 L7
Limerick Cl IP IP1 .... 31 G3
Limes Av RIPW IP8 .... 30 E3
Limes Crs BSF CM23 .... 171 J6
The Limes HSTD CO9 .... 125 G6
  KESG IP5 .... 32 F4
  RCOLE CO7 .... 134 B6 1
  SUD CO10 .... 29 L6
Lime St RCOLE CO7 .... 219 H8
Lime Wk CHLM/GWD CM2 .... 266 E7
Lincoln Av COS CO15 .... 248 F7
Lincoln Cl BSF CM23 .... 170 F8
  IP IP1 .... 31 K2
Lincoln La RCOLW CO6 .... 131 L4
Lincoln Ter FX IP11 .... 7 J4
Lincoln Wy COL CO1 .... 10 F6
Linden Cl CHLM/GWD CM2 .... 266 E6
  COLN CO4 .... 161 G4
  MGTR CO11 .... 135 K2
Linden Dr COS CO15 .... 222 A7
The Lindens BRTR CM7 .... 180 C4 3
  BSF CM23 .... 171 H7
Lindisfarne Cl CHTY IP2 .... 54 C4 1
Lindsell La GTDUN CM6 .... 148 D2
Lindsey Av SUD CO10 .... 5 J8
Lindsey Cl BSF CM23 .... 171 J4
Lindsey Rd BSF CM23 .... 171 H4
  IPNE IP4 .... 32 E6
Linford Ms MAL CM9 .... 271 J6 4
Lingfield Rd IP IP1 .... 31 K1
Ling's La RIPS/CAP IP9 .... 81 G7
Lingwood Rd RCHLM CM3 .... 269 G6
Link Cl COLN CO4 .... 160 A1
Link La RIPS/CAP IP9 .... 77 M7
Link Rd BSF CM23 .... 171 H5
  COS CO15 .... 12 D8
  HSTD CO9 .... 125 M5
  RCOLE CO7 .... 219 J7
  RIPS/CAP IP9 .... 77 J4
  RIPS/CAP IP9 .... 111 J4
Links Av FX IP11 .... 113 J1
Links Dr CHLM/GWD CM2 .... 266 B6
Linksfield KESG IP5 .... 33 G6
Links Rd BRTR CM7 .... 181 L6
  RCOS CO16 .... 248 D7
Links Vw SUD CO10 .... 51 K7
The Link RIPS/CAP IP9 .... 77 M7
Link Wy BSF CM23 .... 171 G7
Linley Gdns COS CO15 .... 12 C8
Linnet Dr CHLM/GWD CM2 .... 266 D7
Linnet Rd CHTY IP2 .... 53 M1 1
Linnets COS CO15 .... 222 B7 2
Linnetts La HVHL CB9 .... 44 C1
Linnet Wy RCOLE CO7 .... 191 M5
Linstead Ct RCOS CO16 .... 249 J1 4
Linton Cl SAFWS CB11 .... 63 H5
Linton Rd CBE/LIN CB1 .... 19 K5
  CBE/LIN CB1 .... 21 H2
The Lintons CHLM/GWD CM2 .... 267 M7
Linwood SBW CM21 .... 227 G3 3
Lionel Hurst Cl SUD CO10 .... 50 E8
Lionfield Ter CHLM/WR CM1 .... 15 L1 1
Lion Meadow HVHL CB9 .... 43 K6
Lion St IP IP1 .... 2 D5
Lion Wk COS CO15 .... 10 E5
Lisle Rd COLS CO2 .... 160 C8
Lister Rd BRTR CM7 .... 180 B5
  IP IP1 .... 31 H4
Lister Tye CHLM/GWD CM2 .... 15 K8
Listonhall Cha HSTD CO9 .... 95 K9
Liston St CHLM/WR CM1 .... 15 H2
Litchborough Pk RCHLM CM3 .... 269 H5
Litchfield HAR CO12 .... 140 A3 1
Litchfield Cl COS CO15 .... 12 E1

Littell Tweed CHLM/GWD CM2 .... 267 J2
Little Baddow Rd MAL CM9 .... 269 L2
  RCHLM CM3 .... 269 G6
Little Bakers FOS CO13 .... 196 C6 1
Little Bentley Rd RCOLE CO7 .... 164 D4
Little Braxted La RCOLE CO7 .... 238 E2
Little Bromley Rd RCOLE CO7 .... 134 C6
  RCOLE CO7 .... 163 G2
Littlebury Gdns COLS CO2 .... 188 E1
Littlebury Green Rd
  SAFWS CB11 .... 61 L2
Little Chishill Rd ROY SG8 .... 58 E5
Little Clacton Rd FOS CO13 .... 223 G3
  RCOS CO16 .... 221 K6
Littlecotes COLN CO4 .... 159 M1
Little Croft St CHTY IP2 .... 54 E2
Little Dorrit CHLM/WR CM1 .... 254 A6
Littlefield Rd COLS CO2 .... 187 L4
Little Flds RCHLM CM3 .... 269 J6
Little Gipping St IP IP1 .... 2 D5
Little Gv RIPS/CAP IP9 .... 77 J5
Little Gulls RIPS/CAP IP9 .... 77 H4
Little Harrods FOS CO13 .... 196 C6
Little Heath RBSF CM22 .... 228 B2
Little Horkesley Rd RCOLW CO6 .... 130 B1
Little Hyde Cl HSTD CO9 .... 70 D3 5
Little Hyde Rd HSTD CO9 .... 70 D3
Little Larchmount
  SAFWS CB11 .... 62 F5 1
Little London Hl BRTR CM7 .... 92 F5
Little London La MAL CM9 .... 257 L8
Little Meadow CHLM/WR CM1 .... 265 J4
Little Mdw MAL CM9 .... 270 A7
Little Nell CHLM/WR CM1 .... 254 A6
Little St Mary's SUD CO10 .... 29 L7
Little's Crs CHTY IP2 .... 2 F9
Little Stile CHLM/WR CM1 .... 265 J5
Little Stone Ct COS CO15 .... 249 L5 1
Little Tey Rd K/T/MI CO5 .... 184 B6
Little Totham Rd MAL CM9 .... 260 E4
Little Tufts RIPS/CAP IP9 .... 77 K4
Little Walden Rd SAFWN CB10 .... 62 F3 2
  SAFWN CB10 .... 62 F3 3
Little Waltham Rd
  CHLM/WR CM1 .... 254 F4
Little Whip St CHTY IP2 .... 2 F8
Little Yeldham Rd HSTD CO9 .... 70 D3
Llewellyn Cl CHLM/GWD CM2 .... 266 F1 1
Lloyd Rd RIPS/CAP IP9 .... 111 J5
Lloyds Av IP IP1 .... 2 F5
The Lloyds KESG IP5 .... 33 L6
Loamy Hill Rd WIT CM8 .... 240 B4
Lobelia Cl CHLM/WR CM1 .... 255 H7
Locarno Rd IPSE IP3 .... 55 K2
Lockhart Av COLW CO3 .... 159 L6
Lockram La WIT CM8 .... 238 C3 4
Lodge Av CHLM/GWD CM2 .... 267 H6
Lodge Cl COS CO15 .... 12 E4
Lodge Ct RCOLW CO6 .... 159 H1
Lodge Crs RCHLM CM3 .... 256 A5
Lodge Farm Dr FX IP11 .... 113 L2
Lodge Farm La RCOS CO16 .... 248 F1 1
Lodge Farm Rd SUD CO10 .... 28 E2
Lodge La COLN CO4 .... 132 F5
  K/T/MI CO5 .... 215 M5
  K/T/MI CO5 .... 216 E4
  RCOLE CO7 .... 133 L7
  RCOLE CO7 .... 218 F6
  RCOS CO16 .... 165 M5
Lodge Rd BRTR CM7 .... 180 B4
  CHLM/WR CM1 .... 265 H6
  HAR CO12 .... 139 L5
  K/T/MI CO5 .... 212 F2
  MAL CM9 .... 260 D6
  RCOLE CO7 .... 219 G6 1
  RCOS CO16 .... 194 B7
Loftin Wy CHLM/GWD CM2 .... 15 L9
Lombard Ct IPNE IP4 .... 3 M3
Lombardy Rd SUD CO10 .... 49 M3
Lonbarn Hl MGTR CO11 .... 137 J3
London Rd BRTR CM7 .... 179 M5
  BSF CM23 .... 14 C9
  CHLM/GWD CM2 .... 31 G8
  CHTY IP2 .... 158 D7
  COLW CO3 .... 158 D7
  COS CO15 .... 12 E2
  IP IP1 .... 2 A5
  K/T/MI CO5 .... 184 E5
  MAL CM9 .... 270 D3
  RCHLM CM3 .... 207 K3
  RCOLW CO6 .... 131 G5
  RCOLW CO6 .... 185 J2
  RCOS CO16 .... 221 M5
  RIPS/CAP IP9 .... 77 J2
  RIPW IP8 .... 53 J4
  ROY SG8 .... 58 B4
  SAFWN CB10 .... 37 L3
  SAFWS CB11 .... 62 F5
  SBW CM21 .... 227 G3
Lone Barn Ct IP IP1 .... 30 F5
Longacre CHLM/WR CM1 .... 265 M6
  COLN CO4 .... 10 A1
Longacre Rd BRTR CM7 .... 181 G7 3
Longacres BRTR CM7 .... 180 C4 4
Long Border Rd RBSF CM22 .... 173 G4
Long Brandocks
  CHLM/WR CM1 .... 265 H4
Long Common MAL CM9 .... 259 H8 1
Longcroft FX IP11 .... 113 G9
  RBSF CM22 .... 173 L6
  SAFWN CB10 .... 66 A5
Long Cft STSD CM24 .... 143 M5
Longcroft Rd COLN CO4 .... 11 K5
Longfellow Rd MAL CM9 .... 271 J4
Long Fld FX IP11 .... 112 F1
Longfield WIT CM8 .... 210 A8 1
Longfield Rd CHLM/GWD CM2 .... 267 G6
  RIPS/CAP IP9 .... 77 J3
Longfields RCOS CO16 .... 248 D1
Long Gn BRTR CM7 .... 181 G6
Long Green La BRTR CM7 .... 149 L3
Longhedges SAFWS CB11 .... 63 G4 1
Long La BRTR CM7 .... 179 H5
  CBE/LIN CB1 .... 19 L4
  FOS CO13 .... 223 L2

SAFWS CB11 .... 61 H8
Longleaf Dr BRTR CM7 .... 180 B5
Longleat Cl CHLM/WR CM1 .... 254 B6
Long Meadow BRTR CM7 .... 179 K8
  BSF CM23 .... 170 F7
Long Mdw HAR CO12 .... 140 B3
Longmeads WIT CM8 .... 239 G8
Longmeads Cl CHLM/WR CM1 .... 265 H4
Longmore Av CHLM/GWD CM2 .... 267 G5
Long Pastures SUD CO10 .... 28 E2
Long Perry RIPS/CAP IP9 .... 77 K4
Longridge COLN CO4 .... 161 H5
Long Rd MGTR CO11 .... 135 L2
Long Rd East RCOLE CO7 .... 134 C2
Long Rd West RCOLE CO7 .... 134 A2
Longship Wy MAL CM9 .... 271 G6
Longshots Cl CHLM/WR CM1 .... 254 C4
Longs La RCHLM CM3 .... 235 H4
Longstomps Av
  CHLM/GWD CM2 .... 266 C7
Longstraw Cl COLW CO3 .... 158 F7
Long St IPNE IP4 .... 3 J7
Lonsdale CBE/LIN CB1 .... 20 A3
Lonsdale Cl IPNE IP4 .... 3 M2
Lonsdale Rd RCOS CO16 .... 194 C3
Looe Rd FX IP11 .... 113 L2
Loompits Wy SAFWS CB11 .... 62 E6
Lophams Cl HVHL CB9 .... 23 H4
Loraine Wy RIPW IP8 .... 30 C4
Lord Holland Rd COLS CO2 .... 188 B2
Lords Av BSF CM23 .... 170 D6
Lordship Rd CHLM/WR CM1 .... 265 K3
Lordsland La BRTR CM7 .... 153 L4
Lordswood Rd COLS CO2 .... 187 L3
Lordswood Vw GTDUN CM6 .... 230 F6
Lorkin's La HSTD CO9 .... 98 D2
Lorkin Wy RCOLW CO6 .... 159 H1
Lott's Rd RCOS CO16 .... 221 K1
Louise Rd WOTN CO14 .... 197 G2
Louse La RCOLE CO7 .... 134 A2
Louvain Rd HAR CO12 .... 140 C4
Love La RCOLE CO7 .... 219 G6
Lover's La RCOLE CO7 .... 192 C6
  RIPS/CAP IP9 .... 109 L1
Loves Wk CHLM/WR CM1 .... 265 K5
Lovetofts Dr IP IP1 .... 30 F3
Love Wy RCOS CO16 .... 221 L7
Lowe Cha WOTN CO14 .... 196 D4
Lowefields RCOLW CO6 .... 127 M8
Lower Anchor St
  CHLM/GWD CM2 .... 14 E5
Lower Barn Rd RIPW IP8 .... 52 C4
Lower Brook St IPNE IP4 .... 2 F6
Lower Dales View Rd IP IP1 .... 31 J5
Lower Downs Slade HVHL CB9 .... 23 J5
Lower Farm Rd COLN CO4 .... 103 K5
Lower Gn RCOLW CO6 .... 128 E4
Lower Harlings RIPS/CAP IP9 .... 111 J5
Lower Holt St RCOLW CO6 .... 127 L7
Lower Houses Rd RIPS/CAP IP9.. 109 M2
Lower King BRTR CM7 .... 180 F4
Lower Langley RCOLW CO6 .... 156 E4
Lower Marine Pde HAR CO12 .... 140 E3
Lower Ml GTDUN CM6 .... 176 A6
Lower Orwell St IPNE IP4 .... 3 G7
Lower Park Crs BSF CM23 .... 171 H8
Lower Park Rd RCOLE CO7 .... 219 G7
Lower Rd BURES CO8 .... 100 D8
  COLS CO2 .... 186 C8
  K/T/MI CO5 .... 214 B4
  K/T/MI CO5 .... 215 M8
  RBSF CM22 .... 199 L6
  SUD CO10 .... 28 D3
  SUD CO10 .... 49 K2
Lower St RCOLE CO7 .... 104 E4
  RIPS/CAP IP9 .... 108 C3
  RIPW IP8 .... 30 C6
  STSD CM24 .... 144 B6 1
  SUD CO10 .... 27 M3
Lowfield SBW CM21 .... 227 G4
Low Rd HAR CO12 .... 140 B4
Lowry Cl HVHL CB9 .... 22 F4
Lowry Gdns IPSE IP3 .... 55 L3 3
Luard Wy COLS CO2 .... 214 C2
  WIT CM8 .... 238 B4
Lubberhedges La GTDUN CM6 .... 148 F2
Lucas Av CHLM/GWD CM2 .... 266 E7
  RCOLW CO6 .... 129 M8
Lucas Rd COLS CO2 .... 10 D9
  SUD CO10 .... 4 F7
Lucas's La RCOS CO16 .... 165 M7
Lucerne Rd RCOLE CO7 .... 162 C7
Lucerne Wy CHLM/WR CM1 .... 265 K5 1
Luces La HSTD CO9 .... 96 B1 3
Luck's La RCHLM CM3 .... 234 B3
Lucy Cl COLW CO3 .... 158 E7
Lucy La North COLW CO3 .... 158 D6
Lucy La South COLW CO3 .... 158 D6
Ludgores La RCHLM CM3 .... 268 F8
Ludham Hall La BRTR CM7 .... 179 M6
Ludlow Cl IP IP1 .... 31 K1
Luff Wy FOS CO13 .... 196 B6
Lufkin Rd COLN CO4 .... 160 B2
Lugar Cl COLN CO4 .... 161 G7
Lukin's Dr GTDUN CM6.. .... 175 M6
Lulworth Av IPSE IP3 .... 55 M2
Lulworth Cl COS CO15 .... 249 L5 2
Lulworth Dr HVHL CB9 .... 23 G6
Lumber Leys RCOS CO13 .... 196 C6
Lummis V KESG IP5 .... 33 L6
Lundy Cl HVHL CB9 .... 23 M6
Lunnish Hl HAR CO12 .... 139 H2
Lupin Dr CHLM/WR CM1 .... 255 H7
Lupin Rd CHTY IP2 .... 54 A1
Lupin Wy RCOS CO16 .... 12 B3
Lushington Av FOS CO13 .... 195 M7
Lushington Rd MGTR CO11.. .... 135 L1
Luther Rd CHTY IP2 .... 2 D9
Lutus Cl SUD CO10 .... 26 C7
Luxford Pl SBW CM21 .... 227 H4
Lydgate Cl MGTR CO11 .... 135 K1
Lydia Dr RCOS CO16 .... 247 J3
Lymington Av COS CO15 .... 222 B5
Lyndhurst Av IPNE IP4 .... 32 E7
Lyndhurst Rd COS CO15 .... 250 E1
Lynmouth Av CHLM/GWD CM2 .... 15 J7

Lynmouth Gdns
  CHLM/GWD CM2 .... 15 J6
Lynne Cl FOS CO13 .... 195 M7
Lynn's Hall Cl SUD CO10 .... 51 H2
Lynton Cl HAR CO12 .... 8 E7
Lynton Dr CHLM/WR CM1 .... 255 G8
Lynwood Av FX IP11 .... 113 K2
Lyon Cl COS CO15 .... 13 K3
Lyons Hall Rd BRTR CM7 .... 152 F5
Lyster Av CHLM/GWD CM2 .... 267 J6

M

Mabbitt Wy COLN CO4 .... 132 D8 3
Maberly Ct SAFWN CB10 .... 62 F3 4
Mabey's Wk SBW CM21 .... 226 D4
Macaulay Rd IP IP1 .... 31 J2
Macbeth Cl COLN CO4 .... 161 H6
Mace Wk CHLM/WR CM1 .... 14 D1
Mackay Ct COLS CO2 .... 188 D3 1
Mackenzie Dr KESG IP5 .... 33 K5
Maclarens WIT CM8 .... 239 J7
Madeira Rd COS CO15 .... 222 F8
Madeline Pl CHLM/WR CM1 .... 254 A7
Madements Rd BRTR CM7 .... 153 L5
Magazine Farm Wy
  CO3 .... 159 J8 1
Magdalen Cl COS CO15 .... 12 E4
Magdalene Cl CHTY IP2 .... 54 B3
Magdalene Crs WIT CM8 .... 209 M2
Magdalen Gn GTDUN CM6 .... 119 J3
Magdalen Rd COS CO15 .... 12 E4
Magdalen St COL CO1 .... 10 F6
Maginley Crs KESG IP5 .... 33 H7 3
Magnaville Rd BSF CM23 .... 199 G1
Magnolia Cl CHLM/GWD CM2 .... 266 D7
  WIT CM8 .... 210 C8 4
Magnolia Dr COLN CO4 .... 161 H5
Magpie Cl RIPW IP8 .... 53 L3 4
Magwitch Cl CHLM/WR CM1 .... 254 B6
Maidenburgh St COL CO1 .... 10 D7 1
Maidenhall Ap CHTY IP2 .... 54 D3
Maidment Crs WIT CM8 .... 238 B5
Maidstone Rd FX IP11 .... 113 G2 6
Mailers La BSF CM23 .... 143 H3
Main Rd CHLM/WR CM1 .... 254 D4
  FOS CO13 .... 223 J2
  HAR CO12 .... 8 E8
  KESG IP5 .... 33 J5
  KIR/NAC IP10 .... 57 H4
  RCHLM CM3 .... 268 C6
  RCOLW CO6 .... 130 B1
  RIPS/CAP IP9 .... 80 C3
  RIPS/CAP IP9 .... 81 G6
Main St CBE/LIN CB1 .... 21 H7
Maitland St STSD CM24 .... 144 A7
Makemores BRTR CM7 .... 179 H3 2
Makins Rd HAR CO12 .... 8 A4
Maldon Ct SUD CO10 .... 5 J6
Maldon Rd COLS CO2 .... 186 C7
  COLW CO3 .... 159 L8
  K/T/MI CO5 .... 211 L4
  MAL CM9 .... 258 B5
  MAL CM9 .... 259 K1 1
  RCHLM CM3 .... 257 K1
  WIT CM8 .... 238 B8
Maldon Wy RCOS CO16 .... 249 K1
Malin Cl HVHL CB9 .... 23 M6
Mallard Cl BRTR CM7 .... 179 L8
  COLS CO2 .... 187 J8
  K/T/MI CO5 .... 211 L2 2
  MAL CM9 .... 262 F3
Mallard Rd CHLM/GWD CM2 .... 266 C8
Mallard Wy CHTY IP2 .... 54 A3
  SUD CO10 .... 50 E8
Mallowhayes Cl CHTY IP2 .... 54 D2 1
Mallows Fld HSTD CO9 .... 126 B4
Mallows Green Rd BSF CM23 .... 142 E3
Mallows La HSTD CO9 .... 94 B2
Malmesbury Cl CHTY IP2 .... 54 C3
Maltese Rd CHLM/WR CM1 .... 266 C1
Malthouse Rd MGTR CO11 .... 135 M1
Malting Farm La RCOLE CO7 .... 133 L3
Malting Green Rd COLS CO2 .... 187 H6
Malting La FOS CO13 .... 195 L4
  SUD CO10 .... 26 D6
Malting Rd COLS CO2 .... 187 L4
  K/T/MI CO5 .... 216 A6
Maltings Cl BURES CO8 .... 100 A4
Maltings Ct WIT CM8 .... 238 B5 2
Maltings La ROY SGB 59 G3
  WIT CM8 .... 238 B5
Maltings Rd CHLM/GWD CM2 .... 267 J8 1
  RCOLE CO7 .... 219 G5
The Maltings BRTR CM7 .... 179 J3
  GTDUN CM6 .... 119 J3
  GTDUN CM6 .... 175 M4
  HAR CO12 .... 139 G5
Maltings Vw BRTR CM7 .... 180 C2 2
Malting Yd RCOLE CO7 .... 189 K5 6
Maltings Park Rd RCOLW CO6 .... 159 H1
Malvern Cl IPSE IP3 .... 55 K1
  KESG IP5 .... 33 H4 2
Malvern Wy RCOLW CO6 .... 131 K6
Malyon Rd WIT CM8 .... 238 B5
Manchester Rd CHTY IP2 .... 53 M3
  COS CO15 .... 223 G7
Mandeville Rd RCOLW CO6 .... 185 G2
  SAFWS CB11 .... 62 F5
Mandeville Wy CHLM/WR CM1.. .... 254 D2
  FOS CO13 .... 196 B6
Mandy Cl IPNE IP4 .... 32 C7
Manfield Gdns RCOS CO16 .... 220 D8
Mangers La CBS CB2 .... 16 F4
Manning Rd FX IP11 .... 7 J5
Mannings Cl SAFWS CB11 .... 63 G6 3
Mannings La RIPS/CAP IP9 .... 80 C3
Mannington Rd IPNE IP4 .... 33 H5 5
Manningtree Rd RCOLE CO7 .... 105 J7
  RCOLE CO7 .... 164 B5
  RIPS/CAP IP9 .... 108 A3
Manor Cl RCOLW CO6 .... 131 L6
  SUD CO10 .... 27 L3 1
Manor Crs RCHLM CM3 .... 234 D8
Manor Dr CHLM/GWD CM2 .... 267 H6
Manor House Wy RCOLE CO7 .... 219 G6

Manor La HAR CO12 .... 140 C3
  RIPS/CAP IP9 .... 108 A3
  SAFWN CB10 .... 37 M3
Manor Links BSF CM23 .... 171 L6
Manor Rd BSF CM23 .... 171 J6
  CHLM/GWD CM2 .... 15 H6
  COLW CO3 .... 159 M6 1
  FOS CO13 .... 223 J2
  FX IP11 .... 7 G8
  FX IP11 .... 83 K7
  GTDUN CM6 .... 147 H8
  HAR CO12 .... 8 D9
  HLWE CM17 .... 226 E8
  HVHL CB9 .... 23 K6
  IPNE IP4 .... 3 G1
  RCHLM CM3 .... 257 L4
  RCOLE CO7 .... 189 L4
  RCOLW CO6 .... 131 G8
  STSD CM24 .... 144 A8
  SUD CO10 .... 4 D2
  SUD CO10 .... 238 C1 3
Manor St BRTR CM7 .... 180 B2
Manors Wy WIT CM8 .... 209 L1
Manor Ter FX IP11 .... 113 G7
Manor Wy COS CO15 .... 223 J7
Manse Cha MAL CM9 .... 271 J4
Mansfield Av IP IP1 .... 31 H3 1
Mansfield SBW CM21 .... 226 C4
Mansfields CHLM/WR CM1 .... 265 H4 1
Manston Dr BSF CM23 .... 171 K4
Manwick Rd FX IP11 .... 7 H6
Maple Av BRTR CM7 .... 179 M3
  BSF CM23 .... 170 F5
  MAL CM9 .... 259 L7
Maple Cl BSF CM23 .... 170 F5
  CBE/LIN CB1 .... 19 K2
  CHTY IP2 .... 54 C2
  COS CO15 .... 12 A5
  HAR CO12 .... 8 F8
  HSTD CO9 .... 126 C3
Maple Dr CHLM/GWD CM2 .... 266 D7
  FOS CO13 .... 195 M7
  WIT CM8 .... 210 C8 5
Maple Gv BSF CM23 .... 170 F5
Maple Hl SUD CO10 .... 25 M3
Maple Leaf K/T/MI CO5 .... 212 E6
Maple Rd SUD CO10 .... 50 D8
Maple Spring BSF CM23 .... 170 E5
The Maples KESG IP5 .... 33 G5
Maple Wy COLS CO2 .... 188 C1 2
Marasca End COLS CO2 .... 188 D6 2
Maraschino Cl COLS CO2 .... 188 C6 1
Marauder Wy RCOLW CO6 .... 155 H3
March Rd SUD CO10 .... 26 D4
Marconi Rd CHLM/WR CM1 .... 15 G1
Marcus Cl COLN CO4 .... 132 D7
  HVHL CB9 .... 23 M6 3
Marcus Rd FX IP11 .... 113 M2
Marennes Crs RCOLE CO7 .... 219 G6
Mareth Rd COLS CO2 .... 187 L3
Margaret Rd COL CO1 .... 10 B4
Margaret St FX IP11 .... 113 G2
Margaretting Rd
  CHLM/WR CM1 .... 265 J5
Margaret Wy SAFWN CB10 .... 62 F4 5
Margate Rd IPSE IP3 .... 55 L7
Marguerite Wy BSF CM23 .... 170 E7
Maria St HAR CO12 .... 9 K4
Marigold Av CHTY IP2 .... 54 A2
  COLN CO4 .... 161 G6
Marigold Cl CHLM/WR CM1 .... 255 H7
Marina Gdns COS CO15 .... 222 E8
  FX IP11 .... 7 H5
Marina Ms WOTN CO14 .... 196 E5
Marina Rd RCHLM CM3 .... 257 J1
Marine Pde HAR CO12 .... 9 J8
Marine Pde East COS CO15 .... 13 G8
Mariners Wy MAL CM9 .... 271 J5
Marion Av RCOS CO16 .... 222 A7
Maritime Av MAL CM9 .... 272 A2 1
Markby Cl CBS CB2 .... 16 F5
Market Cl COLW CO3 .... 10 B5
Market End RCOLW CO6 .... 183 H3
Market Gv HSTD CO9 .... 70 B4
Market Hl HVHL CB9 .... 23 J5
  MAL CM9 .... 271 J2
  RCOLW CO6 .... 183 J3 1
  SUD CO10 .... 4 D6
Market La CBE/LIN CB1 .... 19 K3
Market Pl BRTR CM7 .... 180 B2 4
  GTDUN CM6 .... 175 M4 2
Market Rd CHLM/WR CM1 .... 15 G3
  IP IP1 .... 2 D6
Market Rw SAFWN CB10 .... 62 F4
Market Sq BSF CM23 .... 171 H6
Market St BSF CM23 .... 171 H6 3
  HAR CO12 .... 9 L3
  SAFWN CB10 .... 62 F3
Markhams Cl HVHL CB9 .... 23 H4 5
Marking's Fld SAFWN CB10 .... 63 G3 2
Markland Rd DMAL CM9 .... 271 G4 2
Marks Gdns BRTR CM7 .... 180 E2
Marks Hall Rd RCOLW CO6 .... 155 H6
Markwells RBSF CM22 .... 144 F3
Marlborough Cl BSF CM23 .... 171 H8
  COS CO15 .... 12 B6
Marlborough Dr SUD CO10 .... 4 F5
Marlborough Rd BRTR CM7 .... 180 C1
  CHLM/GWD CM2 .... 14 F7
  IPNE IP4 .... 3 M6
Marlowe Cl BRTR CM7 .... 180 C6 3
  MAL CM9 .... 271 J5
Marlowe Rd COS CO15 .... 249 J4
Marlowe Wy COLW CO3 .... 159 H6
Marlow Rd IP IP1 .... 30 F4
Marne Rd COLS CO2 .... 188 A1
Marney Cl CHLM/GWD CM2 .... 267 G5 1
Marney Wy FOS CO13 .... 196 D7
Marquis Cl BSF CM23 .... 170 D6
Marram Cl COLW CO3 .... 158 D7
Marshall Cl K/T/MI CO5 .... 211 M1 1
  KESG IP5 .... 33 L5 1
Marshalls Piece GTDUN CM6 .... 148 F7
Marshalls Rd BRTR CM7 .... 180 A4

Marshbarns BSF CM23 .... 170 E5
Marsh Crs K/T/MI CO5 .... 189 H5
Marsh Farm La RCOLE CO7 .... 219 M3
Marsh La HLWE CM17 .... 227 G6
Marsh Rd RCOLW CO6 .... 104 B1
Marsh Wy RCOLE CO7 .... 219 G7
Marshy La K/T/MI CO5 .... 189 H6 2
Marston Beck CHLM/GWD CM2 .... 267 J3
Martello La FX IP11 .... 113 M2
Martello Rd WOTN CO14 .... 196 E5
Martens Meadow BRTR CM7 .... 180 F2
Martin End COLS CO2 .... 187 J8
Martingale Dr CHLM/WR CM1 .... 255 H6
Martin Rd CHTY IP2 .... 2 E9
Martin's Rd HSTD CO9 .... 126 A4 3
  SUD CO10 .... 5 K3
Martyns Ri SUD CO10 .... 29 L8
Maryborough Gv COLS CO2 .... 188 D3
Mary La North RCOLE CO7 .... 163 H5
Mary La South RCOLE CO7 .... 163 K6
Mary Mcarthur Pl
  STSD CM24 .... 144 A5 4
Maryon Rd IPSE IP3 .... 55 K5
Mary Park Gdns BSF CM23 .... 199 H1
Mary Warner Rd RCOLE CO7 .... 134 A6
Mascalls Wy CHLM/GWD CM2 .... 267 G6
Masefield Dr COLW CO3 .... 159 H7
Masefield Rd BRTR CM7 .... 180 B5
  MAL CM9 .... 271 J4
Mashay Rd HSTD CO9 .... 70 F1
Mashbury Rd RCHLM CM3 .... 233 H6
Mason Cl COLS CO2 .... 187 K2
Mason Rd COL CO1 .... 10 C3
  RCOS CO16 .... 249 K2
Masons Ct BSF CM23 .... 171 J6
Matching La BSF CM23 .... 170 F5
Matching Rd RBSF CM22 .... 228 D4
Matfield Cl CHLM/WR CM1 .... 254 F6 4
Mathams Dr BSF CM23 .... 170 F8
Mather Wy CHTY IP2 .... 3 G9
Mathews Cl HSTD CO9 .... 126 C2 1
  RCOLE CO7 .... 104 E4
Matlock Cl IPSE IP3 .... 53 L3 5
Matson Rd IP IP1 .... 31 H5 2
Maudlyn Rd COL CO1 .... 11 K9
Maudslay Rd IP IP1 .... 30 E3
Mayberry Wk COLS CO2 .... 188 C2
Maybury Cl RCOLW CO6 .... 185 H2 3
  SS CO15 .... 55 K4
Maybush La FX IP11 .... 113 L4
Maycroft Cl IP IP1 .... 31 J1
Mayda Cl HSTD CO9 .... 125 M4
Mayes Cl BSF CM23 .... 171 M5
Mayes La CHLM/GWD CM2 .... 268 A7
  HAR CO12 .... 139 K4
  RCHLM CM3 .... 269 G7
Mayes Pl GTDUN CM6 .... 119 J7
Mayfield Cl COS CO15 .... 11 J2
Mayfield Pk BSF CM23 .... 198 F2 1
Mayfield Rd CHLM/WR CM1 .... 265 J3
  IPNE IP4 .... 32 E6
Mayflower Av HAR CO12 .... 9 L5
Mayflower Dr MAL CM9 .... 271 J6
Mayflower Gdns BSF CM23 .... 170 D7
Mayflower Wy SUD CO10 .... 4 E1
Mayford Wy RCOS CO16 .... 221 K7
Mayland Cl MAL CM9 .... 271 M1
Mayland Rd WIT CM8 .... 238 C3 5
Maylands Dr RCOS CO16 .... 221 K7
Maylins Dr SBW CM21 .... 226 F3
Maynard Cl GTDUN CM6 .... 175 M4 3
Mayne Crest CHLM/WR CM1 .... 255 H6
Maypole Dr RCOS CO16 .... 248 C1
Maypole Green Rd COLS CO2 .... 187 L4
Maypole Rd K/T/MI CO5 .... 212 E7
  MAL CM9 .... 259 H4
  WIT CM8 .... 239 H8
The Maypole GTDUN CM6 .... 119 H2
May Rd IPSE IP3 .... 55 L3
Maysent Av BRTR CM7 .... 152 B8
May's La RCOLE CO7 .... 134 A1
May St ROY SGB 59 G3
May Wk CHLM/GWD CM2 .... 266 E6 1
  STSD CM24 .... 144 C4
Maze Green Hts BSF CM23 .... 170 E6
Maze Green Rd BSF CM23 .... 170 F6
Mazeo Cl BSF CM23 .... 171 H8
Mazoe Rd BSF CM23 .... 171 H8
Meadgate Av CHLM/GWD CM2 .... 15 L8
Meadow Cl BRTR CM7 .... 151 J6
  COS CO15 .... 222 D6
  FX IP11 .... 83 K5
  HSTD CO9 .... 126 B5
  RCOLE CO7 .... 163 J7
Meadowcroft STSD CM24 .... 144 A6 2
Meadowcroft Wy FOS CO13 .... 196 B6
Meadoword SAFWS CB11 .... 87 H4
Meadow Grass Cl COLW CO3 .... 158 D7 1
Meadowlands BSF CM23 .... 171 J4
  KIR/NAC IP10 .... 83 K2
Meadow La CBE/LIN CB1 .... 19 K3
  K/T/MI CO5 .... 244 D7
  SUD CO10 .... 4 D7
Meadow Rd COLS CO2 .... 187 M4
  SAFWN CB10 .... 37 M2
Meadows Cl RCOLE CO7 .... 162 B7
Meadows Rd RCHLM CM3 .... 269 J7
Meadowside BRTR CM7 .... 152 A8
  CHLM/GWD CM2 .... 15 K2
Meadow Side CHLM/WR CM1 .... 15 G1
Meadowside Gdns IPNE IP4 .... 33 G5
The Meadows BSF CM23 .... 171 G8
  SBW CM21 .... 227 J3
Meadowsweet Cl BSF CM23 .... 170 E7 1
  HVHL CB9 .... 23 G4 3
Meadowvale Cl IPNE IP4 .... 3 M2
Meadow View Cl COLW CO3 .... 159 G8
Meadow View Rd SUD CO10 .... 4 A9
Meadow Wy BRTR CM7 .... 180 E8
  COS CO15 .... 249 H6
  K/T/MI CO5 .... 216 D3
  SBW CM21 .... 227 J4

Mead Pastures MAL CM9 .... 269 M2
Mead Pth CHLM/GWD CM2 .... 14 D8
The Mead GTDUN CM6 .... 119 J2
  GTDUN CM6 .... 175 L3
  SUD CO10 .... 74 D1
Mead Vw BUNT SGB 114 A7
Meadway HSTD CO9 .... 125 G5
  MAL CM9 .... 271 K4
  MGTR CO11 .... 135 J2
Mearns Pl CHLM/GWD CM2 .... 267 H1
Mede Wy RCOLE CO7 .... 189 L2
Medlars Md RBSF CM22 .... 201 H8
Medley Rd BRTR CM7 .... 179 H3
Medway Av WIT CM8 .... 237 M3
Medway Cl CHLM/WR CM1 .... 265 M1
Medway Rd IPSE IP3 .... 55 H3
Meekings Rd SUD CO10 .... 5 J5
The Meers FOS CO13 .... 196 A7
Meeson Mdw MAL CM9 .... 271 G5
Meeting Fld SUD CO10 .... 29 L6
Meeting La HSTD CO9 .... 45 K6
  K/T/MI CO5 .... 245 L3
Megs Wy BRTR CM7 .... 180 D4
Melba Ct CHLM/WR CM1 .... 265 L4
Melbourne Av CHLM/WR CM1 .... 253 M8
Melbourne Cha COLS CO2 .... 188 C4
Melbourne Rd COS CO15 .... 12 D4
  IPNE IP4 .... 32 F6
Melford Cl FX IP11 .... 33 H8
Melford Rd SUD CO10 .... 28 A3
  SUD CO10 .... 49 L3
Melford Wy FX IP11 .... 6 D4
Mellis Cl HVHL CB9 .... 23 H4
Mellis St FX IP11 .... 112 F2
Mellor Cha COS CO15 .... 159 G6
Mell Rd MAL CM9 .... 263 G5
Melplash Cl IPSE IP3 .... 56 A1 2
Melplash Rd IPSE IP3 .... 56 A1
Melrose Gdns COS CO15 .... 222 B8
  IPNE IP4 .... 32 D5
Melrose Rd K/T/MI CO5 .... 244 D7
Melton Cl RCOS CO16 .... 249 J1
Melville Rd IPNE IP4 .... 3 L6
Memory Cl MAL CM9 .... 271 J6 1
Mendip Dr KESG IP5 .... 33 H7
Mendip Rd CHLM/WR CM1 .... 253 M7
Mendlesham Rd RCOS CO16 .... 249 K1
Menin Rd COLS CO2 .... 187 M1
Meon Cl CHLM/WR CM1 .... 254 F7
Mercers Av BSF CM23 .... 198 D1
Mercers Wy COL CO1 .... 10 B4
Mercia Cl CHLM/GWD CM2 .... 267 J3
Meredith Rd COS CO15 .... 12 E6
  IP IP1 .... 31 G3
Merefield SBW CM21 .... 227 G4 2
Meres Cl WIT CM8 .... 238 A4
Merivale Cl MGTR CO11 .... 135 K2
Merivale Rd MGTR CO11 .... 135 K2
Merlin End COLN CO4 .... 161 H4
Merlin Pl CHLM/WR CM1 .... 254 B8 3
Merlin Rd CHTY IP2 .... 53 L2
Mermaid Wy MAL CM9 .... 271 K5 3
Merriam Cl MGTR CO11 .... 106 F5
Merrilees Cr COS CO15 .... 222 F7
Merrion Cl RIPW IP8 .... 53 L3 6
Merrymount Gdns COS CO15 .... 13 M1
Mersea Av K/T/MI CO5 .... 244 D7
Mersea Rd COLS CO2 .... 188 C4
  K/T/MI CO5 .... 216 A8
Mersea Vw RCOS CO16 .... 247 J2
Mersey Rd IPSE IP3 .... 55 H2
  WIT CM8 .... 238 A2
Merstham Dr RCOS CO16 .... 221 L7
Merton Ct COLS CO2 .... 188 C6 2
Messines Rd COLS CO2 .... 187 M1
Meteor Wy CHLM/WR CM1 .... 14 D4
Mews Ct CHLM/GWD CM2 .... 15 G6
The Mews SBW CM21 .... 227 G2 1
Meyrick Crs COLS CO2 .... 160 B8
Micawber Wy CHLM/WR CM1 .... 253 M6
Michaelstowe Cl HAR CO12 .... 139 L3
Michaelstowe Dr HAR CO12 .... 139 L3
Michigan Cl KESG IP5 .... 33 K6
Mickfield Ms FX IP11 .... 112 F2 8
Micklegate Rd FX IP11 .... 7 H6
Middleborough COLW CO3 .... 10 A5
Middlefield HSTD CO9 .... 126 B4
Middlefield Rd MGTR CO11 .... 136 C2
Middle Gn RCOLW CO6 .... 128 E4
Middle King BRTR CM7 .... 180 F4
Middle Mill Rd COL CO1 .... 10 C5
Middle Rw BSF CM23 .... 171 H7
Middle St SAFWS CB11 .... 114 E1
Middleton Cl CHTY IP2 .... 53 M3
  RCOS CO16 .... 221 M7
Middleton Rd SUD CO10 .... 4 A9
Middle Wy SUD CO10 .... 29 M5
Middlewick Cl COLS CO2 .... 188 C4 5
Midguard Wy MAL CM9 .... 271 G6
Midland Cl COLS CO2 .... 188 B1
Midway COS CO15 .... 249 G7
Midway Rd COLS CO2 .... 187 L3
Milburn Crs CHLM/WR CM1 .... 265 M4
Milch La RCHLM CM3 .... 179 G8
Milden Rd CHTY IP2 .... 31 G8
Mildmay Rd CHLM/GWD CM2 .... 15 H7
  IPSE IP3 .... 55 J4
Mildmays RCHLM CM3 .... 268 E5
Mile End Rd COLN CO4 .... 160 A2
Miles Cl COLW CO3 .... 158 E7
Milford Cl RCOLE CO7 .... 189 L4
Military Rd COL CO1 .... 10 E7
The Millars CHLM/WR CM1 .... 254 C2 1
Millbridge Rd WIT CM8 .... 238 B3
Mill Cswy ROY SGB 35 L8
Mill Cha HSTD CO9 .... 126 A3 3
  HVHL CB9 .... 43 L8
Mill Cl BRTR CM7 .... 121 K3
  CHLM/WR CM1 .... 252 C8
  FX IP11 .... 6 F2
  FX IP11 .... 83 K5
  K/T/MI CO5 .... 212 E7
  RBSF CM22 .... 144 E4
  RIPS/CAP IP9 .... 77 G4
Mill Ct GTDUN CM6 .... 174 D6
Millcroft BSF CM23 .... 171 J4
Mill End GTDUN CM6 .... 119 J3

Millennium Wy BRTR CM7....180 E4
Miller's Barn Rd COS CO15....249 J4
Millers Cl BRTR CM7....152 C5
  BSF CM23....170 EB
  CBE/LIN CB1....19 M2
  COLW CO3....158 E7
  GTDUN CM6....204 C1 2
  RCOLW CO6....131 K6
Millers La COLS CO2....158 F7
Millers Md K/T/MI CO5....212 A1
Millers Rw BRTR CM7....67 L7
Mill Fld GTDUN CM6....204 C1
  RIPW IP8....30 D3
Millfield Gdns IPNE IP4....32 C7
Millfields CHLM/WR CM1....265 J4
Mill Flds RCHLM CM3....269 J7
Millfields SBW CM21....227 F8
  STSD CM24....144 A7 1
Millfields Wy HVHL CB9....23 K5
Mill HI BRTR CM7....180 D3
  BSF CM23....143 G8
  HVHL CB9....23 H6
  MGTR CO11....134 F1
  MGTR CO11....135 L1
  RCOLW CO6....101 G7
  RIPS/CAP IP9....77 G4
  STSD CM24....143 M7
  SUD CO10....4 B7
Milliners Wy BSF CM23....198 E1
Mill La BRTR CM7....93 H2
  BRTR CM7....179 G5
  BRTR CM7....180 F7
  BUNT SG9....84 C8
  CBE/LIN CB1....19 L3
  CBS CB2....17 G4
  CHLM/WR CM1....254 C4
  COLS CO2....187 K8
  COLS CO2....214 B2
  FOS CO13....223 G2
  FX IP11....7 H3
  FX IP11....83 J5
  GTDUN CM6....148 F8
  GTDUN CM6....175 M5
  HAR CO12....9 J7
  HSTD CO9....70 C2
  HSTD CO9....97 G5
  HSTD CO9....98 C6
  K/T/MI CO5....184 B3
  MAL CM9....242 D5
  MAL CM9....261 G2
  MAL CM9....271 J4
  MGTR CO11....135 M1
  MGTR CO11....136 F4
  RBSF CM22....228 B1
  RCHLM CM3....205 M6
  RCHLM CM3....207 K6
  RCHLM CM3....236 C2
  RCOLE CO7....105 H6
  RCOLE CO7....162 D1
  RCOLW CO6....127 J4
  RCOS CO16....193 H7
  RCOS CO16....194 B4
  RIPW IP8....30 D4
  RIPW IP8....53 H4
  SAFWN CB10....17 J6
  SAFWN CB10....37 K1
  SAFWN CB10....63 G3
  SAFWS CB11....62 B2
  SBW CM21....227 H2
  SUD CO10....4 B2
  SUD CO10....27 K5
  WIT CM8....238 B3
  WOTN CO14....196 E4
Mill Lane Cl RCOS CO16....193 J7
Mill Park Dr BRTR CM7....180 D4
Mill Piece KIR/NAC IP10....56 D7
Mill Ri RIPS/CAP IP9....79 M8
Mill Rd BRTR CM7....92 F8
  BRTR CM7....121 K3
  CHLM/WR CM1....231 M8
  COLN CO4....132 B1
  COLN CO4....132 C7
  COLN CO4....160 A1
  GTDUN CM6....177 J8
  GTDUN CM6....205 J2
  HSTD CO9....45 G3
  HSTD CO9....68 E2
  HVHL CB9....23 J6
  HVHL CB9....24 C3
  HVHL CB9....42 E5
  IPSE IP3....56 B4
  K/T/MI CO5....244 E5
  MAL CM9....239 M6
  MAL CM9....271 K4
  RBSF CM22....145 G1
  RCOLE CO7....106 A2
  RCOLW CO6....157 M1
  SAFWN CB10....89 J3
  SAFWS CB11....88 C5
  SUD CO10....26 E6
  SUD CO10....28 EB
Mill Side STSD CM24....143 M7
Mills La SUD CO10....49 L1
Millson Bank
  CHLM/GWD CM2....267 J1 3
Mills Rd SUD CO10....5 H5
The Mills IPNE IP4....33 G6
Mill St BSF CM23....171 J8
  COLS CO2....10 E9
  RCOLE CO7....219 J7
  RCOLW CO6....102 C4
  RCOS CO16....248 B1
Mill Tye SUD CO10....74 C1
Mill Vue Rd CHLM/GWD CM2....267 G3
Mill Wk K/T/MI CO5....212 E7 4
Millways MAL CM9....259 K1
Millwrights K/T/MI CO5....212 E7
Milner Rd SUD CO10....5 K4
Milner St IPNE IP4....3 J6
Milnrow RIPW IP8....53 L3
Milton Av BRTR CM7....180 C6
Milton Cl COLW CO3....159 H7
Milton Pl CHLM/WR CM1....254 B8
Milton Rd HAR CO12....9 J7
  MAL CM9....271 J3
  MGTR CO11....135 K3

WIT CM8....210 B8 1
Milton St IPNE IP4....32 C6
Mimosa Cl CHLM/WR CM1....255 H7
Minden Rd SUD CO10....4 E6
Minerva Cl HAR CO12....140 B3
  HVHL CB9....23 M7
Minsmere Dr RCOS CO16....221 L7 5
Minsmere Wy SUD CO10....5 L9
Minster Rd HVHL CB9....23 H4
Minster Wy MAL CM9....271 K5
Mirosa Dr MAL CM9....271 K5
Mirosa Reach MAL CM9....271 J5
Mission La RCOLE CO7....106 D2
Mitchell Av HSTD CO9....126 A4
Mitchell Cir BRTR CM7....93 L7
Mitford Cl IP IP1....31 J1
Mitre Gdns BSF CM23....199 J1 1
Mitton V CHLM/WR CM1....267 H3 4
Moat Farm Cha WIT CM8....238 B2
Moat Farm Cl IPNE IP4....3 L1
Moat Flds RCOLW CO6....129 M7
Moat La BURES CO8....99 J1
Moat Rd HSTD CO9....44 E6
  RCOLW CO6....129 M7
Modlen Rd WOTN CO14....196 O6
Moffat Av IPNE IP4....32 D4
Mole Hall La SAFWS CB11....117 H4
Molehill Green Rbt RBSF CM22....145 L8
Molrams La CHLM/GWD CM2....267 K7
Moneypiece Cl HVHL CB9....23 H4 6
Monkdowns Rd RCOLW CO6....183 K2
Monklands Ct HSTD CO9....125 M4 3
Monks Cl FX IP11....113 M1
Monks Ct WIT CM8....238 A2 4
Monks HI SAFWS CB11....63 H5
Monk's La RCOLE CO7....133 M1
Monks Lodge Rd HSTD CO9....96 F2
Monks Rd RCOLW CO6....127 K6
Monks Wk MAL CM9....263 G5
Monkswood Dr BSF CM23....170 F7
Monkwick Av COLS CO2....188 C4
Monmouth Cl CHTY IP2....54 D4
Mons Rd COLS CO2....187 M1
Montague Rd FX IP11....7 M2
Montana Rd KESG IP5....33 J6
Montbretia Cl COLW CO3....158 F7
Montgomery Cl
  CHLM/WR CM1....255 G6 2
  COLS CO2....188 D1
Montgomery Rd CHTY IP2....54 D4
Monton Ri CHTY IP2....53 M3
Montrose Rd CHLM/GWD CM2....267 H1
Monument Farm Rd
  KIR/NAC IP10....56 E1
Moon Hall La HVHL CB9....23 H8
Moore Rd IP IP1....31 H2
Moorfield Cl KESG IP5....33 L6 4
Moorfield Rd CBS CB2....16 F3
Moorhouse Gn RCOLE CO7....134 A5
The Moorings BSF CM23....171 J7
Moor Pasture Wy HVHL CB9....23 K1
Moor Rd COLN CO4....132 F2
  RCOLW CO6....156 E5
Moors Cl RCOLE CO7....192 A4
Moor's Farm Cha MAL CM9....260 C2
Moorsfield SUD CO10....74 D1 1
Moorside COL CO1....11 H7
Moor's La BRTR CM7....178 F2
  GTDUN CM6....176 F6 1
Mope La WIT CM8....238 F8
Moran Av CHLM/WR CM1....254 D6
Morant Rd COL CO1....160 D8
Morebarn Rd RCOLE CO7....163 G3
Morella Cl RCOLW CO6....192 A6
Morello Ct COLS CO2....188 A6
Morland Rd IPSE IP3....55 H5
Morley Rd HSTD CO9....126 B3 2
  K/T/MI CO5....240 F1
Morleys Rd RCOLW CO6....127 J7
Mornington Av IP IP1....31 H4
Morris Av COS CO15....249 G7
Morris Harp SAFWN CB10....63 G2
Morris Rd CHLM/GWD CM2....15 M4
Morrow La RCOLE CO7....134 C7
Mors End RCOLE CO7....104 F3
Morses La RCOLE CO7....219 H5
Morston Hall Rd FX IP11....83 G4
Morten Rd COL CO1....10 A3
Mortimer Pl SUD CO10....26 D4
Mortimer Rd RCHLM CM3....257 J1
Morton Rd MAL CM9....259 J1
Morton Wy HSTD CO9....126 C2
Mossfield Cl COLW CO3....159 L7
Moss La NHMKT IP6....32 B1
Moss Rd COL CO1....187 G1
  WIT CM8....238 D2
Moss Wy RCOLW CO6....159 G2
Mottram Cl RIPW IP8....53 L3 7
Motts Cl BRTR CM7....180 A1
Mott's La RCOLW CO6....184 F1
  WIT CM8....238 C1
Motts Yd GTDUN CM6....149 G8
Moules La CBE/LIN CB1....19 L7
Moulsham Cha CHLM/GWD CM2....15 K8
Moulsham Dr CHLM/GWD CM2....15 J8
Moulsham Hall La RCHLM CM3....207 G2
Moulsham St CHLM/GWD CM2....14 F8
Moulsham Thrift
  CHLM/GWD CM2....266 C7
Mountain Ash Cl COLN CO4....11 K1
Mountain's Farm Rd
  GTDUN CM6....203 L1
Mountains Rd MAL CM9....239 K7
Mountbatten Cl SUD CO10....4 F1
Mountbatten Dr COLS CO2....188 D2
Mountbatten Rd BRTR CM7....180 D1
  SUD CO10....4 F1
Mountbatten Wy
  CHLM/WR CM1....254 F6
Mount Dr IPSE IP3....56 B4
  STSD CM24....144 A8
Mountfitchet Rd STSD CM24....144 A8
Mount HI HSTD CO9....125 M4
Mounthill Av CHLM/WR CM1....15 M1
Mount Lodge Cha MAL CM9....239 M7
Mount Pleasant HSTD CO9....126 A4
  MAL CM9....271 H3

Mount Pleasant Est MAL CM9....240 A7
Mount Pleasant Rd SAFWS CB11....62 F5
Mount Ri COS CO15....125 M4 4
Mount Rd BRTR CM7....180 C2
  HVHL CB9....23 K3
  RCOLW CO6....183 K3
The Mount COLW CO3....159 H7
  MAL CM9....262 F4
  ROY SG8....58 A4
Mountview Rd COS CO15....13 K1
Moverons La RCOLE CO7....218 D3
Mowlands RIPS/CAP IP9....77 K4
Moy Rd COLS CO2....188 C4
Mulberry Av COLS CO2....188 C1
Mulberry Ct BSF CM23....171 J8
Mulberry Gdns WIT CM8....238 D1 3
Mulberry Wy CHLM/WR CM1....254 F8
Mullins Rd BRTR CM7....152 B7
Mullon Lea CHLM/WR CM1....255 J6
Mumford Cl RCOLE CO7....158 F1
  RCOLW CO6....158 F2
Mumford Rd IP IP1....31 G5
Mumfords La FOS CO13....195 J6
Mundon Rd BRTR CM7....180 F5
  MAL CM9....271 J4
Munnings Cl HVHL CB9....22 F4
  IPSE IP3....55 K5 1
Munnings Dr RCOS CO16....221 M7
Munnings Rd COLW CO3....159 J8
Munnings Wy MGTR CO11....106 D8
Munro Rd WIT CM8....210 B8
Murchison Cl CHLM/WR CM1....254 A8
Murray Cl BRTR CM7....152 A7
Murray Rd IPSE IP3....55 J2
Murrell Lock CHLM/GWD CM2....267 J1
Murrills Rd IPSE IP3....56 B4
Murton Slade HVHL CB9....23 J5 2
Muscade Cl K/T/MI CO5....212 F7 4
Museum St COL CO1....10 D6 2
  IP IP1....2 E5
  SAFWN CB10....62 F3 5
Musgrave Cl HAR CO12....140 B4 1
Musk Cl COLS CO2....158 F6
Mutlow Hill London Rd
  SAFWS CB11....62 B8
Mychett Cl RCOS CO16....221 K7 4
Myland Hall Cha COLN CO4....160 E2
Myneer Pk RCOLW CO6....183 K3 1
Myrtle Gv COLS CO2....160 D8
Myrtle Rd IPSE IP3....3 K9

N

Nabbott Rd CHLM/WR CM1....14 A3
Nacton Crs IPSE IP3....55 K3
Nacton Rd FX IP11....7 G7
  IPSE IP3....3 M9
  KIR/NAC IP10....56 A6
Nails La BSF CM23....171 H6 4
Nalla Gdns CHLM/WR CM1....254 C7
Nancy Smith Cl COLS CO2....160 B8
Nansen Rd COS CO15....222 F7
  IPSE IP3....55 K3
Napier Av COS CO15....248 F7
Narvik Cl MAL CM9....271 J6
Nash Cl COLW CO3....159 K8
  MGTR CO11....106 D8
Nash Dr CHLM/WR CM1....254 C2
Nassau Rd IPSE IP3....55 J3
Nathan Ct COLS CO2....188 D5
Nathan's La CHLM/WR CM1....264 F8
Nats La SAFWS CB11....62 A7
Navarre St IP IP1....2 F4
Navigation Rd CHLM/GWD CM2....15 K3
Nayland Dr RCOS CO16....249 K1
Nayland Rd BURES CO8....100 B5
  COLN CO4....131 M8
  FX IP11....6 D3
  HVHL CB9....23 G7
  RCOLW CO6....102 B4
  RCOLW CO6....130 F7
  RCOLW CO6....131 K5
Nayling Rd BRTR CM7....179 L3
Naze Park Rd WOTN CO14....196 F3
Neale St IP IP1....2 F4
Neasden Av COS CO15....12 C1
Neath Dr CHTY IP2....54 C4
Nelson Crs MAL CM9....271 K5 4
Nelson Gdns BRTR CM7....180 E1
Nelson Gv CHLM/WR CM1....14 D2
Nelson Rd BSF CM23....171 J8
  COLW CO3....159 G6
  COS CO15....12 E9
  HAR CO12....9 H7
  IPNE IP4....32 C6
  SUD CO10....5 H2
Nelson St RCOLE CO7....219 G8
Ness Rd RIPS/CAP IP9....110 C4
Ness Wk WIT CM8....237 M3
Nether Ct HSTD CO9....126 C4
Nethergate St SUD CO10....26 D7
Nether HI HSTD CO9....71 M2
Nether Rd SUD CO10....27 L3
Netley Cl CHTY IP2....54 B5
Neville Rd SAFWN CB10....63 G3
Newark Cl FX IP11....6 C1
New Barn La RBSF CM22....199 L4
Newbarn Rd RCOLW CO6....156 D4
Newbiggen St GTDUN CM6....119 H2
Newbourne Gdns FX IP11....30 F7
Newbourne Rd KIR/NAC IP10....57 K1
New Bowers Wy
  CHLM/WR CM1....255 H7
Newbridge HI RCOLW CO6....158 F3
Newbridge Rd K/T/MI CO5....213 H8
Newbury Rd BSF CM23....171 G6
Newbury Rd IPNE IP4....32 D8
Newby Dr IPNE IP4....33 H8
New Captains Rd K/T/MI CO5....244 D7
Newcastle Av COLW CO3....187 G1
New Church Rd RCOLW CO6....158 F1
Newcomen Wy COLN CO4....132 D7
Newcourt Rd CHLM/GWD CM2....15 M1

Newcroft SAFWN CB10....63 G4 2
New Cut BURES CO8....100 A5
  COLS CO2....187 H8
  RCOLE CO7....192 A5 2
  SUD CO10....28 D2
New Cut West CHTY IP2....3 G8
New Dukes Wy
  CHLM/GWD CM2....267 H1
New Farm Rd COLW CO3....158 F7
Newgate St WOTN CO14....196 E5 5
New House La SAFWN CB10....64 C2
Newhouse Rd RCOLW CO6....155 H1
Newington Gdns COS CO15....222 B5
New Kiln Rd COLW CO3....159 L6
Newland Av BRTR CM7....121 K4 1
Newland Pl WIT CM8....238 C4
Newlands Dr WIT CM8....238 B3
Newlands La RCOLW CO6....102 D4
Newland St WIT CM8....238 C3
New La K/T/MI CO5....184 B8
New Lodge Cha RCHLM CM3....268 D2
New London Rd
  CHLM/GWD CM2....14 E8 1
Newman's Rd SUD CO10....4 D5
Newmarket Rd SAFWN CB10....37 L2
New Meadgate Ter
  CHLM/GWD CM2....15 L7
Newmill La MGTR CO11....107 J4
New Nabbotts Wy
  CHLM/WR CM1....255 G6
Newnham Ct BRTR CM7....180 A3
Newnham Ct CHTY IP2....54 A4
Newnham Gn MAL CM9....271 G2 1
New Pk HSTD CO9....96 B2
New Park St COL CO1....11 H9
Newpasture La GTDUN CM6....177 L1
New Pier St WOTN CO14....196 E5 6
New Pond La SAFWN CB10....62 E3
Newport Cl CHLM/GWD CM2....267 K7
  HAR CO12....140 C4 2
Newport Dr COS CO15....222 C6
Newport Wy FOS CO13....196 C7
Newpots Cl K/T/MI CO5....215 M8
Newpots La K/T/MI CO5....216 A8
Newquay Cl KESG IP5....33 H7 4
New Queens Rd SUD CO10....4 C3
New Rd BRTR CM7....179 H4
  CBE/LIN CB1....21 K7
  CHLM/GWD CM2....267 J7
  CHLM/WR CM1....254 D4
  FX IP11....83 L8
  HSTD CO9....125 G8
  K/T/MI CO5....211 K3
  K/T/MI CO5....212 F8
  MGTR CO11....135 M2
  RBSF CM22....144 D3
  RCHLM CM3....236 E2
  RCHLM CM3....257 J2
  RCOLW CO6....157 K3
  ROY SG8....34 D4
  ROY SG8....59 G1
  SAFWN CB10....17 K7
  SAFWN CB10....63 G4
  SUD CO10....29 K6
Newry Av FX IP11....7 J1
Newson St IP IP1....2 D3
New St BRTR CM7....180 B3 4
  CHLM/WR CM1....15 H3
  GTDUN CM6....175 M5
  HSTD CO9....125 M4
  MAL CM9....271 H3 3
  RCOLE CO7....219 H4
  SBW CM21....227 G2
  SUD CO10....4 C5
New Street Flds
  GTDUN CM6....175 M5 1
New Thorpe Av RCOS CO16....194 C3
Newton Cl BRTR CM7....180 B5 1
Newton Cft SUD CO10....5 G6
Newton Dr SBW CM21....226 F4
Newton Gn GTDUN CM6....175 K4
Newton Rd HAR CO12....8 C9
  IPSE IP3....55 J1
  SUD CO10....4 F6
Newton St IPNE IP4....3 H5
Newton Wy RCOS CO16....220 C8
Newtown Rd BSF CM23....171 H7
New Town Rd COL CO1....10 F9
  RCOS CO16....194 B3
New Wy CHTY IP2....31 H7
  RCOS CO16....247 H2
New Writtle St CHLM/GWD CM2....14 F5
Nicholas Cl CHLM/WR CM1....265 K5
Nicholas Ct WIT CM8....238 B3 3
Nicholas Rd FX IP11....6 C1
Nichols Cl MGTR CO11....135 K2
Nicholsons Ct SUD CO10....51 K7 1
Nickleby Rd CHLM/WR CM1....253 M6
Nickolsons Gv COL CO1....10 F8
Nightingale Cl COLN CO4....161 J5 2
  COS CO15....13 H1
  HAR CO12....140 B4 2
  WIT CM8....238 A5 5
Nightingale HI COLN CO4....104 B7
Nightingale Ms SAFWN CB10....63 H3 4
Nightingale Rd COLW CO3....186 E1 2
Nightingale Rd IPSE IP3....55 J5 4
Nightingale Sq IPSE IP3....55 J5 4
Nightingale Wy COS CO15....13 H1
Nineacres BRTR CM7....180 C4 5
Nine Acres CHTY IP2....54 A4
Noakes Av CHLM/GWD CM2....267 G8
The Nobles BSF CM23....170 F7 1
Nonsuch Meadow SUD CO10....4 C8
The Nook RCOLE CO7....189 L4
Norbury Cl RCOLW CO6....185 H1
Norbury Rd IPNE IP4....32 D6
Norfolk Av COS CO15....223 G2
  K/T/MI CO5....244 F6
Norfolk Cl MAL CM9....271 G4
Norfolk Crs COLN CO4....11 H2
Norfolk Dr CHLM/WR CM1....254 C6
Norfolk Gdns BRTR CM7....180 D1 3
Norfolk Rd IPNE IP4....3 H4
  MAL CM9....271 G4

Norfolk Wy BSF CM23....171 H8
Norman Av BSF CM23....170 F7
Norman Cl FX IP11....113 M1
  RCOS CO16....185 G2
  RCOS CO16....248 C1
Normandie Wy BURES CO8....100 A5
Normandy Av COLS CO2....188 C2
Norman HI RCHLM CM3....236 D3
Norman Rd COS CO15....222 F7
  MGTR CO11....135 M1
Normansfield GTDUN CM6....176 A6
Norman's Wy STSD CM24....144 A6
New Wy COLW CO3....159 K8
  RCOS CO16....247 H2
Norris Cl BRTR CM7....152 E8 1
  BSF CM23....171 L6
Northampton Meadow
  BRTR CM7....121 J3
North Av CHLM/WR CM1....254 B8
  HVHL CB9....23 H6
Northbourne Rd COS CO15....13 H5
North Cl IPNE IP4....32 A5
North Crs HVHL CB9....43 K5
Northcroft SUD CO10....4 C6 1
North Dell CHLM/WR CM1....254 F6
North Dr CHLM/GWD CM2....267 H6
North End Rd HSTD CO9....71 G2
  K/T/MI CO5....17 K5
Northern Rd SUD CO10....5 K6
Northfield Gdns COLN CO4....160 C1
Northfield Rd SAFWS CB11....63 G6 2
  SBW CM21....227 G1
Northgate End BSF CM23....171 H5
Northgate St COL CO1....10 B6
  IP IP1....2 F5
North Hall Rd RBSF CM22....116 D6
  SAFWS CB11....116 C3
North HI COL CO1....10 B6
  RCHLM CM3....256 F7
North Hill Gdns IPNE IP4....3 K4
North Hill Rd IPNE IP4....3 K4
North La RCOLW CO6....185 K1
North Lawn IPNE IP4....32 D5
Northolt Av BSF CM23....171 K4
North Pl HLW CM20....226 C8
North Ri SUD CO10....5 H9
North Rd COS CO15....222 A7
  HSTD CO9....70 B3
  MAL CM9....262 B4
  RBSF CM22....173 L5
  RCOLE CO7....219 H6
  SUD CO10....48 B7
North Station Rd COL CO1....10 B4
North St BSF CM23....171 H5
  GTDUN CM6....175 M4
  HVHL CB9....43 K6
  MAL CM9....241 M8
  MAL CM9....271 K3
  MGTR CO11....135 M1 3
  SUD CO10....4 D5
  WOTN CO14....196 E5 7
  WOTN CO14....196 E4 1
North Street Pde SUD CO10....4 D6 1
North Ter BSF CM23....171 H5
Northumberland Cl
  BRTR CM7....180 D1 4
Northumberland Ct
  CHLM/GWD CM2....267 H1 2
North Wall RCOS CO16....247 H2
Norton Rd CHLM/WR CM1....14 E2
  HVHL CB9....23 G7 2
Norway Crs HAR CO12....8 B8
Norwich Cl COL CO1....10 F5
  RCOS CO16....221 H7
Norwich Rd IP IP1....2 B3
Norwood Av COS CO15....13 M2
Norwood Wy WOTN CO14....196 E4 1
Notcutts RCOLE CO7....106 A4
Notley Dr HVHL CB9....22 D4
Notley Gn BRTR CM7....179 K8
Notley Rd BRTR CM7....180 B3
Nottidge Rd IPNE IP4....3 K6
Nottingham Rd COS CO15....223 G7
Nounsley Rd RCHLM CM3....257 K4
Nunnery St HSTD CO9....95 M1
Nunns Cl RCOLW CO6....183 J3
Nunn's Rd COL CO1....10 B6
Nun's Meadow HSTD CO9....125 G5
Nuns Wk HSTD CO9....70 B4
Nunty's La BRTR CM7....154 B5
Nursery Cl RCOLW CO6....158 E8
Nursery Dr BRTR CM7....152 C8
Nursery Flds SBW CM21....226 F3
Nursery La RCHLM CM3....269 H5
Nursery Ri GTDUN CM6....175 M6
Nursery Rd BSF CM23....171 H7
  CHLM/GWD CM2....15 G7
  SUD CO10....50 D8
Nursery Wk FX IP11....7 K1

O

Oakapple Cl COLS CO2....187 M4
Oak Av COS CO15....249 J3
Oak Bungalows BRTR CM7....180 A2 3
Oak Cl FX IP11....7 G1
  MAL CM9....271 K6
  RCOLW CO6....159 G2
  RCOS CO16....194 C4
Oakdene KIR/NAC IP10....83 K2
Oak Dr SBW CM21....226 E5
Oak Fall WIT CM8....210 D8 6
Oak Farm Rd MAL CM9....269 M3
Oakfield La RCHLM CM3....236 C3
Oakfield Rd RIPW IP8....53 H7
Oak HI BRTR CM7....123 J3
Oak Hill La CHTY IP2....54 D2
Oak Holm COLS CO2....188 C2
Oakland Rd HAR CO12....9 H8
Oaklands Av COLW CO3....159 G8
Oaklands Cl BRTR CM7....179 M5
  BSF CM23....171 K3
Oaklands Crs CHLM/GWD CM2....15 G8
Oaklands Dr BSF CM23....171 K4

Oaklands Pk BSF CM23 ...... 171 K3
Oaklands Wy RCHLM CM3...... 269 G3
Oaklea Av CHLM/GWD CM2 ... 267 G1
Oakleigh Rd COS CO15 ...... 222 B5
Oakley Rd BRTR CM7 ...... 152 B6
  HAR CO12 ...... 139 M4
  MGTR CO11 ...... 138 B8
Oak Lodge Tye CHLM/WR CM1 .. 255 J7
Oakmead Rd RCOS CO16...... 247 J2
Oak Rdg HAR CO12 ...... 139 K6
Oak Rd HSTD CO9 ...... 97 J5
  HSTD CO9 ...... 98 B4
  HSTD CO9 ...... 125 M5
  K/T/MI CO5...... 212 E6
  MAL CM9...... 259 K7
  RCOLW CO6...... 156 D3
  SUD CO10...... 5 K9
  WIT CM8...... 210 E6
Oakroyd Av GTDUN CM6 ...... 176 A5
Oaks Dr COLW CO3 ...... 159 M6
Oaksmere Gdns CHTY IP2 ...... 54 C3
Oaks Pl COLN CO4 ...... 160 A2
The Oaks FOS CO13 ...... 196 B7
Oak St BSF CM23 ...... 171 H7
Oaktree Cl BSF CM23 ...... 171 H6
Oak Tree Rd RCOLE CO7 ...... 190 D5
Oakview HAR CO12 ...... 140 B4
Oak Wk HSTD CO9 ...... 95 M3 5
Oakwood Av COS CO15 ...... 223 G7
  K/T/MI CO5...... 244 F6
Oakwood Cl FOS CO13 ...... 196 A7 5
Oakwood Dr K/T/MI CO5 ...... 244 F6
Oakwood Gdns K/T/MI CO5 ... 244 F6 2
Oasthouse Ct SAFWN CB10 ... 62 F4
Oatfield Cl COLW CO3 ...... 158 F7
Oatlands RCOLE CO7 ...... 162 B7 1
Oban St IP IP1 ...... 2 C3
Oberon Cl COLN CO4 ...... 161 H6
Obrey Wy BSF CM23 ...... 199 G2
Observer Wy K/T/MI CO5 ...... 211 K1
Ockelford Av CHLM/WR CM1 ... 254 B8
Ockendon Wy WOTN CO14 .... 196 C5 1
Octavia Dr WIT CM8 ...... 238 A5 6
Oddcroft RCOLW CO6...... 127 H4
Office La MAL CM9 ...... 240 C8
Old Barn Rd BURES CO8 ...... 100 B7
Old Bell Cl STSD CM24 ...... 143 M7
Oldbury Av CHLM/GWD CM2 ... 267 H6
Old Burylodge La STSD CM24 ... 172 C1
Old Cattle Market IPNE IP4.... 2 F6
Old Church La SUD CO10 ...... 73 H2 1
Old Coach Rd RCOLW CO6...... 11 H6
Old Ct CHLM/WR CM1 ...... 15 L1
Old Court Rd CHLM/WR CM1 ... 15 L1
Oldfield Rd RIPW IP8 ...... 53 K4
Old Forge Rd COS CO2 ...... 187 H8
  RCHLM CM3...... 256 A5
Old Foundry Rd IPNE IP4 ...... 3 G6
Old Hall La MAL CM9 ...... 262 E1
  RIPS/CAP IP9...... 78 B2
  WOTN CO14...... 197 G1
Oldhall Rd RIPS/CAP IP9 ...... 111 K1
Old Haverhill Rd HVHL CB9 ... 23 M1
Old Heath Rd COLS CO2 ...... 188 E1
Old House La COLN CO4 ...... 132 B3
Old House Rd RCOLW CO6...... 131 H5
Old Ipswich Rd RCOLE CO7 ... 133 G6
Old Kirton Rd FX IP11 ...... 83 J5
Old London Rd MAL CM9 ...... 269 M5
  RIPS/CAP IP9 ...... 77 H6
The Old Maltings BSF CM23 ... 171 J6 2
Old Mead Rd RBSF CM22 ...... 144 E1
Old Mill La K/T/MI CO5 ...... 183 M6
  RBSF CM22 ...... 199 K2
Old Mill Rd COLN CO4 ...... 103 L8
  SAFWS CB11 ...... 63 G5
Old Parsonage Wy FOS CO13 .. 196 B8
Old Pier St WOTN CO14 ...... 196 E5
Old River La BSF CM23 ...... 171 H6 5
Old Rd BRTR CM7 ...... 154 A8
  COS CO15 ...... 12 E6
  FOS CO13 ...... 224 B1
  HLWE CM17 ...... 226 E7
  HSTD CO9 ...... 72 F8
  RCOLW CO6 ...... 183 M3
Old Rope Wk HVHL CB9 ...... 23 G6
Old Rose Gdns COLN CO4 ...... 159 M1 1
Old School Cl RCOS CO16...... 248 C1
Old School Ct RCHLM CM3 ... 257 K2 3
Old School Fld CHLM/WR CM1 ... 267 G1
Old School La RCOLE CO7 ...... 162 C7
Old Street HI RBSF CM22 ...... 200 B8
The Old St RIPS/CAP IP9 ...... 77 K4
Old Vicarage CHLM/WR CM1 .. 231 L3
Old Vicarage Rd HAR CO12...... 8 F7
Old Wy FOS CO13 ...... 224 B1
Olive Gv COLS CO2 ...... 187 M3
Oliver Pl WIT CM8 ...... 238 D3 5
Olivers Cl COS CO15 ...... 12 F4
  SUD CO10 ...... 29 M6
Olivers Dr WIT CM8 ...... 238 C6
Olivers La COLS CO2 ...... 187 H6
Olivers Rd COS CO15 ...... 12 F4
Oliver Wy CHLM/WR CM1 ...... 254 B6
Oliveswood Rd GTDUN CM6 ... 175 M6 1
Olympus Cl IP IP1 ...... 30 E3
Onehouse La IP IP1 ...... 31 K4
Ongar Cl RCOS CO16...... 249 K1
Ongark Rd CHLM/WR CM1 ...... 265 K4 2
Ongar Rd CHLM/WR CM1 ...... 264 B6
  GTDUN CM6 ...... 175 M7
Onslow Crs COLS CO2 ...... 188 C4
Opal Av IP IP1 ...... 30 F4
Ophir Rd RCOLE CO7 ...... 219 H8
Orange St GTDUN CM6 ...... 119 J3 1
Orange Tree Cl
  CHLM/GWD CM2 ...... 266 E7
Orchard Av HSTD CO9 ...... 125 M4
Orchard Cl CHLM/GWD CM2 .. 266 E7
  CHLM/WR CM1 ...... 265 K3
  GTDUN CM6 ...... 119 J2
  HAR CO12 ...... 139 J3
  HAR CO12 ...... 166 E2
  HSTD CO9 ...... 45 K7
  HVHL CB9 ...... 23 H6
  MAL CM9 ...... 263 G4
  MAL CM9 ...... 271 H3

RBSF CM22 ...... 227 L5
RCHLM CM3 ...... 257 J1
RCOLE CO7 ...... 162 C7
RCOLW CO6 ...... 185 M3
RCOS CO16 ...... 12 A1
SAFWN CB11 ...... 62 F6
SAFWS CB11 ...... 87 H5
Orchard Dr BRTR CM7 ...... 180 C4
  FOS CO13 ...... 223 J1
Orchard Ga CHTY IP2 ...... 30 E8
Orchard Gv HSTD CO9 ...... 33 J6
Orchard Pightle CBE/LIN CB1.. 19 K6
Orchard Rd BSF CM23 ...... 171 K4
  COL CO1 ...... 10 A4
  K/T/MI CO5 ...... 211 L2
  MAL CM9 ...... 271 H3
  RCOLE CO7 ...... 190 D5
  RIPW IP8 ...... 30 C3
Orchards WIT CM8 ...... 238 B4 1
The Orchards SBW CM21 ...... 227 G3 4
Orchard St CHLM/GWD CM2 .. 15 H5
  IPNE IP4 ...... 3 H5
Orchard Ter CBS CB2 ...... 16 E1
The Orchard GTDUN CM6 ...... 177 L8
Orchard Wy SUD CO10 ...... 28 D2
Orchid Av WIT CM8 ...... 238 A1
Orchid Cl CHTY IP2 ...... 54 A1
Oregon Rd KESG IP5 ...... 33 J7
Orford Crs CHLM/WR CM1 ...... 254 E8
Orford Rd FX IP11 ...... 7 G7
  HVHL CB9 ...... 23 H7
Orford St IP IP1 ...... 2 C3
Oriel Cl BSF CM23 ...... 170 E7
Oriole Wy BSF CM23 ...... 170 E7
Orion Wy BRTR CM7 ...... 180 D1 5
Orkney Cl HVHL CB9 ...... 23 M6
Orkney Rd IPNE IP4 ...... 32 C4
Orlando Cl WOTN CO14 ...... 196 E5 8
Ormonde Cl RCOLW CO6...... 159 G1
Orpen Cl RCOLW CO6...... 158 F1
Orpen's HI COLS CO2 ...... 186 C7
Orvis La RCOLE CO7 ...... 106 A4
Orwell Cl COLN CO4 ...... 161 G4
Orwell Pl IPNE IP4 ...... 3 G6
Orwell Ri RIPS/CAP IP9 ...... 81 H5
Orwell Rd COS CO15 ...... 13 G8
  FX IP11 ...... 7 M2
  HAR CO12 ...... 9 K7
  IPSE IP3 ...... 55 J1
Orwell View Rd RIPS/CAP IP9... 111 K2
Orwell St IP IP1 ...... 2 D3
Osbert Rd WIT CM8 ...... 238 A5
Osborne Cl COS CO15 ...... 222 C6
Osborne Rd IPSE IP3 ...... 55 J1 1
  K/T/MI CO5 ...... 245 G7
Osborne St COL CO1 ...... 10 D8
Osea Rd MAL CM9 ...... 272 D2
Osea Wy CHLM/WR CM1 ...... 255 H8
Osprey Rd HVHL CB9 ...... 23 L6
Ospreys COS CO15 ...... 223 G6
Osprey Wy CHLM/GWD CM2 .. 266 C8 1
Ostler Cl BSF CM23 ...... 198 E1 4
Ostler's Gn SAFWS CB11 ...... 60 D8
Othello Cl COLN CO4 ...... 161 H5
Otley Ct FX IP11 ...... 112 F2 9
Otten Rd SUD CO10 ...... 47 K4
Ottershaw Wy RCOS CO16...... 221 K7
Oulton Cl HAR CO12 ...... 8 B9
Oulton Rd IPSE IP3 ...... 55 G3
Ouse Cha WIT CM8 ...... 237 M3 3
Outpart Eastward HAR CO12 ... 9 L3 4
Overhall HI RCOLW CO6...... 127 L3
Over Hall La SAFWN CB10 ...... 40 F3
Owen Ward Cl COLS CO2 ...... 187 J2
Owl's HI RCHLM CM3 ...... 236 D2
Owls Retreat COLN CO4 ...... 161 H5
Oxborrow Cl FOS CO13 ...... 195 J7 1
Oxcroft BSF CM23 ...... 199 H2
Oxenford Cl HAR CO12 ...... 140 B4 3
Oxford Cl SUD CO10 ...... 5 H9
Oxford Ct CHLM/GWD CM2 ... 267 G3 1
  RCOLW CO6 ...... 127 K7
Oxford Crs COS CO15 ...... 12 F3
Oxford La SUD CO10 ...... 95 L3
Oxford Meadow HSTD CO9 ... 95 M3
Oxford Rd COLW CO3 ...... 159 M7
  COS CO15 ...... 13 G4
  FOS CO13 ...... 196 C8
  HSTD CO9 ...... 125 M4 5
  IPNE IP4 ...... 3 J6
  KESG IP5 ...... 33 J6
  MGTR CO11 ...... 135 M1
Oxley HI K/T/MI CO5 ...... 216 B1
  MAL CM9 ...... 241 J4
Oxlip Rd WIT CM8 ...... 238 A1
Oxney Md CHLM/WR CM1 ...... 265 H5
Oxney Vls GTDUN CM6 ...... 177 M6
Oysterbed Rd FX IP11 ...... 112 B3
Oyster Pl CHLM/GWD CM2 ... 267 H1
Oyster Tank Rd RCOLE CO7... 219 G8
Ozier Ct SAFWS CB11 ...... 63 G6 4
Oziers RBSF CM22 ...... 144 E3

P

Paignton Av CHLM/WR CM1 ... 254 F8
Palace Gdns BSF CM23 ...... 171 G8 1
Pallister Rd COS CO15 ...... 13 G8
Palm Cl CHLM/GWD CM2 ...... 266 E7
  WIT CM8 ...... 210 C8 7
Palmcroft Cl IP IP1 ...... 31 J2
Palmcroft Rd IP IP1 ...... 31 J2
Palmers Cl CBE/LIN CB1 ...... 19 K3
Palmers Cft CHLM/GWD CM2 .. 267 J3 1
Palmers La ROY SG8 ...... 59 L1
Palmerston Ldg
  CHLM/GWD CM2 ...... 267 H6
Palmerston Rd IPNE IP4 ...... 3 J5
  RCOS CO16 ...... 194 C3
Palmerswent Cl SUD CO10 ... 29 M5
Pamela Gdns BSF CM23 ...... 199 H2
Pampas Cl COLN CO4 ...... 160 C1
Panfield La BRTR CM7 ...... 152 A8
Pannels Cl SUD CO10 ...... 28 D1
Pantile Cl WIT CM8 ...... 238 C6
Pantlings La K/T/MI CO5 ...... 183 J8
Panton Crs COLN CO4 ...... 161 G6
Panton Ms BRTR CM7 ...... 180 C5 11
Paper Mill Br RCHLM CM3 ...... 256 F7
Papillon Rd COLW CO3 ...... 159 M6 2
Parade Rd IPNE IP4 ...... 3 J5
Paradise Rd CHLM/WR CM1 ... 265 K5
Pardoe Pl IPNE IP4 ...... 33 J8
Park Av BSF CM23 ...... 199 H2
  CHLM/WR CM1 ...... 14 C1
  FX IP11 ...... 113 K2
Park Bvd COS CO15 ...... 223 G7
Park Cha RCOS CO16 ...... 220 E8
Park Cl SUD CO10 ...... 5 G4
Parkdale RCHLM CM3 ...... 268 E6
Park Dr BRTR CM7 ...... 180 C5
  HSTD CO9 ...... 126 A4
  MAL CM9 ...... 271 K4
  RBSF CM22 ...... 228 D3
  RCOLE CO7 ...... 219 G6
Parker Av FX IP11 ...... 6 A3
Parker Rd CHLM/GWD CM2 .... 15 J6
Parker's Wy RCOLW CO6...... 102 C4
Parkeston Rd FX IP11 ...... 6 F1
  HAR CO12 ...... 8 B4
Parkfields HSTD CO9 ...... 95 M4 2
Parkfield St K/T/MI CO5 ...... 189 H6
Park Gate Rd WIT CM8 ...... 210 C2
Parkhall Rd BRTR CM7 ...... 123 M6
Park HI CBE/LIN CB1 ...... 21 M3
Parklands BRTR CM7 ...... 180 C5
  RCOLW CO6 ...... 183 J3
Parklands Dr CHLM/WR CM1 ... 15 L2 2
Park La BSF CM23 ...... 199 H1
  CBE/LIN CB1 ...... 42 A2
  COLN CO4 ...... 133 G2
  HSTD CO9 ...... 69 K6
  HSTD CO9 ...... 125 H6
  MAL CM9 ...... 241 K2
  RCHLM CM3 ...... 233 H1
  RCOLE CO7 ...... 127 H7
  RCOLW CO6 ...... 127 K7
  SAFWN CB10 ...... 62 F4
  SAFWS CB11 ...... 84 C3
  SUD CO10 ...... 73 H3
Park Lane Cl RCOLW CO6...... 127 K7
Park North IP IP1 ...... 31 M5
Park Rd CHLM/WR CM1 ...... 15 G3
  COLN CO4 ...... 189 J1
  COLW CO3 ...... 159 L7
  COS CO15 ...... 12 D7
  GTDUN CM6 ...... 175 G1
  HAR CO12 ...... 9 K6
  HVHL CB9 ...... 22 F4
  IP IP1 ...... 2 F1
  MAL CM9 ...... 271 H4
  RBSF CM22 ...... 144 F3
  RCOLE CO7 ...... 106 D3
  RCOLE CO7 ...... 163 L5
  RCOLE CO7 ...... 189 K5
  RCOLW CO6 ...... 102 D6
  RCOLW CO6 ...... 103 J2
  SAFWN CB10 ...... 18 A8
  STSD CM24 ...... 144 A7
  SUD CO10 ...... 5 G4
  WIT CM8 ...... 210 C2
Park Side GTDUN CM6 ...... 148 F7
Parkside Av IPNE IP4 ...... 3 G2
Park Sq East COS CO15 ...... 249 H5
Park Sq West COS CO15 ...... 249 H4
Park St GTDUN CM6 ...... 119 J4
Park Vale Cl HSTD CO9 ...... 96 A1
Park View Crs CHLM/GWD CM2 .. 267 H8
Park View Rd IP IP1 ...... 31 J4
Park Wy COS CO15 ...... 249 M4
Parkway CBE/LIN CB1 ...... 21 L7
  CHLM/GWD CM2 ...... 15 H4
  CHLM/WR CM1 ...... 14 F1
  SBW CM21 ...... 227 G4
Parkwood Av RCOLE CO7 ...... 189 K4
Parkwood Dr SUD CO10 ...... 4 C1
Park Wood La MAL CM9 ...... 260 C2
Parliament Rd IPNE IP4 ...... 32 B6
Parmenter Dr SUD CO10 ...... 50 B8
Parnell Cl COLS CO2 ...... 188 C4
  IP IP1 ...... 31 H2
Parnell Rd IP IP1 ...... 31 H2
Parnham Pl IPNE IP4 ...... 33 H8
Parr Cl BRTR CM7 ...... 180 F1
Parr Dr COLW CO3 ...... 187 G1
Parrington Wy MGTR CO11 ... 135 J2
Parry Dr RCOS CO16 ...... 194 E6
Parsonage Cl CHLM/WR CM1 .. 254 C4 2
  FX IP11 ...... 6 F2
Parsonage Farm La
  SAFWN CB10 ...... 61 M1
Parsonage Gv BURES CO8 ...... 100 A5 2
Parsonage La BSF CM23 ...... 171 K5
  GTDUN CM6 ...... 204 F2
  RCHLM CM3 ...... 268 F3
  RCOS CO16 ...... 164 F5
  SAFWS CB11 ...... 114 D2
  STSD CM24 ...... 172 B1
Parsonage Rd RBSF CM22 ... 173 K5
Parsonage St HSTD CO9 ...... 126 B4

Parsonage Wy CBE/LIN CB1 ... 19 M3
Parson's Fld RCOLE CO7 ...... 105 J7
Parson's Heath COLN CO4 ... 161 G3
Parson's HI COLW CO3 ...... 159 J7
Parsons La COL CO1 ...... 11 J9
Parsons Yd MGTR CO11 ...... 135 M1 4
Partridge Av CHLM/WR CM1 .. 254 B7
Partridge Cl HAR CO12 ...... 166 F1
Partridge Dr RCOLW CO6...... 129 M8
Partridge Rd CHTY IP2 ...... 53 M2
Partridge Wy CHLM/GWD CM2 .. 267 G5
Paske Av HVHL CB9 ...... 23 H6
Pasture High RCHLM CM3 ...... 268 F2
Pasture Loates STSD CM24 ... 143 M5
The Pastures IPNE IP4 ...... 33 H8
Paternoster Rw WOTN CO14 .. 196 E5 9
The Path RCOLE CO7 ...... 191 M5
Pathfields Rd COS CO15 ...... 12 D4
Patmore Cl BSF CM23 ...... 170 E8
Patmore Flds RBSF CM22 ...... 116 A7
Patmore Rd COLN CO4 ...... 11 M4
Patricia Gdns BSF CM23 ...... 171 G8
Patten Cl RCOLW CO6...... 185 G2
Pattern Bush St MGTR CO11 ... 106 F5
Patteson Rd IPSE IP3 ...... 3 J9
Pattison Cl WIT CM8 ...... 238 C5
Pattocks La RCOLW CO6...... 156 E3
Pattrick's La HAR CO12 ...... 9 H7
Pauline Cl COS CO15 ...... 222 H7
Pauline St CHTY IP2 ...... 54 E2
Pauls Crs RCOLE CO7 ...... 162 B7
Paul Spendlove Ct COLN CO4 . 161 G4 1
Paul's Rd CHTY IP2 ...... 31 H8
Pawle Cl CHLM/GWD CM2 ...... 267 J6
Paxman Av COLS CO2 ...... 187 J2
Paxton Rd COS CO15 ...... 222 D5
Paycocke Wy RCOLW CO6...... 183 J2
Payne's La RCOLE CO7 ...... 163 L2
Peace Rd COLW CO3 ...... 158 F6
Peacock Av BRTR CM7 ...... 180 B4
Peacocks Cl SUD CO10 ...... 27 L3 2
Peacocks Rd SUD CO10 ...... 27 L3
Peake Av FOS CO13 ...... 195 J7
Peakes Cl K/T/MI CO5 ...... 240 D1
Peal Rd SAFWS CB11 ...... 63 H6 1
Pearce Mnr CHLM/GWD CM2 .. 14 D8
Pearce Rd IPSE IP3 ...... 32 C8
Pearcroft Rd IP IP1 ...... 31 K2
Pearl Rd IP IP1 ...... 30 E5
Pearmain Wy COLW CO3 ...... 186 E1
Pearse Wy IPSE IP3 ...... 56 A4
Pearson Rd IPNE IP4 ...... 32 E8
Pearsons Wy RIPW IP8 ...... 53 H4
Peartree Cl BRTR CM7 ...... 180 C4
  MAL CM9 ...... 261 G7
Peartree HI BURES CO8 ...... 129 J1
Peartree Rd COLW CO3 ...... 186 F1
Peartree Wy RCOS CO16...... 221 L3
Peaslands Rd SAFWS CB11 ... 63 G5
Pebmarsh Cl COLS CO2 ...... 188 C5
Pebmarsh Rd BURES CO8 ...... 99 G4
  RCOLW CO6 ...... 127 H3
Pecockes Cl SUD CO10 ...... 50 B2 2
Pedder's Cl COLW CO3 ...... 187 H2
Pedlars Cl RCHLM CM3 ...... 269 J7
Pedlars Pth RCHLM CM3 ...... 269 J7
Peel Crs BRTR CM7 ...... 180 A2
Peel Rd CHLM/GWD CM2 ...... 267 G1
Peel St IP IP1 ...... 2 E4
Peerswood Rd COLS CO2 ...... 187 M3
Peewit HI FX IP11 ...... 6 F5
Peewit Rd CHTY IP2 ...... 53 L3
Pegasus Wy BRTR CM7 ...... 152 A8
  COLN CO4 ...... 11 K2
Peggotty Cl CHLM/WR CM1 .... 254 B7
Peggy's Wk SAFWS CB11 ...... 62 A2
Peg Millar's La RCHLM CM3 ... 208 E7
Peldon Rd K/T/MI CO5 ...... 216 C5
  K/T/MI CO5 ...... 243 J2
Pelham Cl HAR CO12 ...... 140 B3
Pelham Rd SAFWS CB11 ...... 114 D1
Pelican Cl CHTY IP2 ...... 54 A2
Pelly Av WIT CM8 ...... 238 C5
Pembroke Av MAL CM9 ...... 271 H4
Pembroke Cl CHTY IP2 ...... 54 D2
  COLS CO2 ...... 188 E2 1
Pembroke Gdns COS CO15 ... 223 G7
  SUD CO10 ...... 49 M3
Pembroke Pl CHLM/WR CM1 ... 254 C6
Pendleton Rd CHTY IP2 ...... 53 M4
Penfold Rd COS CO15 ...... 12 F8
  FX IP11 ...... 7 M1
Penlan Hall La RCOLW CO6...... 129 K7
Penn Cl RIPS/CAP IP9 ...... 77 K3
Pennine Rd CHLM/WR CM1 .... 253 M7
Pennington La STSD CM24 ... 143 M5
Penningtons BSF CM23 ...... 170 E8
Penn Ms BRTR CM7 ...... 180 C5 12
Pennsylvania La K/T/MI CO5 ... 212 D8
Penny La IPSE IP3 ...... 32 C8
Penny Meadow RIPS/CAP IP9 .. 77 J4
Pennyroyal Crs WIT CM8 ...... 238 A1 4
Pennyroyal Gdns CHTY IP2 ... 54 A1 3
Penny Royal Rd RCHLM CM3 .. 268 F2
Pennystone Rd SAFWS CB11 .. 63 G5 3
Penrice Cl COLN CO4 ...... 161 G7
Penrose Md CHLM/WR CM1 ... 265 K5
Penryn Rd KESG IP5 ...... 33 H6
Penshurst Pl BRTR CM7 ...... 179 K7 4
Penshurst Rd IPSE IP3 ...... 55 M1
Penticton Rd BRTR CM7 ...... 179 M3
Pentland Av CHLM/WR CM1 ... 254 C7
Pentlow Dr SUD CO10 ...... 28 A4
Pentlow Hawke Cl HVHL CB9 .. 23 K6 2
Penzance Cl CHLM/WR CM1 ... 255 G8
Penzance Rd KESG IP5 ...... 33 J7
Pepper Cl COLN CO4 ...... 10 C1
Peppercorn Wy CHTY IP2 ...... 54 C2
Pepples La SAFWN CB10 ...... 89 J4
Pepys St HAR CO12 ...... 9 K4
Percival Rd FOS CO13 ...... 195 M4
  WOTN CO14 ...... 196 F3
Peregrine Cl BSF CM23 ...... 170 F7
  COS CO15 ...... 222 B7

Peregrine Ct COLN CO4 ...... 161 H5 1
Peregrine Dr CHLM/GWD CM2 .. 266 C8
Perkins Wy IPSE IP3 ...... 55 H4
Perriclose CHLM/WR CM1 ...... 254 F6 5
Perrin Pl CHLM/GWD CM2 ...... 14 E6
Perry HI CHLM/WR CM1 ...... 15 L1
Perry Rd K/T/MI CO5 ...... 212 D8
  WIT CM8 ...... 238 C4
Perry Wy WIT CM8 ...... 238 C6
Persardi Ct COS CO2 ...... 188 C6
Pershore End COLW CO3 ...... 159 G8 2
Perth Cl COS CO2 ...... 188 C4
Pertwee Cl RCOLE CO7 ...... 219 G6
Pertwee Dr CHLM/GWD CM2 .. 267 H7
Pertwee Wy K/T/MI CO5 ...... 216 D3
Pesthouse La HAR CO12 ...... 166 E2
Peter Bruff Av RCOS CO16 ...... 12 B1
Peterfield's La HSTD CO9 ...... 125 G8
Peterhouse Cl CHTY IP2 ...... 54 A3
Petersfield CHLM/WR CM1 .... 254 D7
Petersfield Rd CBS CB2 ...... 16 F5
Peter's Gv RIPS/CAP IP9 ...... 77 J4
Peto Av COLN CO4 ...... 10 C1
Petrebrook CHLM/GWD CM2 .. 267 J2
Petrel Wy CHLM/GWD CM2 ... 266 E7
Petrolea Cl COL CO1 ...... 10 B2
Pettit La BRTR CM7 ...... 209 J1
Petts La SAFWN CB10 ...... 39 G4
Petunia Crs CHLM/WR CM1 ... 255 H7
Petworth Cl BRTR CM7 ...... 179 K6
  RCOLE CO7 ...... 189 L5 4
Pevensey Dr COS CO15 ...... 249 L5
Peverel Av RCHLM CM3 ...... 257 L4
Pewterers Av BSF CM23 ...... 198 E1
Pharos La K/T/MI CO5 ...... 244 E7
Pheasant Ri RIPW IP8 ...... 53 H5
Pheasant Rd CHTY IP2 ...... 54 A2
Philip Av FX IP11 ...... 6 F4
Philip Cl WOTN CO14 ...... 196 C5
Philip Rd CHTY IP2 ...... 54 D2
  WIT CM8 ...... 238 A5 7
Philips Cl BRTR CM7 ...... 179 H3 3
Philips Rd BRTR CM7 ...... 179 H3
Phillip Rd RCOLE CO7 ...... 189 K5
Phillips Cha BRTR CM7 ...... 152 C8
Phillips Field Rd SUD CO10 ... 50 C8
Philpot End La GTDUN CM6 ... 203 K2
Phoenix Gv CHLM/GWD CM2 .. 14 D7
Phoenix Rd IPNE IP4 ...... 32 C6
Piccotts La BRTR CM7 ...... 150 C5
Pickers Wy COS CO15 ...... 223 G6
Picketts Rd FX IP11 ...... 113 L2
Picknage Rd ROY SG8 ...... 58 C3
Pickpocket La BRTR CM7 ...... 179 M7
Pickwick Av CHLM/WR CM1 ... 253 M7
Pickwick Rd CHTY IP2 ...... 31 G7
Picton Av IP IP1 ...... 31 M4
Pierce Gld K/T/MI CO5 ...... 212 E8 1
Pier Gap COS CO15 ...... 13 G8
Pierrefitte Wy BSF CM23 ...... 180 A2
Pigeon's La RIPW IP8 ...... 52 F3
Piggotts Wy BSF CM23 ...... 171 G8
The Pightle BRTR CM7 ...... 92 F7
  HVHL CB9 ...... 23 J5
  RIPS/CAP IP9 ...... 77 K3
Pightle Wy FOS CO13 ...... 196 C6
Pilborough Wy COLW CO3 ...... 187 G2
Pilcox Hall La RCOS CO16...... 164 E6
Pilgrim Cl SAFWN CB10 ...... 37 M3
Pilgrims Cl SAFWN CB10 ...... 37 M3
Pimblett Rw RBSF CM22 ...... 117 H8 1
Pimpernel Rd CHTY IP2 ...... 54 B2
Pincey St STSD CM24 ...... 173 H2
Pinchpools Rd BSF CM23 ...... 143 J2
Pine Av GTDUN CM6 ...... 175 K4
  IP IP1 ...... 31 K4
Pine Cl MGTR CO11 ...... 106 F5
  RCOS CO16 ...... 192 B5
Pinecroft Gdns COLN CO4 ...... 160 D2
Pinecroft Rd SUD CO10 ...... 49 L8
Pinecroft Rd IP IP1 ...... 31 J3
Pine Gv BSF CM23 ...... 171 K7
  K/T/MI CO5 ...... 244 D6
  WIT CM8 ...... 210 C8 3
Pinelands BSF CM23 ...... 171 H4
Pines HI STSD CM24 ...... 143 M8
Pine Rd CHLM/WR CM1 ...... 253 M8
The Pines RCHLM CM3 ...... 237 J8
Pinetree Cl KESG IP5 ...... 33 H6 3
Pine View Rd IP IP1 ...... 31 J5
Pinewood Cl COS CO15 ...... 222 A6
  FOS CO13 ...... 195 M7 2
Pinkeneys ROY SG8 ...... 35 M8
Pinkham Dr WIT CM8 ...... 238 B5
Pink La WIT CM8 ...... 208 F6
Pinkney Cl SAFWN CB10 ...... 89 G3
Pinkuah La SUD CO10 ...... 28 B7
Pin Mill Cl RIPW IP8 ...... 53 L4
Pinmill Rd RIPS/CAP IP9 ...... 81 H5
Pintail Cl CHTY IP2 ...... 54 A3
Pintail Crs BRTR CM7 ...... 179 L2
Pipchin Rd CHLM/WR CM1 .... 254 A7
Piper Rd COLW CO3 ...... 159 K6
Pipers Cl HVHL CB9 ...... 23 L7
The Pippins HSTD CO9 ...... 125 M3 1
  SUD CO10 ...... 28 E1
Pirie Rd RCOLW CO6 ...... 159 G1
Pishiobury Dr SBW CM21 ...... 226 F5
Pitcairn Rd IP IP1 ...... 31 G5
Pit La K/T/MI CO5 ...... 212 E7
Pitmire La BURES CO8 ...... 74 D7
Pitt Av WIT CM8 ...... 238 C5
Pitt Cha CHLM/GWD CM2 ...... 267 G5
Pitts End RCOLE CO7 ...... 105 M2
Plains Farm Cl RCOLE CO7 ... 132 F7
Plains Fld BRTR CM7 ...... 180 F4
Plains Rd MAL CM9...... 240 B7
Plaistow Green Rd HSTD CO9... 125 L8
Plaistow Wy ROY SG8 ...... 59 G3 1
Plampin Cl SUD CO10 ...... 51 K7
Plane Tree Cl CHLM/GWD CM2 .. 266 D7
Plane View Cl COS CO15 ...... 249 K3
Plantation Cl SAFWS CB11 ... 63 G7 1
Plantation Rd RCHLM CM3 ... 256 B4

Planton Wy RCOLE CO7 218 F6
Plashets RBSF CM22 227 L4
Platters Cl IPSE IP3 55 J6
Platters Rd FX IP11 7 H6
Plaw Hatch Cl BSF CM23 171 K5
Players Ct GTDUN CM6 177 L7
Playfield Rd RIPS/CAP IP9 77 K4
Playford La KESG IP5 33 G4
Playford Rd IPNE IP4 32 F6 1
IPNE IP4 33 G6
Playle Cha MAL CM9 259 J1
Pleasant Rd BSF CM23 171 G5
Pleasant Rw IPNE IP4 3 G7
Pleasant Va SAFWS CB11 62 F6
Pleshey Rd RCHLM CM3 233 J1
Plough Dr COLW CO3 159 J8
Plough La SUD CO10 4 B7
Ploughmans Cl BSF CM23 170 E8
Ploughmans Headland
COLW CO3 159 G8 3
Plough Rd RCOLE CO7 192 A5
RIPS/CAP IP9 77 H4
Plough St IPSE IP3 3 K8
Plover Cl FOS CO13 196 A7
Plover Rd CHTY IP2 54 A3
Plume Av COLW CO3 187 J1
MAL CM9 271 H4
Plummers Rd RCOLW CO6 130 A7
Plump Tree La RCHLM CM3 268 F8
Plumptre La RCHLM CM3 268 F8
Plums La BRTR CM7 150 A1
Plumtree Av CHLM/GWD CM2 267 H7
Plymouth Rd CHLM/WR CM1 255 G8
FX IP11 113 H1
Pochard Wy BRTR CM7 179 L8
Pocklington Cl
CHLM/GWD CM2 267 J1 4
Pod's Brook Rd BRTR CM7 179 M4
Pods La BRTR CM7 178 F3
Point Clear Rd RCOS CO16 247 M3
Pointwell La RCOLW CO6 183 J6
Pole Barn La FOS CO13 196 B8
Polecat Rd BRTR CM7 181 H8
Pole La WIT CM8 208 E2
Pollard's Gn CHLM/GWD CM2 267 H3
Pollard Wk RCOS CO16 12 B2
Polley Cl FOS CO13 196 A6 6
Polstead Wy RCOS CO16 249 K1
Pond Cha COLW CO3 187 J1
Pond Cl FX IP11 112 F2
Pond Cross Farm SAFWS CB11 87 J5
Pond Cross Wy SAFWS CB11 87 J5 3
Ponders Rd RCOLW CO6 157 L2
Pondfield Rd COLN CO4 11 M2
Pondholton Dr WIT CM8 238 B6
Pond La RBSF CM22 228 C2
Poney Cha WIT CM8 239 H8
Poole Cl IPSE IP3 55 M2
Poole St HSTD CO9 70 C6
SUD CO10 27 L4
Poore St SAFWS CB11 86 B5
Poperinghe Rd COLS CO2 188 B1
Popes Ct HVHL CB9 24 A8
Pope's La COLW CO3 10 A7
Pope's Rd RCOLW CO6 156 E1
Poplar Av COS CO15 249 J3
Poplar Cl CHLM/GWD CM2 266 E7
COS CO15 249 K3
HSTD CO9 126 B5
HVHL CB9 22 F4
WIT CM8 210 C8
Poplar Grove Cha MAL CM9 259 K6
Poplar La RIPW IP8 53 J2
Poplar Rd SUD CO10 5 J7
Poplars Cl RCOLE CO7 190 D6
The Poplars GTDUN CM6 175 L3 2
MGTR CO11 106 F3
Poplar Wy FOS CO13 195 M7
Poppy Cl CHTY IP2 31 H8
Poppy Gdns COLS CO2 188 E2
Pork La FOS CO13 195 G7
Porter Rd IPSE IP3 56 B4 1
Porters Brook Wk COLN CO4 11 K1
Porter's Cl COLW CO3 158 B3
Porter's La COLW CO3 158 B3
Porters Pk RCHLM CM3 256 C3
Porter Wy RCOS CO16 249 K1
Portland Av HAR CO12 9 H8
Portland Cl BRTR CM7 180 D2 3
Portland Crs HAR CO12 9 G8
Portland Pl BSF CM23 171 H6 6
Portland Rd BSF CM23 171 H6
COLS CO2 10 D8
Port La RBSF CM22 199 K3
Portlight Cl MGTR CO11 136 C1
Portman Rd IP IP1 2 D5
Portman's Wk IP IP1 2 C6
Portobello Rd WOTN CO14 196 E5
Port of Felixstowe Rd FX IP11 6 D3
Portreath Pl CHLM/WR CM1 254 C6
Portsmouth Rd COS CO15 249 L5
Portway CHLM/GWD CM2 267 K1
Portway Ct HSTD CO9 126 B2
Posford Ct COLN CO4 132 B8
Postman's La RCHLM CM3 269 G2
Post Mill Cl IPNE IP4 3 L4
Post Office La MAL CM9 260 D1
Post Office Rd CHLM/WR CM1 254 D5
MAL CM9 270 A8
Potash La RIPS/CAP IP9 78 A5
Pot Kiln Cha HSTD CO9 72 B3
Pot Kiln Rd SUD CO10 5 J9
The Pot Kilns SUD CO10 5 L8
Potters Cl RCHLM CM3 269 J7
Potter St BSF CM23 171 H6
HSTD CO9 96 A6
Pottery La CHLM/WR CM1 254 C8
HSTD CO9 96 B2
Pouch Ml FX IP11 83 K7
Poulk Hall La RCHLM CM3 207 J7
Poulteney Rd STSD CM24 144 A5 5
Poulton Cl MAL CM9 271 J5
Pound Farm Dr HAR CO12 8 B8
Pound Flds CHLM/WR CM1 265 K5
Pound Ga GTDUN CM6 148 F7
Pound La RIPS/CAP IP9 77 H5
RIPW IP8 53 J6
Pound Wk SAFWN CB10 62 F3
Powers Hall End WIT CM8 237 M2
Powling Rd IPSE IP3 55 J3
Pownall Crs COLS CO2 188 B1
Poynter Pl FOS CO13 196 A6 7
Pratts Farm La RCHLM CM3 254 E1
Pratt's La RIPS/CAP IP9 80 C3
Prentice Hall La MAL CM9 262 C5
President Rd COLW CO3 159 G8
Preston Dr IP IP1 31 H3
Preston Rd COS CO15 222 F8
Prestwick Av FX IP11 113 L1
Prestwick Dr BSF CM23 171 K4
Pretoria Rd HSTD CO9 126 B3
Prettygate Rd COLW CO3 159 J8
Pretyman Rd FX IP11 7 H7
IPSE IP3 55 K2
Primley La RBSF CM22 227 L4
Primrose Cl BSF CM23 170 E7
Primrose Hl CHLM/WR CM1 14 D1
CHTY IP2 54 B1
HVHL CB9 23 H6
RIPS/CAP IP9 108 F1
Primrose La K/T/MI CO5 212 E7 5
MGTR CO11 138 C4
Primrose Pl WIT CM8 238 A1 5
Primrose Rd COS CO15 223 G7
Primula Wy CHLM/WR CM1 255 H7
Prince Albert Rd K/T/MI CO5 244 F7
Prince Charles Cl COS CO15 12 B9
SUD CO10 4 E4
Prince Charles Rd COLS CO2 188 B4
Princedale Cl IP IP1 31 J4
Princel La RCOLE CO7 105 H6
Prince of Wales Dr CHTY IP2 54 C3
Prince of Wales Rd WIT CM8 259 J1
Prince Philip Av COS CO15 249 L4
Prince Philip Rd COLS CO2 188 B4
Princes Ct BSF CM23 170 E6 1
Prince's Esp WOTN CO14 196 F5
Princes Gdns FX IP11 7 K2
Princes Ga BSF CM23 170 E6
Princes Rd CHLM/GWD CM2 14 E9
COS CO15 222 F8
FX IP11 7 K3
HAR CO12 8 E8
MAL CM9 271 J3
Princess Anne Cl COS CO15 249 L4
Princess St HAR CO12 8 B4
Princes St CHTY IP2 2 C8
IP IP1 2 F5
Princess Wy HVHL CB9 23 G6
Prince St SUD CO10 4 C5
Princethorpe Rd IPSE IP3 55 L1
Princeton Ms COLN CO4 160 D1 2
Printers Wy HLW CM20 226 C8
Prior Cl HSTD CO9 125 M5
Priors Wy RCOLW CO6 183 J2
Prior's Wood Rd RBSF CM22 173 L6 2
Prior Wy COLN CO4 159 M3
Priory Av HLWE CM17 226 E8
HVHL CB9 23 H6 2
Priory Cl CHLM/WR CM1 14 B4
RCHLM CM3 257 K4
RCOS CO16 248 C7
SAFWN CB10 37 J2
Priory Ct BSF CM23 171 G6
Priory Dr STSD CM24 144 A8
Priory Farm Rd RCHLM CM3 257 K3
Priory Rd COS CO15 12 E6
FX IP11 113 M2 1
RCOLW CO6 156 D2
SUD CO10 4 B2
WIT CM8 240 B2
Priory St COL CO1 10 E7
RCOLW CO6 127 K6
The Priory CHLM/WR CM1 265 K5
Priory Wk SUD CO10 4 C7
Priory Wd HSTD CO9 96 A1
Priory Wood Rbt RBSF CM22 172 C5
Prittlewell Cl CHTY IP2 54 B4
Proctor Cl K/T/MI CO5 216 D3
Proctors Wy BSF CM23 199 J1
Proctor Wy RCOLW CO6 185 G2
Progress Ct BRTR CM7 180 A2
Progress Wy RCOS CO16 221 L4
Promenade COS CO15 248 F7
HAR CO12 140 E3
Promenade Wy RCOLE CO7 218 F8
Prospect Cl RCHLM CM3 257 J2 1
Prospect Hl SUD CO10 74 F2
Prospect Pl SAFWS CB11 63 H4
Prospect Rd IP IP1 2 B4
Prospect St IP IP1 2 A4
Prospero Cl COLN CO4 161 H6
Provence Cl COLW CO3 158 E6
Providence La IP IP1 2 B2
Providence St IP IP1 2 E5
Provident Sq CHLM/GWD CM2 15 J4
Prunus Ct COLS CO2 188 C6 3
Prykes Dr CHLM/WR CM1 14 D3
Pryor Cl WIT CM8 238 C4
Pryors Cl BSF CM23 171 J7
Pudding La COLS CO2 214 D2
ROY SG8 58 C4
The Pudgell ROY SG8 59 G3
Puffinsdale COS CO15 13 H1
Pulpitfield Cl FOS CO13 196 C5 2
Pump Hl CHLM/GWD CM2 267 H7 2
RCOS CO16 248 E1
Pump La CHLM/WR CM1 255 G6
RCHLM CM3 233 G4
Punchard Wy FX IP11 83 L7
Purcell Cl CHLM/WR CM1 265 J4
COLN CO4 161 G7 2
Purdis Av IPSE IP3 56 B4
Purdis Farm La IPSE IP3 56 B3
KIR/NAC IP10 56 E3
Purdis Rd KIR/NAC IP10 56 F3
Purley Wy RCOS CO16 221 K7
Purplett St CHTY IP2 3 G9
Purvis Wy COLN CO4 132 D8
Putticks La RCOLE CO7 106 A2
Pyefleet Cl K/T/MI CO5 189 L7
RCOLE CO7 219 G6
Pyefleet Vw K/T/MI CO5 216 D2
Pyesand FOS CO13 195 L5
Pygot Pl BRTR CM7 180 A1
Pynchbek BSF CM23 199 G2
Pynchon Ms CHLM/WR CM1 15 L2
Pynchon Paddocks RBSF CM22 199 M6

Q

Quadling St IP IP1 2 D7
Quaker's La HVHL CB9 23 J6
Quale Rd CHLM/GWD CM2 267 K1
Quantock Cl KESG IP5 33 H6
Quay La FOS CO13 195 M4
RCOS CO16 194 D1
SUD CO10 4 C8
Quay St MGTR CO11 135 M1
RCOLE CO7 189 K6 2
The Quay HAR CO12 9 K2
Quebec Dr KESG IP5 33 K5
Queech La RIPS/CAP IP9 107 L5
The Queech RIPS/CAP IP9 77 K3 3
Queen Anne Dr K/T/MI CO5 244 F7
Queen Anne Gdns
K/T/MI CO5 244 F7 3
Queen Anne Rd K/T/MI CO5 244 F7
Queenborough La BRTR CM7 179 J4
Queenbury Cl K/T/MI CO5 245 G7 1
Queen Edith Dr HVHL CB9 43 K7
Queen Elizabeth Av COS CO15 249 L4
Queen Elizabeth Wy COLS CO2 188 C4
Queen's Av MAL CM9 271 J4
Queensberry Rd IPSE IP3 55 J4 1
Queensbury Av RCOLW CO6 157 M8
Queenscliffe Rd CHTY IP2 54 C2
Queen's Cl SBW CM21 227 H1
STSD CM24 144 A5
SUD CO10 4 E5
Queens Crs BSF CM23 171 G8
Queensdale Cl IP IP1 31 K4
Queen's Gdns BRTR CM7 151 J6
Queensgate Dr IPNE IP4 32 B5
Queen's Head Rd RCOLW CO6 131 M3
Queensland RIPS/CAP IP9 111 G3
Queensland Crs CHLM/WR CM1 253 M8
Queensland Dr COLS CO2 188 C4
Queens Rd BRTR CM7 152 B8
CHLM/GWD CM2 15 L4
COLW CO3 159 L7
COS CO15 12 B9
FOS CO13 224 B1
FX IP11 7 L2
HAR CO12 140 C3
RCOLE CO7 189 K5
RCOLW CO6 127 K6
RCOLW CO6 158 F2
SUD CO10 4 C4
Queen's Sq IPSE IP3 55 K3
Queens St HVHL CB9 22 E1
HVHL CB9 23 J5
Queen St CHLM/GWD CM2 14 F6
COL CO1 10 D7
FX IP11 113 G1
HSTD CO9 96 B6
HSTD CO9 96 A2
IP IP1 2 E6
MAL CM9 271 J3
RCOLE CO7 219 H7
RCOLW CO6 183 J3
Queen's Wy IPSE IP3 55 K3
Queensway COS CO15 222 F8
HVHL CB9 23 G5
K/T/MI CO5 212 E7
MGTR CO11 135 L1
SUD CO10 50 D8
Queen Victoria Dr
RIPS/CAP IP9 111 K5
Quendon Wy FOS CO13 196 C7
Quentin Cl IP IP1 31 G6
Quickset Rd SAFWS CB11 36 D8
Quilp Dr CHLM/WR CM1 254 B6
Quilter Dr RIPW IP8 53 L4
Quilter Rd FX IP11 113 K3
Quilters Cl COS CO15 223 H7 3
Quince Cl MGTR CO11 106 F4 1
Quinion Cl CHLM/WR CM1 253 M6
Quinton's La FX IP11 113 L2
Quintons Rd RCOLE CO7 105 L2

R

Rachael Gdns WIT CM8 210 A1 3
Radcliffe Dr CHTY IP2 53 M3
Radiator Rd SUD CO10 50 C8
Radleys La RCOLW CO6 101 L1
Radwinter Rd SAFWN CB10 40 D5
SAFWS CB11 63 H4
Raeburn Cl FOS CO13 196 B6 4
Raeburn Rd IPSE IP3 55 H4
Raeburn Rd South IPSE IP3 55 G4
Raglan Ms COS CO15 12 A6
Raglan Rd FOS CO13 196 B8
Raile Wk SUD CO10 29 M5
Railey Rd SAFWS CB11 63 G6
Railway Ap FX IP11 113 J2 1
Railway Sq CHLM/WR CM1 14 F2
Railway St BRTR CM7 180 C2
CHLM/WR CM1 14 F2
MGTR CO11 135 M1
Rainbow Md RCHLM CM3 237 H8
Rainbow Ms MAL CM9 259 H8 2
Rainbow Rd K/T/MI CO5 244 F7
Rainbow Wy RCOLW CO6 127 H4
Raine Av HVHL CB9 22 F5
Rainham Wy FOS CO13 196 D7
Rainsborowe Rd COLS CO2 187 L1
Rainsford Av CHLM/WR CM1 14 C2
Rainsford La CHLM/WR CM1 14 D3
Rainsford Rd CHLM/WR CM1 14 E2
STSD CM24 143 M5
Raleigh Cl SUD CO10 5 G1
Raleigh Rd SUD CO10 5 G1
Rambler Cl COLW CO3 158 F6
Ramparts Cl RCOLW CO6 131 K6
Ramplings Av COS CO15 12 F1
Ramsden Cl COS CO15 13 K2
Ramsey Cl CHTY IP2 54 C4
MAL CM9 271 M1
Ramsey Rd HAR CO12 139 M3
HSTD CO9 125 M5
Ramsgate Dr IPSE IP3 55 K2
Ramshaw Dr CHLM/GWD CM2 267 H2
Rana Ct BRTR CM7 180 B1
Rana Dr BRTR CM7 180 B1
Randall Cl GTDUN CM6 175 M4
Randolph Cl MAL CM9 271 H5 3
Rands Rd GTDUN CM6 203 H5
Rands Wy IPSE IP3 55 K4
Randulph Ter CHLM/WR CM1 15 L1
Randwell Cl IPNE IP4 32 D8
Ranelagh Rd CHTY IP2 31 H8 1
FX IP11 7 M2
Ranger Wk COLS CO2 188 D2
Rangoon Cl COLS CO2 187 K4
Ransome Cl RIPW IP8 30 C7
Ransome Crs IPSE IP3 55 K3
Ransome Rd IPSE IP3 55 K3
Ransomes Wy CHLM/WR CM1 266 D1
IPSE IP3 55 M5
Ransom Rd K/T/MI CO5 212 E8
Ranulf Cl HLWE CM17 226 E7
Ranulph Wy RCHLM CM3 257 K2
Raphael Dr CHLM/WR CM1 255 H6
Ratcliffe Ct K/T/MI CO5 211 K3 2
Ratcliffe Rd COLW CO3 159 G8
Rat Hl RIPS/CAP IP9 110 B4
Ravens Av HSTD CO9 126 B5
Ravensbourne Dr
CHLM/WR CM1 14 A5
Ravens Crs GTDUN CM6 178 A6
Ravensdale COS CO15 222 B7
Ravensfield Rd IP IP1 31 G3
Ravens La RIPW IP8 30 C3
Raven Wy COLN CO4 160 A1
Rawden Cl HAR CO12 8 E7
Rawlings Crs COLN CO4 132 D8
Rawstorn Rd COLW CO3 10 A7
Ray Av HAR CO12 8 D7
Raycliff Av RCOS CO16 222 A6
Raydon Wy SUD CO10 5 L8
Rayfield Cl GTDUN CM6 204 C1
Rayhaven HAR CO12 139 L3
Ray La HAR CO12 111 G8
Rayleigh Cl BRTR CM7 180 E1
COLN CO4 11 G3
Rayleigh Rd IP IP1 31 G4
Ray Md RCHLM CM3 234 B6
Rayment Drift KESG IP5 33 L6 5
Rayne Rd BRTR CM7 179 J3
Rayner Rd COLS CO2 187 K1
Rayner Wy HSTD CO9 126 A4
Raynham Cl BSF CM23 171 L6
Raynham Rd BSF CM23 171 K5
The Ray CHLM/WR CM1 255 G8
Reade Rd RIPS/CAP IP9 79 M7
Readers Ct CHLM/GWD CM2 267 G7
Reading Rd IPNE IP4 32 D6
Reaper Rd COLW CO3 187 J1
Rebecca Gdns WIT CM8 210 A1 4
Rebecca Meade GTDUN CM6 147 H5
Rebow Rd HAR CO12 140 C3
RCOLE CO7 189 K5 7
Rebow St COL CO1 11 G9
Reckitts Cl COS CO15 13 L4
Recreation Cl FX IP11 113 H1 1
Recreation Gnd STSD CM24 143 M7
Recreation La FX IP11 113 H1
Recreation Rd COL CO1 160 D8
COS CO15 13 H5
HSTD CO9 95 M5
HVHL CB9 23 H6
SUD CO10 50 D8
Recreation Wk SUD CO10 50 D8
Recreation Wy IPSE IP3 55 K3
RCOLE CO7 219 H6 1
Rectory Cl HADL IP7 76 A4
RCHLM CM3 234 E7
SAFWS CB11 62 B1 3
Rectory Fld RIPS/CAP IP9 81 G6
Rectory Hl RCOLE CO7 105 L4
RCOLE CO7 189 L4
Rectory La BSF CM23 142 E7
CHLM/WR CM1 266 D1
HAR CO12 139 J4
HSTD CO9 72 E7
K/T/MI CO5 216 B2
KIR/NAC IP10 83 K1
MAL CM9 270 B7
MGTR CO11 107 G4
RCHLM CM3 206 F5
RIPW IP8 52 B2 1
SAFWN CB10 40 C4
WIT CM8 210 C7
Rectory Meadow BRTR CM7 181 L3
Rectory Rd BRTR CM7 153 K6
CBS CB2 16 F5
CHLM/WR CM1 265 K5
CHTY IP2 54 E2
COLN CO4 104 B7
FOS CO13 223 J2
HAR CO12 139 H6
HSTD CO9 95 M4
HVHL CB9 24 D3
K/T/MI CO5 189 G6
K/T/MI CO5 212 E8
MAL CM9 241 L4
MAL CM9 269 M2
MGTR CO11 138 C2
RCOLE CO7 164 A5
RCOLE CO7 189 L3
RCOLE CO7 191 G4
RCOLW CO6 157 H5
RCOLW CO6 185 L4
RCOS CO16 193 J8
RCOS CO16 221 H2
RIPS/CAP IP9 109 L2
SUD CO10 51 K7
SUD CO10 51 J1
SUD CO10 74 A1
SUD CO10 75 K1
Redan St IP IP1 2 C3
Red Barn La HAR CO12 166 D2
Red Barn Rd RCOLE CO7 219 H5
Redbridge Rd COS CO15 222 B5
Redcliffe Rd CHLM/GWD CM2 14 F6
Reddings Cl SAFWS CB11 63 G6 5
Rede Wy SUD CO10 5 L9
Redgate La RIPS/CAP IP9 54 E8
Redgates La SAFWN CB10 63 M1
Redgates Pl CHLM/WR CM1 267 G1 4
Red House Cl FX IP11 83 J5
Redhouse La RCOLW CO6 131 M3
SUD CO10 4 D7
Red House La SUD CO10 74 C1
Red House Wk KIR/NAC IP10 82 A1
Red La RIPS/CAP IP9 77 J5
Redmayne Dr CHLM/GWD CM2 14 D8
Redmill COLW CO3 187 J2
Redricks La HLW CM20 226 B7
Redruth Cl CHLM/WR CM1 255 G8
Redshank Cl HVHL CB9 23 L6
Redshank Dr MAL CM9 259 L8
Red Sleeve RIPS/CAP IP9 77 H4
Redvers Cl BSF CM23 171 J3
Red White & Blue Rd BSF CM23 171 K3
Redwing Cl CHTY IP2 53 M2
Redwood Cl COLN CO4 161 G5
WIT CM8 210 C8 9
Redwood Dr CHLM/WR CM1 265 H4
Reed Cl RCOS CO16 12 B2
Reed Hall Av COLS CO2 187 M2
Reedings Wy SBW CM21 227 H1
Reedland Wy FX IP11 112 F2
Reeds La HVHL CB9 23 J5
Reeve Gdns KESG IP5 33 L6
Reeves Pightle ROY SG8 59 H2
Refinery Rd HAR CO12 110 F8
Regal Cl CHLM/GWD CM2 15 L8
Regency Cl BSF CM23 171 G6
CHLM/GWD CM2 15 M1 1
Regency Ct MAL CM9 259 J8
Regency Gn COLW CO3 187 H1
Regent Cl RCOLE CO7 219 H5
Regent Rd RCOLE CO7 219 H6
Regents Cl COLN CO4 132 E8
Regent St IPNE IP4 3 J5
K/T/MI CO5 189 H5
MGTR CO11 135 M1 5
Regina Cl IPNE IP4 32 D8
Regina Rd CHLM/WR CM1 15 J1
Reigate Av RCOS CO16 221 M7
Reigate Cl IPSE IP3 55 K2 3
Rembrandt Gv CHLM/WR CM1 255 G7
Rembrandt Wy COLW CO3 159 K8 1
Rembrow Rd RIPS/CAP IP9 77 J4
Remembrance Av RCHLM CM3 257 J2
Remercie Rd MGTR CO11 136 C2
Rendlesham Rd FX IP11 112 F2 10
IP IP1 2 B4
Renfrew Rd IPNE IP4 32 E4 2
Rennie Pl CHLM/GWD CM2 267 K2
Rennie Rd CHLM/GWD CM2 15 L5
Renoir Pl CHLM/WR CM1 255 H6
The Retreat RCOLW CO6 159 G2
WIT CM8 238 C4
Reymead Cl K/T/MI CO5 244 E6
Reynard Copse BSF CM23 171 H4
Reynards Cl FOS CO13 195 M7
Reynards Copse COLN CO4 160 C2
Reynolds Av COLW CO3 159 K8
IPSE IP3 55 J5
Reynold's Cl HVHL CB9 22 F4 2
Reynolds Ct FX IP11 112 F2
Reynolds Rd IPSE IP3 55 J5
Rhodes Av BSF CM23 171 H8
Rhugarve Gdns CBE/LIN CB1 19 M3 3
Riby Rd FX IP11 7 J3
Richard Av RCOLE CO7 189 L2
Richard Burn Wy SUD CO10 4 D1
Richardson Pl CHLM/WR CM1 14 D1
Richardson Rd RCOLE CO7 105 M2
Richardsons La RIPS/CAP IP9 80 F6
Richardson Wk COLW CO3 159 H8
Richards Wk RCOS CO16 222 A7 1
Rich Cl RCHLM CM3 207 H6 4
Riche Cl GTDUN CM6 177 K8
Richmond Cl BSF CM23 170 E6 2
Richmond Crs HAR CO12 140 D3
Richmond Dr COS CO15 249 J4
Richmond Rd CHLM/GWD CM2 267 J1
IP IP1 31 H6
K/T/MI CO5 244 F7 4
Rickling Green Rd SAFWS CB11 116 A4
Rickling Rd SAFWS CB11 86 D7
Rickstones Rd WIT CM8 210 C6
Riddiford Dr CHLM/WR CM1 266 B1
Riddles Dr COLN CO4 10 D1
The Ridge RCHLM CM3 269 G3
WOTN CO14 196 D5 3
Ridgeway MAL CM9 271 J5 3
The Ridgeway BRTR CM7 180 C4
CBE/LIN CB1 20 A3
HAR CO12 8 D8
Ridgeway Valley Vw
COLN CO4 160 C1 1
Ridgewell Av CHLM/WR CM1 266 B1
Ridgewell Rd HSTD CO9 45 G3
SUD CO10 45 L4
Ridgewell Wy COLS CO2 188 B4
The Ridings BSF CM23 198 F1
CHLM/GWD CM2 266 F6
Ridlands Cl BRTR CM7 181 G7 4
Ridley Gdns RBSF CM22 144 E3
Ridley Rd CHLM/WR CM1 254 D5
Riffhams Cha RCHLM CM3 268 F4
Riffhams Dr CHLM/GWD CM2 267 H6
Riffhams La RCHLM CM3 268 E5
Rifle Hl BRTR CM7 180 B4
Rigby Av MGTR CO11 136 C2
Riley Av COS CO15 249 G7
Rimini Cl COLS CO2 187 L3
Ringham Rd IPNE IP4 32 C7
Ripley Cl RCOS CO16 221 K7
Ripple Wy COLN CO4 11 H3
Risby Cl IPNE IP4 32 D7
RCOS CO16 249 J1
The Rise COLW CO3 158 C5
Ritabrook Rd CHTY IP2 54 A4
Riverbank Cl SUD CO10 26 E6 1
River Cl HSTD CO9 126 B4
Riverfield La SBW CM21 227 G2 2
River Hl RCHLM CM3 236 D2
River Md BRTR CM7 152 C8
Riverside BRTR CM7 181 M2
BSF CM23 171 H6

GTDUN CM6 ... 176 A4
Riverside Av East MGTR CO11 ... 106 E8
Riverside Av West MGTR CO11 ... 106 E8
Riverside Ct HLW CM20 ... 226 E7
Riverside Rd IP IP1 ... 31 H6
Riverside Wy K/T/MI CO5 ... 211 L4
Rivers St IPNE IP4 ... 3 L3
River Vw WIT CM8 ... 238 C5
River View Rd RIPS/CAP IP9 ... 109 K3
River Wy HLW CM20 ... 226 C8
Rivey Cl CBE/LIN CB1 ... 19 M2
Rivey Wy CBE/LIN CB1 ... 19 M3
Rivish La SUD CO10 ... 29 L6
Roach V COLN CO4 ... 161 G4
Robeck Rd IPSE IP3 ... 55 G4
Robert Cl CHLM/GWD CM2 ... 267 H1
Robert's Hl BURES CO8 ... 129 H2
Roberts Rd COLS CO2 ... 160 B8 1
Robert Wallace Cl BSF CM23 ... 171 H4
Robin Cl RCOLE CO7 ... 191 M5
Robin Crs COLW CO3 ... 186 E1
Robin Dr CHTY IP2 ... 53 M2
Robin Hood Rd RBSF CM22 ... 144 E4
Robinsbridge Rd RCOLW CO6 ... 183 H3
Robinsdale COS CO15 ... 222 B7
Robinson Cl BSF CM23 ... 171 H8
Robinson Rd RCOLE CO7 ... 219 J6
Robin Wy CHLM/GWD CM2 ... 266 D8
SUD CO10 ... 49 L8
Robjohns Rd CHLM/WR CM1 ... 14 A8
Robletts Wy RCOLW CO6 ... 130 A1
Rochdale Wy COLN CO4 ... 161 G7 3
Rochelle Cl GTDUN CM6 ... 119 J2
Rochester Cl BRTR CM7 ... 180 F1
Rochester Wy SUD CO10 ... 4 A1
Rochford Rd BSF CM23 ... 171 K4
CHLM/GWD CM2 ... 15 J5 1
RCOS CO16 ... 248 D1
Rochford Wy FOS CO13 ... 196 C6 2
Rockall Cl HVHL CB9 ... 23 M6
Rockingham Cl COLN CO4 ... 160 F2 2
Rodbridge Hl SUD CO10 ... 49 K1
Roddam Cl COLW CO3 ... 159 L7
Rodney Gdns BRTR CM7 ... 180 E1 5
Rodney Wy CHLM/WR CM1 ... 14 B9
Rogation Cl COLW CO3 ... 158 F8
Rogers Cl FX IP11 ... 113 H1 2
Rokell Wy FOS CO13 ... 196 B7
Rollestons CHLM/WR CM1 ... 265 H4
Rolley La K/T/MI CO5 ... 211 L3
Rolph Cl RCOS CO16 ... 194 C3
Roman Cl MAL CM9 ... 271 H1 1
Roman Ct BRTR CM7 ... 180 E4 2
Roman Ri SBW CM21 ... 226 F3
Roman Rd COL CO1 ... 10 E5
RCHLM CM3 ... 234 D7
Romans Pl CHLM/WR CM1 ... 265 K4 3
Romans Wy CHLM/WR CM1 ... 265 K4
Roman V HLWE CM17 ... 226 E8
Roman Wy FX IP11 ... 113 M1
HVHL CB9 ... 23 M7
RCOS CO16 ... 247 J2
SUD CO10 ... 29 L7
Romford Cl COLN CO4 ... 11 H4
Romney Cl BRTR CM7 ... 152 A7
FOS CO13 ... 196 A6 8
RCOLE CO7 ... 219 G4
RCOS CO16 ... 221 M7
Romney Rd IPSE IP3 ... 55 J5
Romulus Cl COLN CO4 ... 132 B8
Ronald Rd HSTD CO9 ... 126 A5
Rook End La SAFWS CB11 ... 88 D7
The Rookeries RCOLW CO6 ... 185 K1 1
Rookery Cha RCOLE CO7 ... 134 A3
Rookery Cl RCHLM CM3 ... 237 J8 1
SAFWN CB10 ... 37 M2
Rookery La K/T/MI CO5 ... 212 E6
MAL CM9 ... 240 A6
SAFWS CB11 ... 87 G1
The Rookery MGTR CO11 ... 135 L1 2
STSD CM24 ... 144 A5 6
Rookes SAFWN CB10 ... 62 F1
Rookwood Cl RCOS CO16 ... 221 M6
Rookwood Wy HVHL CB9 ... 23 J7
Roosevelt Wy COLS CO2 ... 188 D1
Roos Hill Debden Rd
SAFWS CB11 ... 63 G8
Roots La WIT CM8 ... 259 G1
Ropers La SUD CO10 ... 49 K1
Ropes Dr KESG IP5 ... 33 M5
Rope Wk IPNE IP4 ... 3 H6
MAL CM9 ... 271 J4
Rosabelle Av RCOLE CO7 ... 189 K4
Rosalind Cl COLN CO4 ... 161 H6
Rose Acre RCOLE CO7 ... 76 B7
Roseacres RBSF CM22 ... 173 L6
SBW CM21 ... 226 F2
Rose Av COLW CO3 ... 186 E1
Rosebank HAR CO12 ... 8 C8
Rosebank Rd K/T/MI CO5 ... 244 C7
Rosebay Cl WIT CM8 ... 237 M2
Rosebery BSF CM23 ... 171 L7
Rosebery Av COL CO1 ... 10 F7
Rosebery Rd CHLM/GWD CM2 ... 15 H7
FX IP11 ... 113 K3
IPNE IP4 ... 3 L6
Rose Ct RIPS/CAP IP9 ... 111 H2 1
Rose Crs COLN CO4 ... 159 M3
Rosecroft Cl COS CO15 ... 222 A7
Rosecroft Rd IP IP1 ... 31 J3
Rosefinch Cl HVHL CB9 ... 23 L6
Rose Gdns BRTR CM7 ... 180 C3 3
RCOS CO16 ... 248 D7
Rose Hl BRTR CM7 ... 180 C3
Rosehill Crs IPSE IP3 ... 3 L8
Rosehill Rd IPSE IP3 ... 3 M8
Rose La IPNE IP4 ... 2 F7
MAL CM9 ... 242 D5
RCOLE CO7 ... 189 K6 3
SAFWN CB10 ... 38 A3
Rosemary Av BRTR CM7 ... 180 B1
FX IP11 ... 113 K1
Rosemary Cl GTDUN CM6 ... 175 L4 1
K/T/MI CO5 ... 212 E8 2
Rosemary Crs COS CO15 ... 13 H8
GTDUN CM6 ... 175 L4 2
K/T/MI CO5 ... 212 E8
Rosemary Cresecent
GTDUN CM6 ... 175 L4 3
Rosemary Gdns SUD CO10 ... 4 E1
Rosemary La GTDUN CM6 ... 148 E6
GTDUN CM6 ... 175 L4
HSTD CO9 ... 71 H8
HSTD CO9 ... 126 A3
RCOLE CO7 ... 191 K8
Rosemary Rd COS CO15 ... 12 F7
Rosemary Rd West COS CO15 ... 12 E7
Rosemary Wy COS CO15 ... 249 J6
Rosery Ms FOS CO13 ... 223 J1
Rosewood Cl COLN CO4 ... 160 C1
Roslings Cl CHLM/WR CM1 ... 253 M7
Ross Cl HVHL CB9 ... 23 L6
SAFWS CB11 ... 63 G7 2
Rossdene Gdns GTDUN CM6 ... 230 F6
Rossendale CHLM/WR CM1 ... 14 B6
Rossendale Cl COLN CO4 ... 160 E2
Rossetta Cl RCOLE CO7 ... 189 J3 2
Ross Rd IPNE IP4 ... 32 D4
Rothbury Rd CHLM/WR CM1 ... 265 M4
Rothesay Av CHLM/GWD CM2 ... 14 F7
Rothmans Av CHLM/GWD CM2 ... 267 G7
Rotten Rw SUD CO10 ... 51 J8
Roundacre HSTD CO9 ... 126 A5
Roundbush Rd K/T/MI CO5 ... 213 M4
Round Cl COLW CO3 ... 159 K6
Round Coppice Rd RBSF CM22 ... 172 C5
Roundridge Rd RIPS/CAP IP9 ... 77 K3 4
Roundwood Rd IPNE IP4 ... 32 C6
Routh Av IPSE IP3 ... 56 B4 2
Rover Av COS CO15 ... 249 G6
Rowallan Cl COLW CO3 ... 187 J2
Rowan Cl COLW CO3 ... 186 F1
COS CO15 ... 12 A6
HAR CO12 ... 8 F8
RCOLE CO7 ... 192 B5 1
Rowan Dr MAL CM9 ... 259 L8
Rowanhayes Cl CHTY IP2 ... 54 D2
Rowan Wk SBW CM21 ... 227 G3
Rowan Wy RCHLM CM3 ... 257 J2 2
WIT CM8 ... 210 C8
Rowarth Av KESG IP5 ... 33 L6
Rowell Cl HVHL CB9 ... 23 J3
Rowhedge Ferry Rd
RCOLE CO7 ... 189 J5
Rowhedge Rd COLS CO2 ... 188 F3
Rowherns La RCOLE CO7 ... 192 B1
Rowland's Yd HAR CO12 ... 140 A3
Rowley Cl MGTR CO11 ... 106 F5
Rowley Ct HVHL CB9 ... 24 A8
Rowley Hl HVHL CB9 ... 23 M8
Rowney Av SAFWN CB10 ... 89 G3
Rowney Gdns SBW CM21 ... 226 E5
Rowney Wd SBW CM21 ... 226 E4
Rowntree Wy SAFWS CB11 ... 62 F6
The Row RCOLE CO7 ... 104 E3
Roxburghe Rd RCOS CO16 ... 193 H7
Roxburgh Rd IPNE IP4 ... 32 D4
Roxwell Av CHLM/WR CM1 ... 265 M2
Roxwell Rd CHLM/WR CM1 ... 252 B5
Royal Ct COLN CO4 ... 161 G4 2
MAL CM9 ... 271 J4
Royal Oak Gdns BSF CM23 ... 171 G7
Roy Av IPNE IP4 ... 32 D8
Roy Cl KESG IP5 ... 33 K6
Royston Dr CHTY IP2 ... 53 M3
Royston La SAFWN CB10 ... 36 C5
Royston Rd CBS CB2 ... 16 F2
ROY SG8 ... 58 B2
SAFWS CB11 ... 61 L8
Ruaton Dr COS CO15 ... 12 A3
Rubens Ga CHLM/WR CM1 ... 255 H6
Rubens Rd IPSE IP3 ... 55 J4
Rudkin Rd COLN CO4 ... 132 B8
Rudlands RIPW IP8 ... 53 L4
Rudsdale Wy COLW CO3 ... 159 H8
Ruffels Fld GTDUN CM6 ... 177 G1
Rugby Rd SUD CO10 ... 74 D1
Rugosa Cl COLW CO3 ... 158 E6
Rumsey Flds RCHLM CM3 ... 269 H6
Runnacles St WIT CM8 ... 181 L8
Runnacles Wy FX IP11 ... 112 F2
Runsell Cl RCHLM CM3 ... 269 H6
Runsell La RCHLM CM3 ... 269 H5
Runsell Vw RCHLM CM3 ... 269 H5
Rurik Ct MAL CM9 ... 271 G5
Rushbury Cl IPNE IP4 ... 32 D5
Rushfield SBW CM21 ... 227 G3 5
Rush Green Rd RCOS CO16 ... 249 K2
Rush La RBSF CM22 ... 144 E5
Rushleigh Gn BSF CM23 ... 198 F2
Rushleydale CHLM/WR CM1 ... 255 G8
Rushmere Cl K/T/MI CO5 ... 244 E7
Rushmere Rd IPNE IP4 ... 32 C6
Rushmere St KESG IP5 ... 32 F4
Ruskin Cl FOS CO13 ... 196 A6 9
HVHL CB9 ... 22 F4 3
Ruskin Rd CHLM/GWD CM2 ... 267 G3
IPSE IP3 ... 3 M7
The Ruskins BRTR CM7 ... 179 H4
Russell Rd COS CO15 ... 13 K5
FX IP11 ... 7 J5
IP IP1 ... 2 C7
Russell's Rd HSTD CO9 ... 125 L5
Russet Cl BRTR CM7 ... 180 C4 6
The Rustons CBS CB2 ... 16 F4
Rutherfords CHLM/WR CM1 ... 254 D4
Rutland Av COLS CO2 ... 187 K2
Rutland Gdns BRTR CM7 ... 180 C1 2
Rutland Rd CHLM/WR CM1 ... 254 C7
Rydal Wk IPSE IP3 ... 55 L3
Rydal Wy BRTR CM7 ... 179 L7
Ryde Av COS CO15 ... 222 C6
Rye Cl COLW CO3 ... 158 F8
IPSE IP3 ... 55 M1
RCHLM CM3 ... 257 J2
RCOLE CO7 ... 219 G4
The Rye Fld RCHLM CM3 ... 268 F2
Rye Hills HSTD CO9 ... 126 B5
Rye La COLS CO2 ... 215 J1
Rye Mill La K/T/MI CO5 ... 211 M1
Ryes La RBSF CM22 ... 200 D6
SUD CO10 ... 73 J3
Rye St BSF CM23 ... 171 H4
Rygate Rd COL CO1 ... 10 D6
Rylands RIPS/CAP IP9 ... 77 J3
The Ryle CHLM/WR CM1 ... 265 J5
Rylstone Wy SAFWS CB11 ... 63 H5
Rysley RCHLM CM3 ... 268 F1

S

Sackville Cl CHLM/WR CM1 ... 14 A1
Sackville Wy RCOLW CO6 ... 158 F1
Sacombs Ash La SBW CM21 ... 198 A6
Saddle Ri CHLM/WR CM1 ... 255 G5 1
Sadler Cl COLS CO2 ... 188 D1
Sadlers Cl FOS CO13 ... 195 L7
Saffron Cl BRTR CM7 ... 122 E2 2
Saffron Ct SAFWS CB11 ... 62 F4
Saffron Gdns BRTR CM7 ... 122 D2
Saffron Wk BRTR CM7 ... 122 D2
Saffron Wy K/T/MI CO5 ... 240 E1
Sage Rd COLS CO2 ... 188 C3
Sages RBSF CM22 ... 117 H8
Sages End Rd HVHL CB9 ... 42 C5
St Agnes Wy KESG IP5 ... 33 H7
St Alban's Rd COLW CO3 ... 159 M6
COS CO15 ... 13 J5
St Andrew's Av COLS CO2 ... 11 M8
St Andrew's Av
(Colchester By-pass Rd)
COLN CO4 ... 11 J6
St Andrews Cl IPNE IP4 ... 32 F8 2
RCOLE CO7 ... 190 D6
St Andrew's Dr RIPS/CAP IP9 ... 81 G6
St Andrews Gdns COLN CO4 ... 11 H5
St Andrews Pl RCOLE CO7 ... 219 G4
St Andrew's Ri SUD CO10 ... 49 G8
St Andrew's Rd COS CO15 ... 12 E5
FX IP11 ... 113 J2
HSTD CO9 ... 126 A3
RCHLM CM3 ... 256 B4
RCHLM CM3 ... 257 J1
RCOS CO16 ... 193 H4
SUD CO10 ... 5 H9
St Annes Cl RCOLW CO6 ... 183 K3
St Anne's Rd COLN CO4 ... 11 H4 1
St Anns Rd COS CO15 ... 12 E3
St Anthony's Dr
CHLM/GWD CM2 ... 266 E6
St Aubyns Rd IPNE IP4 ... 32 C8
St Augustine Ms COL CO1 ... 10 E7
St Augustine Rd IPSE IP3 ... 55 M1
St Augustine's Gdn IPSE IP3 ... 55 L2
St Austell Cl KESG IP5 ... 33 J7
St Austell Rd COLN CO4 ... 160 F2
St Austin's La HAR CO12 ... 9 L2 1
St Barbara's Rd COLS CO2 ... 187 M1
St Bartholomew Cl
COLN CO4 ... 160 E2 1
St Bartholomews La SUD CO10 ... 4 B2
St Bernard Rd COLN CO4 ... 160 F2
St Botolph's Church Wk
COL CO1 ... 10 D8 1
St Botolph's St COL CO1 ... 10 D7
St Botolph's Ter
WOTN CO14 ... 196 E5 10
St Botolph's Wy HVHL CB9 ... 23 H5
St Bride Ct COLN CO4 ... 11 L1
St Catherines Cl COLS CO2 ... 187 M4
St Catherine's Ct CHTY IP2 ... 54 A4
St Catherine's Rd
CHLM/WR CM1 ... 14 A4
SUD CO10 ... 29 L6
St Christopher Rd COLN CO4 ... 11 L1
St Christophers Wy COS CO15 ... 249 H6
St Clair Cl COS CO15 ... 222 B5
St Clair's Dr RCOS CO16 ... 220 D8
St Clair's Rd RCOS CO16 ... 220 D8
St Clare Dr COLW CO3 ... 159 J6
St Clare Rd COLW CO3 ... 159 J7
St Clement Rd COLN CO4 ... 160 F3
St Clements GTDUN CM6 ... 119 J3
St Cleres Hall La RCOS CO16 ... 248 D3
St Cleres Wy RCHLM CM3 ... 268 F7
St Columb Ct COLN CO4 ... 160 E3
St Cyrus Rd COLN CO4 ... 160 F3
St Davids Cl COLN CO4 ... 11 K6
St David's Rd IPSE IP3 ... 55 K2
St Denis Cl HAR CO12 ... 140 C4
St Dominic Rd COLN CO4 ... 11 L1
St Edmunds Cl HAR CO12 ... 140 C4 3
St Edmund's Ct COLN CO4 ... 11 J5
St Edmunds Flds GTDUN CM6 ... 176 A3
St Edmund's Hl SUD CO10 ... 74 F7
St Edmunds La BURES CO8 ... 100 B4
GTDUN CM6 ... 176 A3
St Edmund's Pl IP IP1 ... 2 E1
St Edmund's Rd FX IP11 ... 7 H6
IP IP1 ... 2 C1
St Edmund Wy BURES CO8 ... 100 C4
RCOLE CO7 ... 105 M6
SUD CO10 ... 29 M2
St Fabian's Dr CHLM/WR CM1 ... 266 A1
St Faith Rd COLN CO4 ... 11 L1
St Fillan Rd COLN CO4 ... 11 L2
St George's Av HAR CO12 ... 9 G9
HAR CO12 ... 140 E3 1
St George's Cl RCOLE CO7 ... 163 G4
St George's Rd FX IP11 ... 113 L1
St George's St IP IP1 ... 2 E4
St Giles Cl HSTD CO9 ... 96 F3
MAL CM9 ... 271 G3
St Giles Crs MAL CM9 ... 271 G3
St Gregory's Ct SUD CO10 ... 4 B5
St Helena Ms COLW CO3 ... 159 M8
St Helena Rd COLW CO3 ... 159 M8
St Helens Av COS CO15 ... 222 C6
St Helen's Gn HAR CO12 ... 9 L3
St Helen's La COL CO1 ... 10 C6
St Helen's St IPNE IP4 ... 3 J5
St Isidores KESG IP5 ... 33 M6
St Ives Cl KESG IP5 ... 33 J7
RCOS CO16 ... 249 K2
St Ives Rd K/T/MI CO5 ... 216 A7
St James Pk CHLM/WR CM1 ... 265 M1
St James Rd BRTR CM7 ... 152 B8
St James's St HSTD CO9 ... 96 B1
St James Wy BSF CM23 ... 170 D8
BSF CM23 ... 199 G3
St Johns Av BRTR CM7 ... 180 B3
CHLM/GWD CM2 ... 15 G8
COL CO1 ... 10 C8
St John's Cl COLN CO4 ... 160 E1
RCOLE CO7 ... 160 F1
SAFWS CB11 ... 62 F6
St John's Ct MAL CM9 ... 262 E4
St John's Crs STSD CM24 ... 144 A6
St John's Gn CHLM/WR CM1 ... 265 K4 4
St John's La STSD CM24 ... 144 A6 3
St John's Rd CHLM/GWD CM2 ... 15 G7 1
CHLM/WR CM1 ... 265 K4
COLN CO4 ... 160 F2
COS CO15 ... 12 F1
RCOLE CO7 ... 189 L6 1
RCOS CO16 ... 221 K8
STSD CM24 ... 144 A6
St John's St CBS CB2 ... 16 F4
COL CO1 ... 10 B8
MAL CM9 ... 262 E4
St Joseph Rd COLN CO4 ... 160 E2
St Jude Gdns COLN CO4 ... 160 F3
St Judes Cl COLN CO4 ... 11 M1
St Julian Gv COL CO1 ... 10 E8
St Lawrence Rd COLN CO4 ... 160 F3
St Lawrence Wy KESG IP5 ... 33 K5
St Leonards Cl SAFWS CB11 ... 87 J3 1
St Leonard's Rd COL CO1 ... 11 J9
IPSE IP3 ... 55 K2
St Luke's Cha K/T/MI CO5 ... 240 F1
St Luke's Cl COLN CO4 ... 160 F3
St Margaret's Rd
CHLM/GWD CM2 ... 267 G2
St Margaret's St IPNE IP4 ... 3 G4
St Mark Dr COLN CO4 ... 160 F3
St Marks Rd COS CO15 ... 12 E3
St Martins Cl COS CO15 ... 12 E4
GTDUN CM6 ... 229 L6
St Martins Gn FX IP11 ... 83 J5
St Mary's Cl BRTR CM7 ... 151 K6
CHLM/GWD CM2 ... 267 H7 3
FX IP11 ... 83 K7 1
RIPW IP8 ... 30 C4
St Mary's Crs FX IP11 ... 113 G1
St Mary's Dr STSD CM24 ... 144 B7
St Mary's La MAL CM9 ... 271 K3
St Marys Md CHLM/WR CM1 ... 254 C4 3
St Marys Pk KIR/NAC IP10 ... 57 J5
St Mary's Pl GTDUN CM6 ... 176 F6
St Mary's Rd BRTR CM7 ... 180 D2
COS CO15 ... 12 E4
FOS CO13 ... 196 C8
K/T/MI CO5 ... 211 L3
RCOLE CO7 ... 192 B8 1
WIT CM8 ... 210 D6
St Marys Vw SAFWN CB10 ... 63 G1
St Mary's Wk HVHL CB9 ... 43 K7
St Marys Wy NHMKT IP6 ... 32 B1
St Matthew's St IP IP1 ... 2 D4
St Michael's Cha RCOLW CO6 ... 185 M3
St Michael's Cl KESG IP5 ... 33 J7 2
St Michaels Ct MGTR CO11 ... 135 M1 6
St Michael's Dr CHLM/WR CM1 ... 252 C8
St Michael's La BRTR CM7 ... 180 B3
St Michael's Rd BRTR CM7 ... 180 B3
CHLM/GWD CM2 ... 15 G8
COLS CO2 ... 187 L4
HAR CO12 ... 140 D3
RCOS CO16 ... 194 B3
St Mildreds Rd CHLM/GWD CM2 ... 15 G8
St Monance Wy COLN CO4 ... 11 L1
St Nazaire Rd CHLM/WR CM1 ... 254 A7
St Neots Cl COLN CO4 ... 11 M1
St Nicholas Cl WIT CM8 ... 238 B1
St Nicholas Fld BSF CM23 ... 114 D5
St Nicholas Rd WIT CM8 ... 238 B1
St Nicholas St COL CO1 ... 10 D7 2
IP IP1 ... 2 E6
St Nicholas Wy RCOLW CO6 ... 183 J2
St Olaves Rd KESG IP5 ... 33 L5
St Osyth Cl CHTY IP2 ... 54 B5
St Osyth Rd COS CO15 ... 12 A5
RCOS CO16 ... 221 K5
St Osyth Rd East RCOS CO16 ... 221 L4
St Osyth Rd West RCOS CO16 ... 221 K4
St Paul's Rd COL CO1 ... 10 A4
COS CO15 ... 13 J6
St Peter's Av MAL CM9 ... 271 H3
St Peter's Cl BRTR CM7 ... 180 B1 2
St Peter's-in-the-fields
BRTR CM7 ... 180 B1
St Peter's Rd BRTR CM7 ... 180 B1
CHLM/WR CM1 ... 14 A4
K/T/MI CO5 ... 244 D7
RCOLW CO6 ... 183 K2
St Peter's St CBS CB2 ... 16 F5
COL CO1 ... 10 B5
IPNE IP4 ... 2 F6
St Peters Vw HSTD CO9 ... 95 M4 3
St Peter's Wk BRTR CM7 ... 180 B2 5
St Runwald St COL CO1 ... 10 C6 1
St Saviour Cl COLN CO4 ... 11 M1
St Thomas Cl COLN CO4 ... 161 G3 1
St Valery RBSF CM22 ... 173 L6
St Vincent Cha BRTR CM7 ... 152 D8 2
St Vincent Rd COS CO15 ... 249 M4
St Vincents Rd CHLM/GWD CM2 ... 15 G8
Sainty Cl RCOLE CO7 ... 189 L5 5
Salary Cl COLN CO4 ... 161 G4
Salcombe Rd BRTR CM7 ... 180 E4 3
Salcott St MAL CM9 ... 242 D5
Salehurst Rd IPSE IP3 ... 56 A2
Salerno Crs COLS CO2 ... 187 L3
Salerno Wy CHLM/WR CM1 ... 254 A7
Salisbury Av COLW CO3 ... 159 M7
Salisbury Cl BSF CM23 ... 171 H8
Salisbury Rd COS CO15 ... 223 G8 3
IPSE IP3 ... 55 J2
Sallows Cl IP IP1 ... 31 H6 1
Salmon Cl COLW CO3 ... 187 H1
Salmon's La RCOLW CO6 ... 184 C1
Saltcote Maltings MAL CM9 ... 272 A1 1
Salter Pl CHLM/GWD CM2 ... 267 H3 5
Salters BSF CM23 ... 198 E1
Salter's Meadow MAL CM9 ... 261 M1
Salthouse La IPNE IP4 ... 3 G7
Salvia Cl COS CO15 ... 12 B3
Samford Cl RIPS/CAP IP9 ... 79 M6
Samford Pl RIPW IP8 ... 30 D7
Samphire Cl WIT CM8 ... 237 M2
Sampson Dr SUD CO10 ... 29 M5
Sampson's La K/T/MI CO5 ... 244 A1
Samsons Cl RCOLE CO7 ... 219 G5
Samson's Rd RCOLE CO7 ... 219 G4
Samuel Ct IPNE IP4 ... 3 H5
Samuel Mnr
CHLM/GWD CM2 ... 267 H2 3
Sanderling Gdns MAL CM9 ... 259 L8 6
Sanders Dr COLW CO3 ... 159 K6
Sanderson Ms K/T/MI CO5 ... 189 H5
Sandford Cl RCOLE CO7 ... 189 L5
Sandford Mill Rd
CHLM/GWD CM2 ... 267 J3
Sandford Rd CHLM/GWD CM2 ... 15 M2
Sandhurst Av IPSE IP3 ... 3 M9
Sandle Rd BSF CM23 ... 171 J6
Sandling Crs IPNE IP4 ... 33 G8
Sandon Br CHLM/GWD CM2 ... 268 B6
Sandon Cl RCOLW CO6 ... 131 L6
Sandon Hl RCHLM CM3 ... 205 J6
Sandown Cl COS CO15 ... 222 C5
Sandown Rd IP IP1 ... 31 J2
Sandpiper Cl COLN CO4 ... 161 J6
HVHL CB9 ... 23 K6
Sandpiper Rd CHTY IP2 ... 54 A3
Sandpit Cl IPNE IP4 ... 33 H8
Sandringham Cl CHTY IP2 ... 54 B3
Sandringham Dr COLS CO2 ... 188 C1 3
Sandringham Pl
CHLM/GWD CM2 ... 15 K3
Sandwich Cl BRTR CM7 ... 152 A7 3
Sandwich Rd COS CO15 ... 249 M5 2
RCOLE CO7 ... 219 H5
Sandy Cl FX IP11 ... 83 K5
Sandy Hl RCOLW CO6 ... 129 M1
Sandyhill La IPSE IP3 ... 55 G4
Sandy La FRAM/WMKT IP13 ... 33 M1
SUD CO10 ... 49 H8
Sapling Pl IPNE IP4 ... 33 G8 1
Sappers Cl SBW CM21 ... 227 H3
Saran Ct RCOLE CO7 ... 189 J3 3
Sarcel BRTR CM7 ... 153 L7
Sargeant Cl COLS CO2 ... 188 D2 1
Sarre Wy RCOLE CO7 ... 219 G5
Sassoon Wy MAL CM9 ... 271 J4 4
Saul's Av WIT CM8 ... 238 C5
Sauls Bridge Cl WIT CM8 ... 238 C5
Saunders Av BRTR CM7 ... 179 M1
Saunders Cl RBSF CM22 ... 144 E4 1
Savernake Rd CHLM/WR CM1 ... 14 B6
Saville Cl SAFWS CB11 ... 114 D1
Saville St WOTN CO14 ... 196 E4
Savill Rd COLS CO2 ... 188 E3
Sawbridgeworth Rd
RBSF CM22 ... 199 L6
SBW CM21 ... 227 L2
Sawkins Av CHLM/GWD CM2 ... 266 F7
Sawkins Cl CHLM/GWD CM2 ... 266 F7
Sawkins Gdns CHLM/GWD CM2 ... 266 F7
Sawmill La KIR/NAC IP10 ... 56 D7
Sawney Brook CHLM/WR CM1 ... 265 J4
Sawpit La BSF CM23 ... 114 F6
Sawston Cl CHTY IP2 ... 54 C3 5
Sawyers Cl RIPS/CAP IP9 ... 77 J4
Sawyer's Rd MAL CM9 ... 260 E1
Saxmundham Wy RCOS CO16 ... 249 J2
Saxon Bank BRTR CM7 ... 180 D3 2
Saxon Cl COLW CO3 ... 187 H1
FX IP11 ... 113 M1 5
HSTD CO9 ... 126 B3 3
Saxon Dr WIT CM8 ... 238 A2
Saxon La RIPW IP8 ... 52 F5
Saxon Wy CHLM/WR CM1 ... 254 D6
COS CO15 ... 223 H7
MAL CM9 ... 271 K4
SAFWN CB10 ... 62 E4
Sayesbury Av SBW CM21 ... 226 F2
Sayesbury Rd SBW CM21 ... 227 G3
Sayes Gdns SBW CM21 ... 227 H3
Saywell Brook
CHLM/GWD CM2 ... 267 J3 2
Scarfe Wy COLN CO4 ... 161 G7
Scarletts Cl WIT CM8 ... 238 C6
Scarletts Rd COL CO1 ... 160 E8
Sceptre Cl MAL CM9 ... 262 F3
Schneider Cl FX IP11 ... 6 E9
School Cha HSTD CO9 ... 126 A5
School Cl RIPS/CAP IP9 ... 77 J4 2
School Hl COLS CO2 ... 214 C1
RIPW IP8 ... 53 H5
School La CHLM/WR CM1 ... 231 K2
COLS CO2 ... 214 C2
GTDUN CM6 ... 145 M7
HVHL CB9 ... 22 F5
K/T/MI CO5 ... 243 G1
MGTR CO11 ... 106 F4
MGTR CO11 ... 135 J3
MGTR CO11 ... 136 B1
RBSF CM22 ... 117 H8
RCHLM CM3 ... 207 G5
RCOLE CO7 ... 104 F3
RCOLE CO7 ... 105 H6
RCOLE CO7 ... 105 K2
RCOLE CO7 ... 191 J5
RCOLW CO6 ... 101 M8
RCOLW CO6 ... 131 J3
RCOLW CO6 ... 159 G1
ROY SG8 ... 58 C4
SAFWS CB11 ... 60 C6
SAFWS CB11 ... 87 H4
SUD CO10 ... 29 L4
School Rd BRTR CM7 ... 179 G6
CHLM/WR CM1 ... 231 L8
COLN CO4 ... 133 G1
COLS CO2 ... 188 C3
FOS CO13 ... 196 A8 1
HAR CO12 ... 166 E2
HSTD CO9 ... 70 F2
HSTD CO9 ... 72 D8
HSTD CO9 ... 95 M5
HSTD CO9 ... 97 K5
HVHL CB9 ... 24 C3
K/T/MI CO5 ... 212 E4
MAL CM9 ... 259 K2
MAL CM9 ... 260 D3
RCOLE CO7 ... 162 C8
RCOLW CO6 ... 101 M8

RCOLW CO6 185 M3
RCOS CO16 165 G8
RIPS/CAP IP9 78 F4
RIPS/CAP IP9 111 K5
SUD CO10 28 A7
WIT CM8 210 A2
WIT CM8 239 H8
School St SAFWN CB10 37 M3
SUD CO10 4 C7
SUD CO10 28 F7
School View Rd CHLM/WR CM1 14 D1
School Wk BRTR CM7 180 B2
Schreiber Rd IPNE IP4 32 D6
Scofield Ct SUD CO10 5 H8
Scopes Rd KESG IP5 33 L5
Scott Av BRTR CM7 93 L8
Scott Cl BRTR CM7 180 C5
Scott Dr COLW CO3 159 H7
Scott Rd BSF CM23 171 G7
IPSE IP3 55 K4
Scraley Rd MAL CM9 259 L7
Scrip's Rd RCOLW CO6 183 J6
Scrivener Dr RIPW IP8 53 K3
Scurvy Hall La RCHLM CM3 234 D4
Scylla Cl MAL CM9 259 L7
Scythe Wy COLW CO3 187 H1
Seabrook Gdns RCHLM CM3 256 B4
Seabrook Rd CHLM/GWD CM2 267 J7
Sea Cornflower Wy COS CO15 249 J6
Sea Crs COS CO15 249 H7
Seafield Av MGTR CO11 136 D1
Seafield Rd HAR CO12 140 D3
Seafields Gdns COS CO15 222 E8
Seafields Rd COS CO15 222 E8
Sea Flowers Wy COS CO15 249 J6
Seagers MAL CM9 259 K1
Sea Glebe Wy COS CO15 249 J6
Sea Holly Wy COS CO15 249 J7
Sea King Crs COLN CO4 160 D1
Sea Lavender Wy COS CO15 249 J6
Sea Pink Wy COS CO15 249 J7
Searle Wy COLW CO3 158 D4
Sea Rd FX IP11 7 H7
Sea Rosemary Wy COS CO15 249 J6
Sea Shell Wy COS CO15 249 J7
Sea Thistle Wy COS CO15 249 J6
Seaton Cl MGTR CO11 135 K2
Seaton Rd FX IP11 113 G2
Seaview Av HAR CO12 139 L6
K/T/MI CO5 245 G6
Seaview Hts WOTN CO14 196 E6
Seaview Rd RCOLE CO7 219 H6
Seaview Ter RCOS CO16 247 J2
Sea Wy COS CO15 249 H6
Seawick Rd RCOS CO16 248 D7
Sebastian Cl COLN CO4 161 G6
Seckford Cl IPNE IP4 33 H8
Second Av CHLM/WR CM1 254 C8
COS CO15 13 M4
FOS CO13 224 A1
FX IP11 83 K8
HAR CO12 9 H9
HSTD CO9 126 D4
RCOS CO16 193 H5
RCOS CO16 248 E7
SUD CO10 4 F2
WOTN CO14 197 G2
Sedgefield Wy BRTR CM7 180 D4
Sedop Cl SAFWS CB11 62 F6
Selby Cl COLS CO2 187 M4
Seldon Rd K/T/MI CO5 212 F8
Selkirk Rd IPNE IP4 32 E5
Selsey Av COS CO15 249 L5
Selvale Wy FX IP11 7 G1
Selwyn Cl CHTY IP2 2 E9
Serpentine Rd IPSE IP3 55 K3
Serpentine Wk COL CO1 10 B4
Seven Ash Gn CHLM/WR CM1 254 E8
Seven Cottages La KESG IP5 32 E4
Seven Devils La SAFWS CB11 62 F7
Seventh Av CHLM/WR CM1 254 D7
Severalls La COLN CO4 132 E8
Severn Rd COS CO15 13 G2
IPSE IP3 55 H2
Sewell's La SUD CO10 47 J4
Sewell Wontner Cl KESG IP5 33 L5 2
Sexton Cl COLS CO2 188 D5
Sextons La WIT CM8 239 K3
Seymour Rd CHTY IP2 2 E9
COS CO15 249 H4
Seymour St CHLM/GWD CM2 14 E4
Shackleton Cl HAR CO12 140 B4 4
Shackleton Rd IPSE IP3 55 K2
Shadowbush Cl HVHL CB9 23 H4
Shaftenhoe End Rd ROY SG8 58 C4
Shaftesbury Av HAR CO12 8 E7
Shafto Rd IP IP1 31 G5
Shair La RCOLE CO7 192 D3
Shakespeare Cl BRTR CM7 180 C6
Shakespeare Dr MAL CM9 271 J5
Shakespeare Rd COLW CO3 159 H7
IP IP1 31 G1
Shakeston Cl CHLM/WR CM1 265 K5
Shalford Rd BRTR CM7 178 F1
Shamrock Av CHTY IP2 54 A1
Shamrock Cl MAL CM9 262 F3
Shangani Rd BSF CM23 171 H8
Shanklin Cl COS CO15 222 C5
Shannon Cl HVHL CB9 23 M6 4
Shannon Rd IPSE IP3 55 J5
Shardlow Cl HVHL CB9 22 E4 2
Shatters Rd COLS CO2 214 C4
Shaw Cl FOS CO13 196 B6 5
Shaw Dr BRTR CM7 93 L7
Shaw Rd SUD CO10 29 M5
WIT CM8 210 B8
The Shaw RBSF CM22 228 C2
The Shearers BSF CM23 198 D1
Shearers Wy RCHLM CM3 256 B4 2
Shears Crs K/T/MI CO5 244 F8
Sheds La SAFWN CB10 63 G3
Sheepcoates La MAL CM9 260 B3
Sheepcote La BSF CM23 143 G2
Sheepcotes La RCHLM CM3 234 E6
WIT CM8 182 A8
Sheepcot Rd HSTD CO9 96 A2
Sheepen Pl COLW CO3 10 A5
Sheepen Rd COLW CO3 159 M5
Sheering Lower Rd SBW CM21 227 H5
Sheering Mill La SBW CM21 227 H3
Sheering Rd HLWE CM17 227 H8
Sheering Wk COLS CO2 188 B3
Sheerwater Ms COLN CO4 161 J5
Shelborn Br BRTR CM7 181 L1
Shelbourne Cl KESG IP5 33 M6 5
Sheldrake Dr CHTY IP2 54 A3
Shellcroft RCOLW CO6 127 H4
Shellduck Crs BRTR CM7 179 L8
Shelley Av SUD CO10 5 K8
Shelley Cl MAL CM9 271 J5 4
Shelley La RCOS CO16 222 B3
Shelley Rd CHLM/GWD CM2 15 M4
COLW CO3 159 H7
Shelley St CHTY IP2 2 F9
Shenley Rd IPSE IP3 55 K4
Shenstone Dr IP IP1 31 J2
Shepherd Dr RIPW IP8 53 L3
Shepherds Cl BSF CM23 198 E1 5
Shepherds Cft COLW CO3 158 F8
Shepherds Wy SAFWN CB10 63 H3
Sheppard Cl RCOS CO16 221 M7
Sheppard Dr CHLM/GWD CM2 267 J1
Sheppards Wy KESG IP5 33 M6
Sherborne Av IPNE IP4 32 C3
Sherborne Rd CHLM/WR CM1 254 F8
Sherbourne Cl FOS CO13 196 B6 6
Sherbourne Rd COLN CO4 161 H6
Sheriffs Wy RCOS CO16 222 A6
Sherrington Rd IP IP1 2 A1
Sherwood Cl COLN CO4 11 M7
Sherwood Dr CHLM/WR CM1 265 M4
COS CO15 222 A7
Sherwood Flds KESG IP5 33 L6 6
Sherwood Wy K/T/MI CO5 211 M1
Shetland Cl IPNE IP4 32 C5
Shetland Rd HVHL CB9 23 M5
Shillito Cl COLW CO3 187 H1
Ship La MGTR CO11 137 G2
RIPW IP8 30 D4
Ship Launch Rd IPSE IP3 54 F2
Shire Cl CHLM/WR CM1 255 H6
Shire Hall Tard IPNE IP4 3 G7
Shire Hl SAFWS CB11 63 H4
Shire Hill La SAFWN CB10 63 J5
Shirley Cl IP IP1 31 J2
Shoebridge's Hl RCOLE CO7 105 G7
Shop La K/T/MI CO5 246 B2
Shop Rd MGTR CO11 135 K7
Shoreham Rd COS CO15 249 L5
Shore La KIR/NAC IP10 81 K2
MGTR CO11 137 G2
RIPS/CAP IP9 109 J3
Shortcroft BSF CM23 171 M5
Short Cut Rd COL CO1 10 B6
Shortlands CHTY IP2 53 M4
Shortlands Pl BSF CM23 171 H5 2
Shortridge Ct WIT CM8 238 A5 8
Shotley Cl FX IP11 6 F1
RIPW IP8 53 L3
Shotley Wk RIPS/CAP IP9 82 A8
Shropshire Cl
CHLM/GWD CM2 267 H8 1
CHLM/GWD CM2 267 J8 2
The Shrubberies
CHLM/WR CM1 265 H5 1
Shrub End Rd COLW CO3 187 J2
Shrubland Av IP IP1 31 G4
Shrubland Ct COS CO15 13 M1
Shrubland Dr IPNE IP4 33 H8
Shrubland Rd COLS CO2 10 D9
MGTR CO11 136 B2
Shrublands SAFWN CB10 63 G2
Shrublands Cl CHLM/GWD CM2 15 K3
Shums Hl FOS CO13 195 L5
Siam Pl SUD CO10 4 D6
Sidegate Av IPNE IP4 32 C5
Sidegate La IPNE IP4 32 C5
Sidegate La West IPNE IP4 32 B4
Sidmouth Rd CHLM/WR CM1 255 G7 1
Sidney Ter BSF CM23 171 H7
Siena Ms COLS CO2 188 D1
Siggin's La CBE/LIN CB1 19 M7
Silcock Cl COLN CO4 160 E3
Silcott St RCOLE CO7 219 G7
Silent St IPNE IP4 2 F6
Silks Wy BRTR CM7 180 B3
Sillett Cl RCOS CO16 221 M7
Silvanus Cl COLW CO3 159 M7 4
Silverdale Cl IP IP1 31 J4
Silver Hl RIPW IP8 52 C2
Silver Leys RIPS/CAP IP9 78 A7
Silver St BRTR CM7 122 D2
HVHL CB9 22 C1
HVHL CB9 24 D3
MAL CM9 271 H2 2
STSD CM24 143 M7
WIT CM8 209 M1
Silverthorne Cl COLS CO2 188 C2 2
Simmonds Wy RCHLM CM3 269 H5
Simons La COL CO1 11 G8 1
Simpsons La K/T/MI CO5 240 C2
Sims Cl RCOLW CO6 127 K6
Sim's La HVHL CB9 24 F4
Sinclair Cl COLN CO4 160 B3
Sinclair Dr CHTY IP2 54 E2
Singer Av COS CO15 249 G6
Singleton Ct SUD CO10 50 C8 1
Sinnington End COLN CO4 160 E1
Sioux Cl COLN CO4 160 E1
Sirdar Rd IP IP1 2 A4
Sir Isaac's Wk COL CO1 10 B8
Siskin Cl COLN CO4 161 H5
Sittang Cl COLS CO2 187 L4
Sitwell Cl MGTR CO11 135 K1
Siward Rd WIT CM8 237 M5
Six Bells Ct BRTR CM7 152 B8 4
Sixth Av CHLM/WR CM1 254 D7
STSD CM24 172 E2
Skate's Hl SUD CO10 28 D3
Skeins Wy SAFWS CB11 114 E1
Skelmersdale Rd COS CO15 13 H5
Skelton Cl MGTR CO11 135 L1
Skerry Ri CHLM/WR CM1 254 D6
Skiddaw Cl BRTR CM7 179 M6
Skinners St BSF CM23 198 E1
Skipper Ct BRTR CM7 180 B5
Skitts Hl BRTR CM7 180 C3 4
Skreens Ct CHLM/WR CM1 265 M1 1
Sky Hall Hl COLN CO4 103 L6
Skylark La RIPW IP8 53 L3
Skyrmans Fee FOS CO13 196 A7
Sladburys La COS CO15 222 F6
Slade Rd COS CO15 222 E7
Slade St IPNE IP4 3 G7
The Slade SAFWN CB10 39 H6
Slate HSTD CO9 126 B4
Slaters Cl FOS CO13 196 B7
Sleaford Cl CHTY IP2 54 D2
Sloe Hl HSTD CO9 125 L3
Slough Farm Rd HSTD CO9 125 M3
Slough House Cl BRTR CM7 180 F4
Slough La RCOLE CO7 134 A8
RCOLE CO7 161 K7
Slough Rd CHLM/WR CM1 231 K3
MGTR CO11 106 E3
Slushy La RIPS/CAP IP9 109 K2
Smaley La SUD CO10 29 L5
Smallbridge Entry BURES CO8 100 F5
Smallwood Rd COLS CO2 187 K2
Smart St IPNE IP4 3 G7
Smeaton Cl COLN CO4 132 E8
Smeetham Hall La SUD CO10 49 G7
Smithers Cl RIPS/CAP IP9 77 J4
Smithers Dr CHLM/GWD CM2 267 J7
Smith's End La ROY SG8 58 B4
Smiths Fld BRTR CM7 179 H3
COL CO1 160 E8
Smiths Pl KESG IP5 33 M6 6
Smythe Cl RCOS CO16 221 L7 6
Smythies Av COL CO1 10 F7
Snakes La RBSF CM22 144 C3
Snape Cl RCOS CO16 249 J1
Snape Wy FOS CO13 196 B6 7
Sneating Hall La FOS CO13 195 G5
Snelling Gv CHLM/GWD CM2 267 H7
Sniveller's La K/T/MI CO5 210 F2
Snowberry Ct BRTR CM7 180 F1 5
Snowberry Gv COLS CO2 188 C2 3
Snowcroft RIPS/CAP IP9 77 J4
Snowdon Rd CHTY IP2 54 D3 2
Snowdrop Cl BSF CM23 170 E7
CHLM/WR CM1 255 G6 3
WIT CM8 238 A1 6
Snow Hl SUD CO10 26 D4
Soane St IPNE IP4 3 G4
Soft Rd SUD CO10 48 B8
The Soils HAR CO12 139 G8
Somerset Cl COLS CO2 187 K2 2
Somerset Pl CHLM/WR CM1 254 C6
Somerset Rd IPNE IP4 3 L1
Somerset Wy COS CO15 249 H4
Somersham Rd RIPW IP8 30 A1
Somers Rd COLW CO3 187 J1
Somme Rd COLS CO2 187 M1
Sonell Ct RCOLE CO7 189 K3 4
Sorrel Cl CHTY IP2 54 B2
COLN CO4 159 L3
Sorrell Cl MAL CM9 261 G6
RCHLM CM3 234 D7
Southborough Rd
CHLM/GWD CM2 14 E7
Southbrook SBW CM21 227 G4
Southcliff WOTN CO14 196 E6 1
Southcliff Pk COS CO15 13 K3
Southcliff Prom WOTN CO14 196 E6
South Cl HSTD CO9 126 A5
IPNE IP4 3 J1
RCOS CO16 248 D1
Southcote Rd WIT CM8 238 B1 2
Southcroft Cl FOS CO13 195 L7
Southend Rd MAL CM9 269 L8
Souther Cross Rd
CHLM/WR CM1 231 M8
Southey Cl MAL CM9 271 L1 1
Southfield SAFWN CB10 37 J2
Southfields RCOLE CO7 105 H7
Southgate Crs K/T/MI CO5 213 G8
Southgate Gdns SUD CO10 29 L7
Southgate St SUD CO10 29 L7
South Green Rd K/T/MI CO5 217 H2
South Heath Rd RCOLE CO7 220 B2
South Hl FX IP11 7 K4
South House Cha MAL CM9 271 K6
Southland Cl COLN CO4 11 K2
Southmill Rd BSF CM23 171 J7
South Primrose Hl
CHLM/WR CM1 14 D1
South Rd BSF CM23 171 J8
CBE/LIN CB1 18 B2
RBSF CM22 173 L5
SAFWS CB11 63 G4
South Strd MGTR CO11 106 E8
South St BRTR CM7 180 C3
BSF CM23 171 H7
COLS CO2 10 B9
IP IP1 2 C3
MAL CM9 261 M1
MGTR CO11 135 M1
RCHLM CM3 234 A6
SAFWN CB10 37 M3
South Vw GTDUN CM6 175 L5
Southview Dr COS CO15 223 H7 4
WOTN CO14 196 E6
South View Gn RIPS/CAP IP9 78 A7
Southview Rd RCHLM CM3 268 F7
Southway COLS CO2 10 C8
COLW CO3 10 A8
Southwold Wy RCOS CO16 221 J8
Sovereign Cl BRTR CM7 180 F1
Sowerberry Cl CHLM/WR CM1 254 B6
Spalding Av CHLM/WR CM1 254 A8
Spalding Cl BRTR CM7 180 A1
Spalding Wy CHLM/GWD CM2 267 H5
Spanbies Rd RCOLE CO7 104 F4 1
Sparepenny La North
SAFWN CB10 91 J1
Sparepenny La South
SAFWN CB10 91 K1
Sparkey Cl WIT CM8 238 C6 4
Sparks La HSTD CO9 45 J7
Sparling Cl COLS CO2 187 K3
The Sparlings FOS CO13 195 L5
Spa Rd K/T/MI CO5 212 A1
WIT CM8 238 A2
Sparrow Cl HSTD CO9 95 M5
Sparrow Rd SUD CO10 5 K9
Sparrows Cl ING CM4 264 C8
Sparrowsend Hl SAFWS CB11 62 C8
Sparrows Herne COS CO15 222 B7 3
Sparrow's La HLWE CM17 229 G8
RBSF CM22 229 G6
Speckled Wood Ct BRTR CM7 180 A5
Speedwell Cl WIT CM8 237 M2
Speedwell Rd CHTY IP2 54 B1
COLS CO2 188 F3
Spellbrook La East BSF CM23 199 H5
Spellbrook La West SBW CM21 198 F6
Spencer Cl MAL CM9 271 J5 5
RBSF CM22 144 E2 1
STSD CM24 144 A7 2
Spencer Rd RCOS CO16 194 C3
SAFWN CB10 37 M2
Spendells Cl WOTN CO14 197 G3 1
Spenlow Dr CHLM/WR CM1 253 M6
The Spennells RCOS CO16 194 C3
Spenser Rd IP IP1 31 G2
Spenser Wy COS CO15 249 H4
Spicers La SUD CO10 29 L5
Spindle Rd HVHL CB9 22 F5
Spindle Wd COLN CO4 160 C1
Spinks La WIT CM8 238 A4
Spinnaker Cl COS CO15 249 M5 3
Spinnaker Dr MAL CM9 272 A2 2
Spinnel's Hl MGTR CO11 137 K4
Spinnel's La MGTR CO11 137 L7
Spinner Cl IP IP1 30 F5
Spinneyfields K/T/MI CO5 212 F7
The Spinney BRTR CM7 180 E4 4
IPNE IP4 56 B1
SAFWS CB11 87 J6
STSD CM24 144 A8
The Spires CHLM/GWD CM2 267 H7
Spital Rd MAL CM9 270 F6
Sportsmans La RCHLM CM3 257 J3
Sportsway COL CO1 10 D4
Spout La SUD CO10 74 F6
Spratts La MGTR CO11 163 J1
Springbank Av MGTR CO11 135 K2
Spring Cha RCOLE CO7 189 K3
RCOLE CO7 219 G6
Spring Cl COLN CO4 160 E2 2
RCHLM CM3 256 F8
RCOS CO16 12 A1
Spring Elms La RCHLM CM3 269 H2
Springett's Hl BURES CO8 99 M3
Springfield Av FX IP11 113 J1
Springfield Gn CHLM/WR CM1 267 G1
Springfield La IP IP1 31 H5
Springfield Lyons Ap
CHLM/GWD CM2 255 J8 1
Springfield Park Av
CHLM/GWD CM2 15 M3
Springfield Park Hl
CHLM/GWD CM2 15 L3
Springfield Park La
CHLM/GWD CM2 267 G2
Springfield Park Pde
CHLM/GWD CM2 15 M3 1
Springfield Park Rd
CHLM/GWD CM2 15 M3
Springfield Pl
CHLM/WR CM1 254 F8 1
Springfield Rd CHLM/GWD CM2 15 K3
CHLM/WR CM1 15 L2
SUD CO10 4 C2
Springfields BRTR CM7 179 L3
GTDUN CM6 175 L5
RCOLE CO7 219 H7
Spring Gardens Rd RCOLW CO6 128 F6
Springhall La SBW CM21 227 G4
Springhall Rd SBW CM21 227 G3
Spring Hl SAFWS CB11 62 C4
Springhill Cl RCOLE CO7 163 G4
Springhill Rd SAFWS CB11 62 F5
Springhurst Cl IPNE IP4 3 M5
Springland Cl IPNE IP4 32 C7
Springlands Wy SUD CO10 4 F1
Spring La COLW CO3 158 C5
COLW CO3 159 J6
MAL CM9 239 M6
MAL CM9 271 K1
RCHLM CM3 258 B3
RCOLE CO7 189 K3
RCOLW CO6 159 G1
WIT CM8 238 C6
Springmead BRTR CM7 179 M6 1
Spring Meadow NHMKT IP6 33 K1
Spring Pond Cl
CHLM/GWD CM2 267 G5
Spring Rd IPNE IP4 3 K5
K/T/MI CO5 240 E1
RCOLE CO7 219 H6
RCOS CO16 248 C1
RIPW IP8 52 F3
Spring Sedge Cl COLW CO3 158 E6
Springvalley La RCOLE CO7 161 L2
Spring Wy HSTD CO9 96 A4
Springwell Rd SAFWN CB10 38 C8
Springwood Dr BRTR CM7 179 L1
Sprites End FX IP11 83 M8
Spriteshall La FX IP11 83 M8
Sprites La CHTY IP2 53 L3
RIPW IP8 53 L4
Sproughton Rd IP IP1 30 E6
RIPW IP8 30 D6
Spruce Av COLN CO4 11 M5
Spruce Cl K/T/MI CO5 244 D6
WIT CM8 238 C1 4
Spurgeon Cl HSTD CO9 96 A4 2
Spurgeon St COL CO1 11 K8
The Square SBW CM21 227 G3 6
Squires Cl BSF CM23 170 E5
Squirrells Ct CHLM/WR CM1 254 B8 4
Squirrels Cl BSF CM23 171 H5 3
Squirrels Fld COLN CO4 132 B8
The Squirrels RIPS/CAP IP9 77 J3
Stable Cl COLW CO3 158 F7
K/T/MI CO5 245 G6
Stablecroft CHLM/WR CM1 255 G5
Stablefield Rd FOS CO13 196 C6
Stable Ms K/T/MI CO5 245 G5
The Stackyard SAFWN CB10 37 J2
Staddles RBSF CM22 199 K4
Stafford Cl FOS CO13 196 A7
Stafford Crs BRTR CM7 180 F1
Stainers BSF CM23 170 E8
Stalin Rd COLS CO2 188 D1
Stallards Crs FOS CO13 196 A7
Stambourne Rd HSTD CO9 45 H8
HSTD CO9 69 K5
Stambridge Rd COS CO15 12 B3
Stamford Cl CHTY IP2 54 B5
Stammers Rd COLN CO4 160 B1
Standard Av COS CO15 248 F6
Standley Rd WOTN CO14 196 F4
Stane Cl BSF CM23 171 H5
Stane Fld RCOLW CO6 185 G2
Stanes Rd BRTR CM7 152 B7 3
Stanfield Cl COLW CO3 187 G2
Stanley Av IPSE IP3 55 J1
RCOLE CO7 219 G6
Stanley Ri CHLM/GWD CM2 267 H2 4
Stanley Rd COS CO15 12 A7
FX IP11 7 M3
HSTD CO9 125 M3
RCOLE CO7 189 L4
SAFWN CB10 38 A2
SUD CO10 4 D4
Stanleys Farm Rd
SAFWS CB11 63 H5 2
Stanley Wood Av SUD CO10 4 F2
Stanley Wooster Wy COLN CO4 161 G6
Stanmore Cl COS CO15 12 D1
Stanmore Wy RCOS CO16 248 D1
Stannard Wy SUD CO10 5 H9
Stanstead Rd HSTD CO9 126 B5
Stansted Cl CHLM/WR CM1 14 A6
Stansted Rd BSF CM23 171 J5
COLS CO2 188 C4 6
RBSF CM22 144 E4
Stansted Wy FOS CO13 196 C7
Stanstrete Fld BRTR CM7 179 K8 3
Stanton Hughes Wy
MGTR CO11 135 K1
Stanwell St COL CO1 10 C8
Stanwyn Av COS CO15 12 F5
Stapleford Cl CHLM/GWD CM2 14 F5
Staplers Cl MAL CM9 259 K1 2
Staplers Heath MAL CM9 259 K1
Staplers Wk MAL CM9 239 K8
Starfield Cl IPNE IP4 32 D7
Star La GTDUN CM6 175 M4
IPNE IP4 2 F7
Star Md GTDUN CM6 119 J3
Starr Rd RBSF CM22 117 H8
Station Ap BRTR CM7 180 C3
FOS CO13 196 B8
Station Hl BURES CO8 100 A5
Station La HAR CO12 9 H7
Station Rd BRTR CM7 179 H4
BSF CM23 171 H6
BSF CM23 171 J7 2
CBE/LIN CB1 19 K3
COS CO15 13 G6
FOS CO13 195 K7
FX IP11 83 L8
GTDUN CM6 176 A5
GTDUN CM6 177 H6
HAR CO12 8 A4
HSTD CO9 44 F5
HSTD CO9 95 M3
HVHL CB9 23 J5
K/T/MI CO5 211 L2
K/T/MI CO5 240 E1
MAL CM9 242 A8
MAL CM9 262 F3
MAL CM9 271 J2
MGTR CO11 106 D8
MGTR CO11 137 G3
MGTR CO11 138 B2
RBSF CM22 144 E3
RBSF CM22 173 L6
RCHLM CM3 237 H8
RCOLE CO7 189 K5
RCOLE CO7 190 C5
RCOLE CO7 191 J5
RCOLE CO7 191 H7
RCOLE CO7 192 A6
RCOLE CO7 219 G7
RCOLW CO6 127 J6
RCOLW CO6 127 H4
RCOLW CO6 128 F7
RCOLW CO6 128 A6
RCOLW CO6 185 J1
RCOS CO16 194 B5
RIPS/CAP IP9 77 M7
SAFWS CB11 62 A8
SAFWS CB11 62 F5
SAFWS CB11 87 J5
SBW CM21 227 H2
STSD CM24 144 A7 3
SUD CO10 4 E7
SUD CO10 26 B8
SUD CO10 29 L8
WIT CM8 209 H3
WIT CM8 238 C2
WIT CM8 258 E1
Station Rd East CBS CB2 17 G2
Station Rd West CBS CB2 17 G2
Station St CHTY IP2 54 E2
SAFWS CB11 62 F4
WOTN CO14 196 E6
Steam Mill Rd MGTR CO11 136 E5
Stebbing Rd GTDUN CM6 177 K6
Steeds Meadow SUD CO10 29 L5 1
Steele Cl RCOLW CO6 185 H2 4
Steeple Bumpstead Rd
HVHL CB9 42 F5
Steeple Cl MAL CM9 271 M1
Steeple Vw BSF CM23 171 H5
Steerforth Cl
CHLM/WR CM1 253 M6 1
Stella Maris CHTY IP2 30 F8 1
Stennetts Cl FX IP11 83 K7
Stepfield WIT CM8 238 D3
Stephen Cl HVHL CB9 23 H5 2
SUD CO10 29 K8
Stephen Cranfield Cl
K/T/MI CO5 189 J6 1
Stephen Marshall Av BRTR CM7 92 E7

Stephen's Ct IPNE IP4 .... 32 D7 1
Stephenson Rd BRTR CM7 .... 180 C5
  COLN CO4 .... 132 F7
  COS CO15 .... 222 D5
Stephenson Rd West COS CM6 .... 222 C4
Sterling Cl COLW CO3 .... 159 G8
Stevens La GTDUN CM6 .... 178 B7
Stevenson Rd IP IP1 .... 2 C4
Stevens Rd WIT CM8 .... 238 A4
Stewards Cl FOS CO13 .... 196 B6
Stewart Rd CHLM/GWD CM2 .... 266 C7
The Stewarts BSF CM23 .... 171 G6
Stewarts Wy BSF CM23 .... 143 H3
Stewart Young Gv KESG IP5 .... 33 M6 7
Stilemans Wd BRTR CM7 .... 180 F5
The Stiles MAL CM9 .... 272 A2
Stirling Dr HVHL CB9 .... 23 G5
Stirrup Cl CHLM/WR CM1 .... 255 G6
Stivvy's Rd MAL CM9 .... 269 L2
Stock Cha MAL CM9 .... 259 K8
Stockhouse Cl MAL CM9 .... 241 J3
Stockhouse Rd K/T/MI CO5 .... 213 K6
Stockley Cl HVHL CB9 .... 23 L6 1
Stockmers End RIPS/CAP IP9 .... 77 J4
Stockwell COL CO1 .... 10 C6
Stokeash Cl RCOS CO16 .... 249 J2
Stoke Br IP IP1 .... 2 F8
Stoke Hall Rd CHTY IP2 .... 2 E8
Stoke Park Dr CHTY IP2 .... 54 A5
Stoke Rd RCOLW CO6 .... 102 D4
  SUD CO10 .... 26 C7
The Stokes WOTN CO14 .... 196 D4
Stoke St CHTY IP2 .... 2 F8
Stollery Cl KESG IP5 .... 33 L6
Stonebridge Hl RCOLW CO6 .... 126 F6
Stonechat Rd CHTY IP2 .... 53 L2
Stonecrop COLN CO4 .... 159 L3
Stonegrove Rd FX IP11 .... 6 E8
Stonehall Dr RCOS CO16 .... 221 M4
Stonehall La RCOS CO16 .... 165 K4
Stoneham Av RCOS CO16 .... 221 J8
Stoneham St RCOLW CO6 .... 183 H3
Stonehill Rd CHLM/WR CM1 .... 264 B1
Stonehill Wy K/T/MI CO5 .... 244 C6
Stone La K/T/MI CO5 .... 240 B3
  MGTR CO11 .... 138 B1
Stoneleigh SBW CM21 .... 226 F2 1
Stoneleigh Pk COLW CO3 .... 187 H2
Stone Lodge La CHLM/WR CM1 .... 54 C2
Stone Lodge La West CHTY IP2 .... 54 B2
Stone Lodge Wk CHTY IP2 .... 54 B2
Stone Path Dr RCHLM CM3 .... 257 H1
Stone Rd RCOLE CO7 .... 163 K4
Stones Green Rd HAR CO12 .... 165 M3
  HAR CO12 .... 165 M3
Stoney Common STSD CM24 .... 144 A8
Stoney Common Rd
  STSD CM24 .... 143 M8
Stoneyfield Dr STSD CM24 .... 144 A8
Stoney La RCOLE CO7 .... 219 J5
Stopford Cl IP IP1 .... 2 B4
Stores Rd K/T/MI CO5 .... 212 E7
Stortford Hall Pk BSF CM23 .... 171 K5
Stortford Hall Rd BSF CM23 .... 171 K5
Stortford Rd GTDUN CM6 .... 174 D6
  GTDUN CM6 .... 230 C7
  RBSF CM22 .... 228 A1
  SAFWS CB11 .... 114 E1
Stort Ldg BSF CM23 .... 170 F5 1
Stort Ml HLW CM20 .... 226 D7
Stort Rd BSF CM23 .... 171 H7 3
Stort Valley Wy HLW CM20 .... 226 F6
  SBW CM21 .... 227 L3
Stour Av FX IP11 .... 7 H3
Stour Cl HAR CO12 .... 139 M3
  SUD CO10 .... 28 E3
Stourdale Cl MGTR CO11 .... 135 J2
Stour Gdns SUD CO10 .... 74 C1
Stourmead Cl HVHL CB9 .... 24 C3
Stour Rd HAR CO12 .... 9 K5
Stourside RIPS/CAP IP9 .... 111 J5
Stour St MGTR CO11 .... 135 M1
  SUD CO10 .... 4 B7
  SUD CO10 .... 27 L5
Stourton Rd WIT CM8 .... 238 A2 5
Stour V HSTD CO9 .... 44 F2
Stour Valley Pth BURES CO8 .... 100 A3
  HVHL CB9 .... 24 C1
  RCOLW CO6 .... 101 K3
  RCOLW CO6 .... 103 M2
  SUD CO10 .... 46 A1
Stour Valley Rd HVHL CB9 .... 23 K6
Stour Valley Wk SUD CO10 .... 27 L3
  SUD CO10 .... 27 L3
Stourview Av MGTR CO11 .... 136 C1
Stourview Rd MGTR CO11 .... 136 D1
Stradbroke Rd IPNE IP4 .... 32 C6
Straight Rd COLN CO4 .... 132 C1
  COLW CO3 .... 159 G2
  KIR/NAC IP10 .... 56 E5
  MGTR CO11 .... 136 E4
  RCOLW CO6 .... 220 C2
Straight Wy COLS CO2 .... 214 C3
The Strand CHTY IP2 .... 54 E5
Stratford Pl WOTN CO14 .... 196 F5 3
Stratford Rd COS CO15 .... 222 F7
  IP IP1 .... 31 H3
  RCOLE CO7 .... 104 E6
Strattonhall Drift KIR/NAC IP10 .... 82 B3
Strawberry Cl BRTR CM7 .... 180 C4
Strawberry Flds HVHL CB9 .... 22 F6
Strawberry La K/T/MI CO5 .... 241 G2
Strawbrook Hl RCHLM CM3 .... 235 G1
Straw La SUD CO10 .... 4 B7
The Street BRTR CM7 .... 153 K7
  BRTR CM7 .... 179 G4
  BRTR CM7 .... 181 J7
  BRTR CM7 .... 181 M3
  BSF CM23 .... 114 D6
  BSF CM23 .... 143 H3
  CHLM/WR CM1 .... 252 C7
  FOS CO13 .... 195 L4
  FRAM/WMKT IP13 .... 33 M1
  GTDUN CM6 .... 176 F5
  GTDUN CM6 .... 203 G6
  HADL IP7 .... 76 A3
  HAR CO12 .... 139 J4

HSTD CO9 .... 44 D7
HSTD CO9 .... 69 K6
HSTD CO9 .... 98 C6
HSTD CO9 .... 125 G6
K/T/MI CO5 .... 184 A8
K/T/MI CO5 .... 212 F3
KIR/NAC IP10 .... 56 E8
MAL CM9 .... 240 D8
MAL CM9 .... 242 C5
MAL CM9 .... 269 M3
MGTR CO11 .... 107 J4
MGTR CO11 .... 137 G4
RBSF CM22 .... 172 C8
RBSF CM22 .... 227 M5
RCHLM CM3 .... 232 C3
RCHLM CM3 .... 234 D7
RCHLM CM3 .... 236 E2
RCHLM CM3 .... 257 H1
RCOLE CO7 .... 104 E5
RCOLE CO7 .... 105 K3
RCOLW CO6 .... 128 E8
RCOLW CO6 .... 134 A5
RCOS CO16 .... 165 G8
RCOS CO16 .... 193 H4
RCOS CO16 .... 221 L1
RIPS/CAP IP9 .... 54 C7
RIPS/CAP IP9 .... 77 H4
RIPS/CAP IP9 .... 79 M7
RIPS/CAP IP9 .... 109 K3
RIPS/CAP IP9 .... 110 D3
RIPS/CAP IP9 .... 110 F2
RIPW IP8 .... 30 C3
RIPW IP8 .... 52 B5
RIPW IP8 .... 53 H5
RIPW IP8 .... 53 L7
SUD CO10 .... 28 C5
SUD CO10 .... 28 E7
SUD CO10 .... 45 K2
SUD CO10 .... 45 M4
SUD CO10 .... 47 L5
SUD CO10 .... 49 G8
SUD CO10 .... 51 J1
SUD CO10 .... 74 A2
WIT CM8 .... 209 G4
WIT CM8 .... 239 G8
Stretford Ct WIT CM8 .... 209 M2 2
Strethall Rd SAFWS CB11 .... 37 J8
Strickmere RCOLE CO7 .... 104 E3
Strood K/T/MI CO5 .... 244 D6
The Strood K/T/MI CO5 .... 244 D1
Strudwick Cl BRTR CM7 .... 180 B3 5
Strutt Cl RCHLM CM3 .... 257 J1 3
Stuart Cl CHLM/GWD CM2 .... 267 K7
  IPNE IP4 .... 3 L3
Stuarts Wy BRTR CM7 .... 180 D3 3
Stubbs Cl FOS CO13 .... 196 A6
  HVHL CB9 .... 22 F4 4
  IPSE IP3 .... 55 J4
  MGTR CO11 .... 135 K1 4
Stubbs La BRTR CM7 .... 180 E3
Studd's La COLN CO4 .... 159 M1
Stump La CHLM/WR CM1 .... 266 F1
Sturdee Av IPSE IP3 .... 55 K2
Sturmer Rd HVHL CB9 .... 23 L7
Sturrick La RCOLE CO7 .... 191 M4
Stutton Cl RIPS/CAP IP9 .... 108 C3
Stutton Gn RIPS/CAP IP9 .... 108 E4
Stutton La RIPS/CAP IP9 .... 78 E8
Stutton Rd MGTR CO11 .... 107 J3
Styles BRTR CM7 .... 120 F3
Sudbourne Av RCOS CO16 .... 249 J1
Sudbourne Rd FX IP11 .... 112 F2 11
Sudbury Rd BURES CO8 .... 100 B4
  FX IP11 .... 6 D2
  HSTD CO9 .... 126 B2
  SUD CO10 .... 51 J6
Suffolk Av K/T/MI CO5 .... 244 F6
Suffolk Cl COLN CO4 .... 11 H3
  COS CO15 .... 223 G6
Suffolk Coast & Heaths Pth
  FX IP11 .... 113 K4
  IPSE IP3 .... 55 J7
  KIR/NAC IP10 .... 55 M6
  RIPS/CAP IP9 .... 81 G4
  RIPS/CAP IP9 .... 108 E3
  RIPS/CAP IP9 .... 110 B6
Suffolk Crs MAL CM9 .... 271 G4
Suffolk Rd IPNE IP4 .... 3 H3
  MAL CM9 .... 271 G4
  SUD CO10 .... 4 D5
Suffolk St WOTN CO14 .... 196 E5 11
Sugar La HSTD CO9 .... 94 F6
Sullivan Cl COLN CO4 .... 161 G7 4
Summerfield IPNE IP4 .... 32 F5
Summerfields RCOS CO16 .... 96 A4
Summer Hill Rd SAFWS CB11 .... 62 F5
Sunbank GTDUN CM6 .... 176 A5
Sunbeam Av COS CO15 .... 249 G7
Sunbury Wy MAL CM9 .... 271 H5
Sundale Cl COS CO15 .... 223 H7 5
Sunderland Rd FX IP11 .... 6 E9
Sunfield Cl IPNE IP4 .... 32 D7
Sun Lido Square Gdns
  BRTR CM7 .... 179 L3
Sunningdale BSF CM23 .... 171 G2
Sunningdale Av IPNE IP4 .... 32 F8
Sunningdale Dr FX IP11 .... 113 K1
Sunningdale Fall
  RCHLM CM3 .... 257 K1 2
Sunningdale Rd
  CHLM/WR CM1 .... 266 A1
Sunningdale Wy FOS CO13 .... 196 A6
Sunnyfields Rd BRTR CM7 .... 152 F3
Sunny Point WOTN CO14 .... 197 G2
Sunnyside BRTR CM7 .... 180 A2
  STSD CM24 .... 144 A7
Sunnyside Rd RCOLW CO6 .... 129 M8
Sunnyside Wy RCOS CO16 .... 221 L4
Sunray Av FX IP11 .... 113 K1
Sunrise Av CHLM/WR CM1 .... 254 C8
Sun St SBW CM21 .... 227 H4
Surbiton Rd IP IP1 .... 31 H6
Surrey La K/T/MI CO5 .... 240 E1
Surrey Rd FX IP11 .... 7 J2
  IP IP1 .... 2 A6
Sussex Cl RCHLM CM3 .... 256 B5
Sussex Gdns COS CO15 .... 223 G7

Sussex Rd COLW CO3 .... 159 L6
Sutton Acres RBSF CM22 .... 199 M6
Sutton Md CHLM/GWD CM2 .... 267 J1 5
Sutton Park Av COLW CO3 .... 187 J2
Swallow Cl COLS CO2 .... 187 J8
Swallowdale COLS CO2 .... 188 E2 2
  COS CO15 .... 222 B7
Swallow Fld RCOLW CO6 .... 127 K7
Swallow's Rw RCOLE CO7 .... 192 D4
Swallow Wk HSTD CO9 .... 126 B4 2
Swan Cha HSTD CO9 .... 96 A5
Swan Cl COLN CO4 .... 161 G7
  RCHLM CM3 .... 257 H1
Swan Ct BSF CM23 .... 171 H7 4
  MAL CM9 .... 271 K1 2
  MGTR CO11 .... 136 C2 2
Swanfield SUD CO10 .... 29 L6
Swanscomb Rd RCOLW CO6 .... 128 B8
Swansea Av CHTY IP2 .... 54 D4
Swan Side BRTR CM7 .... 180 B2 6
Swan Gv RCOLW CO6 .... 128 E8
Swan Hl RIPW IP8 .... 53 J3
Swan La HVHL CB9 .... 23 J5
  NHMKT IP6 .... 32 A1
  SUD CO10 .... 29 L6
Swan Pas COL CO1 .... 10 D6 3
Swan Rd RCOS CO16 .... 165 M8
Swan St HSTD CO9 .... 96 A4
  RCOLW CO6 .... 156 E2
Swan Yd RCOLW CO6 .... 183 J3
Swatchway Cl IPSE IP3 .... 55 K5 2
Swaynes RCOLE CO7 .... 104 E3
Sweden Cl HAR CO12 .... 8 B7
Sweet Briar BSF CM23 .... 170 D7
Sweet Briar Rd COLW CO3 .... 158 E6
Sweet Md SAFWS CB10 .... 63 G2
Swift Av COS CO15 .... 222 B7
Swift Cl BRTR CM7 .... 180 C5 13
Swinburne Rd IP IP1 .... 31 G2
Swinton Cl CHTY IP2 .... 53 M4
Swiss Av CHLM/WR CM1 .... 266 B1
Sworders Yd BSF CM23 .... 171 H6 7
Sycamore Cl RBSF CM22 .... 173 L6
  RIPW IP8 .... 53 L4
  WIT CM8 .... 210 C8 10
Sycamore Gv BRTR CM7 .... 179 H4 1
Sycamore Pl RCOLE CO7 .... 192 A5 3
Sycamore Rd COLN CO4 .... 11 M4
  MAL CM9 .... 259 K7
  SUD CO10 .... 5 J7
The Sycamores BSF CM23 .... 171 K7
Sycamore Wy CHLM/GWD CM2 .... 266 F7
  COS CO15 .... 12 A6
  FOS CO13 .... 195 M7
  MGTR CO11 .... 106 F5
Sydner Cl CHLM/GWD CM2 .... 267 J8
Sydney Cl COLS CO2 .... 188 D4
  RCOLE CO7 .... 219 H8
Sylvan Cl CHLM/GWD CM2 .... 266 D7
Symmons Cl BRTR CM7 .... 179 H4 1
Symonds La CBE/LIN CB1 .... 19 K2

T

Tabor Av BRTR CM7 .... 180 A2
Tabor Cl RCOLE CO7 .... 219 G6
Tabor Rd COLN CO4 .... 11 K7
Tabors Av CHLM/GWD CM2 .... 267 H6
Tacket St IPNE IP4 .... 2 F6
Tacon Rd FX IP11 .... 7 H7
Talbot Av COS CO15 .... 249 H7
Talbot Rd RCOS CO16 .... 221 L1
  SUD CO10 .... 4 F2
Talbot St HAR CO12 .... 9 J6
Talcott Rd COLS CO2 .... 188 C3
Talisman Cl K/T/MI CO5 .... 212 F7 5
Tallboys Cl KESG IP5 .... 33 L5 3
Tall Trees COLN CO4 .... 160 A2
Tally Ho COLN CO4 .... 160 D1
Tallyho Cnr RCOLE CO7 .... 104 F4 2
Tamarisk Wy COLN CO4 .... 161 G6 3
  COS CO15 .... 249 H7
Tamar Ri CHLM/WR CM1 .... 254 E7
Tambour Cl RCOLW CO6 .... 156 E5 2
Tamworth Cha COLS CO2 .... 188 C3 2
Tangerine Cl COLN CO4 .... 11 M8
Tan La RCOS CO16 .... 194 A8
Tanner Cl RCOS CO16 .... 249 K2 1
Tanners Meadow BRTR CM7 .... 180 F3 3
Tanners Wy SAFWS CB10 .... 63 G4
The Tanyard GTDUN CM6 .... 119 J3 3
Tapley Rd CHLM/WR CM1 .... 254 B7
Tapsworth Cl COS CO15 .... 12 B2
Tapwoods COLW CO3 .... 159 J6
Tara Cl COLN CO4 .... 11 M3
Tarn Hows Cl FX IP11 .... 113 M1 6
Tarragona Ms COLS CO2 .... 188 D1 2
Tarragon Cl K/T/MI CO5 .... 212 E8
Tasmania Rd IPNE IP4 .... 32 F7
Tasman Rd HVHL CB9 .... 23 L6
Taunton Cl IP IP1 .... 31 K1
Taunton Rd CHLM/WR CM1 .... 255 G8
  FX IP11 .... 113 H2
Taverners Wk WIT CM8 .... 238 B1 3
Tavern St IP IP1 .... 2 F5
Tavistock Rd CHLM/WR CM1 .... 254 F8 2
Tawell Ms K/T/MI CO5 .... 212 F8 3
Tawney Cl RIPS/CAP IP9 .... 77 J4
Tawneys Ride BURES CO8 .... 100 C4
Taylor Av CHLM/WR CM1 .... 254 A8
Taylor Cl COL CO1 .... 10 C8
Taylor Dr MGTR CO11 .... 135 L1
Taylors End Rd STSD CM24 .... 173 G4
Taylor's Rd K/T/MI CO5 .... 189 H5
Teal Cl BRTR CM7 .... 179 K8
  CHTY IP2 .... 53 M2
  RCOLE CO7 .... 161 J5
Teal Wy K/T/MI CO5 .... 211 M3
Tedder Cl COLS CO2 .... 188 C1 4
Tees Rd CHLM/WR CM1 .... 254 E7
Teign Dr WIT CM8 .... 237 M3
Telford Rd BRTR CM7 .... 180 C4
  COS CO15 .... 222 D5

Telford Wy COLN CO4 .... 132 F7
Templar Rd BRTR CM7 .... 180 F3
Templars Cl WIT CM8 .... 238 B1 4
Temple Bank HLW CM20 .... 226 D8
Temple Cl CBS CM2 .... 17 G4
  FOS CO13 .... 196 C7
Temple Ct COLN CO4 .... 11 M1
Temple La BRTR CM7 .... 209 L2
Templemead WIT CM8 .... 238 B2 3
Temple Pattle MGTR CO11 .... 106 E6
Temple Rd COLS CO2 .... 187 J3 2
  IPSE IP3 .... 55 L1
Temple Wy MAL CM9 .... 259 H8
Ten Acre Ap MAL CM9 .... 259 H8
Tenby Rd CHTY IP2 .... 54 D4 1
Tendring Rd RCOLE CO7 .... 164 C5
  RCOS CO16 .... 165 H3
Tennyson Cl BRTR CM7 .... 180 B5 2
Tennyson Rd CHLM/WR CM1 .... 254 B8
  IPNE IP4 .... 3 M6
  MAL CM9 .... 271 J4
Tenpenny Hl RCOLE CO7 .... 191 G7
Tenterfield GTDUN CM6 .... 176 A4
Tenter Fld RCOLE CO7 .... 104 F4
Tenterfield Rd MAL CM9 .... 271 J3
Tenterfields SAFWS CB11 .... 87 H4
Tenth Rd KIR/NAC IP10 .... 57 K7
Terling Cl COLS CO2 .... 188 C4
Terling Hall Rd RCHLM CM3 .... 236 B4
Terling Rd RCHLM CM3 .... 237 H7
  WIT CM8 .... 237 J3
Termitts Cha RCHLM CM3 .... 237 H6
  WIT CM8 .... 237 L6
Tern Cl HVHL CB9 .... 23 L6
  K/T/MI CO5 .... 211 M2
Terndale COS CO15 .... 222 B7
Tern Rd CHTY IP2 .... 54 A3
Terrace Hall Cha RCOLW CO6 .... 131 L7
Tew Cl K/T/MI CO5 .... 212 F7 6
Tewkesbury Rd COS CO15 .... 12 F3
Tey Rd RCOLW CO6 .... 127 M7
  RCOLW CO6 .... 157 J5
  RCOLW CO6 .... 183 K2
Tey Road Cl RCOLW CO6 .... 127 L7
Thackeray Cl BRTR CM7 .... 180 C5
Thackeray Rd IP IP1 .... 31 G2
Thames Av CHLM/WR CM1 .... 253 L8
Thames Cl BRTR CM7 .... 180 F4
Thanet Rd IPNE IP4 .... 32 D7
Thatchers Dr RCOLE CO7 .... 162 B7
The Thatchers BSF CM23 .... 170 E8
Thaxted Rd SAFWS CB11 .... 63 H6
Thaxted Wk COLS CO2 .... 188 C5
Theberton Rd IPSE IP3 .... 55 K4
Thetford Rd IP IP1 .... 31 H6 2
Thieves Cnr CHLM/WR CM1 .... 265 H1
Third Av CHLM/WR CM1 .... 254 D8
  COS CO15 .... 13 M4
  FOS CO13 .... 224 A1
  HAR CO12 .... 9 G9
  HSTD CO9 .... 126 D4
  RCOS CO16 .... 248 D6
  WOTN CO14 .... 197 G2
Thirlmere Cl BRTR CM7 .... 179 M6 2
Thirslet Dr MAL CM9 .... 271 L1
Thirtieth St STSD CM24 .... 173 H2
Thirtle Cl RCOS CO16 .... 221 M7
Thistle Cl CHTY IP2 .... 54 B1
Thistledown BRTR CM7 .... 151 J6
  COLN CO4 .... 160 D2
Thistley Cl MAL CM9 .... 261 G7
Thistley Green Rd BRTR CM7 .... 152 D6
Thomas Av FX IP11 .... 83 L7
Thomas Bell Rd RCOLW CO6 .... 127 J7
Thomas Cl CHLM/GWD CM2 .... 267 H3 6
Thomas Rd COS CO15 .... 12 D4
Thomas St RCOLE CO7 .... 219 H7 3
Thomas Wakley Cl COLN CO4 .... 132 B8
Thomas Wk SAFWS CB11 .... 61 H4
Thompson Av COLW CO3 .... 159 H7
Thompson Rd IP IP1 .... 31 H5
Thorley Hl BSF CM23 .... 171 H4
Thorley La BSF CM23 .... 170 D8
Thorley Park Rd BSF CM23 .... 199 H1
Thornbera Cl BSF CM23 .... 199 H1
Thornbera Gdns BSF CM23 .... 199 G1
Thornbera Rd BSF CM23 .... 199 H1
Thornberry Av RCOS CO16 .... 193 H5
Thornbury Rd COS CO15 .... 13 G3
Thornbush La RIPW IP8 .... 30 B5
Thorncroft SAFWS CB10 .... 63 H3
Thorndon Cl RCOS CO16 .... 249 J1 5
Thorne Rd K/T/MI CO5 .... 211 K3
Thorney Rd RIPS/CAP IP9 .... 77 J3
Thornfield Rd BSF CM23 .... 171 G5
Thorn Gv BSF CM23 .... 171 K7
Thornhayes Cl CHTY IP2 .... 54 C2 1
Thornhill Cl FOS CO13 .... 196 B6 8
Thornley Dr IPNE IP4 .... 32 E5
Thornley Rd K/T/MI CO5 .... 113 L3
Thorns Wy WOTN CO14 .... 196 D6
Thornton Dr COLN CO4 .... 10 D1
Thornton Rd RBSF CM22 .... 174 B5
Thorn Wy FX IP11 .... 7 H2
Thornwood COLN CO4 .... 160 B1
Thornwood Cl K/T/MI CO5 .... 244 F7 5
Thoroughgood Rd COS CO15 .... 13 J7
Thorpe Cl FX IP11 .... 83 H5
Thorpe Park La RCOS CO16 .... 194 C6
Thorpe Rd COS CO15 .... 222 B6
  FOS CO13 .... 195 H6
  RCOS CO16 .... 222 B3
Thorpe's Hl RIPW IP8 .... 52 E2
Thorrington Rd RCOLE CO7 .... 191 L5
  RCOS CO16 .... 221 L1
Thracian Cl COLS CO2 .... 187 J3 3
Threadneedle St RCOLE CO7 .... 105 H6
Three Acres RCOS CO16 .... 248 C1
Three Crowns Rd COLN CO4 .... 10 A1
Three Forests Wy GTDUN CM6 .... 229 M5
  RBSF CM22 .... 227 G4
Three Forest Wy RBSF CM22 .... 172 D8
Three Gate Cl HSTD CO9 .... 125 M5
Tremhall Av RBSF CM22 .... 173 H4
Thresher Cl BSF CM23 .... 170 E8

Threshers End COLW CO3 .... 158 F8 3
Through Jollys KESG IP5 .... 33 M5
Thrushdale COS CO15 .... 222 B7
Thurlston Cl RCOS CO16 .... 11 M2
Thurmans La FX IP11 .... 83 K7
Thurstable Cl MAL CM9 .... 263 G3
Thurstable Rd MAL CM9 .... 262 F3
Thurstable Wy MAL CM9 .... 263 G3
Thurston Ct FX IP11 .... 6 D2
Thyme Rd K/T/MI CO5 .... 212 F8 4
Tiberius Cl HVHL CB9 .... 23 M6
Tiberius Gdns WIT CM8 .... 238 A5 9
Tideswell Cl BRTR CM7 .... 180 F1 6
Tideway MAL CM9 .... 271 K5 5
Tidings Hl HSTD CO9 .... 126 A5
Tiffin Dr K/T/MI CO5 .... 213 G8
Tilbury Rd HSTD CO9 .... 45 L6
Tile Barn La MGTR CO11 .... 134 E3
Tile House Rd RCOLW CO6 .... 131 K5
Tilkey Rd RCOLW CO6 .... 183 H1
Timber Hl COL CO1 .... 11 J9 1
Timbers Cl BRTR CM7 .... 179 K6 1
Timperleys RIPW IP8 .... 52 B2
Timsons La CHLM/GWD CM2 .... 267 G1
Tinabrook Cl CHTY IP2 .... 54 A4
Tindal St CHLM/WR CM1 .... 15 H3
Tindon End Rd SAFWN CB10 .... 90 F3
Tinker Av BRTR CM7 .... 93 L7
Tinker St HAR CO12 .... 139 H4
Tintagel Wy MAL CM9 .... 271 G5
Tintern Cl CHTY IP2 .... 54 C3
Tippett Cl COLN CO4 .... 161 G7
Tiptree Hall La K/T/MI CO5 .... 240 D2
Tiptree Rd WIT CM8 .... 239 L4
Titania Cl COLN CO4 .... 161 H6
Tithe Cl WIT CM8 .... 238 A2
Titus Wy COLN CO4 .... 132 D7
Tobruk Rd CHLM/WR CM1 .... 254 B7
  COLS CO2 .... 187 M2
Tofts Cha RCHLM CM3 .... 257 G8
Toga Cl COLS CO2 .... 187 J3
Tofts Wk BRTR CM7 .... 180 B2 7
Tog La RCOLW CO6 .... 131 J2
Tokely Rd RCOLE CO7 .... 191 J2
Tokio Rd IPNE IP4 .... 3 M5
Toller Rd IPSE IP3 .... 55 G2
Tollesbury Rd MAL CM9 .... 262 A1
Tolleshunt D'arcy Rd MAL CM9 .... 261 H2
Tollgate Dr COLW CO3 .... 158 D7
Tollgate East COLW CO3 .... 158 E7
Tollgate West COLW CO3 .... 158 E7
Tolliday Cl RCOLE CO7 .... 189 J3 4
Tolworth Rd IPNE IP4 .... 32 C7
Tomline Rd FX IP11 .... 7 L3
  IPSE IP3 .... 32 C8
Tom's La BRTR CM7 .... 92 C7
Tom Tit La MAL CM9 .... 270 A5
Tony Webb Cl COLN CO4 .... 160 D1
Toppesfield Rd HSTD CO9 .... 70 B5
Top Rd MAL CM9 .... 241 J3
  MAL CM9 .... 269 M3
  SAFWN CB10 .... 65 J8
  SAFWN CB10 .... 89 M2
Torquay Rd CHLM/WR CM1 .... 254 F3
Torrington Cl CHLM/WR CM1 .... 255 G8
Tortoiseshell Wy BRTR CM7 .... 180 A4
Tortosa Cl COLS CO2 .... 188 D1 3
Torver Cl BRTR CM7 .... 179 L7
Totham Hill Gn MAL CM9 .... 240 A7
Totlands Dr COS CO15 .... 222 B6
Tot La BSF CM23 .... 171 M2
Totnes Wk CHLM/WR CM1 .... 255 G7
Totteridge Cl RCOS CO16 .... 12 C1
Toucan Wy COS CO15 .... 222 B7
Toulmin Rd RCHLM CM3 .... 257 J1
Tovell's Rd IPNE IP4 .... 3 M4
Tower Av CHLM/WR CM1 .... 14 C1
Tower Cut RCOLE CO7 .... 219 H7
Tower Mill Rd IP IP1 .... 31 H6
Tower Ramparts IP IP1 .... 2 F4
Tower Rd CHLM/WR CM1 .... 265 H4
  COS CO15 .... 12 F9
  FX IP11 .... 7 K3
  RCOLE CO7 .... 189 K3
Towers Rd MAL CM9 .... 259 L8
Tower St IP IP1 .... 2 F5
  RCOLE CO7 .... 219 H8
Tower Vw CBE/LIN CB1 .... 19 M2
Town Cft CHLM/WR CM1 .... 254 C8 2
Town End Fld WIT CM8 .... 238 A5
Townfield St CHLM/WR CM1 .... 14 F2
Townsend Rd K/T/MI CO5 .... 212 E7
Town St GTDUN CM6 .... 119 J3 4
Towse Cl RCOS CO16 .... 12 A2
Traddles Ct CHLM/WR CM1 .... 254 B7 1
Trafalgar Cl IPNE IP4 .... 3 M4
Trafalgar Rd COLW CO3 .... 159 G7
  COS CO15 .... 12 E9
  SUD CO10 .... 5 H2
Trafalgar Wy BRTR CM7 .... 180 D1
Trajan Cl COLN CO4 .... 132 D7
Tranmere Gv IP IP1 .... 31 H3
Tree Cl COS CO15 .... 222 B6
Trefoil Cl CHTY IP2 .... 54 B1
Trenchard Crs CHLM/WR CM1 .... 254 F6
Trent Rd CHLM/WR CM1 .... 253 L8
  IPSE IP3 .... 55 H3
  WIT CM8 .... 238 A3 4
Trews Gdns CHLM/WR CM1 .... 211 L2
Trimley Cl RCOS CO16 .... 249 K1
Trimley Rd KIR/NAC IP10 .... 83 K2
Trinity Av FX IP11 .... 6 B4
Trinity Cl BSF CM23 .... 171 H7
  K/T/MI CO5 .... 244 E6
  KESG IP5 .... 33 H6
  MGTR CO11 .... 135 M2
  RCOLE CO7 .... 189 L5
Trinity Link HVHL CB9 .... 23 J4
Trinity Ms K/T/MI CO5 .... 244 E6 2
Trinity Rd CHLM/GWD CM2 .... 15 L3
  HSTD CO9 .... 125 M4
  MGTR CO11 .... 135 M2
Trinity St BSF CM23 .... 171 H7 5
  COL CO1 .... 10 C7
  HSTD CO9 .... 125 M4
Trinity Wy BSF CM23 .... 171 H7

Triumph Av COS CO15 .... 249 G6
Troon Gdns IPNE IP4 .... 32 D5
Trotters Fld BRTR CM7 .... 180 D2
Trotwood Cl CHLM/WR CM1 ...... 254 A6
Trunette Rd COS CO15 .... 12 B6
Truro Crs KESG IP5 .... 33 J7 3
Tucker Dr WIT CM8 .... 238 B5
Tucker's Rw BSF CM23 .... 171 H7
Tuddenham Av IPNE IP4 .... 3 J3
Tuddenham La KESG IP5 .... 32 D3
Tuddenham Rd IPNE IP4 .... 3 H3
Tudor Cl COS CO15 .... 249 H4
RCOLE CO7 .... 219 G6 2
RIPS/CAP IP9 .... 111 J4
SUD CO10 .... 4 C2
WIT CM8 .... 238 B5
WOTN CO14 .... 196 F3 3
Tudor Gn COS CO15 .... 249 H4
SUD CO10 .... 4 C1
Tudor Rd SUD CO10 .... 4 C2
Tudor Rose Cl COLW CO3 .... 158 E6
Tudwick Rd K/T/MI CO5 .... 241 G2
MAL CM9 .... 241 G6
Tufnell Wy COS CO15 .... 159 L3
Tufted Cl BRTR CM7 .... 179 L8
Tugby Pl CHLM/WR CM1 .... 254 A7
Tulip Cl CHLM/WR CM1 .... 255 G6 4
Tumulus Wy COLS CO2 .... 187 H3
Tunstall Cl RCOS CO16 .... 220 D8
Turin St CHTY IP2 .... 2 F9
Turkentine Cl SUD CO10 .... 50 F8
Turkey Cock La COLW CO3 .... 158 A7
RCOLW CO6 .... 158 B5
Turkey Oaks CHLM/WR CM1 ...... 15 K2
Turner Cl HVHL CB9 .... 22 F4
RCOLE CO7 .... 189 L4
Turner Gv KESG IP5 .... 33 M5
Turner Rd COLN CO4 .... 10 C1
IPSE IP3 .... 55 J5
Turners Crs BSF CM23 .... 198 E1
Turnpike Cl COLN CO4 .... 133 G6
Turnpike Hl HVHL CB9 .... 22 E1
Turnstone End COLN CO4 .... 161 H5 2
Turpins Av COS CO15 .... 222 E8
Turpins Cl COS CO15 .... 222 E8
Turpins La FOS CO13 .... 196 A6
Turret La IPNE IP4 .... 2 F6
Turstan Rd WIT CM8 .... 238 A5
Tusser Cl WIT CM8 .... 210 D6
Tusset Ms COLW CO3 .... 159 G6 2
Tweed Cl HSTD CO9 .... 125 M6
Twelve Acre Ap KESG IP5 .... 33 K6
Twelve Acres BRTR CM7 .... 180 F2
Twentyfirst St STSD SM24 ...... 173 H3
Twining Rd COLW CO3 .... 187 G1
Twin Oaks CHLM/GWD CM2 ...... 267 J1
Twitty Fee RCHLM CM3 .... 269 J4
Two Acres RIPS/CAP IP9 .... 77 K3
Twyford Bury La BSF CM23 ...... 199 J1
Twyford Cl BSF CM23 .... 171 J8
Twyford Gdns BSF CM23 .... 199 H1
Twyford Rd BSF CM23 .... 171 J8
Tyburn Hl RCOLW CO6 .... 128 C7
Tydeman Cl COLW CO3 .... 186 E1
Tye Green Rd RBSF CM22 .... 144 E6
Tyehurst Crs COLN CO4 .... 160 E3
Tye La RCOLE CO7 .... 190 A2
Tye Rd RCOLE CO7 .... 162 A6
The Tye Rd RCOLE CO7 .... 192 D5
Tyler Av COS CO16 .... 249 K2
Tylers Cl CHLM/GWD CM2 ...... 266 D7
Tylers Gn FX IP11 .... 83 L8
Tyler St CHTY IP2 .... 3 G9
HAR CO12 .... 8 A4
Tylneys Rd HSTD CO9 .... 126 C2
Tyndale Dr COS CO15 .... 249 J4
Tyndales La RCHLM CM3 .... 269 K8
Tynedale Sq COLN CO4 .... 160 D1
Tyrells Cl CHLM/WR CM1 .... 267 G1
Tyrells Wy CHLM/GWD CM2 ...... 267 H6
Tyrone Cl IP IP1 .... 30 F3 1
Tyssen Md RCHLM CM3 .... 256 A5
Tythe Cl CHLM/WR CM1 .... 255 G6
The Tythings HSTD CO9 .... 125 M5 1

U

Ullswater Cl BRTR CM7 .... 179 L7
Ulster Av IP IP1 .... 30 F4
Ulting Hall Rd MAL CM9 .... 258 A6
Ulting La MAL CM9 .... 257 M7
Ulting Rd RCHLM CM3 .... 257 L4
Una Rd HAR CO12 .... 140 A1
Undercliff Rd East FX IP11 ...... 113 J3
Undercliff Rd West FX IP11 ...... 7 M3
Union Rd COS CO15 .... 249 J5
Union St IPNE IP4 .... 3 G5 1
Unity Cl COLS CO2 .... 188 D1
Unity St IPSE IP3 .... 3 K9
Upland Crs K/T/MI CO5 .... 244 E6
Upland Dr COLN CO4 .... 11 K1
Upland Rd IPNE IP4 .... 32 C7
K/T/MI CO5 .... 244 E6
Uplands Crs SUD CO10 .... 4 D2
Uplands Dr CHLM/WR CM1 ...... 254 F6
Uplands Rd COS CO15 .... 12 C9
SUD CO10 .... 4 D2
Upper Acres WIT CM8 .... 210 B8
Upper Barclay St IPNE IP4 ...... 3 G6
Upper Branston Rd COS CO15 ...... 12 C4
Upper Bridge Rd
  CHLM/GWD CM2 .... 14 E7
Upper Brook St IPNE IP4 .... 2 F5
Upper Chapel St HSTD CO9 ...... 126 A3 3
Upper Cha CHLM/GWD CM2 ...... 14 E7
Upper East St SUD CO10 .... 4 E5
Upper Farm Rd SUD CO10 .... 45 M5
Upper Fenn Rd HSTD CO9 .... 126 C3
Upperfield Dr FX IP11 .... 113 K1
Upper Fourth Av FOS CO13 ...... 196 B8
Upper High St IP IP1 .... 2 E3
Upper Holt St RCOLW CO6 .... 127 L7
Upper Mill Fld GTDUN CM6 ...... 176 A6

Upper Moors RCHLM CM3 .... 234 B6
Upper Orwell St IPNE IP4 .... 3 G6
Upper Park Rd COS CO15 .... 12 D6
Upper Rd SUD CO10 .... 75 H5
Upper Roman Rd
  CHLM/GWD CM2 .... 15 H6
Upper Second Av FOS CO13 ...... 196 A8
Upper St RCOLE CO7 .... 104 E4
Upper Third Av FOS CO13 .... 196 A8
Upper Trinity Rd HSTD CO9 ...... 126 A4 4
Upshers SAFWS CB11 .... 63 H5
Upton Cl IPNE IP4 .... 3 K5
RCOLW CO6 .... 158 F1
Urban Rd BSF CM23 .... 171 K6
Usterdale Rd SAFWN CB10 ...... 63 G2
Uxbridge Crs IPSE IP3 .... 55 L4 2

V

Valance Rd SAFWS CB11 .... 85 J6
Vale Cl COLN CO4 .... 161 G3
Vale La RIPS/CAP IP9 .... 107 K1
Valentines Dr COLN CO4 .... 11 J3
Valentine Wy WIT CM8 .... 209 M1
Valfreda Wy RCOLE CO7 .... 189 K4
Valkyrie Cl MAL CM9 .... 262 F3
Valletta Cl CHLM/WR CM1 .... 14 E1
Valley Br CHLM/WR CM1 .... 254 D7
Valleybridge Rd COS CO15 .... 13 J1
Valley Cl COLW CO3 .... 187 G2
  IP IP1 .... 31 L4
  MGTR CO11 .... 106 F4
Valley Crs RCOLW CO6 .... 159 G2
Valley La RIPS/CAP IP9 .... 79 H1
Valley Rd BRTR CM7 .... 180 C1
  COS CO15 .... 13 J1
  HAR CO12 .... 139 M3
  IP IP1 .... 2 C1
  IPNE IP4 .... 31 M4
  RCOLE CO7 .... 189 L5
  SUD CO10 .... 51 G4
Valley Vw BRTR CM7 .... 92 F7
  RCOLW CO6 .... 159 G2
Valley View Cl COLW CO3 .... 160 C1
Valleyview Dr IPNE IP4 .... 56 B1
Vandenbury Cir BRTR CM7 ...... 93 M7 1
Van Dieman's La
  CHLM/GWD CM2 .... 15 K7
Van Dieman's Rd
  CHLM/GWD CM2 .... 15 K7
Van Dyck Rd COLW CO3 .... 159 J8
Vandyck Rd IPSE IP3 .... 55 J5 5
Vane La RCOLW CO6 .... 183 J3
Vanessa Dr RCOLE CO7 .... 189 K4
Vanguard Wy BRTR CM7 .... 180 D1 6
Vanners Rd HVHL CB9 .... 23 J6
Vansittart St HAR CO12 .... 9 K5
Vantorts Cl SBW CM21 .... 227 G3
Vantorts Rd SBW CM21 .... 227 G4
Varden Cl CHLM/WR CM1 .... 254 B7
Vaughan Cl BRTR CM7 .... 179 H3
Vaughan St CHTY IP2 .... 2 F9
Vaux Av HAR CO12 .... 140 B4
Vauxhall Av COS CO15 .... 249 G7
Vauxhall Dr BRTR CM7 .... 179 M3
Vellacotts CHLM/WR CM1 .... 254 D6
Venmore Dr GTDUN CM6 .... 176 A5
Ventnor Dr COS CO15 .... 222 C5
Ventris Cl WIT CM8 .... 30 F8
Vere Gdns IP IP1 .... 31 L3
Vermeer Ride
  CHLM/WR CM1 .... 255 H6 2
Vermont Cl COS CO15 .... 13 K3
Vermont Crs IPNE IP4 .... 3 H3
Vermont Rd IPNE IP4 .... 3 H2
Vernon's Cl RBSF CM22 .... 117 H8
Vernons Rd RCOLW CO6 .... 129 G8
Vernon St CHTY IP2 .... 2 F9
Vernon Wy BRTR CM7 .... 152 B8
Veronica Wk COLN CO4 .... 11 M6
Vesta Cl RCOLW CO6 .... 183 M3
Veyses End RCOLE CO7 .... 104 F3
Viaduct Rd CHLM/WR CM1 .... 14 F3
Viborg Gdns MAL CM9 .... 271 G6 5
Vicarage Av WIT CM8 .... 209 H4
Vicarage Cl BRTR CM7 .... 261 M1 1
  MAL CM9 .... 30 D4
  RIPW IP8 .... 30 D4
Vicarage Crs RCHLM CM3 .... 257 K1
Vicarage Fld SUD CO10 .... 50 D8
Vicarage Gdns COS CO15 .... 12 D8
Vicarage La BSF CM23 .... 114 D5
  GTDUN CM6 .... 119 J2
  RBSF CM22 .... 116 B8
  RCOS CO16 .... 194 B3
  RIPS/CAP IP9 .... 54 D2
  RIPW IP8 .... 30 D4
  SUD CO10 .... 50 D1
  WOTN CO14 .... 196 E5 1
Vicarage Meadow HSTD CO9 ...... 126 A4
Vicarage Rd BRTR CM7 .... 92 F7
  CHLM/GWD CM2 .... 14 F8
  CHLM/WR CM1 .... 252 B8
  FX IP11 .... 6 F2
  RCHLM CM3 .... 233 G3
  SUD CO10 .... 47 J4
Vicars Orch SUD CO10 .... 49 G8
Vicerons Pl BSF CM23 .... 198 F1
Viceroy Cl COLS CO2 .... 188 D2
Victoria Av FOS CO13 .... 195 M5
  SAFWN CB11 .... 63 G6
Victoria Cha CHLM/GWD CM2 ...... 10 A4
Victoria Cl RCOLE CO7 .... 189 K3
Victoria Crs CHLM/WR CM1 ...... 135 L1
  MGTR CO11 .... 135 L1
Victoria Esp K/T/MI CO5 .... 244 F8
Victoria Gdns COLN CO4 .... 160 D2
Victoria Pl COS CO15 .... 11 G8
  RCOLE CO7 .... 219 H7
Victoria Rd CHLM/WR CM1 ...... 15 J2
  CHLM/WR CM1 .... 265 G4
  COLW CO3 .... 159 L8
  COS CO15 .... 13 K4
  FX IP11 .... 7 K3

HVHL CB9 .... 22 F6
MAL CM9 .... 271 J3
RCOS CO16 .... 193 K8
WOTN CO14 .... 196 E5
Victoria Rd South
  CHLM/WR CM1 .... 15 G3
Victoria St BRTR CM7 .... 180 B3
  FX IP11 .... 7 M2
  HAR CO12 .... 9 J6
  IPNE IP4 .... 2 B4
  K/T/MI CO5 .... 244 C7
Victor Rd COL CO1 .... 11 H9
Victory Rd COS CO15 .... 12 D5
  IPNE IP4 .... 32 C6
  K/T/MI CO5 .... 244 C7
Vienna Cl HAR CO12 .... 140 C4
View Point Fx IP11 .... 112 F8
Viking Rd MAL CM9 .... 271 G6
Viking Wy COS CO15 .... 223 H7
Village Cl FOS CO13 .... 195 M6
Village Ga CHLM/GWD CM2 ...... 267 J2
Village Wy FOS CO13 .... 195 M7
Villa Rd COLW CO3 .... 158 E3
Villiers Pl CHLM/WR CM1 .... 256 A4
Villiers-sur-marne Av
  CHLM/GWD CM2 .... 267 J2
Vince Cl K/T/MI CO5 .... 244 F7
Vincent Cl IP IP1 .... 31 G6
Vine Dr RCOLE CO7 .... 189 L2
Vine Farm Rd RCOLE CO7 .... 189 L2
Vine Rd K/T/MI CO5 .... 212 D7
Vinesse Rd RCOLW CO6 .... 130 F4
Virley Cl MAL CM9 .... 271 M1
Vine St BRTR CM7 .... 121 K3 3
The Vineway HAR CO12 .... 8 D7
Vineyard Ga COL CO1 .... 10 C3 1
Vineyard St COL CO1 .... 10 D8
Vint Crs COLW CO3 .... 159 L7
Violet Cl CHLM/WR CM1 .... 255 G6
  CHTY IP2 .... 54 B1
Virgil Rd WIT CM8 .... 210 B8
Virginia Cl COS CO15 .... 249 A4
Virley Cl MAL CM9 .... 271 M1
Viscount Dr COLN CO4 .... 132 E8
Vista Av FOS CO13 .... 195 M4
Vista Rd COS CO15 .... 13 H4
Vitllus Cl COLN CO4 .... 132 D7 3
Vivian Ct WOTN CO14 .... 196 E5
Volwycke Av MAL CM9 .... 271 H5

W

Waddesdon Rd HAR CO12 .... 9 J6
Wade Reach WOTN CO14 .... 196 C5
Wade Rd COS CO15 .... 222 D5
Wade's La RIPS/CAP IP9 .... 81 M7
Wadgate Rd FX IP11 .... 7 G1
Wadhurst Rd IPSE IP3 .... 55 M2
Wagon Md RBSF CM22 .... 228 C2
Wagtail Dr MAL CM9 .... 259 L8
Wainwright Wy KESG IP5 .... 33 M5
Wakefield Cl SAFWN CB10 ...... 37 M2 1
Wakefield Rd COL CO1 .... 10 E5
Wakelin Wy WIT CM8 .... 238 D3 6
Wakes St RCOLW CO6 .... 128 D7
Waldegrave Cl MGTR CO11 ...... 135 M2
Waldegrave Rd MGTR CO11 ...... 135 L2
Waldegraves La K/T/MI CO5 ...... 245 J6
The Waldegraves BURES CO8 ...... 100 B5
Walden Cl MAL CM9 .... 259 J1
Walden House Rd WIT CM8 ...... 239 J8
Walden Rd CBE/LIN CB1 .... 19 K7
  GTDUN CM6 .... 90 B8
  SAFWN CB10 .... 38 A2
  SAFWS CB11 .... 62 B7
Walden Wy FOS CO13 .... 196 C7
Waldgrooms GTDUN CM6 .... 175 L4
Waldingfield Rd SUD CO10 .... 4 F4
Walford Pl CHLM/GWD CM2 ...... 267 H3
Walford Wy RCOLW CO6 .... 183 J3
Walker Cl IPNE IP4 .... 32 E8
Walkers Cl CHLM/WR CM1 ...... 255 H7 4
The Walk COLW CO3 .... 158 C5
  KESG IP5 .... 33 K5
Wallace Binder Cl MAL CM9 ...... 271 H4
Wallace Crs CHLM/GWD CM2 ...... 15 K8
Wallace La RCHLM CM3 .... 205 K6
Wallace Rd IP IP1 .... 31 G5
Wallace's La CHLM/WR CM1 ...... 256 B1
Wallasea Gdns
  CHLM/WR CM1 .... 255 H8 3
Wall Cha RCHLM CM3 .... 205 H6
Waller's Cl ROY SG8 .... 59 H4
Waller's Gv CHTY IP2 .... 54 B1
Wallflower Ct
  CHLM/WR CM1 .... 255 H7 4
Wallis Cl COLW CO3 .... 187 G2
Wall La MGTR CO11 .... 137 M1
The Walls RCOS CO16 .... 247 L7
Walnut Dr BSF CM23 .... 198 F2
  WIT CM8 .... 238 C1
Walnut Gv BRTR CM7 .... 180 A3
Walnut Tree Av SBW CM21 ...... 227 G6
Walnut Tree Crs SBW CM21 ...... 227 G3 3
Walnut Tree La RIPS/CAP IP9 ...... 109 K3
  SUD CO10 .... 4 B6
Walnut Tree Wy COLS CO2 .... 212 E6
  K/T/MI CO5 .... 244 E3
Walnut Wy COS CO15 .... 12 A6
  RCOLE CO7 .... 219 G6
Walsingham Rd SUD CO10 .... 50 B8
Walsingham Rd COLS CO2 .... 10 C8
Walter Radcliffe Wy
  RCOLE CO7 .... 189 L6
Walter Wy WIT CM8 .... 181 L8
Waltham Cl CHTY IP2 .... 54 C3
Waltham Gln CHLM/GWD CM2 ...... 15 J9
Waltham Rd RCHLM CM3 .... 236 B4
Waltham Wy FOS CO13 .... 196 C8
Walton Av FX IP11 .... 113 H5
Walton Rd COS CO15 .... 13 H5
  FOS CO13 .... 195 G3
  RCOS CO16 .... 194 D2
Wantz Cha MAL CM9 .... 271 J3

Wantz Hvn MAL CM9 .... 271 J3 2
Wantz Rd MAL CM9 .... 271 J3
Wapping La RCOLE CO7 .... 218 D3
Warburton Av HSTD CO9 .... 95 M5 1
Ward Crs BSF CM23 .... 171 G7
Warde Cha WOTN CO14 .... 196 D5 4
Wardle Wy CHLM/WR CM1 ...... 254 A6 2
Wardley Cl CHTY IP2 .... 53 M4
Ward Pth CHLM/GWD CM2 ...... 267 K1
Ward Rd RIPW IP8 .... 53 K3
Wards Cft SAFWS CB11 .... 62 F6
Wareham Av IPSE IP3 .... 55 M2
Warehouse Rd GTDUN CM6 ...... 149 H8
Wares Rd CHLM/WR CM1 .... 232 B8
Wargrave Rd COS CO15 .... 12 C4
Warham Rd HAR CO12 .... 140 A4
Warley Cl BRTR CM7 .... 180 E2
Warley Wy FOS CO13 .... 196 D6
Warner Cl BRTR CM7 .... 179 H4
Warners GTDUN CM6 .... 175 M5 2
Warner Wy SUD CO10 .... 51 G5
Warnham Cl RCOS CO16 .... 221 K7 5
Warren Cl CHLM/WR CM1 .... 254 D2 3
  RBSF CM22 .... 173 M6
Warren Heath Av IPSE IP3 ...... 55 M3
Warren Heath Rd IPSE IP3 ...... 55 M3
Warren La COLW CO3 .... 186 D4
  RIPS/CAP IP9 .... 110 E1
Warren Rd BRTR CM7 .... 180 E3
  HSTD CO9 .... 125 M4 6
Warrenside BRTR CM7 .... 180 D5
The Warrens FOS CO13 .... 196 A7
  WIT CM8 .... 239 G8
Warrington Rd IP IP1 .... 2 C2
Warwick Bailey Cl COLN CO4 ...... 159 M3 1
Warwick Cl BRTR CM7 .... 180 C1
  MAL CM9 .... 271 J4 5
Warwick Crs COS CO15 .... 12 E4
  MAL CM9 .... 271 J4
Warwick Dr MAL CM9 .... 271 H4
Warwick Rd BSF CM23 .... 171 K7
  COS CO15 .... 12 D5
  IPNE IP4 .... 3 K4
  RBSF CM22 .... 174 A5
Warwick Sq CHLM/WR CM1 ...... 266 B1
Washford Gdns COS CO15 .... 12 D8
Washington Cl MAL CM9 .... 271 G4 3
Washington Rd HAR CO12 .... 140 C3 1
  MAL CM9 .... 271 H4
Wash La MAL CM9 .... 260 D4
Watch House Rd GTDUN CM6 ...... 149 G8
Waterford Rd IP IP1 .... 30 F3
Water Hall La BRTR CM7 .... 123 H7
Waterhouse La CHLM/WR CM1 ...... 14 B6
Waterhouse St CHLM/WR CM1 ...... 14 C7
Water La BRTR CM7 .... 151 H2
  BRTR CM7 .... 181 L1
  BSF CM23 .... 171 H5
  BURES CO8 .... 100 A4
  COLW CO3 .... 159 L5
  GTDUN CM6 .... 146 E6
  HSTD CO9 .... 98 C6
  HVHL CB9 .... 24 B8
  HVHL CB9 .... 42 E6
  HVHL CB9 .... 43 J7
  RCOLW CO6 .... 102 B5
  SAFWN CB10 .... 65 G6
  SAFWS CB11 .... 87 J4
  SAFWS CB11 .... 88 D3
  STSD SM24 .... 144 A7
  SUD CO10 .... 27 M3
Waterloo La CHLM/WR CM1 ...... 15 H3
Waterloo Rd IP IP1 .... 2 A1
Watermill Rd K/T/MI CO5 .... 212 A1
Waterside RCOLE CO7 .... 219 G6
  STSD SM24 .... 144 A7 4
Waterson V CHLM/GWD CM2 ...... 15 J8
Waterville Ms COLS CO2 .... 188 D2 2
Waterwick Hl SAFWS CB11 ...... 84 D4
Waterworks Cl COLS CO2 .... 215 G1
Waterworks Dr RCOS CO16 ...... 221 K8
Waterworks St IPNE IP4 .... 3 H6
Watery La BSF CM23 .... 142 E4
  GTDUN CM6 .... 203 J3
  RCOLW CO6 .... 182 C4
Watling La GTDUN CM6 .... 119 H1
Watling St GTDUN CM6 .... 119 H2
Watson Rd COS CO15 .... 12 B5
Watts Cl GTDUN CM6 .... 204 D1
Watts Rd COLS CO2 .... 187 K3
Wavell Av COS CO2 .... 187 L1
Wavell Cl CHLM/WR CM1 .... 254 F5 1
Waveney Dr CHLM/WR CM1 ...... 254 E7
Waveney Rd FX IP11 .... 7 H4
  IP IP1 .... 31 G5
Waveney Ter HVHL CB9 .... 23 J6 2
Wavring Av FOS CO13 .... 196 A6
The Wayback SAFWN CB10 ...... 63 G3
Wayside RCHLM CM3 .... 269 G6
Waytemore Rd BSF CM23 .... 171 G8
Wear Dr CHLM/WR CM1 .... 254 F7
Weaver Cl IP IP1 .... 30 F5
Weaverhead Cl GTDUN CM6 ...... 119 J2
Weaverhead La GTDUN CM6 ...... 119 J2
Weavers Cl COLW CO3 .... 159 H8
Weavers Dr SUD CO10 .... 28 D1
Weaversfield WIT CM8 .... 181 L8
Weavers Gn RCOLW CO6 .... 129 M7
Weavers Rw HSTD CO9 .... 126 B4
Weaver St BSF CM23 .... 198 E1
Webbs St KESG IP5 .... 33 L6 7
Webster Cl HSTD CO9 .... 95 M5 2
Weddell Rd HVHL CB9 .... 23 L7
Wedgewood Dr COLN CO4 .... 160 A3
Wedow Rd GTDUN CM6 .... 119 J2
Weeley By-pass Rd RCOS CO16 ...... 193 G4
Weeley Rd RCOLE CO7 .... 192 B8
  RCOS CO16 .... 221 L1
Weggs Willow COLN CO4 .... 11 K6
Weight Rd CHLM/GWD CM2 ...... 15 K3
Weir La COLS CO2 .... 188 D6
Weir Rd COS CO15 .... 189 G5
Weir Pl KIR/NAC IP10 .... 83 K1
Welbeck Cl FX IP11 .... 83 M4 2
Welland Av CHLM/WR CM1 ...... 253 L8
Wellands WIT CM8 .... 239 G8

Wellands Cl WIT CM8 .... 238 F8
Weller Gv CHLM/WR CM1 .... 254 A6
Wellesley Rd COLW CO3 .... 10 A8
  COS CO15 .... 12 F6
  IPNE IP4 .... 3 M6
Well Fld CHLM/WR CM1 .... 265 J4
  HSTD CO9 .... 126 B5
Wellfield Wy FOS CO13 .... 195 M6
Well-green Cl SAFWS CB11 ...... 63 G6 6
Wellington Cl BRTR CM7 .... 180 L1
  CHLM/WR CM1 .... 253 M8
  MAL CM9 .... 271 H3
Wellington Rd HAR CO12 .... 9 L3
Wellington St COLS CO2 .... 10 B8
  IP IP1 .... 2 B3
  RCOLE CO7 .... 219 H7 4
Well La K/T/MI CO5 .... 185 J7
  RCHLM CM3 .... 268 E7
  SUD CO10 .... 26 D6
Wellmeads CHLM/GWD CM2 ...... 15 G7
Wells Cl IPNE IP4 .... 3 J5
Wells Ct CHLM/WR CM1 .... 254 F8
Wells Hall Rd SUD CO10 .... 74 E1
Well Side RCOLW CO6 .... 185 G2
Wells Rd COL CO1 .... 10 F5
Well's St CHLM/WR CM1 .... 14 F2
Well St RCOLE CO7 .... 219 G6
Welshwood Park Rd COLN CO4 ...... 161 G3
Wenden Rd SAFWS CB11 .... 62 D5
Wendy Cl RIPS/CAP IP9 .... 81 H6
Wenham La RCOLE CO7 .... 76 E5
Wenham Rd RIPW IP8 .... 52 F6
Wenlock Rd RCOS CO16 .... 193 H7
Wentford Vw SUD CO10 .... 26 D4
Wentworth Cl RCHLM CM3 ...... 257 K1
Wentworth Crs BRTR CM7 ...... 152 B8
Wentworth Dr BSF CM23 .... 170 F7
  FX IP11 .... 113 L1
  RIPW IP8 .... 53 L3
Wentworth Mdw MAL CM9 ...... 271 H3
Wesel Av FX IP11 .... 6 E3
Wesley End Rd HSTD CO9 .... 68 F2
Wesley Rd COLN CO4 .... 11 K5
West Av CHLM/WR CM1 .... 254 B8
  COS CO15 .... 12 E8
West Belvedere RCHLM CM3 ...... 269 H6
West Bourne Gv
  CHLM/GWD CM2 .... 266 F6
Westbourne Rd IP IP1 .... 31 H4
West Bowers Rd MAL CM9 ...... 269 L1
Westbury Cl RCOLW CO6 .... 157 M8
Westbury Rd FOS CO13 .... 195 J8
  IPNE IP4 .... 32 D5
West Cha MAL CM9 .... 271 H2
Westcott Cl RCOS CO16 .... 221 M7
West Dock Rd HAR CO12 .... 111 G8
West Dr BRTR CM7 .... 122 D2
West End CBS CB2 .... 16 D1
West End La HAR CO12 .... 140 D4
Westend La HVHL CB9 .... 24 D3
West End Rd IP IP1 .... 2 C7
  K/T/MI CO5 .... 240 B2
Westerdale COS CO15 .... 254 F6
Westerfield Rd IPNE IP4 .... 3 G3
Westergreen Meadow
  BRTR CM7 .... 180 A4
The Westerings
  CHLM/WR CM1 .... 267 G7
  RCOLW CO6 .... 102 B3
The Westerlings BRTR CM7 ...... 181 G7
Western Av FX IP11 .... 113 M1
  HVHL CB9 .... 23 G4
Western Cl IPNE IP4 .... 56 B1
  WIT CM8 .... 210 A2
Western La WIT CM8 .... 210 A2
Western Prom RCOLE CO7 .... 218 F8
Western Rd RCOLE CO7 .... 219 G7
  WIT CM8 .... 210 B2
Western's End MGTR CO11 ...... 106 F5
Westfield SUD CO10 .... 26 C7
Westfield Av CHLM/WR CM1 ...... 266 C5
Westfield Cl BSF CM23 .... 171 G6
Westfield Dr RCOLW CO6 .... 183 H2
Westfield Rd BSF CM23 .... 171 G6
West Flds SAFWS CB11 .... 63 G6
Westgate St IP IP1 .... 2 E5
  SUD CO10 .... 29 L3
West Hayes RBSF CM22 .... 228 C2
Westholme Rd IP IP1 .... 31 J4
Westlake Crs RCOLE CO7 .... 189 J3
West Lawn IPNE IP4 .... 32 D5
Westleton Wy FX IP11 .... 112 F2
Westley La SAFWN CB10 .... 38 F8
West Lodge Rd COLW CO3 ...... 159 M7
West Mdw IP IP1 .... 30 E1
West Mill Gn RIPS/CAP IP9 ...... 77 M3
Westminster Gdns
  BRTR CM7 .... 180 D1 7
Westmorland Cl MGTR CO11 ...... 136 D2
Weston Rd COLS CO2 .... 188 D1
Westridge Rd COS CO15 .... 222 C7
West Rd BSF CM23 .... 171 G7
  COS CO15 .... 249 M5
  HSTD CO9 .... 126 A4
  IPSE IP3 .... 56 A5
  SAFWS CB11 .... 62 F5
  SBW CM21 .... 226 D2
  STSD SM24 .... 144 A2
Westropps SUD CO10 .... 29 L8
West Sq MAL CM9 .... 271 G4
West Station Yd MAL CM9 ...... 271 G4
West Stockwell St COL CO1 ...... 10 C6
West St COLS CO2 .... 10 B9
  HAR CO12 .... 9 K3
  MAL CM9 .... 262 D4
  RCOLE CO7 .... 189 K5
  RCOLW CO6 .... 183 G4
  WOTN CO14 .... 196 C5
West View Cl COLN CO4 .... 160 D2 3
Westward Deals HVHL CB9 ...... 24 D3
Westway CHLM/WR CM1 .... 14 B8
  COLW CO3 .... 10 A3
West Wickham Rd CBE/LIN CB1 ...... 21 J2
Westwood Av IP IP1 .... 2 B1
Westwood Dr K/T/MI CO5 .... 245 G7

West Wood Hl COLN CO4 .... 159 K3
West Yd HSTD CO9 .... 126 A5
Wetherby Cl IP IP1 .... 31 K2 1
Wetherfield STSD CM24 .... 143 M6
Wethersfield Rd BRTR CM7 .... 123 G6
   COLS CO2 .... 188 C5
   HSTD CO9 .... 95 L4
Wet La COLN CO4 .... 103 G7
Wetzlar Cl COLS CO2 .... 188 D1 4
Wexford Rd IP IP1 .... 30 F3
Weymouth Cl COS CO15 .... 249 M5
Weymouth Rd CHLM/WR CM1 ..... 255 G7
   IPNE IP4 .... 3 M5
Whalebone Cnr COLN CO4 .... 104 B6
Whaley Rd COLN CO4 .... 11 J6
Wharfedale Rd IP IP1 .... 31 J4
Wharf La BURES CO8 .... 100 B5
Wharf Rd BSF CM23 .... 171 H7
   CHLM/GWD CM2 .... 15 K4
   MAL CM9 .... 272 B1
Wheat Cft BSF CM23 .... 199 G1 2
   CBE/LIN CB1 .... 19 M2
Wheatfield Rd COLW CO3 .... 158 F7
Wheatfields HLWE CM17 .... 226 F7 1
Wheatfield Wy CHLM/WR CM1 ... 14 D2
Wheatlands RCOLE CO7 .... 162 B7
Wheatley Av BRTR CM7 .... 180 E2
Wheatley Cl SBW CM21 .... 226 E4
Wheaton Rd WIT CM8 .... 238 D3
Wheatsheaf Cl MGTR CO11 .... 137 M2
Wheatsheaf La MGTR CO11 .... 137 M2
Wheatsheaf Wy CBE/LIN CB1 ..... 19 M2
Wheeler Cl COLN CO4 .... 161 G7
Wheeler's Hl RCHLM CM3 .... 234 E7
Wheelwrights BSF CM23 .... 198 E1 6
The Wheelwrights FX IP11 .... 83 L7 3
Wherstead Rd CHTY IP2 .... 54 E2
Whinchat Cl CHTY IP2 .... 53 M2
Whinfield Av HAR CO12 .... 140 B4
The Whinneys KESG IP5 .... 33 M5
Whitbreads Farm La
   RCHLM CM3 .... 234 F1
Whitby Rd IPNE IP4 .... 3 L1
White Barns RCHLM CM3 .... 205 K7
Whitebeam Cl
   CHLM/GWD CM2 .... 266 B6 1
White Bear STSD CM24 .... 144 A5 7
Whiteditch La SAFWS CB11 .... 87 H3
White Elm St IPSE IP3 .... 2 F4
Whitefriars Wy COLW CO3 .... 159 J8
Whitegate Rd RCOLE CO7 .... 219 J7
Whitehall Cl COLS CO2 .... 188 E1
White Hall Cl SUD CO10 .... 51 G2
Whitehall Ct WIT CM8 .... 238 C3
Whitehall Gdns CBS CB2 .... 16 B4
Whitehall La BSF CM23 .... 171 H4
   RCOS CO16 .... 193 L2
Whitehall Rd BSF CM23 .... 171 G4
   COLS CO2 .... 188 E2
White Hart La RCOLW CO6 .... 131 G8
White Horse Av HSTD CO9 .... 125 M5
White Horse Cl FX IP11 .... 113 L1 2
White Horse La MAL CM9 .... 271 K3
   SAFWS CB11 .... 87 J4 1
   WIT CM8 .... 238 B2 4
White Horse Rd HVHL CB9 .... 24 C3
   RCOLE CO7 .... 105 M4
   RIPS/CAP IP9 .... 77 K4
Whitehouse Crs
   CHLM/GWD CM2 .... 15 M7
Whitehouse Hl MAL CM9 .... 242 C6
Whitehouse La RCOLW CO6 .... 158 F2
   SUD CO10 .... 5 K7
Whitehouse Rd GTDUN CM6 .... 149 H8
White House Rd IP IP1 .... 30 E2
White Lodge Crs RCOS CO16 ...... 194 E4
White Post Fld SBW CM21 .... 226 F3
Whites Fld RCOLE CO7 .... 105 K2
Whiteshot Wy SAFWN CB10 .... 64 A3 7
Whites La RCHLM CM3 .... 207 G7
White St GTDUN CM6 .... 175 M5
Whitethorn Gdns
   CHLM/GWD CM2 .... 266 E6
Whitethorn Rd IPSE IP3 .... 56 B4 3
Whiteways Ct WIT CM8 .... 238 A2 6
Whitewell Rd COLS CO2 .... 10 C8
Whitland Cl CHTY IP2 .... 54 C5
Whitlock Dr HSTD CO9 .... 70 B4
Whitmore Crs CHLM/GWD CM2 ... 267 K2
Whittaker Wy K/T/MI CO5 .... 244 D6
Whittington Wy BSF CM23 .... 199 G2
Whittle Rd CHTY IP2 .... 53 L7
Whitton Church La IP IP1 .... 31 G1
Whitton Leyer RIPW IP8 .... 30 E3
Whitworth Cl CHTY IP2 .... 53 M3
Whyverne Cl CHLM/WR CM1 ...... 255 G7
Wicken Rd SAFWS CB11 .... 86 B4

Wickfield Ash CHLM/WR CM1 ..... 253 M7
Wickham Bishop Rd
   RCHLM CM3 .... 257 M1
Wickhambrook Ct FX CM1 .... 6 D2
Wickham Crs CHLM/WR CM1 ..... 254 B7
Wickham Hall La WIT CM8 .... 258 E2
Wickham Rd COLW CO3 .... 159 M8
   WIT CM8 .... 238 B5
Wick La HAR CO12 .... 140 D4
   K/T/MI CO5 .... 217 M2
   RCOLE CO7 .... 133 K5
   RCOS CO16 .... 220 E2
Wicklow Av CHLM/WR CM1 .... 253 M6
Wicklow Rd IP IP1 .... 30 F3
Wick Rd COLN CO4 .... 103 L3
   COLS CO2 .... 188 F3
   RCOLE CO7 .... 192 D8
Widford Cha CHLM/GWD CM2 ... 266 B6
Widford Cl CHLM/GWD CM2 .... 14 C9
Widford Gv CHLM/GWD CM2 ... 266 B6
Widford Park Pl
   CHLM/GWD CM2 .... 14 C9
Widford Rd CHLM/GWD CM2 ... 266 B6
Widgeon Cl CHTY IP2 .... 54 B2
Widgeon Pl K/T/MI CO5 .... 211 L3 2
Widleybrook La BRTR CM7 .... 123 H2
Wigborough Rd COLS CO2 .... 215 G3
   K/T/MI CO5 .... 243 L1
Wigboro Wick La RCOS CO16 ..... 248 A3
Wigeon Cl BRTR CM7 .... 179 L8
Wignall St MGTR CO11 .... 135 H2
Wilberforce St IP IP1 .... 2 B4
Wilbye Cl COLS CO2 .... 187 K1
Wilderness Hl RIPW IP8 .... 52 A2
Wilding Dr KESG IP5 .... 33 M6
Wilding Rd RIPW IP8 .... 53 L4
Wilkin Cl COLW CO3 .... 187 J1
Wilkin Dr K/T/MI CO5 .... 212 F8
Wilkinsons Md
   CHLM/GWD CM2 .... 267 J1 6
Willett Rd COLS CO2 .... 187 K2
Willetts Fld SAFWN CB10 .... 91 J2
William Booth Rd FX IP11 .... 112 F2 12
William Boys Cl COLN CO4 .... 11 M3
William Cl RCOLE CO7 .... 189 L1 1
William Dr COS CO15 .... 12 C7
William Groom Av HAR CO12 .... 140 C3
Williams Rd CHLM/WR CM1 ...... 254 D4
William St IP IP1 .... 2 F4
William's Wk COL CO1 .... 10 C6
Willingale Rd BRTR CM7 .... 180 F1
Willingham Wy K/T/MI CO5 .... 161 G6 4
Willoughby Av K/T/MI CO5 .... 244 F7
Willoughby Dr
   CHLM/GWD CM2 .... 267 H3 7
Willoughby Rd CHTY IP2 .... 2 D8
Willoughby's La BRTR CM7 .... 152 E5
Willow Av FOS CO13 .... 195 M7
   RCOS CO16 .... 248 D7
Willow Cl BSF CM23 .... 171 G6
   CHLM/WR CM1 .... 254 D4
   HVHL CB9 .... 22 F4
   RCOLE CO7 .... 132 F7
   RCOLE CO7 .... 218 F7
Willow Crs RCHLM CM3 .... 257 J2
Willowcroft Rd IP IP1 .... 31 J4
Willowdene HSTD CO9 .... 95 M3 6
Willow Gv RCOLW CO6 .... 102 B3
Willow Hall La MGTR CO11 .... 137 M5
Willow Md SBW CM21 .... 227 G4
Willow Mdw HSTD CO9 .... 96 A5 4
Willow Pk RCOLW CO6 .... 158 A4
Willow Ri WIT CM8 .... 210 C8
Willow Springs BSF CM23 .... 170 F5
The Willows COLS CO2 .... 188 C2
   RCHLM CM3 .... 256 A5
   SAFWN CB10 .... 37 M2
Willow Tree Wy RCOLW CO6 ..... 127 K7
Willow Wk K/T/MI CO5 .... 212 E6 2
Willow Wy COS CO15 .... 249 J6
   HAR CO12 .... 140 B3
   HSTD CO9 .... 125 M4
Will's Ayley La SAFWN CB10 ..... 64 A3
Wilmington Rd COLN CO4 .... 160 E3
Wilmslow Dr RIPW IP8 .... 53 L3
Wilshire Av CHLM/GWD CM2 ..... 267 H2
   RCOLE CO7 .... 189 J3
Wilson Marriage Rd COLN CO4 .. 11 J2
Wilson Rd RIPW IP8 .... 53 K4
Wilson's La RCOLW CO6 .... 185 G2
Wilton Cl BSF CM23 .... 171 K6
Wimbish Wk SAFWN CB10 .... 89 G3
Wimborne Av IPSE IP3 .... 55 M1
Wimborne Cl SBW CM21 .... 226 F3
Wimbourne Gdns FOS CO13 ...... 196 B6 9
Wimpole Cl KESG IP5 .... 33 H7 5
Wimpole Rd COL CO1 .... 11 G9

Wincanton Cl IPNE IP4 .... 32 C4
Wincelow Hall Rd SAFWN CB10 .. 65 M4
Winchelsea Dr CHLM/GWD CM2 . 266 F6
Winchelsea Pl RCOLE CO7 .... 219 H5 2
Winchester Cl BSF CM23 .... 198 F1
Winchester Rd COLS CO2 .... 160 C8
   FOS CO13 .... 196 C8
Winchester Wy CHTY IP2 .... 54 B5
Winckford Cl RCHLM CM3 .... 234 D7
Windermere Cl IPSE IP3 .... 55 K5
Windermere Dr BRTR CM7 .... 179 L7
Windermere Rd BRTR CM7 .... 179 L6
   COS CO15 .... 222 E7
   SUD CO10 .... 5 G5
Windham Rd SUD CO10 .... 5 J5
Windhill BSF CM23 .... 171 G7
Windhill Old Rd BSF CM23 .... 171 G6
Winding Piece RIPS/CAP IP9 ...... 77 J4
Windmill Cl COLN CO4 .... 132 B1
   GTDUN CM6 .... 176 A4
   HAR CO12 .... 139 H4
Windmill Ct RCOLW CO6 .... 185 M1
Windmill Flds RCOLW CO6 .... 183 H2
Windmill Gdns BRTR CM7 .... 152 C5
Windmill Hl RIPS/CAP IP9 .... 77 G4
   SAFWN CB10 .... 62 D2
   SUD CO10 .... 29 K3
Windmill Mdw GTDUN CM6 ...... 230 E2
Windmill Pk COS CO15 .... 13 G2
Windmill Rd HSTD CO9 .... 125 M4
   MGTR CO11 .... 136 E4
Windmills RCOLW CO6 .... 156 E5
The Windmills CHLM/WR CM1 .. 254 C2
Windmill Vw K/T/MI CO5 .... 212 E7 6
Windrush Dr CHLM/WR CM1 ..... 254 E7 1
Windrush Rd KESG IP5 .... 33 L5
Windsor Av COS CO15 .... 12 C6
Windsor Cl COLS CO2 .... 188 C2
Windsor Ct RCOLE CO7 .... 219 H7 5
Windsor Gdns BRTR CM7 .... 180 D1 8
   BSF CM23 .... 170 E6
Windsor Rd COS CO15 .... 12 C7
   FX IP11 .... 7 G4
   IP IP1 .... 31 H6
   K/T/MI CO5 .... 244 F6
Winfrith Rd IPSE IP3 .... 55 M1
Wingate Cl BRTR CM7 .... 180 A1 1
Wingfield St IPNE IP4 .... 3 G6
Winnock Rd COL CO1 .... 10 F9
Winsey Cha BRTR CM7 .... 92 E7
Winsford Wy CHLM/GWD CM2 .. 255 K7
Winsley Rd COL CO1 .... 10 F9
Winstanley Rd SAFWS CB11 ..... 63 H6
Winston Av COS CO15 .... 187 K1
   IPNE IP4 .... 32 E5
   K/T/MI CO5 .... 213 G8
Winston Cl BRTR CM7 .... 152 A7 4
   FX IP11 .... 112 F2
Winston Wy HSTD CO9 .... 95 L2
Winstree Rd COLW CO3 .... 158 F7 1
Winstreet Cl COLS CO2 .... 187 H8
Winterbournes WOTN CO14 ..... 196 C6
Winter's Rd K/T/MI CO5 .... 213 M4
Wisdoms Gn RCOLW CO6 .... 183 J2
Wisemans Gdns SBW CM21 ..... 226 E4
Wistaria Pl COS CO15 .... 12 B2
Wiston Rd RCOLW CO6 .... 102 A4
Witch Elm HAR CO12 .... 140 B3
Witch La RCOLW CO6 .... 155 K5
Witchtree La SAFWN CB10 .... 66 B2
Witham Ldg WIT CM8 .... 237 M5
Witham Rd BRTR CM7 .... 180 C7
   MAL CM9 .... 240 E8
   RCHLM CM3 .... 237 G4
   WIT CM8 .... 208 E1
Withersfield Rd HVHL CB9 .... 23 G4
Withipoll St IP IP1 .... 3 G4
Withrick Wk RCOS CO16 .... 220 C8
Witting Cl RCOS CO16 .... 12 C1
Witton Wood Rd FOS CO13 ..... 196 A8
Wivenhoe Rd RCOLE CO7 .... 161 L4
Wix By-pass MGTR CO11 .... 137 K8
Wix Rd HAR CO12 .... 139 H4
   MGTR CO11 .... 137 H5
   RCOS CO16 .... 165 M5
Woburn Av BSF CM23 .... 170 E6
   FOS CO13 .... 195 M6
Woburn Pl CBS CB2 .... 16 B4
Wolmers Hey RCHLM CM3 .... 234 B6
Wolseley Av COS CO15 .... 249 H7
Wolseley Rd CHLM/GWD CM2 .. 14 F4
Wolsey Gdns FX IP11 .... 7 L3
Wolsey St IP IP1 .... 2 E7
Wolton Rd COLS CO2 .... 187 K2
   KESG IP5 .... 33 L6
Wolves Hall La RCOLW CO6 ..... 165 G4
Wood Barn La MGTR CO11 ...... 134 F4
Woodberry Wy FOS CO13 .... 196 D6
Woodbridge Gv RCOS CO16 ..... 249 J1

Woodbridge Rd IPNE IP4 .... 3 M3
   KESG IP5 .... 33 H5
Woodbridge Rd East IPNE IP4 .... 32 E6
Woodcock Cl COLN CO4 .... 161 G7
   HVHL CB9 .... 23 L6
Woodcock Rd CHTY IP2 .... 54 A3
Wood Dl CHLM/GWD CM2 .... 267 G7
Woodfield Cl FOS CO13 .... 196 C6
   STSD CM24 .... 144 A7 5
Woodfield Dr K/T/MI CO5 .... 244 D6
Woodfield La RIPS/CAP IP9 ..... 108 A3
Woodfield Rd BRTR CM7 .... 180 B2
Woodfields STSD CM24 .... 144 A7
Woodfield Ter STSD CM24 .... 144 A7 6
Woodfield Wy RCHLM CM3 ...... 257 J1
Woodford Cl COS CO15 .... 222 B5
Woodhall Cl SUD CO10 .... 4 D3
Woodhall Gv BSF CM23 .... 170 F7
Woodhall Hl CHLM/WR CM1 ..... 253 K2
Woodhall Rd CHLM/WR CM1 ... 254 C6
   SUD CO10 .... 4 C3
Woodham Dr RCHLM CM3 ...... 257 K1 3
Woodham Mortimer Rd
   MAL CM9 .... 270 A5
Woodhill Common Rd
   RCHLM CM3 .... 268 D8
Woodhill Rd CHLM/WR CM1 .... 254 C1
   KIR/NAC IP10 .... 56 E3
Woodhouse La CHLM/WR CM1 . 254 C1
Woodland Cha COLW CO3 .... 158 B4
Woodland Cl RCHLM CM3 .... 237 J8
Woodland Dr COLW CO3 .... 159 H8
Woodland La CHLM/WR CM1 ... 266 C1
Woodlands BRTR CM7 .... 180 D2
   BSF CM23 .... 171 L5
   COLN CO4 .... 161 H4
   COS CO15 .... 249 J4
   HAR CO12 .... 166 D3
   RIPS/CAP IP9 .... 81 G6
Woodlands Cl COS CO15 .... 222 C5
Woodlands Park Dr
   GTDUN CM6 .... 175 K4
Woodlands Ri RCOS CO16 ...... 193 H4 2
Woodlands Rd HADL IP7 .... 76 A3
   RIPS/CAP IP9 .... 79 L6
The Woodlands CBE/LIN CB1 ... 19 K2
   RCOLE CO7 .... 219 G5 3
Woodlands Wy RIPW IP8 .... 30 D1
Woodland Wy HSTD CO9 .... 125 G5 2
   RCOLE CO7 .... 189 K4
Woodpecker Cl BSF CM23 .... 170 E7 2
   COLN CO4 .... 161 H5 3
Woodpecker Rd CHTY IP2 .... 53 M2
Wood Rd MAL CM9 .... 259 K7
Woodroffe Cl CHLM/GWD CM2 . 267 J2
Woodroffe Farm La MAL CM9 .. 263 H3
Woodrolfe Pk MAL CM9 .... 263 H3
Woodrolfe Rd MAL CM9 .... 263 G4
Woodrows La RCOS CO16 .... 221 K8
Woodrow Wy COLN CO4 .... 161 G6
Woodrush End COLW CO3 ...... 158 D7 2
Woodrush Rd IPSE IP3 .... 55 M3
Woodside BSF CM23 .... 171 M5
   FOS CO13 .... 196 D7
   MAL CM9 .... 259 K2
   RCHLM CM3 .... 269 G4
Woodside Cl COLN CO4 .... 161 G4 3
Woodside Wy GTDUN CM6 ...... 175 J4
Woodspring Cl CHTY IP2 .... 54 C3 6
Woods Rd RCHLM CM3 .... 205 K7
Woodstock K/T/MI CO5 .... 244 E6
Woodstone Av IP IP1 .... 31 L4
Wood St CHLM/GWD CM2 ...... 14 D9
Woodview Cl RCOLE CO7 .... 160 F1
Woodview Dr RCHLM CM3 ..... 207 J6
Woodview Rd GTDUN CM6 ..... 175 L5
Woodville Rd IPNE IP4 .... 3 L6
Wood Wy BRTR CM7 .... 179 K7
Woollards Cl IP IP1 .... 2 A5
Woollards Gdns SUD CO10 ...... 29 L5
Woolmers Md RCHLM CM3 .... 233 G3
Woolner Rd RCOS CO16 .... 221 M7
Woolnough Cl HVHL CB9 .... 43 K7
The Woolnoughs KESG IP5 ...... 33 M6 8
Woolpack La FX IP11 .... 152 C8 2
Woolpit's Rd BRTR CM7 .... 150 A4
Woolverstone Cl CHTY IP2 .... 53 M4
Woolwich Rd RCOS CO16 .... 12 A2
Worcester Cl BRTR CM7 .... 180 C4
Worcester Ct
   CHLM/GWD CM2 .... 267 J8 3
Worcester Crs RCOLE CO7 ..... 190 D5

Worcester Rd COL CO1 .... 10 E5
   IPSE IP3 .... 55 J5
Wordsworth Av MAL CM9 .... 271 J5
Wordsworth Crs IP IP1 .... 31 G2 1
Wordsworth Rd BRTR CM7 ...... 152 B6 4
   COLW CO3 .... 159 H7
Workhouse Hl COLN CO4 .... 132 A1
Workhouse Rd RCOLW CO6 ..... 130 E2
Workshop La KIR/NAC IP10 ..... 56 D8
Worlds End La K/T/MI CO5 ..... 211 M2
Worsdell Wy COLN CO4 .... 10 C1
Worsley Cl CHTY IP2 .... 53 M3
Wortham Pl HVHL CB9 .... 23 J5
Worthing Ms COS CO15 .... 249 L5 4
Worthington Wy COLW CO3 ..... 187 H1
Wrabness Rd HAR CO12 .... 139 G2
The Wraglins BSF CM23 .... 171 K8
Wratting Rd HVHL CB9 .... 23 J5
Wren Av CHTY IP2 .... 53 M2
Wrenbrook Rd BSF CM23 .... 171 H8
Wren Cl RCOLE CO7 .... 191 M4 1
Wrendale COS CO15 .... 222 B7
Wren Pk CBS CB2 .... 16 D1
Wright La KESG IP5 .... 33 M5
Wright Rd IPSE IP3 .... 55 L3
Wright's Av BRTR CM7 .... 181 G6
Wright's Green La RBSF CM22 . 199 L6
Wright's Piece RBSF CM22 ..... 117 J7
Writtle Cl RCOS CO16 .... 249 K1
Writtle Rd CHLM/WR CM1 ...... 14 A6
Wroxham Cl COLW CO3 .... 159 K7
Wroxham Rd IPSE IP3 .... 55 H2
Wryneck Cl COLN CO4 .... 160 B2
Wyatts La SUD CO10 .... 74 F5
Wychford Dr SBW CM21 .... 226 E4
Wycke Hl MAL CM9 .... 270 F5
Wycke La MAL CM9 .... 263 G6
Wycliffe Gv COL CO1 .... 10 A3
Wye Rd IPSE IP3 .... 55 J2
Wykeham Rd CHLM/WR CM1 .. 265 K4
Wykes Bishop St IPSE IP3 .... 3 J9
Wyldwood Cl HLWE CM17 ...... 226 E7
Wyncolls Rd COLN CO4 .... 132 E8
Wyndham Crs COS CO15 .... 13 J3
Wynterton Cl IPSE IP3 .... 55 K4
Wynyard Rd SAFWN CB10 ...... 63 G2
Wyse's Rd ING CM4 .... 264 B7

Y

Yale Ms COLN CO4 .... 160 D1
Yardley Hall La GTDUN CM6 .... 89 M7
Yare Av WIT CM8 .... 237 M2
Yarmouth Cl COS CO15 .... 222 A7 2
Yarmouth Rd IP IP1 .... 31 H7
Yarwood Rd CHLM/GWD CM2 . 267 G3
Yeldham Lock
   CHLM/GWD CM2 .... 267 J3 3
Yeldham Pl HVHL CB9 .... 23 J5
Yeldham Rd HSTD CO9 .... 95 L1
Yeoman Rd FX IP11 .... 6 F3
Yeomans Cl BSF CM23 .... 170 F8
Yerril Gdn HVHL CB9 .... 23 G6 4
Yew Cl WIT CM8 .... 210 D8
Yew Ct CHTY IP2 .... 54 C2
Yewlands SBW CM21 .... 227 G4 3
Yew Tree Cl COLN CO4 .... 161 G6
   RCHLM CM3 .... 237 J8
Yew Tree Gdns
   CHLM/GWD CM2 .... 266 F2 3
Yewtree Gv KESG IP5 .... 33 H6
Yew Tree Pl BSF CM23 .... 171 H6
Yewtree Ri RIPW IP8 .... 53 L4
Yew Wy COS CO15 .... 249 H7
Yorick Av K/T/MI CO5 .... 244 E7
Yorick Rd K/T/MI CO5 .... 244 E7
York Cl SUD CO10 .... 4 D3
York Gdns BRTR CM7 .... 180 D1
York Pl COL CO1 .... 10 F5 1
York Rd CHLM/GWD CM2 .... 14 F7
   COS CO15 .... 222 F8
   FX IP11 .... 7 M1
   HVHL CB9 .... 23 G6
   IPSE IP3 .... 55 J1
   RCOLE CO7 .... 219 G2
   RCOLW CO6 .... 127 K7
   SUD CO10 .... 4 D4
York St MGTR CO11 .... 135 M1
Young Cl RCOS CO16 .... 12 B2
Ypres Rd COLS CO2 .... 188 A2

Z

Zambesi Rd BSF CM23 .... 171 H8 2

Index - featured places

Adult Community College
   COL CO1 .... 10 E6
Adult Community College
Chelmsford
   CHLM/WR CM1 .... 14 B3
Alderman Blaxill School
   COLS CO2 .... 187 K2
The Alec Hunter High School
   BRTR CM7 .... 180 E4
All Saints Church
   of England Primary School
   HAR CO12 .... 166 D2
All Saints C of E Junior
Middle & Infant School
   BSF CM23 .... 171 K5
All Saints C of E Primary
School
   HAR CO12 .... 8 C9
All Saints Vc Middle School
   SUD CO10 .... 50 C3

Alpha Business Park
   IP IP1 .... 31 G2
Alresford Business Centre
   RCOLE CO7 .... 190 D5
Alresford Primary School
   RCOLE CO7 .... 190 D6
Alsa Business Park
   STSD CM24 .... 144 B4
Alton Park CP School
   COS CO15 .... 12 C7
Alton Water Sports Centre
   RIPS/CAP IP9 .... 108 D2
Amberfield School
   KIR/NAC IP10 .... 56 E7
Anchor Press Social
   & Sports Club
   K/T/MI CO5 .... 212 F8
Ancient House
   IP IP1 .... 2 F5
Anglia Polytechnic University
   CHLM/GWD CM2 .... 14 F3

Anglia Polytechnic University
   CHLM/WR CM1 .... 254 C2
Anglia University
   CHLM/WR CM1 .... 266 D1
Arena Sports & Leisure Club
   COLS CO2 .... 160 A8
Art Gallery
   GTDUN CM6 .... 148 C1
The Arthur Findlay College
   STSD CM24 .... 144 C8
Ashdon CP School
   SAFWN CB10 .... 40 D4
Ashfield Club House
   GTDUN CM6 .... 202 D3
Audley End
   SAFWS CB11 .... 62 D4
August 12th Art Gallery
   SAFWN CB10 .... 62 F4
Babergh District Council
   SUD CO10 .... 4 C6

Baddow Hall Junior
   & Infant School
   CHLM/GWD CM2 .... 267 J7
Ballingdon Hill
   Industrial Estate
   SUD CO10 .... 49 L7
The Banyards School
   K/T/MI CO5 .... 212 D6
The Barking Dog Theatre Co
   BSF CM23 .... 171 H8
Barley VP School
   ROY SG8 .... 58 C4
Barn Business Centre
   RCOLE CO7 .... 106 A1
Barnes Farm County
   Junior School
   CHLM/GWD CM2 .... 267 J2
Barrack Lane Medical Centre
   IP IP1 .... 2 D4
Barracks
   COLS CO2 .... 10 D9

Bartlet Hospital
   FX IP11 .... 113 K3
Beacon Hill Special School
   CHTY IP2 .... 54 B2
Bearwalden Business Park
   SAFWS CB11 .... 62 A8
Beckers Green County
   Primary School
   BRTR CM7 .... 180 F3
Beckingham Business Park
   MAL CM9 .... 260 F3
Beehive Lane County
   Primary School
   CHLM/GWD CM2 .... 266 E8
Belstead Special School
   RIPW IP8 .... 53 L3
Benbridge Industrial Estate
   MAL CM9 .... 259 J8
Bentalls Industrial Estate
   MAL CM9 .... 259 J8

Bentalls Shopping Centre
MAL CM9 .... 259 K8
Bentfield County
Primary School
STSD CM24 .... 143 M5
Bentley Primary School
RIPS/CAP IP9 .... 78 B6
Birch C of E School
COLS CO2 .... 214 C1
The Birches Medical Centre
KESG IP5 .... 33 K6
Birch Grove Golf Club
COLS CO2 .... 187 K5
Birchwood High School
BSF CM23 .... 171 L5
The Bishops C of E
& RC Primary School
CHLM/WR CM1 .... 255 H7
Bishop's Park Health Centre
BSF CM23 .... 171 H5
Bishops Stortford College
BSF CM23 .... 171 G6
The Bishops Stortford
High School
BSF CM23 .... 199 H1
Bishops Stortford
Town Council
BSF CM23 .... 171 H6
Bishop William Ward School
RCOLW CO6 .... 131 K6
Black Notley Hospital
BRTR CM7 .... 181 M3
Blackwater Leisure Centre
MAL CM9 .... 271 K4
Blackwater Sailing Club
272 ....B2
Blackwater Trading Estate
MAL CM9 .... 271 J1
Blake End Gallery
BRTR CM7 .... 178 C2
Blois Meadow Business Centre
HVHL CB9 .... 43 L6
Bluebridge Industrial Estate
HSTD CO9 .... 126 C4
Blyth's Meadow Surgery
BRTR CM7 .... 180 B2
Bocking Church Street
County Primary School
BRTR CM7 .... 152 B5
The Book Gallery
GTDUN CM6 .... 175 M5
Boreham County
Primary School
RCHLM CM3 .... 256 B5
The Boswells School
CHLM/WR CM1 .... 254 F7
The Box Gallery
RIPS/CAP IP9 .... 78 F6
Boxted C of E Primary School
COLN CO4 .... 103 H6
The Brackenbury
Sports Centre
FX IP11 .... 113 L2
Bradfield Primary School
MGTR CO11 .... 137 G4
Braintree & Bocking
Urban District Council
BRTR CM7 .... 152 B6
Braintree College
BRTR CM7 .... 152 C8
Braintree District Council
BRTR CM7 .... 180 D2
Braintree District Council
BRTR CM7 .... 180 B2
Braintree District Council
WIT CM8 .... 238 C3
Braintree & District
Golf Club Ltd
BRTR CM7 .... 153 J7
Braintree Rugby Club
BRTR CM7 .... 180 F3
Braintree Town Football Club
BRTR CM7 .... 180 E3
Bramford Primary School
RIPW IP8 .... 30 C4
Bramston Sports Centre
WIT CM8 .... 238 B4
Brantham Athletic
& Social Club
MGTR CO11 .... 106 E6
Bridge Hospital
WIT CM8 .... 238 B5
Brightlingsea Infant School
RCOLE CO7 .... 219 G8
Brightlingsea Junior School
RCOLE CO7 .... 219 G7
Brightlingsea United
Football Club
RCOLE CO7 .... 219 H6
Brinkley Grove Gm
Primary School
COLN CO4 .... 132 D8
Britannia Primary School
IPNE IP4 .... 32 D8
Broke Hall CP School
IPNE IP4 .... 33 G8
Brook Craft Market
IP IP1 .... 2 F5
Brookhouse Business Park
CHTY IP2 .... 31 H7
Brooklands School
MGTR CO11 .... 106 F5
Brookside Business Centre
RBSF CM22 .... 199 H4
Brook Street Business Centre
COL CO1 .... 11 GB
Broomfield County
Primary School
CHLM/WR CM1 .... 254 D4
Broomfield Football Club
CHLM/WR CM1 .... 254 D5
Broomfield Hospital
CHLM/WR CM1 .... 254 C2
Broomgrove County
Infant & Junior School
RCOLE CO7 .... 189 K2
Broomhills Industrial Estate
BRTR CM7 .... 179 M3
Broom Hill Swimming Pool
IP IP1 .... 31 J5

Brunel Court Industrial Centre
COLN CO4 .... 132 E8
Bucklesham Primary School
KIR/NAC IP10 .... 57 L5
Bull Hill Industrial Estate
COS CO15 .... 13 H2
Bulmer Road Industrial Estate
SUD CO10 .... 49 L6
Bures C of E Vc
Primary School
BURES CO8 .... 100 B5
Burlington Road Surgery
IP IP1 .... 2 C4
Burrsville County
Junior & Infant School
COS CO15 .... 222 C7
Burton End CP School
HVHL CB9 .... 22 F6
Bus Depot
IP IP1 .... 2 B6
Butter Market Shopping Centre
IP IP1 .... 2 F5
Canfield Cricket Club
GTDUN CM6 .... 202 C4
Cann Hall Primary School
RCOS CO16 .... 221 L7
Capel St Mary School
RIPS/CAP IP9 .... 77 J4
Cardinal Park
IP IP1 .... 2 E7
Car Ferry Terminal
HAR CO12 .... 8 A3
Car Ferry Terminal
HAR CO12 .... 111 GB
Castle Camps Primary School
CBE/LIN CB1 .... 42 A2
Castle Garden Medical Centre
COL CO1 .... 10 F6
Castle Hill Junior
& Infant School
COS CO15 .... 31 J2
Castle Manor Upper School
HVHL CB9 .... 23 G6
Castle Middle School
HVHL CB9 .... 22 F5
The Castle Museum
COL CO1 .... 10 D6
Castle Street Surgery
SAFWN CB10 .... 62 F3
Castle Walk Clinic
STSD CM24 .... 144 B7
The Cathedral Primary School
CHLM/WR CM1 .... 15 J2
The Causeway Business Centre
BSF CM23 .... 171 H6
Causeway Industrial Estate
MGTR CO11 .... 106 D8
Causton County Junior School
FX IP11 .... 112 F1
Cavendish Primary School
SUD CO10 .... 27 L3
Central Health Clinic
CHLM/GWD CM2 .... 15 G4
Central Surgery
FX IP11 .... 113 J2
Central Surgery
SBW CM21 .... 227 G3
Chalkstone Middle School
HVHL CB9 .... 23 J5
Channels Golf Club
RCHLM CM3 .... 255 G2
Chantry Clinic
CHTY IP2 .... 54 A2
Chantry Gallery
SUD CO10 .... 29 L5
Chantry High School
CHTY IP2 .... 54 B2
Chantry Junior & Infant School
CHTY IP2 .... 54 A1
Chapel Hill County
Primary School
BRTR CM7 .... 180 D3
Chappel C of E
(Controlled) Primary School
RCOLW CO6 .... 128 E8
Charterhouse Trading Estate
HVHL CB9 .... 23 L7
Chase Lane Primary School
HAR CO12 .... 140 A3
Chelmer Valley High School
CHLM/WR CM1 .... 254 C3
Chelmer Village Retail Park
CHLM/GWD CM2 .... 267 G3
Chelmondiston CP School
RIPS/CAP IP9 .... 81 G6
Chelmsford Athletics Club
CHLM/WR CM1 .... 254 A7
Chelmsford Cathedral
CHLM/WR CM1 .... 15 H2
Chelmsford College
CHLM/GWD CM2 .... 14 F7
Chelmsford County
High School
CHLM/WR CM1 .... 266 C1
Chelmsford & Essex Museum
CHLM/GWD CM2 .... 14 F8
Chelmsford Golf Club Ltd
CHLM/GWD CM2 .... 266 B7
Chelmsford Lawford
Mead County Junior School
CHLM/WR CM1 .... 253 M8
Chelmsford Road
Industrial Estate
GTDUN CM6 .... 176 B6
Chelmsford Rugby
Football Club
CHLM/WR CM1 .... 267 G1
Chelmsford Squash Club
CHLM/GWD CM2 .... 266 D6
Cherry Tree School
COLS CO2 .... 188 C5
Cherry Tree Surgery
FOS CO13 .... 224 B1
Chief Clerk County Court
COLW CO3 .... 10 B8
Chilton Industrial Estate
SUD CO10 .... 5 J3
Chinese Herbal Medical Centre
CHLM/GWD CM2 .... 15 H5

Chinese Medical Centre
CHLM/WR CM1 .... 14 F2
Chinese Medical Centre
COL CO1 .... 10 B7
Chinese Medical Centre
IPNE IP4 .... 3 G6
Chipping Hill County
Infant School
WIT CM8 .... 238 B2
Chirstchurch Mansion
IP IP1 .... 2 F4
Christchurch Park Hospital
IP IP1 .... 2 E3
Christmas Maltings Surgery
HVHL CB9 .... 23 H5
Church of England
Primary School
SAFWN CB10 .... 37 M3
Civic Centre
CHLM/WR CM1 .... 14 E2
Civic Centre
IP IP1 .... 2 D5
Civic Industrial Estate
HVHL CB9 .... 23 H8
Civic Theatre
CHLM/WR CM1 .... 14 E2
Civil Service Sports Club
KIR/NAC IP10 .... 56 E4
Clacton County High School
COS CO15 .... 13 J4
Clacton Covered Market
COS CO15 .... 13 G7
Clacton & District Hospital
COS CO15 .... 12 E9
Clacton Leisure Centre
COS CO15 .... 13 J3
Clacton on Sea Golf Club
COS CO15 .... 249 L5
Clacton Police Station
COS CO15 .... 12 E8
Clacton Rugby Club
COS CO15 .... 13 J2
Clare Middle School
SUD CO10 .... 26 F5
Clare Primary School
SUD CO10 .... 26 D5
Clarklands Industrial Estate
SBW CM21 .... 199 GB
Clavering Primary School
SAFWS CB11 .... 114 E1
Clements CP School
HVHL CB9 .... 23 G6
Cliff Lane Primary School
IPSE IP3 .... 55 G2
Clifford Road Primary School
IP IP1 .... 3 M6
Coastal Business Centre
COS CO15 .... 12 C6
C of E Primary School
COS CO15 .... 47 J4
Coggeshall Surgery
RCOLW CO6 .... 183 H3
Coggeshall Town
Football Club
RCOLW CO6 .... 182 F4
Colbayns High School
COS CO15 .... 12 C3
Colchester Business Park
COLN CO4 .... 132 E7
Colchester County Court
COLS CO2 .... 10 B9
Colchester County
High School for Girls
COLW CO3 .... 159 K7
Colchester District
General Hospital
COLN CO4 .... 160 A2
Colchester Golf Club
COLN CO4 .... 159 L2
Colchester Institute
COLW CO3 .... 159 M5
Colchester Jamiah Mosque
COL CO1 .... 10 E8
Colchester Mercury
Theatre Ltd
COLW CO3 .... 10 B7
Colchester Museums
COL CO1 .... 10 O6
Colchester Royal
Grammar School
COLW CO3 .... 159 M7
Colchester Rugby
Football Club
COLN CO4 .... 132 C7
Colchester Sixth Form School
COLW CO3 .... 10 B6
Colchester United
Football Club
COLS CO2 .... 187 L1
Colchester Zoo
COLS CO2 .... 186 E4
College Annexe
IPNE IP4 .... 3 G7
The Colne Community School
RCOLE CO7 .... 219 G5
Colne Engaine C of E School
RCOLW CO6 .... 127 J3
Colneis County Junior School
FX IP11 .... 113 K1
Colne Medical Centre
RCOLE CO7 .... 219 G7
Colne View Retail Park
COS CO15 .... 10 F3
Colne Yacht Club
RCOLE CO7 .... 219 H8
Community Care
& Health Centre
COS CO15 .... 249 J5
Community Health Centre
COL CO1 .... 10 D8
Copdock CP School
RIPW IP8 .... 53 H5
Copdock Cricket Club
RIPW IP8 .... 53 H6
Copford C of E
Primary School
RCOLW CO6 .... 185 L3
Copleston High School
IPNE IP4 .... 32 E8

Coppins Green CP School
COS CO15 .... 12 E2
Cornard Surgery
SUD CO10 .... 5 K8
Cornell Estate
CHLM/GWD CM2 .... 15 L4
Corn Exchange
and Film Theatre
IP IP1 .... 2 E5
The Cottage Museum
BRTR CM7 .... 121 J4
Council Offices
COLW CO3 .... 159 L7
County Court
IP IP1 .... 2 E5
County Hall
CHLM/WR CM1 .... 15 G3
County Hall
IPNE IP4 .... 3 H6
County Junior School
CHLM/WR CM1 .... 265 J8
County Primary School
FX IP11 .... 7 H6
County Primary School
FX IP11 .... 83 L8
County Primary School
RCOLE CO7 .... 104 E4
Coupals CP School
HVHL CB9 .... 23 K6
Cramphorn Theatre
CHLM/WR CM1 .... 14 F3
Creffield Road Surgery
COLW CO3 .... 159 M7
Cressing County
Primary School
BRTR CM7 .... 181 G7
Cricket Squash Tennis
& Hockey Club
BSF CM23 .... 170 E5
Crishall C of E Primary School
ROY SG8 .... 59 L2
Crown Pools
IP IP1 .... 2 E4
Crusader Business Park
COS CO15 .... 222 C6
Dabchicks Sailing Club
K/T/MI CO5 .... 244 O6
Dale Hall Primary School
IP IP1 .... 31 K3
Dame Johane Bradbury School
SAFWN CB10 .... 63 H3
Danbury Clinic
RCHLM CM3 .... 269 H6
Danbury Park School
RCHLM CM3 .... 268 E6
D'arcy Gallery
IPNE IP4 .... 2 F6
Deben High School
FX IP11 .... 7 K1
Dedham C of E
(Controlled) School
RCOLW CO7 .... 105 J7
Dedham Sports Club
RCOLW CO7 .... 105 H7
De Vere CP School
HSTD CO9 .... 96 A1
Dickens Place Surgery
CHLM/WR CM1 .... 253 M7
Doctor Child's Surgery
HAR CO12 .... 139 GB
Doucecroft School
K/T/MI CO6 .... 211 L2
Dovercourt Swimming Pool
HAR CO12 .... 140 D4
Downing Primary School
CHTY IP2 .... 54 B3
Drakes Lane Industrial Estate
RCHLM CM3 .... 235 K6
Drapers Sports Club
MAL CM9 .... 259 M8
Dr Guile Surgery
COS CO15 .... 222 C5
Dr Mirza Practice
COS CO15 .... 12 E5
Dukes Park Industrial Estate
CHLM/GWD CM2 .... 267 H1
The Dukes Priory Hospital
CHLM/WR CM1 .... 266 F1
Dunmow C of E Junior School
GTDUN CM6 .... 175 L5
Dunmow County
Infants School
GTDUN CM6 .... 175 M4
Dunmow Sports Centre
GTDUN CM6 .... 175 L2
Duxford C of E
Community Primary School
CBS CB2 .... 16 F4
Earls Colne CP School
RCOLW CO6 .... 127 K7
East Anglian Railway Museum
RCOLW CO6 .... 128 F7
East Bergholt High School
RCOLE CO7 .... 105 M1
East Bergholt Primary School
RCOLE CO7 .... 105 K2
Eastern Angles Theatre Co
IP IP1 .... 2 A3
Eastern Angles Theatre Co
IP IP1 .... 31 H6
East Essex Adult
Community College
MAL CM9 .... 271 H3
East Essex Aviation
Society & Museum
RCOS CO16 .... 247 G1
Eastgate Shopping Centre
IP IP1 .... 2 F5
East Herts District Council
BSF CM23 .... 171 H5
East Herts District Council
SBW CM21 .... 227 G3
Edith Borthwick School
BRTR CM7 .... 152 B5
Eight Ash Green C of E
Primary School
RCOLW CO6 .... 158 B4
Elm Green School
RCHLM CM3 .... 268 F2

Elm Hall County
Primary School
WIT CM8 .... 210 B7
Elmstead Market Surgery
RCOLE CO7 .... 162 C8
Elton Park Business Centre
CHTY IP2 .... 31 G7
Elton Park Industrial Estate
CHTY IP2 .... 31 G7
Elwyn House Felsted School
GTDUN CM6 .... 177 L7
Engaines Primary School
RCOS CO16 .... 221 M3
Enterprise Trading Estate
BRTR CM7 .... 179 H4
Essex County Cricket Club
CHLM/GWD CM2 .... 14 F4
Essex County Hospital
COLW CO3 .... 159 M7
Eversley College
SBW CM21 .... 226 F3
Fairfield Infant School
FX IP11 .... 113 J2
Farnham School
BSF CM23 .... 142 F7
Feering Primary School
K/T/MI CO5 .... 212 A1
Felixstowe International
College
FX IP11 .... 113 L2
Felixstowe Port & Town
Football Club
FX IP11 .... 6 D7
Felixstowe Rugby Club
FX IP11 .... 6 F5
Felsted CP School
GTDUN CM6 .... 177 M6
Felsted Preparatory School
GTDUN CM6 .... 177 K8
Felsted School
GTDUN CM6 .... 177 K7
Fern House Surgery
WIT CM8 .... 238 D1
Finchingfield C of E
Primary School
BRTR CM7 .... 92 F7
Fingringhoe C of E School
K/T/MI CO5 .... 189 H8
Fire Station
IP IP1 .... 2 C7
The Firs Junior School
BSF CM23 .... 171 L7
Fledgelings Pre-school
CHLM/GWD CM2 .... 266 C8
Flitch Industrial Estate
GTDUN CM6 .... 175 M6
Follyfield Felsted School
GTDUN CM6 .... 177 L8
Football Stadium
IPNE IP4 .... 33 J8
Ford End C of E Primary
School
RCHLM CM3 .... 205 K7
Fordham C of E Primary
School
RCOLW CO6 .... 157 M1
Forrester Park Golf
& Tennis Club
MAL CM9 .... 239 L8
Foxearth Primary School
SUD CO10 .... 28 E7
The Foxhall Hospital
KIR/NAC IP10 .... 56 D1
Freshwell Health Centre
BRTR CM7 .... 92 F7
Friars Clinic
SUD CO10 .... 4 C7
Friars Grove Junior
& Infant School
COLN CO4 .... 11 K1
Friends School
SAFWS CB11 .... 63 G5
Frinton Golf Club
FOS CO13 .... 224 A3
Frinton on Sea CP School
FOS CO13 .... 196 A8
Frinton on Sea Lawn
Tennis Club
FOS CO13 .... 224 A2
Frinton Road Medical Centre
COS CO15 .... 222 F7
Frinton Summer Theatre
FOS CO13 .... 196 B8
The Frinton & Walton
Heritage Museum
WOTN CO14 .... 197 G4
Frinton & Walton
Swimming Pool
WOTN CO14 .... 196 F4
Frobisher Primary School
COS CO15 .... 249 K4
Frost Business Centre
BRTR CM7 .... 181 L2
Gainsborough Clinic
IPSE IP3 .... 55 H4
The Gallery
CHLM/GWD CM2 .... 15 H5
The Gallery
COLW CO3 .... 187 G1
The Gallery
IPNE IP4 .... 3 G6
The Gallery
SUD CO10 .... 26 C6
Ganges Museum
RIPS/CAP IP9 .... 111 L5
Gepps House Felsted School
GTDUN CM6 .... 177 K7
Gilberd School
COLN CO4 .... 132 D8
Golds Nurseries Business Park
RBSF CM22 .... 144 D2
Gorse Lane Industrial Estate
COS CO15 .... 222 D5
Gosbecks Junior
& Infant School
COLS CO2 .... 187 J2
Gosfield Lake Golf Club
HSTD CO9 .... 124 E5
Gosfield Primary School
HSTD CO9 .... 125 G6

Gosfield School
HSTD CO9 .... 125 J3
The Gowan Gallery
SBW CM21 .... 227 G3
Grange Paddock
Swimming Pool
BSF CM23 .... 171 H4
Grange Park Industrial Estate
COLS CO5 .... 188 F2
Grange Road Primary School
FX FP11 .... 6 F1
Grange Way Business Park
COLS CO5 .... 188 F2
Great Baddow High School
CHLM/GWD CM2 .... 266 F7
Great Bardfield County School
BRTR CM7 .... 121 K3
Great Bentley CP School
RCOLE CO7 .... 191 M6
Great Bradfords County
Infant School
BRTR CM7 .... 180 D1
The Great Clacton Surgery
COS CO15 .... 222 B7
Great Cornard Middle School
SUD CO10 .... 74 E1
Great Cornard Upper School
SUD CO10 .... 74 D1
Great Dunmow Town Council
GTDUN CM6 .... 175 L5
Great Leighs CP School
RCHLM CM3 .... 207 J6
Great Sampford
County Primary School
SAFWN CB10 .... 91 J2
Great Tey Primary School
RCOLW CO6 .... 156 E4
Great Totham County
Primary School
MAL CM9 .... 239 J8
Great Waldingford Vc
Primary School
SUD CO10 .... 51 H2
Great Waltham C of E School
RCHLM CM3 .... 234 A6
Greenstead Clinic
COLN CO4 .... 161 G5
Greenwich Business Park
IPSE IP3 .... 55 G3
Greenwood School
HSTD CO9 .... 126 B2
The Group Surgery
COLW CO3 .... 159 M7
Grove Lodge Surgery
COS CO15 .... 222 F8
Grove Tennis Club
CHLM/GWD CM2 .... 15 G9
Guildhall & Museum
BRTR CM7 .... 92 F7
Guildhall Surgery
SUD CO10 .... 26 D6
Gusford Primary School
CHTY IP2 .... 53 M4
GX
CHLM/WR CM1 .... 266 A6
GX Superbowl
CHLM/WR CM1 .... 266 A6
Halifax Primary School
CHTY IP2 .... 54 D3
The Hall
SAFWS CB11 .... 117 G1
Halstead Business Centre
HSTD CO9 .... 126 A4
Halstead Hospital
HSTD CO9 .... 126 A2
Halstead Primary School
HSTD CO9 .... 126 B4
Halstead Town Football Club
HSTD CO9 .... 126 A3
Hamford CP School
FOS CO13 .... 196 B6
Hamilton School
COLW CO3 .... 159 M8
Handford Hall Primary School
IP IP1 .... 2 A4
Harwich County
Primary School
HAR CO12 .... 9 L5
Harwich & District Hospital
HAR CO12 .... 8 D9
Harwich Golf Club
HAR CO12 .... 8 A6
Harwich Industrial Estate
HAR CO12 .... 8 B5
Harwich & Parkeston
Football Club
HAR CO12 .... 9 G8
The Harwich School
HAR CO12 .... 140 C3
Harwich Sports Centre
HAR CO12 .... 140 C3
Harwich Town Sailing Club
HAR CO12 .... 9 L3
Haselmere Industrial Estate
BSF CM23 .... 199 J1
Hatfield Heath CP School
RBSF CM22 .... 228 C2
Hatfield Peverel County
Infant School
RCHLM CM3 .... 257 K2
Haven Health Surgery
FX FP11 .... 6 E1
Haverhill Golf Club Ltd
HVHL CB9 .... 24 A7
Haverhill Rovers Football Club
HVHL CB9 .... 23 J7
Haverhill Sports Centre
HVHL CB9 .... 23 K6
Havers Infant School
BSF CM23 .... 171 G8
The Hayward School
CHLM/WR CM1 .... 266 C1
Hazelmere Junior School
COLN CO4 .... 161 G5
Health Service Clinic
COLS CO2 .... 188 C4
The Heathcote School
RCHLM CM3 .... 269 G6
Heath CP School
KESG IP5 .... 33 K6

Heathlands Primary School
RCOLW CO6 .... 131 G8
Heath School
COLW CO3 .... 158 F8
Heathside Special School
IPNE IP4 .... 32 E7
Heavitrees Surgery
CHLM/GWD CM2 .... 14 E7
Heddington Castle
HSTD CO9 .... 96 B1
Hedgerows Business Park
CHLM/WR CM1 .... 255 J7
Hedingham County
Secondary School
HSTD CO9 .... 95 M2
Helena Romanes School
GTDUN CM6 .... 175 L3
Helsinki Health Centre
IPSE IP3 .... 55 M2
Henham & Ugley CP School
RBSF CM22 .... 117 H8
Hertfordshire
& Essex General Hospital
BSF CM23 .... 171 L7
Hertfordshire & Essex
High School
BSF CM23 .... 171 K6
Heybridge CP School
MAL CM9 .... 259 L8
Heybridge House
Industrial Estate
MAL CM9 .... 271 K1
Heybridge Swifts
Football Club
MAL CM9 .... 259 M7
Heydon Grange Golf Club
ROY SG8 .... 34 F4
Highfields County
Primary School
MGTR CO11 .... 135 L1
Highwoods County
Primary School
COLN CO4 .... 160 D1
Highwoods Surgery
COLN CO4 .... 160 D1
Hillmead JMI School
BSF CM23 .... 171 L4
Hillside Primary School
CHTY IP2 .... 54 E2
Hillside Special School
SUD CO10 .... 4 E2
Hilton House Surgery
HSTD CO9 .... 96 A5
Hintlesham & Chattisham
Vc Primary School
RIPW IP8 .... 52 C2
Hm Customs and Excise
IPNE IP4 .... 2 F6
Hoblongs Industrial Estate
GTDUN CM6 .... 176 A7
Hockerill Anglo European
Gm School
BSF CM23 .... 171 K6
Hockerill Sports Club
BSF CM23 .... 171 K8
Holbrook CP School
RIPS/CAP IP9 .... 79 M7
Holbrook High School
RIPS/CAP IP9 .... 79 M7
Holland Haven Primary School
COS CO15 .... 223 G7
Holland Park Primary School
COS CO15 .... 13 L2
Holmwood House School
COLW CO3 .... 158 F5
Holy Family RC
Primary School
WIT CM8 .... 238 B5
Holy Trinity C of E
Primary School
HSTD CO9 .... 125 M3
Holywells High School
IPSE IP3 .... 55 L4
Home Farm CP School
COLW CO3 .... 159 G7
Homestead School
COLN CO4 .... 133 G1
The Honeywood School
RCOLW CO6 .... 183 J2
Howbridge Infants School
WIT CM8 .... 238 B5
Howbridge Juniors School
WIT CM8 .... 238 B5
Howe Green House School
RBSF CM22 .... 199 M3
Hyland House & Park
CHLM/WR CM1 .... 265 L8
Hylands School
CHLM/WR CM1 .... 265 M4
Imperial War Museum
CBS CB2 .... 16 B4
Industrial Centre
CHTY IP2 .... 2 F8
Ipswich Bc Crown Court
IP IP1 .... 2 D5
Ipswich Civic College
IP IP1 .... 2 E4
Ipswich Golf Club
IPSE IP3 .... 56 B3
Ipswich High School for Girls
RIPS/CAP IP9 .... 80 E3
Ipswich Hospital N H S Trust
IPNE IP4 .... 32 E7
Ipswich Museums & Art Gallery
IP IP1 .... 2 E4
Ipswich Regent Theatre
IPNE IP4 .... 3 G5
Ipswich Rugby Union
Football Club
IPNE IP4 .... 32 D3
Ipswich School
IP IP1 .... 2 E2
Ipswich School
IP IP1 .... 31 K5
Ipswich Sports Club
IP IP1 .... 31 K5
Ipswich Town Football Club
IP IP1 .... 2 C6
Ipswich Transport Museum
IPSE IP3 .... 55 L3

Ivry Street Medical Practice
IP IP1 .... 2 D2
Jacques Hall School
MGTR CO11 .... 137 J2
The John Bramston School
WIT CM8 .... 238 B4
John Bunyan Junior
& Infant School
BRTR CM7 .... 180 A1
John Ray CP School
BRTR CM7 .... 180 B5
John Russell Gallery
IPSE IP3 .... 3 H7
Katherine Semar Junior School
SAFWS CB11 .... 63 G7
Kedington Primary School
HVHL CB9 .... 24 C3
Kelvedon St Marys
C of E Primary School
K/T/MI CO5 .... 211 L3
Kendall Primary School
COL CO1 .... 188 E1
Kenneth Mark Practice
SAFWN CB10 .... 62 F3
Kesgrave High School
KESG IP5 .... 33 M4
King Edward Grammar
Sports Ground
CHLM/WR CM1 .... 254 B1
Kingsdale Industrial Estate
CHLM/WR CM1 .... 15 J1
Kingsfleet Primary School
FX FP11 .... 113 L1
Kingsford County
Junior & Infant School
COLS CO2 .... 187 L2
Kings Road Junior School
CHLM/WR CM1 .... 266 B1
Kingsway Hall Art and Theatre
HAR CO12 .... 9 J7
Kingswode Hoe Special School
COLW CO3 .... 159 L6
Kirby Le Soken Primary School
FOS CO13 .... 195 K6
Landseer Business Park
IPSE IP3 .... 54 F2
Langenhoe CP School
K/T/MI CO5 .... 216 C3
Langer Park Industrial Estate
FX FP11 .... 7 H5
Langham Primary School
COLN CO4 .... 133 H1
The Laurels Surgery
RCHLM CM3 .... 256 B5
Lawford C of E Gm
Primary School
MGTR CO11 .... 135 J3
Leas School
COS CO15 .... 12 C7
The Leventhorpe School
SBW CM21 .... 227 G1
Lexden CP School
COLW CO3 .... 159 G7
Lexden Springs School
COLW CO3 .... 159 G6
Lexden Squash Club
COLW CO3 .... 158 F6
Lime Grove Estate
HVHL CB9 .... 23 L8
Links Business Centre
BSF CM23 .... 171 L6
Linton C of E (aided)
Infant School
CBE/LIN CB1 .... 19 L3
Linton Health Centre
CBE/LIN CB1 .... 19 L3
Linton Heights Junior School
CBE/LIN CB1 .... 19 M3
Linton Village College
CBE/LIN CB1 .... 19 K3
Linton Zoological Gardens
CBE/LIN CB1 .... 19 K4
Lionmede Bowling Club & Tennis
Courts
CHLM/GWD CM2 .... 15 M2
Little Bealings CP School
FRAM/WMKT IP13 .... 33 M1
Littlegarth School
RCOLW CO6 .... 102 D6
Little Hallingbury C of E Primary
School
RBSF CM22 .... 199 L5
Little Oakley C of E School
HAR CO12 .... 139 K6
Little Waltham
C of E Primary School
RCHLM CM3 .... 234 D6
London Stansted Airport
RBSF CM22 .... 173 J2
Longfield Medical Centre
MAL CM9 .... 259 N8
Longfield Medical Centre
MAL CM9 .... 271 J3
The Long Melford Practice
SUD CO10 .... 29 L5
Long Melford Primary School
SUD CO10 .... 29 L6
Lord Butler Leisure Centre
SAFWS CB11 .... 63 H5
Lyons Hall County
Primary School
BRTR CM7 .... 180 F1
Magistrates' Court
IP IP1 .... 2 D6
Maidenhall Sports Centre
CHTY IP2 .... 54 E3
Maidstone County
Infant School
FX FP11 .... 113 G2
Malden All Saints
C of E Primary School
MAL CM9 .... 271 J3
Maldon Agricultural Museum
MAL CM9 .... 261 G8
Maldon Court School
MAL CM9 .... 271 H2
Maldon District Council
MAL CM9 .... 271 J3
Maldon Museum
MAL CM9 .... 271 K3

Maldon Primary School
MAL CM9 .... 271 J3
Maldon Town Council
MAL CM9 .... 271 J2
Mallard House
Business Centre
FRAM/WMKT IP13 .... 33 M2
The Maltings
Industrial Estate
SBW CM21 .... 227 H3
Manifest Theatre
MGTR CO11 .... 135 M1
The Manningtree Gallery
MGTR CO11 .... 135 M1
Manningtree High School
MGTR CO11 .... 135 L2
Manningtree Sports Centre
MGTR CO11 .... 135 L1
Manor Fields Jmi School
BSF CM23 .... 170 F8
The Manor of Groves
SBW CM21 .... 226 B3
Manuden CP School
BSF CM23 .... 143 J3
Maple River Industrial Estate
HLW CM20 .... 226 D7
Market Field School
RCOLE CO7 .... 162 C8
Market (Open Air)
IP IP1 .... 2 D5
Marks Hall Arboretum
RCOLW CO6 .... 155 G6
Martells Industrial Estate
RCOLE CO7 .... 133 M8
Mayflower County
Primary School
HAR CO12 .... 8 F7
Meadgate CP School
CHLM/GWD CM2 .... 267 G5
The Medical Centre
K/T/MI CO5 .... 212 F8
Medical Surgery
GTDUN CM6 .... 175 M5
Melbourne House Surgery
CHLM/WR CM1 .... 254 A8
Mersea Community
& Sports Centre
K/T/MI CO5 .... 244 E7
Mersea Island Gm School
K/T/MI CO5 .... 244 E7
The Mersea Road Surgery
COLS CO2 .... 188 C3
Messing CP School
K/T/MI CO5 .... 212 E3
Mid Essex Magistrates Courts
CHLM/WR CM1 .... 15 H3
Milldene School
K/T/MI CO5 .... 212 F7
Millfields (gm) Primary School
RCOLE CO7 .... 189 M4
Mill Road Surgery
COLN CO4 .... 160 A1
Mistley Norman C of E
Primary School
MGTR CO11 .... 136 C1
Monkwick Primary
& Infant School
COLS CO2 .... 188 B3
Monkwick Sports Centre
COLS CO2 .... 188 B3
Montessori School
RBSF CM22 .... 173 K2
Montgomery County
Infant School
COLS CO2 .... 187 L3
Moonhall Business Park
HVHL CB9 .... 23 J8
Morland Primary School
IPSE IP3 .... 55 J5
Moulsham High School
CHLM/GWD CM2 .... 266 D6
Moulsham Infant School
CHLM/GWD CM2 .... 15 H9
Moulsham Lodge Clinic
CHLM/GWD CM2 .... 266 D7
The Mountfitchet School
STSD CM24 .... 172 B1
Mrs Lipmans School
GTDUN CM6 .... 177 K8
M S F Whitehall College
BSF CM23 .... 171 G4
Murrayfield Primary School
IPSE IP3 .... 55 J2
The Museum
SAFWN CB10 .... 62 F3
Myland CP School
COLN CO4 .... 160 A1
Nabbotts County
Junior School
CHLM/WR CM1 .... 255 G6
Nacton Primary School
KIR/NAC IP10 .... 56 E8
Natural History Museum
COL CO1 .... 10 D7
Nayland CP School
RCOLW CO6 .... 102 C4
The Nest Branch Surgery
FX FP11 .... 83 K7
New Cangle School
HVHL CB9 .... 23 H4
Newlands Spring
Primary School
CHLM/WR CM1 .... 253 M6
Newmans Estate
COS CO15 .... 12 C6
Newport CP School
SAFWS CB11 .... 87 H5
Newport Free Grammar School
SAFWS CB11 .... 87 J4
Newport Gallery
SAFWS CB11 .... 87 J4
Newton Green Golf Club
SUD CO10 .... 51 J7
Northchwood Arts Gallery
FX FP11 .... 7 M1
Norchwood Arts Gallery
FX FP11 .... 113 J2
Northgate High School
IPNE IP4 .... 32 B4

Northgate Jmi School
BSF CM23 .... 171 G5
Northgate Sports Centre
IPNE IP4 .... 32 B4
North House Gallery
MGTR CO11 .... 135 M1
North School
COLW CO3 .... 10 A4
Norwich Road Surgery
IP IP1 .... 2 B2
Notley Enterprise Park
RCOLE CO7 .... 76 C2
Notley High School
BRTR CM7 .... 180 B5
Oak Hair & Health Centre
BRTR CM7 .... 180 D3
Oak Industrial Park
GTDUN CM6 .... 176 B6
Oaklands County
Infant School
CHLM/GWD CM2 .... 15 G7
Oaks Hospital
COLN CO4 .... 160 A2
Oakwood Business Park
COS CO15 .... 222 C4
Oakwood County
Infant School
COS CO15 .... 12 C7
Occupational Health Centre
HAR CO12 .... 111 G8
Odeon Cinema
CHLM/GWD CM2 .... 15 J4
Odeon Cinema
COLW CO3 .... 10 B8
Odeon Cinema
IPNE IP4 .... 3 G5
Old Church Surgery
RIPS/CAP IP9 .... 109 L2
Old Customs House
IPSE IP3 .... 3 G7
Old Grammar School
RCOLE CO7 .... 105 H6
Old Heath County
Primary School
COLS CO2 .... 188 E2
Ongar Road Trading Estate
GTDUN CM6 .... 176 A6
Orwell Business Centre
IPSE IP3 .... 55 G3
Orwell High School
FX FP11 .... 113 G2
Orwell Junior School
IPSE IP3 .... 55 H4
Orwell Park School
KIR/NAC IP10 .... 81 K2
Orwell Yacht Club
CHTY IP2 .... 54 E4
Oxford House School
COLW CO3 .... 159 M7
Park Lane Gallery
COL CO1 .... 10 D7
Parkway Middle School
HVHL CB9 .... 22 F5
Parsonage Farm
Industrial Estate
STSD CM24 .... 172 B2
Parsons Heath
Medical Practice
COLN CO4 .... 161 G4
Parsons Heath
Primary School
COLN CO4 .... 161 G3
Peartree Business Centre
COLW CO3 .... 187 G1
Perryfields County
Junior & Infant School
CHLM/WR CM1 .... 254 F7
The Philip Morrant School
COLW CO3 .... 159 K8
Phillips Gallery
CHLM/WR CM1 .... 15 J4
Pinebrook Surgery
RIPW IP8 .... 53 L3
Place Farm School
HVHL CB9 .... 23 H5
The Plume School
MAL CM9 .... 271 H3
Portmans Walk
Industrial Centre
IP IP1 .... 2 B6
Pot Kiln County
Primary School
SUD CO10 .... 5 H8
Powers Hall County
Infant School
WIT CM8 .... 237 M2
Prettygate Junior School
COLW CO3 .... 187 J1
Primary School
HSTD CO9 .... 70 B3
Priory Heath Infant School
IPSE IP3 .... 55 L4
Public Baths
IPNE IP4 .... 3 H7
The Quay Theatre
SUD CO10 .... 4 C8
Queen Street Dental
Health Centre
COL CO1 .... 10 D7
R A Butler Infant
Grammar School
SAFWS CB11 .... 63 G4
Radwinter C of E
Aided Primary School
SAFWN CB10 .... 65 H6
Raeburn Infant School
IPSE IP3 .... 55 H4
Rainsford High School
CHLM/WR CM1 .... 266 A1
Ramsey County
Primary School
HAR CO12 .... 139 H4
Ramsey School
HSTD CO9 .... 126 C3
Ranelagh Primary School
CHTY IP2 .... 31 H8
Ransomes Industrial
Estate Post Office
IPSE IP3 .... 56 A5

Ranworth Surgery
COS CO15 .... 12 E7
Ravenscroft School
RCOS CO16 .... 249 K1
Rayne CP School
BRTR CM7 .... 179 G3
Raynham Road
Industrial Estate
BSF CM23 .... 171 K5
Regency Art Gallery
COLS CO2 .... 10 F9
Register Office
IPNE IP4 .... 3 H6
Rhodes Museum
& Commonwealth Centre
BSF CM23 .... 171 J8
Rice Bridge Industrial Estate
RCOS CO16 .... 194 C6
Richard Whittington
Jmi School
BSF CM23 .... 199 G1
Rickling C of E
Primary School
SAFWS CB11 .... 116 A5
Rickstones School
WIT CM8 .... 210 B7
Ridgewell C of E
(aided) Primary School
HSTD CO9 .... 45 K6
Rivenhall C of E
Primary School
WIT CM8 .... 210 D5
Rivenhall Oaks Golf Club
WIT CM8 .... 238 D1
The Rivermead Gate
Medical Centre
CHLM/WR CM1 .... 266 D1
Riverside Business Park
STSD CM24 .... 143 M7
Riverside Clinic
IPSE IP3 .... 55 G2
Riverside Health Centre
MGTR CO11 .... 135 L1
Riverside Ice & Leisure Centre
CHLM/WR CM1 .... 15 J3
Riverside Industrial Estate
MAL CM9 .... 271 H1
Riverside Industrial Park
CHTY IP2 .... 54 F2
Riverside Retail Park
CHLM/WR CM1 .... 15 K1
Roach Vale Primary School
COLN CO4 .... 161 G4
Rodings Central
Primary School
GTDUN CM6 .... 230 E5
Rolph C of E Primary School
RCOS CO16 .... 194 B4
Rose Hill Primary School
IPSE IP3 .... 55 J1
Rowhedge Surgery
K/T/MI CO5 .... 189 H5
Roxwell C of E Primary School
CHLM/WR CM1 .... 252 C7
Royal Hospital School
RIPS/CAP IP9 .... 108 F2
Royal London Sports Centre
COLN CO4 .... 132 D7
Royal Mail Sorting Office
IP IP1 .... 2 D7
Royal Navy
CHLM/WR CM1 .... 15 G2
Rugby Club
BSF CM23 .... 170 F4
Rush Green Sports Centre
RCOS CO16 .... 249 K2
Rushmere Golf Club
IPNE IP4 .... 32 F7
Rushmere Hall CP School
IPNE IP4 .... 32 D4
Rushmere Sports Club
KESG IP5 .... 33 G4
Saffron Business Centre
SAFWN CB10 .... 63 J3
Saffron Walden County
High School
SAFWS CB11 .... 62 E5
Saffron Walden Golf Club
SAFWN CB10 .... 62 E3
Saffron Walden Hospital
SAFWS CB11 .... 63 J3
Saffron Walden Town
Football Club
SAFWN CB10 .... 62 F3
Sailing Club
RCOLE CO7 .... 219 G8
St Albans RC High School
IPNE IP4 .... 32 F6
St Andrews Church
of England Primary School
RCOS CO16 .... 193 G5
St Andrews C of E
Primary School
RCOLW CO6 .... 185 G2
St Andrews County
Junior School
COLN CO4 .... 11 M7
St Andrews County
Junior School
COLN CO4 .... 161 G6
St Andrews Junior School
RCHLM CM3 .... 257 K2
St Andrews School
SUD CO10 .... 73 H7
St Annes CP School
COLN CO4 .... 11 K3
St Annes Preparatory School
CHLM/GWD CM2 .... 14 F6
St Benedicts College
COLW CO3 .... 159 K7
St Clares Roman
Catholic School
RCOS CO16 .... 249 K1
St Clements Hospital
IPSE IP3 .... 55 H1
St Clements Hospital Lodge
IPSE IP3 .... 32 E8
St Felix RC Primary School
HVHL CB9 .... 22 F6

St Francis RC Primary School
BRTR CM7 .... 180 B1
St Francis RC Primary School
MAL CM9 .... 271 H2
St George's C of E
Primary School
RCOLE CO7 .... 163 G4
St Georges Infant School
COLS CO2 .... 160 C8
St Georges Primary School
COLS CO2 .... 160 C8
St Giles C of E Primary School
HSTD CO9 .... 96 F3
St Gregory V CP School
SUD CO10 .... 4 B7
St Helena School
COLW CO3 .... 159 M5
St Helens Primary School
IPNE IP4 .... 3 J5
St James School
COL CO1 .... 11 G6
St James Surgery
COS CO15 .... 12 E8
St John Payne RC
Comprehensive School
CHLM/WR CM1 .... 254 C7
St John Payne RC School
CHLM/WR CM1 .... 254 B7
St Johns C of E Controlled
Primary School
COLN CO4 .... 160 F1
St Johns C of E Primary School
IPNE IP4 .... 32 C6
St Johns C of E Primary School
RCHLM CM3 .... 269 H6
St Johns Green
County Primary School
COLS CO2 .... 10 C8
St John's Hospital
CHLM/GWD CM2 .... 266 B7
St Johns Industrial Estate
RBSF CM22 .... 174 A6
St John the Baptist
Primary School
HSTD CO9 .... 98 D5
St Josephs College
CHTY IP2 .... 54 C2
St Josephs RC Junior
Middle & Infant School
BSF CM23 .... 170 F7
St Josephs RC
Primary School
HAR CO12 .... 140 D3
St Josephs RC Va
Primary School
SUD CO10 .... 4 B5
St Lawrence C of E
Primary School
RCOS CO16 .... 189 H5
St Leonards Hospital
SUD CO10 .... 4 F6
St Lukes C of E Primary School
K/T/MI CO5 .... 212 F8
St Margarets C of
E V A Primary School
IP IP1 .... 3 G4
St Margarets
Preparatory School
HSTD CO9 .... 124 F5
St Margarets Primary School
HSTD CO9 .... 69 L1
St Marks College
SAFWS CB11 .... 62 C5
St Marks RC Primary School
CHTY IP2 .... 54 B2
St Mary's Business Centre
COLW CO3 .... 10 A8
St Mary's Business Centre
COLW CO3 .... 159 M6
St Marys Catholic School
BSF CM23 .... 171 G6
St Marys C of E
Primary School
RBSF CM22 .... 201 H7
St Marys C of E
Primary School
RCOLE CO7 .... 133 M5
St Marys C of E
Primary School
STSD CM24 .... 144 A6
St Marys Primary School
IPNE IP4 .... 3 L3
St Marys Primary School
SAFWN CB10 .... 62 F3
St Marys School
COLW CO3 .... 159 L6
St Marys School
COLW CO3 .... 158 B8
St Marys School for Girls
COLW CO3 .... 158 B8
St Matthews C of E School
IP IP1 .... 2 C5
St Michaels Hospital
BRTR CM7 .... 180 A2
St Michaels Primary School
BSF CM23 .... 171 G6
St Michaels School
BRTR CM7 .... 179 M3
St Osyth C of E
Primary School
RCOS CO16 .... 248 D1
St Pancras RC
Primary School
IP IP1 .... 31 H3
St Peters C of E
Primary School
HSTD CO9 .... 95 M5
St Peters C of E
Primary School
RCOLW CO6 .... 183 J3
St Peters Hospital
MAL CM9 .... 271 H3
St Philomenas Convent
Day School
FOS CO13 .... 196 B5
St Pius RC Primary School
CHLM/WR CM1 .... 254 B7
St Theresas RC Primary School
COLW CO3 .... 159 G8
St Thomas Moore RC
Primary School
SAFWS CB11 .... 63 G8

St Thomas More RC School
COL CO1 .... 10 F7
Salvation Army
IPNE IP4 .... 3 H7
Samuel Ward Upper School
HVHL CB9 .... 23 K4
Sanatorium Felixstowe
College
FX IP11 .... 113 L3
Sandon School
CHLM/GWD CM2 .... 267 K7
Saracens House
Business Centre
IP IP1 .... 3 G4
Sarbir Industrial Park
HLW CM20 .... 226 E8
Sawbridge Health Clinic
SBW CM21 .... 227 G3
School Street Surgery
SAFWN CB10 .... 37 M3
Severalls Hospital
COLN CO4 .... 132 A8
Severalls Park
Industrial Estate
COLN CO4 .... 132 F7
Sharon Crickitt Complementary
Health Centre
RCOLE CO7 .... 189 K5
Sheepen Road Retail Park
COLW CO3 .... 10 A8
Sheepen Road Retail Park
COLW CO3 .... 159 M7
Sheering C of E
Primary School
RBSF CM22 .... 227 M4
Shotley Primary School
RIPS/CAP IP9 .... 111 H2
Shotley Sailing Club
RIPS/CAP IP9 .... 111 K5
Shrub End Clinic
COLS CO2 .... 187 K2
Shrub End Surgery
COLW CO3 .... 187 J1
Siam Surgery
SUD CO10 .... 4 D6
Sidegate Primary School
IPNE IP4 .... 32 C5
Sikh Temple
IP IP1 .... 2 A5
Silver End County
Primary School
WIT CM8 .... 210 A2
The Silver Tree Craft Gallery
MGTR CO11 .... 135 M1
Sir Charles Lucas School
COLN CO4 .... 161 H6
Sir Charles Lucas School
COLN CO4 .... 161 G5
Snap Theatre
BSF CM23 .... 171 J6
Social History Museum
COL CO1 .... 10 C7
South Street Surgery
BSF CM23 .... 171 H7
South Suffolk Business Centre
SUD CO10 .... 5 G6
Southview School
WIT CM8 .... 210 B7
Spa Pavillion Theatre
FX IP11 .... 113 K4
Spellbrook Jmi School
K/T/MI CO5 .... 199 H6
Springfield County
Primary School
IP IP1 .... 31 G5
Springfield Cricket Club
CHLM/GWD CM2 .... 267 G1
Springfield Junior School
IP IP1 .... 31 H5
Springfield Medical Centre
CHLM/WR CM1 .... 254 F7
Spring Meadow
Primary School
HAR CO12 .... 8 C8
Sprites Junior & Infant School
CHTY IP2 .... 53 L3
Sproughton Business Park
IPNE IP4 .... 30 E6
Sproughton Vc Primary School
RIPW IP8 .... 30 D7
Stansted Clinic
STSD CM24 .... 144 A6
Stanway CP School
COLW CO3 .... 158 E7
Stanway Fiveways CP School
COLW CO3 .... 158 F8
The Stanway School
COLW CO3 .... 158 F8
Stanway Surgery
COLW CO3 .... 158 E7
Stanway Swimming Centre
COLW CO3 .... 158 B8
Station Yard Industrial Park
GTDUN CM6 .... 176 A6
Steeple Bumpstead CP School
HVHL CB9 .... 43 K7
Stoke College
CHTY IP2 .... 45 L2
Stoke High School
CHTY IP2 .... 54 E3
Stonehall Surgery
SUD CO10 .... 26 D6
Stortford Hall Industrial Park
BSF CM23 .... 171 K6
Stort Valley Industrial Estate
BSF CM23 .... 171 K3
Stour Sailing Club
MGTR CO11 .... 135 M1
The Street Industrial Estate
MAL CM9 .... 259 K8
Strumer End Industrial Estate
HVHL CB9 .... 23 K7
Stuarts Industrial Estate
CHLM/GWD CM2 .... 15 L5
Stutton Primary School
RIPS/CAP IP9 .... 108 C3
Sudbury Bowl
SUD CO10 .... 5 H3
Sudbury Business Centre
SUD CO10 .... 4 C6

Sudbury Health Centre
SUD CO10 .... 4 E4
Sudbury Rugby
Union Football Club
SUD CO10 .... 74 D1
Sudbury Town Football Club
SUD CO10 .... 4 C8
Sudbury Tudor
Voluntary Controlled School
SUD CO10 .... 4 E3
Sudbury Uplands Middle School
SUD CO10 .... 4 E3
Sudbury Upper School
SUD CO10 .... 4 E2
Sue Ryder Foundation
SUD CO10 .... 27 M4
Suffolk County Council Offices
IPNE IP4 .... 3 J6
Summercroft Junior
& Infant School
BSF CM23 .... 171 L5
Sutherland Lodge Surgery
CHLM/GWD CM2 .... 15 K7
Tabor High Upper School
BRTR CM7 .... 179 M1
Tabor Middle School
BRTR CM7 .... 180 A2
Takeley Business Centre
RBSF CM22 .... 173 L6
Takeley Gm Primary School
RBSF CM22 .... 173 L5
Tattingstone C of
E V CP School
RIPS/CAP IP9 .... 78 F6
Templars County
Infant School
WIT CM8 .... 210 B8
Templers County
Junior School
WIT CM8 .... 210 B8
Tendring Adult Community
College
COS CO15 .... 12 F5
Tendring CP School
RCOS CO16 .... 165 G7
Tendring Sixth Form College
FOS CO13 .... 196 O6
Tendring Technology
College & Sixth Form College
RCOS CO16 .... 194 B3
Tennyson House Surgery
CHLM/WR CM1 .... 254 B7
Terling C of E Primary School
RCHLM CM3 .... 236 E2
Thaxted Primary School
GTDUN CM6 .... 119 J3
Thomas Lord Audley School
COLS CO2 .... 188 B3
Thomas Rivers Medical Centre
HLW CM20 .... 226 E6
The Thomas Rivers
Medical Centre
SBW CM21 .... 226 E4
Thomas Wolsey School
IP IP1 .... 31 G2
Thorley Hill Jmi School
BSF CM23 .... 199 H1
Thorn Grove Primary School
BSF CM23 .... 171 K7
Threshelfords Business Park
K/T/MI CO5 .... 212 A2
Thurleston High School
IP IP1 .... 31 J1
Thurstable School
K/T/MI CO5 .... 212 F7
Tiptree Heath CP School
K/T/MI CO5 .... 240 D2
Tiptree Sports Centre
K/T/MI CO5 .... 212 F6
Tollesbury CP School
MAL CM9 .... 262 F4
Tollesbury Sailing Club
MAL CM9 .... 263 H3
Tolleshunt Darcy
C of E Primary School
MAL CM9 .... 261 M1
Tooley's & Smarts Almshouses
IPNE IP4 .... 3 G6
Tower Business Park
K/T/MI CO5 .... 212 D6
Tower Ramparts
Shopping Centre
IP IP1 .... 2 F5
Trimley St Martins
County Primary School
FX IP11 .... 83 K3
Trinity Road Primary School
CHLM/GWD CM2 .... 15 L2
Twyford Business Centre
BSF CM23 .... 171 J8
Twyford Business Centre
BSF CM23 .... 199 J1
The Tyrrells CP School
CHLM/WR CM1 .... 255 G8
Uniterian Meeting House
IP IP1 .... 2 E6
Unity Health Centre
SUD CO10 .... 4 D6
University College Suffolk
IPNE IP4 .... 3 J6
University College
Suffolk Annexe
IPNE IP4 .... 3 H5
University of Essex
COLN CO4 .... 161 H7
University of Essex
COLN CO4 .... 189 H1
University Yacht Club
RCOLE CO7 .... 219 H8
Uttlesford District Council
GTDUN CM6 .... 175 M5
Vineyard Gallery
COL CO1 .... 10 D7
Virgin Cinema
IP IP1 .... 2 D5
Walnut Tree Hospital
SUD CO10 .... 4 B6
Walton & Frinton Yacht Club
WOTN CO14 .... 196 E4

Walton Gm Primary School
WOTN CO14 .... 196 E4
Walton Surgery
FX IP11 .... 113 G1
Wardmaster Infirmary
RIPS/CAP IP9 .... 108 F2
Warner Industrial Park
SUD CO10 .... 5 H3
Warren Golf Club
MAL CM9 .... 269 L4
Waterside Business Park
WIT CM8 .... 238 D1
Waterside School
BSF CM23 .... 143 G6
Well Lane Industrial Estate
RCHLM CM3 .... 268 E6
Wells Hall Primary School
SUD CO10 .... 74 D1
Wentworth Primary School
MAL CM9 .... 271 H5
Westbourne High School
IP IP1 .... 31 G4
Westbridge Infant School
IP IP1 .... 2 B4
West Cliff Theatre
COS CO15 .... 12 E9
Westerfield Business Centre
NHMKT IP6 .... 32 A2
Westfield School
HVHL CB9 .... 23 K6
Westlands County
Secondary School
CHLM/WR CM1 .... 265 M4
Westlands CP School
CHLM/WR CM1 .... 14 B3
West Mersea Museum
K/T/MI CO5 .... 244 D8
West Station Industrial Estate
MAL CM9 .... 271 G4
West Station Yard
MAL CM9 .... 271 G4
Wethersfield Primary School
BRTR CM7 .... 122 E2
White Court CP School
BRTR CM7 .... 179 L7
Whitehall Industrial Estate
COLS CO2 .... 188 F2
White House Infant School
IP IP1 .... 30 F4
White House Junior School
IP IP1 .... 30 F4
White Notley C of E
Primary School
WIT CM8 .... 209 H8
Whitton Clinic
IP IP1 .... 31 G3
Whitton Junior & Infant School
IP IP1 .... 31 G2
Widford Industrial Estate
CHLM/WR CM1 .... 14 A9
Widford Lodge
Preparatory School
CHLM/GWD CM2 .... 14 D9
William Julian Courtald
Hospital
BRTR CM7 .... 180 A3
Willis Coroon Building
IP IP1 .... 2 E6
Wimbish CP School
SAFWN CB10 .... 89 L1
Windsor School Clacton
COS CO15 .... 13 M3
The Witham Health Centre
WIT CM8 .... 238 C3
Witham Rugby Union F C
WIT CM8 .... 238 A4
Witham Town Football
& Social Club
WIT CM8 .... 238 A3
Wivenhoe Business Centre
RCOLE CO7 .... 189 L5
Wivenhoe Family
Health Centre
RCOLE CO7 .... 189 K3
Wivenhoe Sailing Club
RCOLE CO7 .... 189 L6
Wivenhoe Town Cricket Club
RCOLE CO7 .... 189 L3
Wix CP School
MGTR CO11 .... 137 K8
Wolsey Theatre
IP IP1 .... 2 D5
Woodford Medical Clinic
RCHLM CM3 .... 268 E6
Woodgreen Animal Shelter
ROY SG8 .... 59 J2
Woodhall Business Park
SUD CO10 .... 50 B3
Woodhall Business
Park Drury Drive
SUD CO10 .... 50 B3
Woodhall County
Primary School
SUD CO10 .... 4 E1
Woodham Walter
C of E Primary School
MAL CM9 .... 269 M2
Woodlands School
CHLM/WR CM1 .... 254 B7
The Working Silk Museum
BRTR CM7 .... 180 B3
Wormingford C of E
Primary School
RCOLW CO6 .... 101 G8
Writtle College
CHLM/WR CM1 .... 265 K2
Writtle Junior School
CHLM/WR CM1 .... 265 J5
The Writtle Surgery
CHLM/WR CM1 .... 265 K3
Wycke Hill Business Park
MAL CM9 .... 271 G5
Wyncroft Surgery
RCHLM CM3 .... 269 H6
Yale Business Park
IPSE IP3 .... 56 B5
Yellow Dot Sports Club
SUD CO10 .... 5 G7

Notes